Media Law

Marie McGonagle

THOMSON ROUND HALL
2003

Published in 2003 by
Round Hall Ltd
43 Fitzwilliam Place
Dublin 2
Ireland

Typeset by
Gough Typesetting Services
Dublin

Printed by
ColourBooks Ltd., Dublin

ISBN 1-85800-272-9

A catalogue record for this book
is available from the British Library

To my parents, Mary and Edward McAllister

MEDIA LAW

AUSTRALIA
Law Book Co.
Sydney

CANADA and USA
Carswell
Toronto

HONG KONG
Sweet & Maxwell Asia

NEW ZEALAND
Brookers
Wellington

SINGAPORE and MALAYSIA
Sweet & Maxwell Asia
Singapore and Kuala Lumpur

Preface to the First Edition

This is not a traditional law book because Media Law is not a traditional law subject. It is only in recent years that it has been offered in University Law Schools in Ireland. Media Law is not confined to law schools of course; it is becoming an important component of the many established and emerging communications and journalism programmes offered at third level and postgraduate level. The fact that it is a new area of study has certain advantages. First, the approach to the subject is not constrained by any set format or long-standing wisdom in the way that Contract Law, for example, has been until recently. Second, courses in Media Law can be designed to take account of the rapid changes occurring in media technology and can examine the relevant law from both an historical and practical perspective.

At a period in our history when law has become all-pervasive in our daily lives, and information a highly-prized commodity in society, it is perhaps fitting to develop a multi- or inter-disciplinary approach to the study of a subject like Media Law. The nature of communications and journalism courses positively invites such an approach. The present text, therefore, aims to facilitate a broad, exploratory study of the subject by adopting a flexible approach to each of the topics covered. It is hoped to give students an understanding of the nature and role of the media in a modern democratic society, to introduce them to the legal framework of the various media (broadcast, print, film, video), and to invite consideration of the content, purpose, scope and impact of legal rules and restrictions on both the day-to-day operations and the development—actual and potential—of the media.

The material in this book has been tried and tested over several years on law students and applied communications students. The aim has been to keep the text itself as simple as possible, but to annotate it to an extent that will provide a starting-point for students wishing to do further research. It is hoped that the text will also be of interest to practising journalists, lawyers and teachers of a variety of media and law related subjects. While it cannot answer all the questions or address all the issues that arise in a media context, it endeavours to point out some of those that have arisen to date and, where appropriate, to indicate proposals for reform.

Reference to cases and materials is necessarily selective. In this field, very many cases are not reported in the official law reports. Some are Circuit Court decisions and there is no written judgment. Others are jury decisions in the High Court, and juries do not have to give reasons for their decision. Reliance is placed, therefore, on accounts of cases published in newspapers, particularly *The Irish Times,* to a lesser extent, the *Sunday Tribune, Irish Independent,* and *Irish Press.* In some chapters, for example Chapter 6 which deals with contempt of court and injunctions, numerous cases are mentioned. The purpose is to give an indication of how legal rules and principles apply in practice and the frequency with which those rules and principles are invoked against the media. It is not that the Irish media are irresponsible, quite the opposite, but rather that rules and principles devised in an earlier period of media development may not take sufficient account of the realities of modern media practice.

The subject-matter of the text is primarily the news and information aspects of the media role, since that is where the law is most developed. The entertainment aspect is touched upon where appropriate, and will, it is hoped, be given greater weight in any future edition. The concept of artistic expression, the developing law on concentration of ownership, changes in copyright law, the nature of publishing, recording, film and retransmission rights will no doubt in the future provide material for extended coverage. In the meantime, this book is offered as a first step in documenting and analysing media law as it pertains in Ireland but within an increasingly globalised context.

At the time of writing a number of important cases are in progress but not yet decided and legislation in certain key areas is in preparation. In particular, the European Court of Human Rights judgment in *Goodwin v UK*, concerning protection of journalists' sources, is eagerly awaited, as is the Irish government's promised legislation on freedom of information. Unfortunately discussion of these will have to wait till another day.

Dóibh siúd atá ag freastal ar chúrsaí faoi dhlí na meán cumarsáide trí Ghaeilge, tá liosta téarmaí ag deireadh an leabhair. Téarmaí oifigiúla dlí atá iontu, chomh maith le leagan Gaeilge de na hailt sin den Bhunreacht a bhaineann leis na meáin chumarsáide.

This book would never have been written were it not for the help and support of so many people, in particular my family, my colleagues in the Law Faculty UCG, especially Liam O'Malley, who as Dean of the Faculty facilitated my research, Tom O'Malley, Denny Driscoll and Gerard Quinn who passed on materials and information and Michael O'Neill and Donncha O'Connell who read proofs of some of the chapters. Law librarian Maeve Doyle answered all my queries, and research students Fiona Fitzpatrick and Niamh Nic Shuibhne painstakingly checked out the references for me. I am grateful also to the staff and research fellows of the Institute for Information Law, University of Amsterdam, where I carried out some of the research and to Professor Bruno de Witte of the Law Faculty, University of Limburg in Maastricht who gave me the opportunity to teach on a comparative media law course there. The National Newspapers of Ireland (NNI), Provincial Newspapers Association of Ireland, National Union of Journalists, Irish Book Publishers Association and many individual publishers, editors and journalists in the print and audio-visual media both in Ireland and abroad have been of great assistance over the years. My thanks are due to all of these but especially to Kevin Boyle, formerly professor of law at UCG, who first suggested Media Law to me as an area of research and who has been very supportive of that research ever since. My work has benefited enormously from his breadth of knowledge and international experience in promoting freedom of expression and human rights generally. Finally, Finola O'Sullivan of Gill & Macmillan and her colleague Deirdre Greenan have been very understanding and helpful throughout.

   Mo bhuíochas fosta do Ghearóid O Casaide, Rannóg an Aistriúcháin, Teach Laighean as diosca ríomhaire de na téarmai dlí a sholáthar dom.

Marie McGonagle
Law Faculty
University College Galway

December 1995

Preface to the Second Edition

When the first edition of this book was published in 1996, the world of the media was a very different place than it is now, a simpler and less crowded arena. Newspapers had gone to colour, the monopoly of public service broadcasting had been broken and a new independent broadcasting sector had emerged. The Internet was in its infancy; digitalisation was just a word for a burgeoning technology; "Big Brother" was still an Orwellian nightmare, and not yet a reality television phenomenon. Media law and regulation, likewise, were much simpler, less extensive and less defined. Key concerns were to update old laws and provide a coherent and principled body of laws and regulation to meet the challenges of the new technologies coming on stream.

Today, media law is a complex area as a result of technological developments and the increasingly international character of the media themselves. This new edition brings the reader up to date on key issues and developments affecting the traditional media and the changes that have taken place in the regulatory framework and media landscape. It also takes a first look at the regulation of the new media: the technological imperatives, the economic and social values, the fundamental rights that need to be safeguarded in this new online, multimedia, interactive world. It is a world in which law, particularly at national level, can play only a limited role.

The new media do not respect physical or conceptual borders; they are instantaneous, they converge, they embrace new technologies with a speed previously unknown; they do not wait for the slow footfalls of the law. Regulation has to be reassessed, therefore, and new forms of regulation have to be considered, either in tandem with, or instead of, law. As the technologies converge, maybe the regulatory bodies need to converge also. If law alone is too slow, too rigid or too cumbersome, maybe co-regulation, self-regulation or even deregulation will provide the answer, or maybe technology will find its own answers. These are the types of question that have arisen and continue to be debated.

Technology aside, there have been many significant developments in media law in Ireland since 1996. The constitutional argument, based on the guarantee of freedom of expression in Article 40.6.1i of the Constitution, was constantly sidelined by judges and lawyers in the 1980s and early 1990s. Now there have been significant decisions from the Supreme Court. A unanimous Supreme Court in 1998, for instance, in *The Irish Times v Judge Murphy*, recognised the vital role of the press in a modern democracy and the need for the courts to embrace the realities of a modern information and technological age. The jurisprudence of the European Court of Human Rights, once dismissed by lawyers proud of their common law heritage, has gained in influence and is set to have an even greater impact following the passage of legislation in June 2003 to incorporate the European Convention on Human Rights into Irish law.

Legislation has also been enacted to update several major areas. The structure of broadcasting, for example, has been revised under the Broadcasting Act 2001. Copyright law has been overhauled, and moral rights and performers' rights included, in the Copyright Act 2000. The enactment of the Freedom of Information Act 1997 was a major step forward in bringing Ireland out of the darkness of official secrets. Regrettably, that brave new venture, which was working well and which had made Ireland a model for access to information legislation in Europe and further afield, was curtailed to a worrying degree by the Freedom of Information (Amendment) Act 2003 and by the subsequent imposition of hefty charges for requests for information and for reviews of decisions.

The long-promised Defamation Bill to update defamation law in Ireland, is still only a promise. The most recent step towards that goal occurred in March 2003 when a Legal Advisory Group established by the Minister for Justice, Equality and Law Reform reported and provided a draft Bill.

Perhaps the most significant development of all in the field, however, since the last edition of this book was in preparation, particularly with regard to the audiovisual and new media, is the centrality of European law and policy. As a result, this edition takes account of law and policy emanating from the various organs of the European Union and the Council of Europe. Such is the vastness and complexity of that corpus of material that it is only possible in a text like this to provide a tentative roadmap for the future, rather than try to tackle any of the myriad issues in an exhaustive manner.

As before, the aim is to keep the text as straightforward as possible but to annotate it to an extent that will provide a starting-point and guide to students or others wishing to engage in further research. The difficulty for researchers nowadays is not a dearth or limited range of information, but the opposite. The challenge is to navigate the unlimited flow of information, most of it reliable, some less so, that is available on all sorts of databases, search engines, websites, CD-ROMs, publications and paper documentation.

As it is not possible to include everything of relevance, one has to be selective and hope to give a flavour of some of the thinking and analysis of issues that is taking place in different countries and different cultures right around the world.

Nor is it possible to keep up to date, to keep pace with research and scholarship on what is now a very wide spectrum of media law issues, ranging from structural to content issues, from concentration of ownership to diversity of output, from physical privacy to data protection, from censorship to news management, and many more. In the days when newspaper production was much slower than now, it was common to have a "stop press" or "latest" news insert. This book can only hope to provide the backdrop to and signpost some of the areas where change is on the horizon. In so doing, and in including a list of core websites in the bibliography, it invites readers to "watch this space" and follow innovations and developments as they occur.

In the first edition of this book, a glossary of Irish-language terms was included to assist those following courses in media or communications law through Irish. That has not been necessary this time, as a dictionary of law in Irish has been published: Leachlain S. Ó Catháin, *Focal sa Chúirt* (Coiscéim, Baile Átha Cliath, 2001).

When contemplating a second edition, I naively thought that it would be an easy task. I learned otherwise and were it not for the help of many colleagues, research assistants, friends and family, it might not have reached fruition. I would like to thank, therefore, my colleagues in the Law Faculty in Galway, particularly Donncha O'Connell for his generosity always in sharing ideas and materials, and Nicola Murphy, who, like Donncha, read some of the draft chapters, and who is a constant source of knowledge on literature and the arts. Research assistants, particularly Suzanne White, in the early stages of the work, and Deirdre Bignell, who has been my lifeline through the drafting and proofing stages, are owed a special thanks for their meticulousness and constant good humour. I appreciate also the help of Arline Broder, the staff of the Faculty office and the staff of the university library.

I am grateful also to the staff and research fellows at the two institutes where much of the research was carried out. The friendliness and support I always receive at the Institute for Information Law (IViR) of the University of Amsterdam, is most appreciated. My time spent at the Programme in Comparative Media Law and Policy (PCMLP) at the University of Oxford was invaluable, and I am grateful in particular to Stefaan Verhulst, who was co-director at the time and to Louise Scott, the administrator of the Programme, both of whom were very helpful. I have also had the pleasure and valuable learning experience of working with a team of experts from other European countries and with Andrew Drzemczewski and his staff at the Council of Europe. My thanks also to David Goldberg, formerly of the University of Glasgow and founding editor of the *Journal of Media Law and Practice*, now *Communications Law*, who has always given me wise advice on research matters. Susanne Nikoltchev and the staff of the European Audiovisual Observatory, for whom I act as Irish legal correspondent, have provided access to much useful information and kindly permitted me to use some material from their publications. Tarlach McGonagle (no relation, of course!) of IViR was the inspiration and driving force behind much of the work and constantly spurred me on to greater precision and higher standards. Mo mhíle buíochas, a Tharlaigh.

And lest I cause a family row, Noel, Conall and Ríona have been most patient and supportive also.

My knowledge and understanding of the media have been greatly informed by those working in the media, by their lawyers and by their representative organisations, NNI, RNAI, NUJ, BCI, RTÉ, the Community Radio Forum, CLÉ (the Irish book publishers association), Let in the Light (the campaign for freedom of information), Women on Air, and all the organisations with which I have been involved in providing training. Eamonn Kennedy, solicitor with RTÉ, kindly read part of my draft and gave me useful insights. Celene Craig of BCI expertly answered my many questions. Therese Carrick, and later David McCartney and Orla Fee, at Round Hall, have been most accommodating and understanding of the need for a little elasticity with deadlines. And, finally, to my students, who may enjoy or suffer the results of my research and teaching, this edition is for you.

Marie McGonagle
July 2003

Table of Contents

Table of Cases

Table of Statutes

CONSTITUTION

IRISH STATUTES

STATUTORY INSTRUMENTS

EU MATERIALS

COUNCIL OF EUROPE

INTERNATIONAL

OTHER JURISDICTIONS

CHAPTER ONE

The Media and Media Law

1.1 INTRODUCTION

To define and understand the subject matter of this textbook, three basic sets of questions are posed at the outset:

1. What are the media, their content and their role?

2. What is law and how is it implemented?

3. What is media law and how does it operate in practice?

This chapter attempts to answer these questions. Students taking communications or journalism courses involving detailed study of the sociology of the media may already be familiar with the first section of this chapter, "What are the media?" Law students and those who have studied the basic principles of law may be familiar with the second section, "What is law?"

1.2 WHAT ARE THE MEDIA?

The term "media" comes from the Latin *medium*, which in the singular form signifies a means, method or way of doing something. The plural form, *media*, in a modern context, signifies ways or means of *communicating*. In this text the term refers to methods or means of communicating with mass audiences and includes the various forms of mass communication in operation today:

- broadcast media – radio, television, including by cable, satellite, MMDS, digital and internet transmission.
- the press or print media – newspapers, magazines, books.
- audio-visual media – film, CD, audio cassette and video, including by traditional and internet delivery.

The oldest of these forms is the print media, which began to take shape as early as the sixteenth century, following the invention of the printing-press. By the middle of the nineteenth century, newspapers had begun to circulate in very large numbers. Increased literacy meant a potentially wider readership, and advances in technology improved printing capacity and reduced unit costs so that mass circulation became possible.

As a result, the term "mass media" was first applied to the print media and only later to broadcasting. Today the term serves two purposes: it distinguishes those media that reach the masses (mass media) from both the older interpersonal media (post, telephone) and some of the newer interactive media that began to develop towards the end of the twentieth century. However, as a result of convergence of the various technologies (telecommunications, broadcasting and computer), the distinction has become blurred. Digital compression technology, in particular, has transformed the media landscape. The telecommunications, broadcasting and computer sectors, which had developed separately and had been regulated separately, have now come together to produce a form of media known as multi-media. The variety and complexities of multi-media services pose new challenges to the role of law and legal regulation. They combine elements of news, information and entertainment in a vast array of guises and packages, which surmount geographic borders and traditional regulatory categories. They add a new dimension to the traditional concept and delivery of entertainment, formerly categorised around theatre, cinematographic film, broadcasting, video and music. Issues of artistic expression and protection, therefore, take on a new significance.

1.3 WHAT IS THE MEDIA'S CONTENT?

1.3.1 News and Information

The essence of the media's role is communication. Because this role has greatly expanded in modern society, the media now serve as the principal source of news and information, opinion, advertising and entertainment in many countries around the world.

Traditionally the media communicated news and information. It was for this purpose that news-sheets, and later, newspapers, were first introduced. For commercial reasons and also because of the paucity of news and difficulty of obtaining it, advertising of local and national products formed a large part of the content. Poor transport meant that news-gathering was a long, slow process, relying on sea travel and horse-based land transport. Nowadays, in contrast, modern technology has made it possible to have almost instantaneous news, not only within a particular landmass, but virtually globally. For some years now, the *International Herald Tribune*, for example, has been published simultaneously in cities across the world on a daily basis. Likewise, technology has made it possible for us to watch and hear events live on radio, television or the internet, as they unfold around the world, where formerly only printed reports or still photographs would have been available some considerable time after the event. Many broadcast networks and newspaper websites deliver news reports and analysis on an up-to-the-minute basis around the clock. The September 11, 2001 terrorist attack on New York and the 2003 war against Iraq are probably the starkest examples of instantaneous audio-visual reporting in recent times.

However, it is not only news that is available to us through the media. We have access to a vast range of information on every conceivable subject. What is the value of the news and information content of the media? It can be said that it leads to a more informed public, to a greater awareness on the part of the readership or audience of the world around them and the major issues of the day. It stirs the public consciousness and allows individuals and groups to react to and have an input into matters that have an impact on their lives. In that sense it encourages and advances participatory democracy. For example, in western democracies the media serve as the main sources of news and information about the world for the vast majority of people. The broadcasting and internet media give up-to-the-minute coverage, visual images and sound; serious newspapers give extended background information, context and detail. All offer some degree of analysis and discussion of the major events of the day and of issues arising in a variety of political and social spheres. Both broadcasting and print media have become indispensable to today's citizen. Each has a function and they should be seen as complementary, not as alternatives. The internet has become not only an important added source of information, but also a new means of delivering information from all manner of sources including broadcast, print and originally-created website material.

In addition to reporting events, keeping the public informed and reflecting society, the media also have a capacity to shape events and determine the issues of the day. The desirability of that function is often criticised on the grounds that the media are not a democratically elected body. That in itself would not be a problem as long as a variety of sources of information exist. Increasingly, however, the media are becoming privatised and power is concentrated in the hands of a few media moguls whose ethic is profit and not always public-spiritedness. At a time when Eastern Europe is emerging from a situation of no-choice, state-run media, the western world, at national and European Union levels, has been increasingly concerned about the risks that privatisation and overconcentration pose to pluralism and diversity.[1]

Rupert Murdoch, for example, controls or has extensive interests in major media outlets all over the world. In Ireland, Tony O'Reilly's Independent News and Media plc now controls or has a significant interest in seven of the eleven national newspapers, the Belfast Telegraph group of newspapers in Northern Ireland, and at least ten of the provincials. In all, it controls over two-thirds of the Irish-published daily titles and nearly 80 per cent of the Irish Sunday newspapers. It has a controlling interest in Newspread, one of the two newspaper and magazine distribution companies in Ireland, as well as a printing company which prints its own titles, and various other holdings. It also has a stake in a number of commercial radio stations, a number of MMDS franchises and cable.[2] In addition it has media interests in the UK, France, Portugal, Australia, New Zealand, South America and South Africa.

The implications of concentration of ownership, including cross-ownership between newspapers and the electronic media, are a cause for concern throughout the world. The risk to diversity in news coverage and views is one of the main reasons put forward to support the introduction of restrictions on ownership of the press. However, the mere fact of multiple ownership does not necessarily mean proprietorial influence over editorial decisions, but as

---

[1] See further Chap.11 below.

[2] For precise details of media ownership in Ireland, see John Horgan, *Irish Media: A Critical History Since 1992* (Routledge, London and New York, 2001).

long as the opportunity for influence is there, the possibility cannot be ruled out.[3] Much depends on the internal structures of media companies; it is possible to ensure a plurality of views within newspapers by creating structures to guarantee editorial independence. That is where editors and journalists have a role to play. Additionally, in a democracy, media organisations themselves must be both responsible in their internal operations and accountable to their public.

1.3.2 Comment – The Expression of Views and Opinions

In the early days of newspapers and broadcasting, there was little comment, analysis or criticism. The function of newspapers was regarded as that of straight reporting. In newspaper parlance, reporting consisted of the five W's: who, what, where, when, why. Criticism was left to the pamphleteers. In time, newspapers came to be prized mainly for their political content, while the function of radio and television broadcasting in its early days was seen primarily as entertainment with a cultural or educational dimension. Current affairs programming, with its emphasis on discussion and expert analysis, came much later. Opinion pieces and gossip and social columns in newspapers emerged as a result of intense competition for sales in a mass-market economy early in the twentieth century.

The essence of media comment and analysis is that it *interprets* news and information. The value of such interpretation lies in the expression of a variety of viewpoints that stimulate public discussion and debate. However, there is a danger that opinions may actually dictate public sympathies, and the range of opinions expressed in the media may be very limited, with little opportunity to air contrary views. In Ireland, it is often said that the so-called "Dublin 4" mentality, reflected in many of the opinion pieces of the national media, is at variance with the more conservative and traditional views that prevail in the rest of the country. This tension may be more apparent than real. At any rate, some degree of tension and airing of differing viewpoints is healthy. It has been said that a good newspaper is a nation talking to itself. There would be a greater problem if there were no diversity in the media and therefore no forum for competing ideas and opinions. It is also unlikely that people would react and form their own opinions to the extent that they do if the media merely reported the news and did not comment or attempt to interpret that news and offer viewpoints on its implications.

The role of the newspaper is somewhat different in this regard to that of the public service broadcaster (such as RTÉ) and private broadcaster (such as TV3). A newspaper can adopt a particular stance or bias; the public knows to expect that and if they do not like it, they can change to another newspaper or to a broadcast channel, as long as a diversity of sources exists. Public service or state broadcasting, on the other hand, was perceived differently. When broadcasting was still a new and uncertain medium and frequencies on the

---

[3] Owen M. Fiss, "Why the State?" in Judith Lichtenberg (ed.), *Democracy and the Mass Media* (Cambridge University Press, Cambridge, 1990).

electromagnetic spectrum were limited, states endeavoured to keep broadcasting as a monopoly within their control and to ensure its operation as a public service. At a time when no alternative audio or audio-visual source was available, radio and television reporting had to be objective and balanced; broadcasters were not to express their own views. Both sides of an issue had to be addressed in a programme, and programmers had to have regard for the cultural and other values of the community.[4] This remained the case even with the advent of the commercial broadcasting stations, which have been saddled with similar requirements of fairness and impartiality.[5] Today, modern technology, offering new delivery systems – digital, webcasting and the like – is making the distinction between commercial and public service broadcasting, and the imposition of any form of control, more difficult, and is rapidly reshaping the form and direction of regulation.[6]

1.3.3 Advertising

Advertising, the main economic base of the Irish media,[7] is a form of "commercial speech". It is largely directed to providing consumer information, although the techniques used and the requirement that it be differentiated from news and information programming or reporting tend to put it into the entertainment category. The nature and impact of advertising, especially when aimed at children, are regarded as so significant that a vast array of legal regulations apply. That is particularly so in the broadcast and audio-visual media, which are regarded as having a greater immediacy than the print media.[8]

---

[4] Broadcasting Authority Act 1960, s.18.

[5] Radio and Television Act 1988, s.9. The public service remit is retained in the Broadcasting Act 2001. The future of public service broadcasting in the face of intense competition from a highly profitable private sector, which can outbid public service broadcasters in the competition for programmes and coverage of sporting and cultural events, has been a major concern at European level and has led, for example, to provision for governments to reserve certain important events for free-to-air broadcasting. See the Television without Frontiers Directive (97/36/EC, O.J. L202/60, July 30, 1997) and the Broadcasting (Major Events Television Coverage) Act 1999 in Ireland. An illustration of the problem was the response to the decision of the Football Association of Ireland in 2002 to award the contract for coverage of Ireland's home soccer games to Sky – see further Chap.11 below.

[6] See, for example, Tom Gibbons, *Regulating the Media* (2nd ed., Sweet & Maxwell, London, 1998).

[7] RTÉ receives its income partly from advertising and partly from licence fees. Advertising was always allowed on RTÉ television, although it was prohibited in broadcasting in some European countries until quite recently. See generally, Euromedia Research Group, *The Media in Western Europe* (2nd ed., Sage Publications, London, 1997); ARTICLE 19, *Information, Freedom and Censorship – World Report 1991* (Library Association Publishing, London, 1991).

[8] Apart from legislation governing advertising, RTÉ and the BCI operate in accordance with a Code of Advertising, drafted in accordance with broadcasting legislation. Note: the Independent Radio and Television Commission (IRTC) was renamed the Broadcasting Commission of Ireland (BCI) and given extended powers by the Broadcasting Act 2001. The Advertising Standards Authority for Ireland (ASAI) operates a voluntary code, which governs all other forms of advertising. Along with similar bodies in other countries, the

Like advertising, and now teleshopping, sponsorship, a form of indirect funding, which has become an important source of finance for programme-makers, is regulated by the European Television without Frontiers Directive and by ministerial and industry codes.[9] Advertising in the print media is governed by general laws (of equality, defamation, sale of goods, passing off, and so forth) and by self-regulatory measures operated by the Advertising Standards Authority of Ireland, which consists of all the main advertising agencies.

1.3.4 Entertainment

All media now have an entertainment role. Media entertainment is a form of communication through the arts; literary, scientific and artistic presentations, stories, drama and music all play a part. Newspaper cartoons, horoscopes, television programme listings, sports results, crosswords, bridge columns and prize games have an appeal of their own and have come to be relied on by people as part of their daily lives. The entertainment value of radio and television broadcasting is firmly established. The role of the law in this sphere is very limited and confined to such requirements as not to offend against public decency, not to defame others, not to encroach unreasonably on their privacy, and not to offend against the State. The value of the entertainment content of the media lies in part in its role in extending the imagination. In German constitutional law, for example, the protection afforded the media extends to its entertainment function, which is regarded as relating to developments in social life.[10]

One might ask if all media content has a value. The content and the sensationalist approach adopted in tabloid journalism are frequently criticised, yet people continue to buy tabloid newspapers in very large numbers. Whether they are bought for content, entertainment, curiosity, or for more salacious reasons is another matter. The large amounts of damages awarded against them by juries in defamation cases are open to interpretation. It is noteworthy that the highest awards made in Ireland by juries to date have been against the *Sunday Independent* (which is not a tabloid format), the *Sunday News* and the *Daily Mirror* (which are tabloids). Tabloids also feature often in claims of intrusion on individual privacy.

ASAI is involved in voluntary regulation on a European-wide basis (see annual reports of ASAI, available at *www.asai.ie*).

[9] Broadcasting Authority Act 1960, s.20(8); Television without Frontiers Directive 1997, Art.17, above, n.5, amending the earlier Directive 89/552/EEC. The text of the Directive is available at *http://europa.eu.int/comm/avpolicy/index_en.htm*. The current code of Broadcast Advertising is that of 1995, updated in 1999. The Broadcasting Act 2001, s.19 makes provision for the Broadcasting Commission of Ireland (BCI), upon being directed by the Minister to do so, to prepare codes of standards, including a code on advertising, teleshopping, sponsorship and other forms of commercial promotion. Sponsored programmes were a feature of radio broadcasting in Ireland from an early date.

[10] Wolfgang Hoffmann-Riem, "Freedom of Information and New Technological Developments in the Federal Republic of Germany: A Case Law Analysis" in Antonio Cassese and Andrew Clapham (eds), *Transfrontier Television in Europe: The Human Rights Dimension* (Nomos Verlagsgesellschaft, Baden-Baden, 1990), p.49, at p.58.

1.4 WHAT IS THE MEDIA'S ROLE?

The importance of a free press or free media is said to lie in its function as a watchdog on government and authority. As a conduit of information, communicating news, views, ideas and analysis, the press offers a safeguard against abuse of power by ensuring accountability. It does so by keeping public opinion informed and by providing a forum for open debate. As John Stuart Mill expressed it in his essay on the liberty of the press:

> "The importance of free discussion ... concerns equally every member of the community. It is of equal value to good government, because without it good government cannot exist. Once remove it, and not only are all existing abuses perpetuated, but all which, in the course of successive ages it has overthrown, revive in a moment, along with that ignorance and imbecility, against which it is the only safeguard."[11]

In a reflection equally applicable today, Francis Holt, in a treatise on the law of libel, published in Dublin in 1812, and a standard work in its time, remarked:

> "[I]t was from the press that originated ... the main distinction of the ancient and modern world, public opinion ... is it possible that a Nero or Tiberius would be suffered to live or reign?"[12]

Whatever the answer may be to that question, there can be no doubt that independent media are the first guarantor of freedom of expression. They have become the main vehicle for the dissemination and exchange of information and ideas, particularly for public discussion and debate of governmental and social policy. As Anthony Lewis, distinguished columnist of the *New York Times*, put it:

> "We value the freedom in part because of its liberating spirit ... but more and more we are concerned with the social function of free speech: to assure that in a political system intended to be responsive to the public will, public opinion is informed. In a word, the purpose is accountability. Government must be accountable for what it does, and there can be no accountability in the dark.
>
> The press and the citizen critic of government need freedom to speak not only as a negative check to prevent corruption or abuse of power. We believe affirmatively that better policy will emerge where there is a choice among possibilities. Wisdom is more likely to come from open debate."[13]

---

[11] John Stuart Mill, "Law of Libel and Liberty of the Press" in John M. Robson (ed.), *Essays on Equality, Law and Education* (University of Toronto Press, Toronto, 1980), p.3, at p.34.

[12] Francis Holt, *The Law of Libel* (1st ed., Reed, London; Phelan, Dublin, 1812), pp.39–40, cited in Mill, above, n.11, at p.18.

[13] Anthony Lewis, "John Foster Memorial Lecture 1987" 9 *London Review of Books*, No.21, 26 (November 1987). See also Anthony Lewis, *Make No Law* (Vintage Books, New York, 1992).

The European Court of Human Rights has repeatedly spoken of the watchdog role of the media. In a 1994 media case, *Jersild v Denmark*,[14] involving a broadcast interview with a group of youths known as the "Greenjackets", who made racist remarks carried in the programme, the Court once again emphasised the important role of the media:

> "Not only does the press have the task of imparting such information and ideas [*i.e.* of public interest], the public also has a right to receive them. Were it otherwise, the press would be unable to play its vital role of 'public watchdog'. ...
> Although formulated primarily with regard to the print media, these principles doubtless apply also to the audio-visual media."[15]

Indeed the court went further and declared that the methods of objective and balanced reporting may vary according to the particular medium and other factors, and that it is not, therefore, for the courts to substitute their own views for those of the press as to what technique of reporting should be adopted by journalists. For instance: "News reporting based on interviews, whether edited or not, constitutes one of the most important means whereby the press is able to play its vital role of public watchdog."[16]

These are important and real functions of the media, and the European Court of Human Rights has adopted a positive and practical attitude to them.

For media critics, however, the reality is that lofty ideals do not always triumph in practice.[17] "How free should the press be?" ran an advertisement in *Times Mirror* in the US some years ago, "Is it [the press] Frankenstein's monster in disguise – a well-meaning but socially disruptive force?"[18] Whatever the answer, technological capabilities and market forces have played a part in reshaping the media. The function of the media nowadays is still communication, but it is communication that increasingly includes entertainment, not just information.[19]

Technological development and the resulting globalisation have brought with them the need for forward planning to cope with the new problems and situations that will arise. The movement away from independence to the interdependence of states, brought about in no small part by media technology, has raised issues of transnational regulation of the media. The imbalance in world communications, identified by the United Nations in the 1970s, has had to be addressed.[20] The concept of state sovereignty over information and the

---

[14] Series A, No.298; (1995) 19 E.H.R.R. 1.

[15] *ibid.* at para. 31.

[16] *ibid.* at para. 35.

[17] See the remarks about the shortcomings of the press by Watergate journalist, Carl Bernstein, *Let in the Light* (Brandon Books, Dingle, 1993), at p.17.

[18] Times Mirror, *We're Interested in What you Think* (The Times Mirror Co., Los Angeles, 1987), p.4; also Times Mirror, *The People and the Press* (The Times Mirror Co., Los Angeles, 1986).

[19] Above, n.10, Hoffmann-Riem.

[20] The MacBride Report, *Many Voices, One World* (UNESCO, New York, 1980), particularly "Issues of Common Concern", p.105; "Communication Tomorrow", p.191.

media has been overtaken by the capabilities of satellite communication and the internet. The opportunity and power to regulate and control content have diminished as satellite transmissions and the worldwide web transcend national boundaries. Technological development, therefore, offers new possibilities, and presents new challenges, but it also necessitates a reappraisal of existing structures, regulations and, consequently, laws.

1.5 WHAT IS LAW?

Law is essentially a body of rules and principles that authorise, guide, dictate, limit or prohibit behaviour in support of certain values or objectives in society. Those rules come from a variety of sources, national and international. In Ireland, Bunreacht na hÉireann, the Constitution of 1937, is the fundamental law of the land and other national laws must conform with it. These include statutes and case law. Statutes (also called legislation or acts of parliament, for example, the Broadcasting Acts) are written law in fixed format passed by the legislature or lawmaking body of the State (in Ireland's case, the Oireachtas). Case law, or judge-made law, comprises rules and principles devised by judges in actual court cases, which are subsequently relied upon and developed by other courts to meet new situations as they arise. For example, the neighbour principle formulated by Lord Atkin in the case of *Donoghue v Stevenson*,[21] which held the manufacturer liable for a faulty product that caused harm to the consumer, was relied on in later cases to impose liability also on suppliers, providers of services, doctors, lawyers, accountants and other professionals on whose skill and advice their clients depended and who suffered if that skill or advice was given negligently. The law of defamation (causing harm to a person's reputation or good name), for example, is made up mostly of judge-made rules derived from court cases and legislation, in particular the Defamation Act 1961.

European Community law has also become an important source of law in recent decades. The EEC Treaty, which formed the framework of the Community and was subsequently developed by the adoption of further treaties, such as the Maastricht and Amsterdam Treaties, is put into effect through legislation, usually in the form of Regulations or Directives. Regulations are automatically applicable rules made in accordance with the Treaty, while Directives are rules that Member States are required to introduce into their domestic law within a period of two years or so. Questions or disputes regarding the Treaty and its implementation are referred to the European Court of Justice in Luxembourg.

International human rights instruments have an impact on national laws too. For instance, Ireland has signed and ratified the European Convention on Human Rights and the International Covenant on Civil and Political Rights. As a result, Ireland has obligations to protect human rights. Those rights include rights to freedom of expression, privacy and fair trial, all of which have implications for the media. (For further discussion, see Chapter 2.)

---

[21] *Donoghue v Stevenson* [1932] A.C. 562.

The law covers the broad spectrum of everyday activities, from road traffic regulations and accidents to shopping and consumer contracts, from health and safety at work to what can or cannot be shown on television. It is also an instrument to determine the structures and functioning of states and governments and to determine agreements and conflicts among nations and the rights of their citizens. Law is therefore wide-ranging and difficult to define with any degree of precision. It can, however, be categorised according to its social function, sphere of application or historical origins.

1.5.1 Divisions of Law

1.5.1.1 Common-Law and Civil-Law Traditions

There are distinct traditions or families of law, principally the common-law and civil-law systems. The common law, which is the system of developing legal rules by following judicial decisions, is native to Britain but has spread to the Commonwealth and most of the English-speaking world. Ireland, as Britain's immediate neighbour, inherited the common-law system. Common law is variously known as "case law" or "judge-made law" because it emanates from judgments delivered in actual court cases.

The rules and principles formulated in the context of judgments in court cases act as precedents that judges hearing later cases rely on to reach their decision. Precedents may be binding or persuasive. The core principle(s) of a case, such as the neighbour principle in *Donoghue v Stevenson* mentioned previously, which is formulated and handed down by a higher court to a lower court in the courts system and which is relevant to the new case at hearing, is binding. On the other hand, decisions of lower courts in the system or of foreign national courts are not binding but may be of persuasive value, to be relied on by judges in subsequent court cases, if helpful to them in reaching a verdict. The laws of the European Community are binding as a condition of membership. The Irish Constitution was amended to provide accordingly (Article 29.4.5). Otherwise, international treaties, sometimes called conventions or covenants, and in essence agreements between nations, are not binding as part of domestic law unless specifically declared to be binding by the Oireachtas in accordance with Article 29.6 of the Irish Constitution.

The other principal family of law is the civil-law tradition, which has its origins in the law of ancient Rome, preserved in codes (written lists of rules) and expounded in the universities of medieval Europe. This is the tradition prevalent in continental Europe today. The codes, which are updated at intervals, remain the central source of legal rules. Decisions in court cases are less important as a source. Ireland, like the countries of mainland Europe and the United States, has a written constitution, setting out the state structures (government, legislature, court system) and guarantees of the fundamental rights of the citizen.

1.5.1.2 Common Law and Equity

Further distinctions are made within the common-law system between common law and equity. The rules of equity, which came to supplement the common law, grew out of appeals to the fairness (*i.e.* "equity") of the situation addressed to the Lord Chancellor, the official known as the keeper of the king's conscience, when the common-law courts failed to provide a remedy. In the early days of its operation, the common law was very rigid. It was based on a writ system, that is, the right to bring a case before the common-law courts depended on a person being able to obtain a writ or order issued in the name of the king, obliging the defendant to appear in court to answer the allegations against him. If the facts of the case did not fit within the terms of an existing writ, one was left without a remedy. In time, new types of writs were made available and the system began to develop and become less rigid. However, to bridge the gaps left in the common-law system, equity developed into a separate area of law with its own remedies and procedures, administered in the Court of Chancery (called after the Lord Chancellor). In the nineteenth century, in a restructuring of the court system under the Judicature Acts, equity merged with the common law but remained the source of remedies such as injunctions. Injunctions are court orders requiring a person to do something or to refrain from doing something. (For a fuller discussion of injunctions, see Chapter 6.)

1.5.1.3 Public and Private Law

Areas of law that impinge on the community at large and in which the community or public has an interest are known collectively as "public law". Public law includes constitutional law, the administration of government and criminal law, where the public interest lies in the detection and punishment of crime, the deterrence of criminal acts and the protection of the community. Private law, on the other hand, refers mainly to relations, agreements and disputes between individuals in which the state or community has no interest.

1.5.1.4 Civil and Criminal Law

The word "civil" is also used to describe private law, in particular to differentiate between civil and criminal law and the different court procedures that apply. Civil law encompasses torts (civil wrongs between individuals) such as trespass, negligence and, of particular interest in media terms, defamation. Criminal law involves the commission of offences, like drunken driving or breach of the peace which are provided for in statute law or common law, which also set out penalties. The main remedy for breach of the civil law is money – referred to as compensation or damages, while fines and imprisonment are the main sanctions imposed by the criminal law. A newspaper or broadcaster found by a court to have defamed an individual may have to pay compensation to that person. A newspaper or broadcaster found to be in contempt of court for publishing material deemed prejudicial to a court case might be subjected to a fine.

1.5.2 How Is the Law Implemented?

1.5.2.1 The Courts System

In Ireland, there is a hierarchical courts system. At the bottom is the District Court, presided over by a single judge, no jury, which deals with minor cases, both civil and criminal. The District Court can award compensation up to a maximum of €6,348.69[22] in civil cases and impose fines of up to €1,904 for each offence along with, or instead of, prison sentences of up to one year in criminal cases. Appeals from decisions of the District Court in minor matters lie to the Circuit Court. More serious cases can begin in the Circuit Court, which also hears both civil and criminal cases. In civil cases heard in the Circuit Court there is no jury, but in criminal cases a jury of twelve people, drawn at random from the electoral register, can bring in a verdict of guilty or not guilty on a unanimous or majority (11 to 1 or 10 to 2) basis. When the Circuit Court is hearing criminal cases, it is known as the Circuit Criminal Court. In civil cases, the Circuit Court can award compensation up to €38,092.14,[23] while in criminal cases, the upper limit for fines and imprisonment is usually laid down in statute by the Oireachtas. Appeals from decisions of the Circuit Court lie to the High Court.

The most serious cases, both civil and criminal, can go directly to the High Court. In civil cases, there is no jury, except in a few tort cases such as defamation, and there is no limit on the amount of compensation that can be awarded. Juries were removed from personal injuries cases by the Courts Act 1988 as a result of intense lobbying by the insurance industry. They were retained in defamation cases in the belief that twelve ordinary people from the real world are better equipped to determine whether words are defamatory than is a single judge. Where there is a jury in civil cases, its function is to answer questions of fact, while questions of law fall to the judge. When engaged in hearing criminal cases, the High Court is known as the Central Criminal Court and a jury is present. The function of a jury in a criminal case is to decide innocence or guilt on the basis of the evidence presented in court. It is the function of the judge to sentence the guilty. Appeals from the decision of the High Court in civil cases are taken directly to the Supreme Court. In criminal cases, appeals lie to the Court of Criminal Appeal and sometimes also to the Supreme Court if there is a particularly important point of law at issue.

The Supreme Court is the highest court in the land and the court of final appeal. It has power to affirm, vary or reverse decisions of the lower courts and can vary the amount of compensation payable. Challenges to statute law or administrative decisions on constitutional grounds are brought in the High Court and, if necessary, to the Supreme Court on appeal. These courts have the power to strike down legislation as unconstitutional. When they do so they create a void that they cannot fill. The courts cannot substitute their own

---

[22] The amount was increased from £5,000 to €20,000 in the Courts and Court Officers Act 2002, Part IV, s.14 but the section has not yet been implemented.

[23] The amount was increased from £30,000 to €100,000 in the Courts and Court Officers Act 2002, Part IV, s.13 but the section has not yet been implemented.

wording for the wording they have found to be unconstitutional. This is because of the doctrine of separation of powers stated in the Constitution. Under that doctrine, power is divided among the three branches of government – the legislature, executive and judiciary – so as to prevent any of them having excessive power.

The High Court also has the power of judicial review, that is, the power to examine and, if necessary, vary or quash decisions of administrative officers, bodies and tribunals. Orders of *certiorari* (to quash a decision), *mandamus* (ordering a lower body to carry out some obligation it has failed to fulfil), *prohibition* (ordering it not to do something) and *habeas corpus* (an order to produce a person being held in detention so that the court can ascertain whether his/her detention is lawful) can be issued. These orders can be directed at government ministers or local authorities with statutory powers or tribunals, such as employment or planning tribunals, which have a judicial, quasi-judicial or administrative function. A decision of RTÉ, the Broadcasting Commission of Ireland or the Broadcasting Complaints Commission, for example, could be judicially reviewed.[24]

1.5.2.2 Procedure

In civil cases which involve individuals, the "plaintiff" is the person who sues, that is, who brings the court action. The person against whom the action is brought is called the "defendant". The plaintiff carries the burden of proving his/her case on the balance of probabilities, *i.e.* that it is more probable than not that the defendant was at fault or committed the wrong of which the plaintiff complained. The usual remedy sought is compensation, but injunctions can also be useful in many situations.

In criminal cases, the person charged with a criminal offence is prosecuted in the name of the people by the Director of Public Prosecutions. The prosecution carries the onus of proving the accused person guilty. Because a guilty verdict results in punishment, which in some cases involves deprivation of liberty, the burden of proof is higher in criminal cases than in civil, where the penalty is only payment of money as compensation for the harm done. In criminal cases, guilt must be proven beyond all reasonable doubt.

1.6 What is Media Law?

Where does media law fit into this overall picture? Media law is not a distinct division of law in the sense that the law of contract or torts is. It derives in part

---

[24] For example, the decision of RTÉ and the IRTC not to allow Gerry Adams's book of short stories, *The Street and Other Stories*, to be advertised on radio or television was judicially reviewed in 1993: *Brandon Book Publishers Ltd v RTÉ* [1993] I.L.R.M. 806; *Brandon Book Publishers Ltd v IRTC*, unreported, High Court, October 29, 1993. The decision of the Broadcasting Complaints Commission (BCC) in a complaint brought by Anthony Coughlan regarding the amount of time allocated to the "yes" and "no" sides in a referendum was judicially reviewed by the High Court in 1998 and its decision appealed to the Supreme Court: *Coughlan v RTÉ and BCC* [2000] 3 I.R. 1.

from all of the sources listed above: Constitution, statute, judicial decisions, European Community law and international conventions and covenants. It does not belong exclusively to the realm of either public law or private law. Instead it comprises elements of both. Similarly, some aspects are dealt with by the criminal law and others by the civil law. In short, media law is that myriad of laws that relate to the media and affect media activities.

1.6.1 The Constitution

The Constitution guarantees media rights and freedoms (Article 40.6.1) but indicates that they are not absolute and therefore authorises their restriction in support of other rights. Thus, the right of the media to convey information and ideas can be restricted in the interests of the good name of the individual (Article 40.3.2), the proper administration of justice (Article 34), public order and morality (Article 40.6.1.i), the authority of the state (Article 40.6.1.i), and so on. There are other rights that are protected by the Constitution but not spelt out in it. These are known as "unenumerated" or "unspecified" rights and are left to the courts to articulate. The source of unenumerated rights in the Constitution is Article 40.3.2. There it is stated that the state shall protect and vindicate "in particular" the life, person, good name, and property rights of every citizen. Use of the words "in particular" signals that other rights are protected in addition to those actually listed. Among the unenumerated rights recognised by the courts to date as entitled to constitutional protection are the rights to have a passport, to travel, to earn a living and to marital privacy.

1.6.2 Statute Law

The Constitution impinges on all areas of law. Statute law, passed in conformity with the Constitution, provides the framework for broadcasting, the setting up of the RTÉ Authority and Broadcasting Commission of Ireland, for example, and the Broadcasting Complaints Commission. Statute law sets out the roles and the procedures to be adopted by these bodies and the regulations and guiding principles for broadcasting. Other statutes, like the Offences against the State Acts 1939-98, or the Prohibition on Incitement to Hatred Act 1989, for example, are not aimed exclusively at the media but either contain specific provisions directed at the media or provisions that are broad enough to encompass the media.

1.6.3 Judge-Made Laws

Judges interpret the Constitution and legislation. It is judges in court cases who determine ultimately the scope of the constitutional guarantees and the application of statutory provisions. When the telephones of two journalists were tapped by order of the Minister for Justice, the journalists took a High Court case to determine that the Constitution protected the right to privacy and that their right to privacy in their telephone conversations had been infringed.[25] When Sinn Féin was refused airtime to make a party political

---

[25] *Kennedy and Arnold v Ireland* [1987] I.R. 587; [1988] I.L.R.M. 472.

broadcast before the general election of 1982, it brought a High Court case alleging that section 31 of the Broadcasting Authority Act 1960, as amended by the Broadcasting Authority (Amendment) Act of 1976, was unconstitutional.[26] The Supreme Court, on appeal, held that the section was constitutional.

Judge-made law is an important source of media law, particularly in those areas that are not governed by statute. For instance, the law on contempt of court is wholly judge-made; there is no contempt of court legislation in Ireland. Defamation is also largely the result of judicial decisions down through the centuries, although there is also an act, the Defamation Act 1961, which incorporates and modifies slightly some of the common-law or judge-made rules.

1.6.4 European Community Law

European Community law impinges on the business activities of the media, and European competition rules apply to media organisations as to other industries. Article 82 (formerly Article 86) of the EC Treaty prohibits the abuse of a dominant position, and was applied in the *Magill* TV listings case (discussed in Chapter 11). National governments and broadcasting organisations may not restrict the access of actual or potential competitors to the market such as in the Flemish television case 1991 and the EBU Eurosport case, 1991 (also discussed in Chapter 11).

Specifically, the EC Television without Frontiers Directive 1989, as amended in 1997, regards broadcasting as a service within the meaning of the EEC Treaty and lays down minimum rules to guarantee freedom of transmission and reception in broadcasting between Member States. The Directive applies only to television but includes transmission by wire, over the air or by satellite, in unencoded or encoded form (Article 1). A majority proportion of transmission time is to be devoted to European works (Article 4); advertising and sponsorship are regulated (Articles 10–18); Member States are to take appropriate measures to ensure that minors are protected from programmes that might seriously impair their physical, mental or moral development; incitement to hatred is specifically prohibited; a right of reply must be provided by all broadcasters in Member States.[27] In accordance with the Directive, provision for a right of reply was made in the Irish Broadcasting Act 1990; a code on advertising was devised by the Minister in 1995, and other requirements of the Directive have been implemented in the Broadcasting Act 2001.[28] Problems concerning the application of the provisions of the Directive, and EC law generally, are dealt with by the European Court of Justice.

---

[26] *State (Lynch) v Cooney* [1982] I.R. 337; [1983] I.L.R.M. 89. See further Chap.10.

[27] Arts 22–3. In comparison, see the European Convention on Transfrontier Television of the Council of Europe, discussed in Chap.11 below.

[28] See Chap.11 below.

1.6.5 International Conventions and Covenants

At the time of writing, Ireland is in the process of incorporating the European Convention on Human Rights into national law. The European Convention on Human Rights Bill, introduced in 2001, was passed in June 2003. Under the Act it will be possible for any person who believes that his/her rights, as protected by the Convention, have been infringed to raise the Convention issues directly in the Irish courts. Previously, it was necessary to exhaust one's domestic remedies in Ireland before making application to the European Court of Human Rights in Strasbourg. The Convention only had the status of guiding principle that our courts ought to follow, but were not obliged to follow. However, if the European Court of Human Rights in Strasbourg decided in a given case that a particular aspect or provision of Irish law was in breach of the Convention, an amendment would be required to bring Irish law into line with the Convention. In the *Norris* case,[29] for instance, the Court found that the criminalisation of homosexual activities between consenting adults in private was a breach of Article 8 of the Convention, which guarantees respect for private and family life, home and correspondence. The Oireachtas was then obliged to bring in amending legislation to give effect to the Court's decision. In *Open Door Counselling v Ireland*,[30] the European Court of Human Rights found that a ban on the provision of abortion information was in breach of the Convention, and Ireland was obliged to give effect to that decision. Indeed, it was a decision of that court also in a case brought by the *Sunday Times* newspaper that led to the passing of the Contempt of Court Act 1981 in Britain.[31] Other decisions of the Court have had major implications for the development of media law and will be discussed in the chapters that follow.

1.7 How does Media Law Operate in Practice?

Media law is implemented through the courts system, in either the civil or criminal courts, depending on the particular subject matter and type of case. As a general rule, minor cases are heard in the District Court. On occasion, journalists and publishers have been fined in the District Court, for breaches of the Official Secrets Act 1963, for example.[32] It would be more usual, however, for cases involving the media to be heard in the Circuit Court or High Court. Defamation cases, for example, are not heard in the District Court. The option for the plaintiff is to have his/her defamation action heard by a judge sitting alone in the Circuit Court with power to award up to €38,092.14 damages or to go for a High Court hearing in which a jury is entrusted to assess damages with no upper limit imposed. One of the relevant factors is, of

---

[29] *Norris v Ireland*, Series A, No.142; (1991) 13 E.H.R.R. 186.

[30] Series A, No.246; (1993) 15 E.H.R.R. 244.

[31] *The Sunday Times v UK*, Series A, No.30; (1980) 2 E.H.R.R. 245.

[32] *DPP v Independent Newspapers* (the Shergar case), reported in *The Irish Times*, February 8, 1984, July 20, 1984; *Irish Independent*, July 31, 1984. *DPP v Independent Newspapers*, (the Brinks-Allied bank robbery case), reported in *The Irish Times*, November 8, 1995, December 16, 1995. See Chap.10 below.

course, legal costs, which are much higher in the High Court. Also the time factor is a consideration. Circuit Court cases take on average one year to come to trial, whereas High Court cases take on average three years (see Chapter 4).

The common-law system administered by judges in court cases has traditionally been plaintiff-oriented. Individual rights protected by the Constitution, including the right to good name, have been zealously safeguarded by the courts and have tended to take precedence over press or media rights to freedom of expression. Legal rules and their implementation seek to achieve a balance between important competing rights: the rights of individuals on the one hand and those of the media or the public at large on the other. How that balance is achieved is important. The vulnerability of the individual in face of the powerful institutions of state, big business and media intrusion, must be recognised. But so, too, must the fact that the media perform a very valuable role on behalf of the public – they are the eyes and ears of the people and are therefore an essential component of a modern democratic society, as repeatedly underscored by the European Court of Human Rights.

The technological capabilities of the media and the centrality of their role make them a very different force today than they were in previous centuries, when many of the legal rules were drawn up. Some legal rules devised in the formative years of the print media (*e.g.* defamation and contempt of court) continue to be applied with little or no modification to the markedly different modern print media and to the audio-visual and electronic media, which were not even envisaged at the time. It is possible therefore that some of those rules have been overtaken by events and become anachronistic or worse, over-restrictive of one of the most vibrant forces in modern society. On the other side of the coin, it could be argued that some of the old rules, which suited a different era, are insufficiently strict and inadequate to protect the individual and public at large from "Frankenstein's monster in disguise".

Such arguments prompt the questions: What should the role of the law be? What are its objectives? It is safe to assume that the role of the law should not be confined to a negative role of curtailment but should have a positive function in promoting fundamental values. A positive regulatory framework for broadcasting, for example, can ensure that a variety of opinions is aired, that minority interests are catered for and so on. If one looks at the purpose of the various laws that affect the media, one sees a number of distinct objectives, which include:

1. Providing a constitution or framework to facilitate media activity, *e.g.* broadcasting

2. Regulating media activities and content in order to protect other rights, *e.g.* a person's reputation or privacy

3. Restricting the zone and nature of activity (time and place regulation) in order to safeguard particular values, *e.g.* the amount of advertising can be restricted so as not to interfere with the integrity of a programme

4. Deterring and punishing, *e.g.* for prejudicing a person's right to a fair trial, and

5. Remedying grievances, *e.g.* where there is a breach of contract or dispute
    as to copyright.

It is important, therefore, to assess the extent to which those objectives are
met in practice. The chapters that follow begin by addressing the nature and
scope of media rights and then sketching in the historical development of media
and law, how the media evolved and the response of law to the media. The
historical dimension contextualises and helps to explain the rationale of
particular legal rules that have survived into the modern era. It is then possible
to begin to assess whether that rationale is still valid and whether the means
used to achieve it are still effective or whether law reform is necessary.

Further Reading

Byrne, Raymond, and McCutcheon, Paul, *The Irish Legal System* (4th ed.,
    Butterworths, Dublin, 2001).
Euromedia Research Group, *The Media in Western Europe* (2nd ed., Sage
    Publications, London, 1997).
Horgan, John, *Irish Media: A Critical History Since 1922* (Routledge, London
    and New York, 2001).
Murphy, Yvonne, *Journalists and the Law* (2nd ed., Round Hall Sweet &
    Maxwell, Dublin, 2000).
Women on Air, *Training Resource Manual for the Independent Radio Sector
    in Ireland*, Module 1 – Law (Marie McGonagle), Galway: Open Learning
    Centre, National University of Ireland, Galway, 1999. Available (text only)
    at *www.irishmedialaw.com*.

CHAPTER TWO

Media Rights

2.1 INTRODUCTION

As discussed in Chapter 1, the role of law in relation to the media is not merely one of restriction. The media have positive rights that are recognised and protected by law. They are essentially rights that all individuals have, but certain of them become particularised to journalists, because of the nature of their work and the function they perform in a democracy on behalf of the citizenry. It is the very essence of human rights that they are universal, although their implementation may be on a national, regional or global basis. In Ireland, for instance, human rights are protected nationally by the Constitution of 1937, regionally by the European Convention on Human Rights 1950 (ECHR)[1] (drafted by the Council of Europe), and globally by the Universal Declaration of Human Rights 1948, the International Covenant on Civil and Political Rights 1966 (ICCPR) and the International Covenant on Economic, Social and Cultural Rights (ICESCR), also 1966, which were drafted under the auspices of the United Nations.

2.2 RIGHTS PROTECTED BY THE IRISH CONSTITUTION

2.2.1 Freedom of Expression

Article 40.6.1 of the Irish Constitution guarantees freedom to express opinions and convictions, subject to considerations of public order and morality:

> "The State guarantees liberty for the exercise of the following rights, subject to public order and morality:–
>
> (i) The right of the citizens to express freely their convictions and opinions.
>
> The education of public opinion being, however, a matter of such grave import to the common good, the State shall endeavour to ensure that organs of public opinion, such as the radio, the press, the cinema, while preserving their rightful liberty of expression, including criticism of Government policy, shall not be used to undermine public order or morality or the authority of the State.

---

[1] The full title of the Convention is: the Convention for the Protection of Human Rights and Fundamental Freedoms, 1950.

> The publication or utterance of blasphemous, seditious, or indecent matter is an offence which shall be punishable in accordance with law."

The formulation of this Article (40.6.1.i) is problematic on a number of fronts. To begin with, the right of the citizens is said to be to express "freely" their convictions and opinions, yet how can they be entitled to express them "freely" if the right is subject to public order and morality, as stated at the very beginning of the Article?[2] Also, if public order and morality are the only overriding interests expressly mentioned, is it intended that the expression of convictions and opinions should be unrestricted except when they endanger public order or morality? In that case, what about opinions based on erroneous information that tend to injure a person's good name or invade his/her privacy or prejudice his/her right to a fair trial, for example? As we shall see, this right to express "freely" one's convictions and opinions is in fact subject to a number of restrictions and considerations in practice. It is a qualified right, not an absolute right.

That said, there is a positive, though limited, right at the core of Article 40.6.1.i, which all citizens have, to express "freely" their thoughts, beliefs and views. It is a freedom to comment. Hence some doubt existed as to whether it included the freedom to express facts or to impart factual information. Some of the courts took the view that it did not and looked elsewhere in the Constitution for protection for factual information. They identified as the appropriate source of protection the unspecified right to communicate in Article 40.3.2.[3]

However, following some further High Court decisions that factual information was included,[4] the Supreme Court resolved the issue. It held in *Roy Murphy v IRTC*,[5] citing Barrington J. in *Irish Times Ltd v Judge Murphy*,[6] that Article 40.6.1.i did include the right to communicate facts. Barrington J. on behalf of the Court stated that Article 40.6.1 is concerned with the public activities of the citizen in a democratic society. The right is a right not only to communicate opinions but also to communicate the facts on which those opinions are based. If that means there is some overlap with the right to communicate implicitly protected by Article 40.3, "... so be it. The overlap

---

2   Costello J. in *AG v Paperlink* [1984] I.L.R.M. 373.

3   Above, n.2, *per* Costello J. at 381–2; Keane J. in *Oblique Financial Services Ltd v The Promise Production Co. Ltd* [1994] 1 I.L.R.M. 74; but see Eoin O'Dell, "Does Defamation Value Free Expression?" (1990) 12 D.U.L.J. 50 and Marc McDonald, "Defamation Report – A Response to the Law Reform Commission Report" (1992) 10 I.L.T. 270.

4   Carroll J. in *AG for England and Wales v Brandon Book Publishers Ltd* [1986] I.R. 597, [1987] I.L.R.M. 135; Geoghegan J. in *Goodman International v Hamilton (No.2)* [1993] 3 I.R. 307; *Burke v Central Television* [1994] 2 I.L.R.M. 161.

5   [1998] 2 I.L.R.M. 360, at 372–3.

6   [1998] 1 I.R. 359, [1998] 2 I.L.R.M. 161 – the Cork drugs case. See Chap.6 below. Indeed, in that case O'Flaherty J., at 395, also accepted that Art.40.6.1 was not confined to convictions and opinions. Denham J., at 399, accepted that it "may" include the publication of information, while Keane J., at 410, reserved the question for a case in which it arose. See also the analysis of the right to freedom of expression by Barrington J., *ibid.* at 403.

may result from the different philosophical systems from which the two rights derive" (at 372). An applicant may therefore be entitled to invoke both. Both, of course, are personal rights and can, in certain circumstances, be limited in the interests of the common good. Interestingly, the Court also held *obiter* that Article 40.6.1 extends to commercial speech. The Court doubted if the guarantee in Article 40.6.1 was confined to those who wished to influence public opinion. Thus an advertisement, though apparently directed at an individual consumer, may be included, whether intended to influence consumers generally or not.

Such clarification from the Supreme Court is welcome, since the formulation of the guarantee in Article 40.6.1.i is at best a tentative and qualified one.[7] The emphasis is on the limitations rather than the right itself. Even before the right is set out in the section, it is stated to be subject to "public order and morality". Those areas of restriction are then repeated in the clause referring to the media, along with such justificatory and qualifying phrases as "the education of public opinion", "the common good" and "their rightful liberty of expression". A further restriction, the authority of the State, is then added, followed at the end of the section by a rider that makes the publication or utterance of blasphemous, seditious or indecent matter an offence punishable in accordance with law.

However, the Supreme Court in *Heaney v Ireland*,[8] in a non-media context, accepted that a test of proportionality must apply in restricting constitutionally-protected rights. The test is one that is frequently adopted by the European Court of Human Rights. It was said by Costello J. in the High Court in *Heaney* (relying on the formulation of the Canadian Supreme Court) to contain "the notions of minimal restraint on the exercise of protected rights, and the exigencies of the common good in a democratic society. ... The objective of the impugned provision must be of sufficient importance to warrant overriding a constitutionally protected right". The means used must be proportionate in that they must:

"(a) be rationally connected to the objective and not be arbitrary, unfair or based on irrational considerations;
(b) impair the right as little as possible; and
(c) be such that their effects on rights are proportional to the objective" (at 607 and 431 respectively).

On the positive side also, the press is specifically mentioned in Article 40.6.1.i. Freedom of the press is acknowledged in Article 40.6.1.i, albeit in a type of parenthesis, in an instruction to the State to ensure that its own authority or public order or morality are not undermined by the press or other media. The

---

[7] "The text of Art.40.6.1 includes enough qualifications to leave in some doubt the commitment of the Constitution to full, democratic, freedom of thought and freedom of speech." – Desmond Clarke, "Section 31 and Censorship: A Philosophical Perspective" (1994) 12 I.L.T. 53.

[8] [1994] 3 I.R. 593, [1994] 2 I.L.R.M. 420 (High Court), [1997] 1 I.L.R.M. 117 (Supreme Court), regarding the right to silence as a "correlative right" to the right to freedom of expression: the right not to speak or communicate (O'Flaherty J. at 123, 126-7).

"rightful liberty" of the press, which includes criticism of government policy, we are told, has to be preserved, but the "education of public opinion" is so important that the onus is on the State to ensure that the organs of public opinion are not used to undermine the important values of public order, morality and the authority of the State. In that formulation, the burden is on the State not so much to safeguard the liberty of the press but rather to regulate its use in support of other specified interests. The formulation is unfortunate and does little to secure media freedoms. The result has been that, until recently, the courts did not pay much attention to the guarantee of freedom of expression, particularly in the media context. Other rights were allowed to take precedence over it. Long-standing common-law rules, such as defamation and contempt of court, were allowed to continue to operate unperturbed.

There were relatively few instances of the courts invoking Article 40.6.1.i in support of media freedom. In *X v RTÉ*,[9] McCarthy J. invoked the guarantee of freedom of expression to refuse an injunction to prevent RTÉ broadcasting a programme on the Birmingham bombings of 1974. Other examples include the High Court's refusal of an injunction to the Attorney General for England and Wales to prevent distribution of a book, *One Girl's War*, about the wartime activities of the British Secret Service, MI5.[10] In *Cullen v Tóibín*,[11] the Supreme Court took the view that a magazine article based on an interview with a witness in a murder case may have been in bad taste but that:

> "There is, however, the matter of the freedom of the press and of communication which is guaranteed by the Constitution and which cannot be lightly curtailed. Such can only be curtailed or restricted by the courts … where such action is necessary for the administration of justice."[12]

In recent years, arguments based on the constitutional guarantee of freedom of expression and the right to communicate have been raised much more frequently. The pleadings in defamation cases, in particular, often refer to the constitutional right to freedom of expression, as well as good name. The significance of the right to freedom of expression has also been addressed by the Supreme Court in cases such as *Irish Times Ltd v Judge Murphy*[13] and *de Rossa v Independent Newspapers*.[14]

---

[9] Supreme Court, March 27, 1990 *ex tempore*: *The Irish Times*, March 28, 1990. See also Raymond Byrne and William Binchy, *Annual Review of Irish Law* (Dublin, The Round Hall Press, 1990), p.534.

[10] *AG for England and Wales v Brandon Book Publishers Ltd* [1986] I.R. 597, at 602; [1987] I.L.R.M. 135, at 137–8.

[11] [1984] I.L.R.M. 577.

[12] *Per* O'Higgins C.J. at 582.

[13] Above, n.6.

[14] [1999] 4 I.R. 432. Indeed, this level of recourse to the constitutional guarantee is one of the biggest developments in media law in Ireland over the last two decades. Prior to that, the constitutional guarantee of freedom of expression was thought inconsequential and rarely raised or relied on, as practitioners and judges retained a preference for the operation of the common law, particularly in defamation cases.

2.2.2 Right to Good Name

While several areas of restriction on freedom of expression or of the press are specified in Article 40.6.1.i, others are not specified in that section. Among the restrictions not specified in Article 40.6.1.i is the right to good name, which is protected by Article 40.3.2 of the Constitution and operates in practice as the principal restriction on the day-to-day workings of the media:

> "The State shall, in particular, by its laws protect as best it may from unjust attack and, in the case of injustice done, vindicate the ... good name ... of every citizen."

Protection of good name is afforded in practice by the law of defamation, which is of common law origin and long predates the Constitution, but has been given a statutory basis in the Defamation Act 1961. The Defamation Act 1961, as a post-1937 statute, enjoys a presumption of constitutionality. However, it is out of date in many respects and amending legislation is long overdue. (See Chapter 4.)

2.2.3 Right to Fair Trial

The restriction of the media in the interests of the administration of justice is not expressly mentioned in Article 40.6.1.i either. O'Hanlon J. in *Desmond v Glackin (No. 1)*[15] considered that it came within the scope of the phrase "public order and morality" in Article 40.6.1.i. Otherwise, it is governed by Article 34.1:

> "Justice shall be administered in courts established by law ... and, save in such special and limited cases as may be prescribed by law, shall be administered in public."

Those "special and limited cases" may authorise the exclusion of the press from attending court cases, or may restrict what they may report in relation to court cases. (For further discussion see Chapters 6 and 7.)

2.2.4 Balancing Conflicting Rights

Normally, when two or more constitutionally-protected rights come into conflict, attempts must be made to harmonise or balance them. However, the restrictions specified in Article 40.6.1.i are presented in such a way as to suggest that they take precedence over the central right. The core value has thus been undermined and there has been a tendency until recently to invoke the restrictions to curtail freedom of expression and media activities, often without due consideration as to their proportionality or justification. That was particularly so in relation to good name, which tended to be given more weight in practice than freedom of expression. The Supreme Court in 1994, however,

---

[15] [1993] 3 I.R. 1; [1992] I.L.R.M. 490.

in *Burke v Central Television*,[16] a case concerning information used to make a television programme about the IRA, indicated that good name is not a trump card that must prevail over other rights.

The courts are often faced with a situation of competing rights. In *Burke*, the Court saw itself as being faced with a choice between rights:

> "The very unusual situation with which the court is faced in this case of choosing between a plausible risk to the lives of persons asserted on the basis that the plaintiffs if given a sight of documents might inform terrorists who would injure the parties identified in the documents on the one hand and the diminution of the capacity of the plaintiffs to protect and vindicate their good names on the other ...".[17]

The Court's decision was that the right to life and to bodily integrity took precedence over the rights to good name and access to documents: "... [I]t is more important to preserve life ... [I]f the right to life is under threat that is a more sacred right than the right of full and untramelled resort to the courts."[18]

One difficulty for the courts is that the Irish Constitution does not provide any mechanism for reconciling competing rights. In its formulation of the rights to good name and freedom of the press, in particular, the Constitution appears to reflect the *status quo*, derived from the long-standing British tradition that attached great importance to good name and relegated freedom of the press to the status of a residual right, to be considered only when all other rights and interests had been accounted for, and to be protected only to the extent that the law did not restrict it.

However, in recent years, due in some measure to the influence of Article 10 of the European Convention on Human Rights and the jurisprudence of the European Court of Human Rights, a more positive attitude to Article 40.6.1.i of the Irish Constitution has developed. The courts now speak much more readily of balancing rights, including the rights to freedom of expression and good name. As Hamilton C.J. stated in *de Rossa v Independent Newspapers*,[19] citing *Hynes-O'Sullivan v O'Driscoll*,[20] the law must "reflect a due balancing of the constitutional right to freedom of expression and the constitutional protection of every citizen's good name. This introduces the concept of proportionality which is recognised in our constitutional jurisprudence." In *Irish Times Ltd v Judge Murphy*, Denham J. said that where there are competing rights the court should give a "mutually harmonious application. If that is not possible the hierarchy of rights should be considered both as between the conflicting rights and the general welfare of society."[21] Following from *D v DPP*[22] and *Z v DPP*,[23] she established that the right to a fair trial and to fair

---

[16] [1994] 2 I.L.R.M. 161.
[17] *ibid.* at 177, Finlay C.J.
[18] *ibid.* at 185, O'Flaherty J.
[19] Above, n.14, at 449.
[20] [1988] I.R. 436, [1989] I.L.R.M. 349.
[21] Above, n.6, at 399, citing *People v Shaw* [1982] I.R. 1, at 56.
[22] [1994] 2 I.R. 465, *per* Denham J. at 474.
[23] [1994] 2 I.R. 476.

procedures is superior to the other rights in the balance. Those "other rights" include the community's right to prosecute, their right of access to the court, to information of the hearing, to the administration of justice in public, the community's freedom of expression and that of the press, and the right to communicate.[24]

In 2002, in a High Court application by two individuals seeking the right to take a case anonymously against the Ansbacher inspectors, McCracken J., in refusing the application, stated, *inter alia*, that if he had to consider a hierarchy of rights in the case – and he took the view that he did not – he had "no hesitation in saying that the right to have justice administered in public far exceeded any right to privacy, confidentiality or good name." Article 40.3 only applied "as far as practicable" and only protected citizens from "unjust attack". It was not an absolute guarantee and could not justify anonymity in court proceedings.[25]

2.2.5 The Right to Communicate

Communication is so central to our very existence and well-being as humans that it has been recognised as a basic human right. In Ireland, it has been recognised by the courts as one of the unspecified personal rights guaranteed protection by the Constitution in Article 40.3. It was first enunciated by Costello J. in *AG v Paperlink*[26] and reaffirmed by him in *Kearney v Ireland*.[27] In *Paperlink*, a case which concerned the state monopoly on postal communications under the Post Office Act 1908, Costello J. held:

> "[T]hat the act of communication is the exercise of such a basic human faculty that the right to communicate must inhere in the citizen by virtue of his human personality and must be guaranteed by the Constitution. ... The exercise of the right to communicate can take many forms ... I conclude that the very general and basic right to communicate which I am considering must be one of those personal unspecified rights of the citizen protected by Article 40.3.1."[28]

Such a right, however, is not absolute:

> "But the right to communicate is obviously not an absolute one. Laws may restrict the nature of the matter communicated (for example, by prohibiting the communication of confidential information or treasonable, blasphemous, obscene or defamatory matter) and laws may also restrict the mode of communication (for example, by prohibiting communication by advertisement contrary to the planning code or by radio contrary to

---

[24] At 399. *Cf.* Hamilton C.J. at 384–5, O'Flaherty J. at 392 and 394, where he speaks also of the right of the accused to have their cases reported in the press.

[25] *The Irish Times*, April 25, 2002. This case is discussed in Chap.6 below.

[26] Above n.2, at 381–2.

[27] [1986] I.R. 116, at 118–9.

[28] Above n.2, at 381.

wireless telegraphy regulations). It follows, therefore, that it is not correct, and indeed, can be misleading, to suggest that the defendants enjoy a right to communicate 'freely'. Along with other citizens they enjoy a right to communicate."[29]

There is a right to communicate, therefore, but it is not a right to communicate freely. The right in whatever form – freedom of expression, freedom to receive and impart information, freedom of the press – is not absolute and can legitimately be curtailed by law in order to protect other interests. The right to freedom of thought (to form and *hold* opinions and ideas)[30] is absolute, but freedom to manifest it through the communication of information and ideas to others is subject to consideration of other prevailing rights, such as the right to good name or fair trial.

There may be a case, however, for distinguishing between private communication and public communication.[31] Private communication occurs where people want to get things off their mind by telling them to others, confiding in them, or by seeking advice from them, and where it is not their wish to spread their opinion widely around. Such communication or expression, according to one leading commentator, requires the highest degree of protection.[32] Public communication, on the other hand, involves the desire to spread ideas or opinions, and includes professional communication by the media, advertisers and others.

The Irish Constitution does not appear to distinguish between private and public communication as such,[33] although it does recognise the need to protect

---

[29] Above n.2, at 382.

[30] See ECHR, Art.9 on freedom of thought: "1. Everyone has the right of freedom of thought, conscience and religion; this right includes freedom to change his religion or belief, and freedom, either alone or in a community with others and in public or private, to manifest his religion or belief, in worship, teaching, practice and observance. 2. Freedom to manifest one's religion or beliefs shall be subject only to such limitations as are prescribed by law and are necessary in a democratic society in the interests of public safety, for the protection of public order, health or morals, or for the protection of the rights and freedoms of others." Art.44.2.1 of the Irish Constitution says that "freedom of conscience and the free profession and practice of religion are, subject to public order and morality, guaranteed to every citizen".

[31] See Henry G. Schermers, "Freedom of Expression" in Liz Heffernan (ed.), *Human Rights: A European Perspective* (The Round Hall Press, Dublin, 1994), p.201. One illustration of such a distinction in our law is that between slander and libel in defamation law (see Chap.4) and also to some extent the common-law qualified privilege as a defence to a defamation action. Thus, communications between husband and wife, employer and employee or secretary are privileged. The distinction between private and public communication is apparent if, as the courts seem to suggest, the qualified privilege defence is available only to limited communication and does not extend to media communication to the world at large – but see further Chap.4 below for discussion of the House of Lords' decision in *Reynolds v Sunday Times* [1999] 4 All E.R. 609.

[32] Schermers, *op. cit.*, at pp.203–5. On the right not to communicate, to keep matters private, see above, n.8, and Eoin O'Dell, "When Two Tribes go to War: Privacy Interests and Media Speech" in McGonagle (ed.), *Law and the Media* (Round Hall Sweet & Maxwell, Dublin, 1997), p.181, at p.242, n.368.

[33] But see the view of the Supreme Court in *Roy Murphy v IRTC* [1998] 2 I.L.R.M. 360 at 372 that Art.40.6.1 is concerned with the public activities of the citizen in a democratic

certain communications, such as reports and publications of the Oireachtas and utterances made in either House thereof, in the interests of frank and open parliamentary debate (Article 15.12). The Supreme Court has also pronounced in favour of Cabinet confidentiality in order to protect internal discussions within government, and an amendment to that effect has been inserted in the Constitution following a referendum in 1997.[34] Cabinet decisions, however, are not protected. Private communications, such as private telephone conversations, are protected as part of the general, unspecified right to privacy in Article 40.3.2 of the Constitution.[35]

The nature of the right to communicate was considered by Barrington J. in *Irish Times Ltd v Judge Murphy.*[36] He concluded that it must include not only the right to communicate facts but also convictions, opinions and even feelings. In some respects, therefore, the rights to communicate and to freedom of expression may overlap and may be complementary but the latter is primarily concerned with the public statements of the citizen.

2.2.6 The Right to be Informed

Denham J. in *de Rossa v Independent Newspapers*[37] also spoke of a "right to information" as one of the "relevant unspecified rights" protected by Article 40.3.1 of the Constitution. While she did not define the right, she did go on to state that the rights protected by Article 10 of the European Convention on Human Rights are similar to the rights of freedom of expression and "freedom to be informed" under the Irish Constitution. She appears therefore to have in mind the right of the public to be informed as a corollary of the right to freedom of expression, and seems to imply that that right under the Irish Constitution is coextensive with the right under Article 10 of the European Convention on Human Rights. Hamilton C.J., in *Irish Times Ltd v Judge Murphy*[38] referred to the public's right to know and be informed by the media but without designating it as an unspecified right in the Constitution in the way that Denham

---

society and that is why the framers of the Constitution grouped the right to freedom of expression, the right to free assembly and the right to form associations and unions in the one subsection. All three rights relate to the practical running of a democratic society. They are part of the dynamics of political change, as Barrington J. stated in *Irish Times Ltd v Judge Murphy*, above n.6, at 404: "They are at once both vitally important to the success of a democracy and potentially a source of political instability. That is why the Constitution and the European Convention both assert and circumscribe them. That is also why it is so important to get the balance right in interpreting them."

[34] *AG v Hamilton (No.1)* [1993] 2 I.R. 250, [1993] I.L.R.M. 81 and 17th Amendment to the Constitution, Art.28.4.3.

[35] *Kennedy and Arnold v Ireland* [1987] I.R. 587; [1988] I.L.R.M. 472.

[36] Above, n.6, at 405-6.

[37] Above, n.14, at 473. The case concerned the quantum of damages in a defamation case and whether guidelines should be given to juries to assist them in arriving at the appropriate amount of damages.

[38] Above, n.6, at 381, 383, 385; *cf.* O'Flaherty J., *ibid.* at 394: "the public are entitled to know what goes on in courts of law", and at 396: "The public have both a right and a responsibility to be kept informed of what happens in our courts." Note also the view of the Canadian Supreme Court that freedom of expression protects listeners as well as speakers: *Ford v Quebec (AG)* [1988] 2 S.C.R. 712, at 767.

J. did in *de Rossa*. Keane J., in the same case, recognised such a right in relation to the courts derived from Article 34.[39] In dealing with the specific issues before her in *de Rossa*, Denham J. went on to say (at 477) that information does not fetter discretion, and that specific information would aid decision-making. Both observations could apply to the broader issue of information being made available to the public.

2.3 RIGHTS PROTECTED BY INTERNATIONAL HUMAN RIGHTS INSTRUMENTS

One of our concerns in the chapters that follow will be the level of recognition and protection afforded the above values in the Irish Constitution and the extent to which they are reflected in legal rules and practice. How strong or effective are the constitutional guarantees and to what extent have they been litigated? How do they compare with the protection provided by the international human rights instruments, the European Convention on Human Rights, the Universal Declaration of Human Rights and the International Covenant on Civil and Political Rights? Is there a similar balance or system for reconciling conflicting rights in those instruments? One thing is clear from the international human rights instruments: the media have certain defined rights but they are far from absolute. They are subject to restrictions that are wide-ranging but narrowly prescribed.

2.3.1 The European Convention on Human Rights

The European Convention on Human Rights (ECHR), which Ireland has ratified and agreed to be bound by, affects Irish law in a number of ways. In the past, it was not part of the domestic law and not directly applicable in Irish courts in the way that European Community law is. A Bill to incorporate it into Irish law was introduced in the Oireachtas in 2001. It lapsed with the General Election of 2002 but was revived and passed in June 2003. The Convention could, however, be referred to in the Irish courts even prior to the Act and relied on by judges for guiding principle. This happened in a number of media cases. In *Desmond v Glackin (No. 1)*,[40] for example, which concerned contempt of court, O'Hanlon J. relied on the Convention and its application in *The Sunday Times (No. 1) v United Kingdom*,[41] a case which challenged the granting of a court injunction to prevent the applicant newspaper publishing articles on the thalidomide drug tragedy and the quest of the victims for compensation. In

---

[39] *Irish Times Ltd v Judge Murphy*, above, n.6, Keane J. at 409: "the right of the public to know what is happening in our courts, a right which is clearly recognised and guaranteed by Article 34."

[40] Above, n.15, at 26–9. In another case in which journalist Barry O'Kelly refused to divulge his sources, the attention of the Circuit Court judge was drawn to the decision of the European Court of Human Rights in *Goodwin v UK*, App. No.17488/90, (1996) 22 E.H.R.R. 123. The Attorney General was invited to present the *Goodwin* arguments. The judge then decided that it was not necessary for the journalist to reveal his sources and that he was not in contempt of court.

[41] Series A, No.30; [1980] 2 E.H.R.R. 245, paras 6–7.

Roy Murphy v IRTC,[42] Geoghegan J. in the High Court stated that regard can and should be had to the Convention "when considering the nature of a fundamental right and perhaps more particularly the reasonable limitations which can be placed on the exercise of that right". Similarly, the Supreme Court in the defamation case *de Rossa v Independent Newspapers*[43] accepted that regard could be had to Article 10.

In that way, the Convention operated as a yardstick to measure the adequacy of the protection for human rights in national laws and to determine an appropriate level of protection where national laws are undeveloped. Second, it operated as a kind of outer layer of protection for Irish citizens who felt aggrieved that their human rights were being infringed and who could not obtain appropriate redress in the national courts. As long as they had exhausted their domestic remedies, they could take their complaint to Strasbourg, initially to the Commission of Human Rights, alleging a breach of the provisions of the Convention.

In recent years, the situation has changed. First of all, the Strasbourg mechanisms have been restructured. Instead of a two-tier process of Commission and Court, the Commission was abolished in 1998,[44] and complaints that satisfy the criteria can now go directly to the European Court of Human Rights. The situation in Ireland is also set to change. Following enactment of the European Convention on Human Rights Act 2003, the Convention will be incorporated into Irish law at sub-constitutional level, on the interpretative model, similar to the Human Rights Act 1998 in the UK. That means that the Irish Constitution will continue to take priority, but that the Convention can be relied on in Irish courts, which can declare that an Irish law or practice is incompatible with the Convention. Where such a finding is made, litigants may receive compensation for breach of their rights under the Convention.

However, under the Act, a finding that a law is incompatible with the Convention will not mean that the law in question will be struck down as invalid or will cease to operate. It will be a matter for the Government to decide whether to amend it or what steps to take to remedy the incompatibility in question. The Convention is not, therefore, being given the force of law in Ireland. A lesser step has been taken and it may well be in some instances that litigants will still find themselves having to take the long and arduous road to Strasbourg to assert their rights. The Government justifies the manner of incorporation of the Bill as being in accordance with the state's dualist doctrine on the giving of effect to international obligations and the primary role of the

---

[42] [1997] 2 I.L.R.M. 467, at 476. The *Murphy* case was appealed to the Supreme Court ([1999] 1 I.R. 12), which upheld Geoghegan J.'s decision. For discussion of the decision of the European Court of Human Rights in the case, see below Chap.8.

[43] Above, n.14. See also *Carrigaline Community Television Broadcasting v Minister for Transport, Energy and Communications* [1997] 1 I.L.R.M. 241. On the status of the ECHR in Irish law, see Donncha O'Connell, "The Irish Constitution and the ECHR: Belt and Braces or Blinkers?" (2000) I.H.R.R. 82.

[44] Protocol No.11 to the Convention, restructuring the control machinery established thereby (European Treaty Series No.155). See generally Clare Ovey & Robin White, *Jacobs & White: European Convention on Human Rights* (3rd ed., Oxford University Press, Oxford, 2002), Chap.24.

Oireachtas in that regard.[45] The Act applies to all organs of the State, a term which is narrowly defined, thus reducing the scope of application. It does not apply to private bodies, and the courts themselves are excluded, ostensibly because they are already mandated to administer justice in accordance with the provisions of the law and the Constitution.

Ireland is the last of the current 45 Member States of the Council of Europe to incorporate the Convention into its domestic law; the United Kingdom did so with the Human Rights Act 1998, which came into force in October 2000, and applies also in Northern Ireland. Under the Belfast Agreement, the Irish Government was committed to bringing forward measures to strengthen and underpin the constitutional protection of human rights in the State, which would draw on the provisions of the European Convention on Human Rights. Under the Agreement these measures were to ensure an equivalent level of protection of human rights as would pertain in Northern Ireland. The provisions of the European Convention on Human Rights Bill 2001 would, according to the introduction to the explanatory memorandum, ensure that there are "two complementary systems" in place in Ireland.

It is important for the media that the Convention be incorporated because of the extent of protection afforded to freedom of expression under Article 10 of the Convention, and the wealth of jurisprudence from the European Court of Human Rights in interpreting and applying it in cases involving the media. Indeed, the Constitution Review Group (CRG), which reported in 1996, recognised the shortcomings of Article 40.6.1.i of the Constitution and recommended that it be replaced by a provision modelled on Article 10.[46]

The article of the Convention that protects media rights is Article 10, which states:

> "1 . Everyone has the right to freedom of expression. This right shall include freedom to hold opinions and to receive and impart information and ideas without interference by public authority and regardless of frontiers. This Article shall not prevent States from requiring the licensing of broadcasting, television or cinema enterprises.

---

[45] For a detailed critique of the Bill see: The Human Rights Commission, *Submission to the Committee on Justice, Equality, Defence and Women's Rights on the European Convention on Human Rights Bill 2001* (June 2002) available at *www.homepage.tinet.ie/~ihrc/echrbill.htm*); The Bar Council's submission (*The Irish Times*, July 12, 2001); Donncha O'Connell, "The Incorporation of the European Convention on Human Rights into Irish Law: Clever and Elegant or Too Clever by Half?" (Brian Walsh Memorial Lecture 2002, Irish Society for European Law, Dublin, November 26, 2002, unpublished).

[46] *Report of the Constitution Review Group* (Dublin, Government Publications, Pn.2632, 1996) at pp.291–304. However, that in itself could be problematic, and it would seem preferable to incorporate Art.10 as it stands, since it is on the wording and *schema* of Art.10 that the comprehensive jurisprudence of the European Court of Human Rights on freedom of expression issues is based. Gerard Hogan, himself a member of the CRG, has stated in "The Belfast Agreement and the Future Incorporation of the European Convention of Human Rights in the Republic of Ireland" (1999) 4 B.R. 205, that Art.10 and the jurisprudence that has grown up around it is "one of the great glories of the European Court" (at p.206).

2. The exercise of these freedoms, since it carries with it duties and responsibilities, may be subject to such formalities, conditions, restrictions or penalties as are prescribed by law and are necessary in a democratic society, in the interests of national security, territorial integrity or public safety, for the prevention of disorder or crime, for the protection of health or morals, for the protection of the reputation or rights of others, for preventing the disclosure of information received in confidence, or for maintaining the authority and impartiality of the judiciary."

The formulation of the right to freedom of expression in the Convention contrasts starkly with that of the Irish Constitution. In the Convention, the right is stated boldly and positively in paragraph 1, unencumbered by any mention of restrictions, other than the power to license particular forms of media. The ambit of the right is clearly set out: it includes factual information, the right to receive and impart information, as well as opinions and ideas. The reference to broadcasting, television and cinema makes it evident that the media are contemplated as coming within the scope of the guarantee and can rely on it for protection. The restrictions on the right are then set out in paragraph two. They are wide-ranging but the reason for them is stated (the duties and responsibilities that exercise of the freedom of expression carries with it), as are the conditions for invoking them (they must be prescribed by law, be necessary in a democratic society, and be invoked in support of the interests specified in the paragraph).

The European Court of Human Rights has consistently interpreted Article 10 in a manner that recognises and values the role of the media in a democratic society. That is not to say that all cases involving the media have been decided in their favour. Much depends on the subject matter of the complaint and the circumstances of the interference with the right to freedom of expression. Commercial expression and artistic expression are less protected than political matters or matters of public concern.[47]

In relation to moral issues, for example, the Court appears to accord states greater scope – a wider margin of appreciation – and is less likely to interfere with their decisions. Several cases illustrating the point will be discussed in later chapters.[48] The same has been true of restrictions invoked in support of state security. The European Court has tended to take the view that states themselves are in the best position to decide the degree of protection they

---

[47] For an analysis of the approach of the Court, and the application of the margin of appreciation, see the cases discussed in Chaps 8 and 9 below, and Paul Mahoney, "Universality versus Subsidiarity in the Strasbourg Case Law on Free Speech: Explaining Some Recent Judgments" [1997] E.H.R.L.R. 364.

[48] See *Gay News Ltd and Lemon v UK* (1983) 5 E.H.R.R. 123; *Choudhury v UK*, App. No.17439/90 (both declared inadmissible by the Commission); *Handyside v UK*, Series A, No.24, (1979) 1 E.H.R.R. 737; *Müller v Switzerland*, Series A, No.133, (1991) 13 E.H.R.R. 212; *Otto Preminger Institut v Austria*, Series A, No.295-A, (1995) 19 E.H.R.R. 34; *Wingrove v UK* (1997) 24 E.H.R.R. 1; *VGT v Switzerland* (2002) 34 E.H.R.R. 4 at para.71.

require. *Purcell v Ireland*,[49] a case concerning section 31 of the Broadcasting Act 1960, as amended, was declared inadmissible by the European Commission on that basis and so did not go forward to the Court for decision. However, in *Spycatcher (The Observer and Guardian v UK)*,[50] the Court for the first time indicated that in certain circumstances government restrictions invoking state security could fall foul of the necessity test in Article 10(2). *Spycatcher* therefore broke new ground but still signalled a minimalist approach on the part of the Court (see further Chapter 10).

Nonetheless, the strength of the media protection can be gauged from cases such as *Handyside v UK*.[51] There the Court acknowledged that national legislatures and courts are the first arbiter and enjoy a margin of appreciation as regards both the framing of national law and its implementation, but went on to emphasise its own supervisory role:

> "The Court's supervisory functions oblige it to pay the utmost attention to the principles characterising a 'democratic society'. Freedom of expression constitutes one of the essential foundations of such a society, one of the basic conditions for its progress and for the development of every man. Subject to Article 10.2 it is applicable not only to 'information' or 'ideas' that are favourably received or regarded as inoffensive or as a matter of indifference, but also to those that offend, shock or disturb the State or any sector of the population. Such are the demands of that pluralism, tolerance and broadmindedness without which there is no 'democratic society'" (para.49).

The direct application of that approach to the media can be seen in a line of cases from *Handyside* to *Jersild v Denmark*.[52] More recently, the Court in *De Haes & Gijsels v Belgium*[53] stressed again that the role of the press as "public watchdog" is essential in a democratic society. Other media issues addressed have included protection of journalists' sources (*Goodwin v UK*[54]) and levels of damages in defamation cases (*Tolstoy Miloslavsky v UK*[55]). The first Irish case involving the media to have been decided in Strasbourg was *Purcell v Ireland*,[56] the case that challenged section 31, the broadcasting ban (above). A decision in *Roy Murphy v IRTC*[57] was given in July 2003. A defamation case, *Independent Newspapers v Ireland*,[58] is pending.

---

[49] (1991) 12 H.R.L.J. 254.

[50] Series A, No.216; (1992) 14 E.H.R.R. 153.

[51] *Handyside v UK*, Series A, No.24; (1979) 1 E.H.R.R. 737.

[52] Series A, No.298; (1995) 19 E.H.R.R. 1.

[53] (1998) 25 E.H.R.R. 1, at para.37.

[54] (1996) 22 E.H.R.R. 123.

[55] Series A, No.316-B; (1996) 20 E.H.R.R. 442; [1996] E.M.L.R. 152.

[56] (1991) 12 H.R.L.J. 254.

[57] Above, n.42.

[58] The case is *de Rossa v Independent Newspapers*, above, n.14. A High Court jury awarded politician, Proinsias de Rossa £300,000 compensation in 1997, a sum that the Supreme Court upheld in 1999 – see further Chap.4. The size of the award is now being challenged in the European Court of Human Rights.

Another Irish case involving freedom of expression in a non-media situation, namely the provision of abortion information, *Open Door Counselling v Ireland*,[59] was decided by the Court, which held that the injunction imposed on the applicant clinics by the Irish courts amounted to a violation of Article 10. The essence of Article 10 is that freedom of expression is the rule – the key value – and limitations on it are the exception. The Court has said that in evaluating a particular restriction it is faced "not with a choice between two conflicting principles but with a principle of freedom of expression that is subject to a number of exceptions which must be narrowly interpreted".[60] The areas of limitation specified in paragraph 2 cover a wide range of competing interests but their application is constrained by the requirements that they:

- be prescribed by law,
- have a legitimate aim, *i.e.* be invoked in support of one of the specified interests (as set out above),
- be necessary in a democratic society.

It is for the Member State invoking a restriction to justify it by reference to these criteria. The European Court of Human Rights first establishes if there has been an interference with the applicant's freedom of expression; if so, it then considers each of the criteria. It is usually only the third of these criteria, the "necessity" requirement, that gives rise to difficulties.

2.3.1.1 Prescribed by Law

In *Sunday Times (No. 1)*[61] the Court interpreted the phrase "prescribed by law" to mean that the law authorising the restriction, whether written or unwritten, needed to be sufficiently clear and accessible, and the penalty reasonably foreseeable. It must be formulated with sufficient precision, the Court said, to enable the citizen to regulate his/her conduct. S/he must be able "if need be with appropriate advice – to foresee, to a degree that is reasonable in the circumstances, the consequences which a given action may entail". That reflects the principle of legal certainty, which is a feature of all legal systems. The Court also indicated that the term "prescribed by law" would include unwritten as well as written law. It would thus include the common law.

2.3.1.2 Legitimate Aim

In addition to being prescribed by law, the measure to be invoked to restrict press freedom must have a legitimate aim and be proportionate to that aim. A measure will be regarded as having a legitimate aim if it is clearly invoked in support of one of those interests specified in Article 10(2). The Court will consider whether the reasons put forward by the national authorities to justify

---

[59] Series A, No.246; (1993) 15 E.H.R.R. 244.
[60] *Sunday Times v UK*, Series A, No.30; (1980) 2 E.H.R.R. 245, at para.65.
[61] *ibid.* at paras 47–50.

the restriction are relevant and sufficient. In doing so, it will look at the case as a whole. Whether or not there was a real need for protection of the interest(s) specified must then be addressed in assessing the "necessity" of the interference.

2.3.1.3 Necessary in a Democratic Society

To be "necessary" in a democratic society, a restriction or limitation on freedom of expression or of the press must correspond to a "pressing social need". It is not enough that the restriction is desirable or reasonable; the necessity of the restriction must be convincingly established. By the same token, it does not have to be imperative or indispensable. In deciding if the interference is necessary, the Court will have regard to the facts and circumstances prevailing in the particular case before it. As well as being necessary, the measure must be proportionate and not overly broad.

In *Handyside*,[62] the fact that the book in question was aimed at children and adolescents weighed heavily with the Court. Similarly, the fact that the book *Spycatcher* had already been published in the United States, and that the information it contained was therefore already in the public domain, led to the Court's decision that an injunction at that stage was not necessary and amounted to a breach of Article 10.[63] National security was not at risk and the right of the press and public to the information outweighed the state's interest in protecting the reputation of its security services.[64] In *Tolstoy Miloslavsky v UK*, the amount of damages awarded in a defamation action was held to be disproportionate.[65]

A good example of the Court's approach in media cases is *Lingens v Austria*.[66] There the Court found that Austrian law, which subjected journalists to criminal penalties for defamation without the benefit of a fair comment defence, was excessively strict. The interference with the applicant's freedom of expression under Article 10 was held unanimously, therefore, to be disproportionate to the legitimate aim pursued. The Court also considered the requirement in Austrian law for the defendant to prove the truth of what were in effect value-judgments. Whereas Article 10 protects both factual information and comment, the Court expressed the view that "a careful distinction needs

---

[62] Above, n.51, at 755–7.

[63] Above, n.50, at 242–3. However, in *Purcell v Ireland*, above, n.56, at 260, the Commission found that the s.31 restriction on the broadcasting of interviews with representatives of and spokespersons for Sinn Féin was "necessary in a democratic society", given "the limited scope of the restrictions imposed ... and the overriding interests they were designed to protect". *Cf.* decision of the Commission in *Brind & others v UK*, App. No.18714/91, May 9, 1994, DR 77, p.42, in relation to a similar British ban affecting Sinn Féin.

[64] Consider also *Weber v Switzerland*, Series A, No.177, (1990) 12 E.H.R.R. 508, a case concerning a press conference held by Mr Weber to complain about how a judge had dealt with a defamation action. The European Court of Human Rights held that the conviction of Mr Weber for disclosing confidential information was an interference with his freedom of expression under Art.10. The interference was not necessary, the Court said, because the interest in maintaining the confidentiality of a judicial investigation no longer existed at the time of the press conference when the applicant revealed the facts.

[65] Above, n.55.

[66] Series A, No.103; (1986) 8 E.H.R.R. 407.

to be made between facts and value-judgments."[67] To penalise value-judgments made in good faith, particularly on political issues, as in *Lingens*, was liable to deter journalists from contributing to public discussion.

Two recurring themes in the Court's jurisprudence on media issues are the recognition of the "pre-eminent role of the press" in a democratic society and the public's right to receive information: "[I]t is ... incumbent on [the press] to impart information and ideas on political issues just as those in other areas of public interest. Not only does the press have the task of imparting such information and ideas: the public also has a right to receive them".[68]

That is particularly so in the realm of political debate:

> "Freedom of the press affords the public one of the best means of discovering and forming an opinion of the ideas and attitudes of their political leaders. In particular, it gives politicians the opportunity to reflect and comment on the preoccupations of public opinion; it thus enables everyone to participate in the free political debate which is at the very core of the concept of a democratic society."[69]

In fact, as a former President of the Court, Judge Ryssdal, observed, the Court has "adopted clearly an activist stand in matters of public criticism of governments and politicians" but "taken a more nuanced attitude in cases relating to contempt of court, trial by newspaper, and similar issues."[70]

The clear distinction made by the Court between politicians and private citizens is reminiscent of the stance taken by the United States Supreme Court. In the United States, the absolutist nature of the press guarantee lies in the First Amendment to the Constitution: "Congress shall make no law ... abridging the freedom of speech, or of the press ...." Based on its understanding of the intentions of the founding fathers in formalising this common-law right, the Court has distinguished between public and private persons in defamation law[71] and substantially relaxed contempt of court laws. Because there are no restrictions on the press specified in the Constitution, the courts in the US have been able to take a bold stand in striking down state restrictions on media activities. The European Court of Human Rights is more constrained, as a result of the restrictions specified in Article 10(2), but nevertheless has been gradually pushing back the boundaries. It is up to the media to present cases to the Court that will allow it to continue in this vein.

2.3.2 The EU Charter of Fundamental Rights

Protection of fundamental rights is a founding principle of the European Union. The EC Court of Justice has consistently held that the EU is bound by the

---

[67] *ibid.* at 420, para.46.
[68] *ibid.* at 418, para.41.
[69] *Castells v Spain*, Series A, No.236; (1992) 14 E.H.R.R. 445, at para.43.
[70] "Freedom of Expression under the European Convention on Human Rights", lecture given by Rolv Ryssdal, President of the European Court of Human Rights, at the Faculty of Law, University College Galway, April 11, 1994.
[71] *New York Times v Sullivan* 376 U.S. 255 (1964), and the line of cases following it.

human rights regime of the European Convention on Human Rights.[72] Article 6(2) of the Treaty on European Union specifically states that the Union shall respect fundamental rights as guaranteed by the Convention, and a new provision inserted into Article 7 by the Treaty of Amsterdam confers powers on the European Council in relation to serious and persistent breaches. A decision was taken in 1999, however, to draft a Charter on Fundamental Rights, whose status would be decided when the process was complete. The draft, which was completed in December 2000,[73] includes provisions on freedom of expression and privacy. Article 7, on privacy, is the counterpart to Article 8 of the Convention, except that the word "correspondence" in the latter is replaced by "communications" to take account of developments in technology. Article 11, on freedom of expression and information, corresponds to Article 10 of the Convention. However, paragraph 2 of Article 11 is new. It states: "The freedom and pluralism of the media shall be respected". According to the explanation accompanying the text, the new provision is based in particular on the case law of the Court of Justice, on the Protocol on the System of Public Broadcasting in the Member States, annexed to the EC Treaty, and on the Television without Frontiers Directive.[74] The present intention is that the Charter on Fundamental Rights will be annexed to the constitution of the EU, which is currently being drafted.[75]

2.3.3 International standards

The rights of the Irish media are also protected at a global level by other international human rights documents containing statements declaratory of various aspects of freedom of expression (or of the right to communicate) and setting out areas of restriction.

The United Nations Universal Declaration of Human Rights refers at Article 19 to the right of everyone to freedom of opinion and expression:

> "Everyone has the right to freedom of opinion and expression; this right includes freedom to hold opinions without interference and to seek, receive and impart information and ideas through any media and regardless of frontiers."

The Declaration itself makes no specific reference to areas of restriction on

---

[72] See, for example, *Nold v Commission* (Case 4/73, [1974] E.C.R. 491, para.13), *Elliniki Radiophonia Tileorassi* (Case C–260/89, [1991] E.C.R. I–2925, para.41), *Commission v The Netherlands* (Case C–353/89, [1991] E.C.R. I–4069, para.30).

[73] [2000] O.J. C 364, December 18, 2000, p.1. On the Government's "cautious" attitude to the Charter, see *The Irish Times*, November 7, 2002.

[74] Particularly, the ECJ case: *Stichting Collectieve Antennevoorziening Gouda and others* (Case C–288/89, [1991] E.C.R. I–4007). The TWF Directive is Council Directive 89/552/EC, as amended; see, in particular, its 17th recital.

[75] See Art.5 of the draft constitution (CONV 528/03), available at *www.europeanconvention. eu.int/bienvenue.asp?lang=EN*; *The Irish Times*, February 8, 2003.

the right.[76] Instead, that is elaborated in the International Covenant on Civil and Political Rights at Article 19:

> "1. Everyone shall have the right to hold opinions without interference.
>
> 2. Everyone shall have the right to freedom of expression; this right shall include freedom to seek, receive and impart information and ideas of all kinds, regardless of frontiers, either orally, in writing or in print, in the form of art, or through any other media of his choice.
>
> 3. The exercise of the rights provided for in paragraph 2 of this Article carries with it special duties and responsibilities. It may therefore be subject to certain restrictions, but these shall only be such as are provided by law and are necessary:
>   (a) For respect of the rights or reputations of others;
>   (b) For the protection of national security or of public order (ordre public), or of public health or morals."

The areas of restriction detailed in paragraph 3 appear to be less extensive than those specified in the European Convention on Human Rights at Article 10(2).[77] The latter are also more specific. A further difference between the two documents relates to the right itself. The guarantee in the Covenant extends to seeking, receiving and imparting information and ideas of all kinds, while the European Convention makes no mention of "seeking" information or "of all kinds". However, the European Commission considered the "seeking" of information to be implicit in the Article since "the right to receive information … envisages first of all access to general sources of information".[78] The Committee of Ministers included the right to seek information in Articles 5 and 8 of its Declaration on the Freedom of Expression and Information.[79] On the second point, the Court has interpreted Article 10 to extend to information and ideas "of all kinds".[80]

The decisions of the United Nations Human Rights Committee in the case of complaints made under the Covenant on Civil and Political Rights, are also

---

[76] It should be noted that the Declaration is not a treaty as such, and therefore is not binding in law, although its widespread acceptance has tended to give it the status of customary law. All of the provisions of the Declaration are subject to a general restriction in Art.30: "Nothing in this Declaration may be interpreted as implying for any State, group or person any right to engage in any activity or to perform any act aimed at the destruction of any of the rights and freedoms set forth herein." *Cf.* ECHR, Art.17.

[77] Though further restrictions are contained in Art.20, while Art.5 prevents abuse of rights.

[78] 43 Eur. Comm. H.R. (1980) 17 *Decisions and Reports* 227 No.8383/78.

[79] Declaration of April 29, 1982.

[80] See, for example, above n.51, at 754, para.49: Freedom of expression is applicable not only to information or ideas "that are favourably received or regarded as inoffensive or as a matter of indifference, but also to those that offend, shock or disturb the State or any sector of the population." The Court has also considered information and ideas in a wide variety of forms from print to audiovisual media, from political expression to artistic and commercial expression.

instructive.[81] The decision in *Ballantyne and Davidson v Canada*,[82] for example, suggests a much greater and decisive protection for commercial information and advertising than has yet emerged from the European Court of Human Rights.[83]

Ireland ratified the International Covenant on Civil and Political Rights in 1989 and accepted the right of individual petition.[84] It was then obliged under Article 40 of the Covenant to submit to the Human Rights Committee periodic progress reports on the protection of human rights in this country. With respect to freedom of expression and the right of access to information, the Committee noted with concern, in response to the 1993 report, that the exercise of those rights was unduly restricted under laws concerning censorship, blasphemy and information on abortion. The prohibition on interviews with certain groups outside the borders by the broadcast media infringed upon the freedom to receive and impart information under Article 19, paragraph 2, of the Covenant.[85]

The Human Rights Committee recommended that:

"[T]he State party take the necessary measures to ensure the enjoyment

---

[81] See, for example, *Gauthier v Canada*, Comm. No.633/1995, regarding access to report Parliament: any accreditation system must be necessary and proportionate to the goal in question and not arbitrary; *Laptsevich v Belarus*, Comm. No.780/1997, regarding a requirement for registration and publication data on every edition of printed periodical publication, found to be a breach of the right to impart information: "The right to freedom of expression is of paramount importance in any democratic society, and any restrictions to the exercise of this right must meet a strict test of justification." (at para.8.2)

[82] Comm. No.359/1989, and *McIntyre v Canada*, Comm. No.385/1989, (1993) 14 H.R.L.J. 171.

[83] See *Markt Intern v Germany* Series A, No.165; (1990) 12 E.H.R.R. 161, where the Court accepted that Art.10 extended to commercial speech (para.26).

[84] First Optional Protocol. For example, see *Patrick Holland v Ireland*, Comm. No.593/1994, UN Doc CCPR/C/58/D/593/1994, November, 22 1996, and *Kavanagh v Ireland* (2001/840 (transcript) June 29, 2001)). Finnegan J. in the High Court in *Kavanagh* held that the views of the Committee are not binding (Irish Times Law Report, October 29, 2001). A subsequent complaint by Kavanagh to the Committee resulted in it upholding the complaint of a violation of ICCPR, Art.26. However, the Supreme Court (2001/194 (transcript) March 1, 2002) held that the decision of the court takes precedence over the "views" of the Committee, and dismissed the appeal. For the rejection by the Committee of the final complaint see Comm. No.1114/2002: Ireland. UN Doc. CCPR/C/76/D/1114/2002/Rev1, November 28, 2002.

[85] Comments of the Human Rights Committee, July 28, 1993, at para.15. The second report is UN Doc. CCPR/C/IRL/98/2, and the list of issues to be taken up as adopted by the Committee is at 2000CCPR/C/69/L/IRL, concluding observations, July 19, 2000. See generally, Deirdre Fottrell, "Reporting to the UN Human Rights Committee – A Ruse by Any Other Name? Lessons for International Human Rights Supervision from Recent Irish Experiences" (2001) 19 I.L.T. 61. See also the Report of the UN Special Rapporteur on Human Rights, E/CN.4/2000/63/Add.2, January 10, 2000, available at *www.unhchr.ch* under "Issues", "Freedom of opinion and expression", "Documents", "Report". The Special Rapporteur *inter alia* noted with concern the chilling effect of libel, the use of section 31 of the Broadcasting Act 1960 (since repealed), the lack of protection for journalists' sources and the continued existence of the censorship acts. He commended the introduction of the Freedom of Information Act 1997, the self-regulatory approach to the internet and the guidelines adopted by the NUJ on racism.

of the freedom of expression as set out in Article 19 of the Covenant. In this regard ... steps should be taken to repeal strict laws on censorship and ensure judicial review of decisions taken by the Censorship on [*sic*] Publications Board."[86]

Since the Human Rights Committee reported in 1993, legislation to allow for abortion information has been passed.[87] The order implementing section 31 of the Broadcasting Authority Act 1960 (as amended) was not renewed, and the section has now been repealed by the Broadcasting Act 2001. Meanwhile, the Freedom of Information Act, passed in 1997, encompasses a right of access to information held by public bodies. The Official Secrets Act 1963 and other censorship legislation have been reviewed, but not yet amended or repealed. They remain, therefore, at odds with the State's obligations under the Covenant.

The Covenant, therefore, while not part of the domestic law of this State, may operate at arm's length to bring about changes in national laws to the benefit of the media. The Committee in its concluding observations on Ireland's first report further emphasised (at para. 18) that the "need to comply with the international obligations should be taken fully into account by the judiciary".

In summary, it is important to appreciate the fact that there is a positive guarantee of media rights in all of these documents and a commitment to those rights built into the enforcement systems. Despite the extensive range of possible restrictions, it is permissible to invoke a restriction to curtail the exercise of the rights concerned only when the restriction is prescribed by law and is necessary in a democratic society. The restriction must be in support of one of the interests listed and the means used must be proportionate to the given aim. It is not clear that the Irish Constitution has an explicit built-in system for prioritising and reconciling competing rights. The international documents and the jurisprudence, in particular that of the European Court of Human Rights, therefore provide a useful yardstick for assessing the legitimacy, reach and efficacy of Irish law in relation to freedom of expression and of the media.

The United Nations Declaration and Covenant and the European Convention all make specific reference to information, while Article 40.6.1.i of the Irish Constitution refers only to convictions and opinions. On the other hand, the Irish Constitution specifically mentions the press, albeit in parenthesis, but, apart from the reference to licensing in Article 10(1) of the European Convention on Human Rights, other international instruments do not. In their case, the media come under the general guarantee of freedom of information. Nevertheless, their freedom is of central importance, as borne out by the jurisprudence of the European Court and the findings of the United Nations Human Rights Committee.

---

[86] *ibid*., at para.21. This was reiterated by the UN Special Rapporteur, above, n.85.

[87] The Regulation of Information (Services Outside the State for Termination of Pregnancies) Act 1995 (following a constitutional referendum, leading to the Fourteenth Amendment to the Constitution, December 1992). This and other developments are set out in Ireland's *Second Report on the Measures Adopted to Give Effect to the Provisions of the Covenant* (Dept. of Foreign Affairs, Dublin, 1998), pp.48–50.

2.4 TOWARDS A REAPPRAISAL OF MEDIA RIGHTS AND FREEDOMS

On a different level, the emergence of new media and the maturing of the older, longer-established media invite a redefinition of related rights and freedoms. The original concept, apparent in the first wave of national constitutions in the nineteenth century, of freedom of expression as the freedom to speak, write and print has become too simple a formulation. The "free communication of thoughts and ideas" of the Declaration of the Rights of Man of the French revolutionaries has taken on a new meaning in the late twentieth and early twenty-first centuries. State monopolies and traditional perceptions of the media have been overtaken by technological developments, which have extended the capacity and capabilities for transmitting print, sound and visual images around the world.

New forms of media have focused attention on the fact that freedom of expression envisages not only the emission of thoughts and ideas but also the freedom to receive them and, therefore, access to the means to receive them. Access, so long restricted by states on the basis of the limitations of the electromagnetic spectrum, has now been opened up by advances in cable and satellite technology and precipitated by computer and digitalisation. The European Court of Human Rights has responded to the challenge. In *Groppera Radio v Switzerland*[88] in 1989, the effect of the phrase in Article 10(1) that "this article shall not prevent States from requiring the licensing of broadcasting, television or cinema enterprises" was declared to be mainly technical and confined to ensuring the orderly control of broadcasting. Licensing must be for technical purposes, the Court said, not content-based purposes, to which Article 10(2) applies.

A reappraisal of media rights and freedoms is underway. Media rights have come to be classified according to the nature and role of the media as institutional and instrumental freedoms;[89] old characterisations and assumptions are being questioned;[90] the relationship between the right to communicate and freedom of expression is still being explored.[91]

As Costello J. stated in *Paperlink*,[92] the right to communicate is viewed as

---

[88] Series A, No.173; (1990) 12 E.H.R.R. 321, at 339, para.61. This was elaborated in *Informationsverein Lentia and others v Austria*, Series A, No.276; (1993) 17 E.H.R.R. 93.

[89] Eric Barendt, "Press and Broadcasting Freedom: Does Anyone Have Any Right to Free Speech?" (1991) 44 C.L.P. 63; Frederick Schauer, "Principles, Institutions, and the First Amendment" (1998) 112 *Harvard Law Review* 84.

[90] See, for example, Geoffrey Marshall, "Press Freedom and Free Speech Theory" (1992) P.L. 40; Marie McGonagle (ed.), *Law and the Media: The Views of Journalists and Lawyers* (Round Hall Sweet & Maxwell, Dublin, 1997); Jack Beatson and Yvonne Cripps (eds), *Freedom of Expression and Freedom of Information* (Oxford University Press, Oxford, 2000); Nicol, Millar, Sharland, *Media Law and Human Rights* (Blackstone Press Ltd, London, 2001).

[91] See, for example, The MacBride Report, *Many Voices, One World* (UNESCO, New York, 1980; 4th ed., 1988); Francis Balle, *Médias et Sociétés* (4th ed., Monchrestien, Paris, 1988) at p.217. See also the articulation and elaboration of both rights in the Irish Supreme Court (above).

[92] Above, n.2, at 381.

part of, or one form of, a wider right to freedom of expression. The concept involves not only the expression of thoughts, ideas and information but also their reception. Its exercise implies the use of a means of diffusion, a medium of communication. It also implies a choice of medium and in that sense is wider than the traditional concept of freedom of the press, but capable of being realised through the element of choice inherent in the new interactive media. Communication concerns the diffusion of material, rather than the content or outcome.[93]

Technology and commercial pressures are conspiring to push for deregulation and a minimisation of restrictions on access to the media. As restrictions are no longer demanded by the limitations of the technology, they must henceforth be justified on the grounds of the activity itself: the extent to which it may encroach on other freedoms.[94] In the past, the focus has been on the limitations rather than the right itself, for example, the formulation in the Irish Constitution. The freedom was a negative freedom, a freedom from, rather than freedom for; a freedom from interference once all other rights had been protected, as opposed to a positive freedom for the media to carry out its functions of informing the public, subject to limitation only in a narrow context and to the minimum extent necessary, where clearly defined interests required it. A new understanding of the media role has emerged, but one which takes cognisance of the entertainment function and profit ethic of the media, as well as their democratic functions:

> "Media freedom is not something that belongs or is of concern only to the press; it is a public freedom in which all have an interest. ... [There is still] a tendency to consider the media as wholly a private and commercial special interest. Undoubtedly it is the case that newspapers, publishers and broadcasters have to make profits otherwise they would fail. But there is more to the media than simply a business and it is that public function which needs to be fostered and recognised in a society concerned to strengthen democracy."[95]

The dangers of manipulation by the media and lack of diversity as a result of concentration of ownership and the profit ethic are very real. One measure to minimise the effects is to ensure that there is an educated and critical public. Technology may find its own solutions in terms of the range of media, number of broadcasting channels available, access to international and global media, for example. Yet, globalisation has led to increased awareness on the part of governments, the EU and international human rights bodies of the importance of ensuring plurality of sources, diversity of content and universal access to the means and channels of information. Positive action through law has proved

---

[93] Above, n.91, Balle, p.219. The results of the European Commission consultation following the Green Paper on Convergence in 1997 indicated the need to separate out transmission and content. See further Chap.11 below.

[94] Above, n.91, Balle, p.223, and Chap.11 below.

[95] Kevin Boyle, "Freedom of Expression and Democracy" in Liz Heffernan (ed.), *Human Rights: A European Perspective* (The Round Hall Press, Dublin, 1994), at p.217.

difficult in practice and is vulnerable to challenge on rights grounds.[96] As a result, increased reliance has been placed in recent years on co-regulation and self-regulation.

Co-regulation envisages co-operation between media and government, through the joint drafting and monitoring of compliance with codes. Self-regulation, which allows the industry itself to set and monitor compliance with its own standards has long been established in the printed press in many countries and is at present the favoured option in relation to the internet. However it is achieved, the need for openness and accountability in the media, for codes of ethics and for avenues of redress for individual complaints is an important counterbalance to media freedoms.[97]

Further Reading

ARTICLE 19: the Global Campaign for Free Expression, *The Virtual Freedom of Expression Handbook*, available at *www.article19.org*.

Barendt, Eric, *Freedom of Speech* (2nd ed., Clarendon Press, Oxford, 1989).

Barendt, Eric and Hitchens, Leslie, *Media Law: Cases and Materials* (Pearson Education Ltd, Harlow, 2000).

Council of Europe, *Case law concerning Article 10 of the European Convention on Human Rights*, H/Inf (2002) 7.

Steiner, Henry J. and Alston, Philip, *International Human Rights in Context: Law, Politics, Morals* (2nd ed., Oxford University Press, Oxford, 2000).

---

[96] See Thomas Gibbons, "Freedom of the Press: Ownership and Editorial Values" (1992) P.L. 279; Eric Barendt, *Broadcasting Law* (Clarendon Press, Oxford, 1993), pp.122–4, and Chap.11 below.

[97] See Kevin Boyle and Marie McGonagle, *Media Accountability: The Readers' Representative in Irish Newspapers* (NNI, Dublin 1995), and Chap.11 below.

CHAPTER THREE

The Historical Development of the Media and the Law

The Times *is one of the greatest powers in the world; in fact, I don't know anything which has more power, except perhaps the Mississippi.*[1]

3.1 INTRODUCTION

The need to communicate is inherent in all civilisations. News was posted on the walls of ancient Rome. Paper was invented in China in the first century AD, and the first book was assembled there in the ninth century. Later, handwritten news circulated in Italy from the commercial centre of Venice in the thirteenth century, but already ecclesiastical censorship (Papal Orders) and official censorship thwarted the authors. It was not until the invention of the printing press by Gutenberg in the middle of the fifteenth century that book publishing in the western world began, with the release of the Gutenberg Bible in 1455. With the development of the postal service around the same time,[2] the news media began to emerge.

3.2 THE DEVELOPMENT OF NEWSPAPERS

Initially printing was reserved for important events, but by the beginning of the seventeenth century, newspapers had begun to appear regularly right across Europe. The first periodical in the world to appear on a regular basis was the *Nieuwe Tijdinger (Les Nouvelles d'Anvers)* (1605), the official chronicle of the French court. A Strasbourg almanac, *Le Mercure Français* (1611), began to be published annually but gradually developed into a monthly, then a weekly and finally a daily, which lasted until the twentieth century. *Le Journal des Savants* (1665) paved the way for literary and scientific journalism. *Le Mercure Galant* published in Paris (1672) was the world's first literary periodical. Book

---

[1] Abraham Lincoln in 1861, cited in *The British Press* (Central Office of Information, London, 1958), at p.3.

[2] The postal service was developed in France in 1464, in England in 1478, in Germany in 1502, in Ireland in 1635; see Jean-Marie Auby and Robert Ducos-Ader, *Droit de l'Information* (2nd ed., Dalloz, Paris, 1982); Robert Munter, *The History of the Irish Newspaper 1685–1760* (Cambridge University Press, Cambridge, 1967), at p.72.

form, however, remained the choice of the philosophers, and pamphlets the choice of the political commentator and critic.[3] All were subject to official censorship, in the form of authorisation, licensing or bans.[4]

The first printing press in England was set up at Westminster by William Caxton in 1476, but it was quite some time before its potential was realised. Because a government licence was required to print, newsletters compiled in London and sent to the provinces were usually handwritten, just as they had been in Italy.[5] It was not until the early part of the seventeenth century that the first printed newspapers began to appear in England, and it was to be another century once the licensing laws had lapsed[6] before the first daily, *The Daily Courant*, began publication in 1702. The first ever daily paper had appeared in Germany in 1660 (the *Leipziger Zeitung*), whereas in most other countries, dailies were unknown until the eighteenth century. It would be a further century before they became a significant force in society. In the United States, for example, regular publications emerged at the end of the seventeenth century, but the first daily, the *Pennsylvania Pocket*, only began in 1784. The forerunners of the modern British newspapers, the *Daily Telegraph* and *The Times*, appeared in 1772 and 1785, respectively. The oldest Sunday paper, the *Observer*, was established in 1791.[7]

In Ireland, newspaper publishing may be said to have begun in the mid-seventeenth century with the publication by the Cromwellians of Cork of the *Irish Monthly Mercury*, followed by a short-lived Dublin weekly. The demand for news was fuelled by tension and war. The Irish postal service began in 1635 and was well established by the end of the century, when a real newspaper press began to emerge. Even then, however, except in times of hostilities, it consisted mainly of news brought from England, with some scant local news and advertisements. Publication depended on the arrival in Irish ports of packet boats bringing foreign letters and dispatches of news. Coffee-houses and ale-houses, the social meeting places of the day, played an important part in circulation, by providing newspapers as an integral part of their service for their patrons. A regular distribution system, based on the postal services, was later developed. It was well into the eighteenth century, however, before provincial papers took off and before the generic term "newspaper" began to be used to describe the myriad of news-sheets and newsletters that had developed.[8] The newspapers at that time were produced by printer-stationers or bookseller-printers.

---

[3]   Above, n.2, Auby and Ducos-Ader, at pp.23–4; Francis Balle, *Médias et Sociétés* (4th ed., Monchrestien, Paris, 1988), at pp.76–7.

[4]   Above, n.2, Auby and Ducos-Ader, at pp.23–4, on the appointment of official censors in France and the banning of a political monthly 1689–91.

[5]   Above, n.1, at p.2.

[6]   The licensing laws were renewed in 1693 for two years and then finally allowed to lapse in 1695.

[7]   Above, n.1 at p.3.

[8]   Robert Munter, *A Handlist of Irish Newspapers* (Bowes and Bowes, London, 1960), at p.vii.

3.2.1 Newspaper Content

Early newspapers in England had been licensed until 1695, with the result that their factual content was rather limited. Investigative journalism, criticism and comment were virtually unknown; advertisements and notices predominated. From the demise of licensing in 1695, indirect controls by way of taxes and stamp duties were used for almost two centuries. Governments sponsored their own newspapers, while threats and inducements to others augmented the state's arsenal against the press.

Developments in Ireland tended to lag behind and mirror those in Britain. Most of the early newspapers were very dull by today's standards, badly produced, containing little apart from news copied from the London papers of the previous weeks or days, with the addition of a few local advertisements and snippets.[9] As in England, however, fear of the power of the press resulted in even greater government control:

> "Hand in hand with the growth and development of the press, both in England and Ireland, was the continuous effort by those in authority to restrict and control this new and dangerous medium".[10]

At first the papers were single sheets, later expanded to four pages. They contained only a minimal amount of home news and no political reporting or comment – that was left to the pamphleteers. In this way, they stayed clear of the wrath of the administration.

The early papers were essentially commercial enterprises undertaken and run by individual stationers. They were one-man operations; the editor had not yet been identified as a distinct functionary bearing legal responsibility; the journalist, if he existed, remained shielded by the printer. William Carey, who produced the *National Evening Star*, described his task in 1792:

> "To preserve my interest with my old advertising friends and to obtain news I had a daily round of visitation to make through the principal street of business. To collect in money due for advertisements, I had also a number of calls out in the day. As I had neither editor nor writer, all the literary labour devolved on me. Besides essays to write I had also to run over the London, Dublin and country Irish papers, to digest the packets, to make extracts, and furnish articles of domestic intelligence and of general observation. I had also to run to the coffee houses to pick up the news of the day, to attend the theatre in the season to give an account of the performance and the parliament house to take down debate. … When I add that I had to correct the proofs, to write letters to country corre-

---

[9] Compare the early papers in France, where one page consisted of French news (court and town, literature, snippets) and the remainder was made up of foreign news: above, n.2, Auby and Ducos-Ader, at p.25.

[10] Above, n.2, Munter, at p.9; Brian Inglis, *Freedom of the Press in Ireland: 1784-1841* (Faber & Faber, London, 1954), p.19 *et seq.*

spondents and to act as my own clerk ... it will appear my hands were pretty full."[11]

Unfortunately, his paper did not last very long, not because his task became too much for him but because of his prosecution for seditious libel (see Chapter 10).

It was only from the beginning of the eighteenth century that the first long-lived newspapers began to appear in Dublin and Belfast. They were in English, a factor that restricted circulation mainly to the English-speaking Protestant population. The *Newsletter* in Belfast, for example, began publication in 1737 and continues to the present day. Early Irish newspapers were prized mainly for their advertisements, which were also the profitable part of the paper and the basis for subscription and therefore competition.

3.2.2 Political Comment

During the eighteenth century, as newspaper advertising caught the imagination of the public and became an important source of revenue, the Irish newspaper changed from a part-time effort to a highly organised undertaking employing full-time workers.[12] Newspapers became part of the daily life of the English-speaking population and as the readership grew with the spread of literacy, so too did the scope of newspaper content, embracing literature, entertainment and educational material. The informational and educative role of the press was established and the scene was set for the introduction of political comment during the political turmoil at the end of the century:

> "Political polemics and public controversy were always dangerous subjects for the press, particularly for the periodic press, while private controversy, to avoid personal implication and even the remote chance of a libel action, was relegated to the advertisement columns."[13]

No outspoken or pro-Catholic press existed until the nineteenth century.[14]

In the first half of the eighteenth century, at least 160 newspapers were published in Dublin, although most of them did not last very long.[15] There were also a few provincial papers. By the middle of the century, Irish politics was becoming more volatile, and the newspapers were beginning to respond with political comment. The government did not like it and reacted by punishing for contempt of parliament. This response of government was not peculiar to Ireland. In Britain and the United States, as in some European countries, the printing-press was tightly controlled; debate and dissent were not tolerated. In the United States, as in Britain and Ireland, parliament was not even open to the public before 1766 and the publication of proceedings was prohibited.

---

[11] R.B. McDowell, "Irish Newspapers in the Eighteenth Century" (1984) 8(2) *Media and Popular Culture, The Crane Bag*, p.40.
[12] Above, n.2, Munter, at p.66.
[13] *ibid.* at p.100.
[14] *ibid.* at p.69.
[15] Above, n.11, at p.40.

Apart from taxes and stamp duties, bribes and threats, the main weapons used against the press were contempt of parliament, contempt of court, and prosecutions for seditious or defamatory libel.

3.2.3 Strict Censorship

Until 1774, Irish newspapers had been free of stamp duties, but not immune from prosecutions. If publishers published anything that might be deemed obscene, blasphemous or seditious, they would be answerable for it in a court of law or before parliament. Such laws were used to "harass and curtail the press with what amounted to a strict censorship".[16] The most adverse effects of such laws were the fear they engendered, the heavy fees payable and the long periods of time for which publishers could be held pending trial, with consequent disruption of their publication.[17] Newspaper offices could be searched and equipment seized and destroyed.

Press offences occupied a regular and prominent slot in parliamentary proceedings. Not only criticism but even the reporting of parliamentary proceedings or of anything relating to them was treated as a breach of privilege and prosecuted until 1772.[18] Once they came to be tolerated by the authorities, reports of parliamentary debates were to form a significant part of many Irish newspapers.

The measure of legislative independence granted to the Irish parliament in 1782 led to a new concentration on home news and politics. The greatest influence of the period, however, was the rise of the Volunteer movement, which brought about a rapid increase in the number of newspapers being published and also a change in their content. The same had happened with the Revolution in France and the War of Independence in America, which were followed, respectively, by the Declaration of the Rights of Man and the United States Constitution, which gave new recognition and status to the press. The first press law in France was enacted in 1791 but censorship, heavy duties and subventions to the loyal press continued unabated until 1830. In Ireland, some of the papers became antagonistic towards government, even scurrilous in their attacks, as when the Volunteers' Journal described the House of Commons as a "den of thieves", a "Gomorrah of iniquity".[19] The government retaliated with prosecutions or threats of prosecutions for seditious libel. Criticism and vehemence were equated with sedition. On the other hand, by the 1820s up to £20,000 a year was being spent on subsidies, proclamations and notices, in a measure designed to keep the press under control.[20] Papers that offered

---

[16] Above, n.2, Munter, at pp.100–1. For a detailed account of the history and development of seditious libel, see Philip Hamburger, "The Development of the Law of Seditious Libel and the Control of the Press" (1985) 37 Stanford L.Rev. 661.

[17] For example, n.2, Munter, at pp.148–9: "It appears that Harding was imprisoned for about six months, for there is a break in the production of his DINL from 6 August 1723 to 18 February 1723/4".

[18] Above, n.2, Munter, at pp.144–156; n.11, at p.42; n.10, Inglis, at p.38.

[19] Above, n.10, Inglis at p.23.

[20] Kevin B. Nowlan, "The Origins of the Press in Ireland" in Brian Farrell (ed.), *Communications and Community in Ireland* (Mercier Press, Dublin and Cork, 1984), p.7, at p.12.

allegiance got more proclamations; those that offered criticism and opposition got little or none.

The judiciary, dependent on the administration for job security and advancement, facilitated repression. Juries could be circumvented altogether or "packed".[21] Sentences imposed were often harsh and out of all proportion to the offence charged. Fines of up to £500 and periods of two years' imprisonment were not unknown. Newspaper proprietors could be attached or held on informations for many months awaiting trial; other publications could not comment on the case lest they be held to be in contempt of court.[22] Some papers went under as a result, but those that survived had become livelier and more varied. The tone and character of Irish newspapers had been changed unalterably.

Nineteenth-century England saw some attempts to liberalise press laws. Pressure from newspapers themselves resulted in some limited reform of the libel laws. The Libel Acts 1843–88 and the Newspaper Libel and Registration Act 1881 provided for defences for newspapers, ranging from apologies to privilege for parliamentary and court reports. Liberalisation of German laws relating to the press began in 1874. In France, the long struggle for press freedom was finally realised with the Press Law of 1881.[23]

3.2.4 Mass Circulation Becomes a Reality

The first news agency had been established in Paris in 1832, followed by Berlin in 1849 and London (Reuters) in 1851. During that period, the press began to reap the benefits of the invention of the telegraph. Improvements in transportation, particularly railways, meant that news was not so stale. As a result, sales which had averaged 2,000–3,000 in the mid-eighteenth century now climbed so rapidly that combined sales of the Dublin dailies in 1871 was over 13,000.[24] In the same year, the London *Daily Telegraph* was able to claim the highest circulation in the world: over 240,000 copies daily.[25] Competition and low sale prices contributed to the process. In England, the popularity among working-class people of the illegal, but cheaper, unstamped press led to the abandonment of stamp duties in 1855 (1870 in France), and mass circulation became a reality, beckoning the heyday of the press and the arrival of the first press barons. In Ireland, as elsewhere, technological developments and improvements in literacy brought about by the introduction

---

[21] In France, there was no jury in press cases until well into the nineteenth century: see above, n.2, Auby and Ducos-Ader, at p.29. In Germany, prior restraint was abolished in 1874 and the competence of the jury re-established, but otherwise strict control of the press continued: *ibid.* at p.45.

[22] Above, n.10, Inglis, at p.46 *et seq.*

[23] Above, n.2, Auby and Ducos-Ader, at p.415 *et seq.*

[24] Circulated through Smith's Dublin office: see L. M. Cullen, "Establishing a Communications System: News, Post and Transport" in Brian Farrell, above, n.20, p.25.

[25] Above, n.1 at p.40. In France, the circulation of one paper had risen from 1,200 in the seventeenth century to 12,000 in the eighteenth, while sales of the daily Paris press increased to one million; see above, n.2, Auby and Ducos-Ader, at p.29. The most rapid expansion, however, was in the US: *ibid.* at p.45.

of formal primary-level education paved the way for mass circulation in the middle of the nineteenth century.[26]

Meanwhile in Ireland, *The Nation*, first published in 1842, with Charles Gavin Duffy as editor, sold more copies than any other newspaper in Ireland before it, selling out its initial print-run of 12,000. It was distributed through reading-rooms and from hand to hand and read aloud, as had been common practice in an age of low levels of literacy.[27] The paper was 16 pages long and had no illustrations. It was suppressed in July 1848 but resumed in 1849.[28] The *Cork Examiner* first appeared in 1841; Belfast's *Irish News* in 1855; *The Irish Times* in 1859. Of the provincials still in operation, the oldest appears to be the *Limerick Chronicle* (1766), followed by the *Derry Journal* (1772), the *Leinster Express* (1831), the *Sligo Champion* (1836), and the *Herald and Western Advertiser*, now the *Tuam Herald* (1837). Elsewhere, the London *Times* had been in operation from 1785 and was already a powerful force when the *New York Times* was established in 1851. By 1866, the French *Le Figaro* had become a daily. By 1887, the *New York Herald Tribune* was producing a European edition.

The rapid technological advances of the twentieth century brought about the greatest changes in the media landscape, with the advent of illustrated and then colour magazines, the invention of new audio-visual media and later computer, satellite and multimedia developments. However, at the beginning of the twentieth century, the era of popularisation in which the British *Daily Express* and *Daily Mirror* were founded, Irish newspapers were still rather dull, with endless columns of print. The news items of the *Daily Independent*, however, were of the titbit variety taken mostly from English papers, with headlines such as "The King on Dancing", "Headless Vicar Suicide".[29] As the visual and content quality improved and circulations increased, the papers became important sources of all kinds of information and political comment. The demand for them and the degree to which people identified with them in their daily lives made them less amenable to control. However, the pattern of censorship and attempts at suppression continued in times of war or strife. The early twentieth century saw military censorship in the aftermath of the 1916 rising and in the Black and Tans era.

3.3 THE DEVELOPMENT OF BOOK PUBLISHING

The book trade in Ireland was also slow to develop. The first book published in Ireland was the *Book of Common Prayer* in 1551, when the "official printer to His Majesty in Ireland" was given a special grant to establish the first printing

---

[26] Up to 1847, 53 per cent of the population was still illiterate; by 1901 the figure had fallen to 14 per cent and newspapers themselves had undoubtedly played a part in bringing about that reduction. See D. McCartney, "William Martin Murphy: An Irish Press Baron and the Rise of the Popular Press" in Brian Farrell, above, n.20, at p.30.

[27] See *The Irish Times*, October 14, 1992, article by Brendan Ó Cathaoir, for further information on the nationalist and campaigning aspects of the paper.

[28] *ibid.*

[29] Above, n.26, McCartney, at p.34.

press in Ireland.[30] Up to the beginning of the eighteenth century, there was only one printer in Dublin producing books on a regular basis, yet in the eighteenth century both the newspaper and book publishing industries flourished.[31] The reasons for the delay in making full use of the printing press were both legal and political. The King's printer had a complete monopoly over the printing and sale of books in Ireland. In other words, book printing was confined by law, through the grant of a patent, to the printing of official matter: books of statutes, grammars, almanacs, proclamations, bibles and such others as the law provided "may or ought to be exposed for sale ... so long as the same are not contrary, repugnant or scandalous to the laws or government or state".[32] It was an offence for anyone other than the King's printer to engage in the publishing of books, with a penalty of ten shillings per copy and rights of seizure.[33] In this way, book publishing was subject to a system of official censorship from its very inception, although it would appear that there was some degree of unauthorised printing. For instance, in 1618, when the Company of Stationers took over the patents, they were authorised to seize "all Popish and prohibited books".[34]

The Star Chamber, which was to be the author of many of the legal rules governing the print media to this day, was established in 1488 to monitor and suppress criticism of church and state. For almost two centuries until its abolition in 1640–1, it concerned itself with seditious and blasphemous libel, and, in order to suppress duelling, defamatory libel. Its concern was with the breach of the peace aspect of libel rather than with reputation as such.[35]

Public peace was also invoked to impose another form of prior censorship in the latter half of the seventeenth century. Copy had to be submitted to the Council of State, which was to vet it for anything "tending to the prejudice of the commonwealth or the public peace and welfare".[36] By this time, printing had begun in Cork, Waterford, Kilkenny and other major cities, but the King's printer as licensor remained responsible to the government for preventing the publication of seditious or scandalous matter throughout Ireland.[37] The struggle to end the King's printer's monopoly continued into the final decades of the seventeenth century. Despite some degree of success, it was not until a hundred years later in 1794 that the Lord Chancellor, Viscount Fitzgibbon, asked: "Has

---

[30] *The Irish Times*, April 17, 2001.

[31] M. Pollard, "Control of the Press in Ireland through the King's Printer's Patent 1600-1800" in (1978–80) 14 *Irish Booklore* (Blackstaff Press, Belfast), p.79; also M. Pollard, "Dublin's Trade in Books 1550–1800", *Lyall Lectures 1986–7* (OUP, Oxford, 1990).

[32] *ibid.* at p.80. Also Hamburger, above, n.16.

[33] *ibid.* at p.81.

[34] *ibid.* at p.82.

[35] The category of obscene libel was not recognised until 1727 in *Curl's Case* (1727) 2 Stra. 788, 93 E.R. 899. The only intention required for criminal libel, whether defamatory, obscene or seditious, was the intention to publish, the reason being that the jury would then have only a minimal say. This was altered by the 1792 Libel Act. The Great Reform Act of 1832 marked the beginning of a more liberal political climate. See *Consultation Paper on the Crime of Libel* (Law Reform Commission, Dublin, 1991), p.7.

[36] Above, n.31, Pollard, at p.84.

[37] *ibid.* at p.89.

the validity of this patent ever been established at law? – I do not know that the Crown has a right to erect a monopoly of that kind".[38]

3.4 THE PRINT AND BROADCAST MEDIA IN THE TWENTIETH CENTURY

3.4.1 From Military Censorship to Moral Censorship

Article 9 of the 1922 Constitution of Saorstát Éireann guaranteed the "right of free expression of opinion … for purposes not opposed to public morality", but despite the guarantee, the media, particularly the print media, suffered in turbulent times. Military censorship was introduced for a period during the Civil War of 1922–3; government advertising continued to be withheld in response to criticism; newspapers supporting the irregulars were banned; editors were called in by the government's Director of Publicity to account for their misdeeds.[39] The period of turmoil in 1927 following the killing of the Minister for Justice saw the introduction of the Public Safety Act 1927, which prohibited publications, including newspapers, connected with illegal organisations (section 9) and allowed for ministerial suppression of seditious publications (section 10). The Act was a temporary measure and was repealed at the end of 1928.

Attention then turned to public morals. For some decades, there had been pressure for censorship on moral grounds.[40] The Censorship of Films Act 1923 was introduced as one of the early pieces of legislation of the new State. Public opinion in Ireland and in most of Europe favoured censorship of publications also. The Geneva Convention for the Suppression of the Circulation and Traffic in Obscene Publications in 1923 had set the scene but legislative action in Ireland awaited the report of the Committee on Evil Literature, established by the Minister for Justice in 1926. The resulting Bill in 1928 implemented some of the Committee's recommendations but did not heed its warnings about attempting to include books: the target should be the unsavoury periodicals and newspapers circulating from abroad, the Committee said, not books, which at any rate were the preserve of the educated. At the time, Ireland was regarded as a newspaper-reading public, not a book-reading public. In any event, the Censorship of Publications Act 1929, which was to blight the Irish literary scene for many decades, was passed. Among its more notorious features were the permanent nature of the bans, the lack of appeal (which is particularly surprising, given that the Censorship of Films Act 1923 did provide for an appeal) and the restrictions on court reporting, some of which are still applicable today (see Chapter 9).

---

[38] *ibid.* at p.93.

[39] John Horgan, "State Policy and the Press" in *Media and Popular Culture, The Crane Bag*, above n.11, p.51; and John Horgan, *Irish Media – A Critical History Since 1922* (Routledge, London, New York, 2001), Chap.1.

[40] This pressure existed despite the fact that there were already a number of nineteenth-century statutes penalising obscene publications: the Obscene Publications Act 1857 and Indecent Advertisements Act 1889, for example. See Michael Adams, *Censorship: The Irish Experience* (The University of Alabama Press, Alabama, 1968), Chap.1.

Although concern with morality endured, political events again came to dominate. The Constitution (Amendment No. 17) Act 1931 established a military tribunal, whose wide-ranging powers included the power to declare any publication seditious and impose unlimited sentences. It was not amenable to the courts and there was no appeal from its decisions. The Act was used to prosecute Frank Gallagher, the editor of the newly founded *Irish Press*, for seditious libel arising out of a series of articles alleging police brutality towards Republican sympathisers.[41] The Act remained in operation until the new Constitution came into force in 1937.

3.4.2 Wartime Censorship

The Second World War brought with it additional censorship, and press and radio, as well as postal and telephone services, were very strictly controlled. Even *Old Moore's Almanac* was seized because of its wartime predictions. Weather reports could be censored because information on the weather was "sensitive" in terms of foreign intelligence. The Emergency Power Order prohibited any material "which could cause offence to the people of a friendly nation".[42] A distinction was made between publications that reflected adversely on Ireland's neutrality and publications that threatened public morality. The Censorship of Publications Act 1929 was regarded as the appropriate mechanism for dealing with the latter, not the emergency legislation under which wartime censorship operated.[43] The wartime censors had the power to silence offending journalists by cutting off their telephones and banning their telegraphed reports, which had to be submitted to the censors in advance of publication.[44] Irish people were not allowed to publish any views on the war; the censors would not allow this sort of controversy to be carried on in the public press. Even school annuals were to be warned to submit proofs before publication, because of announcements in the *Clongownian* in 1944 about past pupils who had been killed when serving with British forces.[45] The *Sunday Times* was among the newspapers temporarily banned, but the only Irish paper seized was the *Enniscorthy Echo* in 1940 because of a report on the bombing of a local creamery.[46] The censors could not legally require newspapers to print anything; they could only order them not to print something, but requests to do so were usually complied with. Photographs, bishops' pastorals and films all came under scrutiny.[47]

The censors had no direct control over radio (see further below): it was left to the Director of the Government Information Bureau to see to it that the

---

[41] Above, n.39, at p.52 and p.31 respectively.

[42] *The Irish Times*, August 10, 1993. Ireland's neutral image was paramount. See the series of articles by Joe Carroll in *The Irish Times*, August 7–13, 1993 and for a detailed account and analysis of the period, see Ó Drisceoil, *Censorship in Ireland 1939–45* (Cork University Press, Cork, 1996).

[43] *The Irish Times*, August 11, 1993.

[44] *ibid.*, August 7, 1993.

[45] *ibid.*, August 9, 1993.

[46] *ibid.*, August 12, 1993.

[47] *ibid.*, August 12–13, 1993.

station was supplied with its material for news. In 1941, after a news bulletin carried remarks made in the Dáil opposing trade union legislation, the minister intervened and ordered that the radio newsroom read over to the censor any doubtful item to seek approval for broadcasting.[48]

Even in neutral Ireland the requirements of war overshadowed the guarantee of press freedom enshrined in the new Constitution of 1937. Anyway, the guarantee of freedom to express convictions and opinions contained only an oblique reference to "organs of public opinion such as the radio, the press, the cinema". Moreover, it was too hedged in by conditions and restrictions to prove an effective bulwark for the media even in times of stability. (The constitutional text was examined in detail in Chapter 2.)

3.4.3 The Post-War Period

The post-war period saw the setting-up of the short-lived Irish Press Agency and of the Government Information Bureau, which heralded the news-management, public relations and spin-doctor era, that was to characterise the final decades of the twentieth century. In the early 1960s, the government set about consolidating many areas of law previously governed by pre-independence statutes and common law. The new Irish statutes included the Defamation Act 1961, the Official Secrets Act 1963 and the Copyright Act 1963. In what was becoming a more prosperous and open society, the Censorship of Publications Act was amended in 1967 to put a 12-year limit on bans imposed by the Censorship Board, the Censorship of Films Act was amended in 1970, and a gradual relaxation of film censorship ensued.[49]

3.5 THE DEVELOPMENT OF RADIO BROADCASTING

Wireless telephones were rapidly developed for military purposes during the First World War, and a short-range broadcast during the Easter Rising in Dublin in 1916 heralded the introduction of radio broadcasting in Ireland.[50] Following the model of the telegraph established in 1851, radio was immediately subjected to control through licensing, though undoubtedly the security situation of the time also played a part.[51] The potential of radio was not really appreciated, but governments ensured they kept control because of the public nature of the airwaves and the limited spectrum. Receivers were expensive and their use

---

[48] *The Irish Times*, August 12, 1993.

[49] On the historical development of film and video, see generally, David Parkinson, *History of Film* (Thames and Hudson, London, 1995); and in Ireland, Ciaran Carty, *Confessions of a Sewer Rat* (New Island Books, Dublin, 1995); Louisa Burns-Bisogno, *Censoring Irish Nationalism* (McFarland & Co. Inc. North Carolina and London, 1997).

[50] In Russia in 1917, radio was used to send messages regarding the resistance, just hours after the presses of two Bolshevik newspapers had been destroyed. In the US, the 1920 presidential election campaign was covered by radio: above, n.3, Balle, at pp.115–116.

[51] *Cf.* France 1923: above, n.2, Auby and Ducos-Ader, at p.320, although some private radio stations did exist prior to the war. See generally, Eric Barendt, *Broadcasting Law: A Comparative Study* (Clarendon Press, Oxford, 1993).

thereby confined. The public service character of radio was recognised, but radio developed initially as an entertainment medium rather than an information medium, as programme schedules in the early years show.[52]

In Britain in 1922, all the companies interested in acquiring a broadcasting licence were brought together to form a separate company, which was to have a monopoly on broadcasting: the British Broadcasting Company. Four years later when the State bought back the company, it became the British Broadcasting Corporation, the BBC, which was later to become the model for public service broadcasting in many countries. In Ireland, a similar move was considered but rejected.[53] The Irish authorities, like their French and German counterparts, decided to keep radio broadcasting within the control of the Department for Posts and Telegraphs.[54]

After the Civil War, when it was realised that radio could play a major role in commercial and cultural progress, a special Dáil committee recommended that broadcasting should be a state service, solely in the hands of the postal ministry. Despite the expressed fears of the radio association which had been formed by enthusiasts in 1923, broadcasting began from the Dublin station, 2RN, in January 1926, under the control of the government department.[55] Broadcasting had already begun in Belfast in 1924 under the BBC, but the aftermath of the Civil War caused the delay in Dublin. The legislative structure for radio broadcasting was provided for in the Wireless Telegraphy Act 1926, which, *inter alia*, made it an offence for anyone else to broadcast or possess broadcasting equipment without a licence. For over six decades, no such licence was forthcoming.

2RN began with what would nowadays be called "wall-to-wall" music from small groups of instrumentalists, solo traditional musicians, singers and amateur choirs, the Army Number 1 Band and the Garda Band. There were some language programmes, talks on poultry-keeping and horticulture but very little news.[56] Radio therefore presented a very minimal threat to the authorities at that time, although some government interference did take place. The Secretary of the Gaelic League was banned from taking part in heritage programmes because he had criticised the Minister for allowing "jazz" and "alien" music on air.[57] Much more severe control was exercised over content, however, by means of the purse strings, leading to indirect censorship. Advertising proved ineffective, and sponsored programmes began to take its

---

[52] See P. Mulryan, *Radio, Radio* (Borderline Publications, Dublin, 1988); R. Cathcart, "Broadcasting – The Early Decades" in Brian Farrell, above n.20, at p.39. See generally, Richard Pine, *2RN and the Origins of Irish Radio* (Four Courts Press, Dublin, 2002).

[53] Several companies including Marconi and Lord Beaverbrook had offered to set up radio stations in Dublin: see "RTÉ Radio: Sixtieth Anniversary" – Special Report, *The Irish Times*, March 28–29, 1986. By "public service broadcasting" is meant a service that is publicly funded but independent of government, that transmits a range of programming available to all, which takes account of social, cultural and democratic values. See further Chap.11 below.

[54] Above, n.3, Balle, at p.117.

[55] Above, n.52, Cathcart, at p.41.

[56] *ibid.* at p.42.

[57] *ibid.* at p.43.

place from the early 1930s.[58] By 1933, a high-power transmitter set up in Athlone provided nationwide coverage, and in 1939 the name of the station was changed to Radio Éireann. Radio Éireann remained in the control of the government but continued to provide a popular educational and entertainment service throughout the 1940s and 1950s, when attention began to turn to television.

3.6 THE DAWN OF TELEVISION

The post-war period had witnessed a greater degree of tolerance than ever before in the history of the press, but the sheer scale of media operations and the emergence of new and more pervasive media brought new challenges and new attempts at control. Such was the level of technical progress, much of it in the US, that by the 1930s regular, though limited, television broadcasting services were already in operation in some countries. By the 1950s, a trans-American service had been developed. BBC Northern Ireland began to operate in 1953; UTV followed in 1959. Twenty-three European countries had television by 1956. From as early as 1950, plans were being made to introduce television broadcasting in Ireland, although it was to take nine years to bring them to fruition.[59] Television was "the most powerful and pervasive medium of mass communication yet devised", as Minister Hilliard said at the time "... its potentialities are indeed incalculable: already it has altered in many respects the pattern of living in those countries where it has most developed. The television set has even become a modern household god".[60]

Following the report of the Television Commission in 1959, the legislature enacted the Broadcasting Authority Act 1960, which invested in a semi-state body, the RTÉ Authority, the sole right to operate broadcasting services.[61] The Act established the structures for television broadcasting and provided for the regulation of programming in terms of both operation and content. It imposed requirements of fairness and impartiality, regard for privacy and cultural aims and gave the minister the right to direct the authority to refrain from broadcasting certain matter (section 31). The government was given the power to appoint the authority and to dismiss it. The 1960 Act thus combined statutory autonomy with government control. The ministerial and governmental powers were later curtailed by amending legislation in 1976 (Broadcasting Authority (Amendment) Act 1976).

---

[58] Above, n.39, Horgan, 2001, at pp.20–1.

[59] Robert J. Savage, *Irish Television – The Political and Social Origins* (Cork University Press, Cork, 1996), p.208.

[60] Minister for Posts and Telegraphs, 52 *Seanad Debates*, Cols 11, 13. See also Muiris Mac Conghail, "The Creation of RTÉ and the Impact of Television" in Brian Farrell, above, n.20, p.64.

[61] For a detailed account of the preparatory period, see above, n.59.

3.6.1 Developments in Television

Cable television became a reality in the 1970s under the Wireless Telegraphy (Wired Broadcast Relay Licence) Regulations 1974, as amended in 1988. The MMDS (Multipoint Microwave Distribution System), used instead of cable in less populated areas, is governed by the Wireless Telegraphy (Television Programme Retransmission) Regulations 1989. There are two types of licence in existence now: the licences issued under the 1974 regulations and those under the Wireless Telegraphy (Programme Services Distribution) Regulations 1999, which cover both cable and MMDS and are directed towards the introduction of digital television.

A problem arose in the early 1990s when unlicensed deflector services, relaying mainly British television stations to local communities at a fraction of the MMDS price, began to operate. Cable and MMDS companies, who had apparently obtained exclusive licences for their franchise areas, objected and several court cases ensued.[62] The issue was resolved in the short-term by granting licences to the deflector operators until the term of exclusivity would conclude. The issue is now addressed by the Wireless Telegraphy (UHF Television Programme Retransmission) Regulations, as amended in 2001.[63] Meanwhile, the Irish licence for satellite channels was secured in 1986 by Atlantic, owned by the American Hughes Communications Corporation, and RTÉ began to broadcast across Europe and the United States on the Astra satellite, as well as selling programmes to cable channels. In 1989, RTÉ also began to operate a new station, Atlantic 252, in conjunction with Radio Luxembourg, but later sold its shareholding due to financial pressures.

The pattern in Ireland was not unlike that in a number of other Western European countries. RTÉ television was established at arm's length from government, under the control of a semi-state authority. Under the 1960 Act, it had a monopoly but was saddled with public service obligations. That means that in providing programming it had a public responsibility, and was required to take account of national culture, the need for fairness and impartiality, the right to privacy, good taste, concern for the whole community and the need for understanding and peace. It was required to maintain balance, impartiality and fairness in its news and current affairs coverage. RTÉ was obliged to treat election candidates fairly, although that did not mean that it had to treat them equally.[64] It was prohibited also from broadcasting material likely to incite to crime or to undermine the authority of the State. The fact that certain powers

---

[62] For example, *Southcoast Community Television Broadcasting v Ireland* (*The Irish Times*, November 11, 1995) and *Carrigaline Community Television Broadcasting v Minister for Transport, Energy and Communications* [1997] 1 I.L.R.M. 241.

[63] S.I. No. 348 of 1999. The Regulations provide for annual renewal of the licences and permit a maximum of four frequency channels in respect of any single location. See further *www.odtr.ie* (the Office of the Director of Telecommunications Regulation, now the Commission for Communications Regulation, ComReg).

[64] See *The State (Lynch) v Cooney* [1982] I.R. 337, [1983] I.L.R.M. 89; *Madigan v RTÉ* [1994] I.L.R.M. 472, where the court accepted that past election performance could be *one* of the criteria used by RTÉ in allocating broadcasting time to candidates, but not the only one.

were reserved to the government and minister, including the power to appoint and remove from office the members of the RTÉ Authority, proved problematic in practice and led to the introduction of amending legislation in 1976.

The Broadcasting Authority (Amendment) Act 1976 also established the Broadcasting Complaints Commission (BCC) with power to investigate and adjudicate complaints within specified categories, including the operation of section 31 and the fairness and impartiality requirements; also advertisements and material published by RTÉ. The only sanction provided was that RTÉ must publish the particulars of any complaint when requested to do so by the BCC and in an agreed manner. Reports of decisions are published in the *RTÉ Guide* and usually in the national newspapers. The BCC produces annual reports, which are laid before both Houses of the Oireachtas. One problem with the BCC over the years has been its low level of visibility: it is a part-time commission, meeting only when complaints arise and operating until recently from a box number.

The role of the BCC was expanded in 1988 to allow it to deal with complaints against the commercial stations also.[65] There is now an obligation on television broadcasters, under the EC Television without Frontiers Directive of 1989, to provide a right of reply to viewers.[66] That obligation was addressed in the Broadcasting Act 1990, which provides for complaints by any person to the Broadcasting Complaints Commission (BCC) regarding broadcasts containing inaccurate facts or information, which constitute an attack on that person's honour or reputation (section 8(1)). It also obliges RTÉ to broadcast the decisions of the BCC which find in favour of the complainant, in whole or in part, at a time and in a manner corresponding to that of the offending broadcast (section 8(2)). The role of the BCC has been extended again by the Broadcasting Act 2001. (See Chapter 11 below.)

3.7 PRIVATE COMMERCIAL RADIO AND TELEVISION BROADCASTING

The 1960 Act provided a new framework for radio as well as television and gave RTÉ a monopoly over both forms of broadcasting. Nonetheless, illegal pirate radio stations continued to flourish, with up to 80 or more operating up to 1988 when the Broadcasting and Wireless Telegraphy Act finally forced them off the air, if they were to be eligible to apply for the new commercial licences. Over the decades there had been repeated attempts to use the Wireless Telegraphy Act 1926 against the pirate stations but without success. Constitutional challenges in the High Court by two of the stations did not succeed in having the 1926 legislation set aside as unconstitutional.[67] The applicants in both cases were "pirate" stations whose premises had been raided and equipment seized by employees of the Department of Posts and Telegraphs.

---

[65] Radio and Television Act 1988, s.11.

[66] EC Directive 89/552/EEC, October 3, 1989, Art.23, as amended in 1997.

[67] *Nova Media Services Ltd v Minister for Posts and Telegraphs* [1984] I.L.R.M. 161 and *Sunshine Radio Productions Ltd v Minister for Posts and Telegraphs* [1984] I.L.R.M 170. See also above n.39, Horgan, 2001, at pp.124–7.

They claimed that the Wireless Telegraphy Act 1926, which prohibits broadcasting or the possession of broadcasting equipment except under licence, was unconstitutional in that it infringed their freedom of expression guaranteed by Article 40.6.1.i of the Constitution. The High Court accepted that a stateable case had been made on the constitutional argument but refused the relief sought, namely an interlocutory injunction restraining further raids and seizures.[68]

By the time the *Nova* and *Sunshine Radio* cases were taken, the 1926 Act was hopelessly out of date and totally ineffective in curbing the pirate stations, which by then numbered 80 or 90. The fines that could be imposed under the Act were ludicrously small. In one case, a station with a turnover of several hundred thousand pounds was fined a paltry £20.[69] Pirate stations were able to operate, therefore, beyond the reach of the law, unencumbered by section 31 restrictions or worries about public responsibility, privacy or taste. For the most part, though, they were music stations. Nonetheless, it was a major failing on the part of the legislators that for over 60 years no one in the State with the exception of RTÉ could broadcast lawfully within the State. The Act had made provision for licensing by the Minister, but in all that time no licences were forthcoming. The 1988 legislation was therefore long overdue.

The Broadcasting and Wireless Telegraphy Act 1988 obliged pirate stations interested in acquiring a broadcasting licence to go off the air by midnight on December 31, 1988. The Radio and Television Act 1988 then provided for a system of licensing. It established the Independent Radio and Television Commission (IRTC) (section 3), with powers to grant licences (section 4), initially for a period of seven years, and then subject to review. The Act set out the criteria to be applied by the IRTC in granting licences. For example, it had to have regard to the quality, range and type of programmes proposed, to what extent they would cater for the Irish language, culture and minority interests or provide opportunities for Irish talent in music, dance and entertainment (section 6).

The principles of objective and impartial reporting of news and treatment of current affairs, imposed on RTÉ by the Broadcasting Authority Acts 1960-76, were imposed also on the commercial stations by the Radio and Television Act 1988, as were obligations not to broadcast anything that might "reasonably be regarded as offending against good taste or decency, or as being likely to promote, or incite to, crime or as tending to undermine the authority of the State", and to ensure that "the privacy of any individual is not unreasonably encroached upon" (section 9). The new stations were required to include a minimum level of news and current affairs (20 per cent) in their daily programme schedule, and this was monitored by the IRTC (section 9). This requirement was much criticised at the time because of the expense involved in terms of staff, planning and resources. It was also argued that such requirements belong to the realm of public service broadcasting not commercial

---

[68] The court applied the balance of convenience test, a test which, arguably, is no longer acceptable in freedom of expression cases following the European Court of Human Rights decision in *Spycatcher: Observer and the Guardian v UK*, Series A, No.216; (1992) 14 E.H.R.R. 153.

[69] The penalties were increased by the Broadcasting and Wireless Telegraphy Act 1988.

broadcasting. However, experience has shown that for most stations provision of news is not an undue burden and audiences have a huge appetite for local news. Some local stations experienced teething troubles, however, while the national commercial radio station, Century Radio, collapsed, to be replaced eventually in 1998 by Today FM. The national commercial television station, TV3, was required to carry a "reasonable" amount of news.

In addition to the requirement of a minimum amount of news and current affairs in the Radio and Television Act 1988, an upper limit had been placed on the amount of advertising that could be carried (section 10): not more than 15 per cent of the total programming or ten minutes per hour.[70] As the new stations struggled financially to establish themselves, measures were introduced to cap the advertising revenue earned by RTÉ (Broadcasting Act 1990). However, the measures adopted proved unworkable and were abolished by the Broadcasting Authority (Amendment) Act 1993.

The section 31 ban was also extended by the Radio and Television Act (section 12) to the new commercial stations and the IRTC had the task of preparing guidelines for the commercial stations on how the section was to be applied.[71] In 1993, Brandon Book Publishers sought judicial review of the IRTC's decision not to allow advertisements for Gerry Adams's book of short stories to be carried on the commercial stations.[72] In January 1994, when the government allowed the section 31 order to lapse, the IRTC drew up new guidelines, which were regarded as more flexible than those of RTÉ. They contained a strong endorsement of free speech and a strong presumption against prior restraint.[73] The local stations are also governed by section 9 of the 1988 Act, the equivalent of section 18 of the Broadcasting Authority Act, prohibiting the broadcasting of matter likely to promote or incite to crime or tending to undermine the authority of the State. The IRTC's guidelines offered an interpretation of section 9, which was to be taken to relate to identifiable harm.[74]

---

[70] The Broadcasting Act 1990, s.3, imposed severe restrictions on the amount of advertising that RTÉ could carry (7.5 per cent of daily programming), but this was replaced by the Broadcasting Authority (Amendment) Act 1993, s.2, which allowed the RTÉ Authority to fix the total daily times for broadcasting advertisements and the maximum amount of advertising per hour "subject to the approval of the Minister". The EC Television without Frontiers Directive (above, n.66) also lays down detailed rules governing television advertising in Arts 10–21. Article 18 says that the amount of advertising shall not exceed 15 per cent of daily transmission time, or 20 per cent if it includes teleshopping spots and other forms of advertising. Advertising spots and teleshopping spots within a given clock hour shall not exceed 20 per cent.

[71] There were instances of members of Sinn Féin being barred from the local stations; see *The Irish Times*, December 16, 1989.

[72] *Brandon Book Publishers Ltd v IRTC*, unreported, High Court, Carney J., October 29, 1993; *cf. Brandon Book Publishers Ltd v RTÉ* [1993] I.L.R.M. 806.

[73] IRTC Guidelines, January 17, 1994: *The Irish Times*, January 18, 1994, and Eamonn Hall, "The Majestic Guarantee – Freedom of Speech" (1995) *Dlí, The Western Law Gazette*, No. 9, 79. RTÉ also issued new guidelines in January 1994: *Broadcasting Authority Acts 1960-93, Guidance for Staff on Observance of Section 18(1) of the Broadcasting Authority Act 1960.*

[74] Above, n.73, Hall, at p.83; Colum Kenny, "Section 31 and the Censorship of Programmes" (1994) 12 I.L.T. 50. For a philosophical analysis of s.31, see Desmond Clarke, "Section 31 and Censorship: A Philosophical Perspective" (1994) 12 I.L.T. 53. The Ministerial

In this and other matters the IRTC (now the BCI[75]) has a monitoring function to ensure that the local stations are complying with the terms of their licence. For instance, the BCI can review the news content of a particular station's output and can, if satisfied that there is sufficient diversity of news and current affairs in the locality, reduce the 20 per cent figure. It can also order stations to change their schedule, where they are not providing sufficient local programming, for example.[76] The ultimate sanction is to withdraw the licence, as it did in the case of Radio Limerick One.[77]

The transition from a government-controlled monopoly to a private commercial market was difficult. In the beginning, the strength of RTÉ's position in the market was problematic for the new challengers. Advertising was limited and restrictions were imposed on content and on mode of transmission. The planned third national television station was initially to be carried on MMDS, the multi-point microwave distribution system, which had been tested in Canada and was thought suitable for rural Ireland, where cable was impractical. However, TV3 had difficulty meeting the IRTC's terms in order to take up their licence and the commission decided to withdraw it. In the case that followed, *TV3 v IRTC*,[78] an order of *certiorari* was granted quashing the decision of the IRTC to withdraw the licence from TV3. The order was granted on the grounds of natural justice, as the commission had not given notice of its intention to withdraw the licence or given TV3 an opportunity to be heard, that is, to make its case. An appeal to the Supreme Court by the IRTC was dismissed.[79] Discussions between the two parties continued throughout 1994 and the licence was eventually restored to the consortium. TV3 began broadcasting as the third national station in 1998.[80]

In time, the commercial stations established themselves on the local and national media landscape and became stronger financially. The IRTC also began to grant licences for community broadcasting. A government green paper on the future of broadcasting was published in 1995, followed by the heads of a Bill in 1997.[81] After much discussion on the future of broadcasting, it eventually

---

orders invoking s.31 were not renewed after 1994 and the s.31 provision has now been repealed by the Broadcasting Act 2001.

[75] The IRTC was restructured and renamed the Broadcasting Commission of Ireland under the Broadcasting Act 2001.

[76] This happened, for example, when two companies operating stations in the Cavan/Monaghan and Roscommon/Longford areas merged. They were ordered to retain separate stations and distinctly local programming: *The Irish Times*, January 17, 1995.

[77] [1997] 2 I.L.R.M. 1 (Supreme Court).

[78] Unreported, High Court, Blayney J., May 4, 1992.

[79] Supreme Court, October 26, 1993; *The Irish Times*, October 27, 1993. On the whole saga of TV3, see Colum Kenny, "TV3 and the Regulation of Competition in Broadcasting" in Marie McGonagle (ed.), *Law and Media: the Views of Journalists and Lawyers* (Round Hall Sweet & Maxwell, Dublin, 1997), p.39.

[80] In addition, a new Irish language television station, Teilifís na Gaeilge, became operational in 1996. For reasons of time and convenience, it was set up temporarily under the Broadcasting Authority Acts as part of RTÉ. The Broadcasting Act 2001 now makes provision for Teilifís na Gaeilge (since renamed TG4), to operate as an independent station.

[81] Green Paper, *Active or Passive? Broadcasting in the Future Tense* (Government

led to the passing of the Broadcasting Act 2001. That Act forms the basis for the restructuring of broadcasting and the introduction of digital services in Ireland (see Chapter 11).

3.8 THE DEVELOPMENT OF THE INTERNET AND MULTI-MEDIA

The internet is a network of networks, a global web of linked networks and computers. It is a decentralised, unrestricted global medium of communications. It began as a network established by the Defense Department in the United States in 1969.[82] The first bulletin boards emerged in 1978. Large commercial services began offering gateways to the internet in 1989, and web browsers were introduced in 1995. Given the range and scope of the technology and the pace of technological development, the question of whether and how to regulate the internet became an issue that was not easily resolved.[83] By the end of the twentieth century, mobile telephony, internet access, online newspapers, teletext services on television and webcasting were well established. Digital and interactive services were coming on stream.

3.9 CONCENTRATION AND CONVERGENCE IN THE LATE TWENTIETH CENTURY

The late twentieth century, therefore, saw a period of exceptional growth in the range and scope of the print and broadcast media.[84] It witnessed the development and maturing of television, the beginnings of the new computer-based media and a resultant converging of the various technologies involved. Newspaper owners had begun to invest in radio and television operators, and vice versa. Both print and broadcast media had set their sights on the opportunities for expansion and the potential for new services offered by the newest technologies. The market was gradually coming to be dominated by fewer, bigger players.

The demise of the Irish Press group afforded an opportunity for Independent Newspapers to take an even greater share of the newspaper market in Ireland. The matter of increasing their financial interest in the *Sunday Tribune* and of their loans to the ailing Press Group, were both referred to the Competition

---

Publications, Dublin, 1995); *Clear Focus – The Government's Proposals for Broadcasting Legislation* (Pn 3648, The Stationery Office, Dublin, 1997).

[82] See, for example, Raymond Wacks, "Privacy in Cyberspace: Personal Information, Free Speech, and the Internet" in Peter Birks (ed.), *Privacy and Loyalty* (Clarendon Press, Oxford, 1997), p.93, at p.95.

[83] See Denis Kelleher, "The Regulation of the Internet" (1998) 3 B.R. 408.

[84] After a period of relative calm in the newspaper market, changes in technology, events in Northern Ireland and competition from the British newspapers, particularly the tabloids, all contributed to change and a period of growth and expansion. The *Sunday World* had been launched in 1973 to take on the British tabloids. It published a northern edition also. See above, n.39, Horgan, 2001, pp.108–9. *Magill* magazine was launched in 1977, the *Sunday Tribune* in 1980, the *Star* in 1988, and the *Sunday Business Post* in 1989.

Authority.[85] The Authority recommended against both, as being likely to prevent or restrict competition and as an abuse of a dominant position.[86] A new Sunday newspaper, *Ireland on Sunday*, eventually emerged in 1997, to take the place of the sports newspaper, *The Title*, which had been set up following the demise of *The Sunday Press*.[87]

The demise of the Press group and the growth of Independent Newspapers led to concern as to the future of the newspaper industry in Ireland. As a result, the Government set up a Commission on the Newspaper Industry in 1995. The Commission reported in 1996 and made a number of recommendations, including reform of the defamation laws, protection of privacy, and the establishment of a newspaper ombudsman.[88] None of those have yet been acted upon; the Government's response to the wider issues was to seek a review of the Commission's report by the Competition and Mergers Review Group of the Department of Enterprise, Trade and Employment. That Group reported in June 2000, with suggestions for inclusion in Competition legislation.[89] Meanwhile, consolidation and concentration of ownership continued. Independent Newspapers continued their expansion into Northern Ireland, buying the *Belfast Telegraph*, while the Belfast *Newsletter* became part of the British Mirror group. Scottish Radio Holdings expanded its interests in the Irish local newspaper and broadcast markets, while UTV took over two Cork local radio stations.[90] As the twenty-first century dawned, there was considerable concern in Ireland, as in other countries, at the impact such expansion and consolidation would have on plurality of ownership and diversity of viewpoint in the media, principles much valued in a democratic society.

Further Reading

Adams, Michael, *Censorship: The Irish Experience* (The University of Alabama Press, Alabama, 1968).
Hall, Eamonn, *The Electronic Age: Telecommunication in Ireland* (Oak Tree Press, Dublin, 1993).

---

[85] Competition Authority, *Report of the Investigation of the Proposal whereby Independent Newspapers plc would Increase its Shareholding in the Tribune Group from 29.9% to a possible 53.09%* (The Stationery Office, Dublin, 1992), and Competition Authority, *Interim Report of Study on the Newspaper Industry* (The Stationery Office, Dublin, 1995).

[86] Above, n.85, *Report*, 1992, at para.6.17; *Report*, 1995, at para.8.62.

[87] It was taken over in 2000 by Scottish Holdings Ltd: above, n.39, Horgan 2001, pp.164–5.

[88] Commission on the Newspaper Industry, *Report* (Pn 2841, The Stationery Office, Dublin, 1996).

[89] Competition and Mergers Review Group, *Final Report*, Pn 8487 (Department of Trade and Enterprise, Dublin, 2000). The Competition Act 2002, s.23 now makes specific provision for media mergers.

[90] For details of changes in ownership during this period, see above n.39, Horgan, 2001, pp.164–5. For an overview of the Irish media landscape, see *www.ejc.nl/jr/emland/ireland.html* (European Journalism Centre, Maastricht). More recent developments in the media in Ireland are addressed in Chap.11 below.

Horgan, John, *Irish Media – A Critical History Since 1922* (Routledge, London and New York, 2001).

Inglis, Brian, *Freedom of the Press in Ireland 1784–1841* (Faber and Faber, London, 1954).

Munter, Robert, *The History of the Irish Newspaper 1685–1760* (Cambridge University Press, Cambridge, 1967).

Jones, Derek, (ed.), *Censorship: A World Encyclopedia* (Fitzroy Dearborn, London and Chicago, 2001 (4 volumes)).

Ó Drisceoil, Donal, *Censorship in Ireland 1939–45* (Cork University Press, Cork, 1996).

Pine, Richard, *2RN and the Origins of Irish Radio* (Four Courts Press, Dublin, 2002).

Savage, Robert J., *Irish Television – The Political and Social Origins* (Cork University Press, Cork, 1996).

CHAPTER FOUR

Defamation

To deny any advantage to censure ... is to give an undue preponderance to praise.[1]

4.1 INTRODUCTION

A person's good name is priceless. The Bible makes various references to good name, which is more important than "great riches".[2] Shakespeare in *Othello* refers to good name as the "jewel" of the "soul", the "purest treasure mortal times afford".[3] Originally conceived as a form of property, which could be acquired or earned, good name or reputation developed a close affinity with concepts of honour (status and personal identity) and dignity (social respect and civility).[4] Its essence, however, is not fame or distinction; it is not character or personality or image, but rather how one is judged by the public.[5] Irrespective

---

[1] John Stuart Mill, "Law of Libel and Liberty of the Press" in John M. Robson (ed.), *Essays on Equality, Law and Education* (University of Toronto Press, Toronto, 1980), p.3 at p.16.

[2] For example, Proverbs 22:1.

[3] Act III, scene iii, 155–61. Yet "Reputation is an idle and most false imposition; oft got without merit and lost without deserving." Othello II. iii. 259-64. Is the seeming contradiction a case of ambivalence, as Barendt says in "What is the point of Libel Law?" [1999] 52 *Current Legal Problems* 110, at p.114, or is a distinction being made between good name and reputation?

[4] Robert C. Post, "The Social Foundations of Defamation Law: Reputation and the Constitution" (1986) 74 Cal.L.Rev. 691, at pp.703,707. Barendt, above, n.3, at p.117, points out, however, that libel law protects reputation, not dignity, which is too vague and amorphous a concept to provide a basis for a legal cause of action: "its place is in a constitution, rather than in the law of torts which is concerned to provide redress for clear and demonstrable injuries." See also Thomas Gibbons, "Defamation Reconsidered" [1996] 16 *Oxford Journal of Legal Studies* 587 at p.592: a reputation is not a fixed attribute of the individual but rather an appraisal based on the facts which are known about the person and on the social values which are considered relevant; therefore a reputation is socially contingent. It depends on others' views and assessments and it does not represent in itself a personal interest, which the law can defend. It is not necessarily, or even mainly, dependent on moral evaluations. Gibbons concludes that what is required is a means of dealing with the important concern, indirectly associated with reputation, that individuals should not be judged by false information.

[5] Van Vechten Veeder, "The History and Theory of the Law of Defamation – Part II" (1904) 4 Colum. L. Rev. 33. In medieval times, a person without a good reputation could not serve as a witness or bring a case as a plaintiff. In feudal society, the right to hold land depended on a reputation for faithfulness, while under Roman law one's rights as a citizen could be lost if one gained a reputation for bad moral conduct: see Solveig

of possessions, land, money or social status, a person can have his/her good name among friends, neighbours, colleagues, clients and community.

Freedom of expression, however, is also priceless: the freedom to communicate our thoughts, opinions and criticisms; to receive and impart information; to engage in dialogue and in public and private debate. The modern media play an important role in that information and communication process.

The first questions that arise are how to protect both good name and freedom of expression, and what is to happen if these two priceless values come into conflict? What happens if public debate reflects adversely on the good name of an individual or company? Must public debate give way to the concerns of that individual or company, or should good name take second place to the interests of society in open public debate? The problem boils down to how two conflicting values are reconciled. How a society resolves that conflict sheds a great deal of light on its character.

A second series of questions in the media context concerns the extent to which existing laws take account of, regulate or underpin the important role and function of the media in today's society. In the common-law world the tool devised to protect good name or reputation (the esteem in which others hold us) is the civil law of defamation and, in particularly serious cases, the law of criminal libel. This chapter deals with the civil law as it affects the media; criminal libel will be dealt with in Chapter 8 (prosecutions for defamatory libel), Chapter 9 (obscene and blasphemous libel) and Chapter 10 (political and seditious libel).[6]

4.2 WHAT IS DEFAMATION?

"Defamation" is the generic term for two torts or civil wrongs, libel and slander. "Libel" refers to publication in any lasting or permanent form, and "slander" refers to publication in a passing or transient form, usually the spoken word. The distinction is purely historical and serves no useful purpose today.[7] In the

---

Singleton, "Privacy versus the First Amendment" [2000] 11 Fordham Intell. Prop. Media & Ent. L.J. 97, at p.130, citing Diane L. Zimmerman, "Requiem for a Heavyweight: a Farewell to Warren and Brandeis's Privacy Tort" (1983) 68 Cornell L. Rev. 291.

[6] For a fuller treatment of defamation, see Marc McDonald, *Irish Law of Defamation* (2nd ed., The Round Hall Press, Dublin, 1989); Sir Brian Neill and Richard Rampton, *Duncan and Neill on Defamation* (Butterworths, London, 1983); Peter Frederick Carter-Ruck *et al.*, *Carter–Ruck on Libel and Slander* (5th ed., Butterworths, London, 1997); P. Milo and E.G. Rogers (eds), *Gatley on Libel and Slander* (9th ed., Sweet & Maxwell, London, 1998).

[7] W.S. Holdsworth traces its history and calls it an "unfortunate distinction": "Defamation in the Sixteenth and Seventeenth Centuries" (1924) 40 L.Q.R. 397. Various attempts to abolish the distinction between libel and slander were made in England, including the 1816 Brougham Bill, 1834 Daniel O'Connell Bill, 1843 Lord Campbell Bill: above, n.5, Van Vechten Veeder at p.55. Various law reform bodies since then have recommended its abolition. See, for example, Irish Law Reform Commission, *Report on the Civil Law of Defamation* (LRC 38–1991) at p.5; Australian Law Reform Commission, *Unfair Publication: Defamation and Privacy*, 1979, at para.76; Faulks Committee, *Report of the Committee on Defamation* (Cmnd 5909, London, 1975), Chap.2. Today libel is still

media context, therefore, the terms "defamation" and "libel" tend to be used interchangeably, and "slander" for the most part does not apply except, for example, where a journalist says something defamatory when interviewing someone for a story or in a personal capacity, in which case it is not a media issue. Section 15 of the Defamation Act 1961 specifies that defamation occurring in broadcasting is to be treated as publication in permanent form, that is, as libel rather than slander. The internet, too, despite its "chat" rooms and constant changing and updating, is of an enduring nature and has a global reach, such as to bring it within the rubric of libel. As such, the courts, in the absence of specific legislation, endeavour to apply traditional defamation law rules to online defamation.

Libel can also be prosecuted as a crime in some circumstances (see Chapter 8). Prosecutions nowadays are rare, particularly in the case of the media. In recent times, however, there have been some prosecutions for libel on the internet.[8] Civil actions for damages, on the other hand, are frequent.[9] Civil actions, or suits, may be taken in the Circuit Court or High Court, seeking compensation (damages) or possibly an injunction. In the Circuit Court there is no jury and the upper limit on compensation is currently €38,092.14; in the High Court there is still a jury in defamation cases and there is no upper limit on damages, which are said to be "at large".[10]

---

regarded as much more serious than slander and this difference is reflected in the amounts of compensation awarded. The amounts for slander remain low, although a recent case resulted in an award of €12,500: *Kane v Clarke* (*The Irish Times*, February 8, 2002).

[8] For example, an allegation that a teacher was a paedophile resulted in a two-and-a-half year prison sentence, with a recommendation that it be served in the Central Mental Hospital: *The Irish Times*, December 21, 1999, January 15, 2000; also *DPP v Kenny*, Circuit Court, March 27, 2001, *The Irish Times*, March 28, 2001: a businessman was convicted of libelling a business competitor (female) on the internet. He had placed a notice on the internet indicating that she was providing prostitution services. Following conviction, the defendant had to pay £30,000 compensation to the victim and was put on probation (*The Irish Times*, May 19, 2001). Examples of civil actions for defamation relating to the internet include: *Forbes v Barnes and Noble* (*The Sunday Times*, June 6, 1999): sample chapter of the book *The Committee* about the role of security forces in N. Ireland on the internet; *Trimble v Amazon.com (UK)* (*The Sunday Times*, June 6, 1999, *The Irish Times*, June 14, 1999): the defendants were the distributors of the same book in the UK.

[9] An examination of High Court records in defamation cases revealed that the total number of cases set down for hearing in the five-year period 1986–90 was more than double that of 1981–85. The number for 1990 alone was more than double that for 1986 and more than four times that for 1980. See Kevin Boyle and Marie McGonagle, *A Report on Press Freedom and Libel* (NNI, Dublin, 1988), and "Defamation – The Path to Law Reform" in Marie McGonagle (ed.), *Law and the Media* (Round Hall Sweet & Maxwell, Dublin, 1997), p.57. Statistics, where quoted and not otherwise attributed, are from those two sources.

[10] The Law Reform Commission has, however, put forward proposals for changes to the law of defamation (above, n.7), and a private member's bill, incorporating most of those changes was introduced in the Oireachtas in February 1995. The government put a stay of nine months on it, with a view to bringing in its own proposals. At the time of writing, a new Defamation Bill is still promised – see further below; also Barry O'Halloran, "All the news that's Fit to Print?" (1999) 93(4) *Law Society Gazette* 16.

4.2.1 Historical Development

Defamation and *scandalum magnatum* (1275) – the inventing or spreading of false news about the monarch, royal ministers or chief peers and the "great men of the realm", were already offences in sixteenth-century England, when the king's courts took over jurisdiction from the earlier secular and ecclesiastical authorities.[11] The press was licensed, and by the end of that century, various publications were banned, including all publications of satire.[12] Up to the seventeenth century, when the tort of defamation was first developed (1670), the usual course of conduct if someone insulted you or said something to injure your good name was to resort to violence or challenge him to a duel. A more peaceable solution had to be found in the interests of public order. In 1609, the Star Chamber, a court comprising the highest dignitaries of church and state, established to suppress the rising tide of public opinion, invoked provisions of Roman criminal law.[13] It offered the possibility of prosecuting and punishing the offender as an alternative to duelling. The likelihood of a breach of the peace was a central concern, but the importance of defamation lay also in the nature of the political structures and Christian teachings of the period. Politics took place at court, where personalities and social status counted more than policies and "nothing sapped legitimacy more effectively than the literature of libel".[14] Christian teaching emphasised the moral obligation not to expose one's neighbour's failings, and the church courts treated defamation as a violation of "harmony and charity within the Christian community".[15] There was thus an overlap between Christian values and the secular code as to the sacredness of a gentleman's good name.[16]

If the scandal was in writing, it was regarded as being particularly serious and past any justification. Writing had been so rare an accomplishment that much weight was attached to anything written.[17] As a result, truth was not a defence to defamation in either ecclesiastical or common law.[18] In time, private

---

[11] See Debora Shuger, "Civility and Censorship in Early Modern England" in Robert C. Post (ed.), *Censorship and Silencing: Practices of Cultural Regulation* (The Getty Research Institute, Los Angeles, CA., 1998), pp.93, 97.

[12] *ibid.* at 89.

[13] Van Vechten Veeder, "The History and Theory of the Law of Defamation – Part I" (1903) 3 Colum. L. Rev. 546, at 562-3. The Star Chamber was abolished in 1640-1.

[14] Above, n.11, at p.96, n.32. See also Lois G. Forer, *A Chilling Effect – The Mounting Threat of Libel and Invasion of Privacy Actions to the First Amendment* (W.W. Norton, New York and London, 1987), pp.52–4. Shugar, above, n.11, at p.92 says: Character assassination remains an effective tactic today, but it would have been particularly so in an era without reliable, independent sources of news and without the "hard" evidence of fingerprinting and photographs. Such lies presented a serious political danger because they would have been virtually impossible to refute.

[15] Above, n.11, at p.98; n.13, at pp.550–1: the Church punished defamation as a sin; the usual ecclesiastical penance was acknowledgment of the baselessness of the imputation and an apology to the person defamed.

[16] Above, n.11, at p.99, although, as Holdsworth says, above, n.7, at p.409, defamation, which alleged offences cognizable only in the Ecclesiastical Courts, and unaccompanied by temporal damage, was not actionable at common law.

[17] Above, n.13, at p.566.

[18] Above, n.11, at p.98.

prosecutions for defamation in the courts became so popular and numerous, often dealing with trivial matters, that they had to be discouraged. Since truth was not a defence to a criminal prosecution, those with something to hide preferred to prosecute rather than run the risk of a civil action in which the defence of truth might succeed against them. Besides, damages were less important to the rich and powerful than revenge and restoration of honour through a successful prosecution and consequent punishment of the perpetrator of the libel. It was not money they wanted (although in a hierarchical society, money could "ennoble") but rather the satisfaction of having the offender fined or imprisoned.

From 1697 on, prosecutions could only be brought for written defamation, and from 1888 the Newspaper Libel and Registration Act made it more difficult to prosecute newspaper proprietors, publishers and editors, by requiring the leave of a judge in chambers to do so. After 1835, a more liberal regime existed and State prosecutions for political or seditious libels were discontinued. However, the crown law officers were still willing to take up criminal libel actions started by individuals against newspapers and were even willing to intervene in civil actions brought by individuals in order to ensure a fine and prison sentence.[19]

Criminal prosecutions in Britain and Ireland eventually gave way in the twentieth century[20] to civil actions for damages, in contrast to other European countries, like France and Germany, where criminal prosecutions, though rare by comparison, remained the norm. That is so for a variety of reasons, including the fact that in Germany, in particular, money damages were not regarded as an appropriate remedy for injury to good name or reputation. It was regarded as demeaning to reduce a person's reputation to money terms.[21]

During the nineteenth century, cases of civil defamation usually involved private individuals rather than the press. For example, in Ireland there were the notorious cases of a Father O'Keeffe who sued the cardinal for punishing him under canon law. He was punished, he said, because he had remained faithful to his oath of allegiance to the crown and had refused to recognise the temporal supremacy of the pope. A few years prior to that, Fr O'Keeffe had also sued the bishop for slander, for which he had been suspended, so he sued the vicar general of the diocese for libel and slander in suspending him. At one stage he was awarded one farthing but that verdict was set aside and the case never came before the courts again.[22]

It was not unknown, either, for newspaper proprietors to settle their differences, which often spilled over into their papers, by means of civil actions

---

[19] See, for example, Brian Inglis, *The Freedom of the Press in Ireland: 1784–1841* (Faber and Faber, London, 1954), p.225. (The Attorney General intervened in a civil suit to procure the publisher of *The Pilot* a three-month prison sentence and fine, even though the libels complained of were not particularly offensive.)

[20] This occurred from the time of the Second World War in Britain; see J.R. Spencer, "Criminal Libel – A Skeleton in the Cupboard", Parts 1 and 2, [1977] Crim. L.R. 383, 465, at p.389.

[21] See Professor Werner Lorenz, "Privacy and the Press – A German Experience", *Butterworth's Lectures*, 1989-90, (Butterworths, London, 1990).

[22] The Archbishop of Dublin, "The O'Keeffe Cases" (1913) 1 Ir. Eccles. Rec., pp.113–31.

for defamation. The most notorious civil actions for libel during that period, however, were taken by Orangemen against the *Evening Mail* and the *Evening Post*, which had expressed disgust at the selection of one of them as subsheriff of Monaghan. A jury in each case awarded what for the time were heavy damages (£250, £300).[23]

4.2.1.1 Rules Laid Down by Statute

The first statute in which defamation was mentioned was in 1285.[24] Various statutes followed. Since then, the rules governing the tort of defamation were formulated over a long period by judges in the common-law courts. Some of those rules were then modified or clarified by statutes dating from 1792 to 1888. Nineteenth-century England saw the introduction of a number of measures designed to ease the situation for the press. Those legislative measures came about as a result of intense lobbying by the newspapers themselves, aided by the fact that a number of newspaper proprietors were then in parliament.

In 1843, Lord Campbell's Libel Act provided for the publication of apologies as a remedy for libel, which was a significant step forward. It also provided for payment of money into court by the defendant before a hearing as an incentive to the plaintiff to settle or run the risk of having to pay his own legal costs. In defamation cases, the winner took all; so if the defendant lost the case, s/he had to pay his/her own legal costs and those of the other party, unless the amount of money s/he had paid into court beforehand was higher than the amount of damages awarded by the court, in which case the plaintiff, even though successful, had to pay his/her own costs. The idea of payment into court, therefore, was to even up the risk to the two parties and encourage them to settle their dispute. The aims of the 1843 Act were very much in the press's favour but, in some respects, they proved problematic in practice and the Act was amended in 1845.

If newspapers had a legal privilege to report certain matters, they could not be sued for defamation arising out of those reports. Section 2 of the Newspaper Libel and Registration Act 1881 extended privilege to reports of public meetings. It was repealed by the Law of Libel (Amendment) Act 1888, which re-enacted the privilege, but in a narrower form, by giving lists of those particular types of meetings that would be covered by privilege. The 1888 Act also made provision for privilege in respect of reports of parliament and court proceedings. It required leave to be obtained from a judge for the institution of criminal proceedings against newspapers.

The main provisions of those statutes were then incorporated, with slight modifications, into the Defamation Act 1952 in Britain (1955 in Northern Ireland), which deals exclusively with civil defamation, and the Defamation Act 1961 in Ireland, which closely followed the British Act, but deals with both civil and criminal defamation. Both Acts therefore reflect the technology

---

[23] Above, n.19, at p.225: *Gray v Evening Post* (£250), *Jones v Evening Mail* (£300).
[24] 13 Edward I, c.1 – see above, n.13, at p.551.

and media practice of the 1950s. The British have updated aspects of the 1952 Act in the Defamation Act 1996 but, in Ireland there has been no statutory intervention since 1961, despite repeated calls and recommendations for reform.[25]

Defamation, therefore, is an area of law made up of common-law rules and statute law. However, in the Irish context, there is a further important dimension: the constitutional protection of good name and of freedom of expression, including that of the press.

4.2.1.2 Constitutional Dimension

In Britain, freedom of speech is only a common-law principle, not a constitutional right, although it now has the protection of Article 10 of the European Convention of Human Rights to the extent that the Convention is incorporated into English law by the Human Rights Act 1998. In Ireland, as in other European jurisdictions and the United States, which have written constitutions, freedom of speech is a constitutional right. With the possible exception of the United States, however, that right is not absolute. Quite the contrary, it is subject to a host of other considerations and consequent restrictions.

The Irish Constitution of 1937 characterises the right as one to express freely one's convictions and opinions but includes a reference to the "rightful liberty of expression" of the media "including criticism of government policy". That liberty shall not be used to undermine public order or morality or the authority of the State. Furthermore, the publication or utterance of blasphemous, seditious or indecent matter shall be punishable in accordance with law (Article 40.6.1.i). The constitutional recognition of the media's freedom of expression, therefore, appears rather weak. It could be argued, however, that the Constitution accepts that the media are entitled to extensive freedom to publish, and merely points out that that freedom is subject to certain limitations. The subsection of the article that deals with freedom of expression and the media does not actually mention defamation as a limitation.

However, in Article 40.3.2 the Constitution specifically guarantees the right to good name. Following a guarantee to respect and defend the personal rights of the citizen in Article 40.3.1, the Constitution states:

> "The State shall, in particular, by its laws protect as best it may from unjust attack and, in the case of injustice done, vindicate the ... good name ... of every citizen". (Article 40.3.2)

Because the Constitution is paramount and all other laws must comply with it, the question arises as to whether the tort of defamation, which was in existence for centuries before the Constitution came into force, adequately reflects and

---

[25] See Law Reform Commission, above, n.7; *Report of the Commission on the Newspaper Industry* (Pn 2841, Stationery Office, Dublin, 1996); Report of the Special Rapporteur on Freedom of Expression in Ireland (1999), E/CN.4/2000/63/Add 2, at para.84, available at *www.unhchr.ch*. See further below.

implements the constitutional guarantees. Does it protect the good name of every citizen from unjust attack and vindicate it in the case of injustice done to it? Does it offer adequate protection and appropriate vindication to the individual whose good name is attacked? Does it make adequate provision for the protection of the media's freedom of expression? Is it possible that defamation law actually goes beyond what the Constitution requires and protects good name not only from unjust attack but from any or all attacks? If so, what is the effect of defamation rules on freedom of expression and on the media?

The Constitution itself does not provide a mechanism for deciding which right is to prevail when two constitutionally protected rights come into conflict. The courts strive for a harmonious interpretation of the Constitution. In weighing conflicting rights, guidance can be obtained from the European Convention on Human Rights, which is now being incorporated into Irish law by legislation (see Chapter 2 above.) Article 10 of the Convention prioritises freedom of expression. Freedom of expression is the core value and it can only be restricted to the extent necessary in a democratic society to protect other specified rights and interests. Among those rights and interests is reputation, or good name.

In Ireland the constitutional statement on freedom of the press has tended to be considered too weak to have any real impact on the common-law approach to defamation. In direct contrast, the United States Constitution, with its strong First Amendment commitment to freedom of the press, has dominated and reshaped the tort of defamation in that country. In Ireland, as a consequence of following developments in Britain, which had no such guarantee, the tort of defamation continued to operate along common-law lines as if the Constitution did not exist. It is arguable that at least some of those common-law rules and how they affect the media could be challenged successfully under Article 10 of the European Convention on Human Rights.[26]

For decades the constitutional argument based on freedom of the press was not often advanced, and when it was, it was not embraced with any great enthusiasm by the courts. Judges showed a reluctance to introduce constitutional jurisprudence into an area that for centuries had been dealt with at common law, with only relatively minor statutory modifications. When they did address the constitutional dimension, they tended to refer only to Article 40.3, the right to good name.[27] The underlying assumption was that the common law of defamation, partly codified in the Defamation Act, had got the balance right. The Constitution Review Group, reporting in 1996, said: "[T]he essential question is whether the defamation laws effect a fair balance between the right

---

[26] See, for example, *Lingens v Austria*, Series A, No.103; (1986) 8 E.H.R.R. 407; *Oberschlick v Austria*, Series A, No.204; (1991) 12 H.R.L.J. 238, (1995) 19 E.H.R.R. 389; *Schwabe v Austria*, Series A, No.242-B (1992); *Tolstoy Miloslavsky v UK*, Series A, No.316-B; (1995) 20 E.H.R.R. 442; [1996] E.M.L.R. 152. For cases decided in the UK under the Human Rights Act 1998, see Andrew Nicol, Gavin Millar, Andrew Sharland, *Media Law and Human Rights* (Blackstone Press Ltd, London, 2001).

[27] Academic commentators over the last decade or so have advocated a new approach based on the Constitution; see, for example, above, n.6, McDonald; n.9, Boyle and McGonagle, O'Dell, "Does Defamation Value Free Expression?" (1990) 12 D.U.L.J. 50, and "Reflections on a Revolution in Libel" (1991) I.L.T. 181.

of free speech on the one hand and the need to protect individual reputations on the other".[28]

But do the defamation laws effect a fair balance? Is the law of defamation sound? Given Ireland's history of dispossession and poverty, it is understandable that human dignity and good name should occupy a special place in the value system. This may go some way to explain why a jury will sometimes award higher damages for reputation than they would for physical injuries. It is also a fact of life that the higher a person's material wealth and standing in the community, the higher the amount of damages likely to be awarded. The more ordinary the person, the lower the damages – if the person can afford to bring an action in the first place, because free legal aid is not available in defamation cases.[29] It is incongruous that good name should be so highly valued and yet no legal aid provided to enable less well-off individuals access to the courts to seek a remedy for attacks made on their good name.

The Irish Constitution speaks of protection for, and vindication of, good name. The protection provided for good name by defamation law lies partly in the availability, in limited circumstances, of injunctions, but mainly in the threat of damages. The threat of damages awards to the very survival of some of the indigenous media can be so acute that some stories are simply not published, reports are so watered down as to be almost unrecognisable, and cases that ought to be fought in the courts are settled out of court for sizeable sums of money. Research has shown that of every 100 cases commenced in the courts against the media, approximately 80 are settled out of court or during the hearing, in most instances with some monetary payment. Of the remaining 20, approximately 15 are won by the plaintiffs and five by the media.[30] Some

---

[28] *Report of the Constitution Review Group* (Pn. 2632, Government Publications, Dublin, 1996), p.295. See also the Law Reform Commission, *Consultation Paper on the Civil Law of Defamation*, 1991, p.194: "A defamation action is unusual in that there are three interested parties. The plaintiff who perceives himself to be a victim of an attack upon his reputation wishes to assert his constitutional right to protection of his good name. The defendant who has made the statement at issue is appealing to a countervailing constitutional guarantee of free speech. The delicate balancing exercise necessitated by attempting to reconcile these important interests is complicated by the fact that expression of any kind plays a vital role in democracy and there is therefore a large public interest at stake. ... We believe that current Irish defamation law fails to serve each of these interests satisfactorily in many areas." *Cf.* the Faulks Committee, above, n.7 at para. 19: "The law of defamation has two basic purposes: to enable the individual to protect his reputation, and to preserve the right of free speech. These two purposes necessarily conflict. The law of defamation is sound if it preserves a proper balance between them."

[29] Defamation is expressly excluded under the Civil Legal Aid Act 1995, s.28(9)(a)(i). This is despite the recommendations of the Pringle Committee in 1977: *Report of the Committee on Civil Legal Aid and Advice* (Prl. 6862, Government Publications, Dublin, 1977). In the UK, the Access to Justice Act 1999, s.6, Schedule 2, para.1, makes provision for funding for defamation cases through the Community Legal Services Fund, or the Legal Aid Fund. See, however, *McVicar v UK*, App. No.46311/99, (2002) 35 E.H.R.R. 22, where it was held by the European Court of Human Rights that, in the specific circumstances of the case, the absence of legal aid did not constitute a violation of the Convention. The applicant, a journalist, was well-educated and would have been well able to represent himself before the court.

[30] Above, n.9. The problem is particularly acute for small publications and book publishers. See, for example, the *Sunday Tribune*, October 23, 1988 and *The Irish Times*, November

newspapers and books are read from cover to cover by lawyers before publication to try to detect possible libels.

The Constitution puts the onus on the State to vindicate the good name of every citizen, but does an award of damages when a case finally comes to court some three years after publication actually vindicate a person's good name? Perhaps more immediate remedies would be appropriate in many circumstances. Furthermore, if the remedy is court-based, it is questionable whether every citizen's good name can be vindicated in the absence of legal aid. There is an inequity also in the fact that the State may pay the costs of civil servants and other State employees who sue for defamation in respect of their official role. If they win, they keep their damages; if they lose, the State pays their costs.[31]

All of these issues and more were addressed by the Law Reform Commission in its *Consultation Paper* and *Report on the Civil Law of Defamation* in 1991. To date its recommendations have not been acted upon, although a private member's bill based on them was introduced in 1995, and successive governments have included libel law reform in their programmes for government. The courts have also intimated, that, with respect to constitutional rights, good name is not a "trump" card that takes precedence over all other rights.[32] This may have signalled the first step towards a new balance or constitutionalising of the tort of defamation.[33] For the present, it is necessary to examine the existing rules, with the constitutional requirements in mind.

11, 1989. (Gill & Macmillan, for example, had paid out well over £100,000 in out-of-court settlements and costs in the previous 18 months and had to discontinue libel insurance as it could not afford the premiums demanded.) Libel cases are believed to have led to the demise of the *Irish Statesman* in 1928 *(Clandillon v Irish Statesman,* High Court, November 14, 1928, a case that arose out of a review of a book of folk songs, *Lon Dubh a' Chairn); The Leader* in 1955 *(Kavanagh v The Leader,* unreported, Supreme Court, March 4, 1955, a reference in a literary article to poet Patrick Kavanagh); the Irish language newspaper *Amárach* in 1983 *(Lindsay v Amárach,* reported in *The Irish Times,* February 15, 1983, a reference to how a government minister was allocating state money). More recently, libel actions were reported to have caused the sale of the *Cavan Leader (Sunday Tribune,* November 17, 1991).

[31] See, for example, *Cole v RTÉ (The Irish Times,* May 3–13, 1989); *Holloway v Business and Finance* [1987] I.L.R.M. 790, [1988] I.R. 494, *The Irish Times,* December 1, 1990. In the latter case, the articles complained of were published in 1985 but the case was not disposed of until 1990. State employees constitute the third largest group of people suing for libel. Business and professionals constitute the largest; see above n.9 at para. 6.14 and p.99, respectively.

[32] *Goodman v Hamilton (No.2)* [1993] 3 I.R. 307; *Burke v Central Television* [1994] 2 I.L.R.M. 161; Chap.2 above.

[33] See discussion on Constitution, Chap.2 above. The tort of defamation has been constitutionalised in the United States *(New York Times v Sullivan* (1964) 376 U.S. 254, and following cases) and in Australia (where the High Court confirmed that the common law of defamation must conform to the freedom of expression guarantee implicit in the constitution: *Lange v Australian Broadcasting Corporation* (1997) 145 A.L.R. 96; and the earlier cases of *Theophanous v Herald and Weekly Times Ltd* (1994) 68 A.L.J.R. 713; *Stephens v West Australian Newspapers Ltd.* (1994) 68 A.L.J.R. 765. See further discussion below on the defence of qualified privilege.

4.3 KEY ELEMENTS IN PROVING DEFAMATION

There is no statutory definition of defamation and therefore it is necessary to fall back on judicial dicta to formulate one. A working definition, based on such dicta, is:

"Defamation consists of the wrongful publication of a false statement about a person, which tends to lower that person in the eyes of right-thinking members of society or tends to hold that person up to hatred, ridicule or contempt, or causes that person to be shunned or avoided by right-thinking members of society".[34]

While such a definition is not rigid and must not be parsed and analysed with the precision due to a statutory definition, it does nonetheless pinpoint the elements of the tort and offer a structure in which to discuss and assess the rules. Each of the main elements of that definition will be discussed in turn.

4.3.1 Wrongful Publication

For present purposes the word "wrongful" indicates publication of a kind or of matter prohibited or not exempted by law. "Publication" refers to the making or communicating of a statement about a person to a third party, that is, someone other than the person himself/herself. Because the essence of defamation is the harm done to the esteem in which a person is held by others, the defamatory remarks must have been made to others, even one other, but not just the person they concern: "If a plaintiff loses the respect for his reputation of some or even one right-thinking person he suffers some injury".[35]

In a media setting, publication is almost always present. Communication to others is fundamental to the media's function, whether in the pages of a newspaper, on radio or television, on video, film or other medium.

Defamation cases have arisen also from publication on the internet, by placing defamatory material on bulletin boards, in e-mails and on websites. Given the nature of the technology, proving publication on the internet may be somewhat more difficult than in the traditional media, as it can easily be

---

[34] See Bryan McMahon and William Binchy, *Irish Law of Torts* (3rd ed., Butterworths, Dublin, 2000, p.882); also *Quigley v Creation Ltd* [1971] I.R. 269, *Berry v The Irish Times* [1973] I.R. 368.

[35] McLoughlin J. in *Berry*, above, n.34. Thomas Starkie explained that defamation law exists to compensate "temporal" losses, not "spiritual grievances, which cannot be estimated in money ... [A]nd so, a mere injury to the feelings without actual deterioration of person or property, cannot form an independent and substantive ground of proceeding": Thomas Starkie, *A Treatise on the Law of Slander, Libel, Scandalum Magnatum and False Rumours xx*, New York 1826, cited in Robert C. Post, "The Social Foundations of Defamation Law: Reputation and the Constitution" (1986) 74 *California Law Review* 691 at p.695. However, Anglo-Saxon law from which the common law of defamation evolved was particularly concerned with insults addressed by one person to another. The requirement that the communication be published to a third party emerged only gradually: Post, *ibid.*, p.710 at n.112.

removed, and evidence such as times and dates can easily be tampered with. The opportunity for accidental publication is also present, as when codes affixed to photographs, or transitional steps taken towards placing material on the web, can result in momentary availability of material not intended for publication, or which, although initially intended, might almost instantaneously be removed. In the case of accidental publication, it is likely that the old common-law rules would apply,[36] and no liability would result in the absence of negligence. In the case of momentary publication, the defendant could dispute publication and the onus would lie with the plaintiff to prove that in the circumstances publication did occur, and that publication was by the defendant. There are, however, two aspects of publication that are of particular significance for the media.

In law, publication by the media is in permanent form, and therefore constitutes libel.[37] Libel can be in the form of words, visual images, gestures and other methods of signifying meaning.[38] Thus print, photographs, drawings, cartoons, film, music and satire can all give rise to libel actions. The capacity for internet material to endure and to be very widely accessed in written, photographic, or audio-visual form puts it into the same category, and general defamation principles apply. In the UK, the Defamation Act 1996 specifically excludes from liability as "publishers" service providers and others who are not in a position of control over content. In such circumstances, they can raise the defence of innocent dissemination, but only where they have no knowledge of the defamation. In *Godfrey v Demon Internet Ltd*,[39] the defendants had been told of the defamatory content and therefore could not claim lack of knowledge. The case was settled out of court.

4.3.1.1 Who Is Liable?

Because publication refers to the making or communicating of defamatory matter, everyone in the publication process is technically liable and can be pursued for damages. That may include the reporter, sub-editor, editor, proprietor, publisher, printer and distributor, and in appropriate circumstances the letter writer, advertiser, or public relations firm, even the caller to a radio talk show. No one is immune, although employees (reporter, sub-editor and printer, for example) may be indemnified by their employer. In other cases, the individual might not have enough money to be worth pursuing. With regard

---

[36] See McMahon and Binchy, above, n.34 at p.884.

[37] Defamation Act 1961, s.15, includes broadcasting as libel. The reference is only to civil libel; broadcasting is not included in Part 1 of the Act dealing with criminal libel.

[38] Defamation Act 1961, s.14(2).

[39] [2000] 3 W.L.R. 1020. Following the *Godfrey* case, the position of Internet Service Providers (ISPs) was addressed in the UK in the Electronic Commerce (EC Directive) Regulations, 2002 (liability to attach only where actual knowledge and ISP does not act quickly to remove offending material). See also, English Law Commission, *Defamation and the Internet* (Scoping Study No.2) December 2002; Paula Mulooly, "Liability for Defamatory Statements on the Internet: a Comparative Overview" (2000) 1 *Hibernian Law Journal* 202; Eugene R. Sullivan II, "Lost in Cyberspace: A Closer Look at ISP Liability" [2001] ENT. L.R. 192.

to the internet, an added complication is that the defamer may be anonymous and not traceable. Anonymous remailers, for example, receive messages, strip them of their identity and forward them to the intended recipients. Trolling is another possibility, where someone posts a message on the internet and makes it look as if the message has come from someone else.[40] There is a limited common-law defence available to distributors, who are not liable unless they knew or ought to have known that material they were distributing was defamatory, and their lack of knowledge was not due to negligence on their part. The essence of the defence is control, or lack of it. Distributors nowadays may handle many thousands, if not millions, of titles, and therefore the opportunity for control, or knowledge of content, is very limited. However, the common law defence for distributors is not available to printers, and in this and other respects, the law is outdated and fails to take account of modern technology. Unlike their predecessors, printers nowadays are often just contract printers who receive copy online and have little or no opportunity to check content. For that reason, a defence for printers, who are not themselves the authors of the defamatory matter, is included in the Defamation Act 1996 in the UK.

That Act also extends the defence to Internet Service Providers (ISPs). Again, the key question is essentially one of editorial control. Some degree of internal monitoring and good "netiquette" (terms of service, guidelines, policy statements and such like) can go some way to regulating internet content, but the ability to instantaneously transmit messages, including anonymous messages, to thousands of people around the world makes the opportunity to monitor or control much more difficult than in the case of the traditional media.[41] It also makes the potential harm significantly greater. While ISPs have some of the same characteristics as telephone and telegraph companies, regarded as "common carriers" and not liable for content, except where they have knowledge of content, there are also some significant differences. In some ways they are akin to rebroadcasters (cable or MMDS services, for example) in that they merely relay content generated by others; they are mere conduits, retransmitting without review matter supplied by third parties – except that the opportunity to respond in cyberspace is much greater, and that some services are interactive, not merely passive. Courts in the United States appear, therefore, to have adopted a standard reflecting a sliding scale of editorial control.[42] A practical consideration is not in effect to penalise ISPs who take steps to exert editorial control, as that would provide an incentive to ISPs not

---

[40] See, for example, the US case *Zeran v America Online, Inc.* 958 F. Supp. 1124, 1127 (E.D.Va.), 129 F.3d 327 (4th Cir. 1997), 118 S.Ct. 2341 (1998).

[41] In the US, the right to communicate anonymously has been recognised since 1960 in *Talley v California* 362 U.S. 60 and has since been extended to cyberspace.

[42] See *Daniel v Dow Jones & Co.* 520 N.Y. S. 2d 334 (Civ. Ct. 1987) – online service analogous to a distributor; *Cubby, Inc. v CompuServe, Inc.* 776 F. Supp. 135 (S.D.N.Y. 1991) – online service analogous to a distributor, no opportunity to review, no duty to monitor, therefore no liability, otherwise an undue burden on the free flow of information, impractical; *Stratton Oakmount, Inc. v Prodigy* 23 Media L. Rep. (BNA) 1794 (N.Y. Sup. Ct. 1995) – bulletin board, control through automatic software screening and enforcement of guidelines, therefore regarded as publisher for purposes of liability.

to exert control and thus escape liability. To address that problem, the Communications Decency Act 1996 contains a provision that ISPs are not to be treated as publishers.[43] It does not specifically say that they cannot be treated as distributors, but later courts have interpreted it as giving absolute immunity.[44] Absolute immunity, however, can leave a defamed person without a remedy. The objective must be to encourage responsibility and self-regulation, without engendering fear of liability that will cause ISPs to remove postings at the slightest hint of defamation.

There has been some discussion also as to the approach likely to be taken to defamation on the internet by the European Court of Human Rights.[45] In any event, the European E-Commerce Directive (2000/31/EC) harmonises the position across Europe. Under Article 12, ISPs will not be liable for defamatory information transmitted on their sites, provided they do not initiate the transmission, select the recipient or modify the information contained in it. Under Article 14, they will not be required to monitor content but if defamatory matter on it is brought to their attention, they will be required to remove it. The E-Commerce Directive was transposed into Irish law by the Electronic Commerce Act 2000. Section 23 of the Act provides that all provisions of existing defamation law shall apply to all electronic communications within the State, including the retention of information electronically. Regulations introduced in February 2003 under the Directive limit the liability of ISPs, including liability for defamation, where the service they provide is as a mere conduit for the transmission of information or where they simply cache or store information temporarily to make it easier for users to access it, or where they unknowingly host or store information relating to an unlawful activity.[46]

It is quite common in Ireland for plaintiffs to sue some or all of the people involved in the publication process, depending on their relative ability to pay. For instance, in the case of a small book publisher or the publisher of a small-circulation magazine, it might be felt that the distributor would be a better mark financially. Thus, Easons, as distributors, have on occasion been sued

---

[43] S.230(c)(1). The Act was declared unconstitutional by the US Supreme Court in *Reno v A.C.L.U.* 117 S.Ct. 2329 (1997), but not s.230(c)(1).

[44] *Zeran* (above, n.40); *Blumenthal v Drudge* 992 F. Supp. 44 (D.D.C. 1998) – electronic report; *Doe v America Online, Inc.* 729 So. 2d 390 (Fla. 1999) – obscene material; *Lunney v Prodigy Services Co.* 683 N.Y.S. 2d 557 (App.Div. 1998) – offensive e-mail. See further, Steven M. Cordero, "Damnum Absque Injuria: *Zeran v AOL* and Cyberspace Defamation Law" (1999) 9 Fordham Intell. Prop. Media & Ent. L.J. 775, and Nancy W. Guenther, "Good Samaritan to the Rescue: America Online Free from Publisher and Distributor Liability for Anonymously Posted Defamation" (1998) *Communications and the Law* 35.

[45] See, for example, Dragos Cucereanu, "Cyberlibel Cases before the European Court of Human Rights: Estimating Possible Outcomes," *Netherlands Quarterly of Human Rights*, Vol. 19/1, 5-20, 2001. Following the settlement of a defamation claim by British ISP, Demon (over £200,000), there were a number of website closures in Britain. It was reported (*The Irish Times*, April 17, 2000) that a UK magazine had threatened to sue over intended content on Outcast's website, which led to the website being closed down, and that the case was to go to the European Court of Human Rights on the basis of a violation of Article 10 on freedom of expression.

[46] S.I. No.68 of 2003. EC Directive 2001/29/EC (below, Chap.11) classifies ISPs as "intermediaries".

either along with, or instead of, the publisher.[47] It is also open to a plaintiff to sue one publication for offending matter and not sue others who carried the same material.[48] Moreover, it is also possible to have a number of actions arising from the same defamatory matter, either because more than one individual is affected or because there is republication, a new edition of a book, for example, or the rebroadcasting of a programme. Likewise, various media may be sued by the same person arising out of the same story.[49] At the time of his death, Robert Maxwell had taken out numerous writs for libel, and Sonia Sutcliffe, wife of the Yorkshire Ripper took numerous cases against the British media. Because repetition of defamatory matter is itself actionable, it is possible to sue for something that was unchallenged in the past. It should be remembered also that libel actions in Ireland can be commenced at any time up to six years after publication,[50] while in the UK the period has been reduced to one year.

[47] *Dempsey v The Phoenix and Easons* (*The Irish Times*, February 8, 1996); *Coffey v The Phoenix and Easons* (*The Irish Times*, May 14, 1999) – in that case the printers were also sued. Older cases include: *Fitzgibbon v Eason & Son* (1910) 45 I.L.T.R. 91; *Ross v Eason & Son, and The Winning Post* (1911) 2 I.R. 459, 45 I.L.T.R. 89; *O'Brien v Eason & Son* (1913) 47 I.L.T.R. 266; *McDermott v Eason & Co.*(1914) 48 I.L.T.R. 1. That is not to say that small outfits will not be sued also. Students should note that many third level student publications and radio stations have had brushes with the law of defamation in recent years. For example, the Students' Union in UCC was sued when a student publication described five security officers as having the intelligence of a retarded turnip, when one of them, for example, had an MA (*The Irish Times*, March 8, 1996, April 16, 1996).

[48] In *O'Connor v The Kerryman* (*The Irish Times*, February 22, 1991), the plaintiff sued the *Kerryman* newspaper but not *Kerry's Eye*, which carried the same story, albeit in a slightly different form.

[49] See above, n.6, McDonald, at p.75 (multiple publication), at p.267 (on joinder of parties); *Duffy v Newsgroup Newspapers* [1992] 2 I.R. 369, [1992] I.L.R.M. 855, re consolidation of actions. The *Duffy* test was applied in *Murphy v Times Newspapers* (known as the "Slab" Murphy case), by the Supreme Court (October 21, 1997), which ordered separate trials in the case of two brothers, Thomas and Patrick Murphy, alleged in a newspaper article in June 1985 to be members of the IRA and engaged in the Brighton bombing. The newspaper had not intended to refer to the second brother, Patrick. He was awarded £15,000 plus costs in 1990; the defence of justification succeeded in respect of Thomas and his case was dismissed; both appealed, a retrial was ordered by the Supreme Court: *Murphy v Times Newspapers Ltd & Ors* [1996] 1 I.R. 169. Thomas Murphy eventually lost his case. See *The Irish Times*, May 17, 1996, April 30, 1998, May 16, 1998. The action by Patrick Murphy (see *(Patrick) Murphy v Times Newspapers* [2000] 1 I.R. 522) was resolved eventually at the High Court on the eve of the action (*The Irish Times*, November 20, 2001).

[50] Statute of Limitations 1957, s.11. Contrast other jurisdictions, *e.g.* UK, where the period was reduced to three years (Limitation Act 1980) on the recommendation of the Faulks Committee (above, n.7) and to one year (Defamation Act 1996) on the recommendation of the Neill Committee (Supreme Court Procedure Committee, *Report on Practice and Procedure in Defamation*, 1991). The period was reduced to two years in New Zealand (Defamation Act 1992). The Irish Law Reform Commission has recommended a three-year period (Law Reform Commission, *Report on the Civil Law of Defamation* (LRC 38–1991), para.13.1). See also discussion in LRC, *Consultation Paper*, above, n.28, para.524.

4.3.1.2 Repeating a Libel

Because repetition of a libel is itself a libel, to publish defamatory remarks made by someone else can incur liability. The common law rule is that anyone who republishes defamatory matter "adopts" it as his own and is liable in equal measure to the original defamer.[51] Both the original speaker and those who repeat it, often media carrying the original speaker's remarks, can be pursued, unless the publication involves an official report to which the defence of qualified privilege applies.[52] Sometimes the plaintiff will decide to ignore the original speaker and simply go after the media. For example, remarks made by a politician outside the Dáil or Seanad and by officials at private meetings, as well as extracts from press releases have given rise to actions against the media.[53] Stories "lifted", in whole or in part, from other sources, as well as facts published elsewhere and reprinted, even by arrangement, have resulted in actions by aggrieved plaintiffs.[54] In 1996, Sinn Féin Councillor, Christy Burke, successfully sued both the *Sun* newspaper and RTÉ, arising out of a caption in the *Sun* over a photograph of Burke and the Rev. Ian Paisley shaking hands on the steps of a public building in Dublin.[55] The caption read "Handshake with devil", and RTÉ, in its morning radio summary of the day's papers ("It Says in the Papers"), referred to the *Sun's* photograph and repeated the caption. The plaintiff was awarded £15,000 in the Dublin Circuit Court.

In this regard, it is no defence to say that the remarks were made by someone else, whether named or not.[56] Neither is it a defence in itself to preface the remarks with such phrases as "it is believed that", "it is widely rumoured that", or "it has been alleged that". Use of the conditional tense, of "could have" or "might have" will not save a person from liability. Even for the journalist to state that the allegations are strongly refuted or not believed will not necessarily provide a defence, although it may take some of the sting out of it. In *Boyle v*

---

[51] But see Lord Nicholls in *Reynolds v Times Newspapers* [1999] 3 W.L.R. 1010 (H.L.), at 1027.

[52] See, for example, *DPP v Woods and Independent Newspapers* (*The Irish Times*, July 10, 1986). See further discussion below.

[53] See, for example, reports headed "Deputy accuses teacher unions" and "Keating condemns teacher strikes" in *The Irish Times*, November 27, 1985, which led to a defamation action: *Mulvey v The Irish Times, Irish Press and Keating* (*The Irish Times*, July 15, 1986). The case was compromised on the basis of an acknowledgment by the defendants that the plaintiff had always acted in a proper and professional manner. Further proceedings were stayed. The matter complained of in *Ryan v The Irish Times* (*The Irish Times*, June 11, 1993), came from a press release, that the journalist had taken steps to verify. A press release issued by or on behalf of the then Minister for Enterprise and Employment in 1996 also led to a defamation case being taken by Irish Press Publications against the State (below, n.153). For developments in the UK in relation to press releases that form part of press conferences, see *Turkington v Times Newspapers* [2000] 3 W.L.R. 1670, [2001] 2 A.C. 277.

[54] For example, *The Irish Times* was jointly sued with the BBC when it republished extracts from *The Listener* magazine in 1983. The case resulted in a settlement: *Sloan v The Irish Times and BBC* (*The Irish Times*, October 24, 1985).

[55] *The Irish Times*, May 9, 14, 24, 1996.

[56] See, for example, *Doyle v The Economist* [1981] N.I. 171. But see further below regarding instances of qualified privilege.

The Irish Times,[57] a journalist quoted the remarks of a French rugby star to the effect that the disciplinary hearing which suspended him was a "stitch-up": "After all I was being heard by Irishmen in Ireland a week before we play Ireland". The journalist added the words "Not quite true. The Frenchman's case was heard by a three-man committee under the chairmanship of Ireland's Peter Boyle, with one representative from England and Wales respectively". Despite the journalist's intervention, a High Court jury found that Mr Boyle, a solicitor, had been defamed and awarded him £50,000 and costs. It accepted that the article meant that Mr Boyle was guilty of corrupt, biased and unjust conduct.

In contrast, the European Court of Human Rights in *Thoma v Luxembourg*[58] said that punishing a journalist for assisting in the dissemination of statements made by another person (a fellow journalist in this case) would seriously hamper the contribution of the press to the discussion of matters of public interest and should not be envisaged unless there were particularly strong reasons for doing so. Also, a requirement for journalists to distance themselves systematically and formally from the content of a quotation that might defame or harm a third party was not reconcilable with the role of the press in providing information on current events, opinions and ideas. The journalist in this case had indicated that he was quoting from a press article and had also interviewed a third party about the credibility of the allegations it contained.

The Irish Law Reform Commission in 1991 stated that a defendant could mitigate damages by showing that he had repeated material from another source and had disclosed that source in the publication. That proposition was accepted by Keane J. in *Browne v Tribune Newspapers plc*,[59] but while it may mitigate damages it will not relieve the defendant of liability altogether.

In defamation law, it is the act of publishing, of passing on the defamatory matter to others, even one other, that incurs liability. Because publication need only be to one other or a small number of people, circulation or audience figures are largely irrelevant, although they may influence the size of damages awarded. Circulation figures did not seem to have any effect in 1991 in *Morgan and others v Independent Newspapers*,[60] when an award of £75,000 was made against the *Dundalk Argus*, a local weekly newspaper with a circulation of about 8,000 copies. The paper, in reference to late-night trouble and vandalism in the mall in the town, had published a report that "Garda want 'killing fields' closed down", along with a picture of "the offending chip vans". The three owners of the chip vans sued and were awarded £25,000 each for defamation.

---

[57] *The Irish Times*, July 12–14, 2001.

[58] *Thoma v Luxembourg*, App. No.38432/97, 29 March 2001, at paras 62–64; see also *Bladet Tromso v Norway*, May 20, 1999, (1999) 29 E.H.R.R. 125. The House of Lords in *Reynolds* (above, n.51) at least went half-way and accepted that a newspaper could raise queries or call for an investigation and not adopt allegations as statements of fact – at 1027. The Court of Appeal in *Loutchansky v Times Newspapers Ltd (No.2)* [2002] 1 All E.R. 652, extended the *Reynolds* privilege to mitigate the rule on repetition: see Robertson and Nicol, *Media Law* (4th ed., Penguin Books, London, 2002), at pp.xxv-xxvi.

[59] [2001] 1 I.R. 521; [2001] 2 I.L.R.M. 424.

[60] *The Irish Times*, February 22, 27–28, 1991.

The use of quotation marks will not normally provide protection either.[61] Indeed, use of quotation marks carries a dual responsibility:

(i) to publish the words *verbatim*, as any deviation or inaccuracy could lead to a defamatory meaning and leave one open to suit by the speaker, and

(ii) to ensure that the words quoted are not defamatory of another identifiable person because that person could sue both the speaker and the media who carried them.

Take for example, the following headline that appeared over a court report: "Peace Commissioner 'refused to honour £700 bet'". The part of the headline in quotation marks suggests that it is a direct quote from a person or document. However, in the court report that followed this particular headline, there was no such statement. Moreover, the amount of money referred to in the report was £500 not £700. In addition, the evidence given in court and referred to in the report was that the bookmaker had refused to "accept" the bet, which is very different from refusing to "honour" the bet. The inaccuracy in the headline led to a defamation action. Incidentally, it was true that the bookmaker concerned happened to be a peace commissioner.[62]

4.3.2 Of a False Statement

Theoretically, it is only the publication of *false* statements that is actionable. As it is the reputation of a person or the esteem in which a person is held by others that the law of defamation is designed to protect, it follows that there should be no protection against the publication of true statements about a person. A person's reputation is entitled to be assessed on the basis of the truth and there is no entitlement to protection for a good reputation not warranted by truth. Truth, therefore, is a complete defence to an action for defamation (see para. 4.5.2 below), but it is not as simple as that in practice. On the contrary, the defence is rather a double-edged sword. If truth can be proved to the satisfaction of the court, then the plaintiff will have no remedy no matter how hurtful or harmful the publication may have been to him/her, morally, financially or otherwise. That is so no matter how private the details given or how long ago the events recounted occurred. It is so even if there is no public interest involved in publication. In one sense that is how it should be; it should not be a function of defamation law to protect privacy. There should be separate protection for one's private life and family. In the absence of such privacy protection, however, it seems harsh that a person harmed by the publication of

---

[61] Unless the words form part of a fair and accurate report of a public matter listed in the Schedule of the Defamation Act as having qualified privilege. Even then, the privilege attaches to the report, not the headline.

[62] See *Irish Independent*, January 9, 1986. The defamation case was later dismissed on the application of the plaintiff: *Doran v Independent Newspapers* (*The Irish Times*, February 10–11, 1989). Inaccurate headlines over court reports can also lead to contempt of court proceedings (see Chap.6).

true but harmful details should have no legal remedy. (Privacy will be considered in Chapter 5.)

4.3.2.1 The Presumption of Falsity

In practice, however, it may not be too difficult for the plaintiff to succeed in an action for defamation. That is so because Irish law retains the old common-law presumption of falsity.[63] That means that when a plaintiff goes to court alleging defamation, the court proceeds on the basis that what was published about him/her was false, and it is then up to the (media) defendant to prove that it was in fact true. The plaintiff does not have to satisfy the court that what was published concerning him/her was false, only that it was defamatory. Indeed, the issue of truth or falsity will not even arise unless the defendant seeks to rely on the defence of truth, called "justification".

The reality for the media is that every statement published in whatever form is potentially actionable. Every statement challenged is, in law, false, unless or until proven otherwise. The onus of proof is on the defendant, in contrast to all other torts where the onus is on the plaintiff to prove the elements of the tort. In the tort of negligence, for example, if the plaintiff alleges negligent driving or negligent medical care, s/he must first establish that the defendant owed him/her a duty of care, that the defendant had breached that duty, and that as a consequence of the breach the plaintiff suffered damage. In defamation, on the other hand, it is only necessary for the plaintiff to establish that the matter was published by the defendant, that it referred to the plaintiff and that it had a defamatory effect. Damage is presumed; fault is not in issue. Defamation is a strict liability tort, so the degree of care taken by the journalist or media organisation and the reason or motive for publishing is irrelevant.[64]

Like all presumptions, the presumption of falsity can be rebutted, in this case by a showing of truth on the part of the defence. In practice, that can prove exceedingly difficult for a media defendant because of the journalistic practice of promising confidentiality to those who provide information – usually referred to as journalists' sources. Sources, even if not promised anonymity or confidentiality, may be unwilling to appear in court to testify against a plaintiff. It is often easier for plaintiffs to get friends and associates to come into court to testify on their behalf than it is for the media to get witnesses to come into court to testify against a plaintiff as to truth. In a case against the *Phoenix* magazine in 1986, for instance, an accountant was accused of being a "hatchet-man" and "Captain Bligh" because of his alleged cost-cutting of "luxuries such as functioning typewriters … even toilet rolls that the pampered staff had become accustomed to". In his subsequent defamation action, his wife and a

---

[63] The presumption of falsity was abandoned in the US in *Philadelphia Newspapers Inc. v Hepps* 475 U.S. 767 (1986). The Irish LRC was divided on the issue of removing the presumption but by a majority recommended its abolition: above n.7, LRC at paras 7.28–7.35.

[64] The presumption of falsity is therefore a separate issue from fault but has the effect of putting the onus on the defendant to prove the truth of the allegations: above, n.50, *Paper*, at p.46 and *Report*, at p.55.

friend gave evidence in court. His wife gave evidence of the distress and hurt involved. She told the court of an occasion when her husband was late for an after-work drink and someone remarked that he must have stayed back in the office to count the sheets of toilet paper.[65]

It is not so easy for the media defendant to get people to come into court to say that someone was indeed a hatchet-man or similar.[66] However, witnesses do need to be produced in court, as other evidence such as journalists' notes and out-of-court statements are likely to be inadmissible. In legal terms, notes may amount only to "hearsay" but are nonetheless useful and should be retained by journalists. For instance, when an allegation of defamation is made against a newspaper, it is important that journalists' notes be available to check out how the remarks complained of came to be published. Similarly, outcuts or footage from television programmes should be retained. The information they provide may be crucial to the newspaper, broadcaster or the lawyers in deciding whether to defend an action or settle out of court. Difficulties in the past have led some newspapers to take the precaution of getting sworn affidavits from witnesses before they decide to publish.[67]

If the defendants fail in their defence of truth (justification), aggravated damages may be awarded against them. As a result, plaintiffs may sometimes succeed in defamation cases even though the matter complained of was true, simply because the media could not, for one or more of the above reasons, rely on the defence of truth. Alternatively, the media may be reluctant to plead the defence because of the consequences if they should fail to establish it to the satisfaction of the court. The degree of proof required is proof on the balance of probabilities, that it is more likely than not that the matter was true. This may not appear to be a very exacting standard but it can be in practice. In other cases, the defence may simply not be open because what was published was inaccurate or untrue.

In the United States, the presumption of falsity has been removed and public plaintiffs must prove malice, namely that the defendant knew or ought to have known that the matter was false, or was reckless as to whether it was true or not.[68] Private plaintiffs have to prove negligence, that the defendant was careless as to whether the matter was true or false.[69]

---

[65] *Kavanagh v The Phoenix* (*The Irish Times*, November 5, 1986), arising out of an article published in *The Phoenix* magazine, April 11, 1986.

[66] It was most unusual in *Murphy v Times Newspapers* (*The Irish Times*, May 16, 1998) that a garda chief superintendent was willing to give evidence on behalf of the defendants to the effect that the plaintiff was a member of the IRA.

[67] An example is the *Sunday Tribune*, December 4, 1994, when the paper decided to name the swimming coach alleged to have sexually abused some of the children under his care.

[68] *NY Times v Sullivan* 376 U.S. 254 (1964), *Gertz v Robert Welch Inc.* 418 U.S. 323 (1974).

[69] *Philadelphia Newspapers Inc. v Hepps* 475 U.S. 767 (1986). The European Court of Human Rights has also drawn a clear distinction between public and private plaintiffs and between facts which are susceptible to proof and value judgments which are not: see *Lingens*, above n.26; *Dalban v Romania* (2001) 31 E.H.R.R. 39: "a journalist should not be debarred from expressing critical value judgments unless he or she could prove the truth" (at para.49).

4.3.2.2 Inaccuracy and Error

Not every false publication will lead to an action for defamation. To incur liability, the publication must also refer to the complainant and be defamatory, in the sense of adversely affecting his/her reputation. Some inaccuracies may be inconvenient, embarrassing or hurtful, but not defamatory and, therefore are more appropriately handled by a correction, clarification or retraction system, such as is operated by the readers' representative in Irish newspapers or by the Broadcasting Complaints Commission.[70] Other inaccuracies, though apparently trivial, can be defamatory and can found a successful action.

Mistakes resulting from human error, even though understandable, can also result in sizeable damages. For example, a transcription error, which resulted in a reference to "the Clarke family" rather than "Mrs Clarke's family", led to an award of £47,500 in *Clarke v Independent Newspapers*.[71] A typesetting error in which it was stated that a solicitor might "willingly" rather than "unwittingly" give information to an illegal organisation led to substantial undisclosed damages in *Rice v The Irish Times*.[72] The name John Browne, spelt with an "e", carried a price tag of £75,000 in *Browne v Independent Newspapers*,[73] even though the piece in question had a disclaimer at the end to the effect that the names used were fictitious and not intended to refer to any living person. The report, about bribery and corruption in the planning and by-law process in the Dublin area, assigned the fictitious names of John Black, John White and John "Browne" to three builders. There was only one builder named "John Browne" in the area at the time and he sued.

In another case, a photograph of two men was to be used by the *Evening*

---

[70] See recommendations of the LRC in this regard: above, n.50, *Report*, Chap. 9; also Kevin Boyle and Marie McGonagle, *Media Accountability: The Readers' Representative in Irish Newspapers* (NNI, Dublin, 1995); Kevin Boyle and Marie McGonagle, above, n.9, *Law and the Media*, 1997. Corrections would also seem to be the most appropriate remedy where inaccuracies occur in court reporting. In relation to tribunals of inquiry, it has been suggested that if the legislature has set up a tribunal with its attendant publicity, it should take steps to minimise the risk of damage to reputation. The step recommended is an order for correction. That would require an amendment to s.17 of the Defamation Act 1961 to provide that publication of an ordered correction would be admissible in evidence in mitigation of damages, and an amendment to s.8 that no criminal prosecution for libel would be taken where an ordered correction had been published. See Rory Brady, "Inquiries: the Rights of Individuals, Privacy and Confidentiality, Reform of the Law of Tribunals" (1999) B.R. 443, at p.444. It is in everyone's interests that the media report accurately and correct mistakes or inaccuracies. Indeed, orders for correction or rectification are common in many European countries. However, it is submitted that there should be provision in any such scheme of ordered corrections for a correction not just to mitigate damages but to end the matter in appropriate circumstances, and also that an ordered correction would only apply where the mistake was of some significance, and not just trivial. The dangers of pursuing the media for trivial matters have been seen in the practice of contempt of court in Ireland over the decades, but less so in recent years. See Kevin Boyle and Marie McGonagle, "Contempt of Court: The Case for Law Reform" in McGonagle (ed.), above, n.9, *Law and the Media*, 1997, p.127. See also Chapter 6 below.

[71] *The Irish Times*, February 1, 1991.

[72] *ibid.*, December 6, 1991.

[73] *The Irish Times*, November 12–19, 1992.

Press to show the defendant in a court case. The picture was cut in half to eliminate the second person but the wrong half was published. It resulted in an award of £50,000.[74] The positioning of an unrelated photograph beside a story on the maltreatment of horses led to a £20,000 settlement by *The Star*.[75] Likewise a photograph of the wing of a prison where sexual offenders are held beside a story of a man convicted of unrelated charges resulted in an award of £60,000 against the *Examiner* newspaper.[76]

As some of the above cases illustrate, court reporting is an area that requires particular caution. While there can be practical difficulties, with the acoustics in court houses and the availability of information on court cases, for example (see further Chapter 7), a reporter who gets a name wrong, or confuses details of the charges, or who makes an incorrect assumption, may well find himself/ herself sued for defamation. To publish a report that "Jim" Murphy was convicted of charges when it was actually his brother Tim or cousin Tom or some other Murphy will likely lead to a defamation action, to which the reporter will probably have no defence. To report that someone has been convicted of more serious charges than in actual fact has also been known to result in an award of damages, albeit usually of a smaller amount.[77] To make wrong assumptions or to link people convicted of charges to others is extremely dangerous, as it can result in a defamation action or indeed contempt of court (Chapter 6 below). In one such case, a person convicted of disorderly behaviour was stated to be the son of a District Court judge of the same name, when the two were not related.[78]

It may be argued that an individual's good name must be protected against inadvertent error as well as deliberate error or error arising from negligence. After all, the effect on the individual's reputation is the same, regardless of how the error arose. Indeed, that is the rationale behind the strict liability nature of the tort of defamation. On the other hand, the media role in modern society in providing information, in reflecting public opinion and in stimulating debate is so important that, it could be argued, some allowance should be made for the time pressures under which the media operate. Both arguments can be accommodated by making provision for remedies of correction, clarification and declaration, in addition to what is at present virtually the sole remedy of damages.

To what extent the present law engenders caution and promotes accuracy

---

[74] *O'Kelly v Evening Press* (*The Irish Times*, May 23–28, 1992). *Cf. Doyle v Irish Press* (*The Irish Times*, December 6, 1984, cited in McDonald, above, n.6, at p.22); *Wren v RTÉ*, in which a photograph of a former Garda Commissioner was included in a montage on international crime (*The Irish Times*, June 21, 1994).

[75] *Glennon v The Star* (*The Irish Times*, July 1, 1992). However, in *de Valera v Independent Newspapers* (*The Irish Times*, December 14, 1984), the plaintiff failed to show that the placing of her photograph alongside an unrelated story was defamatory.

[76] *Hill v Examiner Publications* (*The Irish Times*, November 18, 2000, and October 26, 2001, regarding appeal on grounds that award was grossly excessive. The Supreme Court upheld the award: [2001] 4 I.R. 219).

[77] *Latham and Byrne v Independent Newspapers and Irish Press* (*The Irish Times*, May 9, 1986), see further below, n.89. But see also *Hill v Examiner Publications*, above n.76.

[78] *Hussey v Irish Press* (*The Irish Times*, January 14, 1995).

is open to question. There is no doubt that it penalises inaccuracy, and that one of the few self-help options open to the media under the present law is to take steps to ensure the highest possible degree of accuracy, and in the event of inaccuracy, to be prepared to correct or clarify it at the earliest possible opportunity. If the individual concerned still proceeds to court, the fact that a correction or clarification was published should be seen as mitigating damage.

On the question of accuracy, particular attention needs to be paid to the spelling of people's names, as in the *Browne* case[79] and to their title or rank. Research has confirmed that people are very sensitive about how they are portrayed in the media and can be upset and angered by inaccuracies concerning them.[80] The greatest percentage of defamation actions relate to factual inaccuracies, as do the greatest percentage of complaints to the readers' representatives of the national newspapers, for example.[81] Business or professional reputation is a real concern to individuals because of what they see as possible consequences to their livelihood.

Journalists are so familiar with media coverage and their own input into it that they can become blasé about how they portray others. They too, however, are sensitive about their own reputations when editors want to publish apologies about their work[82] or when they become the subject matter of someone else's story – a fact borne out by statistics on defamation actions against the media, which show journalists themselves as five per cent of plaintiffs.[83] As regards the exercise of their own profession, it is important for journalists to realise that getting facts right about identifiable people is essential. In the first place it is essential for avoiding libel; it is also essential if they are sued and want to be able to rely on the defences of justification or fair comment (which will be discussed later in this chapter). The answer is careful checking of factual details about identifiable people, their activities, business or professional undertakings. If the journalist or reporter preparing the story does not assume responsibility for that, then the chances of someone further down the line in the sub-editing

---

[79] Above, n.73. *Cf. Merrill v Sunday Newspapers Ltd* (*The Irish Times*, June 9–10, 1989), in which the *Sunday World* confused the very similar names of two Americans prominent in the art world and living in Ireland around the same time. Publication of a photograph of the wrong man in relation to a conviction for theft resulted in a jury award of £35,000. Judgment was reserved (*The Irish Times*, February 6, 2003) in an application to strike out an intended libel action by Brighton bomber, Patrick Magee, against the publishers of the *Sunday Mirror.* It was contended that they had got the wrong Magee when they reported that the plaintiff had threatened to kill Sinn Féin President, Gerry Adams, for allegedly "surrendering to" the peace process. There was a different Magee in the prison mentioned in the report.

[80] See above, n.70, Boyle and McGonagle, 1995, at p.24.

[81] *ibid.* at pp.24–5. See also the annual reports of the Australian Press Council and the British Press Complaints Commission.

[82] There have been cases in England and elsewhere in which journalists have sued their papers because of apologies published concerning their work (see, for instance, *Press Gazette*, October 19, 1991 (UK)). However, where the paper is threatened with a libel action arising out of what the journalist has written, a published apology should be covered by the privilege for self-defence; see *Willis v Irish Press* (1938) 72 I.L.T.R. 238.

[83] Boyle and McGonagle, above, n.9.

or publication process being able to do so, when not in possession of the facts that were at the journalist's disposal, will be greatly lessened.

4.3.2.3 Fact and Comment

The definition of defamation given at the outset speaks of a false *statement*. A statement of fact or facts about a person is therefore normally at issue in a defamation action. That does not mean that all comment, *i.e.*, expression of opinions as opposed to facts, is free and immune from suit. One measure of the law's regard, or lack of regard, for freedom of expression is the amount of latitude accorded to comment. As indicated in Chapter 2, the freedom to form or *hold* opinions is absolute and cannot be restricted. The right to comment, that is to *express* opinions, one would imagine, should also be largely untrammelled. The law of defamation does attempt to effect a balance between the protection of reputation and freedom of expression in this regard. Unlike the European Convention on Human Rights,[84] however, it does not provide that all comment is free except to the extent that it encroaches on reputation, but rather provides a defence of fair comment, which will be discussed later in this chapter.

The distinction between fact and comment is more developed in the United States. There, following the *Gertz*[85] decision, opinion was taken to be immune, and the *Ollman*[86] test was developed to distinguish between fact and comment. It involved a four-part inquiry as to the common usage or meaning of the specific language, the verifiability, context and location. However, it has been held since then by the Supreme Court that no federal constitutional privilege exists for opinion.[87] The essence of the new test is verifiability: regardless of whether the imputation is presented as fact or opinion ("Jones is a liar" or "In my opinion, Jones is a liar"),[88] assertions of facts that can be proved false are actionable; everything else is not.

4.3.3 About a Person

Defamation concerns the wrongful publication of a false statement about a person. The fact that the person is not actually named is not necessarily a bar to taking an action. A person may just as easily be identified by description, reference to locality or other information. If, however, a person cannot show that the statement concerned him/her, then s/he will not be able to sue successfully on it. There are several issues involved here.

---

[84] *Oberschlick v Austria (No.2)*, judgment of July 1, 1997, Reports of Judgments and Decisions, 1997-IV, (1998) 25 E.H.R.R. 357, for example, where a journalist called a politician an idiot.

[85] *Gertz v Robert Welch Inc.*, above, n.68; *cf. Hustler Magazine Inc. & Flint v Falwell* 485 U.S. 46 (1988): no distinction between false statements of fact and opinions.

[86] *Ollman v Evans* 471 U.S. 1127 (1985).

[87] *Milkovich v Lorain Journal Co.* 497 U.S. 1 (1990).

[88] *ibid.* at 18-19.

4.3.3.1 Individuals and "Legal" Persons

First of all, a "person" is any individual human being (including infants, bankrupts, lunatics, foreigners, convicted prisoners)[89] or any "legal person", a "legal person" being a company or other incorporated body, or a body such as a local authority. These are creatures of the law and have a legal status of their own, which allows them to sue or be sued. Thus, a company could sue for defamation in its own right, separately from the rights of its directors or members.[90] Companies are the plaintiffs in approximately 7.5 per cent of defamation cases in Ireland. If the defamatory imputations are likely to have financial implications for the company, the amount of damages awarded may be greater than in the case of an individual.[91] In England, in *Derbyshire County Council v Times Newspapers*,[92] the court decided that a local authority could not sue for defamation in respect of its collective or official reputation. Similarly, a political party cannot sue.[93] The position in Ireland regarding local authorities remains unchanged, although cases taken by them are rare. Trade unions can also sue in Ireland.[94]

---

[89] See above, n.6, McDonald, ch.12. Two men convicted of receiving stolen cigarettes successfully sued in 1986 when newspaper reports stated that they had been charged with possessing arms with intent to endanger life. They had been charged with robbery but the robbery charge had been dropped. They were awarded £2,000 each: *Latham and Byrne v Independent Newspapers and Irish Press*, above, n.77; also *Hill*, above, n.76. Re foreigners, see the decision of the European Court of Justice in *Shevill v Presse Alliance*, Case C–68/93, March 7, 1995; [1995] 2 W.L.R. 499, [1995] E.C.R. I-415.

[90] Post, *California Law Review*, above, n.4, at 696, says that the fact that corporations and other inanimate entities can sue for defamation can only be understood by reference to the concept of reputation as property.

[91] In 1994, a court in England awarded £1 million sterling to a company engaged in yacht design as a result of an unfavourable criticism of one of its designs: *Walker and Wingsail Systems v Yachting World* (*The Irish Times*, July 9, 1994, August 23, 1995). The company director and his wife received separate awards, bringing the total to £1.45 million. The size of the award to the company would appear to reflect the plaintiff director's contention that the criticism in the yachting magazine was designed to put the company out of business. A settlement for a much lower sum was reached shortly before the appeal was due to be heard.

[92] [1993] 2 W.L.R. 449 (H.L.) 1993. For a critique see, Eric Barendt, "Libel and Freedom of Speech in English Law" (1993) P.L. 449 and Ian Loveland, "Privacy and Political Speech: an Agenda for the 'Constitutionalisation' of the Law of Libel" in Peter Birks (ed.), *Privacy and Loyalty* (Clarendon Press, Oxford, 1997), p.51, at p.56.

[93] *Goldsmith v Bhoyrul* [1998] Q.B. 459; [1997] 4 All E.R. 268.

[94] Trade unions cannot sue in the UK: see Geoffrey Robertson and Andrew Nicol, above n.58, at p.91. In Ireland, they can do so; see above, n.6, McDonald, at pp.57, 278–80: they have "pseudo-corporate status ... by virtue of statutory control". See, for example, *ATGWU v Cork Examiner* (*The Irish Times*, November 7, 1987). Trade unions, however, are immune from liability in tort in certain circumstances by virtue of s.4 of the Trade Disputes Act 1906 and the Industrial Relations Act 1990 (see *The Irish Times*, November 23, 1994). See LRC, *Paper*, above, n.50, at p.411, *Report*, at para. 12.21. Cases involving other bodies include *Royal College of Surgeons v Sunday World* (*The Irish Times*, February 8, 1989).

4.3.3.2 Living Persons

Only the living can sue for defamation. If a person dies, the action, like other actions in tort, dies with him/her. Since reputation is a personal right, it is deemed to die with the person, so that no right of action accrues to the next of kin. This position has been upheld under the Constitution in *Hilliard v Penfield Enterprises*,[95] an application to bring a prosecution for criminal libel (see Chapter 8). Similarly, relatives or associates cannot sue in respect of defamatory publication concerning a person who is already dead. Otherwise history could never be written. If, however, the relatives or associates of the deceased are themselves defamed by the remarks about the deceased, a cause of action will lie.[96]

While Irish law seems clear, it is not universally accepted that one's reputation, *i.e.* the esteem in which one is held by others, dies with one.[97] In the United States, the common law rule against recovery by the next-of-kin or estate prevailed until recently. In 1998, the Supreme Court expressly rejected the assumption that there is no cause of action for defamation of the dead, that an individual's reputation dies with him.[98] It is true that a deceased person will not feel the hurt or shame and will not be affected personally or financially, although the business or estate may well be. To allow claims by the next of kin or relatives of a deceased person would place a heavy burden on historians and on the media. However, the memory in which the deceased is held endures and may be worthy of protection. Some reform bodies have recommended a period of three to five years following the death during which close relatives could sue.[99] Damages would not be available; only a declaratory order, or where appropriate, an injunction to prevent repetition of the defamation.

---

[95] [1990] 1 I.R. 138. Another example is *Buckley v 98FM* (*The Irish Times*, June 17, 1994, December 12, 1994). The case arose out of remarks made on a radio show presented by Fr Michael Cleary. As he died, the action against him was discontinued, but it proceeded against the station. A retrial was ordered (*The Irish Times*, March 9, 1995) but the case was eventually settled and struck out with no order as to costs.

[96] *Hilliard, ibid.*; see also above, n.6, McDonald, at pp.281–4; n.50, *Paper*, at p.401; n.50, *Report*, at p.83.

[97] The personality right in Art.2 of the German Constitution expires on death but the dignity right in Art.1 endures. The law protects the dignity of the deceased for at least ten years: Gregory Thwaite and Wolfgang Brehm, "German Privacy and Defamation Law" [1994] 8 E.I.P.R. 336. See also Richard P. Mandel and Renee Hobbs, "The Right to a Reputation after Death" (1991) 13 C & L 25 (US).

[98] *Swidler & Berlin v United States* 524 U.S. 399, 118 S.Ct. 2081.

[99] The LRC recommended a period of three years: see above, n.50, *Report*, at p.92. In Rhode Island, a 1974 statute provided a right of action where the defamation was contained in an obituary or similar account within three months of the death. The fact that in 25 years there had not been a single reported case under it suggests that it either is not necessary, that it is too narrow or that it provides a sufficient deterrent. Arguments for and against a cause of action for the next-of-kin and estate have arisen from the concept of reputation as property but have tended to stress honour and dignity. For an argument advocating a civil cause of action especially now that criminal libel has fallen into desuetude, see Raymond Iryami, "Giving the Dead Their Day in Court: Implying a Private Cause of Action for Defamation of the Dead from Criminal Libel Statutes" (1999) 9 Fordham Intell. Prop. Media & Ent.L.J. 1083.

4.3.3.3 Groups

There is no group action as such for libel or defamation. However, the key factor is identification. Therefore, if the group mentioned is relatively small, individual members may be able to succeed by showing that they are personally identifiable. There is no fixed number for the size of the group.[100] In *Dineen v Irish Press*,[101] the newspaper had published details of a letter critical of the expenses incurred by officers of the Irish Medical Organisation, and referring to a meal and drinks on a particular occasion. The plaintiff, who was one of only three such officers and who was not present on the occasion mentioned, was awarded £77,000 damages by a High Court jury.

4.3.3.4 Identification

In the case of any defamation plaintiff, the key question is identification. The plaintiff must prove that the defamatory reference complained of would be taken by others to refer to him/her. If the person is named, there is usually no problem, except where there is more than one person of the same name (see next subsection for further discussion) or confusion of similar names as in *Merrill v Sunday Newspapers Ltd*.[102] If the person is not named, it is still possible that s/he is sufficiently identified by details of location, by description or by use of photographs, images or other information given in the publication, as in *Cusack v RTÉ*,[103] in which no names were given during a radio interview but the locality was mentioned. The woman interviewed on the "Liveline" programme about her husband's suicide referred to the fact that he had received letters from the revenue sheriff before his death. There were only three revenue sheriffs in the locality mentioned and one of them sued successfully and was awarded £40,000. Similarly, in *Moore and Byrne v Irish Press*,[104] the plaintiffs

---

[100] In *O'Brien v Eason and Son* (1913) 47 I.L.T.R. 266, a member of the Ancient Order of Hibernians sued, but as the matter complained of did not concern him personally over and above the other members, and as the order had about 100,000 members, the action failed: see above, n.6, McDonald, at p.57. *Cf. Gallagher and Shatter v Independent Newspapers* (*The Irish Times*, May 10, 1980), where the solicitors were held not to be personally identifiable. In another case, *Black v Northern Whig* (1942) 77 I.L.T.R. 5, concerning a government report on "grave scandals" in a Northern Ireland hospital, 10 members of the 15-member statutory committee that ran the hospital sued, and the court held that each was so closely identified with the board as to be personally associated with the offending remarks. Each was awarded £50, plus costs: see above, n.6, McDonald. McDonald, at pp.57–8, also cites a case in 1975 when the High Court held that 24 companies had each shown a *prima facie* claim against Independent Newspapers. An article had suggested that a number of companies involved in the beef-processing industry were falsifying returns in order to claim EC intervention money. For individual members of a group to succeed, the defamatory statement must reflect on them in a personal way and not just on the group or organisation. The decision was appealed on other grounds. See also *The Irish Times*, July 9, 1998, regarding a case taken by 15 county councillors against RTÉ, 14 of whom settled.

[101] *The Irish Times*, June 22–30, 1989.

[102] *ibid.*, June 9–10, 1989 and above, n.79, *Merrill*.

[103] *ibid.*, November 15–16, 1989.

[104] *The Irish Times*, December 4, 1986. A reference in a *Sunday Business Post* article to "a senior Fianna Fáil politician" as having accepted £50,000 from a developer through an

were not named in the publication complained of, but the article at various points revealed that the subjects were two senior executives in the construction division of AnCo (the semi-state employment training authority at the time) based in Dublin. Two men who met the description sued and were awarded £23,000 each. Likewise, a report on the hustings in an election referred to a fuel merchant in a named town who had close links with a particular political party. The description was so specific that the plaintiffs, two brothers who were fuel merchants, though not named, would have had little difficulty meeting the burden of proof. The case was settled without going to court.[105] In *Cooney v Sunday World*,[106] identification was by photograph. In *Fullam v Associated Newspapers Ltd*,[107] there was evidence of jeering by the crowd at a football match to indicate that the plaintiff was identified as the person referred to in a sports report in the newspaper as only being able to kick with one foot.

The test is whether reasonable people would take the reference to be to the plaintiff. If no name is given and only vague details, then it is unlikely that anyone will be able to prove that others took the reference to be to him/her. On the other hand it is possible that more than one person could sue if the details given were sufficiently imprecise to lead people to think they referred to a second or other persons not intended by the reporter or publisher. That is so even if the publication was intended to be fictitious and the details were different in some respects, as in *Sinclair v Gogarty*.[108] Oliver St John Gogarty was sued for a reference to two Jews in his book, *As I Was Going Down Sackville Street*, even though the occupation and street of business of the plaintiffs differed from those of the two Jews in the book. It should be noted that there is no defence in defamation law for fiction as such. If the plaintiff is able to satisfy the court that the reference would be taken to be to him/her, that is sufficient, even if a disclaimer has been published.

The burden of proof on the plaintiff is not very exacting. It is usually sufficient to bring in friends or acquaintances as witnesses to say that they took the reference to be to the plaintiffs.[109] For example, in *Sinclair v Gogarty*, Samuel Beckett, who swore an affidavit, admitted in cross-examination that his aunt was married to the plaintiff's brother, who, it was also claimed, was referred to in the book and was the subject of the verse: "But Willie spent the sesterces/ And brought on strange disasters/ Because he sought new mistresses/ More keenly than old Masters".

---

intermediary in the car park of the Burlington Hotel was taken to be the Taoiseach, Bertie Ahern. Mr Ahern sued the Cork businessman who had made the allegations: *Ahern v O'Brien* (*The Irish Times*, July 11, 2001). He was awarded £30,000, the maximum available in the Circuit Court, plus costs. He did not sue the newspaper.

[105] *Ryan v Irish Times* (*The Irish Times*, June 11, 1993).

[106] *The Irish Times*, November 8, 1978, cited in McDonald, above, n.6, at p.40. The question has arisen in the UK as to whether a photograph, which was not a true photograph of the claimant, but of someone she strongly resembled, and which appeared in an advertisement for a pornogaphic ISP, gave her a cause of action in defamation: *Kerry O'Shea v MGN* [2001] E.M.L.R. 40, discussed in Jonathan Coad, "'Pressing Social Need' and Strict Liability in Libel" [2001] ENT. L.R. 199.

[107] [1953–4] Ir. Jur. Rep. 79; [1955–6] Ir. Jur. Rep. 45.

[108] [1937] I.R. 377.

[109] See above, n.65.

This verse had appeared only in the American edition,[110] and anyway by the time of the court case, Willie was dead and could not sue. The other witnesses in the case were also relatives, employees or acquaintances, who had only read the book when prompted to do so by the plaintiff. The award against Gogarty in 1937 was £900 plus costs. The total came to £2,000 and sales of the book were also affected.[111]

4.3.4 Which Tends to Lower That Person

4.3.4.1 Tends to

Libel is actionable *per se*. Except in cases where special damage is claimed, proof of actual harm arising from a defamatory publication is not required. Harm to reputation is presumed, and all that it is necessary to show is that the matter complained of would tend to make people think less of the plaintiff. It is sufficient for witnesses to say that they thought less of the plaintiff as a result of the publication or broadcast, and it is not permissible for witnesses to be asked their interpretation of the matter complained of. That becomes a question for the jury in the High Court or judge in the Circuit Court. The judge decides whether the matter is capable of being defamatory and it is for the jury then to decide whether it was defamatory in fact. The standard is an objective one: the effect on "right-thinking" members of society. However, such a standard is problematic since community viewpoints can vary widely and be sharply divided.[112]

One problem that arises from the fact that harm is presumed and that actual harm need not be shown is that plaintiffs may sometimes receive compensation even though they suffered no injury to their reputation. Put another way, the media may have to pay compensation even though the publication has not actually harmed the plaintiff. This is a serious concern, because large awards of compensation can cripple some of the smaller media organisations. Should the plaintiff be obliged, therefore, to prove actual harm to his/her reputation?[113] In reality, most plaintiffs do offer some indication of harm: snide remarks made by others, crowds booing a footballer, a fall-off in trade and such like. However, to require all plaintiffs to prove actual harm to the satisfaction of the court might be unfair because injury to reputation could be very difficult to assess or prove in some cases.

4.3.4.2 Lower that Person

A statement is defamatory if it tends to lower the person in the eyes of right-thinking members of society, to hold the person up to ridicule, odium or

---

[110] Ulick O'Connor, *Oliver St. John Gogarty* (Mandarin Paperbacks, London, 1990), at p.278.
[111] *ibid.*, pp.284-5.
[112] See above, n.50, *Report*, at pp.6–7.
[113] See David A. Anderson, "Reputation, Compensation and Proof" (1984) 25 *William and Mary Law Review* 747.

contempt or to cause the person to be shunned by right-thinking members of society. However, social values and attitudes are peculiar to particular cultures and subject to change, with the result that what is regarded as defamatory varies with time, place and circumstance. For instance, to call someone a landgrabber or an informer might have had connotations in Ireland at particular periods of our history that they would not have now or elsewhere.[114] The significance of words like "gay", "rebel" or "fenian" would depend very much on time and circumstance.[115] In *Burke v The Sun and RTÉ*,[116] the journalist claimed in evidence that since the James Cagney film "Shake Hands with the Devil", filmed in Dublin in the 1950s, the phrase "handshake with the devil" had taken on a new meaning. He claimed that since then it meant "make peace with your enemy". However, the Circuit Court judge who heard the case took the view that it connoted evil or wrongdoing, and awarded the plaintiff £15,000. Decided cases, particularly older ones or those from other jurisdictions, are, consequently, of limited value in indicating what will be regarded as defamatory.

Also, very few defamation cases are included in official law reports, unless they are appealed to the Supreme Court, because there are no written judgments given in the Circuit Court and juries in the High Court do not give reasons for their decisions. Thus the only source for details of the pleadings, evidence, and decision is newspaper reports of cases at the time of the hearings. An added problem is that approximately 80 per cent of defamation cases are settled out of court and accordingly only scant details, if any, are reported in the media.

In *Barrett v Independent Newspapers*,[117] one of the few defamation cases to go to the Supreme Court, an allegation that an elected representative had pulled at a journalist's beard and made a triumphalist remark about the outcome of a party leadership crisis was accepted as defamatory. Counsel for the plaintiff contended that it amounted to a very serious allegation that the TD had assaulted the journalist, but the Supreme Court advised that the jury should have been told to consider where the allegation would fall on the scale of seriousness of allegations that might be levelled at a politician. The jury award of £65,000 was considered excessive by the Supreme Court and a new trial was ordered.

---

[114] See Ó Dálaigh C.J. in *Berry v The Irish Times* [1973] I.R. 368, where he held that the label "Twentieth-century Felon Setter" was not defamatory but that if the word "informer" had been used instead, it might have been. The law of defamation reflects community values, a certain ethos, which varies widely between cultures and tells us a lot about them; but defamation is about more than community values, abstract ideas or rights. It is about real people, injury to their reputations and the anger, hurt, frustration and embarrassment that often accompany it.

[115] The term "gay bachelor" was found to be capable of being defamatory in *Reynolds v Malocco t/a 'Patrick' magazine* [1999] 2 I.R. 203; [1999] 1 I.L.R.M. 289. Remarkably, the court made a distinction between the meaning accorded to the term "gay" in 1968 as contrasted with 1998, but then went on to rely on a 1975 English case, which found that the term was likely to be defamatory, as representative of the legal position in Ireland in 1998. See further below, n.355, and generally, Elizabeth M. Koehler, "The Variable Nature of Defamation: Social Mores and Accusations of Homosexuality" (1999) 76 J&MC Quarterly 217.

[116] Above, n.55.

[117] [1986] I.R. 13, [1986] I.L.R.M. 601.

In *McDonagh v Newsgroup Newspapers*,[118] however, seven years later, the Supreme Court held that a jury award of £90,000 was at the top end of the scale but not excessive. In that case, the *Sun* newspaper had alleged that an unnamed representative of the Irish government at the Gibraltar inquest into the death of three IRA volunteers was, *inter alia*, "a lefty spy". In *Prior v Irish Press*,[119] where the allegation was that the plaintiff, a local farmer, was involved in a kidnapping, the Supreme Court upheld an award of £30,000. The farmer had been arrested but later released. The newspaper published an apology as soon as his release became known.

In *Egan v BBC*,[120] a character in a television play uttered words to the effect that the plaintiff garda had tortured local suspects. The fact that the words were uttered in a play or docu-drama did not negate their defamatory effect and damages were awarded. In *Lynch v Irish Press*,[121] it was held to be defamatory to say that an actor (Joe Lynch, alias Dinny Byrne of the long-running television series "Glenroe") had "left the punters in the lurch" when he failed to turn up for a cabaret booking, of which he said he had no knowledge. A High Court jury awarded him £25,000 compensation. The earlier case of *Fullam v Associated Newspapers*[122] had decided that a remark to the effect that a professional footballer did not use his left foot because he could not was defamatory. Likewise in *Quigley v Creation Ltd*,[123] a remark that a well-known actor had left the country, not to further his art but to fill his pockets, was held to be defamatory. A Northern Ireland court in *Doyle v The Economist*[124] awarded £50,000 to Judge Doyle when *The Economist* suggested he had been appointed to the bench solely because he was a Catholic. A similar sum each was awarded to a prominent Northern politician and barrister when the *Sunday World* reported that the two had had words about which of them had been first to see the last chocolate eclairs in a baker's shop.[125]

Decided cases show that it is enough that the plaintiff was held up to ridicule and made to look a fool or a laughing-stock. That was the complaint in *Madigan v Irish Press*,[126] which involved an allegation in a light-hearted column that the plaintiff, a local councillor, had bought a map of an island owned by his party leader, believing it to be an original. The jury award of £30,000 was upheld on appeal. In *Agnew v Independent Newspapers*,[127] a report of the plaintiff's wedding elicited a similar complaint, while an error which resulted in the wrong TD being named in a local newspaper report of a television programme on betting taxes was also held to be defamatory.[128]

---

[118] Irish Times Law Report, December 27, 1993.
[119] *The Irish Times*, February 25–26, 1987; *The Irish Times*, October 24, 1989.
[120] *ibid.*, December 12, 1980.
[121] *ibid.*, February 8–11, 1989.
[122] Above, n.107.
[123] [1971] I.R. 269.
[124] [1981] N.I. 171, above, n.56.
[125] *Boal and McCartney v Sunday World* (*The Irish Times*, October 14–19, 1988).
[126] *The Irish Times*, November 19–20, 1987 (HC), February 11, 1989, March 4, 1989 (SC).
[127] *ibid.*, June 29, 1985.
[128] *McSharry v Waterford Post* (*The Irish Times*, May 1, 1985).

The issue involved is the tendency to make one look ridiculous to others, not the embarrassment caused to oneself or the hurt to one's feelings, although a perusal of defamation cases and, in particular, the apologies often read in court following settlements suggests otherwise. The essence of good name or reputation is the esteem in which others hold one and not self-esteem.[129] In defamation law it is the defamatory effect that is important, not the intention of the speaker.[130] Vulgar abuse is not regarded as defamatory. This is particularly so with regard to verbal abuse uttered in the heat of the moment. In the case of written abuse, which is more considered, less hasty and more lasting, it is less likely that remarks would be dismissed as mere vulgar abuse.[131]

4.3.5 In the Eyes of Right-thinking Members of Society

Who or what are "right-thinking" members of society and how or what do they think? The phrase is used to indicate that not all persons or groups will be regarded as an acceptable barometer of defamatory meaning or effect. To say that someone is a police informer, for example, may lower his/her reputation in the eyes of wrongdoers, criminals and terrorists. However, it would not be regarded as defamatory in law, because the law is not concerned with the esteem or lack of it in which those elements of society hold an individual. There are thus moral connotations and a censorious note to the phrase "right-thinking members of society" that are not present in the normal legal standard of the "reasonable person". It would appear that the standard of the reasonable person is perfectly adequate in defamation, as in other torts, and that there is nothing to be gained from applying a different standard. Indeed, in modern defamation practice, the standard adopted appears to be that of the reasonable person, particularised as the reasonable reader, listener or viewer.[132] The concept of reasonableness can accommodate different community values and viewpoints.

---

[129] Gannon J. in *Hilliard v Penfield Enterprises* [1990] 1 I.R. 138. That is one of the reasons why the courts have been reluctant to allow the tort of intentional infliction of emotional suffering to spill over into the realm of defamation law. See the US case of *Hustler Magazine Inc. & Flint v Falwell* (above, n.85) and the Irish case *Thomas v Independent Newspapers* (*The Irish Times*, July 26, 1988), where a 12-year-old boy, suing through his parents, claimed that publication of his name as a witness to an armed robbery amounted to the intentional infliction of emotional suffering. The claim was rejected.

[130] See above, n.50, LRC, *Paper*, at pp.10–11.

[131] *ibid.* at p.11. The issue of ridicule has been considered in the UK in cases such as *Berkoff v Burchill* [1996] 4 All E.R. 1008 (suggestion that actor was particularly ugly) and *Norman v Future Publishing* [1999] E.M.L.R. 325 (opera singer caught in swing doors wrongly reported to have said when advised to turn sideways: "Honey, I ain't got no sideways").

[132] See, for example, Griffin J. in *Barrett*, above, n.117, at 30: "typical readers of reasonable intelligence", and Geoghegan J. in *Foley v Independent Newspapers* [1994] 2 I.L.R.M. 61, at 65: "any ordinary reader". On the role of the jury see *Barrett* (above, n.117), and on the question of striking out a case see *Conlon v Times Newspapers Ltd* [1995] 2 I.L.R.M. 76.

4.3.6 Innuendo

A statement can be defamatory on its face or by innuendo. It can be defamatory in its ordinary and natural sense or it can be defamatory because of some secondary or hidden meaning. Some imputations are obviously capable of being defamatory in their ordinary everyday sense. For example, to say wrongly that a person has unlawfully evaded tax liability and is a fugitive from justice would be defamatory.[133] Likewise, it would be defamatory in the ordinary sense to say that someone was involved in drugs or with the IRA, was racist, accepted bribes or that a nurse would not attend bomb victims because she was sympathetic to the bombers.[134] As a good example of the complexity of defamation law, however, one can point to the fact that there are two kinds of innuendo, confusingly called: (a) false or popular innuendo and (b) true or legal innuendo.

4.3.6.1 False or Popular Innuendo

By false or popular innuendo is meant a secondary meaning that derives from the words themselves, a case of "reading between the lines". For example, in *Campbell v Irish Press*,[135] a review of a snooker exhibition complained that "the table told lies". The plaintiff pleaded an innuendo that this meant he was incompetent in organising the exhibition. Other examples include *Kavanagh v The Leader*,[136] *Fisher v The Nation*,[137] and *Kenny v The Freeman's Journal*.[138] In *Kennan v Irish Press*,[139] a statement was made, in the course of a long interview, by the new incumbent of the office of Director of Restrictive Practices, that he might have acted differently from his predecessor. Such a statement might not appear defamatory on its face but could imply that his predecessor in office had not acted in an appropriate manner.

4.3.6.2 True or Legal Innuendo

By true or legal innuendo is meant a secondary meaning of the words complained of, not drawn from the words themselves, but from extrinsic facts. Such an innuendo must be pleaded specifically. Examples include *Bell v*

---

[133] *Boland v RTÉ (The Irish Times*, July 1, 1989).

[134] *Corrigan v The Cork Examiner (The Irish Times*, June 30, July 1, 1989).

[135] (1955) 90 I.L.T.R 105.

[136] Unreported, Supreme Court, March 4, 1955.

[137] [1901] 2 I.R. 465.

[138] (1892) 27 I.L.T.R. 8. See above, n.28, *Paper*, at p.16, re innuendo and ordinary meaning. To say that an actor failed to turn up for an engagement and left the patrons in the lurch suggests that he is unreliable (above, n.121, *Lynch v Irish Press*). To say that a man who had committed suicide had been sent letters by the revenue sheriff suggested, according to plaintiff's counsel, that the sheriff had abused his powers, was unfit to hold public office, had murdered the deceased, was guilty of dishonourable, cruel and inhumane tactics and conduct in the discharge of his duties and that his inhumane actions caused or contributed to the man's death by terrorising him to the extent that he committed suicide (above, n.103, *Cusack v RTÉ*).

[139] *The Irish Times*, February 3, 1984.

Northern Constitution,[140] in 1943, in which a bogus birth announcement was telephoned through to a newspaper. The two people mentioned in it as the parents, who knew each other but were not married, pleaded an innuendo to the effect that they were immoral and were having sexual relations with each other outside of marriage.[141]

Where justification, or truth, is pleaded in defence, it must meet the innuendo.[142] The situation regarding innuendos and the pleading of innuendos is unduly complex and begs the question as to whether there is any need to retain the distinction between the two types and distinct rules regarding pleading or whether a simpler procedure might not be found.[143]

4.4 Practical Issues Regarding Defamation

4.4.1 Who Sues?

In practical terms, the more important question is often not who can sue but who is likely to sue.[144] A study of High Court cases reveals that the majority of libel plaintiffs are male, and are businessmen or professionals whose primary concern is for their business or professional reputation and for possible financial harm rather than personal reputation. The next largest category of libel plaintiff is that of State employees, followed by lawyers and politicians. Women represent only 10–15 per cent of plaintiffs, although that marks an increase over the previous five-year period studied.[145] In the past, women who sued usually did so jointly with a spouse or male colleague; they rarely did so on their own.[146] Women were much more likely to use the readers' representative or voluntary complaints system on their own initiative.[147] This may be in part because procedures are so much simpler under the latter system. If so, that might strengthen the argument in favour of simpler procedures and remedies for defamation also. Journalists themselves make up five per cent of plaintiffs

---

[140] [1943] N.I. 108.

[141] *Cf. Cassidy v Daily Mirror* [1929] 2 K.B. 331. In 1994, *The Irish Times* published an apology to the family of a deceased woman because a death notice, which should have read "beloved of James her late husband", had contained the word "and" after "James": see *The Irish Times*, June 25, 29, 1994.

[142] See above, n.50, *Paper*, at pp.46–7.

[143] The LRC makes some recommendations in this regard; see above, n.50, *Report*, at pp.9–10.

[144] See above, n.58, Robertson and Nicol at p.89, and the pragmatic approach adopted by British newspapers and broadcasting companies, detailed in Russell L. Weaver and Geoffrey Bennett, "New York Times Co. v Sullivan: The "Actual Malice" Standard and Editorial Decision-Making" (1993) 14 J.M.L.P. 2.

[145] See above, n.9, Boyle and McGonagle. The figure is gradually increasing.

[146] Exceptions include *Campbell-Sharpe v Magill* (*The Irish Times*, June 29, 1985); *Agnew v Independent Newspapers* (*The Irish Times*, June 29, 1985); *Ní Chiaráin v Evening Herald* (*The Irish Times*, June 25, 1986); *McAleese v Independent Newspapers* (*The Irish Times*, November 18, 1988); *Corrigan v Cork Examiner* (*The Irish Times*, June 30, 1989); *Dineen v Irish Press* (*The Irish Times*, June 30, 1989); *Flanagan v The Star* (*The Irish Times*, March 3, 1990).

[147] See above, n.70, Boyle and McGonagle, 1995, at p.18.

who sue the media.[148] Companies or corporations make up approximately 7.5 per cent of plaintiffs, often suing along with individual directors.

It is also becoming more common for foreign nationals to sue for defamation in the Irish courts. That may reflect the increasingly transnational, even global, reach of the media. It may also reflect the strictness of the libel laws or the availability of sizeable damages here. In some instances, the plaintiff may have Irish connections and be particularly concerned about their reputation in this country. Invariably, questions of jurisdiction arise (see below). Some US plaintiffs have sued successfully in Ireland and the UK, but US courts have refused to enforce judgments for damages awarded to them.[149] They have done so on the basis that the awards were contrary to public policy or would violate the First and Fourteenth Amendments to the United States Constitution.

4.4.2 Why Do They Sue?

The reason so many people sue for defamation may be related to the very high value put on reputation in our society. On the other hand, it may be just a reflection of the general climate of litigiousness that characterises society today. The media are seen as wealthy, as a source of easy money. A study of defamation plaintiffs suing the media in the US[150] found that people sued to get even with the media or because there was no other remedy available. The study made the case for simpler, more immediate remedies, for the creation of a climate of correction and clarification. This is already part of the media culture of other EU countries, which provide rights of rectification and reply to aggrieved readers. The EC Television without Frontiers Directive 1989 led to the introduction of a right of reply in this country also, but only in relation to television.[151] National newspapers have operated to varying degrees a voluntary system of correction through the readers' representatives scheme, introduced in 1989.

---

[148] For example, see *Devine v Magill* (*The Irish Times*, January 30, 1986, *Sunday Tribune*, February 2, 1986); *Ward and Ní Fhlatharta v Independent Newspapers* (*The Irish Times*, June 29–July 7, 1989); *O'Rourke v Independent Newspapers* (*The Irish Times*, May 3, 1995), *Finucane v Independent Newspapers* (*The Irish Times*, February 29, 1996), *Kenny v Sunday Independent* (*The Irish Times*, August 3, 1997), *Dervan v Independent Newspapers* (*The Irish Times*, May 8, 12, 1999), *Clarke v Coogan and Ireland on Sunday* (*The Irish Times*, November 16, 2001), *Waters v Sunday Times* (*The Irish Times*, May 2, 2002).

[149] *Telnikoff v Matusevich* 347 Md. 561, 702 Atlantic 2d 230 (Md. Ct. App. 1997) and *Bachchan v India Abroad Publications, Inc.* 154 Misc. 2d 228, 585 N.Y. Supp. 2d 661 (Sup. Ct. N.Y. Co. 1992). See Kyu Ho Youm, "The Interaction between American and Foreign Libel Law – US Courts Refuse to Enforce English Libel Judgments" (2000) 49 I.C.L.Q. 131.

[150] The Iowa study: Randall P. Bezanson, Gilbert Cranberg and John Soloski, *Libel Law and the Press: Myth and Reality* (The Free Press, New York, 1987), at pp.79–94.

[151] The remedy intended to meet the requirement of a right of reply was included in the Broadcasting Act 1990. See below Chap.11.

4.4.3 Who Is Sued?

Technically, any individual, legal person or anyone involved in the publication process can be sued. In the print media that means anyone from the reporter, editor and proprietor through to the printer, distributor and even, possibly, the seller. In the broadcast media it means everyone from presenter, editor, producer to broadcasting authority. The reason for including printers and distributors, in particular, is twofold. First, there is the concern to ensure that someone will be able to meet an award of damages. If the publisher is small and relatively impecunious, or a fly-by-night operator, or a person or persons unknown, the defamed plaintiff should not have to suffer the consequences. However, the inability to pay of those directly responsible would not of itself seem sufficient grounds to impose liability on others whose involvement is removed from the harmful act.

The key issue, therefore, would seem to be control. When the laws were devised, media operations were essentially one-man commercial operations, run by printer/stationers. Thus the printer fulfilled all of the obligations now shared by reporter, editor, proprietor, printer and distributor/seller. Accordingly, he had complete control over content at every stage of the process and could therefore be held legally responsible for any libel arising from his publications. Over time, as media operations developed and separate roles of reporter, editor and sub-editor emerged, the common law conceded the diminished responsibility of distributors, who had now begun to handle large numbers of publications from various printing houses. A defence of reasonable care was introduced, whereby a distributor, who did not know, and who had no way of knowing that a particular publication contained a libel, would not be liable for it, provided his lack of knowledge did not stem from an absence of reasonable care. Nowadays, with distributors handling enormous numbers of publications and with an increased use of technology, control over content is minimal. Checking for libel is unduly burdensome, if not impossible, and, therefore, even the requirement of reasonable care is problematic. What constitutes reasonable care in the case of a distributor handling in excess of half a million titles per year?

A defence of reasonable care was not recognised in the case of printers, who were deemed still to have control and to be a good financial mark. Nowadays, the picture is quite different. Direct input by computer means that usually the printer has no control whatsoever over content. Often, the printer no longer sets up the type or corrects proofs marked for correction by the publisher. For these reasons, reform bodies have recommended a defence for printers.[152] In the case of broadcasters also, the guiding principle for reform of the law should be control. In that way, account could be taken of the impact of technology on the roles of those involved in the various stages of programme production and broadcasting.

Defamatory matter can occur in any section of a newspaper (birth or death notices, advertisements, business to sports pages). It can occur in any type of broadcast programme (not only news or current affairs but documentaries,

---

[152] See above n.50, *Paper*, at p.417; *Report*, at p.87.

docu-dramas, drama, film – including those that are foreign-produced, satirical programmes, advertisements). It can occur in any book, whether factual or fiction, and in any other media. As a result, everyone in the business needs to be on his/her guard. Also, since the repetition of defamatory remarks is actionable, particular care must be taken with press releases,[153] open letters,[154] extracts from other publications, reports of what politicians and others have said outside of the Dáil or Seanad; even editorial comment.[155]

4.4.4 Public/Private Plaintiff Distinction

At present the Irish law of defamation makes no distinction between public and private plaintiffs. The traditional view taken by the common-law courts was expressed by Raymond L.C.J. in his speech in the trial of Thomas Woolston in 1729:

> "Even a private man's character is not to be ... scandalized.... And much less is a magistrate, minister of state, or other public person's character to be stained, either directly or indirectly. And the law reckons it a greater offence when the libel is pointed at persons in a public capacity, as it is a reproach to the government to have corrupt magistrates, etc. substituted by his majesty, and tends to sow sedition, and disturb the peace of the kingdom".[156]

With the dawn of democracy, attitudes to public persons changed. In an Irish case in 1866, Monahan C.J. stated that "The right to comment upon the public acts of public men is the right of everyone".[157] Public persons have come to be regarded as public property, as fair game for criticism: "Anyone who throws a hat into a public arena must be prepared to have it mercilessly, though not maliciously, trampled upon".[158] Public discussion and criticism must not be

---

[153] For example, *Ryan v Irish Times* (above, n.53): the information about fuel merchants allegedly giving money and fuel in exchange for votes had come from a press release issued by a political party. A ministerial press release also gave rise to allegations of defamation of a company: *Irish Press Publishers v Bruton and Gleeson* (*The Irish Times*, October 21, 1997).

[154] In *O'Connor v The Kerryman* (above, n.48), fishermen, who had allegedly been verbally attacked from the altar by a priest, responded through an open letter from their solicitors and a paper that published it was sued. *Maronek v Slovakia*, App. No.32686/96, Judgment April 19, 2001, also concerned an open letter, which the European Court of Human Rights found: "undeniably raised issues capable of affecting the public interest" (at para.56), and taking the letter as a whole, the statements did not appear excessive. The Court, therefore, found that there had been a violation of Art.10.

[155] *Donoghue v Irish Press and Sunday Tribune* (*The Irish Times*, October 20–22, 1990), concerned, respectively, remarks in an editorial about the handling of a court case and remarks made by the defence solicitor to a journalist outside the court.

[156] 94 E.R. 113; Holt, *The Law of Libel* (Reed, London, Phelan, Dublin, 1812) p.55, cited in above, n.1, at p.29.

[157] *Kane v Mulvaney* (1866) I.R. 2 C.L. 402.

[158] Above, n.58, Robertson and Nicol, 3rd ed. at p.85. See also Lord Lester, "Defaming Politicians and Public Officials" (1995) P.L. 1, and "Private lives and public figures: freedom of political speech in a democratic society" (1999) 4 *Communications Law* 43.

stifled. The doctrine that the governed must not criticise their governors is now obsolete. In *New York Times v Sullivan*,[159] the United States Supreme Court went further.[160] There must be free debate and a breathing space for error, the Court said, because error is inevitable in free debate. Inadvertent error should not be penalised. The media in fulfilling their central and fundamental role in society should not have to compensate a public official because of an error they did not make deliberately or recklessly. In other words, in order to succeed in a defamation action against the media, a public person must prove malice, *i.e.* that the offending remarks were published knowingly or recklessly, without regard to their truth or falsity.

The *New York Times* decision was regarded as a major breakthrough for freedom of speech, but its practical effect was somewhat negated in the years that followed by a relaxation of standards on the part of the press no longer threatened by the likely success of multi-million dollar suits from public officials, and by further court cases seeking to refine and develop the *New York Times* decision.[161] That decision should extend not only to public officials but to public figures, said the courts, because both:

(a) have significantly greater access to the channels of communication and therefore a better chance of correcting or counteracting false statements about them than have private individuals, and

(b) have voluntarily sought the public gaze by assuming roles of power and influence in society and must, as a consequence, accept the increased risk of criticism.

Private persons have not done so and therefore require greater protection, it is argued. However, as inadvertent error must be tolerated, so the argument runs, the private individual must at least prove negligence on the part of a media defendant. In Ireland there is no such hurdle as malice or negligence for public or private plaintiff. Libel is a strict liability tort and even a typesetter's error or a wrong caption on a photograph, or two stories transposed, can result in sizeable awards of damages. The *New York Times* decision has not solved all the problems, even in the United States, however. It has not solved basic problems of high awards and costs, but it has lessened the chilling effect of libel actions for the media.[162] There is now a huge volume of pre-trial

---

[159] Above, n.68.

[160] For a detailed analysis of *New York Times v Sullivan*, see Anthony Lewis, *Make No Law* (Vintage Books, New York, 1992); also Anthony Lewis, "Law and the Press: A Deadly Embrace?" (1998) xxxiii Ir. Jur. 34.

[161] *Gertz v Welch* (above, n.68), which extended the ruling to public figures, including limited purpose public figures, that is, those who "thrust themselves to the forefront of particular controversies in order to influence the resolution of the issues involved" (at 345).

[162] See, for example, above, n.144, Weaver and Bennett, at p.9, on how few threats of libel actions the media in the US receive in comparison with the media in the UK. The extension of the public official category to public "figures" in subsequent cases created further problems of classification, which has led some courts to refine the "public figure" category to exclude "limited-purpose public figures" – see *Foretich v Capital Cities/*

proceedings in the US, so much so that some plaintiffs, particularly public plaintiffs, cannot get to a defamation hearing at all. To place the hurdle so high might well amount to a denial of the plaintiff's right of access to the courts.[163]

The European Court of Human Rights in *Lingens v Austria*[164] also recognised the distinction between public and private plaintiffs. The case arose out of the publication by a journalist of criticism of the attitude of the Austrian federal chancellor to national socialism and the participation of Nazis in the governance of the country. The court emphasised the importance of a free press, in that it affords the public one of the best means of discovering and forming an opinion of the ideas and attitudes of political leaders. Freedom of political debate is at the very core of the concept of a democratic society. It follows, therefore, the Court said, that the limits of acceptable criticism are wider as regards a politician as such, than as regards a private individual. The politician inevitably and knowingly lays himself open to close scrutiny of his every word and deed by both journalists and the public at large, and he must consequently display a greater degree of tolerance. Everyone is entitled to have his/her reputation protected, including politicians, but in their case that protection has to be weighed in relation to the interests in open discussion of political issues. To fine a journalist for political comment was a censure likely to deter journalists from contributing to public discussion of issues affecting the life of the country and to hamper the press in its role as purveyor of information and public watchdog.[165]

The European Court has maintained and elaborated the public/private distinction in subsequent defamation cases.[166] In *Lopes Gomes Da Silva v Portugal*,[167] the Court restated the principles applicable to politicians, who must display a greater degree of tolerance, particularly when they themselves make public statements that are susceptible of criticism. In *Nikula v Finland*,[168] it added that in some circumstances the limits of acceptable criticism may be wider with regard to civil servants also when exercising their powers.

ABC, Inc., 37 F.3d 1541 (4th Cir. 1994), which set out a five-part test for determining whether a plaintiff is a "limited-purposes public figure".

[163] See, generally, Roy V. Leeper, "Refocusing Libel Law: Gross Irresponsibility and *Naantaanbuu v Abernathy*" (1998) *Communications and the Law* 67. For arguments in support of a public figure defence, see Helen Searls and Daniel Lloyd, "The Case for a Public Figure Defence" [1999] ENT. L.R. 1.

[164] Above, n.26.

[165] *ibid.*, *Lingens* at 419–20.

[166] *ibid.* Also *Thorgeirson v Iceland*, Series A, No.239; (1992) 14 E.H.R.R. 843; *Castells v Spain*, Series A, No.236; (1992) 14 E.H.R.R. 445. The Court also held in *Colombani v France* (App. No.51279/99, June 25, 2002) that a law under which *Le Monde* newspaper was found to have defamed a foreign Head of State did not conform to the practice and conception of modern politics: it "cannot be reconciled with modern practice and political conceptions", since its effect was to afford them immunity from criticism solely because of their function or status, irrespective of whether that criticism was justified. In the Court's view, that privilege went beyond what was necessary to achieve the objective (paras 68–70).

[167] App. No.37698/97, September 28, 2000, at para. 30ii, citing also *Oberschlick v Austria (No.2)*, above, n.84, at para.29.

[168] App. No.31611/96, judgment of March 21, 2002, at para.48.

The Court's approach is likely to influence our law either directly, through cases being brought against Ireland, or indirectly, insofar as there is a presumption that our law is in conformity with the Convention, which operates as a yardstick in relation to our domestic law, pending incorporation. In the UK, the House of Lords in *Reynolds v Sunday Times*[169] has developed the common-law defence of qualified privilege to address some of the issues (see further below). The public/private distinction should therefore not be ignored in Ireland, even though the Law Reform Commission did not recommend its introduction.[170]

4.4.5 Limitation Periods

In Ireland, the limitation period in respect of libel remains six years. Such a long period of time may have been justifiable in the early days of newspapers before the introduction of the postal service and transport systems. In those days when publication was erratic and distribution was haphazard, it could happen that a person would not discover defamatory content for quite some considerable time after publication. In contrast, it is impossible to justify a period of six years in today's world of almost instantaneous transmission of information and images on a global basis. In the UK, the six-year period was reduced initially to three years and then under the Defamation Act 1996 to one year. In most European jurisdictions, the period is three to six months. Any longer period creates problems for the media in terms of keeping journalists' notes, tapes, and other records. In Ireland, the reality is that most cases are commenced within three months of publication, and only one or two out of nearly 800 cases in the past five years have been commenced more than three years after publication.[171]

4.4.6 Absence of legal aid

Legal aid is not available in defamation cases, despite recommendations that it should be.[172] Its absence means that a defamation action remains the privilege of the rich, unless lawyers choose, as some do in practice, to take cases on a "no foal, no fee" basis, that is, agreeing not to charge fees unless the client

---

[169] Above, n.51. The New York gross irresponsibility standard advocated in Leeper, above, n.163, has some similar hallmarks to *Reynolds*: gross irresponsibility relates to action taken "without due consideration for the standards of information gathering and dissemination ordinarily followed by responsible parties", at 571. As in *Reynolds*, it puts the emphasis on the nature of the content rather than the public/private status of the plaintiff.

[170] LRC *Report*, above, n.7.

[171] Boyle and McGonagle, *Survey of High Court Defamation Cases 1995–2000* (not yet published). The Government in 2001 announced its intention to bring in a new defamation bill, which would, *inter alia*, reduce the period of limitation to three years, as recommended in 1991 by the LRC (see *The Irish Times*, December 19, 2001). See also the Report of the Legal Advisory Group on Defamation 2003 (below).

[172] See above, n.29 and n.7, LRC.

succeeds in obtaining compensation in the action. It could be argued that the absence of legal aid amounts to a breach of the constitutional right to one's good name and a breach of the European Convention on Human Rights. However, the European Court of Human Rights has held in *McVicar v UK*[173] that in the particular circumstances of that case, the plaintiff's rights were not violated by the absence of legal aid. In two libel cases against the *Sunday Times* and *Magill* magazine in 2002, legal aid was refused by the High Court in Belfast. Mr Justice Kerr said he did not consider that the absence of legal aid amounted to a violation of the plaintiff's human right to a fair hearing under the European Convention on Human Rights.[174]

4.4.7 Jurisdiction

The fact that the media operate in many cases on a transnational or even global level means that issues of jurisdiction arise much more frequently than in the past. One of the most noticeable developments in defamation cases in Ireland in the 1990s, for instance, was the number of cases taken against the Irish media by plaintiffs in Northern Ireland and further afield. In many such cases, the issue of jurisdiction arose. The preliminary question was whether the Irish courts had jurisdiction to hear the case and, in that regard, whether the case was being pursued in any other jurisdiction. Normally, the plenary summons contains an endorsement asserting the court's power under the Jurisdiction of Courts and Enforcement of Judgments (EC) Act 1988, which implemented the Brussels Convention 1968, and confirming that no proceedings are pending between the parties in any other contracting state in relation to the same cause of action. Occasionally, however, jurisdiction is contested.

In *Shevill v Presse Alliance*,[175] the European Court of Justice held that a person defamed may bring an action against the publisher either in the country in which the publisher is established or has his main place of business, or in each of the countries where the publication has been distributed and where the victim claims to have suffered damage. If the plaintiff sues in the country where the publisher is established, s/he can claim there for all the damage ensuing from the publication. If s/he sues in another state(s) where the publication is distributed, s/he can only claim there for the harm caused in the state in question. In the particular case, the plaintiff sued a French magazine in Britain, even though the magazine, which had a circulation of some 200,000 copies in France, only sold some 230 copies in England, and only 10 of them in Yorkshire where the plaintiff lived. English courts, however, demand that

---

[173] Above, n.29.

[174] *Lynch v Sunday Times*, *Lynch v Magill* (*The Irish Times*, June 19, 2002).

[175] Above, n.89. By analogy, in the case of satellite or transfrontier broadcasting, jurisdiction should lie for all the harm in the State where the broadcaster is established, or in the place(s) of reception to the extent that the plaintiff's reputation has been injured there. For a detailed approach to the issues, see David I. Fisher, *Defamation via Satellite – A European Law Perspective* (Kluwer Law International, The Hague, 1998), and for the application of *Shevill* in Ireland, see T.P. Kennedy, "Defamation across borders in the EU" *Eurlegal, Law Society Gazette*, May 2000.

the plaintiff have more than just a tenuous link with that jurisdiction in order to sue there.[176]

In *Ewins v Carlton UK Television Ltd and Ulster Television plc*,[177] a television documentary on the IRA made by Carlton in the UK and transmitted by ITN, including UTV, could be received in Ireland and was viewed by as many as 111,000 viewers here. The High Court in Dublin held, approving *Shevill*, that in those circumstances the plaintiffs could sue for defamation in Ireland for the harm done to their reputation in this state.

The question of the jurisdiction of the Irish courts arose also in *Hunter and Callaghan v Duckworth & Co. Ltd and Louis Blom-Cooper.*[178] The plaintiffs were two of the Birmingham Six and the alleged libel was contained in a booklet published and distributed in England. Kelly J. in the High Court held that the Brussels Convention did not intend to depart from the common-law rule that the original publisher of a defamatory statement is liable for its republication by another person where the republication of the words to a third party was the natural and probable result of the original publication. Hence, where an original publication, made in a contracting state, is subsequently republished in Ireland, the appropriate question to be considered is whether or not the republication was such a natural and probable consequence of the original publication. If it was, the Irish courts had jurisdiction to determine the claim for damages for harm done in this state. Given the issues discussed in the book, the proximity of England to Ireland and the interest that was likely to be shown in the topic in Ireland, it was almost inevitable that publication would occur here, the judge said, and this must have been the natural and probable consequence of allowing the booklet to be published in the first instance on the agreed written terms. The Irish courts, therefore, had jurisdiction.

Given the nature of the internet and its worldwide reach, complex issues of jurisdiction can arise. The question as to which courts have jurisdiction in the case of an internet libel has arisen in the United States and Australia, and plaintiffs have sued successfully in their home states, although the defamatory material was posted on websites elsewhere.[179]

---

[176] See David Hooper, "Forum Shopping in Libel Actions" (1999) *Yearbook of Copyright and Media Law* 124; Alan Reed, "Multistate Defamation Jurisdiction: A Comparative Analysis of Prevailing Jurisprudence in the United States and the European Union" (1996) *Communications and the Law* 29.

[177] [1997] 2 I.L.R.M. 223. The court also held that in terms of a television or radio broadcast there is no distinction between publication and distribution where both happen simultaneously.

[178] Irish Times Law Report, January 17, 2000. The booklet was *The Birmingham Six and other Cases*, published in 1997. The High Court in Dublin was asked initially to determine whether the first defendant was entitled to the protection of the guarantee of freedom of expression in the Irish Constitution, under EU law and the ECHR. Ó Caoimh J. said that the issues canvassed were "novel" in the Irish context, that they raised the issue of the primacy of one right over another, freedom of expression over good name, points which gave rise to a defence not previously recognised in this State. On that basis, the Attorney General was asked if he wished to be a party. (*The Irish Times*, December 7, 2001.) Ó Caoimh J. decided (High Court, July 31, 2003) that the case should proceed.

[179] See, for example, *Berezovsky v Michaels* [2000] 1 W.L.R. 1004, *Gutnick v Dow Jones*

4.5 DEFENCES

There are a number of defences specific to defamation, in addition to those available in tort cases generally. The defences specific to defamation are: justification; fair comment; and privilege, both absolute and qualified. If established, they are complete defences to defamation. The offer of amends for unintentional defamation can serve as a bar to an action if accepted, or as a defence if offered in accordance with the conditions laid down in the Defamation Act 1961, section 21, but not accepted. An apology on its own is not a complete defence but may be pleaded in mitigation.

4.5.1 General Tort Defences

The general tort defences include the defences of consent and self-defence. Consent in the defamation context means consent to publication, where a person volunteers a statement for publication or broadcast, enters into a publishing contract or expressly waives his/her rights to sue. The consent must relate to the actual libel published, not just to agreement to appear on a programme or be interviewed.[180] Self-defence is a general defence to tort actions and applies equally to defamation. A person whose reputation is attacked is entitled to respond to defend and protect it. However, just as a person who is physically attacked may not use more force than is necessary in self-defence, so in defamation the response must be proportionate in the extent of its content and in the medium used. Thus, a person responding to a defamatory allegation

---

[2001] V.S.C. 305, *www.austlii.edu.au/au/cases*; also *Young v Tribune Newspapers* and *Gutnick v Barron's Financial Weekly* referred to in Carl S. Kaplan, "A Libel Suit May Establish E-Jurisdiction" *New York Times*, May 27, 2002. In both cases, the plaintiffs sued successfully in their home states of Virginia and Victoria respectively, as neither had any connection with the states in which the libellous material was posted on the internet, *i.e.* Connecticut and New York. The High Court of Australia in *Gutnick* ruled (*Dow Jones & Co Inc v Gutnick* [2002] H.C.A. 56, December 10, 2002; *The Guardian*, December 11, 2002) that he could sue in Melbourne, as an internet article is published wherever it is read, rather than where the publisher is based. The magazine had only 14 subscribers in Australia, of whom five were in Victoria, but the number of online subscriptions using Australian credit cards was 1,700 and that was sufficient to allow the case to be heard in Victoria. Publishers are not obliged to publish on the internet, the court said, so, if the potential reach is uncontrollable then the greater the need to exercise care in publication. However, a claim could only be brought in Australia if the plaintiff had a reputation there. The decision has serious implications for the media and internet publishing in general, which will have to be worked out. See "Australian Net Libel case highlights need for harmonising laws" *The Irish Times*, November 8, 2002, which also states that fears of the possibility of defamation cases led the Irish government to decide not to publish the Ansbacher report (on off-shore accounts) on the internet. See also Harvey L. Zuckman, "The Global Implications of Defamation Suits and the Internet: The US View" [2001] ENT. L.R. 53; Patrick O'Callaghan, "Libel on the Internet" (2003) 8 B.R. 15 and Peter Bartlett, "Jurisdiction on the Internet: Addressing Cross-Border Defamation" (2003) *International Legal Practitioner* 5.

[180] Under the Civil Liability Act 1961, as interpreted by the Supreme Court in *O'Hanlon v ESB* [1969] I.R. 75, consent is not established by contract alone; it must be expressly communicated.

must not introduce irrelevancies that would defame others and must confine his/her response to those to whom the original remarks were addressed.

In relation to defamation, self-defence is usually treated under the defence of privilege which is discussed in detail at para. 4.5.4.2 below. Self-protection affords a ground for the plea of privilege, as illustrated by the case of *Willis v Irish Press*.[181] In *Willis*, the paper was threatened with a libel action in relation to a journalist's articles on sporting events, which had appeared in the paper. In response to the threat, it published an apology. The journalist then sued for defamation on the grounds that the apology harmed his reputation, but the publication of the apology was held by the Supreme Court to be privileged and the apology itself a privileged communication. The question of malice was then a matter for the jury. The decision was based both on the duty element of qualified privilege and on the ground of "reasonable purpose of self-protection", following the English Court of Appeal decision in *Adam v Ward*.[182] The *Willis* decision should be noted by journalists, some of whom have sued their papers in the past for publishing apologies concerning their work. The apologies, they claim, undermine their professional reputation as journalists. Apologies or corrections should, therefore, be published in consultation with the journalist concerned. Furthermore, journalists concerned about the form of a proposed apology reflecting on their work should probably obtain independent legal advice.

Does the self-defence privilege extend to the protection of others or to the protection of property? The English case *Bowen-Rowlands v Argus Press Ltd*,[183] cited in *Willis*, is instructive. There it was held that a letter, written by the daughter of a deceased, complaining of a story about him quoted in a book review in the newspaper, was privileged. However, it is not clear whether the privilege stemmed from self-protection on the part of the daughter, whose feelings the story was "clearly calculated to injure", or from protection of the memory of the father. At any rate, it was held that the publication of the letter in the newspaper, which had published the book review, was privileged. The form of apology printed in *Willis*, accepting that the statements published contained "accusations and imputations of dishonourable and unprofessional conduct ... wholly unfounded", though agreed at the time by the parties' solicitors and settled by counsel, would probably not be countenanced by media lawyers today. The court held that the newspaper had a duty to put right the injury caused by the published articles and that there were no means open to it to do so other than by publishing the apology.

4.5.2 Justification

John Stuart Mill has said:

> "[I]f there are cases in which a truth unpleasant to individuals is of no advantage to the public, there are others in which it is of the greatest;

---

[181] (1938) 72 I.L.T.R. 238. See also above, n.6, McDonald, at p.146.

[182] [1917] A.C. 309; see also discussion in 4.5.4.2, Qualified Privilege.

[183] *The Times*, February 10, 1926, March 26, 1926.

and that the truths which it most imports to the public to know, are precisely those which give most annoyance to individuals, whose vices and follies they expose".[184]

Justification is the old term used to signify the defence of truth. It stems from the belief that if the allegations were true, their publication was justified in the sense that a person is entitled only to his true reputation, not to a good reputation that is false and therefore undeserved. Truth is a complete defence to an action for defamation.[185] To rely on it the defendant must be able to prove substantial truth, enough to take the sting out of the defamation. At common law, the defendant had at one time to prove the precise truth of the allegation and, where there were two or more distinct allegations, prove that each and every allegation complained of was substantially true. The Defamation Act 1961 modified the old rule. It provides that where there is more than one allegation, it is not necessary to prove the truth of every single one, provided that any words not proven true do not materially injure the plaintiff's reputation, given the truth of the others:

> "[I]n an action for libel or slander in respect of words containing two or more distinct charges against the plaintiff, a defence of justification shall not fail by reason only that the truth of every charge is not proved, if the words not proved to be true do not materially injure the plaintiff's reputation having regard to the truth of the remaining charges". (Defamation Act 1961, section 22)

Section 22 also has the effect of modifying the old common-law rule on partial justification.[186] Even with this mitigation of the old common-law rules, the defence is a difficult one to sustain in practice and is pleaded on its own in only five per cent of cases. The application of section 22 arose in the case of *Beverly Cooper-Flynn v RTÉ, Charlie Bird and James Howard.*[187] In that case, the jury decided that RTÉ had established the truth of one allegation, namely that the plaintiff had advised or encouraged a number of investors to participate in an investment scheme the purpose of which was to evade tax. The jury was not satisfied, however, that RTÉ had discharged the onus of proof in relation to another allegation that the plaintiff had encouraged the third-named defendant to do so. Nonetheless, the jury decided that the allegation not proven true did not materially damage the plaintiff's reputation, given the allegations that had been proven true. Accordingly, the jury awarded no damages.[188]

---

[184] Above, n.1, at p.15.

[185] Subject, in the UK, to the limitation of the Rehabilitation of Offenders Act 1974.

[186] See above, n.50, *Paper*, at p.48; n.6, McDonald, at pp.100–110.

[187] *The Irish Times*, March 24, 2001. The earlier discovery stage of the proceedings is reported at [2000] 3 I.R. 344, [2001] 1 I.L.R.M. 208. See also *Murphy v Times Newspapers* [2000] 1 I.R. 522, where Keane J. in the Supreme Court considered the issues of justification and partial justification.

[188] A high standard of truth is required by the courts and the position in this country is still a very far cry from the American case *Lakian v Boston Globe (Time Magazine,* August

Truth must be proven on the balance of probabilities: that the words complained of are more probably true than not. That degree of proof may not appear very high or onerous; yet the defence is difficult to set up in practice. That is particularly so for media defendants, who often rely for their information on sources to whom they promise confidentiality or witnesses who may be unwilling to appear in court. The allegations must be proved true in any reasonable sense contended by the plaintiff. Where an innuendo is pleaded, the words must be proven true according to the sense arising out of the innuendo. Doubts remain as to whether evidence of previous convictions can be used to justify imputations of criminal activities, although it can be used as evidence of general bad reputation, as Murphy J. stated in the Supreme Court in *Hill v Examiner Publications*.[189]

One of the difficulties for the media defendant lies in the fact that aggravated damages may be awarded if justification is pleaded but fails. Such an award of aggravated damages signals that the conduct of the defendant has added to the harm. The rationale behind an award of aggravated damages where a plea of justification fails is that the defendant, in standing over the story and asserting that it was true, has "persisted in a lie". Not only has s/he impugned the plaintiff's reputation in the first instance but s/he has maintained throughout the pre-trial and trial stages that the allegations were true, thus adding to the harm to the plaintiff's reputation. The defence is therefore a dangerous one. The possibility of an award of aggravated damages acts as a deterrent to defendants to rely on the defence.[190] As well as aggravated damages, there may be occasions when punitive damages will be awarded.

The primary task of juries in assessing damages is to compensate the injured party for the harm done, not to punish the defendant. Nevertheless, the Supreme Court in *McIntyre v Lewis*[191] supported the retention of punitive damages in

---

19, 1985), in which the jury found that five paragraphs of a newspaper story were false and defamatory but the gist of it true and awarded no damages. *Cooper-Flynn v RTÉ*, however, is a good example of the operation of section 22, although the case is under appeal to the Supreme Court (*The Irish Times*, May 12, 2001). See also *Sherwin v Independent Newspapers* (*The Irish Times*, November 21–28, 2001, December 6–14, 2001). In the UK, the Court of Appeal in *Tancic v Times Newspapers Ltd* (*The Times*, January 12, 2000) held that particulars of justification should be strictly confined to those matters which are essential to the proper disposal of the real issues between the parties. See (2000) 5 *Communications Law* 70–1.

[189] Above, n.76 at 224. See also above n.50, *Paper*, at pp.52–4; the "Slab" Murphy case, above n.49 (evidence of garda) and *Chambers v Times Newspapers Ltd* [1999] 1 I.L.R.M. 504: allegations that plaintiff was a leading member of the IRA, defence of justification on basis that plaintiff had been convicted of five offences in the Special Criminal Court (SCC); book of evidence and transcript of trial in SCC sought; non-party discovery refused but would be considered favourably if documents not forthcoming on discovery from plaintiff; importance of documents to defence recognised. With regard to discovery, see also: *McDonnell v Sunday Business Post* (High Court, February 2, 2000).

[190] CLÉ, the Irish Book Publishers Association, in its submission on defamation to the Law Reform Commission in 1991, argued that the defendant should not be penalised for exercising his/her right to plead justification. Far from the original injury being repeated and increased by it, failure of the plea effectively and in a very full manner repudiates and lays to rest the defamatory statement, providing the plaintiff with the fullest vindication of reputation, CLÉ argued.

[191] [1991] 1 I.R. 121.

certain circumstances in defamation cases. This decision has, however, clarified the issue and laid down criteria to apply.[192] Where punitive damages are awarded, they tend to be much greater than the compensatory award. For instance, in the English case of *Elton John v Sunday Mirror*,[193] £75,000 was awarded as compensation and £275,000 as punitive or exemplary damages. In Scotland, where juries are seldom used in defamation cases and compensation levels are low, punitive damages are not part of the law.[194]

The defence of justification is therefore problematic on a number of fronts. However, it relates only to facts, as only facts can be proved true or false. There is a separate defence for comment. In practical terms, journalists who want to stand over what they have reported, need to be satisfied not only that they have got their facts right and that what they have said was true, but also that they would be able to prove it true in court. Journalists need to be careful when describing or commenting on a single incident not to give the impression that it is a habitual occurrence, in which case the defence of truth may not be satisfied. They need to be careful not to ascribe motives or reasons for behaviour, unless they are sure those motives or reasons can also be proven true in court. For instance, to say that a solicitor did not raise the matter of diplomatic immunity in court because he had forgotten to bring the documentation with him resulted in an award of £30,000 in the Circuit Court against two newspapers. It was true that the solicitor did not raise the matter of immunity, but he was able to satisfy the court that his decision not to do so was deliberate and not the result of forgetting the documents.[195]

It can be dangerous also to draw inferences from facts. In *Prior v Irish Press*,[196] for example, a local farmer had been arrested during a search for kidnappers, and the inference was drawn that he was one of the kidnappers. In fact, he merely happened to be passing and was in the wrong place at the wrong time. Such an inference brings the allegation into the realm of fact. The formulation in *Campbell v Spottiswoode*[197] of the law regarding imputations of dishonourable motives is somewhat unclear, and there do not appear to be

---

[192] *ibid.*, McCarthy J. at 138, O'Flaherty J. at 139–41.

[193] *Elton John v Mirror Group Newspapers* (*The Guardian*, November 5, 1993). The amount was later reduced on appeal to £75,000: [1996] 2 All E.R. 35. For an explanation of the terms "exemplary" and "punitive" damages, see above n.191, at 133–5, 139–41.

[194] See Jean McFadden, "£350,000 libel damages for Elton John – why it could not happen in Scotland" (1994) 15 J.M.L.P. 13. The highest damages award in Scotland for defamation in a non-jury trial was £7,500. There had been only one jury trial in the last 40 years, and it resulted in an award of £50,000. Since then, in *Clinton v MGN Ltd* and *Barry v MGN Ltd* (1999) S.L.T. 590, 1999 S.C. 367, concerning allegations of a long-term affair between a priest and a female acquaintance, £45,000 was awarded to the priest and £120,000 to the woman. Also, where economic loss results to a business, *e.g. Baigent & others v BBC* (Inner House of the Court of Session, October 25, 2000), in which five members of a family running a nursing home were awarded a total of £170,000; see generally Tom Crone, *Law and the Media* (4th ed., Focal Press, Oxford, 2002), p.289.

[195] See above, n.155.

[196] Above, n.119.

[197] (1863) 3 B.&S. 769: if you impute wickedness, you must prove that the implications are true.

any Irish authorities on the subject except *Black v Northern Whig*[198] and *Foley v Independent Newspapers*,[199] in which Geoghegan J. in the High Court was satisfied that *Campbell v Spottiswoode* was still good law in this jurisdiction.

In order to avail of the defence of justification, journalists need to have evidence that would stand up in court. They need to be able to rely in part on witnesses who would be willing to testify. Journalists depend on confidential sources and therefore have no alternative in some cases but to settle or forego their defence. Even when sources have not been promised confidentiality they may not be willing to appear, and the availability of witnesses who are willing to testify is often a difficulty for the media in defending a case.[200] Journalists also rely on their own detailed notes of the story and of the checks they ran. Their notes and tape-recordings have a value. They are useful to lawyers in determining whether a case should be fought or settled. Where they record events first-hand, they may also have an evidential value in court. To that end, journalists should be encouraged or required by their employers to date notes as they make them and keep them for a reasonable period of time.[201] Where they merely record what others said, journalists' notes might not be admissible in evidence in court on the grounds that they amount to "hearsay". The same applies to tape-recordings and video evidence. It is for the courts to decide on admissibility in accordance with the law of evidence.

Most important, for all aspects of the media, is the creation or promotion of a climate of carefulness and checking. This will remain the key to avoiding defamation, even if law reform along the lines proposed by the Law Reform Commission becomes a reality. If the Commission's proposals are acted upon, negligence or absence of reasonable care will be the test applied in claims for general damages. The media will no longer be liable to pay damages in all cases of defamation but only in those where it is established that there was a failure to take reasonable care. In this respect, our law would be brought more into line with that of the United States (malice and negligence standards) and most European countries *(bonne foi* in France, for example). The idea behind a defence of reasonable care is to allow some latitude to the media, a breathing-space for error, as the United States Supreme Court put it in *New York Times v Sullivan*,[202] while at the same time encouraging careful research in journalism.

---

[198] (1942) 77 I.L.T.R. 5; see also above, n.50, *Paper*, at pp.68-71.

[199] [1994] 2 I.L.R.M. 61. The defence plea was fair comment.

[200] The absence of witnesses was a problem for the defendants in *Ryan v Irish Times* (above, n.105) and *O'Connor v The Kerryman* (above, n.48), for example.

[201] Technically, a libel action in this country can be brought up to six years after publication, but in reality the vast majority of cases are commenced within the first month or two (above, n.171). However, in *Mangan v Independent Newspapers* (*The Irish Times*, February 20, 2002) the plaintiff did not commence proceedings until 17 months after publication. There have been also a few exceptional cases even in recent years in which the plaintiff has begun proceedings just a matter of weeks or days before the six-year deadline.

[202] Above, n.68. See also Úna Ní Raifeartaigh, "Fault Issues and Libel Law – A Comparison between Irish, English and United States Law" (1991) 40 I.C.L.Q. 763. For a practical perspective on *New York Times v Sullivan* see Thomas Kane, "Malice, Lies, and Videotape: Revisiting *New York Times v Sullivan* in the Modern Age of Political Campaigns" (1999) Rutgers L.J. 755.

It may be argued that promotion of standards or of media accountability is not, and should not be, the purpose of defamation law. Nonetheless, reasonable care is the standard demanded by tort law of all other professions; negligence is the test of their liability and is preferable to the strict liability situation under current defamation law.[203]

4.5.3 Fair Comment

Fair comment is the defence most often relied on by the media, with limited success. To establish the defence of fair comment, the defendant must show:

(a) that the words complained of were comment, as opposed to fact,

(b) that the comment was fair, in the sense of being honestly held, and

(c) that the comment was made on a matter of public interest.

4.5.3.1 Comment as Opposed to Fact

The greatest difficulty with the defence of fair comment lies in distinguishing between fact and comment. "Comment" is the expression of opinion, whereas "fact" is the statement of verifiable information.[204] In practice, however, it can be difficult to separate the two, which are often intertwined. For instance, if a restaurant review states that "the sausages were swimming in grease" or that "the peas were frozen on the plate", is that fact or comment?[205] If the words are prefaced by phrases such as "in my opinion" or "it seems to me that", does that necessarily signal that what follows is comment as opposed to fact? If that were so, journalists and publishers would have very great scope indeed and could use the device to cover all kinds of insinuations and inferences. Would that necessarily be a bad thing? After all, the other two requirements of the defence, honest opinion and public interest ((b) and (c) above) would still apply as "brakes". The legal position is that the use of such phrases will normally signal comment,[206] but it is open to the court to decide if that is so in the particular case. However, it might be inimical to good journalism to use

---

[203] See *Reynolds v Times Newspapers Ltd* (above, n.51, discussed under 4.5.4.2 "Qualified privilege at Common Law" below) and more particularly, the Art.10 case law of the ECHR, discussed below and in Chap.2 above. Tom Crone, *Law and the Media*, above, n.194, at pp.283–4, gives a list of UK cases where aspects of defamation law have been tested for their compatibility with Art.10. On a defence of "reasonable publication" see *Khumalo and Others v Bantubonke*, Constitutional Court of South Africa (June 14, 2002) and Report of the Legal Advisory Group on Defamation (below).

[204] Since the fairness of the comment is not really a factor in the defence, the word "fair" in the title of the defence is inappropriate. The Law Reform Commission and other reform bodies have recommended renaming the defence simply as "comment" or "comment based on fact". See above, n.50, *Report*, recommendation 14.3.

[205] The LRC has put forward criteria for distinguishing fact and comment; see above, n.50, *Paper*, at pp.281–4; *Report*, at pp.40–43. Duncan and Neill, 2nd ed., 1983, para. 12.13, pp.61–3. See, generally, Úna Ní Raifeartaigh, "Defences in Irish Defamation Law" (1991) 13 D.U.L.J. 76.

[206] They are indicative, not decisive, see LRC, *ibid.*

such phrases, because of the impact they have on the authoritativeness or readability of the material.[207] Who would want to read or listen to a story or review peppered with "in my opinion"? The reader knows when s/he reads an editorial that it is the expression of the views of the newspaper. The reader knows that a review is only the reviewer's opinion and assessment. How much weight readers or listeners place on editorials or reviews depends largely on what the newspaper is, or who the particular reviewer is.

Newspaper editorials are normally accepted as comment but can be sued upon successfully, as seen in *Donoghue v Irish Press*.[208] In that case, editorial comment referred to a so-called "passports for sale" case, in which an official at the Irish Embassy in London, who had been accused of "selling" Irish passports, was allowed to go free. The editorial stated that the "slip-up over diplomatic immunity" was difficult to understand and that "if the case had been properly handled in the first place ... no embarrassing second attempt would be needed". A lawyer from the Chief State Solicitor's Office, who was in charge of the case, sued successfully, although he had not been named. An editorial is by its very nature a comment, but in the eyes of the law, to say that there had been a "slip-up" is verifiable, and therefore more in the realm of fact than comment. To reduce the analysis of the language used to this degree of particularity is, however, artificial and can distract from the overall impression of the piece.[209] At any rate, while the comment in *Donoghue* was on a matter of public interest, the Circuit Court judge did not accept that it was fair comment.

In *Lopes Gomes Da Silva v Portugal*,[210] a case which also concerned an editorial in a newspaper, the European Court of Human Rights found that the conviction of a journalist for defamation was a violation of his freedom of expression. It held that there was a factual basis for the comments made in rather trenchant terms about the political beliefs and ideology of a candidate chosen to stand in city council elections. The situation clearly involved a political debate on matters of general interest, the Court said, an area in which restrictions on freedom of expression should be interpreted narrowly. Were there no factual basis, the opinion could appear excessive, but that was not the case here. In *Donoghue*, on the other hand, there may have been a factual inaccuracy in relation to the so-called "slip-up", but whether that would be sufficient for the comments to "appear excessive" is debatable. In any event the particularity and artificiality of the fact/comment divide used in the common law courts is not always helpful.

---

[207] See above, n.6, McDonald, at p.211.

[208] Above, n.155. The editorial in the *Irish Press* had appeared on October 3, 1987.

[209] This is the kind of situation in which a right of reply or rectification would seem appropriate. That is the remedy available to public officials in other European countries such as France, Germany, Belgium, Greece. See above, n.50, *Paper*, paras 470–71; n.70, Boyle and McGonagle.

[210] Above, n.166. See also *Feldek v Slovakia* (App. No.29032/95, judgment of July 12, 2001), where the Court said that it could not "accept the proposition, as a matter of principle, that a value judgment can only be considered as such if it is accompanied by the facts on which that judgment is based.... The necessity of a link between a value judgment and its supporting facts may vary from case to case in accordance with the specific circumstances." (at para.86)

In the same way, opinion pieces in the "op. ed." pages, diary pieces, book, theatre and restaurant reviews are normally expected to be comment pieces but can be sued upon. A diary piece on army evidence in a case in which a soldier had been convicted of child sexual abuse gave rise to an action in *Foley v The Irish Times*.[211] A Circuit Court award of £5,000, which is low by defamation standards, reflected the fact that a prompt apology was published in the diary. The case of *Ward and Ní Fhlatharta v Independent Newspapers*[212] arose out of a column piece which commented on the voting on an abortion motion by delegates to an NUJ conference. The High Court jury found that the facts were substantially true but that the comment was not fair comment. In *Harkin and Kendricks v The Irish Times*,[213] the Circuit Court awarded £15,000 to the plaintiffs based on a restaurant review. The judge was persuaded by the not inconsiderable influence and propensity to cause harm that critics have, most notably the theatre critic of the *New York Times*. Nonetheless, the judge's view that a restaurant critic should visit a restaurant on at least two separate occasions before writing about it is simply not practical. Customers are unlikely to visit twice before deciding if they like it or not. The High Court, on appeal, found part of the review inaccurate but not defamatory and reversed the decision. Costs, nonetheless, were awarded to the plaintiffs, which meant that in financial terms at least it was a hollow victory for the newspaper.

Letters to the editor, a mechanism to allow readers to express opinions or to react to coverage, are also vulnerable and require particular scrutiny. If they can be shown to be written in self-defence or if absence of malice can be proved, then they may not incur liability in certain circumstances.[214] Headlines are even more problematic. They will seldom be treated as fair comment, which precludes the use of that defence. Equally they are unlikely to be regarded as "reporting" to come within the protection of the defence of privilege, which the Defamation Act 1961 provides for fair and accurate reports. The only possible defence in respect of headlines, therefore, is justification.[215]

It can be so difficult to distinguish between fact and comment or to predict how a court will distinguish between them, especially in the early stages of an action, that the practice has developed of lawyers pleading the "rolled-up" plea:

> "[I]nsofar as the words complained of consist of allegations of fact, they are true in substance and in fact, and insofar as they consist of opinion they are fair comments made in good faith and without malice upon the said facts, which are matters of public interest".

The only advantage of this plea is that it allows defence lawyers to buy time.

---

[211] *The Irish Times*, November 13, 1991. The case arose from a piece in "An Irishman's Diary" in the paper on January 17, 1990.

[212] *The Irish Times*, June 29–July 7, 1989.

[213] *The Irish Times*, April 1–2, 1993.

[214] For the position in US law, see Kyu Ho Youm, "Letters to the Editor and US Libel Law" (1992) 13 J.M.L.P. 220.

[215] See D. McLean, "Libel Consequences of Headlines" (1989) 66 J.Q. 924; *Charleston v News Group Newspapers Ltd* [1995] 2 W.L.R. 450 (HL).

In order to keep their options open in case the court will find that the words contain facts rather than, or in addition to, comments, defence lawyers must further plead justification. This must be pleaded separately because the rolled-up plea relates to the defence of fair comment only. Confusion arose in *Campbell v Irish Press*,[216] the case about the snooker exhibition (above, para. 4.3.6.1) and the remark that "the table told lies". Despite evidence that the plaintiff had lost money on subsequent exhibitions, the jury assessed damages at "nil", for which the Supreme Court substituted £1, since a finding of libel carries a right to at least nominal damages.[217] The defendants, who had published an apology withdrawing their remarks, later tried to stand over them in court. They pleaded the "rolled-up plea", but the trial judge was of the opinion that the article complained of contained no comment, only facts. Therefore, the defence of fair comment was not open to them. As a result, the rolled-up plea, which covers only facts on which comment is based, for the purposes of the defence of fair comment, was not available to them. They should have pleaded justification as well.

It is an element of the defence of fair comment that, even when the words complained of are established as comment rather than fact, the comment must be shown to be based on true facts, either expressly stated or readily accessible to the reader, listener or viewer, as the case may be. The truth of every fact need not be proven, just sufficient facts to support the comment:

> "In an action for libel or slander in respect of words consisting partly of allegations of fact and partly of expression of opinion, a defence of fair comment shall not fail by reason only that the truth of every allegation of fact is not proved, if the expression of opinion is fair comment having regard to such of the facts alleged or referred to in the words complained of as are proved". (Defamation Act 1961, section 23)

The rationale of section 23 is that opinions based on facts that are not true mislead rather than inform the public. Indeed, Justice Rehnquist in the US Supreme Court in *Keeton v Hustler Magazine Inc.*[218] stated that false statements of fact harm both the subject of the falsehood and the readers of the statement. If the supporting facts are not shown to be true, it is possible that aggravated damages could be awarded.[219] The rule in *Mangena v Wright*[220] established

---

[216] Above, n.134. See also *Burke v Central Television* [1994] 2 I.L.R.M. 161, where disclosure of documents used to make a television programme about the IRA was refused because of the risk to life. The court found that the statements complained of were facts, not comments. The rolled-up plea had been pleaded but it is a plea of fair comment, not justification. In the circumstances, the defendants were given liberty to deliver an amended defence.

[217] In *Reynolds v Times Newspapers Ltd* (above, n.51) the jury found that the plaintiff had been defamed but awarded no damages. The trial judge substituted the amount of one penny.

[218] 104 S.Ct. 1473 (1984), at 1479.

[219] See *Campbell v Irish Press* (above, n.134); *McIntyre v Lewis* (above, n.191). Fleming advocates a right of reply remedy for opinion based on untrue facts, and if those facts are stated, a retraction remedy. See John G. Fleming, "Retraction and Reply: Alternative Remedies for Defamation" 12 U.B.C. Law Review 15, at pp.22–3.

[220] [1909] 2 K.B. 958.

that the defence will still be available even if the supporting facts are untrue but were spoken on an occasion of privilege. This is an exception to the general rule and the extent of its application is unclear.[221]

Despite the fact that the right to comment, to express one's opinions and convictions, is expressly protected by Article 40.6.1.i of the Constitution, Irish courts appear to take a very narrow and static approach to the defence of fair comment. The courts have not shown any willingness to develop the defence or to allow it to expand to accommodate the role of the media in commenting on and criticising standards in society generally. Book, cinema, theatre, even restaurant, reviews are a valid part of media content and should be given a wide latitude. They have a potential to cause harm, and therefore should be answerable in law where they are actuated by spite or other wrongful motive. However, the present distinction between fact and comment becomes totally artificial in practice (as shown by the previous examples) and means that the defence is rarely successful. An easier and more meaningful test would be to ask was the remark an expression of the journalist's opinion, or to take an overview of the language used, as the European Court of Human Rights did in *Lopes Gomes Da Silva v Portugal.*[222] Otherwise, it is possible that reviews will cease to be part of media content and will be replaced by an uncritical litany of praise, courtesy of the public relations industry. That industry has a very valid role but it should not become a substitute for criticism and analysis in the media. The European Court of Human Rights in *Lingens v Austria*[223] and following cases has made a clear distinction between fact and opinion and has held that the requirement that the defendant prove the truth of an allegedly defamatory opinion infringes his/her right to impart ideas as well as the public's right to receive ideas, under Article 10 of the Convention:

> "[A] careful distinction needs to be made between facts and value judgments. The existence of facts can be demonstrated, whereas the truth of value-judgments is not susceptible of proof. ... As regards value-judgments, this requirement [to prove truth] is impossible of fulfilment and it infringes freedom of opinion itself".[224]

In *Dichand & others v Austria,*[225] the Court held that criticism, even in strong

---

[221] See above, n.50, *Paper*, at p.265; n.50, *Report*, at p.37; n.6, McDonald, at p.215; n.58, Robertson and Nicol, at p.123.

[222] Above, n.166.

[223] Above, n.26. See also *Schwabe v Austria*, Series A, No.242-B (1992); *De Haes & Gijsels v Belgium* (1998) 25 E.H.R.R. 1, at para.47; *Prager & Oberschlick v Austria* (1995) 21 E.H.R.R. 1, at para.37, where it has been held that there must be a sufficient factual basis for the expression of the opinion.

[224] *Lingens*, above, n.26, at para.46.

[225] App. No.29271/95, Chamber Judgment of February 26, 2002; *cf. Oberschlick v Austria (No.2)*, above, n.84; *Lopes Gomes Da Silva v Portugal*, above, n.166, following *Prager and Oberschlick v Austria*, above, n.223, p.19, para.38, "journalistic freedom also covers possible recourse to a degree of exaggeration, or even provocation", and *Feldek*, above, n.210 at para.86. In *Dichand*, the Court found a violation of Article 10, even though there was only "a slim factual basis" for one of the value judgments (at para.52). The requirement of supporting facts may vary depending on the context.

and polemical language, of the strategies and overlap of interests of a politician-lawyer were value-judgments, had an adequate factual basis and represented a fair comment on issues of general public interest. The concept of value-judgment as espoused by the European Court is wider than mere comment in that it embraces assessment and analysis of facts as well as opinion.[226]

4.5.3.2 An Opinion Honestly Held

To establish the defence of fair comment it must be shown that the comment was fair in the sense of being an opinion honestly held. The test is not subjective,[227] but rather an objective test as to whether a commentator, however biased or irrational, however exaggerated or extreme the language used, could honestly have held such an opinion given the truth of the facts on which it was based.

Confusion arises, however, because malice is also relevant to the defence of fair comment and the test of malice is subjective, although the question of malice is only relevant if the elements of the defence have been established. This and other distinctions and nuances that have developed in relation to the defence make it very confusing for juries, in particular.

The essence of the defence of fair comment is the factual basis for the comment. The expression of the opinion need not be fair. Intemperate, exaggerated or vehement language may be used, since the defence protects "the honest views of the crank and the eccentric", as much as those of any other, but not when they are based on dishonest statements of fact.[228] As Mill said, ridicule and invective should be tolerated: "They may stimulate partizans, but they are not calculated to make converts".[229]

In theory, the trenchancy or irrational nature of the comment, or the vehemence of the language used, will not destroy the defence. Only a finding of malice will do so. Malice here means some wrongful motive: spite, ill will, personal vendetta or want of good faith. The onus is on the plaintiff alleging it to establish malice. Evidence of a concerted campaign against the plaintiff may be sufficient to establish malice. A failure to retract a statement or apologise for it will not usually be taken as proof of malice, but it depends on the circumstances. As the Supreme Court said in *Barrett v Independent Newspapers*,[230] the conduct of the media from publication right through the trial process can be taken into account. Repetition of the comment, or publication of an inadequate or damaging apology, may be taken as evidence of malice. A particular difficulty arises where the matter complained of has

---

[226] See Nicol, Millar, Sharland, above, n.26, at p.80. See also *UII v Austria*, App. No.28525/95, Chamber Judgment of February 26, 2002.

[227] See above, n.6, McDonald, at p.209; the dangers of a subjective test can be seen in *Herbert v Lando* 441 U.S. 153 (1979).

[228] See above, n.58, 3rd ed., Robertson and Nicol, at p.82. The test is objective: whether a person, however prejudiced or obstinate, could honestly hold the view expressed, however exaggerated, prejudiced, wrong or substantially unfair it may be: *Telnikoff v Matusevitch* [1991] 4 All E.R. 817, affirming the decision of the Court of Appeal.

[229] Above, n.1, John Stuart Mill, at p.15.

[230] Above, n.117.

come unsolicited, for example, in a letter to the editor. What if the author was actuated by malice, unknown to the editor or publisher? The law is not altogether clear, but it seems that the malice of the author will not deprive the publisher of the defence.[231]

While the language used is not fatal to the defence, it should be noted that, unlike other jurisdictions, there is no defence in Irish law for criticism as such, whether in the form of literary criticism, humour, satire, irony or hyperbole.[232] These are merely factors to be considered in deciding whether the words complained of are defamatory or whether any of the defences, such as fair comment, are established. To penalise them would make for very dull copy in an area where readers or audiences expect opinion and, indeed, originality or individuality on the part of the reviewer. Reviewers need latitude to "gild the lily", even if it means that the publisher of the work reviewed ultimately loses sales as a result.[233] As the United States Supreme Court asserted, ideas and opinions should be corrected not by judges and juries but by the competition of other ideas.[234] Likewise, the European Court of Human Rights has held that there must be room for exaggeration, even provocation.[235]

4.5.3.3 Public Interest

The question of the public interest is a matter for the judge to decide. Judges have consistently stated that the public interest is not the same as the interest of the public. Other than that, they have not given any detailed guidance as to what constitutes the public interest, or any great support for media appeals to the public interest. It is therefore a nebulous concept of uncertain scope.[236] In

---

[231] See above, n.50, LRC, *Report*, p.91; n.58, Robertson and Nicol, p.111; *Telnikoff v Matusevitch* [1990] 3 All E.R. 865, [1991] 4 All E.R. 817 (HL); "Fair comment defence – proper and improper motives – a fair balance?" (2001) 6 *Communications Law* 195.

[232] See the cases discussed above in relation to defamatory effect that involved humour, satire, poking fun. In *Mangan v Independent Newspapers* (*The Irish Times*, February 20, 28, 2002) a District Court judge, described in a "semi-mocking", "light-hearted", "sardonic" article about the reactions of various judges to mobile phones (one judge had jailed a journalist whose mobile phone went off in court) as a "mobile phone freak" was awarded €25,000 by a High Court jury. The defence of fair comment had been advanced but was withdrawn from the jury who did not therefore have the opportunity to consider it. Because the award was lower than the High Court threshold, he was awarded €100,000 in costs calculated at Circuit Court level. An appeal by Independent Newspapers was unsuccessful (Irish Times Law Report, March 3, 2003).

[233] This point was made by book publishers themselves in the CLÉ (Irish Book Publishers Association) submission on the law of defamation to the LRC in 1991.

[234] Holmes J. in *Abrams v US* 250 U.S. 616 (1919).

[235] For example, *Oberschlick*, above n.26, n.84; *De Haes et Gijsels v Belgium*, above, n.223, at para.46; *Nilsen and Johnsen v Norway* (1999) 30 E.H.R.R. 878, *Dalban v Romania* (2001) 31 E.H.R.R. 39, at para. 49 and *Lopes Gomes Da Silva v Portugal* (2000), above, n.166. Some commentators base their claim for protection of humour, satire and parody on the freedom of artistic expression, which is included in ECHR, Art.10, in ICCPR, and in the German Constitution. As forms of artistic expression, they have recognition in the laws of copyright.

[236] *Gatley on Libel and Slander*, 8th ed., paras 732–46 lists topics of public interest, which are quoted in LRC *Paper*, above, n.28, at pp.71–2; David Parsons, "The meaning of 'public interest'" (2001) 6 *Communications Law* 191, reviews its history and definition.

the context of the fair comment defence, however, comment on a wide range of public as opposed to private matters is envisaged, from arts and restaurant reviews to comments on national and local issues.

In *Thorgeirson v Iceland*,[237] the European Court of Human Rights held that media reporting and comment on matters of public interest are entitled to the same degree of protection as political discussion. The case concerned two articles on police brutality for which the journalist had been fined in the Icelandic courts. Individual police officers were not named in the articles, but there were references to "brutes in uniform" and allegations of serious assault. The issue was a matter of public concern, the Court of Human Rights held, and the articles had the legitimate purpose of promoting reform of the system for investigating complaints against the police. The articles were based on public opinion following the recent conviction of a police officer for brutality. In those circumstances, although the articles relied heavily on rumours, stories and the statements of others, they related to an important matter of public interest and the journalist should not be required to prove the factual basis for those statements. It would seem, therefore, that where media comment is based on public opinion on an important matter of public interest it will be given wide protection in the same way as political criticism and comment.[238]

A number of Irish cases might well have come under the *Thorgeirson* rubric. An *Irish Times* diary piece, for example, commenting on the prosecution of a brothel keeper, criticised the witnesses who had given evidence against her, referring to them as "ticks" and suggesting that giving evidence against her was "ten times more odious than using her house".[239] A garda who had given evidence in the case claimed that he had been defamed, but the opening sentence of the diary column had intimated that the gardaí were only doing their job. The Circuit Court judge found that there was no defamation involved. It would appear also from the circumstances of the case that a defence of fair comment could have succeeded.[240]

4.5.3.4 Malice

The question of malice in relation to the defence of fair comment has always been vexed, both in theory and in practice.[241] As outlined above under the

---

In German law, opinions except malicious insults are free, whether reasonable or not, unless abusive. If fact and opinion are mixed, the test is whether it refers to concrete events which can be proven/disproven or contains primarily opinion; generally the courts prefer to treat remarks as opinion, and a high level of protection is given to matters of public interest. See above, n.97, Thwaite and Brehm, at p.344.

[237] Above, n.168.

[238] *ibid.* at para.64. See also *Thoma v Luxembourg*, above, n.58.

[239] *Fields v The Irish Times* (*The Irish Times*, January 26, 1995).

[240] The newspaper report of the case does not disclose whether the defence of fair comment was pleaded.

[241] See above, n.6, McDonald; n.50, LRC, *Report*; n.58, Robertson and Nicol, pp.109–112. The question has recently been addressed by Lord Nicholls on behalf of the court in a Hong Kong case, *Albert Cheng v Tse Wai Chun Paul*. The judgment, however, is problematic. Apart from saying that malice does not bear the same meaning in all respects for the defences of fair comment and qualified privilege (and therefore the textbooks

other requirements for the defence, it requires a showing that the defendant did not have an honest belief in what was published. Normally, the lack of an apology or retraction will not be sufficient to establish malice.

4.5.4 Privilege

There are two forms of privilege applicable to defamation: absolute privilege and qualified privilege. The former stems from the Constitution and from statute, while the second has its roots in the common law and statute.

4.5.4.1 Absolute Privilege

The Constitution speaks only of privilege, the adjective "absolute" is not used, but the privilege is nonetheless regarded as absolute, *i.e.* it is not destroyed by malice. Under Article 13.8.1 of the Constitution, the President of Ireland has absolute privilege in respect of the exercise and performance of the powers and functions of his/her office. Article 15.12 of the Constitution accords privilege to all official reports and publications of the Oireachtas or of either House thereof and to utterances made in either House wherever published: "All official reports and publications of the Oireachtas or of either House thereof and utterances made in either House wherever published shall be privileged".

The Irish language version "táid saor ar chúrsaí dlí cibé áit a bhfoilsítear" makes clear the absolute nature of the privilege. The privilege has been extended to committees of the Oireachtas by section 2 of the Committees of the Houses of the Oireachtas (Privilege and Procedure) Act 1976. Doubts[242] as to whether it extended to witnesses appearing before committees of the Oireachtas, and indeed Commissions and Tribunals of Inquiry established by the Oireachtas, were put to rest by legislation.[243]

---

are wrong), Lord Nicholls also said that knowledge or reckless indifference to the truth (the *New York Times v Sullivan* test) would constitute malice such as to defeat the defence of fair comment, and that the presence of an ulterior motive will not amount to malice: "Honesty of belief is the touchstone. Actuation by spite, animosity, intent to injure, intent to arouse controversy or other motivation, whatever it may be, even if it is the dominant or sole motive, does not of *itself* defeat the defence. However, proof of such motivation may be evidence, sometimes compelling evidence, from which lack of genuine belief in the view expressed may be inferred." (Court of Final Appeal of the Hong Kong Special Administrative Region, November 13, 2000). Van Vechten Veeder (above, n.5, pp.35–6) says that malice can be traced back to the ecclesiastical courts. It was part of *injuria* of Roman law; the matter was looked at from a moral, not a legal, point of view.

[242] See above, n.50, *Paper*, at p.76, para.97; *Report*, at para.14.10 (4).

[243] Select Committee on Legislation and Security of Dáil Éireann (Privilege and Immunity) Act 1994; the Committees of the Houses of the Oireachtas (Compellability, Privileges and Immunities of Witnesses) Act 1997. The latter at s.11(1) states that a person giving evidence to a committee or providing a document "shall be entitled to the same privileges and immunities as if the person were a witness before the High Court." S.11(2) then states that "If a person who is giving evidence to a committee in relation to a particular matter is directed to cease giving such evidence, the person shall be entitled only to qualified privilege in relation to defamation in respect of any such evidence as aforesaid

By virtue of section 18(1) of the Defamation Act 1961, absolute privilege attaches to fair and accurate reports of court proceedings published contemporaneously:

> "A fair and accurate report published in any newspaper or broadcast by means of wireless telegraphy as part of any programme or service provided by means of a broadcasting station within the State or in Northern Ireland of proceedings publicly heard before any court established by law and exercising judicial authority within the State or Northern Ireland shall, if published or broadcast contemporaneously with such proceedings, be privileged".

The requirement of contemporaneity means that only reports published during the hearing or immediately after the hearing are privileged. That means that rebroadcasts or republication at a later date may not have the benefit of the privilege. Moreover, the privilege is confined to the more immediate news media; it attaches only to newspaper and broadcast reports, not to film, video or book publishing.[244] The reason for confining the privilege to contemporaneous reports is that matter given in evidence in court, whether by way of charge or countercharge, may subsequently be refuted or proven groundless. If such charges can later be repeated at will under the protection of privilege, the person concerned may suffer undue harm. Nonetheless, it may be argued that the requirement of contemporaneity is not necessary, as the need to ensure that a report is fair and accurate will of itself provide adequate protection for the parties. It follows that for a court report to be considered fair and accurate if published some weeks, months or years later, both sides of the evidence would have to be given with the outcome of the case, if completed. Besides, only reports of cases are covered by privilege; comments on cases are not covered, although it may be possible to rely on the defence of fair comment instead.

It also appears to be something of an anachronism to exclude "any blasphemous or obscene matter" from the privilege, if that is the intended effect of section 18(2): "Nothing in subsection (1) of this section shall authorise the publication of any blasphemous or obscene matter".[245]

While tabloid journalism, with its emphasis on the unseemly and the

---

given after the giving of the direction unless and until the committee withdraws the direction." The Ethics in Public Office Act 1995, s.32(11) states that documents, reports of the Commission, wherever published, and statements at meetings or sittings of the Commission by its members or officials wherever published shall be absolutely privileged. The Tribunals of Inquiry (Evidence) (Amendment) Act 1997, s.2, amends s.1 of the principal Act by inserting after subsection 3: "A person who produces or sends a document to any such tribunal pursuant to an order of that tribunal shall be entitled to the same immunities and privileges as if he or she were a witness before the High Court."

[244] The other media therefore have to fall back on common-law qualified privilege; see above, n.50, *Paper*, at pp.250–253.

[245] "Seditious" matter, which is usually included with blasphemous and obscene matter, in Art.40.6.1 of the Constitution, for example, is not mentioned in s.18.2; *cf.* Libel Amendment Act 1888, s.3.

sensational, is not to be encouraged, it is at least arguable that to deliberately exclude any blasphemous or obscene matter from a court report could render the report unfair or inaccurate and cause it to lose the privilege altogether. How could cases such as *Corway v Independent Newspapers*[246] (alleged blasphemy in a cartoon) or *DPP v Fleming*[247] (a criminal libel case about obscene remarks written on telephone boxes) ever be reported, if the inclusion of the allegedly blasphemous or obscene remarks would not attract privilege and would leave the reporter open to charges? The privilege for reporting court cases here or in Northern Ireland (Defamation Act 1961, section 18) is regarded as absolute privilege and will not be defeated by a showing of malice. Reports of cases heard in foreign courts, however, are governed by qualified privilege only (Defamation Act 1961, section 24 and Schedule), as discussed in section 4.5.4.3.

4.5.4.2 Qualified Privilege at Common Law

Common law qualified privilege arises on occasions when:

(a) the speaker has a duty, whether legal, moral or social[248] to publish the information complained of, and

(b) the person to whom the information is addressed has a reciprocal duty or interest in receiving it.

The privilege rests on this notion of duty or common interest. The purpose behind the privilege is to allow business and commerce and the activities of daily life to operate without the constant threat of libel actions. The privilege is conferred where communication takes place for honest purposes, and is therefore destroyed by malice or any wrongful motive. It does not matter if the allegations made on a privileged occasion turn out to be unfounded as long as they are made honestly and without malice.

The privilege can be lost if there is excess of publication, if the statement contains irrelevant allegations, for example, or if it is addressed to someone who has no interest in receiving it. An example would be a complaint made to the wrong body, as in *Hynes-O'Sullivan v O'Driscoll*.[249] There a solicitor, unhappy with the behaviour and fees charged by a doctor for attendance in court, complained to the wrong medical body.[250] To attract the privilege, the communication must be confined to the particular matter in which the parties have a legitimate common interest, *i.e.* it must not be excessive in terms of either content or circulation. In *Doyle v The Economist*,[251] the court held that

---

[246] [1999] 4 I.R. 484. See Chap.9 below.

[247] *The Irish Times*, November 23, 1989. *Cf.* restrictions on court reporting in Censorship of Publications Act 1929. See also the discussion in Chap. 8.

[248] See *Willis v Irish Press*, above, n.82.

[249] [1988] I.R. 436, [1989] I.L.R.M. 349.

[250] See discussion of *Adam v Ward* in Robertson and Nicol, above, n.58 at p.135, stating that the "right of reply" privilege is one of general application.

[251] Above, n.56. See also *Lindsay v Maher*, *The Irish Times*, February 4, 1984 (the defendant was an elected representative of the farming community and therefore had a duty to

there was no such interest involved in the publication of the opinion of unnamed barristers that the plaintiff judge had been appointed to the bench for reasons other than merit.

Where the only effective mode of discharging the duty or protecting the interest which gives rise to the privilege is to insert a notice or advertisement in a newspaper, one might expect that such notice or advertisement would attract the privilege so as to protect the advertiser and the paper. In *O'Connor v The Kerryman*,[252] solicitors representing fishermen, who had allegedly been attacked in a sermon at Mass, issued an open letter on their behalf. Was there excess of publication in that case? If Mass can be regarded as an open forum, it is arguable that the open letter was privileged also, provided its content did not go beyond what was necessary to defend the clients. On that argument, the media that carried the letter would then have privilege too, at least if it had been published verbatim without comment. Where the matter is of general public interest and it is the duty of the defendants to publish it, privilege will apply.

It has long been established that the defence of qualified privilege with its insistence on duty or common interest is wide enough to encompass self-protection. If the initial attack was made in a newspaper or broadcast, use of the same medium to counteract the attack entitles both the respondent and the newspaper or broadcast which carries the response to privilege.[253] In *Nevin v Roddy and Carty*,[254] the Supreme Court said: "[A] man who appeals to the public through the medium of the press cannot complain if those whom he has attacked reply to him through the same public medium".

The court went on to state that "where a party publishes in a public newspaper statements reflecting upon the conduct or character of another, the aggrieved party is entitled to have recourse to the public press for his defence and vindication".[255]

---

defend farmers. When they were attacked in open court, he also had a right to use an "open" forum and was entitled to choose a newspaper interview).

[252] Above, n.48. The case was settled out of court. The argument advanced here is therefore a general one and not intended to reflect on the merits of the particular case.

[253] Above, n.82, *Willis v Irish Press*. McMahon and Binchy, above, n.34, at p.934, say that publication to the world at large may be justified where the defendant is merely responding to an accusation through the same medium in which the initial attack was made.

[254] [1935] I.R. 397 at 410. Fitzgibbon J. in the Supreme Court in *Nevin* took the view that if "the writer of the letter [answering the original allegations published in the paper] had lawful justification and excuse for writing and publishing it, it is difficult to see any ground for holding that the innocent proprietor of the newspaper to which it was sent for publication is liable for damages" (at 422). "But if a man is protected in law in making an appeal to the public through the columns of the public press I can see no ground for holding that the printer and publisher of the paper in which his appeal appears … is liable in damages for the publication, at least until it is proved to the satisfaction of a jury that the publisher or printer, as the case may be, was himself actuated by express malice" (at 423).

[255] *ibid.* at 414, quoting *O'Donoghue v Hussey* I.R. 5 C.L. 124. It may be noted that in *Lindsay v Maher* (above, n.251) and *O'Connor v The Kerryman* (above, n.48), the plaintiffs did not publish their original criticisms in a newspaper, therefore those cases can be distinguished from *O'Donoghue v Hussey*.

In *O'Brien v The Freeman's Journal Ltd*,[256] it was held that, to establish legitimate self-defence, it must be shown that the alleged libels were published to refute attacks and charges publicly made and that there was an intimate connection between them. The key is vindication: the defendants, said the court, are entitled to vindicate themselves against false aspersions on them by the plaintiff: "Their privilege was to defend themselves against an attack made upon them by the plaintiff, not to make an independent attack upon the plaintiff unconnected with and irrelevant to the attack made by the plaintiff upon them".[257]

Sufficient facts must therefore be shown in the plea to establish the necessary connection and relevance and to show that the charges being refuted were defamatory or false, as there would be no privilege if they were true.[258] The privilege is to defend a character already aspersed, not to assume the initiative in attack.[259] It therefore enables defendants to meet the charges brought against them, not to bring further accusations.[260] It is a "right of reply privilege"[261] and, insofar as it enables a reputation to be vindicated, is in keeping with the constitutional guarantees expressed in Article 40.3. It is for the judge to decide whether the occasion is privileged. It is for the jury, if necessary, to decide any questions of fact that may be in dispute. Once an occasion is shown to be privileged, it is for the plaintiff to prove malice in order to destroy the privilege. Proof of lack of belief that the matter is true may be regarded as malice, unless the speaker was under a duty to pass on the information and did not endorse it.[262]

To date, however, the courts have been reluctant to acknowledge the availability of the common-law qualified privilege defence to the media. They have been unwilling to recognise a general media duty to inform or a general public right to be informed. It might be easier to establish such a duty and right in a specialised newspaper, periodical or broadcast, or on a local level where circulation is limited. It is very difficult for a national newspaper or broadcaster to establish the privilege. In their case, it might be necessary to establish, in addition to a duty and right to be informed, that the media publication was the only option available. Beyond that, the best that can be said is that the courts have been reluctant to recognise a media qualified privilege but that the application of the duty/interest formula should be argued for, depending on the particular circumstances of the case.

A turning-point may have been reached in *Reynolds v Times Newspapers*,[263] a case taken in the London courts by Albert Reynolds, a former

---

[256] (1907) 41 I.L.T.R. 35.

[257] *ibid.*, Andrews J. at 37.

[258] *ibid.* at 38.

[259] *Magrath v Finn* (1877) I.R. 11 C.L. 152. "The privilege is in fact a shield of defence, not a weapon of attack", *per* May J. in *O'Donoghue v Hussey*, (above, n.255) cited in *Nevin* (above, n.254), at 418.

[260] *O'Brien*, above, n.256, at 38, Wright J.

[261] See above, n.250, Robertson and Nicol.

[262] See above, n.50, *Paper*, at p.101.

[263] [1999] 3 W.L.R. 1010 (HL); [1999] 4 All E.R. 609, and above n.51. Mr Reynolds was referred to as a "gombeen man" and accused of telling lies in the Dáil.

Taoiseach (Irish prime minister) against the *Sunday Times*. There, the House of Lords declined to introduce a generic qualified privilege that would have protected political reporting. It did so on the grounds, *inter alia*, that it would leave politicians too vulnerable to unsourced and unfair attacks, and that political reporting did not merit separate protection. Instead, the Law Lords decided to develop the common-law qualified privilege. They did so to the extent that they recognised that the two-part duty and reciprocal interest criteria of the common law could apply as between the media and the public at large. It could do so in situations where the media are reporting on matters of serious public concern, provided they report in a responsible way.[264] In a sense, the decision brings libel law more into harmony with traditional tort law by focusing on the defendant's conduct. It introduces an element of negligence (reasonable care), rather than strict liability, but it sets the hurdle so high as to make it likely to be difficult to avail of in practice, or at least to engender caution on the part of journalists and publishers.[265]

One could argue in relation to the approach of the House of Lords in *Reynolds* that it is not the role of defamation law to set and apply standards of responsible journalism but only to weigh up factors that would destroy privilege. As Barendt[266] says, libel law imposes a degree of discipline on the media; it civilizes the standards of public discourse – but those are more appropriate to criminal law and should not be objectives of defamation law. In New Zealand, the court in *Lange v Atkinson (No. 2)*[267] said the steps taken in preparing the

---

[264] *ibid.* at 1027B. The court provided ten indicators to determine responsibility in reporting.

[265] There have been decisions both for and against the media in the UK since the *Reynolds* decision, *e.g. Saad Al-Fagih v HH Saudi Research and Marketing UK Ltd* [2002] E.M.L.R. 215, *Gaddafi v Telegraph Group Ltd* [2000] E.M.L.R. 431 (upheld right of journalists to protect their sources while still maintaining a qualified privilege defence), *Grobbelaar v MGN Ltd.* [2001] 2 All E.R. 437; HL, October 24, 2002 and *Loutchansky v Times Newspapers Ltd* [2001] 3 W.L.R. 404, a case involving allegations of money laundering and associations with the Russian mafia, where the court elaborated on the *Reynolds* dicta but held against the newspaper. However, another Court of Appeal in *Loutchansky v Times Newspapers Ltd (No.2)* [2002] 1 All E.R. 652 extended the application of the *Reynolds* privilege to neutral reportage and mitigated the "repetition of a libel" rule: see discussion of the rule above, and Robertson and Nicol, above n.58, at pp.xxv-xxvi. The NZ court in *Lange v Atkinson* [2000] 3 N.Z.L.R. 385 at 399 decided to stand over its approach in *Lange v Atkinson and Australian Consolidated Press NZ Ltd.* [1998] 3 N.Z.L.R. 424, opining that *Reynolds* would only add to the uncertainty and chilling effect of the existing law, and that it blurred the distinction between the *occasion* of privilege and its *misuse*. The New Zealand Law Commission had criticised *Lange*: NZLC Preliminary Paper 33, *Defaming Politicians: A Response to Lange v Atkinson* (NZLC, Wellington, 1998) and Report 64, 2000; also the Privy Council in *Bonnick v Morris* [2002] 3 W.L.R. 820 (standard to be applied in a practical and flexible manner (at paras 24–8)).

[266] Above, n.3, at 112; *cf.* n.150, Bezanson. See also Ian Loveland, "A New Legal Landscape? Libel Law and Freedom of Political Expression in the UK" (2000) E.H.R.L.R. 476, at p.489, regarding the right result but the wrong test. In *Miami Herald Publishing Co. v Tornillo* 418 U.S. 241 (1974) at 256, the US Supreme Court stated that a "responsible press is an undoubtedly desirable goal, but press responsibility is not mandated by the Constitution and like many other virtues it cannot be legislated."

[267] [2000] 3 N.Z.L.R. 385; also *Lange v Atkinson (No.1)* [1998] 3 N.Z.L.R. 424. The reasonableness test was favoured in *Lange* and in *Theophanous*: see *Lange v Australian*

story and such like were not relevant to the existence of the privilege, although they might be to its abuse.[268]

The House of Lords in *Reynolds*, nonetheless, goes some way to adopting the approach of the European Court of Human Rights, in that it recognises the importance of the freedom of expression of the media and the public's right to know:

> "The press discharges vital functions as a bloodhound as well as a watchdog. The court should be slow to conclude that a publication was not in the public interest and, therefore, that the public had not a right to know, especially when the information is in the field of political discussion. Any lingering doubts should be resolved in favour of publication".[269]

The European court has consistently endorsed the media role and supported responsible or "good faith" journalism, but it has expressly stated that it will not second-guess journalists,[270] and has refrained from laying down rules for responsible journalism. It has said that the methods of objective and balanced reporting may vary considerably, depending, among other things, on the media in question. However, in determining whether a restriction on a journalist was necessary and proportionate, it will look at all the facts of the case, including the publication in question and the circumstances in which it was written.[271] Thus, it may look at the potential impact of the medium concerned, the manner in which the programme was prepared, its contents, the context in which it was broadcast and the purpose of the programme.[272]

One can contrast with the common law approach decisions of the European Court of Human Rights, where even the failure of the journalist to seek the views of those about whom the allegations were being made did not outweigh their right to freedom of expression,[273] and where an allegation of fact was found to have no basis in truth, but the Court acknowledged in other value

---

Broadcasting Corporation (1997) 145 A.L.R. 96; and the earlier cases of *Theophanous v Herald and Weekly Times Ltd.* (1994) 68 A.L.J.R. 713; *Stephens v West Australian Newspapers Ltd.* (1994) 68 A.L.J.R. 765.

[268] *Cf.* Lord Lester's fallback position in *Reynolds* that the House of Lords also rejected, *i.e.* that political information should be protected unless the plaintiff could show want of care on the defendant's part. The question of privilege is a matter for the judge; the question of abuse of privilege is a matter for the jury. Paul Mitchell, "Malice in Qualified Privilege" [1999] P.L. 328, suggests that in light of *Reynolds* it is perhaps more appropriate now for the courts to switch the emphasis from the historical focus on the defendant's motive to the public interest in receiving the information.

[269] *Reynolds*, at 1027H.

[270] *Jersild v Denmark*, Series A, No.298; (1995) 19 E.H.R.R. 1, at para.31. In *Lopes Gomes Da Silva v Portugal*, above, n.166, the court said (at para. 30iii) that its task was to monitor, under Art.10 "and in the light of the whole case" the decisions delivered by the national courts by virtue of their power of appreciation. In that case, it also gave weight to the fact that the journalist had "acted in accordance with the rules governing the journalistic profession" (at para.35).

[271] *Lopes Gomes Da Silva v Portugal*, above, n.166, at para.32.

[272] *Jersild*, above, n.270, at para.31

[273] *Tromso v Norway* (1999) 29 E.H.R.R. 125, at paras 63–66.

judgments the right "to hit back in the same way".[274] In *Bergens Tidende v Norway*[275] also, the Court held that the complaints of dissatisfied patients, although expressed in graphic and strong terms, were essentially correct and accurately recorded by the newspaper. Reading the articles as a whole, the Court did not find that the statements were excessive or misleading, and held unanimously that the damages award against the newspaper in the Norwegian courts constituted a breach of the newspaper's right to freedom of expression. In an important statement, the Court said:

> "By reason of the "duties and responsibilities" inherent in the exercise of freedom of expression, the safeguard afforded by Article 10 to journalists in relation to reporting on issues of general interest is subject to the proviso that they are acting in good faith in order to provide accurate and reliable information in accordance with the ethics of journalism". (para. 53)

The Court thus recognises a zone of activity within which journalists are the decision-makers in accordance with the ethics of journalism and where the standard required is that they act in good faith in pursuit of the aims of providing accurate and reliable information for the public. It may be argued that the House of Lords in *Reynolds* starts from the premise that the defence is only available if key factors are met, whereas the European Court starts from the premise that freedom of expression requires the defence unless in the totality of the situation certain key factors exist or are missing such as to cause the loss of the defence.

Whatever its shortcomings,[276] *Reynolds* will have a value in Ireland as persuasive precedent, particularly when the effects of incorporation of the European Convention on Human Rights begin to be addressed in Ireland.[277] The real value of *Reynolds*, one could argue, was that it signalled the likely effects of incorporating the Convention in the UK under the Human Rights Act 1998. "The starting-point is now the right to freedom of expression", Lord

---

[274] *Thorgeirson v Iceland* (above, n.168 – article on police brutality); *Nilsen & Johnsen v Norway* (1999) 30 E.H.R.R. 878 – response to "brutal criticism of the police" (at para.52).

[275] [2001] 31 E.H.R.R. 16.

[276] See Marie McGonagle, "Lords' Verdict in Reynolds Case Leaves Political Writing in Limbo" (*The Irish Times*, November 1, 1999), Sallie Spilsbury, "Bloodhounds and Watchdogs – Qualified Privilege, Malice and the Publication of Material in the Public Interest" [2000] ENT. L.R. 43 (indicating problems regarding malice, burden of proof, etc.), Kevin Williams, "Defaming Politicians: The Not So Common Law" (2000) 63 M.L.R. 748 (pointing out that the House of Lords approach is concerned with the nature of the message, and the conduct of the messenger (at p.754); that there is little indication of what weight is to be attached to individual factors; that there is no explanatory comment on the requirement to verify information, no definition of matter of public concern (at p.754); it has moved British libel law in the direction of fault-based liability (at p.755); checking processes etc. will be under scrutiny (at p.755)), and Jonathan Coad, "The Irrelevance of Truth and Falsity in the New Law of Defamation" [2002] ENT. L.R. 95.

[277] Ó Caoimh J. in *Hunter* (above, n.178) accepted the relevance of *Reynolds* (High Court, July 31, 2003). It has also been accepted as "authoritative guidance" in Scotland (*Adams v Guardian Newspapers*, Court of Session, May 7, 2003).

Steyn said (at 1030), while Lord Nicholls (at 1027) said: "Above all, the court should have particular regard to the importance of freedom of expression". Also important in that regard is the Law Lords' reliance on the jurisprudence of the European Court of Human Rights,[278] and their elaboration of the language of the European court regarding the role of the press "as a bloodhound as well as a watchdog" (at 1027). Furthermore, they accepted that any lingering doubts should be resolved in favour of publication (at 1027). At the end of the day though, despite the rhetoric and expansion of the defence of qualified privilege, it did not avail the *Sunday Times* in the circumstances of the case against Albert Reynolds, which was eventually settled.

Meanwhile in Ireland, the issue of public interest qualified privilege, *i.e.* a duty on the part of the defendant to impart the information in question, formed part of the original defence in *McDonald v RTÉ*.[279] The case concerned a radio broadcast of April 1992, which the plaintiff, although not named, alleged connected him with the murder of a farmer in Co. Louth. The case came before the Supreme Court in 2001 on the issue of whether certain documents were privileged from disclosure. At the time of writing, the case has not been fully disposed of, and so the opportunity exists for an Irish court to address the issues of public interest and the right of the public to know in the light of *Reynolds* and the European Convention on Human Rights.

4.5.4.3 Statutory Qualified Privilege

There is also a specific media qualified privilege provided by statute. It is contained in section 24 of the Defamation Act 1961 and elaborated in the second schedule to the Act. Unlike the privilege for court reporting contained in section 18 of the Act, the section 24 privilege is a qualified privilege only and will be lost if there is a showing of malice.

It is a privilege that attaches first to fair and accurate reports of the proceedings in public of foreign legislatures, international organisations of which Ireland is a member or at which Ireland is represented, the International Court of Justice, foreign courts, extracts from public registers, notices, and such like.[280]

Second, provision is made for a privilege that is "subject to explanation or contradiction". In this case, the privilege is lost if the publisher is requested by the plaintiff to publish a reasonable statement by way of explanation or contradiction and refuses or neglects to do so or does so in a manner not adequate or not reasonable having regard to all the circumstances (section 24(2)). This type of privilege extends to fair and accurate reports of the findings or decision of certain stated types of bodies and associations in the State or Northern Ireland; the proceedings at public meetings *bona fide* and lawfully

---

[278] For example, *De Haes & Gijsels v Belgium*, above, n.223; *Goodwin v UK* (1996) 22 E.H.R.R. 123 (paper's unwillingness to reveal sources not to count against it). See generally, Barendt, "The Human Rights Act 1998 and Libel Law: Brave New World" (2001) 6 Media and Arts L. Rev. 1.

[279] [2001] 1 I.R. 355; [2001] 2 I.L.R.M. 1.

[280] For more detail see Defamation Act 1961, Part 1, Second Schedule.

held on matters of public concern, whether admission is general or restricted; meetings of local authorities, statutory commissions and tribunals; reports or summaries of official notices issued for the information of the public by government, local authority or garda, and their counterparts in Northern Ireland.[281] In all cases, the privilege protects only matter that:

(a) is not prohibited by law

(b) is of public concern, and

(c) the publication of which is for the public benefit (section 24(3)).

The case of *Ahern v Cork Evening Echo*[282] is a good example of this kind of privilege and of the limited circumstances in which the law accepts a media duty to inform the public. The case concerned the publication of a warning issued by gardaí about the activities of bogus charity collectors. The plaintiff, a *bona fide* charity collector, claimed that the reference would be taken to be to him. The newspaper published a clarification. In court it was accepted that the newspaper had qualified privilege. It had acted on information received in good faith and had taken the necessary steps to safeguard the plaintiff's reputation. There was no liability.

The privilege, while useful to the media, is limited in a number of ways. It applies, rather incongruously, to newspapers and broadcasting only, thus creating a difficulty for book publishers and other media defendants who are not included. It does not extend to coverage of press conferences, which are a major forum nowadays for making information available to the public. In the UK, the House of Lords has held that press conferences come within the rubric of "public meetings" in the relevant statute. In a Northern Ireland case, *Turkington and others v Times Newspapers Ltd*,[283] a press conference had been organised following the unsuccessful appeal of Private Lee Clegg, who had been convicted on criminal charges relating to the shooting dead of two young joyriders in Belfast. During the course of the press conference, criticism was levelled at the solicitors who had represented Lee Clegg. The solicitors sued for libel. The defence successfully raised the argument that a press conference was a public meeting and should be covered by the statutory provisions that accorded privilege to fair and accurate reports of public meetings. The Lords held unanimously that:

> "A meeting is public if those who organise it ... by issuing a general invitation to the press, manifest an intention or desire that the proceedings of the meeting should be communicated to a wider public. Press representatives may be regarded ... as the eyes and ears of the public to whom they report" (at 923).

---

[281] For more detail see Defamation Act 1961, Part 2, Second Schedule.

[282] *The Irish Times*, March 2, 1989.

[283] [2000] 3 W.L.R. 1670; [2000] 4 All E.R. 913; [2000] N.I. 410. For reports of various stages of this and related cases taken by the plaintiffs, see *The Irish Times*, May 15, 21, 1996, September 12, 1996, October 15, 1996, October 24, 1998, November 14, 1998. See also Kevin Williams, above, n.276.

The House of Lords also held that the contents of the press release issued at the press conference "were as much part of the proceedings of the press conference as if they had been read aloud during the meeting" (at 924). The test is whether, assuming the meeting to have been public, the contents of the written press release formed part of the materials communicated at the meeting to those attending.[284] The media in the UK, therefore, have qualified privilege for fair and accurate reports of press conferences and press releases that form part of the materials of a press conference. The Irish Law Reform Commission in 1991 recommended widening the categories of privileged statements but favoured including only a limited range of press conferences, whereas the Newspaper Commission in 1996 recommended including press conferences without stipulating any limitations.[285]

In the US, a newsworthiness or neutral report privilege attaches to reports which satisfy the following criteria: responsible and prominent speaker, public-figure plaintiff, fair and dispassionate coverage, matter of public concern.[286] The neutral report privilege is seen as a way of balancing the need for the public to receive information with the need to minimise regulational harm. By reducing the media's fear of liability, provided the report is fair and dispassionate, it encourages them to provide more information to the public. Many states also recognise a wire service privilege, which allows the media to republish without fear of liability for defamation any news stories originally reported by a reliable news service, as long as the republisher had no knowledge of the story's falsity.[287]

4.6 REMEDIES

4.6.1 Damages

The principal remedy for defamation is damages. Damages are a sum of money intended to compensate the plaintiff. Compensation can be claimed for damage to reputation, and special damages for pecuniary or material loss that is quantifiable can also be claimed. In certain circumstances aggravated or punitive damages may be awarded.[288] Compensation is a notional remedy, as Denham J. pointed out in *de Rossa* v *Independent Newspapers*: "The defamed does not cease to have been defamed after an award of damages. An order of damages

---

[284] *ibid.*, Lord Bingham, at 924.

[285] Above, n.50, *Paper*, at pp.242–5; *Report*, at pp.28–35; *Report of the Commission on the Newspaper Industry* (Pn 2841, The Stationery Office, Dublin, 1996), para. 7.53. See also New Zealand Defamation Act 1992, which expressly includes press conferences in the privilege.

[286] See generally, Committee on Communications and Media Law, "The Neutral Report Privilege" (1999) *Communications and the Law* 1.

[287] *e.g. Zetes v Richman* 447 N.Y.S. 2d 778 (N.Y. App. Div. 1982). That issue arose in Ireland in *Boyle v The Irish Times* (above, n.57), where a journalist quoted the remarks of a French rugby star, carried by the AFP newsagency.

[288] See above nn.191, 193. See also *Kennedy and Arnold v Ireland* [1987] I.R. 587; [1988] I.L.R.M. 472 (damages were awarded in addition to a declaration that the plaintiffs' consititutional rights to privacy had been infringed).

is an artificial form by which a court gives a remedy to an injured person".[289]

One of the difficulties with damages is that jury awards tend to be unpredictable. Juries are given no guidance on how to assess damages. The Supreme Court in *Barrett v Independent Newspapers*[290] said that they should be given guidelines. The plaintiff was entitled to be compensated for the damage to his reputation and also for the hurt, anxiety and distress, the Chief Justice said.[291] The judges offered specific guidelines as to how a jury might arrive at a suitable figure: in the context of *Barrett*, by taking into account that the plaintiff was a full-time politician[292] and the effect on him in the particular circumstances of the case, and by fitting the allegation into its appropriate place on the scale of defamatory remarks to which the plaintiff as a politician might have been subjected.[293] Damages should be compensatory and should therefore be reasonable, fair and bear a due correspondence with the injury suffered.[294] The Court also said that juries should take into account such matters as the plaintiff's position and standing in the community, the nature of the libel, the absence or refusal of any retraction or apology, any social disadvantages that may result or be thought likely to result from the wrong done to the plaintiff, the injury to his feelings, *i.e.* the natural distress he may have felt at having been spoken or written of in defamatory terms, the whole conduct of the defendants from the time of publication down to the moment of their verdict and the conduct and attitude of the plaintiff himself.[295]

---

[289] [1999] 4 I.R. 432, at 478. Even in the US, where few cases reach trial and damages when awarded are usually overturned on appeal, celebrities and high-profile people continue to take defamation cases seemingly as a way of airing their grievance and claiming a moral victory: see R.A. Smolla, *Suing the Press* (Oxford University Press, New York, Oxford, 1986). Often their concern is more with their public image (created, promoted or facilitated by the media in the cult of the personality and the "star") than their reputation as such.

[290] Above, n.117 at 23. In *Sutcliffe v Pressdram* [1991] 1 Q.B. 153, Lord Donaldson at 178, said that the question of guidelines for juries is a matter of practice, not substantive law.

[291] *ibid.* at 19.

[292] *ibid.* at 20, Finlay C.J.

[293] *ibid.* at 23–4, Henchy J.

[294] *ibid.* at 24, Henchy J. Damages are intended as a "once and for all" award. It is not possible to go back to court to revisit the award. Thus, if a media organisation pays out an award of damages and it subsequently emerges that the publication was true, it cannot oblige the plaintiff to return the damages, except by suing for fraudulent misrepresentation, deceit or such like. Following the interim report of the Flood Tribunal, the *Sunday Independent* said it was withdrawing its apology to Mr Joseph Murphy Jnr and would sue for the return of the £70,000 paid to him in July 2001 in settlement of a libel action. The company was also to apply to the High Court to have two other claims by the plaintiff struck out as "an abuse of process": *The Sunday Independent*, September 29, 2002, *The Irish Times*, September 30, 2002. In the UK, Jeffrey Archer, who was found to have committed perjury during his successful libel action in 1987, had to return the £500,000 damages, plus costs and interest (*The Times* (London), October 3, 2002).

[295] *ibid.* at 30, Griffin J. The English Law Commission suggested that aggravated damages should be renamed "damages for mental distress": *Aggravated, Exemplary and Restitutionary Damages* (Law Commission Report No.247, 1997), 183, Rec. 2, Draft Bill, clause 13.

The issue of damages arose again before the Supreme Court in *McDonagh v News Group Newspapers Ltd*[296] and in *de Rossa v Independent Newspapers*.[297] In both cases, the amount of damages, £90,000 and £300,000 respectively, was upheld. *McDonagh* involved a barrister who had represented the Irish government at the inquest into the deaths of the Gibraltar Three. In a newspaper article he was referred to as "a lefty spy".

The plaintiff in *de Rossa* was Proinsias de Rossa, then a TD, who had been leader of the Workers' Party and later formed Democratic Left. In 1992, he was in negotiations with other parties to try to form a government when the *Sunday Independent* carried an article by Eamon Dunphy which made reference to "special activities", which "served to fund the Workers' Party". The activities were said to be criminal, involving armed robberies and forgery of currency. De Rossa sued for defamation. The matter was finally decided by a jury after three hearings. The first in November 1996 ended after eight days with the jury being discharged following an article in the *Sunday Independent*, which it was believed might mislead or confuse the jury. The second in March 1997 ended after 15 days when the jury failed to reach a verdict. The third in July 1997 resulted in a verdict for the plaintiff and damages assessed by the jury at £300,000.

The case was appealed to the Supreme Court on the issue of damages: first, that the award was excessive, wholly disproportionate to the damage done, so high as to amount to a restriction on freedom of expression of the defendant and therefore in breach of Article 10 of the European Convention on Human Rights; second, that the law or practice restraining counsel or judge from giving specific guidance as to the appropriate level of damages was inconsistent with the Constitution; and finally, that the trial judge misdirected the jury.

The majority of the Court took the view that the traditional approach to the assessment of damages should not be altered; nor should the practice of appellate courts in only interfering with jury verdicts where the award is so disproportionate to the injury suffered and wrong done that no reasonable jury would have made such an award. In view of the seriousness of the charges made against the plaintiff, its potential effect on his career (it is immaterial that he went on to become a government minister and subsequently a member of the European Parliament), and the fact that the plaintiff had to endure three trials, as well as the failure of the newspaper to print a retraction, the award was not deemed disproportionate. In arriving at those conclusions, the Court laid considerable emphasis on the traditional importance of the role of the jury in the assessment of damages in defamation actions. Having revisited the case law on that role, the Chief Justice said (at 458) that neither the Constitution nor the Convention requires that the guidelines to be given to juries should be changed.

Denham J. in her dissenting judgment agreed with and adopted the views expressed by Henchy J. in *Barrett* in support of providing guidelines to juries.

---

[296] Unreported, Supreme Court, November 23, 1993.
[297] Above, n.289.

In principle it is open to the court to provide guidelines: "No law precludes the giving of guidelines". "Information does not fetter discretion" (at 477). Indeed, guidelines would help juries and the administration of justice. They would assist in achieving consistent and comparable decisions, which would enhance public confidence in the administration of justice. In *McCartan, Turkington and Breen v Times Newspapers Ltd*,[298] the Lord Chief Justice in the Court of Appeal in Northern Ireland had stated: "It is of limited assistance to tell them [the jury] that the level of damages must be proportionate, for it gives them no more practical guide than telling them to be reasonable". Denham J. went on to find that the award made in *de Rossa* was excessive and stated that she would have reduced the amount to £150,000 (at 483).

In the later case of *O'Brien v Mirror Group Newspapers*,[299] a jury award of £250,000 to Esat and 98FM chairman, Denis O'Brien, was overturned on appeal to the Supreme Court. Mr O'Brien had claimed that the articles in the *Irish Mirror* meant that he had paid £30,000 as a bribe to former government minister, Ray Burke, to get a radio licence for 98FM.[300] The Supreme Court found that the award of damages was disproportionately high and ordered a retrial on the issue of damages only. However, four of the five judges refused to reconsider their decision in *de Rossa* (above) that guidelines on the assessment of damages should not be given to juries. The sole dissent on the question of guidelines came from Mrs Justice Denham, who said there was a real issue as to whether the scope of judicial control at the trial and on appeal offered adequate and effective safeguards against disproportionately large awards of damages.

In England the issue of assessing damages has been under scrutiny for a considerable period of time, led by the Court of Appeal and prompted at least in part by the decision of the European Court of Human Rights in *Tolstoy Miloslavsky v UK*.[301] Some judges there have been rather colourful in their approach, telling juries in assessing damages not to think of football pools or telephone numbers but to think of a figure somewhere between the price of a house and a clapped-out Volvo.[302]

---

[298] [1998] N.I. 358 at 381; see also, above, nn.53, 283.

[299] *The Irish Times*, November 11, 1999 (HC), October 26, 2000 (SC), [2001] 1 I.R. 1. See also *Hill v Cork Examiner Publications* (above, nn.76, 189), in which the Supreme Court applied *de Rossa* and *O'Brien*, stating *inter alia* that "there would appear to be insuperable difficulties for any judge to assemble the appropriate body of information on which to base such guidelines" and that the assessment by a jury of damages in a defamation action had an "unusual and emphatic sanctity" and an appellate court should be slow to interfere with it (at 227, Murphy J.).

[300] The articles were based on an anonymous note said to have been shown to a journalist by a senior politician. There was evidence given that after seeing the note, the journalist attempted to contact a number of relevant people, including the public relations firm acting for Mr O'Brien. Mr O'Brien said he had sought a retraction from the newspaper but had not received a word of apology.

[301] Series A, No.316-B; (1995) 20 E.H.R.R. 442. For a comparison between *de Rossa* and *Tolstoy Miloslavsky*, see Patrick Leonard, "Irish Libel Law and The European Convention on Human Rights" (2000) B.R. 410; Michael Kealey, "Irish Developments in Defamation" (1999) 4 *Communications Law* 194.

[302] *The Sunday Times*, April 1, 1990 (*Linley v Today*). Or the price of a night out at his favourite night club where a bottle of champagne costs £55, or the price of a car, or the

Because of the unpredictability of juries and the prospects of high damages and even higher costs,[303] media defendants might be inclined to settle cases at an early stage. But if they do so, they come to be recognised as "an easy touch", which in itself encourages more claims and perpetuates the problem. If they hold out and go to court, their chances of winning are very small,[304] and there is the possibility of high jury awards, factors that encourage plaintiffs not to settle unless an offer of a considerable sum of money is made.

If the media go to court, the plaintiff has nothing to lose, because of present rules regarding payment into court. Payment into court is a mechanism that ensures that a defendant will not have to pay plaintiff's costs if the damages awarded are less than the sum lodged with the court. It is not available to the defamation defendant under Order 22, r.1(3) of the Rules of the Superior Courts, unless the defendant first admits liability, in which case, the only matter to be resolved is the level of damages to be awarded. The defendant who has admitted liability will not then be able to rely on a defence. Legal costs are also very high, often much higher than the damages awarded, with the result that small publishers are invariably advised to settle cases for a fixed sum, rather than face the uncertainty of a court case with the possibility of a large award of damages and costs that could destroy the company. Book publishers and smaller and newer periodical and newspaper publishers are particularly vulnerable because they usually have no libel insurance, either because it is not available or because the premiums are too high. Payment into court, when available without admission of liability, simply evens up the risk, so that there is an incentive to both sides to try to settle the case. The operation of the rule in Ireland contrasts with the UK, where a similar rule was abolished in 1933–

---

price of a house (*Sunday Tribune*, February 4, 1990) (*Neil v Worsthorne*). On libel awards in the UK generally, see Julie Scott-Bayfield and Jane Swann, "Libel Damages: The Beginning of the End?" in Eric Barendt and Alison Firth (eds), *The Yearbook of Copyright and Media Law* (Oxford University Press, Oxford, 1999), p.104. The Court of Appeal, in taking steps to lower the size of damages awards, indicated in *Sutcliffe v Pressdram*, above, n.290, that some guidance for juries was required to assist them to appreciate the real value of large sums, and later in *Elton John v MGN* [1996] 2 All E.R. 35 at 54 (above, n.193), expressed the view that it was "offensive to public opinion" to recover higher damages for defamation than for serious physical injuries. The English case law is considered by the Supreme Court in *de Rossa*. In the US, CJR March/April 1997 reported that juries had awarded a quarter of a billion dollars over the past six years, although in almost half of them, the awards were vacated on appeal.

[303] In *Sherwin v Independent Newspapers* (*The Irish Times*, November 21–28, 2001, December 6–14, 2001), the plaintiff, who was national organiser of Fianna Fáil, was awarded only £250 by the High Court jury. As a result he was entitled only to costs on the Circuit Court scale. He was awarded costs of £5,000 and ordered by the High Court to pay costs estimated at about £100,000 to Independent Newspapers. He also had to meet his own costs – *The Irish Times*, December 14, 2001. The case was appealed to the Supreme Court. In *McDonalds Corp. v Steel*, [1995] 3 All ER 615, the case taken in the UK by McDonald's fast-food restaurants against two environmentalists, the award against the two was £57,500, while costs of the 314 day trial, the longest in English legal history, were estimated at £10m ([1999] E.W.C.A. Civ. 1144; *The Irish Times*, January 13, 1999).

[304] Beverly Cooper-Flynn, above, n.187, was a rarity in this respect and in *Browne v Tribune Newspapers*, above, n.59, the Supreme Court ordered a retrial.

4.[305] However, the Irish High Court has stated in a non-media defamation case that there is no convincing reason to justify a differentiation between defamation and other torts when it comes to the question of payment into court.[306]

The highest sum ever awarded in Ireland for defamation against the media was £300,000 in *de Rossa* v *Independent Newspapers*.[307] That sum equates to about 20 times the average annual industrial wage at the time. The allegations were of a very serious nature and would "tend to" make others think less of the plaintiff. In defamation, damage is presumed (actionable *per se*), so the plaintiff does not have to prove actual damage and may receive money damages even if the allegations did not actually harm his reputation, or if nobody believed them. Barendt describes the presumption of damages as an anomaly and argues that a plaintiff should be obliged to prove injury to reputation (not just "tends to").[308]

Prior to *de Rossa*, the highest award was £275,000 in *Denny* v *Sunday News*.[309] In that case, the plaintiff, a County Monaghan soldier, was named in an article with a huge headline: "British 'spy' was Irish Soldier". An army investigation after publication of the story cleared the soldier of any involvement. The paper did not contest the case and the only issue in court was the amount of damages. In 1986, the Supreme Court clarified its position in relation to substituting its own award of damages in an appeal for those of a

---

[305] For example, a payment of £5,005 was lodged in *Reynolds* (above, n.263) without an admission of liability. The Circuit Court Rules 2001 (O.15, r.9) allow "any defendant" to make a lodgment: see *O'Rourke v Sunday World*, March 12, 1999, Smithwick J. (1999) 16 I.L.T. 255.

[306] *Norbrook Laboratories Ltd and Norbrook Laboratories (Ireland) Ltd v Smithkline Beecham (Ireland) Ltd t/a Smithkline Beecham Animal Health* [1999] 2 I.L.R.M. 391 at 396. The case also examines the issues of partial justification and separate causes of action in respect of each innuendo, where several are pleaded.

[307] Above, n.289. £515,000 was awarded in a non-media case *Dawson and Dawson t/a A.E. Dawson & Sons v Irish Brokers Association* (*The Irish Times*, July 5, 1996) but was overturned on appeal (SC, February 27, 1997).

[308] Above, n.3, at 123. He quotes Powell J. in *Gertz*, above, n.68 at 349, to the effect that the doctrine of presumed damages invites the jury to punish unpopular opinion rather than compensate individuals for injuries they have sustained as a result of the defamatory publication. If one cannot prove injury to reputation, it is probably a case of wounded feelings and there could be a separate remedy for that (at 125). In the Irish case *McDaid v The Examiner* (*The Irish Times*, November 17–18, 1999), for example, there was evidence of abusive telephone calls, etc. as evidence of actual harm.

[309] *The Irish Times*, November 14, 1992. Prior to that, the largest award by an Irish court had been £135,000 plus costs in *McNamee v Mirror Group Newspapers* (*The Irish Times*, November 30, 1989, December 2, 1989). In a report of the trial on terrorist charges of the plaintiff's brother, the *Daily Mirror* had mistakenly included the words "of his" in a reference to two brothers involved in IRA activities, thus associating the plaintiff with the IRA. An apology had been published but the judge considered it unsatisfactory. In another case in Northern Ireland, a jury, after a 25-day hearing, awarded £450,000: *Eastwood v McGuigan* (*The Irish Times*, February 11–March 10, 1992). On the question of the size of awards, it may be noted that the award of £65,000 in *Barrett* was five times the average annual industrial wage and that circulations in Ireland are relatively small.

lower court or jury.[310] However, in the defamation cases that have come before it since then the Court has usually upheld the jury award or occasionally ordered a retrial.[311] In England the Court of Appeal has exercised its right to substitute its own award rather than order a new trial. In *Rantzen v Mirror Group Newspapers*,[312] the Court reduced the award from £250,000 to £110,000. The European Court of Human Rights in *Tolstoy Miloslavsky v UK*[313] generally supported the Court of Appeal's attempts to ensure that damages awards were proportionate and held that an award of £1.5 million was so disproportionately large as to constitute a violation of the plaintiff's right to freedom of expression under Article 10 of the Convention.[314]

It is difficult to gauge the part played by emotional distress in jury cases. It is often alluded to in evidence as a major consequence of the offending publication.[315] The celebrity cases suggest also that the status of the particular defendant may be a factor in determining the size of the award. It appears that awards against tabloid newspapers, which publish emotional and sensational stories, are likely to be significantly higher than those against non-tabloid newspapers or public service broadcasters.[316] There may be some significance in the fact that the highest awards in Ireland were against the *Sunday Independent* (a broadsheet newspaper but one that is not only powerful but also controversial and hard-hitting), the *Sunday News* (a Northern Ireland tabloid newspaper, now owned by Independent Newspapers) and the *Daily Mirror* and *Sun* (both British tabloids with Irish editions). Alternatively, it may be that the highest awards were totally attributable to the seriousness of the allegations. [317]

---

[310] *Holohan v Donoghue* [1986] I.L.R.M. 250.

[311] *Prior v Irish Press* (*The Irish Times*, October 24, 1989) – award of £30,000 upheld; *Madigan v Irish Press* (*The Irish Times*, March 4, 1989) – award of £30,000 upheld; *McDonagh v News Group Newspapers* (Irish Times Law Report, December 27, 1993) – award of £90,000 upheld. The Supreme Court also upheld an award of £70,000 in *Campbell-Sharpe v Independent Newspapers* (*The Irish Times*, July 23, 1998). In *Barrett*, which pre-dated the 1986 *Holohan* decision, and in *Browne v Tribune Newspapers plc t/a The Sunday Tribune* (above, n.59), and *O'Brien v MGN Ltd* (above, n.299), it ordered a retrial. In *Hill* (above, n.76) it upheld an award of £60,000.

[312] *The Times*, April 6, 1993, [1993] 3 W.L.R. 953, [1993] 4 All E.R. 975.

[313] Above, n.26.

[314] *ibid.* at para.51. See also *Maronek v Slovakia*, above, n.154: the domestic courts lacked sufficient reasons to justify the relatively high amount of compensation awarded to the claimants.

[315] Barendt, above, n.3, at p.117, says that he thinks in some instances libel law is used to provide a remedy for wounded feelings and a loss of self-esteem, where there is no indication that any loss to reputation has occurred. In practice the issue of emotional distress may have a bearing on whether a case is settled or fought in court.

[316] That may bear out Barendt's thesis (above, n.3, at p.120) that libel law in some instances is not so much vindicating a right to reputation as protecting a right to dignity against media excesses. Hugh Oram in *Paper Tigers* (Appletree Press, Belfast, 1993), p.32, states that the *Sunday World* had a lot of libel actions in 1980s so had to move away from the ultra-sensational investigative story that was winning them readers but costing them money.

[317] With the exception of *O'Brien*, all of the cases involved allegations of links with paramilitary activity. A study of High Court records for the period 1990–2000 shows

The greatest obstacle to reform of defamation law is the reliance on the damages remedy.[318] Reliance on damages harks back to the notion of reputation as property, an asset capable of being earned through one's labours and therefore having a monetary value in society.[319] However, despite its origins, reputation has long since become more associated with honour and dignity.[320] Unlike property, honour and dignity inhere in the individual; they cannot be earned, but can be lost. They cannot be compensated or restored through money damages. They therefore need to be protected and "compensated" by remedies other than money damages. Viewed as an attack on honour, the essential objective of defamation law must be conceived as the restoration of honour[321] – what the Irish Constitution terms "vindication". Viewed as dignity, the objective is rehabilitation, re-establishing respect in the community.[322] Remedies other than damages need to be explored. As long as damages remain the central remedy for defamation, however, there is little incentive for plaintiffs or defendants to try other remedies and little room for reform.

4.6.1.1 Possible Alternatives to Damages

The provision of simpler, swifter remedies as alternatives to damages was one of the key proposals of the Law Reform Commission, and, indeed, of many similar bodies elsewhere, including the US and Australia.[323] Retractions,

---

that a high number of libel cases against the media during that period arose out of allegations of involvement in or connection with the IRA or other paramilitary activity.

[318] See above, n.219, John G. Fleming: "The preoccupation of our law of defamation with damages has been a crippling experience over the centuries. The damages remedy is not only singularly inept for dealing with, but actually exacerbates, the tension between protection of reputation and freedom of expression, both equally important values in a civilized and democratic community."

[319] Robert C. Post, above, n.4, at p.695: "Unjustified aspersions on character can thus deprive individuals of the results of their labors of self-creation, and the ensuing injury can be monetarily assessed." Injurious (or malicious) falsehood is a closely related tort, which is unequivocally addressed to the protection of property interests like chattels, trademarks, copyrights, and patents (*ibid.* at p.699). It involves harm to corporate goodwill (*ibid.* at p.741). As a result, the law on injurious falsehood does not presume damage from the fact of publication and the plaintiff has to prove damage.

[320] *ibid.* at p.700.

[321] *ibid.* at p.703. Post also uses the term "vindication".

[322] *ibid.* at p.713. Post, at p.715, identifies two distinct functions of defamation law derived from the concept of dignity: the rehabilitation of individual dignity and the maintenance of communal identity.

[323] See above, n.50, *Paper*, at pp.365–83. In Germany, a right of reply must be sought within two weeks of publication from a newspaper, three months from a magazine. A reply and/or retraction are regarded as primary remedies; damages are only secondary. They are available only after a full hearing and are low. Punitive damages are unknown. The focus of the law is on the rectification of error, not money. The criminal law is reserved for the unusual or flagrant case: see above, n.97, Thwaite and Brehm, at p.350. In *Sutcliffe v Pressdram*, above, n.290, Lord Donaldson regarded the assessment of damages as a social rather than a judicial function and pointed to the need for damages to vindicate the plaintiff's good name in the eyes of the public. However, the idea that the plaintiff could point to an award of damages as evidence that the allegations were untrue, could be achieved just as well by publication of the court judgment or declaration. See also the suggestion of a "vindication action" as an adjunct to existing remedies, in

corrections, clarifications, declaratory proceedings and judgments should be made available to those who want to vindicate their good name, quickly and effectively, rather than having to go through a court case to obtain damages some three years after publication of the harmful matter.[324] In the UK, the Defamation Act 1996 now makes provision for fast-track procedures, where the media are prepared to publish a correction and apology on realizing their mistake (sections 2–4), and where the matter is of a trivial nature (sections 8–10).[325] In the first of those circumstances, the publication of a correction and apology constitutes vindication of good name, which, it is submitted, would be perfectly in harmony with the Irish Constitution. In the second, disposal of trivial matters is by judge alone, without a jury, which is authorised by the Irish Constitution in the case of minor offences, and which, in practice, is already the situation in defamation cases heard in the Circuit Court in Ireland. The English courts have taken further steps to reduce the length and expense of libel actions. For example, the Court of Appeal has held that particulars of justification should be restricted to essential matters.[326]

4.6.2 Mitigation

Certain factors may be taken in mitigation of damages.[327] The most common is the publication of an apology (Defamation Act, section 17), but factors such as circulation figures, the conduct of the plaintiff and evidence of previous bad reputation[328] are also relevant. In *Browne v Tribune Newspapers*,[329] the

James H. Hulme, "Vindicating Reputation: An Alternative to Damages as a Remedy for Defamation" (1981) 30 American University LR 375.

[324] On retraction and right of reply, see John G. Fleming, above, n.219; Marie McGonagle, "A Right to Reply", in Manfred Wichmann (ed.), *Freedom of Expression and Human Rights Protection* (Friedrich Naumann Foundation, Brussels, 1997). On the appropriateness of mediation in libel cases, see Richard Shillito, "Mediation in Libel Actions" (2000) 150 N.L.J. 122. There are many instances of libel plaintiffs stating that they sued reluctantly and only because there was no alternative remedy.

[325] See William Bennett, "Defamation: summary disposal, summary judgment and a judge's power to rule that statements are only capable of being defamatory" (2001) 6 *Communications Law* 115. In the UK, there is now a Pre-Action Protocol for Defamation (August 2000, available at *www.lcd.gov.uk/civil/procrules_fin/contents/protocols/prot_def.htm*, which aims to improve pre-action communication between the parties with a view to increasing the number of pre-action settlements.

[326] *Tancic v Times Newspapers Ltd.* (*The Times*, January 12, 2000), *per* Lord Justice Brooke. In Ireland, defamation cases can be subject to significant delays particularly at the pleadings stage and with discovery and other measures can take several years to dispose of. Recently a case was struck out because of delays: *Ewins v Independent Newspapers* (*The Irish Times*, March 7, 2003). The case concerned two articles published in the *Irish Independent* in April 1995. See also related case, above, n.177. See also *Doyle v. Independent Newspapers* [2001] 4 I.R. 594 regarding "particulars".

[327] See above, n.50, *Paper*, at p.117.

[328] See the rule in *Scott v Sampson* (1882) 8 Q.B.D. 491 and the exceptions to the rule. The circumstances of the publication or character of the plaintiff cannot be pleaded in mitigation unless notice is given seven days in advance (RSC 1986, Ord. 36, r.36). For discussion of the rule, see McDonald, n.6, at pp.248–50 and *Hill*, above, n.76, Supreme Court.

[329] Above, n.59.

plaintiff was a detective superintendent in the Garda Síochána in Co. Cavan when a shooting incident took place there. The jury in the High Court found that the *Sunday Tribune* article, which suggested that the garda had neglected and omitted to investigate a serious complaint of possession of firearms prior to the shooting, was true in substance and in fact. However, the plaintiff had been cross-examined as to monies recovered by him in four other libel actions he had taken, but which were not connected to the libel action at issue. On appeal, the Supreme Court considered that reference to unrelated libel actions could be relevant only, if at all, to the issue of damages. It considered at length section 26 of the Defamation Act 1961, which states:

> "In any action for libel or slander the defendant may give in evidence in mitigation of damage that the plaintiff has recovered damages, or has brought actions for damages, for libel or slander in respect of the publication of words to the same effect as the words on which the action is founded, or has received or agreed to receive compensation in respect of any such publication".

Keane, C.J., with whom Denham and Geoghegan JJ. concurred, said that the law in Ireland regarding mitigation of damages is as set out in the Law Reform Commission's Consultation Paper on Defamation (1991). In mitigation of damages, therefore, it is permitted to show:

(a) that the plaintiff had a general bad reputation prior to the publication in question;[330]

(b) that the plaintiff had recovered damages or brought actions for damages for libel or slander in respect of words to the same effect as the words on which the action is founded or had received or agreed to receive compensation in respect of any such publication (Defamation Act 1961, section 26);

(c) that the defendant had made or offered an apology to the plaintiff before the commencement of the action or as soon afterwards as he had an opportunity of doing so, in case the action was commenced before there was an opportunity for making or offering such an apology (Defamation Act 1961, section 17);

(d) evidence of retractions or corrections by the defendant, or the offer of a right of reply;[331]

---

[330] Particularly the rule in *Scott v Sampson* (1882) 8 Q.B.D. 491 to the effect that general evidence of a bad reputation was admissible but not evidence of particular facts, rumours or suspicions tending to show the character and disposition of the plaintiff. The Law Reform Commission in its *Report on the Civil Law of Defamation* (LRC 38-1991) recommended that the law should be clarified to permit the defendant to introduce in mitigation of damages any matter, general or particular, relevant at the date of trial to that aspect of the plaintiff's reputation with which the defamation was concerned; cf. above, n.7, Faulks Committee in England. See also *Hill* (above, n.76) at 227 (SC).

[331] There is no specific mention of the defendant's state of mind being taken in mitigation. Contrast France where a finding of good faith on the part of the journalist can relieve

(e) evidence of the conduct of the plaintiff;

(f) evidence of the circulation of the libel;

(g) repetition (of the libel) and disclosure of source.[332]

The Supreme Court ordered a retrial on all the issues.

4.6.3 Apologies

The apology provided for in section 17 of the Defamation Act is intended as a means of mitigating damage. The apology must be made or offered to the plaintiff before the commencement of the action or as soon afterwards as s/he has an opportunity of doing so. To avail of the section, it is necessary to give prior notice in writing of an intention to do so. An apology is not therefore a complete defence to a libel action but it can in certain circumstances ward off a court action.[333]

In other circumstances, where the case proceeds to court, if the apology is accepted as wholehearted and fulsome by the court, it can mitigate damage and lead to a reduction in the amount of compensation payable. See, for example, *Bowman v Connaught Telegraph*,[334] where the judge acknowledged that the defamatory remark was the result of a typesetting error and took account of the fact that an apology had been published. He awarded £1,000. Likewise in *Foley v The Irish Times*[335] allowance was made for the publication of an apology and £5,000 awarded. On the other hand, if the apology is regarded as half-hearted, it may only compound the original injury, as was claimed in *McSharry v Waterford Post*[336] and could conceivably lead to a higher award of damages. In *Boland v Independent Newspapers*,[337] an article alleged that the plaintiff, a former government minister, had been involved in the Arms

---

him/her of liability altogether. Note also the weight given by the European Court of Human Rights to good faith on the part of the journalist and his/her compliance with journalistic ethics. Above n.167, *Lopes Gomes Da Silva v Portugal* and n.275, *Bergens Tidende*.

[332] See above, n.50, *Paper*, at p.126, para.132. However, the LRC does not elaborate on this or cite any cases in support.

[333] See, for example, the *Magill* allegation that Tánaiste, Mary Harney, had been ordered by the Flood Tribunal to make extensive disclosure of her financial records. The matter ended without the need to go to court when the plaintiff accepted an unreserved apology and acknowledgment, *inter alia*, that the story was "wholly untrue and without any substance or foundation", was seriously defamatory of her and particularly damaging to her and her party, coming as it did during the general election campaign. Ms Harney's legal costs were paid by *Magill*, as well as a sum of €25,000 to a charity of her choice (*The Irish Times*, May 11, 2002).

[334] *The Irish Times*, May 16, 1986.

[335] Above, n.211.

[336] *The Irish Times*, May 1, 1985. *Cf. Campbell-Sharp v Magill* (*The Irish Times*, June 29, 1985); *McConville v Kennelly* (*The Irish Times*, January 27, 1984); *Agnew v Independent Newspapers* (*The Irish Times*, June 29, 1985). Robertson and Nicol, above, n.58, at p.141, recommend that when the media agree to publish an apology, they should seek a disclaimer of further legal action as a condition of publishing the apology.

[337] *The Irish Times*, March 7–9, 1996.

Trial and had been dismissed from the cabinet by then Taoiseach Jack Lynch. Both allegations were incorrect and Independent Newspapers duly published a follow-up piece by way of correction and apology. The piece stated that Independent Newspapers accepted that Kevin Boland "was not involved in this trial" and that he had resigned on principle from government. The plaintiff claimed that this "apology" only aggravated the matter, since it implied that although he was not involved in the Arms Trial, he had been involved in some other trial. A High Court jury awarded him £75,000.

Another difficulty with apologies is that they are often taken to be an admission of liability. If that happens, then the defendant may find that s/he cannot rely on any of the defences to defamation and is totally at the mercy of the jury. It becomes simply a matter of how much money the jury will award. In *McDaid v The Examiner*,[338] the defendants published a story that Government Minister Jim McDaid had received the report of the barrister appointed to inquire into allegations of sexual abuse of young swimmers by their coaches but had not revealed the names of the perpetrators to the gardaí. It emerged that the minister had received the report, but that it did not contain the names and therefore he could not have passed them on to the gardaí. The *Examiner* immediately carried a front-page apology. The apology was raised in mitigation but the jury nonetheless awarded the Minister £90,000. There was evidence that despite the apology the minister had received abusive telephone calls for weeks after the publication.

4.6.4 Unintentional Defamation and the Offer of Amends

Many defamatory publications are unintentional, but that does not mean that they will not attract liability. Defamation is a strict liability tort. That means that, once the elements of the tort are proved, *i.e.* publication by the defendant, reference to the plaintiff, defamatory nature, the publisher is liable, regardless of motive or intent unless s/he can establish one of the defences provided for in the Defamation Act 1961 or at common law. The only remedy provided in the case of unintentional defamation is the offer of amends in section 21 of the Defamation Act 1961. This was devised by parliament as a remedy for the harshness of the situation encountered in Britain in cases such as *Hulton v Jones*[339] and *Newstead v London Express*.[340] In the former, it turned out that there was a barrister of the same name as a fictitious church warden referred to in a light-hearted sketch about sober Englishmen living it up on the other side of the Channel. In the second, an accurate court report was sued upon by the plaintiff, who happened to have the same name and come from the same locality as a man convicted of bigamy.

The remedy devised by parliament was intended to provide a form of right of reply, a method of setting the record straight. The aim was admirable, because the most sensible way to clear up confusion is to publish a clarification, rather

---

[338] Above, n.308.
[339] [1910] A.C. 20.
[340] [1940] 1 K.B. 377.

than proceeding to court for damages. A clarification published immediately or soon after the event can undo any possible damage in a way that an award of money some years later can not. In fact, it is quite common nowadays for newspapers and broadcasting stations to publish clarifications in such circumstances and the people concerned are usually satisfied.[341] In some cases at least, a clarification is a better vindication of reputation, as required by the Irish Constitution, Article 40.3, than damages.

In that sense, the offer of amends should provide a remedy for fiction and many other areas of unintentional defamation. However, the offer of amends in section 21 of the Defamation Act 1961 is applicable in only a very limited category of unintentional defamation. It applies where a person who has published words alleged to be defamatory of another person claims that "the words were published by him innocently in relation to that other person". Even then, it can be availed of only if the publisher:

(a) did not intend to publish them about that other person and did not know of circumstances by which they might be understood to refer to him; or

(b) the words were not defamatory on their face and the publisher did not know of circumstances by virtue of which they might be understood to be defamatory of that other person

and, in either case, the publisher "exercised all reasonable care in relation to the publication" (section 21(5)). "Publisher" in this instance includes any servant or agent concerned with the contents of the publication.

If the publisher meets these conditions, s/he may offer to publish a suitable correction of the words complained of and a sufficient apology. S/he must also take such steps as are reasonably practicable to notify persons to whom copies have been distributed that the words are alleged to be defamatory of the party aggrieved (section 21(3)). If the offer is accepted and duly performed, the publisher will incur no further liability. Any question arising, following acceptance, will be determined by the High Court (section 21(4)). If the offer is not accepted, it may be possible for the publisher to rely on the making of the offer as a defence (section 21(1)(b)). However, a number of difficulties arise. The defence will not be available if the party aggrieved proves that s/he has suffered special damage, usually financial damage (section 21(6)). Nor will it be available to a publisher who is not the author of the offending words unless s/he proves that the words were written by the author without malice (section 21(7)). Moreover, there are practical difficulties involved in setting up the defence. The offer must have been expressed to have been made for the purpose of the section (that is, section 21 of the Act). It must have been made as soon as practicable after the defendant received notice of the alleged defamation. It must not have been withdrawn (section 21(1)(b)). It must be accompanied by an affidavit specifying the facts relied upon to show that the words were published innocently of the plaintiff (section 21(2)); and no evidence other than evidence of facts specified in the affidavit shall be

---

[341] See above, n.70, Boyle and McGonagle, 1995, at pp.25–7.

admissible on behalf of the publisher to prove that the words were so published (section 21(2)).

The section relating to the offer of amends has seven subsections, four of which are further subdivided into paragraphs (a) and (b); it spans two and a half pages of print. While there is some evidence to suggest that it can dispose of defamation cases if accepted,[342] it has proved impractical as a defence. Two of the difficulties encountered with the offer of amends are the requirement of reasonable care and the requirement of an affidavit.

The requirement of reasonable care is a stumbling block to the use of the offer of amends in either guise, as a complete remedy or as a defence. What constitutes, in journalistic terms, reasonable care? While the concept of reasonable care in relation to manufacturers, professionals, local authorities and other such bodies is well developed in tort law, its application to journalists and media is less certain. The House of Lords in *Reynolds* (above) has suggested 10 indicators, while the European Court of Human Rights has said that it depends on the medium used, and gives weight to compliance with journalistic ethics. A case such as the previously cited *Browne v Independent Newspapers*[343] might have been the kind of case where one would expect the offer of amends to provide a remedy. The circumstances of the case may have been such that the requirement of reasonable care would not have been met. At the most basic level, a perusal of the relevant telephone directory would presumably have provided the information that a builder of that name operated in the locality. The problem was further compounded by the fact that unlike the other "colour" surnames used (White and Black) Browne was spelt with an "e". The publisher may have felt that the publication of a disclaimer and categorisation of the names used in the article as fictitious would prevent liability. However, a jury awarded the plaintiff £75,000.

In the case of the media, reasonable care must necessitate at least the checking of sources and facts. In the English case of *Ross v Hopkinson*,[344] the requirement was not met as the name chosen for the fictitious actress was the same as that of a leading West End actress. An indication of what might constitute reasonable care in journalistic terms can be gleaned from the standard imposed on the private plaintiff in the United States to show negligence and from the French concept of *bonne foi*. In the US, public plaintiffs, such as politicians and public figures, must show malice on the part of the media, whereas private plaintiffs must show negligence.[345] The steps taken by the journalist and media organisation in the pre-publication stages come under scrutiny. As in the test proffered in *Reynolds* (above), the steps taken by the

---

[342] Lawyers for the *Cork Examiner*, for example, reported that they had used the offer of amends successfully in one case.

[343] Above, n.73, para. 4.3.2.2.

[344] *The Times*, October 17, 1956. See also Libel Act 1843, s.2 and cases thereon in above, n.6, McDonald, at pp.230–31.

[345] Above, n.68. See also Randall P. Bezanson *et al.*, above, n.150, at pp.122–7 and *passim*; John Soloski and Randall Bezanson (eds), *Reforming Libel Law* (The Guilford Press, New York, 1992), pp.8-10, 333-4; Frederick Schauer, "Reflections on the Value of Truth", reproduced in Raymond Wacks (ed.), *Privacy* (Dartmouth, Aldershot, 1993), at p.407.

journalist and the state of the defendant's mind becomes relevant. In *Herbert v Lando*,[346] the US Supreme Court held that the plaintiff was entitled to enquire into the editorial process and even to rummage through journalists' research notes, paperwork and unused film to gauge their state of mind at the time of publication. The effect of the decision was to encourage the creation of a paper trail: to stop issuing critical internal memos and issue positive statements approving and commending the journalists' work instead.

In France, journalists can plead *bonne foi*, *i.e.* that they acted in good faith. The court will then look to see if certain criteria are met: was there a legitimate purpose in publishing the story, an absence of personal animosity, serious and objective investigation, prudent expression? For instance, in 1993 the Cour de Cassation (equivalent of our Supreme Court) decided that an allegation that a doctor was profiting from AIDS by offering illusory treatment for financial gain was capable of being defamatory. However, it found that the purpose in publishing the article was to inform the reader on a matter of public interest and that the journalist had researched the story thoroughly, contacting doctors and experts with opposing views, so that *bonne foi* was established and there was no liability.[347] In contrast, the BBC in 1983 settled a case taken by a Harley Street slimming expert against the "That's Life" programme, which he said portrayed him as "a profiteering, unscrupulous quack". The case, *Gee v BBC*,[348] had been running in the High Court in London for 89 days when the BBC agreed to pay £75,000 damages, plus the doctor's share of the total legal bill, estimated at £1.2 million. The trial began with a jury but they were later discharged when the hearing, which was largely taken up with detailed medical evidence, became too complex for them.

The second stumbling block to the use of the offer of amends is the requirement of an affidavit. The most obvious difficulty with this requirement stems from the conditions attaching to it by virtue of section 21(1)(b) and section 21(2). An offer of amends must be made as soon as practicable, must be accompanied by an affidavit and only the facts set out in the affidavit can then be relied on if the case goes to court. The problem, therefore, is that if the media delay in making the offer of amends in order to check out the facts thoroughly, they run the risk that the offer will not be considered to have been made as soon as practicable.[349] On the other hand, if they make the offer "as soon as practicable", there is a danger of overlooking facts that would be important for their defence but that could not then be raised in court because only facts contained in the affidavit are admissible. The usefulness of the section

---

[346] Above, n.227.

[347] Cour de Cassation, March 17, 1993. *Cf.* German law: Section 193 of the German Criminal Code recognises that pressure of time or lack of resources leaves the press without adequate means to verify the truth of a statement before publication; therefore, there will be no liability if there is a legitimate interest involved and either reliable sources were referred to or the information received and the person supplying it were thoroughly checked (*Kant v Der Spiegel*, 1990); above, n.97, Thwaite and Brehm, at p.346.

[348] *The Irish Times*, April 24, 1985, October 20, 1986. See also (1986) 136 N.L.J. 515.

[349] See, for example, *Ross v Hopkinson* (*The Times*, October 17, 1956, cited in above, n.58, Robertson and Nicol (3rd ed., at p.94), where a period of seven weeks after publication did not meet the requirement).

is further reduced by the fact that it does not apply in cases where special damage is proved. It is also exceedingly burdensome to expect the publisher of letters to the editor, works of fiction and so on to prove absence of malice on the part of the author in order to be able to rely on the offer of amends. In sum, the statutory remedy envisaged by section 21 is good in theory but virtually impossible to avail of in practice. Reform bodies in a number of countries have recommended overhauling it or replacing it entirely.[350]

4.6.5 Injunctions

Injunctions are and should be an infrequent remedy for defamation. The purpose they serve in defamation law is to prevent publication in the first instance, or to prevent repetition of material already published. Given the importance of freedom of expression and the far-reaching effects of any form of prior restraint, they should be used and available for use only in exceptional and very limited circumstances. The Irish Law Reform Commission has pointed out that injunctions against allegedly defamatory publications are subject to constitutional restrictions.[351] In defamation cases, injunctions will be refused if the defendant newspaper or broadcaster demonstrates an intention and ability to plead any of the defences available, *i.e.* justification, fair comment or qualified privilege.[352] For example, an application was made to prevent RTÉ transmitting certain allegedly defamatory material in a programme that was to name the real Birmingham bombers. The Supreme Court, upholding the decision of Costello J. in the High Court, refused the injunction. There must be very exceptional circumstances for the courts to intervene by means of an injunction to stop a threatened publication that is defamatory, Costello J. said.[353]

Nonetheless, an interlocutory injunction was granted restraining publication in *Reynolds v Malocco t/a "Patrick" magazine.*[354] The case involved two main allegations, namely that the plaintiff permitted the sale of drugs in his nightclubs and that he was a homosexual, since he was referred to as a "gay bachelor". Kelly J. in the High Court considered the general rules regarding the granting of injunctions but recognised that, in a case such as this, freedom of expression was an important consideration.[355] The decision was based largely on the fact that justification was not pleaded in relation to the second allegation

---

[350] Faulks Committee, above, n.7, at pp.76–8; n.50, Supreme Court Procedure Committee (Neill Committee) 1991; n.50, LRC, *Paper*, at pp.327–35. The Defamation Act 1996 in the UK attempted to simplify the procedures but some uncertainty remains: see Robertson and Nicol, above, n.58, at pp.140–1.

[351] *Consultation Paper on Contempt of Court,* 1991, at p.273, citing *X v RTÉ* (Supreme Court, March 27, 1990, affirming High Court, Costello J.; see also discussion in LRC *Consultation Paper on the Civil Law of Defamation* 1991, at paras 136–9.

[352] See above, n.6, McDonald, Chap. 11; *X v RTÉ* (above, n.351; *The Irish Times*, March 28, 1990).

[353] *The Irish Times*, March 29, 1990.

[354] Above, n.115.

[355] In that regard, Kelly J. made a passing reference to the ECHR. He also pointed out that, while the grant of injunctive relief is always discretionary, it is a jurisdiction of a delicate nature and the court must be circumspect to ensure that it does not unnecessarily interfere with the right to freedom of expression.

and that damages were unlikely to be available in the circumstances of the case, and therefore would be an inadequate remedy.[356] In a later case, a company was granted a temporary injunction against the *Examiner* newspaper to prevent publication of any defamatory matter relating to the company's title to its housing project.[357]

4.7 LAW REFORM

Even with the refinements and improvements carried over into the Defamation Act 1961, defamation law in Ireland has proved less than satisfactory. The Act has not stood the test of time; it does not take account of modern technological realities in the media field and needs to be replaced with an updated law. Libel law at present is unduly complex, a "mad jumble", as one commentator has called it,[358] and many would argue that it manages to achieve the worst of two worlds: it does little to protect reputation and it does much to deter speech and hinder the media. As the Law Reform Commission said, current defamation law fails to serve either the plaintiff, defendant or public.[359] It fails to give due respect to the constitutional provisions. Many of the problems stem from lack of clarity and lack of certainty, which create a chilling effect on media reporting.[360]

Consequently, the Commission made a number of substantive recommendations to be included in a new Defamation Act.[361] A private member's bill, based on the LRC's recommendations was introduced in 1995, and the government in response announced its intention to bring in its own proposals. Since then, reform of the libel laws has been on the programme of successive governments, but has yet to be acted upon.[362] There has been very little statutory

---

[356] Justification was pleaded in relation to the first allegation but the court found that there was no admissible evidence to support it. Preference in this regard was expressed for the approach to a plea of justification taken by the Supreme Court in *Cullen v Stanley* (1926) I.R. 73, rather than that in *Gallagher v Tuohy* (1924) I.L.T.R. 134. For a critical comment on the case, see Neville Cox (1998) 20 D.U.L.J. 246 and, regarding injunctions in defamation cases, Kevin Feeney, "Restraining the Publication of Allegedly Defamatory Material" (1998) 4 B.R. 261.

[357] *Astra Construction Services Ltd. v Examiner Publications (Cork) Ltd. and Denis O'Brien* (*The Irish Times*, February 22, 27, 2001).

[358] Marcel Berlins, cited in Marie McGonagle, "Practical Aspects of Defamation Law" *Dlí – The Western Law Gazette*, Spring 1991, at p.17. Robertson and Nicol, above, n.58, at p.103, state that Irish defamation law is "antediluvian" and that the Republic is a "fly-trap" for English publishers.

[359] See above, n.50, *Paper*, at p.194.

[360] *ibid*. For discussion of the chilling effect of the libel laws in England, see Eric Barendt and others, *Libel and the Media – the Chilling Effect* (Oxford University Press, Oxford, 1997), pp.186–197.

[361] For responses to the LRC, see O'Dell, "Reflections on a Revolution in Libel" (1991) I.L.T. 181, at p.214; Marc McDonald, "Defamation Reform – A Response to the LRC Report" (1992) I.L.T. 270.

[362] The outline of a bill was circulated at the end of 2001, in advance of the general election of June 2002 (*The Irish Times*, December 19, 2001). Fine Gael while in opposition in 2001 also published a position paper outlining its proposals for reform. In October

intervention in the area of defamation law in recent years and the effect of what little there has been has simply been to extend the application of the existing law. The Electronic Commerce Act 2000, as outlined above, contains a provision extending the law of libel to electronic publication and the Broadcasting Act 2001 (section 15(d)) states, for the avoidance of doubt, that neither the transmission company nor the multiplex company (established for the purpose of providing digital television), which accepts a supply of programme material, shall be regarded for the purposes of the law of defamation as having published the material.[363]

If the government implements the Law Reform Commission's proposals of 1991, and takes account of the more salient developments in defamation law in other jurisdictions in recent years, and particularly the European Convention on Human Rights jurisprudence, many of the difficulties experienced with current defamation law, as outlined above, will be lessened or removed. The focus will no longer be on damages alone, and there will be an incentive to try other means, such as correction or declaratory orders, to vindicate reputation. The extension of the common law defence of qualified privilege, if carefully drafted and implemented, will give the media the incentive to maintain high standards of care and accuracy in the preparation and presentation of stories of importance to the public interest.

The Legal Advisory Group established by the Minister for Justice in 2002 reported in 2003.[364] Among its main recommendations was a defence of reasonable publication, which would be available where a defendant could show that the publication in question was made in the course of, or for the purposes of, the discussion of some subject of public interest, the public discussion of which was for the public benefit (para.12). A number of factors to determine reasonableness are set out (para.13) and the defence would be lost if the publication was actuated by spite, ill-will or improper motive (para.14). The Group also recommended that juries continue to assess damages in the High Court but that the judge give directions and that there be a statutory provision to make clear that the Supreme Court on appeal could substitute its own assessment of damages (paras 18, 20). It did not recommend removing the presumption of falsity but did propose that all plaintiffs be required to file an affidavit verifying the particulars of their claim (para.22). Other proposals generally support and update those of the Law Reform Commission of 1991, particularly those that would provide a range of possible remedies and encourage early settlement of actions. A one year limitation period is favoured (para.53).[365]

Even with reform, journalists will still carry a heavy responsibility in preparing and checking stories, so as not to unjustifiably encroach on the good

---

2002 the Minister for Justice announced the setting up of an Advisory Body to look at issues such as the burden of proof and the defence of qualified privilege, with a view to bringing a new Defamation Bill before the Dáil in mid-2003. See further below.

[363] The Broadcasting Act 2001 is discussed in Chap.11 below.

[364] *Report of the Legal Advisory Group on Defamation*, March 2003, available at *www.justice.ie* under "publications".

[365] In accordance with its terms of reference, the Group also put forward proposals for the establishment of a statutory press council. See further Chap.11 below.

name of the individual. To that end, the following "checklist" is offered to journalism students as a practical guide to avoiding libel.[366] However, it is only a checklist, not a substitute for being familiar with the rules of libel law, discussed in this chapter.

Checklist for journalists

In preparing your story:

1. Have you named, or otherwise identified, any individuals or company? Could anything you have said point to, or reasonably be taken to refer to, any group small enough that its individual members might be identifiable?

2. Have you checked out and stated accurately all the facts about them that you intend to include in the publication? Have you sought the other side of the story?

3. Can you prove all those facts through witnesses, documents that will stand up in court and notes of the checks that you have made?

4. Is anything you have said capable of being regarded as defamatory, either in its ordinary sense or by virtue of an innuendo?

5. Will you have a defence?

Further Reading

ARTICLE 19, *Defining Defamation: Principles on Freedom of Expression and Defamation* (ARTICLE 19, London, 2000; also available in English and French at *www.article19.org*).

Binchy, William, "Some Unanswered Questions in Irish Defamation Law" in Sarkin, Jeremy and Binchy, William (eds), *Human Rights, the Citizen and the State* (Round Hall Sweet & Maxwell, Dublin, 2001), p.243.

Boyle, Kevin, and McGonagle, Marie, "Defamation: the Path to Law Reform" in *Law and the Media: the Views of Journalists and Lawyers* (Round Hall Sweet & Maxwell, Dublin, 1997), p.57.

Law Reform Commission, *Consultation Paper on the Civil Law of Defamation*, 1991, and *Report on the Civil Law of Defamation* (LRC 38–1991, Dublin, 1991).

Legal Advisory Group on Defamation, *Report* (March 2003, available at *www.justice.ie* under "publications").

Loveland, Ian, *Political Libels: A Comparative Study* (Hart Publishing, Oxford, 2000).

McDonald, Marc, *Irish Law of Defamation* (2nd ed., The Round Hall Press, Dublin, 1989).

---

[366] This checklist, devised by the author, formed part of a training programme initiated by the *Irish Times* and has been included in an *Irish Times* staff booklet. The author is grateful to the *Irish Times* for permission to reproduce it here.

McHugh, Damian, *Libel Law – A Journalist's Handbook* (2nd ed., Four Courts Press, Dublin, 2001).

Murphy, Yvonne, *Journalists and the Law* (2nd ed., Round Hall Sweet & Maxwell, Dublin, 2000)

Robertson, Geoffrey, and Nicol, Andrew, *Media Law* (4th ed., Penguin Books, London, 2002).

CHAPTER FIVE

Privacy

5.1 INTRODUCTION

In *Martin Chuzzlewit*, Dickens had the newsboys in New York shouting:

> "The *New York Sewer*. Here's the Sewer's exposure of the Washington gang and the Sewer's exclusive account of a flagrant act of dishonesty committed by the Secretary of State when he was eight years old, now communicated, at a great expense, by his own nurse".[1]

Dickens was alluding to the capacity of some elements of the press to intrude on personal privacy without any recognisable public value. He calls into question the boundaries of media reporting but in doing so points up some of the uncertainties that still bedevil this area of law.

While there is widespread acceptance of the need to protect privacy, there is some doubt as to what should be protected and how. For instance the right to privacy is protected in the legal systems of continental Europe in some instances by their constitutions or by the incorporation into their law of the European Convention on Human Rights (Article 8) and given effect by their civil and criminal codes. In contrast, the common-law jurisdictions have never seen privacy as a central value to be protected in any systematic or comprehensive way by law. There is no specific tort of invasion of privacy, and only certain aspects of the wider right are criminalised.

5.2 WHY PROTECT PRIVACY?

Awareness of the need for effective protection of the private lives of individuals against intrusion by state authorities was intensified by the atrocities of Nazism and the Second World War. The need for protection specifically aimed at intrusion by the media has been fuelled by the capabilities of modern technology and the growth of the "yellow" or tabloid press, its appeal to prurience and focus on intimate details and events of people's lives. Throughout the common-law world, there have been movements in recent decades to put in place specific privacy laws to curb media intrusion into people's private lives.

In the UK, for example, the Younger Committee on Privacy in its 1972 report recommended against a blanket declaration of a right to privacy on the

---

[1] Cited in Anthony Lewis, "John Foster Memorial Lecture 1987", 9 *London Review of Books* No.21, 26 (November, 1987).

grounds that it would introduce uncertainties into the law and affect freedom of information.[2] In the media field, the Committee's recommendations were confined to improvements in the structure and operation of the Press Council and Broadcasting Complaints Commission. The Committee did, however, favour the introduction of a generally applicable tort of disclosure or other use of information unlawfully acquired (at para. 632). In the meantime, a number of private members' bills were introduced in parliament but without success.

Almost 20 years after the Younger Report, the case of *Kaye v Robertson*[3] in 1990 confirmed that in English law there was no right to privacy as such and accordingly no right of action for breach of a person's privacy. The case arose from the intended publication of a *Sunday Sport* article and photographs of well-known actor Gordon Kaye in his hospital bed, seriously ill after a car crash. It prompted the British Government to establish the Calcutt Committee, which reported in 1990.[4] It recommended against the introduction of a tort of invasion of privacy (para. 12.5) but in favour of the creation of specific criminal offences of entering or placing surveillance on private property and of taking photographs of or recording the voice of an individual who is on private property without consent and with intent to obtain personal information with a view to publication (para. 6.33). The press was to be given one final chance to make self-regulation work. The Press Council was abolished and replaced by a Press Complaints Commission (PCC) with a narrower remit to implement a Code of Practice drawn up by newspaper editors. Calcutt reviewed the situation in 1993 and concluded that the operation of the PCC was not satisfactory and that a statutory regime was needed and should not await the introduction of a statutory tort of privacy.[5]

Since then, a number of privacy complaints against the press in the UK have been addressed by the PCC and privacy cases have begun to be taken in the courts there under the Human Rights Act 1998.[6] Newsreader Anna Ford

---

[2] Kenneth Younger (Chairman), Committee on Privacy, *Report of the Committee on Privacy* (Cmnd. 5012, HMSO, London, 1972).

[3] [1991] F.S.R. 62 (C.A.). That view has since been questioned, for example, in *Shelley Films Ltd v Rex Features* [1994] E.M.L.R. 134, and was distinguished in the 1995 case in which an injunction was granted to prevent the *Mirror* publishing further photographs of Princess Diana in the gym (*The Times*, February 9, 1995). See generally, Mark Thomson, "Privacy and Prior Restraint after the Human Rights Act" (2000) 5 *Communications Law* 54.

[4] Sir David Calcutt, Calcutt Report, *Report of the Committee on Privacy and Related Matters* (Cmnd. 1102, HMSO, London, 1990).

[5] Sir David Calcutt, *Review of Press Self-Regulation* (Cmnd. 2135, HMSO, London, 1993). Privacy as a constitutional right, supplemented by rights of action to protect particular aspects of it, is supported by Barendt, "Privacy as a Constitutional Right and Value" in Peter Birks (ed.), *Privacy and Loyalty* (Clarendon Press, Oxford, 1997) p.1.

[6] There is now a positive right to privacy in the UK under the Human Rights Act 1998. See generally, Basil Markesinis (ed.), *Protecting Privacy* (OUP, Oxford, 1999); Tom Crone, *Law and the Media* (4th ed., Focal Press, Oxford, 2002), pp.87–126; Myles Jelf, "Not with a Bang but a Whimper? A Right to Privacy and the End of Voluntary Self-regulation of the Press" [1999] ENT. L.R. 244; Jonathan Griffiths, "The Human Rights Act 1998, Section 12 – Press Freedom Over Privacy?" [1999] ENT. L.R. 36; Mark Thomson, above, n.3; Jonathan Coad, "Privacy – Article 8. Who Needs It?" [2001] ENT. L.R. 227.

complained to the PCC about publication of photographs taken of her and her companion on a beach. The PCC rejected her complaint and she sought judicial review of the PCC decision in the High Court but it was refused.[7] A case taken by model Naomi Campbell, who claimed breach of privacy when photographs showing her leaving a drugs and alcohol treatment clinic were published in the *Daily Mirror*, was upheld in the London High Court in March 2002 but overturned on appeal.[8] Section 12 of the Human Rights Act, which deals with the right to privacy, requires the courts to have particular regard to freedom of expression.

There is a growing concern in Ireland, too, that media organisations are pushing back the boundaries of privacy and offensiveness. This may be in response to competition, primarily from the British press, which has made significant inroads into the Irish market, with offices in this country and separate Irish editions.[9] It was the activities of the tabloid press in Britain that led to calls for the introduction of privacy legislation there. Indeed, it was the excesses of the American yellow press that prompted jurists Warren and Brandeis to try to formulate a right to privacy in their seminal article in the Harvard Law Review over a century ago.[10] The capabilities of modern technology to intrude on people's private lives have brought the issue centre-stage once more.

5.3 What to Protect?

It is relatively easy to identify specific facets of a right to privacy but extremely difficult to define the scope and contours of the right. The problem of definition has occupied jurists for decades. The Warren and Brandeis concept of the "right to be let alone", captures the idea of a zone of privacy but is perhaps too broad and simplistic to aid definition. As members of a community network, people cannot be completely isolated, yet the more intrusive the network and media spotlight become, the greater the need for a recognised retreat or zone of privacy in people's lives. A more modern approach to the problem is encapsulated, therefore, in the concept of the right to freedom from "unwarranted" or "unjustified" intrusion. The use of the word "unwarranted" takes account of the realities of a complex information society, where some degree of intrusion is inevitable, and of advances in the technology of

---

[7] *Anna Ford v Press Complaints Commission* [2001] E.W.H.C. Admin 683. Other high profile complainants include the Beckhams, who were granted an injunction preventing the *Mirror* from publishing photographs of their new home: *David and Victoria Beckham v MGN* (unreported, 2001).

[8] *Campbell v MGN Ltd* (2002) H.R.L.R. 28, [2002] E.W.C.A. Civ. 1373. The Court of Appeal found that the publication was justified in the public interest. Costs, which will have to be paid by the plaintiff, are estimated at £750,000: *The Irish Times*, May 3, 2002, October 15, 2002. Linda Clarke, "Privacy, breach of confidence and the press: where are we now?" (2002) 7 *Communications Law* 78, considers this and related cases.

[9] See *Report of the Commission on the Newspaper Industry*, (Pn 2841, The Stationery Office, Dublin, 1996), at para.7.21, and generally the Law Reform Commission, *Consultation Paper* (1996) and *Report on Privacy: Surveillance and the Interception of Communications Privacy* (LRC, Dublin, 57–1998).

[10] Warren and Brandeis, "The Right to Privacy" 4 Harv. L.R. 193 (1890).

communication, where the opportunities for intrusion are endless. For example, in the telephone tapping case, *Kennedy and Arnold v Ireland*,[11] the President of the High Court upheld the journalists' constitutional right to privacy in respect of their telephone conversations. He pointed out, however, that inadvertent interference from time to time had to be endured as an inevitable incidence of telephonic technology.[12] Recognising that some intrusion is inevitable, the Council of Europe has spoken of "the right to live one's own life with a minimum of interference"[13] but has also said that in view of "the new communication technologies, which make it possible to store and use personal data, the right to control one's own data should be added to this definition".[14]

In the internet age, when technology has advanced to the stage where all kinds of personal data can be collected and distributed instantaneously and globally, even via a mobile phone, absolute privacy cannot be guaranteed by law and a precise legal definition of privacy is exceedingly difficult to achieve. Attempts to date have tended to focus on either the *methods* used to obtain information on people's private lives – deception, eavesdropping, "bugging" and the use of technological devices[15] – or on the *form* of intrusion – publishing embarrassing private facts or pictures,[16] intruding into grief and benefiting commercially from using a person's public attributes or persona.

In the US for example, Professor Prosser[17] disagreed with Warren and Brandeis about the existence of a general right to privacy in American law and instead identified four separate privacy-based torts, which he said the law protected:

(a) intrusion into another's seclusion

(b) appropriation of another's image or person for trade or commercial purposes

---

[11] [1987] I.R. 587, [1988] I.L.R.M. 472.

[12] *Cf.* the argument advanced by Eamonn Hall, *The Electronic Age: Telecommunication in Ireland* (Oak Tree Press, Dublin, 1993), at p.429, that constitutional guarantees "should not be shackled on mere technological grounds".

[13] Resolution 428(1970) of the Consultative (Parliamentary) Assembly of the Council of Europe. The resolution then went on to identify certain aspects of the right: private, home and family life, physical and moral integrity, honour and reputation, avoidance of being placed in a false light, non-revelation of irrelevant or embarrassing facts, unauthorised publication of private photographs, protection from disclosure of information given or received by the individual confidentially.

[14] "Right to Privacy", Resolution 1165 (1998) of the Parliamentary Assembly. The Assembly states that the rights to privacy and to freedom of expression are neither absolute nor in any hierarchical order, since they are of equal value (para.11).

[15] For the position in the United States, see Michael W. Richards, "Tort Vision for the New Millennium: Strengthening News Industry Standards as a Defense Tool in Law Suits over Newsgathering Techniques" (2000) 10 Fordham Intell.Prop., Media & Ent.L.J. 501.

[16] For an account of the ECHR case law on the taking and use of pictures, see S.H. Naismith, "Photographs, Privacy and Freedom of Expression" [1996] E.H.R.L.R. 150.

[17] Dean Prosser, "Privacy" 45 Calif. L. Rev. 383 (1960), discussed in Diane Zimmerman, "Requiem for a Heavyweight: A Farewell to Warren and Brandeis's Privacy Tort" 68 Corn. L.R. 291, in Raymond Wacks (ed.), *Privacy* (Vol. 2, Dartmouth, Aldershot, 1993).

(c) portrayal of another in a false light (knowingly or recklessly) and

(d) publication of private facts.

However his analysis, too, is problematic. The first two of these torts are concerned with property or financial interests and are not aimed particularly at the media. The third, false light, involves portraying someone as a different kind of person than s/he is. It may be to ascribe to the person a characteristic or view that s/he does not hold and finds offensive. False light is closely linked to defamation but goes beyond it in encompassing false but non-defamatory statements as well as false and defamatory statements. By encompassing statements that are not defamatory, it imposes a heavy burden on the media in terms of detecting the problem. The fourth tort, insofar as it protects true facts lawfully obtained, is susceptible to attack on constitutional grounds, given the strong commitment to freedom of the press in the First Amendment to the US Constitution. In fact, the case law has narrowed considerably the scope of the tort and only state interests of the highest order will warrant imposing liability on the media.[18]

In Britain the former Press Council, a self-regulatory, non-statutory body, established in 1953, attempted to delimit privacy in its Declaration of Principle on Privacy 1976[19] and in its Code of Practice 1990. The Council was replaced by the Press Complaints Commission, which operates a code of practice, drawn up by and subscribed to by editors. On the issue of privacy, Article 3 of the Code says:

> "(i) Everyone is entitled to respect for his or her private and family life, home, health and correspondence. A publication will be expected to justify intrusions into any individual's private life without consent.
> (ii) The use of long-lens photography to take pictures of people in private places without their consent is unacceptable.
>
> *Note* – Private places are public or private property where there is a reasonable expectation of privacy".

---

[18] See Robert C. Post, "The Social Foundations of Privacy: Community and Self in the Common Law Tort" (1989) 77 Calif. L.R. 957; Harvey L. Zuckman, "The American Torts of Invasion of Privacy" [1990] 5 ENT. L.R. 173. In most cases involving the four privacy torts, the standard is reasonableness: whether the invasion is unreasonable. See, for example, "Privacy, Technology, and the California 'Anti-Paparazzi' Statute" (1999) 112 *Harvard Law Review*, No.6, 1367–1384. The Irish LRC voiced difficulties with the reasonableness standard but did embrace the concept of a "reasonable expectation" of privacy (*Report*, above, n.9, at paras 2.10–2.23). The four torts are also "personal" in the sense that they only apply to living persons, although some states in the US have statutes that provide for the survival of privacy tort actions, see, for example, Cal. Civ. Code para.3344.1 (West, 2000).

[19] See Noel Paul, *Principles for the Press* (The Press Council, London, 1985), at p.183; Code of Practice, March 15, 1990; see News Section [1990] 2 ENT. L.R., E–30; The Press Council, *The Press and the People* (The Press Council, London, 1984), Chap.7, p.290, at p.291. The Declaration stressed that the public interest involved must be a "legitimate and proper public interest and not only a prurient or morbid curiosity".

The code was amended and the privacy provisions strengthened following the death of Princess Diana in 1997, when attention focused on the intrusive role of the "paparazzi", freelance photographers who pursue celebrities. The code also has articles on harassment by journalists and photographers; intrusion into grief or shock; children; children in sex cases; listening devices and hospitals.[20]

5.4 TOWARDS A LEGAL DEFINITION OF PRIVACY

It is generally accepted that there is a core and penumbra of privacy, but there has been little consensus on actual content, how to determine that content, what objectives to follow and indeed the value or values to be protected. Should concern lie with the effects of the intrusion on the individual concerned or on the readership or audience? Is it the embarrassment and hurt to the victim or the sense of outrage and offensiveness felt by the audience that is to be addressed?[21] Are privacy and public decency separate issues or are they aspects of the same sense of moral values? For instance, experience in Ireland has shown that complaints of invasion of privacy against the media are few and do not come from the victim. Occasionally they come from relatives and friends, but most often they come from unconnected third parties.[22] These third parties express rage and outrage at what they perceive to be the consequences of the publication or broadcast for the individual concerned. They speak of falling standards in Irish journalism and bemoan the way the media portray aspects of Irish life by covering subjects that they, the readers or viewers, believe should not be aired in public. Is it possible then that what is talked about under the umbrella of privacy is in fact two separate issues: (a) the right to individual privacy and (ii) the preservation of public morals and ethical standards? The two are related but separate issues. Privacy considerations in this chapter will therefore be confined to the effect on the individual, that is, individual privacy. (The public morals aspect will be discussed in Chapter 9.)

5.4.1 The Right to Individual Privacy

When speaking of individual privacy, further questions need to be addressed. For instance, should a distinction be made between the *neutral* concept of

---

[20] The full text of the code is available at *www.pcc.org.uk*. The National Newspapers of Ireland (NNI) also have a code specifically on privacy dating from 1997, details at *www.nni.ie*. The NUJ Code also has provisions on privacy, details at *www.nuj.org.uk* or *http://indigo.ie/~nujdub*.

[21] Post (above, n.18, at 958), citing Thomas Emerson, "The Right of Privacy and Freedom of the Press" (1979) 14 Harv. C.R.–C.L. Rev. 329, 333, and case law: the tort of invasion of privacy is usually said to be protecting the "subjective" interests of individuals against "injury to the inner person" and its stated purpose is to provide redress for injury to a plaintiff's emotions and mental suffering. An intrusion on privacy is intrinsically harmful because it is defined as that which injures social personality (Post, at p.964).

[22] See Kevin Boyle and Marie McGonagle, *Media Accountability: The Readers' Representative in Irish Newspapers* (NNI, Dublin, 1995), at p.27.

privacy (*i.e.* that the publication of private facts is wrong whether they are true or false, bad or good; it is the very publication of them that is wrong, not their character) and the *moral* concept of personal dignity (*i.e.* that only those facts that adversely affect a person's dignity are worthy of protection)? If the moral concept is to be adopted, is the appropriate test a subjective or objective one?

 In the search for a theoretical basis for privacy, many theses and analyses have been advanced.[23] Some focus on the functions of privacy and the interests it protects. From these, it can be said that the core of privacy is intimacy,[24] the intimate nature of certain details, activities, ideas or emotions that people generally do not want to share with others or only with close family members or friends. Such a core of intimacy would embrace family life, home, correspondence, telephone conversations, and sexual relations. In this context, the reporting of intimate details in family law cases could be restricted, for example.

Other facets of the intimacy element of privacy would fall to the courts to determine in accordance with contemporary norms and standards, in an approach similar to that adopted by the European Court of Human Rights (discussed later in this chapter). A defence of public interest could apply,[25] and the public/private divide that has found favour with the US Supreme Court and European Court of Human Rights could also be accommodated – that is, a public person would still be entitled to protection against publication of the intimate details of family life that did not impinge on his/her public functions.[26] Following Professor Gerety's analysis, intimacy is the core of the right to privacy but at least two other functions of privacy are also deserving of protection: first, autonomy – keeping control of one's destiny – and second, identity – allowing a person to develop his/her own potential as an individual. This is where false light, copyright, and similar issues fit into the overall concept of privacy, even though they are closely related to property rights. For Post,[27] the core is human dignity and the harm is loss of respect needed for social life (civility).

The concept of privacy is gradually becoming clearer but the problem of legal definition remains unresolved. However, that should not operate as a barrier to effective protection of privacy. After all, defamation has not been defined either in Irish law; there is no statutory definition of defamation, only

[23] See Thomas Emerson, above, n.21; Frederick E. Schauer, "Reflections on the Value of Truth", in Raymond Wacks, above, n.17, at p.407; Eoin O'Dell, "When Two Tribes Go to War: Privacy Interests and Media Speech", in McGonagle (ed.), *Law and the Media* (Round Hall Sweet & Maxwell, Dublin, 1997), p.181. For theories of privacy as a personal, moral and social value and its application to cyberspace, see Katrin Schatz Byford, "Privacy in Cyberspace: Constructing a Model of Privacy for the Electronic Communications Environment" [1998] 24 *Rutgers Computer and Technology Law Journal* 1.

[24] See Tom Gerety, "Redefining Privacy" (1977) 12 Harv. C.R.-C.L. Rev. 233, cited in Emerson, above, n.21, at p.338.

[25] Most European jurisdictions have a public interest defence, the notable exception being France: see ARTICLE 19, *Press Law and Practice* (ARTICLE 19, London, 1993), at p.67.

[26] See, for example, the Report of the Newspaper Commission 1996, paras 7.13–7.16.

[27] Post, above, n.18.

the dicta of individual judges in court cases. Privacy, however, presents another difficulty: to find an appropriate remedy for invasion of privacy. Damages can only compensate after the event when the harm has already been done.[28] Retractions and corrections are likely to be of little help. They can minimise the harm done in defamation cases, where the offending statement is shown or admitted to be false; but in privacy cases, the details are likely to be true, otherwise the defamation remedy would be available. Injunctions, too, are of limited value. They pose dangers to the freedom of the press from prior restraint and can only be sought when it is known that private facts are to be published. Non-legal bodies such as press councils have proven largely ineffective in protecting or defending privacy. There are few, if any, sanctions that they can apply, apart from censuring the publication concerned and having that censure carried in the media.

5.4.2 What Is the Legal Basis for the Right?

5.4.2.1 The Constitution

In Ireland it has been accepted by the courts that the Constitution does recognise the right to privacy, even though that right is not spelt out in the text.[29] It remains, therefore, for the courts to identify the right and particular aspects of it, as they did in the *McGee* case[30] in respect of marital privacy and in *Kennedy and Arnold v Ireland*[31] in respect of telephone conversations. In *Kennedy*, the private telephones of two journalists working as political correspondents with two national newspapers were tapped by order of the Minister for Justice. The court declared the right to privacy to be one of the personal, unspecified rights contained in Article 40.3 of the Constitution. It is not an absolute right and can be restricted in the interests of public order, morality and the common good:

> "The nature of the right to privacy must be such as to ensure the dignity and freedom of an individual in the type of society envisaged by the Constitution, namely, a sovereign, independent and democratic society".[32]

In an earlier case, *AG v Norris*,[33] which concerned the rights of homosexuals

---

[28] For Post, above, n.18, the harm is intrinsic and damages are meant to reaffirm the plaintiff as a member of the community from which the show of disrespect has excluded him or her.

[29] Art.40.3.2. The US Constitution does not contain the word "privacy" either but does protect the right implicitly: the Fourth Amendment guarantees individuals the right to be secure in their persons, houses, papers, and effects against unreasonable searches and seizures. The Ninth Amendment, which protects unenumerated rights, has also been invoked to acknowledge the right to privacy and its importance to individual dignity and autonomy. The California Constitution on the other hand specifically guarantees an "inalienable right to privacy". See generally (Note), "Privacy, Photography and the Press" (1998) 111 Harv. L. Rev. 1086.

[30] *McGee v Attorney General* [1974] I.R. 284.

[31] Above, n.11. Journalist Vincent Browne was later awarded £95,000 in an out-of-court settlement for the tapping of his telephone as far back as 1975.

[32] *ibid.* at 593 and 477 respectively *per* Hamilton P.

[33] [1984] I.R. 36.

not to have their private behaviour criminalised, Henchy J. identified the right
to privacy that "inheres in each citizen by virtue of his human personality".
The right to privacy, he said, is

> "a complex of rights, varying in nature, purpose and range, each
> necessarily a facet of the citizen's core of individuality within the
> constitutional order. ... Other aspects of the right ... [have] yet to be
> given judicial recognition. ... It is sufficient to say that they would all
> appear to fall within a secluded area of activity or non-activity which
> may be claimed as necessary for the expression of an individual
> personality, for purposes not always moral or commendable, but meriting
> recognition in circumstances which do not endanger considerations such
> as state security, public order or morality, or other essential components
> of the common good".[34]

There have been few cases as yet in this jurisdiction in respect of privacy as a
restriction on media reporting,[35] other than in the context of court reporting
and the reporting of tribunals (see discussion in Chapter 7). The freedom of
expression clause, Article 40.6.1.i, does not specifically mention privacy as a
restriction on the freedom of the press. That is not to say that such a restriction
does not exist, but it does point to the need to preserve freedom of the press
and not undermine it by according undue weight and scope to the restrictions
on it.

This issue arose in *Maguire v Drury*,[36] where a woman sought an injunction
to prevent further publication concerning her alleged affair with a Catholic
priest on the grounds that such publication would infringe her constitutional
right to privacy. O'Hanlon J. in the High Court decided, *inter alia*:

(a) that the case did not concern the intimacies of married life or marital
    communications but rather the husband's allegations of an extra-marital
    affair,

---

[34] *ibid.* at 71–72 (Henchy J. dissenting). Privacy as a constitutional right is a personal right
of living persons only, not of the dead or of institutions: see, *inter alia, Hilliard v Phoenix*
(Chap.8 below), and see also *The Irish Times*, July 31, 2002, regarding the advice of the
Attorney General to the Laffoy Commission that the names of dead people identified as
child abusers could be published.

[35] In *NIB v RTÉ* [1998] 2 I.R. 465; [1998] 2 I.L.R.M. 196, the Supreme Court considered
the right of bank clients to privacy or confidentiality in their dealings with banks. It held
that freedom of expression should prevail because of the public interest in exposing
wrongdoing. Research has shown that very few complaints of invasion of privacy are
made against the Irish media: see above, n.22, and the annual reports of the Broadcasting
Complaints Commission. However, in relation to the printed press, there have been
several high profile cases in recent years, where intrusion on privacy has been an issue.
In the absence of a press council or press ombudsman in Ireland to whom a formal
complaint could be made, there was extensive media discussion of press ethics in such
situations. See, for example, Damien Kiberd "The Impact of Law and Ethics on the
Practice of Journalism in Ireland" in Eoin Cassidy & Andrew G. McGrady (eds), *Media
and the Marketplace – Ethical Perspectives* (IPA, Dublin, 2001), p.154.

[36] [1995] I.L.R.M. 108.

(b) that other remedies, such as libel, were available in appropriate circumstances to deal with such a situation and

(c) that freedom of the press should not be curtailed merely to avoid the distress caused by publication of matters which show up a parent in a sordid or unfavourable light.[37]

In any event, maximum publicity had already been given to the husband's version of events, and the ultimate decision was likely to be that it was quite lawful to publish, in which case, an injunction, if granted, would encroach in a significant manner on the freedom of the press.

5.4.2.2 The European Convention on Human Rights

Article 8 of the European Convention on Human Rights states:

> "1. Everyone has the right to respect for his private and family life, his home and his correspondence.
>
> 2. There shall be no interference by a public authority with the exercise of this right except such as is in accordance with the law and is necessary in a democratic society in the interests of national security, public safety or the economic well-being of the country, for the prevention of disorder or crime, for the protection of health or morals, or for the protection of the rights and freedoms of others".

The Convention protects both freedom of expression (Article 10) and privacy (Article 8). Within their respective articles, freedom of expression and privacy are the core values, which may only be restricted to the extent necessary in a democratic society in support of certain specified interests. However, it is not altogether clear which right would prevail if, for example, an individual complained that legislation or a court decision giving priority to freedom of expression breached his/her right to privacy under the Convention. To date, no case has arisen where a conflict between the two has been contested before the court, although several decisions have been taken at Commission level.

In *N v Portugal*,[38] the Commission held that there was no violation of Article 10 when a magazine publisher was convicted of defamation and invasion of privacy for publication of a number of photographs of a well-known businessman engaging in sexual activities with a variety of young women. In *Spencer v UK*,[39] a case concerning the brother and sister-in-law of Princess Diana, the Commission would not exclude the possibility that the absence of an actionable remedy, in relation to the publications of which the applicants

---

[37] *ibid.* at 113–5. On the interaction of privacy and freedom of expression see the views of Stefan Walz, cited in FGB Aldhouse, "Data protection, privacy and the media" (1999) 4 *Communications Law* 8, at pp.11–12.

[38] App. No.20683/92, decision of February 20, 1995. See also *Winer v UK*, App. No.10871/84, decision of July 10, 1986, re private matters revealed in a book, where a defamation action was considered sufficient.

[39] App. No.28852/95 (1998) 25 E.H.R.R. C.D. 105.

complained, could show a lack of respect for their private lives. In that respect it would have regard to the duties and responsibilities that go with the right to freedom of expression in Article 10 of the Convention, and to the obligation on contracting states under Article 8 to provide a measure of protection for the right to privacy of an individual affected by others' exercise of their freedom of expression (at 112). The issues were not teased out, however, as the complainants were found not to have exhausted their domestic remedies, since they could have taken an action for breach of confidence in the English courts (at 117–8).

The English courts have begun to address the privacy issue under the Human Rights Act 1998, which enables them to apply the European Convention on Human Rights principles. In *Theakston v MGN Ltd*,[40] the court decided, *inter alia*, that a brothel was not a private place and that the relationship between a prostitute and a client was not one of confidentiality. The court granted an injunction prohibiting the publication of photographs taken in the brothel without the plaintiff's consent, but allowed the publication of the story. In *Venables and Thompson v News Group Ltd*,[41] the case involving the two boys convicted of the murder of toddler Jamie Bulger, the courts granted injunctions preventing media identification and providing for new identities for the boys, who were now young adults and about to be released. In that case, there was deemed to be a real and serious risk of revenge attacks and therefore the right to life took precedence over the rights of the media.

It should be noted, however, that while Article 8(2) refers to interference by a "public authority" only and does not mention the media, the European Court of Human Rights has accepted that the State could have positive obligations under Article 8(2).[42] It has also been emphasised that in cases involving the mass media, Article 10 must be taken into account.[43] Article 10(2) does not expressly mention privacy as a ground for restricting freedom of the press, although it does refer to "the rights of others" and to the disclosure of information received in confidence. Most countries that protect privacy allow a public interest defence, so that if it can be shown that there was a

---

[40] [2002] E.M.L.R. 22. In *A v B plc* [2002] 2 All E.R. 545, concerning details of a married footballer's affair, the Court of Appeal in Britain set out guidelines as to how in future cases the line should be drawn between an individual's right to privacy and the competing right to freedom of expression: see (2002) 7 *Communications Law* 63–5.

[41] [2001] 2 W.L.R. 1038. The *Manchester Evening News* subsequently breached the injunction, though not intentionally. The President of the Family Division of the High Court (December 4, 2001) found the newspaper to be in contempt of court, fined the publisher £30,000 and ordered it to pay £120,000 in costs. *Cf.* child killer Mary Bell [2003] E.W.H.C. 1101, May 21, 2003.

[42] *e.g. X and Y v The Netherlands*, Series A, No.91, judgment of March 26, 1985. On the horizontal effect of Art.8 (that is, its application to private parties such as the press), see also the Parliamentary Assembly of the Council of Europe (Resolution 1165 (1998)) para.12: ECHR, Art.8 "should not only protect an individual against interference by public authorities, but also against interference by private persons or institutions, including the mass media", and see the view of the English court in *Douglas v Hello! Magazine* [2001] 2 W.L.R. 992.

[43] *e.g. N v Sweden*, App. No.11366/85, decision of October 16, 1986.

public interest involved in revealing the private information, there will be no liability in law.[44]

5.5 WHAT PROTECTION IS THERE AT PRESENT?

5.5.1 Person and Property

In Ireland, little or no attempt has been made to define privacy, particularly as regards the media. It is accepted that the Constitution protects it as a right but the common law is characterised by its fragmented approach and provides little in the way of systematic privacy protection. Tort law could be said to offer incidental or haphazard protection at best, and is notable for its gaps, particularly the lack of a specific tort of breach of privacy.[45] Incidental protection may be offered in certain situations by the torts of trespass to person, land or goods and the tort of nuisance. They can provide a remedy, for example, in the case of unwanted telephone calls, persistent harassment or use of surveillance equipment. For instance, Jeremiah Locke, the man at the centre of the Kerry Babies case in 1985,[46] took an action against two ITN reporters who, he claimed, had been harassing him, calling at his home, telephoning him incessantly, and shouting through the letter-box. His tort action for trespass and nuisance yielded damages of £100. He also obtained an injunction restraining the journalists from entering his property and watching or besetting him.[47] In *Thomas v Independent Newspapers*,[48] the plaintiff (a young boy), whose name and address were published in the newspaper as a witness to a bank robbery, sued unsuccessfully for the tort of intentional infliction of emotional suffering. This is a tort that the courts created in order to address a particular situation[49] and have been very reluctant to develop it to meet what are in effect defamation or privacy situations.[50]

---

[44] For the protection of privacy in other countries, see ARTICLE 19, *Press Law and Practice* (above, n.25), and *The ARTICLE 19 Freedom of Expression Handbook* (London, 1993), pp.162–4; *Report of the Committee on Privacy and Related Matters* (Calcutt Report, Cmnd. 1102, HMSO, London, 1990) Chap.5, and LRC, above, n.9, *Paper*, at pp.192–7, *Report*, at pp.82–100.

[45] See Bryan McMahon and William Binchy, *Irish Law of Torts* (3rd ed., Butterworths, Dublin, 2000). See also reference to privacy in the "territorial" sense in Paul Gallagher, "Tribunals and the Erosion of the Right to Privacy" (1999) B.R. 406.

[46] *The Irish Times*, October 31, 1985.

[47] An injunction for the same pupose was granted in the case of a Cork doctor (*The Irish Times*, March 5, 1996) but lifted a few days later. The right to privacy was not absolute; publicity might be uncomfortable or unpleasant for Dr Barry but there was no evidence to support a continuing injunction and there was also a danger that the effect of granting it would be to suppress reportage.

[48] *The Irish Times*, July 26, 1988.

[49] *Wilkinson v Downton* [1897] 2 Q.B. 57.

[50] See *Hustler Magazine Inc. & Flint v Falwell* 485 U.S. 46 (1988), a case concerning a cartoon that depicted a politician in a very unfavourable light.

5.5.2 Confidentiality

The Courts of Equity in Britain developed an action for breach of confidence to fill a gap in the common-law protection. However, until recently, its use has been confined mostly to commercial or national security situations. It was relied upon in *Spycatcher*[51] in an attempt to restrain a former member of the Secret Service from revealing in his memoirs details of the Service's operations. The action is more in the nature of a disciplinary measure. The concern in *Spycatcher*, for example, was to discourage civil servants from breaching their contract of employment with the government, which required them to be bound by the Official Secrets Act. At stake in such cases is not the right to personal or individual privacy but rather state secrecy *versus* the public interest in disclosure. In confidence cases generally, it is the breach of the obligation of confidence which is at the heart of the matter, rather than breach of privacy as such, which often arises in the absence of any such obligation.

The use of an action for breach of confidentiality as a remedy for invasion of individual privacy by the media arose in *Spencer v UK*.[52] The case concerned the publication of articles regarding the admission to a clinic of Princess Diana's sister-in-law. The European Commission of Human Rights found that the breach of confidence remedy was available and should have been sought in the English courts before a complaint was taken to Strasbourg. In other words, the complainants had not exhausted their domestic remedies and therefore their complaint was inadmissible. Confidentiality also arose in a number of other cases, including the decisions in *Douglas v Hello!*[53] and in *Venables and Thompson v News Group Ltd*.[54]

Breach of confidence (along with negligence, breach of contract, and privacy) as a remedy for invasion of individual privacy by the media, was relied on in a Dublin High Court action taken by a former swimmer, who was interviewed in a BBC radio programme broadcast in 1995. The programme dealt with allegations of child sexual abuse perpetrated by a former coach. The swimmer, who claimed to have been a victim, had agreed to be interviewed following assurances that his identity would not be revealed. When his identity was revealed, liability was admitted by the BBC and the only issue for the

---

[51] *The Observer and the Guardian v UK*, Series A, No.216; (1992) 14 E.H.R.R. 153.

[52] Above, n.39. For the views of various law reform bodies on the distinction and relationship between confidentiality and privacy, and particularly the argument that the law of confidence should not be used merely as a peg on which to hang a right of privacy, see above, n.9, LRC, *Paper*, at paras 4.33–4.63.

[53] Above, n.42; Peter Carey, "Hello to Privacy?" [2001] ENT. L.R. 120.

[54] Above, n.41. See also *Creation Records Ltd v News Group Newspapers Ltd* [1997] E.M.L.R. 444, where an injunction was granted to prevent publication of photographs taken during a photo shoot for the cover of a new record by the rock group Oasis; *Mills v Newsgroup Newspapers Ltd* (High Court, June 4, 2001), where an injunction was refused in light of the fact that the plaintiff had courted publicity over the years and because there was no apprehended harm to her; *A v B plc* (above, n.40), where an injunction was granted restraining publication of details of a sexual relationship between a married professional footballer and two other women, as this was an area of private life and there was no public interest. See discussion in Patrick Leonard, "Recent Developments in Privacy and Breach of Confidence" (2001) 7 B.R. 102.

court was the assessment of damages. An award of £90,500 was made. The harm caused was of a psychological and emotional nature.[55]

Protection of confidentiality has arisen in Ireland in a number of other spheres. For example, in *AG for England and Wales v Brandon Book Publishers Ltd*,[56] an injunction was refused by Carroll J. in the High Court. The material contained in the book *One Girl's War*, about the activities of MI5 some 40 years earlier, did not pose any threat to the authority of the Irish State, which under our Constitution was the only justifiable reason for restricting freedom of expression in such a case. In 1992, however, the Supreme Court, by a majority, held in favour of Cabinet confidentiality, by analogy with the constitutional immunity from suit for any statement made in either House of the Oireachtas:

> "[Cabinet confidentiality] extends to discussions and to their contents but it does not of course extend to the decisions made and the documentary evidence of them. ... It is a constitutional right ... which goes to the fundamental machinery of government, and is, therefore, not capable of being waived by any individual member of a government, nor ... are the details and contents of discussions at meetings of the government capable of being made public ... by a decision of any succeeding government".[57]

In a dissenting judgment, McCarthy J. expressed the view that freedom of government discussion did not require an absolute constitutional right of confidentiality and that any defamatory statements made in the course of discussion would attract qualified privilege unless they were made maliciously, in which case they should be actionable.[58] The implications of the Supreme Court's decision gave rise to concern but the Government decided to hold a referendum to amend the Constitution, rather than having the matter examined by the Commission established in 1995 to review the Constitution. A more proportionate measure, it is submitted, was the provision to allow information to be refused on the basis of cabinet confidentiality, which was inserted in the Freedom of Information Act 1997 (see chapter 10 below).

In *ACC v Irish Business*,[59] an injunction was granted to prevent publication on the basis of breach of confidence and copyright. Likewise, in *The Council of the Bar of Ireland v Sunday Business Post*,[60] a temporary injunction was granted on grounds of breach of confidence to prevent publication of a letter

---

[55] *FW v BBC* (*The Irish Times*, March 19, 20, 26, 1999).

[56] [1986] I.R. 597; [1987] I.L.R.M. 135.

[57] *AG v Hamilton (No.1)* [1993] 2 I.R 250, [1993] I.L.R.M. 81, Finlay C.J. at 100.

[58] *ibid.*, McCarthy J. at 275–92; 103–117. In a defamation case being taken by Irish Press Publications against the State, arising out of a press release issued on October 24, 1996 by or on behalf of Minister for Enterprise and Development, Richard Bruton, certain documents sought by them were found by Carroll J. to be covered by cabinet confidentiality: *Irish Press Publications Ltd v Minister for Enterprise and Employment* [2002] I.E.H.C. 104, October 15, 2002, available at *www.irlii.org*. The case is proceeding nonetheless (*The Sunday Times*, November 10, 2002).

[59] *The Irish Times*, August 9, 1985.

[60] Unreported, High Court, March 30, 1993.

and statement submitted to the Council's inquiry into the conduct of a barrister. The documents were said to contain information of a sensitive and private nature. The presiding judge accepted that publication could lead to irreparable damage to the Council and its system of investigation of professional misconduct. In that regard, he was protecting the system, rather than individual privacy as such. The disciplinary inquiry had been held *in camera* and a rule of the Professional Practices Committee required absolute confidentiality.[61]

However, absolute rules of that nature may be open to scrutiny on constitutional grounds. A more nuanced approach, which examined both the constitutional imperatives and the approach of the European Convention on Human Rights, was adopted in *Barry v Medical Council*.[62] The case concerned a doctor who was facing a disciplinary inquiry and wished to have the proceedings conducted in public. The terms of the Medical Practitioners Act 1978 were such that, in the courts' view, the Fitness to Practice Committee had a discretion to hold the hearing in private or in public. Barrington J. for the Supreme Court emphasised that the case only concerned the first stage of a three-stage process, which also involved the High Court if a decision was taken to remove the doctor from the register. Reference was made to the case law of the European Court of Human Rights, which had stated in *Diennet v France*:[63] "Lastly, while the need to protect professional confidentiality and the private lives of patients may justify holding proceedings *in camera*, such an occurrence must be strictly required by the circumstances".

The complaints in *Barry* were said by the Supreme Court to raise matters "of the gravest and most intimate nature relating to the private lives of a number of patients". The Committee, therefore, was justified in holding its inquiry in private.[64]

In *NIB v RTÉ*,[65] the Supreme Court in a majority decision affirmed an order of the High Court discharging an injunction against RTÉ. RTÉ had obtained information about certain bank accounts apparently used to evade tax. The Court acknowledged the public interest in the maintenance of confidentiality between banker and customer, on the one hand. On the other hand, there is also a public interest in defeating wrongdoing and where the publication of confidential information may be of assistance in defeating wrongdoing then "the public interest in such information may outweigh the public interest in the maintenance of confidentiality".[66] In such circumstances, the information should be furnished to the authorities, especially if sought by them. However, since the allegation was one of serious tax evasion, this was a matter of genuine interest and importance to the general public, especially the vast majority who are law-abiding tax payers, and therefore it was in the public

---

[61] *The Irish Times*, March 6, 1993.

[62] [1998] 3 I.R. 368. The judgments of Costello J. in the High Court and of Barrington J. in the Supreme Court are both instructive.

[63] (1995) 21 E.H.R.R. 554, at 567, para.34.

[64] See also *EHB v The Fitness to Practise Committee of the Medical Council and Dr Moira Woods* [1998] I.R. 399. For other relevant cases, though not directly concerning the media, see Gallagher, above, n.45, at pp.407–412.

[65] Above, n.35.

[66] *ibid.*, Lynch J., at 494, I.L.R.M. at 204.

interest that the general public should be given this information.[67] Apart from warning RTÉ of the possibilities of a serious libel if it published the names of innocent account-holders, the Court held in favour of publication.[68]

A few months later the issue of whether the constitutional right to privacy extended to the confidentiality of an individual's banking transactions was addressed by the Supreme Court in *Haughey and others v Moriarty and others*.[69] The case arose out of a challenge to the Moriarty Tribunal of Inquiry, established by government in accordance with the Tribunal of Inquiry (Evidence) Acts 1921–1997. The Court accepted that encroachment on the right to privacy could be justified by the exigencies of the common good but only to the extent necessary for the proper conduct of the inquiry. Fair procedures were therefore important, particularly the giving of notice and an opportunity to make representations.[70]

Another aspect of confidentiality of direct interest to the media is the confidentiality that relates to journalists' sources. That issue is considered in detail in Chapter 6.

5.5.3 Copyright

The law of copyright is not primarily concerned with privacy but rather with property rights in one's creative work. It can, however, operate incidentally to protect privacy or provide a remedy for its breach. It can, for example, protect against the unauthorised use of a photograph.[71] It was the remedy relied on when nude photographs of Belfast's Lord Mayor and his girlfriend were published in the *Sunday World* and the *Star*.[72] In the Irish courts, Carroll J.

---

[67] *ibid.* at 495; I.L.R.M. at 205.

[68] *ibid.* at 495; I.L.R.M. at 205. See also the dissenting judgment of Keane J., with whom Hamilton C.J. concurred. The essential issue, he said, was whether RTÉ had established a public interest in the disclosure of the information which outweighs the public interest in confidentiality and, if so, the extent of the disclosure which is legitimate. Since some of the account-holders might be innocent of any wrongdoing, RTÉ should be confined to disclosing the information to the Revenue Commissioners, save in certain listed circumstances. See, generally, Paul Lavery, *Commercial Secrets: the Action for Breach of Confidence in Ireland* (Round Hall Sweet & Maxwell, Dublin, 1996).

[69] Case No.103/98, July 28, 1998.

[70] *Cf. Redmond v The Sole Member (Flood Tribunal)*, unreported, Supreme Court, January 6, 1999 (*The Irish Times*, January 7, 1999). The Supreme Court held unanimously that the exigencies of the common good, when such inquiries are necessary to preserve the purity and integrity of public life, outweighed the constitutional right to privacy. The tribunal had not exceeded its jurisdiction or failed to observe fair procedures. See Louis Blom-Cooper, "The role and functions of Tribunals of Inquiry – an Irish perspective" [1999] P.L. 175; Gallagher, above, n.45.

[71] See, for example, above, n.5, Chap.9. See also *Krone Verlag Gmbh & Co.KG v Austria*, App. No.34315/96, Chamber Judgment, February 26, 2002, where use of the Copyright Act in Austria to restrain publication of a photograph of a politician in connection with an article on his salaries, was held to be a violation of ECHR, Art.10, since the photographs did not disclose any details of his private life.

[72] *Wilson v Sunday World and the Star* (*The Irish Times*, October 10, 2000). The couple claimed that the photographs, taken of them on holiday in France and published in May 1996, had been stolen. A High Court settlement was reached.

accepted in *Brandon Book Publishers*[73] that freedom of expression could be restricted in the interests of copyright or confidential information, although there was no breach of either in the particular case before her.

5.5.4 Legislative Protection

Legislation protects privacy in a number of areas. It imposes restrictions on court reporting in the interests of privacy. These range from family law cases being held *in camera*, to the names of victims of rape and sexual assault being withheld. (For further discussion see Chapter 6.) Section 18 of the Broadcasting Authority Act 1960, as amended by section 3(1)(a) of the Broadcasting Authority (Amendment) Act 1976 and incorporated in the Radio and Television Act 1988, section 9(1)(e), requires broadcasters to ensure that the privacy of the individual is not unreasonably encroached upon. The 1976 Act established the Broadcasting Complaints Commission, with powers to handle complaints concerning, *inter alia*, invasion of privacy. An examination of the Commission's decisions, however, indicates that most complaints concern bias, lack of fairness or impartiality and not privacy. A complaint that did concern privacy was brought by a consultant child psychologist in relation to a programme on child sexual abuse where the children were clearly identifiable and their names given. The decision to uphold the complaint was unanimous.[74] A right of reply for those whose legitimate interests, in particular reputation and good name, have been damaged by incorrect facts, was included in the Broadcasting Act 1990, as required by the EC Television without Frontiers Directive.[75]

The Data Protection Act 1988 gives individuals a right of access to personal information concerning them, where the information is held by agencies on automated systems. They are entitled to have data corrected or erased. The Act also imposes certain obligations on the holders of personal data, including the obligation to register with the Data Protection Commissioner, but it applies to automated systems only, not to manual systems.[76] The Data Protection

---

[73] Above, n.56, at p.602, 137. Various articles in the issues of the *Technology & Entertainment Law Journal* (T.E.L.J., Round Hall Sweet & Maxwell, Dublin) address aspects of privacy, including privacy and intellectual property law. See also Lee A. Bygrave, "The Technologisation of Copyright: Implications for Privacy and Related Interests" [2002] E.I.P.R. 51.

[74] Broadcasting Complaints Commission, Ninth Annual Report, 1987; and Eamonn Hall, above, n.12, p.299. A subsequent complaint by the same complainant was dismissed. He complained that the inclusion in a news item of the fact that a young boy killed while on a train journey had been returning to reform school amounted to an infringement of the boy's right to privacy. The Commission considered the fact that the boy was dead and the question of supervision of children going and coming from State institutions to be relevant factors (Fifteenth Annual Report, 1993–4).

[75] 89/552/EEC, [1989] O.J. L298/23. The amending Directive is 97/36/EC [1997] O.J. L202/60.

[76] The Freedom of Information Act 1997 provides for access to "records" containing personal information held by public bodies, whether on automated or manual systems (Chap.10 below). The Data Protection Regulations introduced in April 2002 provide that transfers of data to countries outside the EEA cannot take place unless one of a number of clear conditions designed to protect people's privacy rights are met. These include: approved contractual safeguards, the clear consent of data subjects, or the

(Amendment) Act 2003 will extend the Act to manual data also.[77] The Act was introduced to transpose into Irish law the European Directive on Data Protection (Directive 1995/46). In addition, the EU (Data Protection) Regulations (S.I. No. 626 of 2001), dealing mainly with the transfer of data outside the State, became law in April 2002. The legislation provides for general protection of personal data and is not specifically aimed at the media. It does, however, contain special exemptions for literature, journalism and art.

As a result of developments in data protection, it has been argued that the concept of privacy has shifted from privacy as a civil and political rights issue (motivated by polemic ideology) to a consumer rights issue (underpinned by the principles of data protection and by the law of trading standards), and from an issue of societal power relationships to one of strictly defined legal rights.[78]

Other legislation, such as the Postal and Telecommunications Services Act 1983 and Interception of Postal Packets and Telecommunications Messages (Regulation) Act 1993, has made it an offence to intercept telephone conversations or correspondence, except in specified circumstances.[79] In 1993, a number of print and radio journalists were fined under the Postal and Telecommunications Services Act 1983 for disclosing or using a telephone conversation between prominent politicians which was intercepted illegally by means of a scanning device. Publication had caused the politicians "embar-

---

approval of such a country for such purposes by the EU. The Data Protection Commissioner has said that the new regulations should make life a lot easier for responsible organisations whose business involves the transfer of personal data overseas (*The Irish Times*, January 11, 16, 2002).

[77] See generally, Karen Murray, "The Changing Face of Data Protection" (2002) 7(4) B.R. 2; Robert Clark, *Data Protection Law in Ireland* (The Round Hall Press, Dublin, 1990); Robert Clark, "Data Protection in Ireland" (1996) 1 J.I.L.T. at *www.elj.warwick.ac.uk/ jilt*. Also, European Directive on Data Protection adopted in 1995: Directive on the Protection of Individuals with regard to the Processing of Personal Data and on the Free Movement of such Data, 95/46/EC, [1995] O.J. L281/31. See also the European Convention on the Protection of Individuals with regard to Automatic Processing of Personal Data (ETS 108 and Protocol ETS 181). The main changes to the 1988 Act relate to definitions, new rights for data subjects, new responsibilities for data controllers, new rules regulating the registration process and new powers and functions of the Data Protection Commissioner. The Act includes both automated and manual data. It also contains the right to be informed, improved rights of access, employment rights, the right to object, to block certain uses of data and freedom from automated decision-making. It clarifies or makes firmer the responsibilities related to the handling of personal data and contains special exemptions for journalistic, artistic and literary processing – compare the Data Protection Act 1998 in the UK, and see discussion of same in FGB Aldhouse, above, n.37. Detailed information on both the Regulations and the Act is available on the Data Protection Commissioner's website: *www.dataprivacy.ie*.

[78] Simon G. Davies, "Re-engineering the Right to Privacy: How Privacy Has Been Transformed from a Right to a Commodity", in Philip E. Agre and Marc Rotenberg (eds), *Technology and Privacy: The New Landscape* (The MIT Press, Cambridge, Mass. and London, England, 1997), p.143. In the same book, Robert Gellman, "Does Privacy Law Work?" (at p.194), refers to data protection as "an important subset of privacy law" and observes that privacy law and policy throughout the world have converged around fair information practices.

[79] *The Irish Times*, July 29, 1993. The LRC, above, n.9, deals primarily with surveillance and interception of communications.

rassment", the judge said. Embarrassment is not necessarily the same as invasion of privacy; the real issue is the right to hold telephone conversations in private.

That right has come under threat with the revelation that the Government in April 2002 instructed telecommunications operators to store traffic information about every telephone, mobile, fax, e-mail and internet use for a period of three years. The discussion was covered by Cabinet confidentiality and was only revealed when the Data Protection Commissioner gave details of the instructions. The commissioner favoured the six-month period of retention which he and other European Data Commissioners regard as "adequate and proportionate". "Once privacy rights are surrendered", he said, "they are quite hard to recover".[80] The measures were taken under the Postal and Telecommunications Services Act 1983, but a new Data Retention Bill is in preparation. The justification being advanced for the Bill is that the information is needed by the gardaí for criminal investigations.

5.5.5 Privacy versus Defamation

The embarrassment, hurt or humiliation that a person suffers on the exposure of private personal facts results from the divergence it causes from the image s/he wants to project of himself/ herself.[81] It is this divergence that is the essence of the injury, and therefore it can be caused by the publication of true facts, just as readily as by false statements.

Because the publication of true facts can be just as damaging to a person's privacy as the publication of false facts to his/her reputation, truth is not a defence to a breach of privacy. As Barendt put it: "The whole point of protecting privacy is to keep some information away from public exposure, even if it is true".[82] Nonetheless, there is an overlap and the boundaries between libel and privacy are uncertain. There is a paradox in common law in that defamation is

---

[80] See *The Irish Times*, February 25, 2003, March 14, 2003. The secrecy of the process and the nature and length of the retention put in place in 2002 raise serious questions as to its constitutionality and compatibility with ECHR, Art.8. A recent survey shows that the average length of retention in Europe is 12 months and that Ireland is "way out ahead with 3 years" (*www.statewatch.org/news/2003/jan/12eudatret.htm*). On the issue of data retention at EU level, see Directive 2002/58/EC, [2002] O.J. L201/37 on privacy and electronic communications, amending earlier Directives 97/66/EC and 95/46/EC. See, in particular, Recital 11 (on States carrying out lawful interception of electronic communications: such measures must be appropriate, strictly proportionate to the intended purpose and necessary within a democratic society and should be subject to adequate safeguards in accordance with the ECHR), and Art.15(1), which permits States to restrict the scope of the rights provided for "when such restriction constitutes a necessary, appropriate and proportionate measure within a democratic society to safeguard national security (*i.e.* State security), defence, public security, and the prevention, investigation, detection and prosecution of criminal offences or of unauthorised use of the electronic communication system. ... To this end, Member States may, *inter alia*, adopt legislative measures providing for the retention of data for a limited period justified on the grounds laid down in this paragraph ...". Communication is defined in the Directive to exclude broadcasting, except in the case of identifiable subscribers or users (Article 2(d)).

[81] See above, n.17, Zimmerman.

[82] Eric Barendt, *Freedom of Speech* (Clarendon Press, Oxford, 1989), at p.190.

heavily and systematically protected, while privacy is only accorded incidental protection.[83] As a result, defamation actions sometimes act as a "surrogate for privacy".[84] In addition, current defamation laws apply to both print and broadcast media, while the obligation to respect privacy is a feature of broadcasting legislation (Broadcasting Authority Act 1960, section 18) but has no direct application to the print media. As far as the print media are concerned, privacy is protected only indirectly and incidentally by tort law, although it is also a feature of journalists' codes of ethics.[85]

The European Convention on Human Rights speaks of the right of everyone to respect for his private and family life, home and correspondence (Article 8), while the International Covenant on Civil and Political Rights states that no one shall be subjected to arbitrary or unlawful interference with his privacy, family, home or correspondence, nor to unlawful attacks on his honour and reputation (Article 17). In other words, the Covenant links the rights to privacy and reputation, much as the German Constitution does in its concept of a right to one's dignity and personality *(das Personlichkeitsrecht)* of which the private sphere or zone *(Privatsphäre)* is just one component.[86]

5.5.6 Self-Regulation

Forms of self-regulation, such as press councils and media ombudsmen, have been adopted in many countries, usually as a result of pressure and threats of intervention from government. Press councils, financed by the industry, have existed since the early part of the century (Sweden 1916, Norway 1928, Britain 1953), but many have since disappeared or been replaced.[87] The British Press

---

[83] The reverse is true in France, where photographs taken without consent and the publication of an article about a divorce and liaison were regarded as an invasion of privacy and resulted in an award of FF60,000 and an order to publish the court's findings (unreported, July 5, 1993, C.A., Paris). The French courts will not restrain publication, however, on the basis of a perceived danger of invasion of privacy (Tribunal de Grande Instance de Paris, October 26, 1992). See also Sir Louis Blom-Cooper, "The Right to Be Let Alone" (1989) 10 J.M.L.P. 53, at p.57: "The first thing to do is to acknowledge the imbalance in the one (that is the law of defamation) and then to address the omission in the other (a law of privacy)".

[84] Barendt, "What is the point of libel law?" [1999] 52 *Current Legal Problems* 110 at p.117, where he also (at p.122, n.44) opines that the Elton John case (*John v MGN Ltd* [1996] 3 W.L.R. 593, [1996] 2 All E.R. 35) really concerned an invasion of the plaintiff's privacy.

[85] The NUJ Code of Conduct, for example, and the NNI Code of Privacy (1997). Regarding the broadcast media, see *RTÉ Programme-Makers' Guidelines* (RTÉ, Dublin, 2002), p.15.

[86] The UN Declaration on Human Rights of 1948 said: "No one shall be subjected to arbitrary interference with his privacy, family, home or correspondence, nor to attacks upon his honour and reputation. Everyone has the right to the protection of the law against such interference or attacks" (Art.12).

[87] For example, the National News Council in the United States, established in 1973, ceased to operate in 1984, due to a general lack of acceptance. However, a number of European countries have established forms of complaints mechanisms over the past ten years. Indeed, France and Greece seem to be the only western European countries that have never considered introducing a press council. Some central and eastern European countries now have self-regulatory bodies also. An Alliance of Independent Press Councils of

Council, for example, came under a great deal of criticism for having no teeth and was spurned by tabloid editors. It was replaced in 1991 by the Press Complaints Commission, designed to implement a code of practice drawn up by a committee of editors. Codes of practice have become a popular means of self-regulation and can be useful in providing guidance and standards. They are also media or journalist-driven, rather than government-led or court-led. They often have two main drawbacks, however: their power is mainly moral, in that they do not contain sanctions; and they are often ignored and fall into disuse.

Alternatively, there is a growing practice of co-regulation, between government and media, whereby codes are drafted in accordance with legislation or are given a status in law. In the UK, under section 12(4)(b) of the Human Rights Act 1998, which incorporated the European Convention on Human Rights, the courts must have regard to any relevant privacy code. Likewise, various broadcasting codes and the PCC code have been designated relevant codes for the purposes of the Data Protection Act 1998 under a 1999 Order. The effect of the order is that the codes, which have been observed on a voluntary basis, become in effect enforceable by the courts. Whether that is a desirable development is open to question: it is not that journalists should be entitled to operate above or outside the law, but rather that codes have more to do with ethics than with law and therefore should remain the preserve of journalists themselves. Rather than self-regulation, it becomes a form of co-regulation or implied devolution of power by the government.[88]

There is no press council as such in Ireland but all the national newspapers have had readers' representatives since 1989. It is their task to receive complaints from readers and provide an appropriate avenue of redress. In the case of complaints of inaccuracy or misleading reporting, corrections or clarifications are published. Complaints of invasion of privacy are few, and when they do occur they are brought to the attention of the editor or relevant department. In *Maguire v Drury*,[89] the evidence showed that once the editor was aware that photographs of the children of the family had been taken by deception, he gave an assurance that the photographs would not be used. Provincial newspapers, because they are at the heart of the community, can usually handle complaints at a personal level. Their reliance on the community is the best guarantor of protection of privacy. In the case of the broadcast media, the Broadcasting Complaints Commission hears complaints, and if it upholds them, its findings must be carried by the broadcaster under the right

---

Europe has been formed in recent years. It has 27 members, including Ireland, which does not yet have an industry-wide press complaints mechanism, but has plans to introduce one: see *www.aipce.org*.

[88] See generally, Colin Munro, "Self-regulation in the media" [1997] P.L. 6; Thomas Gibbons, *Regulating the Media* (2nd ed., Sweet & Maxwell, London, 1998), pp.274–284; Robert Pinker, "Press freedom and press regulation – current trends in their European context" (2002) 7 *Communications Law* 102; Carmen Palzer, "Co-Regulation of the Media in Europe: European Provisions for the Establishment of Co-regulation Frameworks," *IRIS plus* 2002:6; Tarlach McGonagle, "Co-Regulation of the Media in Europe: The Potential for Practice of an Intangible Idea," *IRIS plus* 2002:10.

[89] Above, n.36.

of reply requirement of the Broadcasting Act 1990, in accordance with the EC Television without Frontiers Directive.

5.5.7 Privacy, Computers and the Internet

Self-regulation remains the preferred option for regulating the internet and new communications media generally.[90] That is so for a variety of philosophical reasons, including the principle of access to information, and for practical reasons, such as the global nature of the medium, which makes it difficult to control. However, the potential to intrude on individual privacy in particular has led to a variety of legal responses as well. As Gellman[91] has observed, the battle over privacy in the twentieth century was a struggle over adapting privacy principles to constant technological advances. New technology was the principal catalyst for more formal legal responses to privacy invasions. Issues range from wiretapping, instantaneous photography, computer-assisted digital manipulation of photographs,[92] to databanks and the increasing inter-nationalisation of activities involving personal data. In *Dustin Hoffman v Capital Cities/ABC, Inc.*,[93] for example, a manipulated image of the actor was held by the court to have exploited him and robbed him of his dignity, professionalism and talent. He was violated by technology, the court said.

The main problems, according to Gellman,[94] are that, to be effective, privacy laws need regular oversight and enforcement. The response to date has been to combine self-regulation with self-help (technological devices to assist users, such as encryption, fire walls, walled gardens to protect children, and various other data security techniques), legislation and the extension of common law principles. Self-regulation, which may take the form of privacy codes or principles, advisory boards and such like, may not always be sufficient on its own, due to lack of commitment or weak enforcement measures. Self-help requires awareness and education. Legislation tends to be slow and lags behind technological developments; it also tends to be sectoral and deals with specific aspects of privacy, for example, surveillance or child pornography or data protection. Common law principles were not designed to deal with the internet and while they can sometimes accommodate specific problems, they do not

---

[90] See, for example, Council of Europe, Resolution No.2 of the 5th European Ministerial Conference on Mass Media Policy, Thessaloniki, December 1997; Monroe Price and Stefaan Verhulst, "The Concept of Self-Regulation and the Internet," in J. Waltermann & M. Machill (eds), *Protecting our Children on the Internet: Towards a Culture of Responsibility* (Bertelsmann Foundation Pubrs, Gutersloh, 1999), p.133; *Illegal and Harmful Use of the Internet* (First Report of the Working Group, The Stationery Office, Dublin, 1998, available at *www.justice.ie*).

[91] Above, n.78, Gellman, at p.203.

[92] See Gyong Ho Kim and Anna R. Paddon, "Digital Manipulation As New Form of Evidence of Actual Malice in Libel and False Light Cases" (1999) *Communications and the Law* 57: In digital technology, scanners break down the image into geographic picture elements known as pixels. The pixels represent different characteristics of the image, and the digital scanning device operator can manipulate the pixels in a variety of ways: colours can be changed, brightness or shadow added, elements of the picture removed entirely, or elements from other images added.

[93] 1999 U.S. Dist. LEXIS 506, at *1.

[94] Above, n.78, at p.213.

provide comprehensive protection.[95] In *Michaels v Internet Entertainment Group Inc.*[96] the court granted a preliminary injunction to prevent an adult entertainment internet content provider from distributing a video of celebrities Bret Michaels and Pamela Anderson engaged in sexual activity. It did so on the basis of privacy and copyright, but in particular on the grounds of appropriation and unreasonable publicity given to their private life.

Internet spoofing and cyberstalking are also causes of concern, as are the collection,[97] storage, manipulation and dissemination of personal information. Privacy in cyberspace takes on critical importance because information lies at the core of the cyberspace social order.[98] The territorial view of privacy has no application and the interconnectivity of cyberspace not only increases the accessibility of personal information but also monitoring and exploitation. Reality television, such as the "Big Brother" and "Survivor" shows, usually accompanied by nothing-spared 24 hour-a-day webcasting, attract the voyeuristic side of audiences, and seem to belie the need or desire of individuals for privacy protection in their chosen pursuit of fame.[99] Thus the myriad ways in which personal space and personal data can be invaded increase rapidly as the technology advances, and with a wireless world-wide web, the all-pervasiveness of the medium and universal access to it, it poses new challenges to lawmakers.[100]

Following the terrorist attacks of September 11, 2001, the privacy of internet users has come under threat from a number of quarters. In Europe, the European Parliament has approved a Directive that will allow governments to oblige internet service providers and telephone companies to retain data on users for a limited period. Law enforcement agencies would then be able to demand access to the data when investigating crimes.[101] The most important safeguard

---

[95] Hence the need to combine elements of all four forms of response (self-regulation, self-help, legislation and common law). See Debra A. Valentine, "Privacy on the Internet: The Evolving Legal Landscape" (2000) 16 *Santa Clara Computer and High Technology L.J.*, No.2, 401.

[96] 5 F. Supp. 2d 823 (C.D. Cal. 1998).

[97] For example, via cookies, or by hackers, crackers or telemarketers, which Friedman has called the "little brother" phenomenon, as opposed to the government-instituted "Big Brother" of Orwell's novel, *1984*: see Thomas L. Friedman, "Little brother" *New York Times*, September 26, 1999.

[98] See above, n.23, Katrin Schatz Byford.

[99] A number of countries have adopted self-regulatory measures to safeguard human dignity in response to the "Big Brother" phenomenon. See, for example (2001) *IRIS*-9 (Strasbourg: European Audiovisual Observatory), p.12, re Portugal and Poland and Statement (2002) 1 of the Standing Committee on Transfrontier Television (Council of Europe, T–TT (2002) on human diginity, with particular reference to programme formats (available at *www.humanrights.coe.int/media/topics/broadcasting/transfrontier/ TTTinfo(A).rtf*).

[100] See Prof. Dorothy Glancy, "At the intersection of visible and invisible worlds: United States Privacy Law and the Internet" (2000) 16 *Santa Clara Computer and High Technology L.J.*, No.2, 357. The role of law and regulability of cyberspace have been analysed extensively by Harvard law professor, Lawrence Lessig: see, for example, "The Law of the Horse: What Cyberlaw Might Teach" (1999) 113 *Harvard Law Review*, No.2, 501–549.

[101] Directive 20002/58/EC. *The Irish Times*, June 3, 2002, *The Sunday Tribune*, June 9, 2002.

will be the requirement for such measures to be proportionate and in accordance with the European Convention on Human Rights and rulings of the European Court of Human Rights.

5.6 A STATUTORY REGIME?

Although invasion of privacy by the media has not been a problem in Ireland in the past, there has been considerable concern expressed at a number of privacy-invasive stories which have appeared in the last few years. Economic pressures and competition from the British media circulating in Ireland were largely blamed. By the late 1990s, the British media were firmly established in the Irish newspaper and broadcast markets. Some had set up their own editorial offices and printing facilities in Ireland and the process of buying up indigenous Irish newspapers and investing in radio stations had begun. In addition to those and other changes in the media landscape, the capabilities of modern technology have made it so much easier to invade individual privacy than before. Also the appetite of the public for the sensational, the seedy and the intimacies of people's lives, particularly those of film stars, pop stars, political leaders and other public personalities, appears to encourage it.

In the overall context of the dangers posed by new technology, the Law Reform Commission favoured introducing a narrowly defined statutory regime. In its *Consultation Paper*[102] and *Report*[103] on privacy, it points out that growth of the internet and of surveillance have stretched both the concept of privacy and the range of its application. Hence the need for a more focused and effective statutory approach, rather than relying on the existing patchwork of laws.[104]

As the Law Reform Commission appreciated, the difficulty in devising any such regime is to decide not only what is to be protected but also how to build in a deterrent element that will be effective and yet not undermine the freedom of the press. Much has been written in the United States on both elements. One test that has been put forward for determining what should be protected is the "plain view" test: what happens in plain view is not private. The test effectively sorts out what is in the private sphere and what is in the public. What is done in plain view has already ceased to be part of the plaintiff's private life.[105] The second element, deterrence, has become more problematic with rapid advances in technology.[106] Where privacy laws have been introduced they have tended to focus on personal autonomy or personal information, while many are specific and context-dependent. Wacks, for example, speaks of a trinity of "informational privacy", "relational privacy" and "decisional privacy".[107]

---

[102] Above, n.9; Chap.8, p.172 deals with the media.

[103] Above, n.9, LRC 57–1998.

[104] *ibid.* at paras 1.100–1.101, where the LRC states, *inter alia*, that "One should not be forced to torture the form of defamation to suit the substance of a claim in privacy."

[105] See Deckle McLean, "Plain View: A Concept Useful to the Public Disclosure and Intrusion Privacy Invasion Torts" (1999) *Communications and the Law*, 9.

[106] See Gellman above, n.78, and other articles referred to elsewhere in this chapter.

[107] Raymond Wacks, "Privacy in Cyberspace: Personal Information, Free Speech and the

What approach have other countries taken? In New Zealand, a common-law jurisdiction, several cases involving the media have established the existence of a tort of invasion of privacy and the courts have now gone on to consider its ambit.[108] In France, where privacy protection is well developed, the French Civil Code and Article 35 of the Press Law of 1881 protect privacy: "Everyone has the right to respect for his private life". The Penal Code makes it a criminal offence to engage in any conduct that deliberately infringes the private life of another person by overhearing, recording or communicating words spoken privately or confidentially, without the person's consent.[109] The protection offered by the law of privacy includes references to a person's love life, family life, disclosure of the private address or telephone number of a public figure or an individual's salary. The last-mentioned restriction was successfully challenged under Article 10 of the European Convention on Human Rights in 1999 in *Fressoz and Roire v France*.[110] The satirical newspaper, *Le Canard Enchaîné*, had published details of a pay increase to the chairman of the Peugeot car company, at a time when the workers were in dispute with the company over pay. The Court said, however, that the information contributed to public debate on a matter of public interest (para. 50) and therefore the conviction, in this case, for possession of copies of tax documents, amounted to a breach of Article 10.

In France, a large number of court actions are taken for breach of privacy. The deterrent value of the law, therefore, is slight. The primary remedy is damages, but the amount awarded is moderate compared with defamation damages in common-law jurisdictions. In 1985, Marlene Dietrich was awarded the equivalent of €1,500 when 40 lines of the foreword to a book were found

---

Internet," in Peter Birks (ed.), *Privacy and Loyalty* (above, n.5), p.93, at p.94; Raymond Wacks, "Towards a new legal and conceptual framework for the protection of Internet privacy" (1999) 3 (1) I.I.P.R. 1. (This particular issue of IIPR focuses on privacy and privacy-related matters in both the Irish and international contexts.) COPPA, the Children's Online Privacy Protection Act in the US, for example, protects children's informational privacy – see discussion in Laurel Jamtgaard, "Big Bird Meets Big Brother: a Look at the Children's Online Prvacy Protection Act" (2000) 16 *Santa Clara Computer and High Technology L.J.* 385 and Joshua Warmund, "Can COPPA Work? An Analysis of the Parental Consent Measures in the Children's Online Privacy Protection Act" (2000) 11 Fordham Intell. Prop., Media & Ent. L.J. 189.

[108] See Rosemary Tobin, "The New Zealand Tort of Invasion of Privacy" (2000) 5 *Communications Law* 129, at nn.4, 5 (particularly reference to *P v D & Independent News Ltd* [2000] 2 N.Z.L.R. 591, Nicholson J.). In Australia, the High Court was asked in *Lenah Meats Pty Ltd v Australian Broadcasting Corporation* (2001) H.C.A. 63, to consider if Australian law recognised a tort of privacy. The majority declined to do so. For aspects of the law in Australia and various other jurisdictions, see above n.9, *Paper*, at pp.222–233, 248–54.

[109] Art.226–1. Previously, Art.368 of the code made it a criminal offence to listen to, record or transmit by means of any machine, words spoken by a person in a private place without the consent of that person or to fix or transmit by means of any machine a picture of a person in a private place without the person's consent. However, it was amended in 1994, *inter alia*, to take account of developments in technology. *Cf.* the recommendations in the Calcutt Report, above, n.4, para.6.35; LRC *Report*, above, n.9, at pp.101–4.

[110] Judgment of January 21, 1999 (2001) 31 E.H.R.R. 2.

to contain references to her relationships with several people. Brigitte Bardot received damages of one franc when she complained about a photograph showing her in her underwear.[111] Nonetheless, French laws of privacy continue to be strengthened. Tougher restrictions have been placed on the use of pictures by the media as part of an overhaul of the criminal justice system aimed at preserving the presumption of innocence.[112]

In Germany, Articles 1 and 2 of the Basic Law *(Grundgesetz)* together recognise a "personality right", protecting the dignity, freedom and self-determination of the individual. Privacy and defamation are aspects of that general right and are shaped by it, although given separate recognition in the Codes. Privacy is protected under both the civil and criminal law. The public/ private distinction is applied. Indeed, the public category contains a further distinction between public persons who have voluntarily entered the public arena on a permanent basis and those who have become involved in particular issues.[113] The degree of protection varies, but as far as family and home are concerned, all categories enjoy a high degree of protection. Article 5, which protects freedom of the press, provides a defence to a breach of privacy if the breach discloses information of significant interest to the public.[114]

By comparison with other European countries, therefore, Irish law cannot be said to protect privacy in a systematic way. There is quite considerable protection in Irish law for various aspects of privacy, but it adds up to something of a patchwork. The theoretical basis and justification for protection has not been addressed in a comprehensive manner. If a right to privacy is to be developed, then it ought to be developed in a systematic way in accordance with the Constitution and with the guidance of the international human rights instruments. All of this was recognised by the Law Reform Commission, although its deliberations concerned a specific aspect of privacy, namely privacy-intrusive surveillance.

Having considered all of the above issues and more, the Law Reform Commission's core recommendation was for the enactment of a tort of privacy-invasive surveillance, and not a general privacy tort.[115] It also recommended

---

[111] *The Irish Times*, June 20, 1985, April 15, 1986. See also *Bardot v Daily Express* J.C.P. 1966 II 14 521. The actor, Robert de Niro, was awarded FF80,000 (approx. €12,000) for defamation and privacy when two articles were published in *France Soir* connecting him to a prostitution ring (*The Irish Times*, May 21, 1998).

[112] See *The Guardian*, June 1, 2000.

[113] See Gregory Thwaite and Wolfgang Brehm, "German Privacy and Defamation Law" [1994] 8 E.I.P.R. 336.

[114] *ibid.* at p.340. On the issues of human dignity and moral integrity see the following by David Feldman: "The Developing Scope of Article 8 of the European Convention on Human Rights" [1997] E.H.R.L.R. 265, "Privacy-related Rights and their Social Value" in Peter Birks, above, n.6, "Human Dignity as a Legal Value" (2 parts) (1999) P.L. 682, (2000) P.L. 61. For an American view, see Jonathan Kahn, "Bringing Dignity Back to Light: Publicity Rights and the Eclipse of the Tort of Appropriation of Identity" [1999] 17 Cardozo Arts & Ent L.J. 213.

[115] The new tort would protect a "reasonable expectation" of privacy, which would involve a consideration of a number of different factors, including the place, object or occasion of the surveillance, the purpose, means, status or function of the person, conduct and overall context (at para.7.08). *Note: all the paragraph references given are to the Report* (LRC 57–1998).

the enactment of a related tort of harassment, analagous to the criminal offence of harassment under section 10 the Non-Fatal Offences against the Person Act 1997).[116] The main ancillary recommendation was for new torts of unjustified disclosure or publication of material obtained by, or as a result of, privacy-invasive surveillance or harassment (at 8.01). In the latter case, and importantly for the media, there would be no liability where the publication was justified by overriding considerations of the public interest.[117]

A new remedy, which would have implications for the media, would be a "privacy order". This order, a form of preventive injunction, could be sought to "forestall" publication of material obtained as a result of, or by means of, privacy-invasive surveillance or harassment (at 8.14). A public interest defence would apply.[118] As a form of prior restraint, such a measure would require serious scrutiny under Article 10 of the European Convention on Human Rights, but the Law Reform Commission believes that by confining it to instances of privacy-invasive surveillance or harassment it would fall within Ireland's margin of appreciation and thus survive challenge.[119]

The Law Reform Commission also recommended new criminal offences relating to installing surveillance devices and trespassing for the purpose of surveillance, with provision for a wide range of defences. In the case of the media and the practice of newsgathering, use of the criminal law spells danger. Police powers of arrest could lead to great difficulties in practice, as police could be called to any scene to remove reporters or camera crews, in circumstances which might later be thrown out of court.[120] Genuine news-gathering, or newsgathering involving privacy-invasive surveillance but where a genuine public interest warrants it, could thus be seriously hampered.

Not surprisingly, since protection of privacy is the essence of both the

---

[116] *ibid.* at para.7.17. In both cases, damages would be available (at 7.29) and the right of action would survive the death of the victim (at 7.35). The offence of harassment set out in s.10 of the Non-Fatal Offences against the Person Act includes the use of the telephone and covers acts, intentional or reckless, which seriously interfere with a person's peace or privacy or cause alarm, distress or harm to that person. Penalties are severe: up to seven years imprisonment on indictment.

[117] *ibid.* at 8.10. Four specific aspects of the public interest are instanced: the detection and prevention of crime; the exposure of illegality or serious wrongdoing; informing the public on a matter of public importance; preventing the public from being misled by the utterances of public figures (broadly defined), where private beliefs and behaviour are directly at variance with same (at 8.11). It is stated that the list is not exhaustive.

[118] The LRC saw it as involving "a balance between two perishables – privacy or news" but came down on the side of privacy (at 8.15). It did note, however, the element of prior restraint involved with such an order.

[119] *ibid.* at Annex 1, paras 1.73, 1.211. The margin of appreciation is the measure of discretion permitted under the ECHR.

[120] *Report*, Chap.9. Robertson and Nicol, *Media Law* (Penguin Books, London, 2002), at p.285, state, with reference to English law, that the criminal offences proposed by the Calcutt Committee, despite their public interest defence, were misconceived and have given police unparalleled powers to arrest reporters and television camera crews as they went about their ordinary business. The LRC also proposes to disallow the public interest defence in respect of the publication of material or information obtained by privacy-invasive surveillance which involved any of the acts set out in relation to the criminal offences (at 9.16).

proposed civil and criminal actions, the Law Reform Commission envisages a discretion to hold proceedings *in camera* and/or to place "tailored" restrictions on publication where "on balance privacy so warrants" (at 9.34). The prior restraint and *in camera* provisions are among the more worrying aspects of the Law Reform Commission's proposals. Both are aimed at preventing invasions of privacy. The first, the privacy order, is directed at prevention in advance of any such intrusion, when the impending intrusion is known. The second, the *in camera* provision, is directed at the reporting of any court case arising out of such intrusion. There is a danger that privacy orders would be used as "gagging-orders" by the rich and powerful in society. Restrictions on court reporting can lead to an information deficit, which means that the public is deprived of knowledge of the extent of the problem and of how justice is being done in its name.[121] Past experience has shown[122] that both measures, unless very carefully drafted and delimited, could be used to hamper the newsgathering and publication processes.

In all, while the Law Reform Commission's recommendations are not solely or directly aimed at media surveillance or publication, they have the purpose and effect of catching them. The civil measures at least are legitimate restraints, to the extent that they are designed to protect an aspect of a right to privacy, to date ill-defined but nonetheless recognised at both constitutional and international level. They must be taken seriously as existing law fails to offer a clear and workable framework for protection of privacy in the context of surveillance. They also have the advantage that they are based on an independent analysis by the Commission of the essence of the rights involved.[123] They are proposed in their own right and not as appendages to other laws, such as defamation, or strained applications of torts of trespass, nuisance, confidence, and so forth. Provided they are narrowly drafted, therefore, and construed to give full weight to the countervailing right to freedom of expression and to allow scope for ethical media practice, the civil measures are unobjectionable in principle. It is true that if imposed in the present climate, they would add another burden to that currently imposed on the media by the unreformed nature of the defamation laws. But that is an argument for reforming defamation laws rather than stymying the development of efficient privacy laws.

Existing broadcast guidelines and press and journalists' codes,[124] as well

---

[121] This is the basis of an argument for a reappraisal and refining of the *in camera* rule in general. See further Chs 6 and 7 below.

[122] See Chs 6 and 7 below.

[123] The LRC provides a closely-argued assessment of the theoretical and policy bases and implications, as well as testing them against the jurisprudence of the European Commission and Court of Human Rights on Art.8 and Art.10 ECHR.

[124] See RTÉ, *Programme-Makers' Guidelines*, 2002, "Privacy" and "Surreptitious Recording and Use of Hidden Cameras". Broadcast guidelines are in response to a statutory obligation contained in the Broadcasting (Authority) Acts and therefore might be more accurately described as a form of semi-self-regulation or co-regulation. See also the various sets of guidelines produced by the IRTC (now the BCI) under the Radio and Television Act 1988 (*www.bci.ie*). The NNI Code on Privacy 1997 and NUJ Code of Conduct are self-regulatory measures, developed by the bodies themselves without any input from government.

as editorial guidelines in individual newspapers, already address the issues in greater practical detail. However, the remedies they provide for victims of invasions of privacy at present are very limited.[125] The newspapers have pinpointed the defamation laws as the main stumbling-block to the establishment by the industry of a Complaints Commissioner or Commission.[126] The debate on protection of privacy, in what form and at what level, is set to continue, particularly in the context of the incorporation of the European Convention on Human Rights into Irish law.

Further Reading

Barendt, Eric (ed.), *Privacy* (Ashgate Publishing Ltd, Aldershot, 2001).

Clayton, Richard & Tomlinson, Hugh, *Privacy and Freedom of Expression* (Oxford University Press, Oxford, 2001).

Kuner, Christopher, *European Data Privacy Law and Online Business* (Oxford University Press, Oxford, 2003).

Lorenz, Professor Werner, "Privacy and the Press – a German Experience", *Butterworths Lectures* 1989-90 (Butterworths, London, 1990).

Markesinis, Basil S., *Protecting Privacy* (Oxford University Press, Oxford, 1999).

Ó hAnnracháin, Fachtna, "Privacy and Broadcasting" (1971) 105 I.L.T. 225.

Rosenbaum, Joseph I., "Privacy on the Internet: Whose Information Is It Anyway", 38 Jurimetrics J. 565–573 (1998).

Schauer, Frederick, Intenet Privacy and the Public Private Distinction", 38 Jurimetrics J. 555–564 (1998).

Tugendhat, Michael & Christie, Iain (eds), *The Law of Privacy and the Media* (Oxford University Press, Oxford, 2002).

---

[125] In the case of broadcasting, whether public service (RTÉ) or commercial (BCI), complaints can be made to the Broadcasting Complaints' Commission.

[126] See *www.aipce.org* for details of such independent press bodies in Europe. The NNI has taken steps to establish such a body but views it as the *quid pro quo* of defamation law reform. In October 2002, the Minister for Justice established an advisory group to advise him on specific aspects of defamation law but also on the establishment of a statutory press council or complaints' body (see above, Chap.4). Robertson and Nicol, above, n.119, at p.285, however, state with reference to English law: "Law should not be used actively to suppress publication of the truth. It can, however, usefully work to *deter* publication of unimportant private truths if it provides an effective remedy for victims of invasion of privacy. An effective remedy – the right to bring a civil action, legally aided where appropriate, and to obtain compensation and damages – is precisely what English law does not, at present, offer, and self-regulation through the Press Complaints' Commission is a hollow pretence." See further Chap.11 below.

CHAPTER SIX

The Principle of Open Justice:
The Media and the Courts

6.1 INTRODUCTION

The relationship between the media and the courts can be difficult. The courts are concerned with safeguarding the administration of justice and the right to a fair trial. They do not always regard the media as an integral part of the process and sometimes treat journalists as an intrusion, particularly when inaccurate or misleading reporting is seen to obstruct the administration of justice or prejudice a fair trial. Nonetheless, the Irish Constitution (Article 34) provides for a system of open justice. Justice is administered on behalf of the public and the public has a right to attend. The media, by extension, have a right to report on court proceedings. "The actual presence of the public is never necessary", according to Walsh J. in *In re R*,[1] "but the administration of justice does require that the doors of the courts must be open so that members of the general public may come and see for themselves that justice is done." The opportunity for public access must be real and not illusory.[2] Referring to the preconstitutional position, Walsh J. said:

"The primary object of the courts is to see that justice is done and it was only when the presence of the public or public knowledge of the proceedings would defeat that object that the judges had any discretion to hear cases other than in public. It had to be shown that a public hearing was likely to lead to a denial of justice...."[3]

This principle was made part of the fundamental law of the State by Article 34 of the Constitution. As the Supreme Court held in *Beamish and Crawford Ltd v Crowley*,[4] apart from the exceptions permitted by law, publicity is inseparable from the administration of justice. Nowadays the case can be put even more strongly. The media have become such a central part of people's lives that their role in court reporting has taken on a greater importance. It is from the media that most people get their knowledge of the court system and court proceedings. Most people do not read official law reports written in technical

---

[1] [1989] I.R. 126 at 134.
[2] See *Riepan v Austria*, European Court of Human Rights, App. No.35115/97, judgment of November 14, 2000.
[3] Above, n.1, at 135.
[4] [1969] I.R. 142.

legal language by barristers. They read their newspaper, listen to the radio, or watch television for the lay person's account of what is happening. The value of the journalist's account, therefore, should not be underestimated, but it should be remembered that journalists cannot be expected to report with the precision and level of technical detail that characterises official law reports. They can, however, be expected to strive for high levels of accuracy in reporting in the interests of the public.

The importance of the principle of open justice and role of the media in reporting the courts were recognised and clearly articulated by the Supreme Court in the case of *Irish Times Ltd v Judge Murphy*.[5] The decision was unanimous and all five judges issued judgments. The case arose from a ban on contemporaneous[6] reporting imposed by the trial judge in a drugs case in Cork, which involved a number of non-nationals accused of importing a large consignment of cocaine. The ban was challenged in the High Court and on appeal to the Supreme Court. The two issues in the appeal related to the principle of open justice and whether the trial judge had a right to impose such a ban.

In relation to open justice, Hamilton C.J. stated:

> "Justice is best served in an open court where the judicial process can be scrutinised. In a democratic society, justice must not only be done but be seen to be done. Only in this way, can respect for the rule of law and public confidence in the administration of justice, so essential to the workings of a democratic state, be maintained."[7]

The obligation to administer justice in public is not discharged by conducting a trial, to which the public, including the media, are admitted but in respect of which there is in force an order prohibiting the media from contemporaneous reporting of the proceedings, since such an order deprives the wider public of knowledge of the proceedings.[8] The public nature of the administration of justice and the right of the wider public to be informed by the media of what is taking place are matters of the greatest importance, the Chief Justice said.[9] However, such rights are not absolute and can be restricted in support of competing rights, in particular the right of an accused person to a fair trial and fair procedures, which incorporate the requirement of trial by a jury unprejudiced by pre-trial publicity.[10] However, fair and accurate reporting by the media will rarely interfere with that right, and the trial judge in the particular case was not entitled to assume that the reporting of the proceedings would be other than fair and accurate.[11] A concern of the trial judge, which led to the

---

[5] [1998] 1 I.R. 359.

[6] The issue of contemporaneous reporting is of particular significance for the media, not least because if contemporaneous reporting is prohibited, reporting after the case has finished may not attract the privilege for contemporaneous reporting conferred by s.18 of the Defamation Act 1961.

[7] Above, n.5, at 382.

[8] *ibid.* at 383.

[9] *ibid.* at 383.

[10] *ibid.* at 384. It had already been established in *D v DPP* [1994] 2 I.R. 465 and *Z v DPP* [1994] 2 I.R. 476 that the right to a fair trial is a superior right.

[11] *ibid.* at 386.

imposition of the ban, was inaccurate reporting by a local radio station in a previous case. If subsequent reporting did turn out to be unfair or inaccurate, it could be dealt with under contempt of court or by giving appropriate directions to the jury.

Denham and Keane JJ. placed the issue firmly in the present: we live in a modern democracy in the age of information technology, when the reality is that most people learn about the courts from the press. The press are the eyes and ears of the public,[12] and any curtailment of the press must be viewed as a curtailment of the access of the people to the administration of justice.[13] Besides, it is an important protection for accused persons that their case be heard in public.[14] The most benign climate for the growth of corruption and abuse of powers, whether by the judiciary or members of the legal profession, is one of secrecy.[15]

The principle of open justice also meant that the plaintiffs in *Roe v Blood Transfusion Service Board*[16] and in the Ansbacher accounts case[17] were not permitted to take a court case under an assumed name. It also formed the basis for a decision of the President of the High Court when he addressed a problem that reporters had been voicing for many years, namely the position when court documents are not read out but are formally entered into the court record. Are such documents to be regarded as public so that reporters may report on them and use information contained in them? Mr Justice Finnegan said that judges who read papers in private, albeit to save court time for all concerned, were not strictly administering justice in public. He said the watchdog of the public was very often the press representative in court, and when sworn affidavits of evidence were not read in open court it meant that basically no one other than the parties had any idea what was going on. In a statement of considerable importance to the media, he said that affidavits read in such a

---

[12] *ibid.* at 401 and 409 respectively. See also Louise Arbour J., Supreme Court of Canada, "Exposing Truth while Keeping Secrets: Publicity, Privacy and Privilege" [2000] 35 Ir. Jur. 17 on the relationship between the media and the courts, which she describes as a symbiotic one, since one often possesses information vital to the other and provides safeguards for the other in healthy democracies.

[13] Above, n.5, at 398.

[14] *ibid. at* 401. In a subsequent case, following argument from counsel on behalf of a number of newspapers and RTÉ, citing *Irish Times Ltd v Judge Murphy*, a Circuit Court judge lifted his ban on reporting (*The Irish Times*, December 1, 2000).

[15] Above, n.5, Keane J., at 409. See also his views on judges subjected to the spotlight of media attention (*Law Society Gazette*, May 2000).

[16] [1996] 3 I.R. 67.

[17] Application by two individuals to take an anonymous case: *The Irish Times*, April 25, 2002. McCracken J. in the High Court stated that the identification of the parties seeking justice "is a small price to be paid to ensure the integrity and openness of one of the three organs of the State, namely the judicial process, in which openness is a vital element .... It is often said that justice must not only be done but must also be seen to be done, and, if this involves innocent parties being brought before the courts in either civil or criminal proceedings and wrongly accused, that is unfortunate, but it is essential for the protection of the entire judicial system." He also said that if he had to consider a hierarchy of rights in the case – and he took the view that he did not – he had "no hesitation in saying that the right to have justice administered in public far exceeded any right to privacy, confidentiality or good name."

way should be treated as read in open court and "may in such circumstances be made available to the press".[18]

Because they perform a vital public function, court reporters should be viewed as a positive rather than negative force. Courts should be keen to ensure accuracy in reporting, in their own interest, as well as that of the public, and be prepared to facilitate reporters to that end. The court system, personnel, litigants and the administration of justice itself would be the beneficiaries. In general terms, the situation in Irish courts has improved with the development of the Courts Service, the introduction of computerisation and improved media liaison.[19] Nonetheless, there are still aspects of law and practice that need to be scrutinised. The courts, rightly scrupulous in their protection of the administration of justice and the right to fair trial, have tended in the past to turn first to the law to punish inaccurate or misleading reporting, rather than taking positive steps to encourage understanding and a high level of accuracy. One of the principal measures adopted and invoked by the courts to that purpose has been the law of contempt of court.

6.2 CONTEMPT OF COURT

6.2.1 Constitutional and Common-Law Origins

The Irish Constitution guarantees freedom of expression and of the press in Article 40.6.1. It also specifies a number of areas of limitation or restriction on that freedom: public order and morality and the authority of the State. It does not specifically mention protection of the courts or the administration of justice as a limitation, yet, in practice, the freedom of the press to report or comment on court proceedings is restricted in a number of ways.

The basis for these restrictions in the interests of the administration of justice is thought to stem, therefore, from Article 34 of the Constitution, which provides for open justice, and Article 38 which provides, *inter alia*, for due process and fair trial.[20]

---

[18] *The Irish Times*, September 17, 2002.

[19] The need for improvement and the situation that prevailed prior to the formation of the Courts Service (*www.courts.ie*) were addressed in the first edition of this book and in Boyle and McGonagle, "Contempt of Court: The Case for Law Reform", *Law and the Media* (Round Hall Sweet & Maxwell, Dublin, 1997), p.127, at pp.131–2. For developments since then, see the reports of the Courts Commission, in particular, *Third Report, Towards the Courts Service* (Stationery Office, Dublin, 1996, on computerisation of the courts), and *A Working Paper on Information and the Courts* (Stationery Office, Dublin, 1997, available at *www.justice.ie*, on the establishment of an information office and access to public documents for *bona fide* journalists).

[20] In an incest case, *DPP v WM* [1995] 1 I.R. 226, Irish Times Law Report, March 13, 1995, Carney J. in the High Court appeared to accept Art.34 as the constitutional basis for such restrictions. On the other hand, O'Hanlon J. in *Desmond v Glackin (No.1)* [1993] 3 I.R. 1, at 28; [1992] 1 I.L.R.M. 490, at 513, considered that the phrase "public order or morality or the authority of the State" in Art.40.6.1 was "sufficiently wide to comprehend a restriction on the right to freedom of expression so far as may be necessary for maintaining the authority and impartiality of the judiciary, corresponding to that in Art.10(2) of the European Convention on Human Rights."

Whatever their formal basis, restrictions, in practice, take two main forms:

(a) denying or limiting access to the courts, and

(b) imposing restrictions on the content of reports of court proceedings.

Both are provided for by statute and will be discussed in Chapter 7. However, the common law of contempt of court is more far-reaching. Over the years, most of the top Irish broadcasters, including Gay Byrne, Pat Kenny and Gerry Ryan, have had to appear in court in relation to contempt. In fact, Gerry Ryan and RTÉ were fined as a result of a radio interview with an alleged rape victim when the case against the accused was pending.[21] The concern of the courts was for the accused's right to a fair trial, *i.e.* that the trial should not be prejudiced by media coverage. It has been a regular occurrence, though less so in recent years, for the national media to be summoned before the courts because of the perceived risk to a fair trial occasioned by inaccurate headlines, background or colour pieces on cases that have not been finally disposed of, or mistakes made in reporting evidence.[22]

Contempt law, which empowers courts to impose fines and imprisonment or the sequestration of assets in response to prejudice or interference with the judicial process, enables the courts to maintain a high level of protection around the courts themselves and the administration of justice. Whether the courts need such a high level of protection today has been called into question, as have the long-held assumptions that the media have the capacity to cause serious prejudice to court cases or that juries, in particular, are susceptible to influence by the media.[23] There is an argument to be made that the public, including juries, are media-wise, having grown up in a media environment, and that the courts should reflect that in their handling of, and response to media reporting.[24] As Denham J. said in *Kelly v O'Neill and Brady*, jurors are robust and capable of hearing cases fairly even where there has been pre-trial publicity.[25]

---

[21] *The Irish Times*, April 3, 1990.

[22] See above, n.19, Boyle and McGonagle, 1997. In 1992 alone, there were at least 17 such instances, mostly attributable to misunderstanding, inadvertent mistakes or human error. In most of these, the court was satisfied with an apology, but in some instances, the decision was taken to put back for hearing to the next court term the trial that was believed prejudiced and for the media to pay the costs involved. The decrease in the number of such incidents may be attributable in part at least to successive Supreme Court decisions in favour of information and the public right to know. See, for example, *Irish Times Ltd v Judge Murphy*, above, n.5; *NIB v RTÉ* [1998] 2 I.R. 465; *Kelly v O'Neill and Brady* [2000] 1 I.R. 354, [2000] 1 I.L.R.M. 507; and in relation to pre-trial publicity, *D v DPP* [1994] 2 I.R. 465, *Z v DPP* [1994] 2 I.R. 476, [1994] 2 I.L.R.M. 481.

[23] See, in particular, above, n.22, *D v DPP, Z v DPP, Kelly v O'Neill and Brady* (particularly, Denham J.) and generally, Boyle and McGonagle, 1997, above, n.19.

[24] See the arguments raised in other jurisdictions, for example, Geoffrey Marshall, "Press Freedom and Free Press Theory" (1992) P.L. 40; Robert Martin, "Contempt of Court: The Effect of the Charter", in Anisman and Linden (eds), *The Media, the Courts and the Charter* (Carswell, Toronto, 1986), pp.208–210; Robert Martin and G. Stuart Adam, *A Sourcebook of Canadian Media Law* (2nd ed., Carleton University Press, Ottawa, 1994), and more generally, Robert Martin (ed.), *Expression and the Law in the Commonwealth* (Irwin Law, Toronto, 1999).

[25] Above, n.22, [2000] 1 I.R. 354, at 367; [2000] 1 I.L.R.M. 507, at 521–2.

It is true that, historically, the emerging press was viewed with apprehension. The courts feared its potential and its effect on public confidence in the justice system, and so resorted to contempt of court as a control mechanism. In the early days, criticism in the press of any of the state institutions was not tolerated and was often equated with sedition. Respect for the courts had to be maintained. Criticism, it was believed in that pre-democratic age, would promote disrespect and cause people to lose confidence in the courts. It had to be quelled. For instance, the editor of the *Dublin Evening Post* in 1785 used his paper to criticise the manner in which he had been treated by the courts in a libel action against him, and was duly sentenced to one month's imprisonment for contempt of court, fined £5, and ordered to enter into securities to keep the peace.[26] In 1798 he was jailed again, this time for six months, for criticising the Court of King's Bench.[27] The purpose of contempt of court was disciplinary, to uphold the authority of the courts – the King's courts. Initially it was aimed at court officers, parties and witnesses appearing in court, but with the emergence of the printed press the jurisdiction was extended to prevent criticism and interference from outside the court.

6.2.2 Contempt of Court in Other Jurisdictions

Contempt of court law is unique to common-law jurisdictions. It is unknown in civil-law countries, where specific criminal offences set out in the penal codes protect the independence and impartiality of the judiciary and the administration of justice. There, the system in criminal cases is inquisitorial rather than adversarial, and it may be argued that proceedings in court, because they are not so dependent on oral testimony, do not need the same degree of protection from media reporting as do our courts. Nonetheless, there is something to be said for the clear and defined scope of a statutory offence, as opposed to the imprecise scope of the contempt power.[28]

All the major international human rights instruments proclaim the right to a fair trial but none of them include protection of the administration of justice among the legitimate areas of restriction on freedom of expression. The European Convention on Human Rights does, however, include "maintaining the authority and impartiality of the judiciary" as an area of restriction in Article 10(2). This was included in response to pressure from the United Kingdom in support of its contempt laws. It was under the heading of "maintaining the

---

[26] Brian Inglis, *The Freedom of the Press in Ireland, 1784-1841* (Faber and Faber, London, 1954), p.32.

[27] *ibid.* at p.77.

[28] In Canada, for example, the Law Reform Commission, *Working Paper*, No.20, 1977, p.48, recommended that the whole field of offences against the administration of justice, particularly the rules of contempt, become part of the criminal code. However, contempt was to remain largely uncodified, the criminal code mainly authorising its continuance, providing for an appeal and the operation of the *sub judice* rule in respect of certain specified offences. See generally, above, n.24, Martin and Adam, and Robert Martin, *Media Law* (Irwin Law, Ontario, 1997). For a comparative analysis of the common law of contempt and French law, see Michael Chesterman, "Contempt: in the common law but not in the civil law" (1997) 46 I.C.L.Q. 521.

authority and impartiality of the judiciary" that the European Court of Human Rights considered contempt of court law in *Sunday Times v UK*,[29] the thalidomide drug case, although the court concluded that the common law of contempt was much wider than the restriction in Article 10(2).

In *Nikula v Finland*,[30] the Court found that the conviction of a defence lawyer for defamation for criticising the public prosecutor in court was a violation of his freedom of expression under Article 10. The court reiterated that the special status of lawyers gives them a central position in the administration of justice as intermediaries between the public and the courts, and as such it is legitimate to expect them to maintain public confidence in the administration of justice. However, interference with a lawyer's freedom of expression, the Court said, could have implications for the accused's right to a fair trial under Article 6 of the Convention. The Court further noted in support of the lawyer that his criticisms were confined to the courtroom, as opposed to being voiced in the media.

In *News Verlags GmbH and CoKG v Austria*,[31] the European Court of Human Rights stated that the duty of the press to impart information and ideas on all matters of public interest extends to the reporting and commenting on court proceedings, which, provided they do not overstep the bounds (as set out in the judgment), contribute to their publicity and are thus perfectly consonant with the requirement of Article 6(1) of the European Convention on Human Rights that hearings be public.[32] As in *Jersild v Denmark*,[33] the Court said that Article 10 of the Convention protects not only the substance of information and ideas but also the form in which they are presented, and it is not for the courts to substitute their own views as to what reporting techniques should be adopted by journalists (para. 39).

As with defamation and privacy, a problem arises as to how to reconcile conflicting rights. The approach of the common law has been to give precedence to protection of the courts and the right to a fair trial over freedom of reporting and information. Indeed, it could be said that in this respect the common-law approach is at odds with, if not diametrically opposed to, that espoused by Article 10 of the European Convention on Human Rights. There the question is not one of "a choice between two conflicting principles, but with a principle of freedom of expression that is subject to a number of exceptions which must be narrowly interpreted".[34] The Court in *Sunday Times v UK* recognised that the administration of justice "requires the co-operation of an enlightened public":

---

[29] Series A, No.30, (1979) 2 E.H.R.R. 245.

[30] App. No.31611/96, judgment of March 21, 2002.

[31] App. No.31457/96, judgment of January 11, 2000.

[32] *ibid.* at para.56. The limits of permissible comment on pending criminal proceedings may not extend to statements which are likely to prejudice, whether intentionally or not, the chances of a person receiving a fair trial or to undermine the confidence of the public in the role of the courts in the administration of justice (at para.56, citing *Worm v Austria*, judgment of August 29, 1997, (1997) 25 E.H.R.R. 454, at para.38).

[33] (1995) 19 E.H.R.R. 1.

[34] Above, n.29, at para.65.

"There is general recognition of the fact that the courts cannot operate in a vacuum. Whilst they are the forum for the settlement of disputes, this does not mean that there can be no prior discussion of disputes elsewhere, be it in specialised journals, in the general press or amongst the public at large. Furthermore, whilst the mass media must not overstep the bounds imposed in the interests of the proper administration of justice, it is incumbent on them to impart information and ideas concerning matters that come before the courts just as in other areas of public interest. Not only have the media the task of imparting such information and ideas; the public also has a right to receive them."[35]

Article 6 of the Convention, which provides for the right to a fair and public hearing, stipulates that the press may be excluded from the courts in the interests of morals, public order and certain other specified interests or when the court considers it "strictly necessary" in special circumstances where publicity would prejudice the interests of justice.[36] It does not, however, refer to reporting restrictions; it is Article 10 that does so. How then would the European Court of Human Rights decide a case, taken under Article 6, alleging that a trial had been unfair because of extensive and prejudicial media coverage? In *Sunday Times v UK*, the Court emphasised that the expression "authority and impartiality of the judiciary" had to be understood "within the meaning of the Convention". For this purpose, the Court said, "account must be taken of the central position occupied in this context by Article 6, which reflects the fundamental principle of the rule of law".[37]

In Britain, following recommendations of the Phillimore Committee in 1974[38] and especially the decision of the European Court of Human Rights in *Sunday Times v UK*, the law of contempt is now governed by statute — the Contempt of Court Act 1981. In Ireland, contempt remains wholly common law; legislation merely provides for its extension to certain tribunals. As in other jurisdictions, particularly Canada and Australia, there has been dissatisfaction with the uncertainty of the common law and the Law Reform Commission has published proposals for reform.[39] Before addressing questions of reform, however, it is necessary to understand the ground rules.

6.3 FORMS OF CONTEMPT

The term "contempt of court" is somewhat antiquated and inaccurate in so far as it suggests conduct that brings the courts into disrepute or holds them up to ridicule. It does cover such conduct but it also covers much more. There are two principal forms of contempt: (a) civil contempt and (b) criminal contempt, although the distinction between them has become more and more blurred in

---

[35] *ibid.*

[36] *Cf.* Art.14.1 of the International Covenant on Civil and Political Rights (ICCPR).

[37] Above, n.29, at para.55.

[38] *Report of the Committee on Contempt of Court* (Cmnd. 5794, HMSO, London, 1974).

[39] *Report on Contempt of Court* (LRC 47–1994).

recent decades, particularly with the emergence of a number of "hybrid" cases
(to be discussed later).

6.3.1 Civil Contempt

Civil contempt, according to Ó Dálaigh C.J. in *Keegan v de Búrca*,[40] "usually
arises where there is a disobedience to an order of the court by a party to the
proceedings and in which the court generally has no interest to interfere unless
moved by the party for whose benefit the order was made."

"Civil" contempt is so-called, therefore, because it involves breach of an
order issued as part of the civil side of the court's jurisdiction, not because it
relates solely to civil cases or because it gives rise to a civil action. In fact, it is
in many respects criminal. For instance, breach of a court order can result in
imprisonment. The purpose of civil contempt is coercive rather than punitive,
that is, it aims to persuade the person to obey the order, and that seemingly is
the justification for the indefinite terms of imprisonment which may result. A
court may sentence defaulters to imprisonment *sine die*,[41] that is to say, for an
unspecified period, until such time as they purge their contempt by agreeing to
or taking steps to obey the order. For instance, a Kerry couple who had planted
trees on land over which their neighbours had turf-cutting rights were
imprisoned *sine die* when they failed to comply with a court order to remove
the trees. They were released later following negotiations. Similarly, a woman
in Achill was imprisoned for failure to obey a court order to get rid of a noisy
rooster that was disturbing her neighbours. Eventually, the rooster died and
solved that problem, but the woman was back in prison for failure to pay a fine
imposed by the District Court for harassing a neighbour by playing excessively
loud radio music.[42]

The object of civil contempt is, therefore, to prompt compliance with court
orders and in that way to preserve the authority and dignity of the courts. The
Law Reform Commission has recommended retaining the *sine die* sanction
but looking at the feasibility of accruing, or *per diem* (daily), fines as in the
United States, Netherlands and Norway, as an alternative. The Commission
did not favour substituting definite terms of imprisonment for *sine die*.[43]

Civil contempt does not have any major implications for the media. From
time to time, individual journalists may be restrained by court injunction from
entering certain premises, hounding someone for a story or publishing certain
information. Breach of such an injunction would constitute civil contempt.
More often, media cases are either exclusively criminal contempt or "hybrid'"
versions, *i.e.* where breach of the court order restraining publication is civil
contempt but the fact of publishing the story which the order concerns is
criminal contempt. In a case involving the *Irish Press*,[44] publication of extracts

---

[40] [1973] I.R. 223, at 227.
[41] A Latin term meaning "without naming the day".
[42] *The Irish Times*, May 7, 1999.
[43] LRC, *Consultation Paper on Contempt of Court*, 1991, pp.380–88; *Report on Contempt of Court*, (LRC 47-1994), at pp.52–3, 72–3.
[44] *The Irish Times*, October 25–26, 1991.

from a report, which was subject to a court order, amounted to civil contempt. An order had been made under the Companies Acts prohibiting publication of the report to anyone other than the government minister who had commissioned it. The court accepted that there had been a misunderstanding as to the legal position and no intention on the part of the journalist or editor to commit contempt and, therefore, accepted their apology. In this particular case, as breach of the order had already occurred and was unlikely to recur, the *sine die* punishment would not have been appropriate. Nonetheless, counsel argued that breach of the order clearly constituted civil contempt and that the publication of the information was bordering on criminal contempt also. However, Costello J. in the High Court did not make an order against the journalist and editor for contempt, nor did he require them to identify their sources, but he did require them to hand up notes of the extracts from the report.[45]

In 1985, RTÉ was found guilty of contempt in stating the fact of a bankruptcy in a "Today Tonight" programme on friendly societies and fringe banks.[46] An order prohibiting publication of the bankruptcy had been made a few months earlier. The President of the High Court accepted that RTÉ was not aware of this prohibition but found that this fact did not excuse them. It was RTÉ's responsibility to make all reasonable inquiries, he said.[47] Nonetheless, he accepted an apology. Publication in breach of the court order constituted civil contempt and it was feared also that it would jeopardise the man's chances of making an arrangement with his creditors inside the bankruptcy. A more recent example is the "Baby A" case, an unlawful custody case, in which the *Irish Independent* disclosed the names of some of those involved. An application was made on behalf of the pregnancy-counselling agency at the centre of the case to attach and commit the editor, health correspondent and chief executive for contempt of court by breaching the court order.[48]

6.3.2 Criminal Contempt

Criminal contempt is of much greater consequence for the media. Ó Dálaigh C.J. said in *Keegan v de Búrca* that it:

> "consists in behaviour calculated to prejudice the due course of justice, such as contempt *in facie curiae*, words written or spoken or acts calcu-
> lated to prejudice the due course of justice or disobedience to a writ of

---

[45] *ibid.*

[46] *The Irish Times*, March 16, 1985.

[47] *ibid.*

[48] *In the matter of an inquiry pursuant to Article 40.4.2 of the Constitution and in the matter of Baby A, an infant: Eastern Health Board v E, A and A* [2000] I.R. 430. In another case, also involving children, a judge was critical of Independent Newspapers for publishing photographs of the parents of four young children found home alone. The parents' solicitor said that the paper was aware of the judge's order when it reproduced photographs of the parents for a second time. No action was taken (*The Irish Times*, March 29, 2001). See further Chap.7 below.

habeas corpus by the person to whom it is directed – to give but some examples of this class of contempt. ... Criminal contempt is a common law misdemeanour and, as such, is punishable by both imprisonment and fine at discretion, that is to say without statutory limit – its object is punitive...."[49]

Each of the types of prejudicial behaviour identified by Ó Dálaigh C.J. can be considered in turn.

6.3.2.1 Contempt In Facie Curiae *(in the face of the court)*

Contempt *in facie curiae*, according to O'Higgins C.J. in *The State (DPP) v Walsh and Conneely*,[50] "consists of conduct which is obstructive or prejudicial to the course of justice, and which is committed during court proceedings". This form of contempt can occur in a variety of ways, such as courtroom demonstrations, insulting court personnel, impeding access to the courtroom and so on. However, its most important aspect from the media point of view concerns the refusal of journalists to disclose their sources of information when called to give evidence in court.

(i) Journalists' sources

If a journalist refuses to answer a relevant question put to him/her, s/he is in contempt of court. There has been no recognition of journalists' privilege by the Irish courts, and newspaper proprietors, editors and journalists have been fined or have gone to jail on occasion rather than disclose their sources.[51] In *O'Brennan v Tully*,[52] the editor of the *Roscommon Herald* was fined £25 on the spot for refusing to identify the author of a letter to the paper, which criticised the plaintiff, a county councillor and member of Dáil Éireann. The editor's offence was to refuse to answer a "relevant" question.[53]

The leading case is *In re Kevin O'Kelly*.[54] Kevin O'Kelly was an RTÉ journalist, called as a witness in the trial of Seán Mac Stiofáin for membership of the IRA. O'Kelly refused to identify the voice on a tape-recording as that of Mac Stiofáin and was sentenced to three months imprisonment by the Special Criminal Court. He appealed to the Court of Criminal Appeal, where his prison sentence was quashed and a fine of £250 imposed instead. O'Kelly considered that to answer the question would be a breach of confidence between himself

---

[49] Above, n.40. On contempt in general, see Gerard McCormack, "Corrupting the Criminal Process" (1985) 1 I.L.T. 6 and Hugh Mohan, "Contempt of Court and the Media" (2002) (7) B.R. 384.

[50] [1981] I.R. 412, at 421.

[51] For example, see above, n.26, at p.143.

[52] (1933) 69 I.L.T.R. 116.

[53] In 1934, Joe Dennigan, the political correspondent of the *Irish Press* was sent to prison for one month by the military tribunal for refusing to reveal his sources for an article on the banning of the Young Ireland Association (the Blueshirts); see John Horgan, "Case Made History for Journalism" (*The Irish Times*, April 24, 1992) and Horgan, *Irish Media: a Critical History since 1922* (Routledge, London, 2001), at p.34.

[54] (1974) 108 I.L.T.R. 97.

and his source, which would not only put his own position as a journalist in jeopardy but would also make it difficult for other journalists to promote the public good by fostering the free exchange of public opinion. Walsh J., who delivered judgment in the appeal, sympathised with the role of journalists but said that:

> "journalists or reporters are not any more constitutionally or legally immune than other citizens from disclosing information received in confidence ... [and the fact that] a communication was made under terms of expressed confidence or implied confidence does not create a privilege against disclosure."[55]

It is interesting to note that Walsh J. did not expressly inquire into the relevance of the particular question put to O'Kelly or the necessity for answering it. He made a passing remark that the obligation to give "relevant" testimony did not constitute harassment of journalists, and proceeded to quash the prison sentence on the grounds, *inter alia*, that O'Kelly's refusal to answer the question "while perhaps adding some little extra difficulty to the case, did not effectively impede the presentation of the prosecution's case".[56] In other words, O'Kelly's answer was not necessary, yet a fine was imposed. The offence is, therefore, primarily disciplinary, to maintain the authority of the courts and, as such, is a strict liability offence.

A few years prior to *O'Kelly*, however, Lord Denning in an English case, *AG v Mulholland and Foster*,[57] had held that a judge should require a journalist to answer only when the question was relevant, proper and necessary in the course of justice to be put and answered. The Contempt of Court Act 1981 in Britain further narrowed and refined the test. A person in that jurisdiction will not be in contempt of court for refusing to disclose his/her sources of information (section 10) unless it is established to the satisfaction of the court that disclosure is necessary in the interests of justice or national security or for the prevention of disorder or crime. The Act was introduced in Britain to give effect to the decision of the European Court of Human Rights in *Sunday Times v UK*,[58] which found aspects of the common law of contempt to be in breach of the Convention.

The improved protection for journalists (and others) envisaged in the Act did not prove very effective in practice, however. Despite a promising decision in *AG v Lundin*[59] when a journalist was held not to be in contempt for refusing to answer because his answers were not necessary "in the interests of justice", the phrase "the interests of justice" was widely interpreted in later cases, *e.g. British Steel Corporation v Granada Television*[60] and *Re Goodwin*.[61]

---

[55] *ibid.* at 101.
[56] *ibid.* at 102.
[57] [1963] 2 W.L.R. 658, [1963] 1 All E.R. 767.
[58] Above, n.29.
[59] (1982) 75 Cr. App. R. 90, [1982] Crim. L.R. 296, D.C.
[60] [1982] A.C. 1096.
[61] [1990] 1 All E.R. 608 (Ch D), *X v Morgan Grampian Publishers Ltd and Others* [1990]

The latter case concerned a journalist, Bill Goodwin, who received information that a leading software company, Tetra Ltd, was experiencing financial difficulties. When he contacted the company to check the information, the company sought a court injunction to prevent him publishing the information and an order seeking disclosure of the identity of the source of his information. Goodwin refused to identify his source and was fined £5,000 for contempt. The case was pursued to the Court of Human Rights (*Goodwin v UK*[62]), which held that the combined interests of the company did not outweigh the journalist's interest in protecting his source. The Court held that protection of confidential sources was an essential means of enabling the press to perform its important function of public watchdog and should not be interfered with except in exceptional circumstances where vital public or individual interests were at stake:

> "Protection of journalistic sources is one of the basic conditions for press freedom. ... Without such protection, sources may be deterred from assisting the press in informing the public on matters of public interest. As a result, the vital public watchdog role of the press may be undermined and the ability of the press to provide accurate and reliable information may be adversely affected. Having regard to the importance of the protection of journalistic sources for press freedom in a democratic society and the potentially chilling effect an order of source disclosure has on the exercise of that freedom, such a measure cannot be compatible with Article 10 of the Convention unless it is justified by an overriding requirement in the public interest." (para. 39)

Following *Goodwin*, the English Court of Appeal, in a case involving Elton John,[63] stressed that disclosure will only be ordered in exceptional circumstances. Lord Woolf also held that before the courts require journalists to break what they consider to be a very important professional obligation to protect a source, "the minimum requirement is that other avenues should be explored".[64] Since then, the Human Rights Act 1998 has come into operation in the UK (October 2000), and there have been cases going both ways.[65] A

---

2 All E.R. 1, where Bridge and Oliver L.JJ., in particular, emphasised the public importance of protection of sources and further refined the "necessity" test for disclosure.

[62] (1996) 22 E.H.R.R. 123. See also Robert D. Sack, "*Goodwin v United Kingdom*: An American View of Protection for Journalists' Confidential Sources under UK and European Law" (1995) 16 J.M.L.P. 86; Bina Cunningham, "Journalists' privilege from a European perspective" [1995] 1 ENT. L.R. 25.

[63] *John v Express Newspapers plc* [2000] 3 All E.R. 257. See also reference to *Goodwin* in *Reynolds v Times Newspapers* [1999] 3 W.L.R. 1010 at 1041. The Irish Law Reform Commission in its *Report on Privacy: Surveillance and the Interception of Communications* (LRC 57–1998) stated that the effect of *Goodwin* was not to create an absolute right and did not foreclose a reasoned balancing exercise, but the true force of it was "to place a very heavy onus on States to justify laws forcing disclosure" (at p.220).

[64] *John v Express Newspapers plc.*, above, n.63, at p.265. For a brief discussion of the issues, see Daniel Pickard, "Disclosure of Journalists' Sources – Sir Elton John v Express Newspapers" [2000] ENT. L.R. 200.

[65] See Robertson and Nicol, *Media Law* (Penguin Books, London, 2002), pp.260–270,

recent application of section 10 of the Contempt of Court Act in the UK led to a finding that an internet service provider could obtain an order requiring website operators to disclose the identity of the source of defamatory material posted by an anonymous contributor to a discussion board.[66]

The *Goodwin* judgment of the European Court of Human Rights has been further developed at European level, both by the court itself,[67] and by the other organs of the Council of Europe.[68] Most specific is the Committee of Ministers Recommendation R(2000) 7 on the right of journalists not to disclose their sources of information.[69] Principle 1 of the Recommendation stipulates that "domestic law and practice in member states should provide for explicit and clear protection of the right of journalists not to disclose information identifying a source" in accordance with Article 10 of the European Convention on Human Rights. Principle 3 provides that states shall pay particular regard to "the right of non-disclosure and the pre-eminence given to it in the case-law of the European Court of Human Rights", and may only order a disclosure if "there exists an overriding requirement in the public interest and if circumstances are of a sufficiently vital and serious nature". Other principles deal with limits and conditions, the rule in *de Haes and Gijsels*,[70] surveillance, search and seizure, and protection against self-incrimination.[71]

---

and Thomas Gibbons, "Protection of Journalistic Sources" (2002) *Communications Law* 124; *Ashworth Special Hospital v MGN Ltd.* [2002] U.K.H.L. 29; *Interbrew SA v Financial Times & others* [2002] E.M.L.R. 446.

[66] *Totalise plc v Motley Fool and Another, The Times*, March 15, 2001, judgment Q.B.D., February 19, 2001. In *R v Central Criminal Court, ex p. Bright* [2001] E.M.L.R. 4, however, the Divisional Court quashed an order against *The Guardian* requiring it to surrender an e-mail sent to it by David Shayler, a former MI5 officer, charged with offences under the Official Secrets Act 1989 (UK).

[67] At least in the particular circumstances of the cases before it. For example, in *de Haes and Gijsels v Belgium*, judgment of February 24, 1997, (1998) 25 E.H.R.R. 1, it upheld the right of journalists not to disclose their source in a defamation case arising from their criticism of some members of the judiciary. In *Fressoz and Roire v France*, judgment of January 21, 1999, (2001) 31 E.H.R.R. 2, it held that the public's interest in being informed outweighed the duties and responsibilities the journalists had under Art.10 as a result of the suspect origin of the confidential tax documents that had been sent to them. Further cases, involving searches of news desks or the homes of journalists, have been declared admissible before the Strasbourg court: *Roemen and Schmit v Luxembourg* (March 12, 2002), *Ernst & others v Belgium* (June 25, 2002) – see Dirk Voorhoof, "The Protection of Journalistic Sources: Recent Developments and Actual Challenges" (2003) 1 *Auteurs & Media* 9. In *Roemen and Schmit* the Court on February 25, 2003 found the searches disproportionate, a breach of Art.10, and reiterated the importance of the protection of journalists' sources for press freedom. In *Ernst*, the Court on July 15, 2003, held unanimously that there had been a violation of both Arts 10 and 8.

[68] See, for example, the Resolutions of the Ministerial conferences on Mass Media Policy, available at *www.coe.int/media*.

[69] March 8, 2000, DH-MM (2000) 2, 125–128, *www.humanrights.coe.int/media*.

[70] Above, n.67.

[71] A good example of the latter is a Russian case, in which a journalist was threatened that if he did not disclose his source he would be charged with assisting in a kidnapping. As Andrei Richter points out ("Protection of Sources in Russian Media Law", Conference paper, Luxembourg, September 30, 2002 available at *www.coe.int/MediaLuxembourgE*), such criminal charges would have had a reverse effect, since an accused person has a constitutional right not to testify against himself and to decline to testify at all.

The *Goodwin* decision has also had repercussions in other European states,[72] including Ireland. Although not binding on Irish courts, since the decision was against the UK and the ECHR had not yet been incorporated into Irish law, it has proved to be of considerable persuasive value. In 1996, Barry O'Kelly, a journalist with the *Star* newspaper, refused to reveal his sources when called as a witness in a civil action in the Dublin Circuit Court. The court's attention was drawn to the ruling of the European Court in *Goodwin* and the Attorney General's office was invited to put the *Goodwin* arguments. As a result, the judge found that it was not necessary for the journalist to disclose his sources and that he was not in contempt of court.[73] Although the case was heard in a lower court, and so does not form a binding precedent, it is nonetheless an indication of the likely attitude to the *Goodwin* principles in Irish courts.

(ii) Journalists' notes, photographs and film footage

Another offshoot of the protection of sources, despite *Goodwin*, is the increasing pressure on journalists to surrender photographs and film footage of public events, particularly where those events have led to civil unrest, football hooliganism and such like. The purpose is to identify the perpetrators of the violence. It has been argued that this is a separate issue from that of confidential sources of information. Even if that argument is correct, there is great unease among the journalistic community about being obliged to hand over, for the purpose of criminal investigation, material collected in the pursuit of journalism. While journalists are like other citizens and have the same responsibilities as citizens, their role as journalists requires them to be independent of all authorities and organs of the state.[74]

---

[72] See Dirk Voorhoof, above, n.67. Some countries, such as Spain, Portugal and Macedonia protect sources in their constitutions; others do so in legislation, while a few (Belgium, The Netherlands), have no specific law on sources but offer some level of protection in their case law. Ireland is out on a limb in not doing so.

[73] *The Irish Times*, November 27–28, 1996, December 20, 1996, January 14, 1997. The judge stated that his decision was based on two English authorities and that the position in law remained as in the *Kevin O'Kelly* case in 1973, namely that journalistic privilege did not exist. In Irish law there is no privilege for journalists and their sources, although a qualified privilege has been recognized in other relationships: priests/penitents (*Cook v Carroll* [1945] I.R. 515); lawyers/clients (see Nuala Jackson and Thomas Courtney, "Without Prejudice or without Effect?" (March, April 1991) G.I.L.S.I. 49, 119); police/informers (Paul A. O'Connor, "The Privilege of Non-Disclosure and Informers" (1980) 15 Ir. Jur. 111); Marc McDonald, "Some Aspects of the Law on Disclosure of Information" (1979) 14 Ir. Jur. 229); marriage-counsellor/client (*ER v JR* [1981] I.L.R.M. 125, but not between a member and counsellor of the Church of Scientology (*Johnston v Church of Scientology* [2001] I.R. 682); doctors/patients (Henchy J. in *Hynes v Garvey* [1978] I.R. 174, at 187; Lynch J. in *NIB v RTÉ* [1998] 2 I.R. 465, at 494); and bankers/customers (*NIB v RTÉ, ibid.*).

[74] The view is well articulated in the dissenting opinions of McLachlin J. in *CBC v Lessard* [1991] 3 S.C.R. 421 and *CBC v New Brunswick (AG)* [1991] 3 S.C.R. 459 and in the principle that if the press is informally and involuntarily impressed into the service of law enforcement agencies as a subsidiary fact-gathering agent, it will lose its credibility as being the independent eye and ear of the citizenry – cited and discussed in Arbour, above, n.12, at 25–6.

Apart from Irish legislation such as the Offences against the State Acts and Official Secrets Acts, which are seldom used against journalists, there is British legislation which contains provisions that can be used to require journalists, including Irish journalists operating in the jurisdiction, to hand over notes or material which will sometimes risk divulging sources. In 1992, Channel Four and independent programme makers, Box Productions, were fined £75,000 for contempt for refusing to reveal their sources for a programme on loyalist death squads in Northern Ireland. The powers conferred by the Prevention of Terrorism Act 1989 were invoked to require them to hand over files, documents and other material relating to the programme.[75] The North's emergency legislation and the Criminal Law Act 1976 were used to seize footage from television companies, including RTÉ, following the killing of two British army corporals in Belfast.[76]

The same legislation was used in 1999 to try to force journalist Ed Moloney, northern editor of the *Sunday Tribune*, to hand over to the police in Northern Ireland records of interviews he had conducted in relation to the murder in 1989 of solicitor Pat Finucane.[77] The journalist refused to comply with a court order for the records on the grounds that it would jeopardise his career as a journalist and would be a breach of journalistic ethics. In a decision which clarified and extended the scope of legal protection for the confidentiality of journalists' sources, at least in the context of the relevant legislation, the Belfast High Court held that the onus was on the police to show that the notes would be likely to contain material which would advance the investigation into the murder. The police must show "something more than a possibility" that the

---

[75] *DPP v Channel Four Television Co. Ltd* [1993] 2 All E.R. 517; *The Irish Times*, April 30, 1992, July 28, 1992. The approach of the court has since been questioned in light of the Human Rights Act 1998 in the UK – see Robertson and Nicol, above, n.65, pp.395–6.

[76] *The Irish Times*, March 25, 1988. Since then the Irish government announced an end to the state of emergency (*The Irish Times*, February 7, 1995). In 1995 a Northern Ireland court ordered the BBC, UTV and RTÉ to hand over unbroadcast television film of a stand-off in Portadown between police and Orangemen. The application was brought by the RUC under the 1989 Police and Criminal Evidence Order (*The Irish Times*, August 30, 1995). On the use of the North's emergency legislation against the media and on the likely effects of the Human Rights Act, see Ruth Costigan, "Human Rights and Police Seizure of Journalists' Material" (2000) 5 *Communications Law* 197.

[77] *In the matter of an Application by Ed Moloney for Judicial Review*, unreported, High Court (NI), Carswell J., October 27, 1999, *http://indigo.ie/~nujdub/judgment.htm*. Moloney had entered into an agreement with his source, William Stobie, not to identify him or reveal details of his allegations unless he was ever charged with Pat Finucane's murder. When that happened, Moloney identified Stobie and wrote a detailed report on his claims that he had alerted the RUC about the intended murder. However, as the *Sunday Tribune* (October 31, 1999) pointed out in an editorial following the High Court decision in favour of Moloney, confidentiality extends beyond the naming of a source. It applies to notes of interviews as well. "A journalist cannot hand these over for use in a police investigation, not just because it would be a betrayal of the source but because they may be used as support for a prosecution (in which the journalist could be called as a witness). Newspapers have no part to play in the gathering of evidence in police investigations or to assist in criminal proceedings. Journalists act in the public interest by gathering and publishing information that would not otherwise reach the public domain". William Stobie was later acquitted but was shot dead shortly afterwards.

material would be of some use. They must "establish that there are reasonable grounds for believing that the material is likely to be of *substantial* value to the investigation". Following the Omagh bombing, the Terrorism Act 2000 was passed, which gave the RUC wide-ranging powers to seek film and pictures, whether or not it had been transmitted or published. The RUC used the legislation to seek film and newspaper pictures of riots in Belfast in July 2001.[78]

(iii) Journalists' Sources and Tribunals

There is no legislation in Ireland equivalent to the British Contempt of Court Act 1981, although a bill was introduced in 1995 and a private member's bill to amend the defamation laws also contained provisions to protect journalists' sources.[79] Neither was enacted. The latter provisions in the bill were included in response to the case of *DPP v O'Keeffe*,[80] in which a Granada Television journalist was prosecuted for, in effect, contempt of a tribunal of inquiry. A programme on irregularities in the beef processing industry in Ireland had prompted the government to establish a Tribunal of Inquiry. Journalist Susan O'Keeffe was asked by the tribunal to identify her sources and hand over documentation used in the preparation of the programme. She refused. The chairman of the tribunal, under the terms of the Tribunals of Inquiry (Evidence) Acts 1921–79, sent a file to the DPP with a view to prosecuting her for refusing to "produce any documents … in [her] power or control legally required by the Tribunal … or to answer any question to which the tribunal may legally require an answer" (section 1(2)(b), as amended). There is no defence provided in the Act, although it would have been open to her to prove that the documents sought by the tribunal were not in her "power or control", belonging as they did to Granada Television. She could also have argued the case as to whether the tribunal, not being a court of law, could "legally require" an answer to the question put to her.[81] The case eventually collapsed due to lack of evidence.[82]

In another case arising out of the Beef Tribunal, *Kiberd and Carey v Tribunal of Inquiry into the Beef Industry*,[83] the High Court upheld the right of the tribunal to make an order pursuant to section 4 of the 1979 Act obliging two journalists to appear before it to tell the tribunal the source of the information

---

[78] *The Irish Times*, August 1, 2001.

[79] Defamation Bill (No.5 of 1995), ss.43–5. The Bill pre-dated the *Goodwin* judgment. It sought to incorporate the provision of s.10 of the Contempt of Court Act 1981 in Britain, to the effect that contempt will arise only where disclosure of sources is necessary in the interests of justice, national security or for the prevention of disorder or crime. The onus of proving necessity in support of any of these interests was to rest on the prosecution (s.43(2)). The provision was to be extended to Tribunals of Inquiry by s.44. A separate Contempt of Court Bill (No.2 of 1995) was also introduced with the aim of protecting journalists' sources.

[80] *The Irish Times*, January 28, 1995. The issue also arose in *Burke v Central Television* [1994] 2 I.L.R.M. 161, in which discovery of documents relating to IRA activities, used to make a television programme, "The Cook Report", was refused because of the risk to life involved.

[81] On this and related problems, see above, n.43, *Paper*, Chs 9 and 17.

[82] *The Irish Times*, January 28, 1995.

[83] [1992] I.L.R.M. 574.

on which two articles published in the *Sunday Business Post* were based and the identity of the person or persons from whom the information had been obtained.[84] The articles concerned matters due to come before the tribunal. They were based on material given to the tribunal in confidence, and the chairman feared that, if the matter were not inquired into, other witnesses might not come forward and documents might be withheld. The High Court held that, apart from this, the order was necessary in the circumstances because the tribunal had to take steps to ensure that no further articles would be published based on material submitted in confidence to it. Although the right to make the order was upheld, no charges were brought against the journalists for refusing to divulge their sources.[85]

Constant leaking of confidential information has plagued the Flood Tribunal (planning matters) and Moriarty Tribunal (payments to politicians).[86] In some instances the matters were referred to the gardaí for investigation,[87] in others journalists were ordered to produce certain documents.[88] The Saville Tribunal of Inquiry (the Bloody Sunday inquiry) in Derry also led to a number of requests to journalists to disclose their sources.[89] The tribunal found *Daily Telegraph* journalist, Toby Harnden, in contempt and referred the matter to the High Court in Belfast.[90] In some instances, the requests for disclosure related to programmes and articles that had been instrumental in the setting up of the inquiry and counsel for the tribunal stated that it would be a supreme irony if the tribunal were to take the view that it was not necessary to obtain the source of the very information which had in part led to its establishment in the first place.[91] However, counsel for Channel 4 counter-argued that the fact that Channel 4 reports played a substantial part in the setting up of the Bloody Sunday inquiry is an argument for journalistic confidentiality, not against it.[92]

Journalists depend on sources but they need to be circumspect in their

---

[84] The chairman did not use the power given by the Act to treat the contempt as if it had been contempt of the High Court and punish the journalists himself. This power has been questioned on constitutional grounds by the LRC, *Paper*, above, n.43, at p.422.

[85] *The Irish Times*, October 15, 1994. In the case of the *Irish Press* publishing extracts from a report, in breach of a court order (above, n.44), Costello J. in the High Court recognised that a free and fearless press with access to sources was important for society to function properly and did not think that it was necessary for the sources to be revealed in the particular case before him (*The Irish Times*, October 26, 1991).

[86] *The Sunday Tribune*, April 25, 1999. On the subject of politicians and their sources, particularly in the case of the Morris tribunal regarding allegations of garda corruption in Donegal see Chap.7.

[87] *The Irish Times*, April 23, 1999.

[88] *The Sunday Business Post*, April 4, 1999.

[89] See, for example, *The Irish Times*, April 27, 1999, September 30, 1999, October 2, 1999, April 14, 2000, May 2, 2002.

[90] *The Irish Times*, April 14, 2000. The judge's ruling that, having regard to the right to a fair trial as enshrined in the ECHR, the proceedings should be regarded as criminal, thus affording Mr Harnden additional legal rights at his trial, was appealed to the Court of Appeal in London. The appeal was dismissed (*The Irish Times*, February 15, 2003).

[91] See *The Irish Times*, October 10, 1999. The same could be said for the Beef Tribunal, but as is argued above, the purpose of the tribunal was to discover and deal with the *substance* of the information, not the source.

[92] See Mary Holland, "Saville has implications for media," *The Irish Times*, May 2, 2002.

dealings with them and in their use of information that has been leaked for a purpose. Their role is not that of public relations consultants or advertising agents; they need to consider the public interest involved in publishing leaked documents and information. Nonetheless, if it is accepted that all sources are not wrongdoers and do not act out of personal spite or rancour, the need to identify them becomes secondary to the need to preserve the free flow of information.

In the United States, a majority of states have "shield laws", providing journalists and their sources with varying degrees of protection. Under these laws, journalists are usually only required to answer questions or provide documentation if the information is vital to the trial of a serious offence and is not available from any other source. In an interesting development in 1991, the US Supreme Court held in *Cohen v Cowles Media*[93] that a source who had been promised confidentiality by a newspaper journalist but whose name had been revealed in the paper could sue the newspaper for breach of contract on the basis of the promissory estoppel principle, that is, the newspaper would be stopped from going back on the promise given by the journalist. The source, who was the campaign manager for a candidate, had planted damaging information about an opponent in the run-up to an election. The newspaper editor took the decision, in those circumstances, to name the source. The *Cohen* decision has opened the door to a growing number of successful lawsuits against the American media for factually correct reports in which liability arises only from the means used to gather the underlying truthful information.[94] The situation in *Cohen* is not akin, of course, to identifying a source in a court of law. A journalist who did so could hardly be sued for conforming to a legal requirement. However, the practical effect would be the same. The journalist would lose the confidence of other potential sources and the flow of information to him/her and to other journalists would dry up. A journalist's ability to inform the public depends on the maintenance of confidential relationships, yet Irish law has so far refused to recognise any right to protect confidential sources.

6.3.2.2 Contempt by Scandalising the Court

The second form of criminal contempt indicated by Ó Dálaigh C.J. was: "words written or spoken ... calculated to prejudice ... justice".[95] The form of "words written or spoken" could otherwise be described as "constructive" contempt, *i.e.* contempt committed outside the court. It can be further broken down into

---

[93] 501 U.S. 663 (1991). See Jens B. Koepke, "Reporter Privilege: Shield or Sword? Applying a Modified Breach of Contract Standard When a Newspaper 'Burns' a Confidential Source" (1990) 42 F.C.L.J. 277.

[94] See Michael W. Richards, "Tort Vision for the New Millennium: Strengthening News Industry Standards as a Defense Tool in Law Suits over Newsgathering Techniques" (2000) 10 Fordham Intell.Prop., Media & Ent.L.J. 501, at p.506. Richards suggests that it is time for the industry to establish standards of newsgathering, which would serve as evidence of reasonableness and a counterweight to the distrust of the media (*ibid.* at pp.512–3).

[95] Above, n.40.

two categories: (i) words that amount to scandalising the court, for example criticism of a judge or court if the criticism imputes partiality or corruption, and (ii) words that are likely to prejudice a fair trial, for example reference to other offences or past convictions, publication of matter deliberately kept from the jury or publication of photographs where identification is in issue. Again the distinctions have become less marked in recent years but are a convenient vehicle for analysing the nature and range of activities that can amount to criminal contempt.

On the question of scandalising, O'Higgins C.J. in *The State (DPP) v Walsh and Conneely*,[96] stated:

> "Contempt by scandalising the court is committed where what is said or done is of such a nature as to be calculated to endanger public confidence in the court. ... It is not committed by mere criticisms of judges as judges, or by the expression of disagreement – even emphatic disagreement – with what has been decided by a court. ... Such contempt occurs where wild and baseless allegations of corruption or malpractice are made against a court. The right of citizens to express freely, subject to public order, convictions and opinions is wide enough to comprehend such criticism or expressed disagreement. Such contempt occurs where wild and baseless allegations of corruption or malpractice are made against a court so as to hold the judges '... to the odium of the people as actors playing a sinister part in a caricature of justice.'"[97]

Therefore, to constitute contempt by scandalising, the attack must be on a court or on a judge acting in his or her judicial capacity and must amount to more than mere criticism. However, tolerance and what is regarded as "mere criticism" may vary from one era or culture to another, or even from one court to another,[98] although, in fairness, it must be said that Irish judges do take account of freedom of expression and the right to criticise. Since contempt occurs when "baseless" allegations are made, it would appear that justification or truth is a defence.[99]

Many of the cases which have arisen in Ireland have concerned criticism of the operations of the Special Criminal Court. To accuse it of "conducting a mock trial" was regarded as contempt,[100] as were two letters imputing improper and base motives and bias to the judges of that court.[101] Criticism of the establishment of the court or the retention of the death penalty or the provisions

---

[96] Above, n.50.

[97] Quoting Gavan Duffy P. in *AG v Connolly* [1947] I.R. 213.

[98] Compare, for example, *AG v O'Kelly* [1928] I.R. 308, *AG v Connolly* [1947] 1 I.R. 213, *AG v O'Ryan and Boyd* [1946] I.R. 70 with the other cases cited in the text. For examples of earlier cases when newspaper proprietors were fined and imprisoned for "reflections on the court", "false accounts of the proceedings", and so on, see Inglis, above, n.26, at pp.77, 80, 103.

[99] See Yvonne Murphy, *Journalists and the Law* (2nd ed., Round Hall Sweet & Maxwell, Dublin, 2000), at p.134.

[100] *AG v Connolly*, above, n.97.

[101] *In re Hibernia National Review* [1976] I.R. 388.

of the Offences against the State Act under which the court is set up would not be contempt because they are matters that can validly be debated in public.[102]

In the case of *In re Kennedy and McCann*,[103] a journalist reported on a child custody case and implied that justice could not be obtained in an Irish court in our "sick" and "hypocritical" society. The report, said the courts, contained a gross misstatement of how the court had dealt with the case, which had been held *in camera*. The journalist and editor apologised and were heavily fined. The judge told them that if they had not apologised, they would have received a substantial prison sentence. The case also raised issues of privacy and the right to report (see further discussion in Chapter 7).

The classic case on scandalising the court was *The State (DPP) v Walsh and Conneely*,[104] involving once again an attack on the Special Criminal Court. Following the conviction and sentence of two people for capital murder, *The Irish Times* published a statement issued on behalf of the Association for Legal Justice. The statement condemned the sentences meted out by a court "composed of government-appointed judges having no judicial independence which sat without a jury and which so abused the rules of evidence as to make the court akin to a sentencing tribunal".[105] The case raised important questions as to the boundaries of fair criticism, the role of the courts themselves in deciding whether a court has been scandalised and, in particular, the use of summary trial (*i.e.* without a jury) in contempt cases.

For some time now in Britain, although not in some other Commonwealth countries,[106] contempt by scandalising has fallen into disuse. In Ireland, it has still emerged from time to time, but judges nowadays are more tolerant, more accustomed to media criticism and comment and, therefore, less likely to punish for scandalising. *Desmond v Glackin (No.1)*[107] involved media statements made by a government minister and the inspector he had appointed to inquire into a property acquisition, which had been the subject of considerable public controversy. O'Hanlon J. in the High Court relied on the context of the statements, in finding that they did not exceed the bounds of fair and permissible criticism.[108] A statement made by the Minister, that the High Court "certainly facilitated Mr Desmond in blocking the enquiry", was the kind of statement that might once have been regarded as scandalising. However, it was taken, in the context of the interview, to refer to the expedition with which the application had been processed by the High Court and which had resulted in the inquiry

---

[102] *ibid.*, Kenny J., at 391.

[103] [1976] I.R. 382.

[104] Above, n.50.

[105] *ibid.* at 420. The case against *The Irish Times* was dropped. The other two defendants were given suspended sentences of 18 and 12 months imprisonment. See J.M. Kelly, *The Irish Constitution* (Gerard Hogan and Gerry Whyte (eds), 3rd ed., Butterworths, Dublin, 1994), p.935.

[106] A Canadian journalist, who was local bureau chief of the *Far Eastern Economic Review*, was jailed in Malaysia in 1999 for scandalising the court. He had criticised the court for fast-tracking a case brought by the wife of an appeal court judge on behalf of her son, seeking £2 million damages for discrimination against him when he was dropped from a school debating team (*The Irish Times*, October 11, 1999).

[107] Above, n.20.

[108] *ibid.* at 17.

being halted, which the Minister deplored. This is, it is submitted, a reasonable and common-sense approach, especially as the remarks were made in a radio interview shortly after the event and followed the issuing of a press release on behalf of Mr Desmond by a public relations firm.[109]

The decision in *Desmond v Glackin* continued a trend in recent years of courts no longer feeling threatened by the media but accepting that the media have a legitimate role in commenting on and criticising the operation of the courts. This development is to be expected as the media and public mature together. It is not that the courts have abandoned the notion of contempt or are any less zealous in protecting their authority but rather that they allow more latitude and are less inclined to punish. Relying on the dicta in *In re Kennedy and McCann* (above), Carroll J. in *Weeland v RTÉ*[110] said:

> "I do not see why a judgment cannot be criticised, provided it is not done in a manner calculated to bring the court or the judge into contempt. If that element is not present there is no reason why judgments should not be criticised. Nor does the criticism have to be confined to scholarly articles in legal journals. The mass media are entitled to have their say as well. The public take a great interest in court cases and it is only natural that discussion should concentrate on the result of cases. So criticism which does not subvert justice should be allowed."

Further evidence of that trend can be seen in *McCann v An Taoiseach*.[111] RTÉ admitted that their reporting of the case, which had sought to prevent a broadcast by the Taoiseach in advance of a referendum on the Maastricht Treaty,[112] was careless and inaccurate, imputing remarks to the judge that he had not made. This was a serious contempt, the judge said, but no action was required because it was not intentional or malicious and was immediately and fully repaired.[113] Where the contempt is unintentional, as studies show it almost invariably is,[114] then, as Carney J. recognised, the most effective remedy is rectification or retraction.[115] This was recognised also in a manslaughter case in which inaccurate reports were published by two newspapers and a radio station. Budd J. accepted the explanation that the inaccuracy was due to a transmission error and recommended that no action be taken as corrections had been published and broadcast promptly.[116] The Law Reform Commission[117] has recommended that a court should be empowered to order the pub-

---

[109] The role and influence of public relations firms are a recent phenomenon, requiring scrutiny. They were a significant factor in the handling and coverage of the Beef Tribunal, for example.

[110] [1987] I.R. 662, at 666, referring to the dicta of O'Higgins C.J., above, n.103, at 386.

[111] High Court, June 22, 1992, Carney J.; *The Irish Times*, June 23, 1992.

[112] The government intended to use s.31(2) of the Broadcasting Authority Act 1960 to allow the Taoiseach to make the broadcast.

[113] Above, n.111.

[114] See Kevin Boyle and Marie McGonagle, above, n.19, at p.178.

[115] Above, n.111.

[116] *The Irish Times*, December 6, 1994.

[117] Above, n.43, *Report*, at p.32; *Report on the Civil Law of Defamation* (LRC 38–1991).

lication of an apology and/or a correction in cases of scandalising, similar to the orders recommended in their *Report on the Civil Law of Defamation.*

It is possible to take this view a step further and ask whether, in this day and age, there is any need for this form of contempt at all. It is true that judges cannot readily defend themselves in the media but is there any reason, other than an organisational or economic one, why the courts should not, like other institutions of state, become part of the media age, and establish their own press office or media relations officer to explain procedures, summarise judgments and generally enhance accuracy in reporting and public knowledge? Courts in other jurisdictions have done so, most notably in Canada and Australia.[118] The Courts Service, which has taken over the management of the Irish courts, has made great strides in this direction.[119]

However, it must be pointed out that the Law Reform Commission[120] did not recommend abolishing contempt by scandalising completely. They recommended retaining it for imputing corrupt conduct to a judge or court and for publishing to the public a false account of legal proceedings, but only on proof of intention or recklessness and where there is a substantial risk of the administration of justice or the judiciary or any particular judge(s) being brought into serious disrepute. Truth would be a defence. The onus of proving corruption would rest with the defence, that of proving the falsity of an account of legal proceedings, with the prosecution.

6.3.2.3 Contempt by Prejudicing a Fair Trial

Contempt by prejudicing a fair trial is the form of contempt that most affects the media. It consists of the publication of matter calculated to prejudice ongoing or pending cases, criminal or civil. The perceived danger is of influencing the jury, where there is one. Judges have usually contended that because of their experience and training, they would not be susceptible to media comment or pressure and do not need protection.[121] An offending

---

[118] See Robert J. Sharpe, "The Role of a Media Spokesperson for the Courts – The Supreme Court of Canada Experience" (1990) 1 Media Comm. L. Rev. 271; Australian Law Reform Commission, *Discussion Paper*, No.26, 1986, referring to the establishment of a media liaison bureau in Victoria.

[119] The Working Group on a Courts' Commission in its *Working Paper*, above, n.19, examined the media and information provisions in a number of other countries and advised the setting up of an Information Office with a media liaison function. It is worth noting that in the US the function is seen as one of facilitating competent coverage of the courts. In Northern Ireland, one of the functions mentioned is that of regulating film access to court houses.

[120] Above, n.43, *Report*, at Chap.5.

[121] See *Cullen v Tóibín* [1984] I.L.R.M. 577, at 581 (O'Higgins C.J.); *Weeland v RTÉ* [1987] I.R. 662, at 666 (High Court, Carroll J.); *Wong v Minister for Justice* (High Court, Denham J.) July 30, 1992. Haugh J. in *The People (DPP) v Haughey* (unreported, High Court, June 26, 2000) referred to two schools of thought regarding juries: one, that juries can be relied upon virtually no matter what the circumstances; the other, that the assumption that prejudicial effects can be overcome by instructions to a jury is a naïve assumption and an unmitigated legal fiction. See also the Supreme Court in *Irish Times Ltd v Judge Murphy*, above, n.5.

publication could entail a reflection on an accused person so as to jeopardise his chances of a fair trial or it could relate to a civil action, for defamation, for example, and adversely affect the position of one of the parties. In *Desmond v Glackin (No. 1)*,[122] the alleged contempt related to judicial review proceedings. Indeed, as *Desmond* shows, there can be an overlap between the various forms of contempt and one set of facts can give rise to contempt by scandalising and contempt by prejudicing a trial.[123]

Other examples from the case law include newspaper criticism of the Special Criminal Court while it was conducting a murder trial;[124] a letter to a newspaper criticising the Special Criminal Court while an appeal in the case was pending;[125] an article revealing details of *in camera* hearings;[126] an article proclaiming that an accused's statements had not been made voluntarily;[127] and a newspaper report on organised crime in Dublin, referring to a Mr Daly, who, it turned out, was due before the courts the next day on armed robbery charges.[128] In the last-mentioned case, the jury was discharged and the trial put back to the next court term because of the risk that the jury could be influenced by the report.

The jury was discharged also when a lead story in an evening newspaper risked causing prejudice by mentioning the family relationship between the accused in an ongoing drugs trial and a convicted drugs dealer with the same surname.[129] A case against Gay Byrne in 1989 over remarks he had made in a newspaper article about a case he was taking against a number of accountants was eventually dismissed in 1992.[130] It was always unlikely that there would be a jury involved, and in any event, the case was subsequently withdrawn, so that to pursue the contempt issue was purely academic, "an exercise in futility",

---

[122] Above, n.20.

[123] Both were rejected in *Desmond*.

[124] *AG v Connolly*, above, n.97.

[125] *The State (DPP) v Walsh and Conneely*, above, n.50.

[126] *In re Kennedy and McCann*, above, n.103.

[127] *The State (DPP) v Irish Press Ltd*, unreported, High Court, December 15, 1976. For further examples of prejudicial publications, see Boyle and McGonagle, 1997, above n.19. In the UK case of *HMA v Beggs* [2002] S.L.T. 139, the court had to consider whether prejudicial material appearing on a website could amount to contempt of court. The material, which referred to previous convictions of the accused, including a murder conviction, which had been quashed on appeal, was contained in articles from the website of *The Guardian*, extracts from an American Internet publication and material appearing on the websites of *The Sunday Times* and the *Sunday Herald*. Lord Osborne considered that there was publication, that proceedings were "active" (Contempt of Court Act 1981, s.2(3)) but, given that the material in question would have to be downloaded from the archives, as opposed to a random search, his Lordship took the view that the publication would not amount to a substantial risk of serious prejudice (the test applicable under the 1981 Act). In those circumstances, it did not constitute contempt of court.

[128] *The Irish Times*, March 1, 15, 1988, *Sunday Tribune*, March 6, 1988, where an apology was also published. In Britain there is a "warned list" which alerts the media to cases that are coming on for hearing, so that the risk of inadvertently prejudicing pending cases is lessened.

[129] *DPP v Dunne* (*Evening Herald*, July 10, 1986, *The Irish Times*, July 12, 1986).

[130] *The Irish Times*, March 26, 1992.

as Carroll J. said in the High Court.[131] Gerry Ryan and RTÉ were fined £200 and £500, respectively, in 1990 following a radio interview with the alleged victim of a rape while the accused's trial was pending before the courts.[132] Other forms of publication can be seen as contempt as well. The publication of photographs can constitute contempt where identification is an issue[133] as can inaccurate headlines, even when the text of the report or article itself is accurate.[134] Reference to previous convictions[135] and to confessions[136] has led to a finding of contempt. Even a song by Christy Moore about the Stardust tragedy amounted to contempt.[137]

(i) "Trial by Media"

Criminal investigations undertaken by the media run the greatest risk of being in contempt of court. So-called investigative journalism can lead to what is frequently denounced as "trial by the media", which was identified by Lord Diplock in the *Sunday Times* case as one of three main forms of prejudice, in that the media usurp the functions of courts of law without the safeguards of legal rules of evidence regarding admissibility and override the presumption of innocence.[138] The argument has taken on a new dimension with the televising of "celebrity" trials in the United States, for example, the Kennedy-Smith, Bobbitt, Louise Woodward, and O.J. Simpson trials. There has been widespread comment and speculation on the likely effects of television on these cases, but the real impact has yet to be assessed (see further discussion in Chapter 7). The counter-argument to the "trial by media" assertion is that the media do not "try" anyone in the sense that no sanction is imposed except through the courts.

---

[131] *ibid.*

[132] Above, n.21, *The Irish Times*, April 3, 1990.

[133] *In re MacArthur* [1983] I.L.R.M. 355.

[134] *The Irish Times*, December 11, 1992, referring to an *Irish Independent* headline "Girl (13) sexually assaulted by man (55)" which implied the guilt of the accused. The editor was later granted leave to seek an order prohibiting the Circuit Court judge from proceeding with a trial for contempt for want of jurisdiction to hold a summary trial (*The Irish Times*, December 19, 1992). See also *The Irish Times*, October 22, 1994, referring to a headline in the *Star*; the editor was given leave to challenge the order fining him £10,000 for contempt (*The Irish Times*, November 8, 1994). In another case, difficulties arose over the use of the word "drugs" in headlines in several newspapers, when the evidence in court was to "substances" (*The Irish Times*, October 27, 1994). Tabloid-style headlines, such as "brute" in the *Irish Mirror* during a murder trial, can undermine the presumption of innocence and may lead to contempt (*The Irish Times*, January 22, 2000).

[135] A good example is the Australian case *Hinch v AG* (1987) 164 C.L.R. 15, concerning a programme broadcast in Australia about a priest charged with child molesting. Also *DPP v Independent Newspapers & Others* (*The Irish Times*, January 25, 2003), below, n.215.

[136] See, for example, *The Irish Times*, July 25, 1996, on the leaking of evidence of a confession to the media in the Bambrick murder trial two months before it was proven in court, although in the particular case the trial judge did not seek action against any of the reporters involved.

[137] *The Irish Times*, August 28, 1985.

[138] *AG v Times Newspapers* [1973] 3 All E.R. 54 (HL) at 72–3.

The televised cases in the US have no direct counterpart in this jurisdiction, where cameras are not allowed in court. Thus concern here has been mainly with pre-trial publicity and with inaccurate or misleading reporting in the media after the day's hearing in court.

(ii) Sensational Media Coverage

In recent years, concern has also been expressed at the trend to sensationalise court proceedings, particularly those concerned with sexual offences. The practice of publishing ever larger and more dramatic photographs of accused persons appearing in court has also raised questions about the value of the presumption of innocence.[139] In a murder trial, *DPP v Nevin*, the trial judge banned the publication of photographs of the accused in newspapers but not on television.[140] The trial had attracted a great deal of public interest and an immense amount of media coverage, including much comment on Mrs Nevin's demeanour, dress, make-up and reading matter. The coverage led to an application by the defence to stay the proceedings on the grounds that the accused would not get a fair trial.[141] The application was refused on the basis of the "real risk" test. In imposing the ban on photographs and comment on the accused in the printed press, the judge's concern was for Mrs Nevin's

---

[139] In a murder trial, *DPP v Sweetman and Palmer* (*The Irish Times*, February 12, 1997), the jury was discharged following publication of two "prejudicial" photographs. The photographs had shown an altercation between a photographer and a man accompanying one of the accused. The trial judge criticised the "undesirable" practice of publishing photographs of accused persons unless or until they are convicted. See Marie McGonagle, "News Photographs and the Right to a Fair Trial", *The Irish Times*, February 12, 1997. See also John Horgan, "Sensationalising Court Proceedings may be Unfair", *The Irish Times*, August 26, 1999. In *The People v Davis* [2001] 1 I.R. 146; [2001] 2 I.L.R.M. 65, photographs showing a murder accused being brought to and from court in handcuffs were held to be prejudicial and in contempt of court. The court's concern was for the presumption of innocence and the dignity of the individual. It referred to the Rules for the Government of Prisons 1947 to the effect that prisoners being brought to court should be exposed to public view as little as possible. However, the evidence against the accused was so overwhelming that publication of the photographs did not affect the outcome of his trial. In *DPP v Dunleavy* (*The Irish Times*, April 30, 2002) the jury was discharged because of the publication in the *Evening Herald* of a photograph showing the accused in handcuffs. The judge ordered the editor of the *Evening Herald* to appear before him concerning the publication of the photograph, which was also wrongly captioned with the name of a defendant in a separate case. The Court of Criminal Appeal in *DPP v McCowan* quashed a conviction on a number of grounds, including that the accused man was seen in handcuffs by potential jurors (March 31, 2003, Hardiman J., *The Irish Times*, April 1, 2003).

[140] *The Irish Times*, February 10, 2000. Miss Justice Carroll did not impose a ban on the broadcast media, apparently because no complaint had been made against them. Compare the decision of the European Court of Human Rights in *News Verlags v Austria* (above, n.31), particularly paras 39, 58–9. See also Simon McAleese, "A step too far? Reporting restrictions on the *Nevin* case" *Law Society Gazette* (May 2000) 16; Paddy Dillon-Malone, "Mrs Nevin's Pictures – A European Gloss" [2000] 5 B.R. 510; Úna Ní Raifeartaigh, "The European Convention on Human Rights and the Irish Criminal Justice System" (2001) 7 B.R. 111, at 114.

[141] Two juries had been discharged but not through any fault of the media (*The Irish Times*, April 12, 2000).

dignity as a human person and the presumption of innocence. A number of colour pieces had commented on Mrs Nevin's clothing, hairstyle, fingernails and choice of reading material, in terms that were "at times cruel, at times titillating and always intrusive".[142] An *Evening Herald* profile of a District Justice linked to the case was regarded by Ms Justice Carroll as having trespassed on the role of the jury to decide the credibility of witnesses and as having brought in extraneous comment on matters relevant to the trial.[143] An *Irish Mirror* headline ran "Sex Secrets of the Black Widow" and a graphic in the *Irish Times* distorted her image to that of an ogre.[144]

In contrast, the European Court of Human Rights in a somewhat similar case, *News Verlags GmbH v Austria*,[145] found that a ban on a particular newspaper from publishing photographs (though not comment) of a person charged in connection with letter bomb offences was not necessary in a democratic society and was disproportionate. It went further than was necessary to protect the accused person against defamation, invasion of privacy or violations of the presumption of innocence. The Court acknowledged that there could be good reasons for prohibiting the publication of a suspect's picture in itself, depending on the nature of the offence at issue and the particular circumstances of the case (para. 58). However, such is the public interest where criminal proceedings are involved that relevant and sufficient reasons must be adduced to justify a prohibition of that nature. The ban on publishing photographs in *News Verlags* did not in any way restrict the applicant company's right to comment on the criminal proceedings, but it did restrict its choice as to the presentation of its reports, while other media were free to continue to publish the photographs. Since it was not the pictures by themselves, but only in combination with the text, that interfered with the accused's rights, the absolute prohibition on publication of them went further than was necessary to protect the accused (para. 59). Publication was banned not only in connection with a text that was prejudicial but, even more restrictively, in connection with reports on the criminal proceedings, irrespective of the accompanying text (para.22).

In light of the judgment of the European Court in *News Verlags*, and the prior restraint aspect of such a ban, it would appear that a lesser measure, such as a warning to the press, would have been more proportionate in the circumstances of *Nevin*. Such warnings at an earlier stage in the trial might have obviated the need for such a ban in the first place, although it must be remembered that this was the third attempt, as two previous trials had been aborted, and the trial judge had previously dismissed complaints about colour

---

[142] *The Irish Times*, February 10, 2000.

[143] *The Irish Times*, April 12, 2000.

[144] See *The Sunday Times*, April 23, 2000.

[145] Above, n.31. Despite the fact that the comments on the accused were insulting and contrary to the presumption of innocence, with references to "Nazi" and "terrorist for the Führer", the Austrian courts had not banned them, only the photographs. The ban in *Nevin* was therefore more extensive than the one found to be contrary to Art.10, ECHR in *News Verlags*. Since comment had not been banned in *News Verlags*, the Court did not have to decide on that issue; however, the *test* to be used in so deciding is clear from the judgment.

pieces and said she would direct the jury not to read newspaper accounts nor to pay attention to radio or television reports of the trial for its duration. In any event, the appeal court in *Nevin* said that the trial had been conducted fairly and that the various rulings made by the trial judge in dealing with the publicity issues were within her discretion to make and were proper rulings. Geoghegan J. pointed out, however, that the perception that following *Z v DPP* (see below), that a trial could not be stopped on the grounds of adverse publicity was completely wrong. Trial judges must have a discretion on that matter and the appeal court should not interfere with that discretion unless it was exercised wrongly. Even then, there would be other factors to consider, including whether the media disclosed previous convictions. There was a big difference, he said, between a one-day trial taking place after adverse publicity and a 40-day trial such as this.[146]

(iii) Pre-trial publicity

Another area of concern in recent years has been the effect of pre-trial publicity on the right to a fair trial. In recent years there have been a number of attempts in Ireland to stop trials altogether on the basis that the accused could not get a fair trial, due to saturation media coverage of events prior to the trial. The test applied by the Irish Supreme Court in *Z v DPP*[147] was one of a "real" risk of an unfair trial. It was on the basis of that test that the Court allowed the trial of the man at the centre of the *X* case[148] to proceed. The *X* case was a case which took place in 1992 when a court injunction was obtained to prevent a 14-year-old girl going to Britain for an abortion. The man accused of offences against

---

[146] It is true that the ban on comment and photographs in the print media was a lesser measure than staying the proceedings, which had been requested. However, it was still an extensive restriction, even more restrictive than the ban in *News Verlags*, and therefore susceptible on proportionality grounds. There is also the issue of its discriminatory nature, applying, as it did, only to the print media. Following Mrs Nevin's conviction, her appeal to the Court of Criminal Appeal on numerous grounds, including the effects of media coverage on the right to fair trial, was heard in February 2003. Judgment was reserved (*The Irish Times*, February 15, 2003) and the appeal finally dismissed on all counts on May 14, 2003 (*The Irish Times*, March 15, May 15, 2003). The appeal court was satisfied that it had been a fair and orderly trial. The court considered it unlikely that any of the jury had been prejudiced and was impressed by the length of time the jury had deliberated – a total of 26 hours and 36 minutes (*The Irish Times*, February 13, 2003).

[147] Above, nn.10, 22. See Gordon Duffy, "Pre-trial Publicity; Prejudice and the Right to a Fair Trial" (1994) 4 I.C.L.J. 113 and 141.

[148] *AG v X* [1992] 1 I.R. 1. The High Court in *Z v DPP* had spoken of a "real or serious" risk. Prior to that, a number of major trials in both England and Ireland had collapsed because of pre-trial publicity, for example *R v Taylor* (1993) 98 Cr. App. R 361, *The Times*, June 15, 1993, *The Irish Times*, December 7, 1994; *R v Cullen* (*The Times*, May 1, 1990, the case in which the convictions of the "Winchester Three" were quashed because of remarks made by Lord Denning and Secretary of State for Northern Ireland, Tom King, about the right to silence). There had also been cases in Ireland where extradition to Britain was refused because of media coverage in that country: *Magee v O'Dea* [1994] I.L.R.M. 540, and the decision of the Attorney General in the Fr Patrick Ryan case (*The Irish Times*, December 14, 1988).

the girl had contended that his trial should not proceed because there had been extensive media coverage of the case in 1992.

The same issue arose in *DPP v Haugh*[149] when a former Taoiseach, Charles Haughey, was facing a criminal trial for obstructing the McCracken Tribunal, which was investigating payments to politicians and political parties. In December 1999, Mr Haughey sought to have his trial postponed until the publicity surrounding the tribunal had died down. He claimed that there was a real risk that he would not get a fair trial until such time as the "fade factor" had taken effect and the effects of the adverse publicity had abated. The question is whether by warnings and directions to the jury or by other less restrictive measures than abandoning or postponing the trial indefinitely, the judge can ensure that the accused person gets a fair trial. In the *Haugh* case, the respondent, who had been the trial judge, had decided to take the additional step of sending a questionnaire to prospective jurors to assess whether they were prejudiced against Mr Haughey. All three judges who reviewed his decision held that there was no express or implied statutory power or inherent jurisdiction to support such an approach.[150]

The same test, whether there was a "real" risk, was subsequently applied by Haugh J. in the later stage of the case, *The People (DPP) v Haughey*.[151] In the circumstances of the case at that time, however, the judge was satisfied that "at present" there existed "a real and substantial risk that the accused, a former Taoiseach, would not receive a fair trial" and stayed the proceedings indefinitely, though not permanently (he made an order "staying all further proceedings on this indictment without leave of this Court"). The offending matter was an interview given by the Tánaiste and the circulation of a leaflet about a proposed public demonstration. The DPP appealed the decision and Carroll J. found that the order made by Haugh J. was an order of adjournment, and not an order prohibiting the trial or effectively imposing a permanent stay on the trial. She said it was open to the DPP to apply to Haugh J. at any time for a date for a new trial, and it would be up to Mr Haughey to prove that there was at that stage a real risk that he could not get a fair trial.[152]

In June 2002, former Dublin City Manager, George Redmond, applied for an order prohibiting his trial on corruption charges. He claimed that because of extensive adverse media coverage of his affairs it would not be possible for him to be tried by an impartial and unbiased jury. He was not seeking to have his trial prohibited permanently, but rather, as in the *Haughey* case above, he wanted it prohibited until "the prejudice that pertains at this time is spent".[153] However, the court held that it was not satisfied that there was a real risk which could not be obviated by suitable warnings. While there was some risk,

---

[149] [2000] 1 I.R. 184.

[150] The relevant legislation was the Juries Act 1976, s.15(3). See further John L. O'Donnell, "The Jury on Trial: Reflections on *DPP v Haugh*" [2000] 5 B.R. 470, which also discusses the issue of post-trial publication.

[151] Unreported, High Court, June 26, 2000.

[152] *The Irish Times*, November 4, 2000.

[153] *The Irish Times*, June 7, 2002. The DPP was also reported to be seeking the imposition of reporting restrictions on the application, although it was not clear on what basis or to what purpose: *The Irish Times*, June 7, 2002.

it could be avoided by appropriate warnings and directions from the trial judge both before a jury was empanelled and during the trial itself. Kearns J. warned, however, that any further publication of salacious or prejudicial material, either about the impending trial or about Mr Redmond, could leave open the possibility of another application for postponement of the trial.[154] On the other side of the fence, Patrick Holland, a convicted drug dealer, sought to overturn a decision of the prison authorities refusing him the right to communicate with the media.[155]

6.3.2.4 Acts Calculated to Prejudice the Course of Justice

Acts aimed at influencing juries, interfering with witnesses or abusing the parties to a case are included in this category of contempt. Chequebook journalism runs a high risk of falling within such a category. The Supreme Court has ruled also that jury deliberations should always be regarded as completely confidential and should not be published after a trial.[156] In Britain, the Contempt of Court Act 1981 makes it an offence to solicit or disclose jury deliberations. One author described this as an extraordinarily wide provision, which applies in all cases and does not take account of the particular circumstances of the individual case; it interferes with *bona fide* research into jury deliberations and may seriously impede public discussion of the merits of the jury system.[157]

Arguments for and against jury disclosures are set out in the Law Reform Commission's *Consultation Paper on Contempt of Court*.[158] In its final recommendations in 1994, the Commission concluded "that it is beyond argument that there could be no absolute rule of secrecy" and instead recommended a "considerable range of secrecy".[159] *Bona fide* research would be permitted subject to prior approval and such conditions as may be specified by the Chief Justice or President of the High Court or Circuit Court, as

---

[154] *The Irish Times*, October 31, 2002. Media attention was one of the issues addressed by the High Court in the attempt by Cork doctor, James Barry, to prevent his trial on charges of indecent and sexual assault of a number of his female patients. While the media attention was distressing and caused a great deal of anxiety, there was no evidence to suggest that it in any way inhibited him in dealing with the garda investigation, apart from a period of about three months when he left the jurisdiction to avoid the media (*The Irish Times*, February 15, 2003).

[155] *The Irish Times*, June 11, 2002. Judgment was reserved (*The Irish Times*, April 4, 2003).

[156] *The People (DPP) v O'Callaghan* [1993] 2 I.R. 17, at 26, O'Flaherty, J.

[157] Eric Barendt, *Freedom of Speech* (Clarendon Press, Oxford, 1989), at p.216. See also Paul Robertshaw, "Leaking the Secrets of the Jury Room" (1993) 12 J.M.L.P. 114; Robertson and Nicol, above, n.65, at pp.392–4. Both the Lord Chancellor and the Royal Commission for Criminal Justice believe the law should be changed to enable research to be carried out into how juries reach their verdicts (*The Times*, May 1, 1995). The European Commission on Human Rights rejected a complaint regarding the secrecy of jury deliberations in *Associated Newspapers Ltd v UK* (App. No.24770/94, November 30, 1994). See, however, *Sander v UK*, judgment of May 9, 2000 (jury not impartial) and *Young* (1995) 2 Cr. App. R. 379 (four jurors tried to communicate with the murder victim by means of a Ouija board).

[158] Above, n.43, at pp.364–74.

[159] *ibid., Report*, at para.7.15.

appropriate.[160] Were it to be otherwise, research could not be carried out even to test the assumption that juries are likely to be prejudiced by media reports.

6.3.2.5 *Disobedience to a Writ of Habeas Corpus*

Ó Dálaigh C.J. included disobedience to a writ of *habeas corpus* as an example of criminal contempt. Others have argued, however, that since it involves disobedience to a court order it should be classified as civil contempt. There are clearly borderline cases and cases in which an overlap between civil and criminal contempt occurs. Disobedience to a writ of habeas corpus is therefore discussed in that broader context below.

6.3.3 "Hybrid" Cases: Civil and Criminal Contempt

To the categories of civil and criminal contempt outlined above, a third could be added: mixed or "hybrid" cases of contempt. Civil contempt, as we have seen, is committed by disobedience to a court order, whereas criminal contempt can be committed in a variety of ways that cause interference with, or prejudice to, the administration of justice in court hearings. A "hybrid" case involves both civil and criminal contempt. In the media context, it could involve breach of a court order not to publish certain information, which amounts to civil contempt, while the fact of publishing it could constitute interference with, or prejudice to, a court hearing and therefore amount to criminal contempt.

The principal distinctions between the two forms historically were, first, that in the case of civil contempt the court moved at the instance of the party whose rights had been infringed (*i.e.* the party who was suffering harm as a result of the breach of the court order) not of its own volition, and second, that the indefinite term of imprisonment for civil contempt could not be commuted or remitted in the way that a definite term in a criminal matter could (see Article 13.6 of the Constitution). Both distinctions have been eroded. In *In re MacArthur*,[161] a criminal case, for instance, an *ex parte* application was made by the accused in respect of criminal contempt, although Costello J. thought it undesirable, at least in the circumstances of the particular case. Problems have also arisen with indefinite terms of imprisonment and intervention is often necessary.

The Phillimore Committee[162] in Britain recommended fixed terms in all cases of contempt, and the Contempt of Court Act 1981 in Britain now reflects that recommendation. It may also be noted that since proceedings for civil contempt can result in imprisonment, the degree of proof required is proof beyond reasonable doubt, the standard in a criminal case, and a person charged with civil contempt cannot be compelled to incriminate himself.[163] As a result,

---

[160] *ibid.* at paras 7.14–19.

[161] [1983] I.L.R.M. 355. MacArthur, who had been charged with murder, sought to have the then Taoiseach, Mr Haughey, attached for contempt arising from remarks he made at a press conference.

[162] Above, n.38.

[163] *State (DPP) v Irish Press Ltd*, unreported, High Court, December 15, 1976; *In re Mac Arthur*, above, n.161.

there has been some confusion. In *Keegan v de Búrca*,[164] for instance, Ó Dálaigh C.J. listed disobedience to a writ of *habeas corpus* as a criminal contempt, whereas Henchy J. in *The State (DPP) v Walsh and Conneely*[165] thought that this was perhaps only a civil contempt now. *Keegan* was an extraordinary case in that, at the hearing of a motion seeking an order for attachment for breach of an injunction (civil contempt), the defendant refused to answer a question put to her (criminal contempt). After allowing counsel an opportunity to explain the position to his client, the President of the High Court made an order committing her to prison *sine die*, *i.e.* he treated it as civil contempt. The Supreme Court, on appeal, held that the contempt was in fact criminal and therefore should be punished by a definite term of imprisonment. McLoughlin J.[166] in his dissenting judgment, acknowledged that "contempts have been classified as criminal contempts and civil contempts, but there does not seem to be any clear dividing line".

Another hybrid case arose during the course of the Beef Tribunal in 1991, when *Sunday Business Post* editor, Damien Kiberd, was called upon to reveal his sources. He refused to do so, which could have been punished as an offence under the Tribunals of Inquiry (Evidence) (Amendment) Act 1979 or as contempt in the face of the tribunal. In addition, as the chairman pointed out, the editor's remark to him "you are trawling for information" might itself be punishable there and then as *in facie* contempt.[167]

In *The State (Commins) v McRann*,[168] Finlay P. was invited by counsel effectively to abolish whatever distinction remained between civil and criminal contempt. He declined to do so, holding himself bound by, and in agreement with, the definition given by Ó Dálaigh C.J. in *Keegan*.[169] It is submitted, nevertheless, that by upholding the summary process (trial by judge alone, without a jury), Finlay P. in effect eroded the distinctions even further. Since then, however, the Law Reform Commission recommended against abolishing the distinction.[170] The Phillimore Committee in Britain in 1974 found the distinction "more apparent than real" and recommended abolishing the few remaining vestiges of distinction.[171]

In the case of the media, the distinction is largely irrelevant. Because breach of an injunction or other court order by the media will normally entail publication, it is likely to constitute both civil and criminal contempt and to be punished, if at all, as criminal rather than civil contempt. In 2001, a sexual abuse trial was halted after five newspapers named the accused, apparently in breach of an order made by the judge that the man not be named outside the court. The order had been made to protect the identity of the alleged victims. Breach of the order would constitute civil contempt; however, the judge ruled

---

[164] Above, n.40.
[165] Above, n.50.
[166] Above, n.40, at 235.
[167] *The Irish Times*, February 26, 1992.
[168] [1977] I.R. 78.
[169] Above, n.40.
[170] Above, n.43, at paras 2.7, 8.1.
[171] Above, n.38, paras 170–76.

that it was a criminal contempt because the accused's name and photograph had been published and affected his right to a fair trial. Three of the newspapers had also linked the accused man to his brother who, the judge said, was a person of some notoriety. Three of them obtained leave to seek judicial review of the decision.[172]

The issue was addressed directly by the Supreme Court in 2001 in *The Sole Member of the Tribunal of Inquiry into Certain Planning Matters and Payments v Lawlor.*[173] The facts were such that contempt of court was being pressed into action to perform both a coercive and a punitive function, that is to coerce Mr Lawlor to comply with the orders and to punish him for so blatantly and persistently failing to do so. The case, therefore, called into question the separate roles and rationales that had developed over the years in relation to civil and criminal contempt. It was not simply a case of civil contempt in the terms in which Ó Dálaigh C.J. had articulated it in *Keegan v de Búrca*,[174] in that it was not only the private interests of a litigant that were at issue in this case. As Keane C.J. stated, there was also a public interest in the proper and expeditious investigation of the matters within the remit of the tribunal and the need to ensure that, not merely the appellant in this particular case, but all persons who are required by law to give evidence to the tribunal comply with their obligations fully and without qualification.[175]

The distinction between civil and criminal contempt also bears on the sanction to be imposed, whether a fine or imprisonment for a fixed or indefinite (*sine die*) period. The determination of which form of sanction is appropriate rests with the particular facts of the case and the objective or goal to be achieved, whether coercion or punishment and deterrence, or both. The Supreme Court appears to accept that contempt of court can be used in the one set of circumstances to achieve both. The failure of Mr Lawlor to comply with the orders amounted in the first instance to civil contempt, while the manner in which he did so, brought it into the realm of criminal contempt.[176] The decision of the Supreme Court and the fixed term of imprisonment imposed suggests

---

[172] *The Irish Times*, May 22, 23, 30, 2001. The hearing was adjourned (*The Irish Times*, May 31, 2001). In a similar case, the editors of two newspapers as well as the director of programming at TV3, were fined for contempt for breaching an order to preserve the victims' anonymity in the case of a Dublin man jailed for15 years on rape and torture charges against his wife and daughter (*The Irish Times*, July 14, 29, 2000). Photographs of the former family home had appeared in two of the papers and on television and photographs of the defendant with his eyes blacked out had appeared in all of the papers. In another case, involving an article published during a murder trial, the *Sunday World* was given leave to seek judicial review of the DPP's successful District Court application to proceed against it by way of indictment before the Circuit Criminal Court (*The Irish Times*, August 30, 2000). The accused had pleaded guilty to manslaughter but not to the charge of murder, on which he was tried in 1996. The jury, in a unanimous verdict, acquitted him.

[173] December 12, 2001.

[174] Above, n.40.

[175] At pp.46–8 of the transcript.

[176] Fennelly J., for instance, spoke of Mr Lawlor as having "defied" the order and having sworn at least one affidavit that was so incomplete as to "entail deliberate deception" (at 1–2). See Cathal Murphy, "Contempt for Failure to Make Discovery following *The Sole Member v Lawlor*" [2002] 7 B.R. 160.

that the distinction between civil and criminal contempt is no longer useful, and that contempt of court, if it is to continue, should do so in a unified form, which allows the courts to tailor it to the particular facts and the goal(s) to be achieved.[177]

6.4 ELEMENTS OF CONTEMPT

After considering the various types of contempt, questions arise as to the elements necessary to constitute contempt.

6.4.1 Degree of Prejudice

The question as to what degree of prejudice is required to amount to contempt has exercised the courts over a long period. Kenny J. in *R v Dolan*[178] had put forward a two-fold test: was the publication calculated to prejudice the fair trial of the accused and, if so, was the contempt of so serious a character as to call for the intervention of the court. Madden J. in the same case pointed out that the danger to the administration of justice must be real and not imaginary.[179] It was not necessary, however, that actual prejudice be proved, just that the publication was calculated to cause prejudice. Gavan Duffy J. in *AG v Connolly*[180] also recognised a two-limb test, namely the question of whether the matter was calculated to produce a public mischief and, if so, whether that mischief was a grave one. The question was decided in Britain in the Contempt of Court Act 1981, section 2.2: "a publication which creates a substantial risk that the course of justice in the proceedings in question will be seriously impeded or prejudiced".

In that formulation, the degree of risk is qualified, as is the degree of prejudice. It is not enough that the publication presents a slight risk of serious damage, or, for that matter, a high risk of marginal damage. In practice, however, the English courts appeared to interpret the word "substantial" in the Act to mean a risk other than a remote one. This was a low threshold, and one that did not prove very helpful to the media.[181]

One advantage of the British formulation is that it eliminates the notion of "calculated", which is problematic, in that it is difficult to define. Does it mean simply that the publication is likely to cause prejudice or is of a kind that would cause prejudice, or does it suggest deliberation or premeditation? Morris J. in a High Court case in 1993 said that it had to be established to his satisfaction beyond all reasonable doubt that the contents of the radio interview in question "were calculated, in the sense that it would tend to" prejudice the impartiality

---

[177] However, the case for specific, narrowly tailored offences set out in statute might be preferable: Boyle and McGonagle, above, n.19.

[178] [1907] 2 I.R. 260, at 268.

[179] *ibid.* at 275.

[180] Above, n.97, at 221.

[181] For example, see *AG v English* [1983] 1 A.C. 116, Lord Diplock, at 141–2; *AG v News Group Newspapers* [1986] 2 All E.R. 833, Donaldson, M.R., at 841.

of potential jurors in the action.[182] As noted above, the test now applied by the Irish Supreme Court as formulated in *D v DPP*[183] and *Z v DPP*[184] is one of a "real risk" of an unfair trial.

The issue was revisited by the Supreme Court in *Irish Times Ltd v Judge Murphy*.[185] The court reiterated its view that a jury should be discharged only where the risk of an unfair trial could not be avoided by appropriate rulings and directions. The test devised by the court is two-fold: (i) was there a real risk that the accused would not receive a fair trial if it was held in public and (ii) was the real risk unavoidable or could it be avoided by appropriate rulings and directions? Simply put, the test is one of "a real and unavoidable risk".[186] Furthermore, Denham J. made a point that may be of importance for the media. She said that when there is a question of banning reporting, the two-fold test should be applied "after hearing evidence and submissions from the parties and any relevant representatives" (at 400). While the media are not actually a party to the case, they are directly affected by such a ban and therefore should have a right to be heard.

6.4.2 Mens Rea

The question of intention is vexing. In the past, Irish courts have accepted the definition of constructive contempt (*i.e.* contempt out of court) put forward by Lord Eldon in *Ex parte Jones*[187] as contempt "depending upon the inference of an intention to obstruct the course of justice". Thus, if the publication met the requirement of being "calculated" to interfere with the proceedings, an intention to interfere was imputed by the courts. In *AG v Cooke*,[188] however, Sullivan P. separated the two limbs of the test and held that the article in question was not intended to interfere with the court's decision in pending criminal proceedings and was not calculated to do so. It is not clear how he would have resolved the matter had he found the article calculated to interfere but not intended to. In *AG v Connolly*,[189] Gavan Duffy J. appeared to favour the strict liability rule, *i.e.* liability regardless of intention. He held that the offending article was calculated to produce a grave public mischief and that it was no defence in law to say that the defendant intended nothing wrong.[190]

---

[182] *The Irish Times*, June 26, 1993.

[183] Above, n.10.

[184] Above, n.10. The massive media attention and emotion were cited as reasons for transferring from Galway to Dublin the trial of a man accused of soliciting two men to murder his wife (*The Irish Times*, October 2, 1996).

[185] Above, n.5.

[186] *ibid.*, Denham J., at 400. O'Flaherty J. also said that a judge should have confidence in the jury to understand and comply with such directions, to disregard any inadmissible evidence and to give a true verdict in accordance with the evidence. He also took the view that applications were being made too frequently, on very tentative grounds, to have juries discharged (*ibid.* at 387, 389). His view would appear to be supported by research carried out on contempt cases, Boyle and McGonagle, above, n.19, at p.164.

[187] Cited by Meredith J. in *AG v O'Kelly*, above, n.98, at 324.

[188] (1924) 58 I.L.T.R. 157.

[189] Above, n.97, at 219.

[190] *ibid.* at 221. In Britain, the 1981 Act provides for a strict liability offence but creates

It would appear, therefore, that it is the effect of the publication that is important, and that the question of intention or motive only arises in relation to sentencing. According to Finlay P. in *The State (DPP) v Irish Press*,[191] the test is an objective one, *i.e.* whether the publication is likely to interfere with the due and fair trial of pending proceedings:

> "the motive or intention or the *mens rea* of the party or parties responsible for the making of the publication is not relevant. A man may therefore publish what does in law constitute contempt of court in this category inadvertently but that does not mean ... that he is liable if it was caused by inadvertence to be punished for it."

In *Daly*, for example, when a prejudicial article appeared in the *Sunday Tribune*, there was no intention to cause prejudice but the paper was still held to be in contempt.[192] The jury was discharged; the trial was put back to obviate any possible prejudice, and an apology was accepted. Costello J. in *MacArthur*[193] seemed to sum up the view of the courts when he said that if

> "the words were spoken inadvertently ... and ... immediate steps were taken to avoid any possible prejudice that the words might give rise to and if it can be shown ... that any possible prejudice can be obviated by the direction which the trial judge can give to the jury, then it seems to me to be highly unlikely that the court would exercise its extraordinary punitive powers and punish such a person for contempt...."

The approach of Morris J.[194] in an application brought by six gardaí, following a Gay Byrne radio interview with Osgur Breathnach, on the subject of the Sallins mail robbery and its aftermath, was refreshing. Not only did he show a media awareness himself, he also credited the Irish public with the same degree of maturity and a healthy, even sceptical, attitude to what they see and hear. He considered the interview in context, as a human-interest piece, and recognised that even views expressed by broadcaster Gay Byrne would not necessarily find universal support. Many would be unaffected by those views and ignore them; some might even oppose them simply because they were Gay Byrne's.[195] Over the last few years there have also been a number of

---

certain defences (ss.3–5). It continues common law (s.6). An intention to prejudice or subvert the course of justice is not required.

[191] Above, n.127, at p.2 of the typescript (as case unreported).

[192] Above, n.128.

[193] Above, n.133, at 356. It has been pointed out, however, that, if tried and convicted, a conviction will still stand and could have repercussions at a later stage if the publisher were to be charged again; see Sally Walker, "Freedom of Speech and Contempt of Court: The English and Australian Approaches Compared" (1991) 40 I.C.L.Q. 583, at p.589. Keane J. in the Supreme Court in the Liam Lawlor case, above, n.173, considered, citing Lord Denning in *Re WB (an infant)* [1969] 1 All E.R. 594, that the court has a discretion, analagous to a suspended sentence in the criminal courts, to do what is just in all the circumstances.

[194] *The Irish Times*, June 26, 1993.

[195] *ibid.*

instances where the court has accepted an apology but ordered the media to pay a sum of money towards the costs of the trial.[196] In the introduction to a report of a court case on a radio programme, an inadvertent error in confusing the evidence against two accused led to the trial being halted and RTÉ being ordered to pay £5,000 towards the costs of the trial.[197] Since this form of contempt is a criminal offence, the notion of strict liability sits uneasily with the safeguards of the criminal law.[198] However, the European Court of Human Rights, applying Article 6 of the European Convention on Human Rights (right to a fair trial), stated in *Worm v Austria*[199] that the limits of permissible comment on pending criminal proceedings may not extend to statements which are likely to prejudice "whether intentionally or not", the chances of a person receiving a fair trial.

6.4.3 Restricted Comments and the *Sub Judice* Rule

When proceedings are ongoing or pending, they are said to be *sub judice* and therefore comment on them is restricted. But when are proceedings to be regarded as "pending"? The current position is that proceedings are pending from the issue of a writ in civil cases and the laying of charges in a criminal case.[200] Comment is then restricted, but not prohibited. However, as the risk of prejudice is high, the media must exercise the utmost caution. The rule has been open to abuse by those wishing to stifle comment. For example, it has happened that a politician or public figure, finding himself or herself in hot water, has taken out a writ and informed the media that s/he has done so, in order to silence them. This process of issuing "gagging-writs" was helped by the long time-lag from the issue of a writ to the actual court hearing (in the case of the High Court a period, on average, of three years). The case could be dropped by the politician at any stage, but the media would have been silenced until the danger was over. It is possible for the media also to hide behind the *sub judice* rule and not publish anything on the grounds that the matter is *sub judice*. The rule can even be used to stifle comment on important matters of public interest.

6.4.3.1 Sub Judice *in the Dáil*

Dáil debates on an issue are sometimes refused because the matter is *sub judice*. Under the doctrine of separation of powers in the Constitution, the Dáil must

---

[196] *e.g.* Boyle and McGonagle, above, n.19, pp.165–179 (summary of cases). See *The People (DPP) v Haughey*, unreported, High Court, June 26, 2000, where Haugh J. stated *obiter* that "the motive or intention of a publisher ... would be a relevant consideration on a motion to attach or commit for contempt, as would any withdrawal or explanation made thereafter".

[197] *The Irish Times*, October 13, 1992. See also *The Irish Times*, July 30, 1992.

[198] The Law Reform Commission suggests a test of negligence in relation to "active" proceedings, above, n.43, *Report*, at para.6.10.

[199] Above, n.32.

[200] See above, n.43, *Paper*, at pp.86–7, regarding the relevance of *R v Beaverbrook & Associated Newspapers Ltd* [1962] N.I. 15 to the question of "imminent" proceedings.

not encroach on the courts. In 1986, for example, a government minister issued a writ for libel against *Magill* magazine over allegations about his business interests. The *Sunday Tribune* sought clarification of the scope and application of the *sub judice* rule and was able to publish an editorial and article on the effects of the rule on press freedom.[201] The Minister was subsequently asked to resign by the Taoiseach and questions were tabled in the Dáil. They were refused on the grounds that the matter was *sub judice*. There is a Dáil convention, as there is in England, to avoid debate that could constitute parliamentary interference with judicial decisions. In a bizarre incident in 1991, the clerk of the Seanad was subpoenaed to appear as a witness at the trial of a defamation action taken by the Cathaoirleach of the Seanad, Seán Doherty, against the *Sunday Times*. A motion had to be passed to permit this to happen but no debate was allowed because the matter was *sub judice*.[202] Standing Orders (S.O. 56) now provide that a member shall not be prevented from raising in the Dáil any matter of general public importance, even where court proceedings have been initiated, unless, *inter alia*, it relates to a case where notice has been served and the case is to be heard, or is being heard, by a jury, or where a matter is raised in such an overt manner that it appears to be an attempt by the Dáil to encroach on the functions of the courts or a judicial tribunal.

6.4.3.2 *The* Sunday Times *Case*

The question of the operation of the *sub judice* rule arose in Britain in the *Sunday Times* case, which went to the European Court of Human Rights.[203] In that case, the perceived prejudice arose from a deliberate attempt on the part of the newspaper to influence the settlement of pending proceedings by bringing pressure to bear on a party to the case, Distillers Ltd, the manufacturers of the thalidomide drug, which when taken by pregnant women had caused their babies to be born with abnormalities. Publication of an article had been restrained by injunction on the grounds that it would amount to contempt of court because its purpose was to enlist public opinion to exert pressure on Distillers to make a more generous settlement to the victims. The Court of Appeal discharged the injunction on the grounds, *inter alia*, that the public interest in discussion outweighed the potential prejudice to a fair trial or settlement of the action.[204] The House of Lords, however, reinstated the injunction holding that the proposed article would pre-judge the issues and amount to trial by newspaper.[205] Subsequently the European Court of Human

---

[201] *Sunday Tribune*, September 7, 1986.

[202] *Doherty v Sunday Times* (*The Irish Times*, February 15, 1991). A Dáil motion was passed on April 8, 1993 to relax the *sub judice* rule. See above, n.43, *Report*, at p.43, and now Dáil Éireann Standing Orders, 2002, available at *www.irlgov.ie/oireachtas*.

[203] Above, n.29.

[204] *AG v Times Newspapers* [1974] A.C. 273, [1973] 1 All E.R. 815 (C.A.). *Cf. Hinch v AG* (1987) 164 C.L.R. 15, an Australian case in which a balancing test was proposed: if the publisher sought to serve, and did serve, a public interest that outweighs the prejudicial effect of the publication, the publisher is not guilty of contempt of court.

[205] Above, n.138.

Rights, in a majority decision, decided that the injunction was not justified under Article 10(2) of the Convention.[206] Although it was prescribed by law and imposed for a legitimate purpose (maintaining the authority of the judiciary), the restriction was not justified by a pressing social need and could not therefore be regarded as "necessary" within the meaning of Article 10(2). As a result of the Strasbourg decision, the legislature in Britain intervened and passed the Contempt of Court Act 1981.

6.4.3.3 Time Limits and the Rule

One of the purposes of the 1981 Act in Britain was to impose time limits on the operation of the *sub judice* rule. Henceforth, applicable proceedings would be classed as "active" (section 12). Civil proceedings would be "active", not from the issue of the writ but from the date of setting-down for trial or when a date for the hearing was fixed (section 13). Proceedings would remain active until disposed of, discontinued or withdrawn. Criminal proceedings would be active from the relevant initial step, whether arrest, the issue of a summons to appear, the service of an indictment or other document specifying the charge or the making of an oral charge (section 4). They would remain active until concluded by acquittal, sentence, discontinuance or other final verdict (section 5). Appellate proceedings would also be considered active (section 15).

The advantages of the legislative changes in Britain are two-fold: they impose precise, if arbitrary, time limits and they reduce the time span in which the media can be silenced. While it can take three years in Ireland from the date of issue of a writ for a civil case to come to court, it is usually only a matter of months from the date of setting-down. A similar change in Irish law would be beneficial. In relation to criminal proceedings, the Phillimore Committee in Britain,[207] whose recommendations formed the basis of the new legislation, had suggested the date of charge as the appropriate time for the *sub judice* rule to begin to run. However, while the new legislation was in preparation, the so-called "Yorkshire Ripper" was finally caught by police. The nature and extent of media coverage of his apprehension and arrest prompted the government to change its mind with regard to the appropriate time to curtail media comment in a criminal case. The date of arrest rather than charge was adopted.

Another aspect of the British legislative changes that might be questioned is whether it is necessary for the *sub judice* rule to apply during appellate proceedings, where there will not be a jury involved. This need has been discounted by the Supreme Court in *Cullen v Tóibín*.[208] In that case, the plaintiff had been convicted in the Central Criminal Court of murder and malicious damage. His appeal to the Court of Criminal Appeal was based on the insufficiency of evidence of an accomplice, which was the only evidence against him. While his appeal was pending, *Magill* magazine entered into a contract

---

[206] Above, n.29.
[207] Above, n.38.
[208] Above, n.121.

with the accomplice to publish her version of the story. The plaintiff applied for an injunction to prevent publication. The injunction was granted by Barrington J. in the High Court,[209] but the Supreme Court lifted it,[210] stating first, that the courts should only interfere with freedom of expression and of communication guaranteed by the Constitution in Article 40.6 where it was necessary for the administration of justice, and second, that the Court of Criminal Appeal could not be prejudiced by publication because it would be dealing with pure issues of law. Also, the Court noted that the plaintiff could always sue for defamation afterwards. In the High Court, Barrington J. had acknowledged that it was a serious piece of investigative journalism but added that if it had been published before the trial in the Central Criminal Court, it would clearly have been contempt of court.[211] The Supreme Court suggested that it was in bad taste but that freedom of the press should prevail.[212]

In Ireland, the issue of time limits in relation to the *sub judice* rule has also arisen. In *The State (DPP) v Independent Newspapers*,[213] the High Court adopted the date of charge as the appropriate starting time in criminal cases. In that case, the *Evening Herald* had published a story that the DPP intended bringing indecency charges against a local councillor. The story referred to the political party to which the councillor belonged, but did not name him or the local authority. At the time the story was published, no charges had been brought, although they were brought two days later. Did the publication constitute contempt of court? O'Hanlon J. took the view that if publication had taken place after the preliminary examination of the case against the accused in the District Court, section 17 of the Criminal Procedure Act 1967 would have applied to restrict reporting. However, as no one had actually been charged in the case and no court actually had seisin of it, the DPP's application for an order of attachment for contempt must be refused. The countervailing importance of freedom of expression would not allow such an extension of the law of contempt, the judge said, and it was undesirable from the point of view of the accused that proceedings for contempt with the attendant publicity should be in progress at the very time when the criminal prosecution against him would be coming on for hearing.[214]

---

[209] *ibid.* at 578–81.

[210] *ibid.* at 582.

[211] *ibid.* at 579.

[212] *ibid.* at 581. The Australian Law Reform Commission, above, n.118, recommended that no restrictions should apply between the jury verdict and an order for a retrial. The Irish Commission departed from its provisional recommendation of 1991 and decided that it "would be unduly restrictive to extend the operation of the *sub judice* rule to appellate proceedings, which are invariably decided by non-jury courts" (above, n.43, *Report*, at para.6.14).

[213] Unreported, High Court, O'Hanlon J., May 28, 1984.

[214] *ibid.* at p.5 of typescript. Despite the clarity of that decision, confusion surrounded RTÉ's proposed "Today Tonight" programme in 1989 on the Dublin property developer Patrick Gallagher, who had earlier pleaded guilty to false accounting and company theft charges in Belfast. RTÉ received conflicting legal advice as to whether the programme could go ahead, even though at the time no charges had been brought against Gallagher in the State (*The Irish Times*, November 30, 1989). Doubts have been cast on O'Hanlon J.'s decision in *The State (DPP) v Independent Newspapers* (above, n.213), however,

The date of charge was the deciding factor in the case brought by the DPP against a number of Irish newspapers and their editors, as well as RTÉ and the producer of the Gerry Ryan Show, in 2003. Following a road accident, which claimed the lives of a taxi driver and a youth, two 16-year-olds were charged. The names and photographs of the two were published in some of the media, as were an address and references to previous convictions and proceedings that had been heard *in camera* in the Children's Court. Kelly J. held that material published before the youths were charged was not punishable as contempt of court.[215]

The position as to whether the *sub judice* rule applies between conviction and sentence has been addressed by the Supreme Court, which pointed out the uncertainties in the law and the need for legislation to give clarification. In *Kelly v O'Neill and Brady*, known colloquially as "the case of all the Kellys", because applicant, judge, barrister and reporter were all called Kelly, the Circuit Court fined the editor of *The Irish Times* and a reporter £5,000.[216] After a three-week trial by jury, Eamonn Kelly had been convicted of possession of £500,000 worth of cocaine for supply and remanded for sentence. Before sentence was passed *The Irish Times* published an article, indicating that the gardaí believed Kelly was involved in other crimes ranging from violent crime to fraud and drug smuggling. Counsel for Kelly described the article as false and irrelevant. The article was held to be in contempt. The paper was fined but appealed the ruling. The contempt issue was referred to the Supreme Court on two points:

(i) whether [following the decision of the Supreme Court in *Cullen v Tóibín*] it can be a contempt of court to publish the article complained of after a criminal trial has passed from a jury and where the remainder of the hearing

---

by the Law Reform Commission (above, n.43, *Paper*, at pp.86–7), which points to the fact that O'Hanlon J. did not refer to *R v Beaverbrook & Associated Newspapers Ltd* [1962] N.I. 15 in his judgment. Kelly J. in *DPP v Independent Newspapers & Others* (below, n.215), took the view that adoption of the "imminent" formula (*i.e.* that the *sub judice* rule would begin to run from the time that charges are imminent) would give rise to "huge uncertainty" and could lead to possible undue cramping of the media in their coverage of public affairs and newsworthy events, thus improperly interfering with the freedom of the press (*The Irish Times*, March 8, 2003).

[215] *DPP v Independent Newspapers & Michael Roche (managing editor), Sunday Newspapers Ltd & Colm McGinty (editor, Sunday World), Independent Star Ltd & Gerard Colleran (editor, Irish Star), RTÉ & Alice O'Sullivan (producer, Gerry Ryan Show)*. The youths were charged at 10.30 on January 13, 2003. See *The Irish Times*, January 25, 2003. A preliminary ruling was given on January 28, 2003 and was followed by a written judgment of March 7, 2003. See pp.16–41 of the typscript, approving O'Hanlon J. (above, n.213). Publication of names and photographs or other identifying information did constitute contempt, as did reference to the fact that at the time of the trial the youths were awaiting trial on other charges, because of the interference with the presumption of innocence and right to a fair trial. Sunday Newspapers Ltd were fined €20,000, Independent Newspapers, €15,000, and Independent Star €10,000. The editors of the *Sunday World* and *Irish Star* were also found to be in contempt but no additional penalty was imposed on them personally. Contempt proceedings against RTÉ were dismissed (*The Irish Times*, January 29, 2003).

[216] *Kelly v O'Neill and Brady*, above, n.22; considered in Pauline Walley, "Criminal Contempt of Court: the *Eamonn Kelly* Case Considered" (2000) B.R. 295.

will take place before a judge sitting alone [*i.e.* when the only person who could be affected was the trial judge who was considering the sentence (the trial judge had said his concern was for the expert witnesses who had still to appear before him)], and

(ii) whether, given the constitutional right to freedom of expression of the press, the publication of the article complained of could ever constitute a contempt of court when published after conviction and before sentencing?[217]

The Supreme Court eventually gave its ruling in 1999.[218] The judges were unanimous in their view that the article could constitute contempt but the question of whether it actually did so in practice was a matter for the High Court to determine. Given the absence of an intention to interfere with the administration of justice on the part of the editor and reporter, the offence of criminal contempt may not have been committed at all, according to Keane, J. In any case, he said, the circumstances of the case would clearly have called for the imposition of no more than a modest penalty and the respondents might have been found innocent of any contempt.[219]

Incidentally, Kelly was jailed for 14 years but appealed the sentence. His conviction was quashed by the Court of Criminal Appeal and a retrial ordered because of reports in the *Star* and *Sunday World* during the trial. The former had named Kelly in a reference to "cocaine kingpins"; the latter had published a photograph of him and referred to another man who had absconded as an "arms dealer". This amounted to prejudicial content, the court said, and therefore the trial judge should have acceded to applications to discharge the jury.[220]

In another case, involving a Newry man convicted of importing £1.5 million worth of ecstasy, sentencing was adjourned because a *Sunday Times* article, published four days after conviction and before sentencing, claimed that garda sources had provided information that the man had previous IRA links.[221] An added concern in this case was the risk of the man's family being targeted.

In a subsequent case, a Circuit Court judge hearing evidence before sentencing in a sexual assault case sought to impose a full media ban on the proceedings. Six media groups applied to have the ban lifted on the grounds that it violated the public's constitutional right of access to the courts. The

---

[217] *The Irish Times*, November 23, 1993, February 10, 1994, March 8, 1994. The article complained of had been published in *The Irish Times* on May 17, 1993, two days after Eamon Kelly had been convicted but before sentencing.

[218] On December 2, 1999. See *The Irish Times*, December 3, 1999, and McGonagle, "SC [Supreme Court] Ruling's Call for Law on Contempt may Help", *The Irish Times*, December 6, 1999.

[219] Above, n.22, at 380 and 538. See the judgments regarding the view that judges could be prejudiced, and that in the case of any doubt, the balance should be tipped in favour of the administration of justice. A key factor was the proximity of the court process. *Cf.* the views expressed by Haugh J. in *The People (DPP) v Haughey*, above, n.121.

[220] *The Irish Times*, February 10, 1994.

[221] *The Irish Times*, May 12, 1999.

judge said the sentence he was to impose on a man convicted of sexual abuse might be influenced if he knew it was going to be reported by the media. He said that if a convicted man was going to be given serious publicity that might be a punishment in itself. After further legal argument, he amended the order to allow reporting except identification of the accused and victim. However, the victim asked that the abuser be named. Her application was rejected by the judge, on the basis that he did not think it was in her best interests. He banned the media from reporting the reasons why he thought that was so. The judge imposed a three-year suspended sentence.[222] One of his concerns was that the publicity would deter other victims from coming forward. He had taken a similar stance in response to similar requests from victims in other sexual abuse cases.[223] Judicial review of the decision was sought by the *Star* newspaper, which the victim and her parents had contacted to say they wanted the perpetrator named.[224] The High Court duly quashed the Circuit Court order.[225] The *Star* had argued that under the Criminal Law (Rape) Acts, the trial judge did not have jurisdiction to make such an order. Kearns J. in the High Court said that any rights the accused might have were dealt with by the legislation, which was quite explicit in removing the protection of his identity following a conviction. Kearns J. also accepted that the question as to whether victims might be less inclined to come forward if the prohibition were lifted was clearly a matter of policy and not a reason to sustain the making of the order.[226]

6.4.3.4 The Scope of the Rule

The cases of *Desmond v Glackin (No. 1)*[227] and *Wong v Minister for Justice*[228] raise further questions about the scope and application of the *sub judice* rule. O'Hanlon J. in *Desmond* said that quite apart from any effect of media comment on judge or jury, the law of contempt is concerned with the potentially harmful effects that may flow from unbridled comments made in a public manner concerning the subject matter of legal proceedings pending before the court or the parties involved in such proceedings.[229] On the facts of the case, however, he found that the *sub judice* rule had not been breached. The remarks of the second defendant, Des O'Malley had been "injudicious and indiscreet", but he was entitled to a right of reply in the circumstances as his remarks had been

---

[222] *The Irish Times*, December 1, 2, 2000, *Sunday Independent*, December 3, 2000.

[223] *The Irish Times*, March 11, 2000, *Sunday Independent*, December 3, 2000.

[224] *The Irish Times*, April 27, 2001, May 29, 2001, October 25, 2002.

[225] *Independent Star Ltd v His Honour Kieran O'Connor* [2002] I.E.H.C. 109 (November 1, 2002), available at *www.bailii.org/ie/cases*, *The Irish Times*, November 2, 2002. In any event, the purpose of the provisions in the Act is to protect the victim, not the perpetrator (paras 32–3). The decision is in accordance with the overall position as indicated by the Supreme Court's ruling in *Irish Times Ltd v Judge Murphy* (1998), above, n.5.

[226] *The Irish Times*, November 2, 2002.

[227] Above, n.20.

[228] [1994] 1 I.R. 223.

[229] Above, n.20, at 20.

"a response to serious allegations made against him by Mr Desmond which had already been well-publicised".[230] The balance had to be struck in favour of freedom of expression. Nonetheless, the uncertainty that surrounds the scope of the rule is unsatisfactory for the media; the legislature should intervene to clarify it. Denham J. in *Wong* said that, while the trial judge would be unlikely to be prejudiced, the linking of the plaintiff to the Chinese Triad underworld was prejudicial to the administration of justice "as a result of a litigant in mid-trial being held up to such public obloquy",[231] and thus constituted a contempt, purged by an apology.[232] Her fear was the effect of the allegations on how her decision would be viewed. If her decision was favourable to the plaintiff, people who had read the allegations might think the judgment perverse, thus undermining public confidence in the justice system. In that respect, the form of contempt involved in the case is closer to contempt by scandalising the court.[233]

6.5 DEFENCES

The question of appropriate defences to charges of contempt of court has been addressed in a number of jurisdictions. The Contempt of Court Act 1981 in Britain provided for a number of defences, in addition to any that might already be available at common law.[234] The new defences included innocent publication or distribution (section 3) and discussion of public affairs if the risk of impediment or prejudice to particular proceedings is merely incidental to the discussion (section 5). The Australian Law Reform Commission also favoured a defence of innocent publication and a public interest defence.[235] The Irish Commission has proposed a defence of reasonable necessity to publish,[236] but not a public interest defence. The fact that a publication involves a matter of public interest cannot, the Commission says, justify prejudicing legal proceedings.[237] It went on to say that a similar defence to that available for media reports of court cases should be available in relation to proceedings of the Oireachtas. There should, the Commission said, be an express statutory defence for fair and accurate reports published contemporaneously or within a reasonable time after the proceedings.[238]

---

[230] *ibid.* at 33–4.

[231] Above, n.228, at p.22 of typescript.

[232] *Cf. Lovell and Christmas v O'Shaughnessy* (1934) 69 I.L.T.R. 34.

[233] See above, n.43, *Paper*, at pp.310–313; *Report*, at para.6.23.

[234] The position regarding common-law defences is not clear; see (1981) 1 *Current Law Statutes Annotated*, No.49.

[235] See above, n.118.

[236] Above, n.43, *Report*, at para.6.24.

[237] *ibid.* at para.6.25.

[238] *ibid.* at paras 6.26–32.

6.6 PERSONS LEGALLY RESPONSIBLE FOR PUBLICATION

In the decided cases, it has sometimes been the reporter and editor who have been pursued for contempt, sometimes the editor and proprietor, occasionally the author or company alone. As to who should be legally responsible for the publication of prejudicial matter, the Law Reform Commission[239] suggested a test centring on three separate (though at times overlapping) criteria: authorship, control and proprietorship. It concluded that:

(a) the author of material which offends against the *sub judice* rule should in general be liable where the material appears in the publication unamended

(b) in cases where the offending material was derived from information supplied by a person, whether a journalist or otherwise, such person should be capable of being held responsible for *sub judice* contempt if he or she, in all the circumstances, ought reasonably to have anticipated the publication of the information without correction

(c) a person may be found guilty of *sub judice* contempt even though what was published represents an amalgamation or cumulation of contemptuous material contributed by himself or herself and another person if, in isolation, the contemptuous material for which he or she is responsible would constitute *sub judice* contempt

(d) those in control of newspapers and other media, such as editors, should be capable of being criminally responsible for *sub judice* contempt to the extent that, by the exercise of that control, they ought to have prevented the publication of the offending material

(e) the proprietors of newspapers should be vicariously liable for *sub judice* contempts published in their newspapers. Only fines should be imposed on proprietors by way of punishment.[240]

6.7 EXTENSIONS OF THE CONTEMPT POWER

From time to time, new situations present themselves for which the contempt power is pressed into action. Its use can be justified in some cases by reference to the overall objectives of contempt; in others it marks a departure from the norm and an extension of the power.

---

[239] Above, n.43, *Paper*, at pp.336–340; *Report*, at paras 6.33–6.36. Some statutes now set out the person(s) who are to be held responsible in certain areas; see further Chap.7 below. In some European countries, such as Sweden, the role of the Editor-in-Chief, who assumes full legal responsibility, is seen as an important safeguard for editorial freedom.

[240] Above, n.43, *Report*, rec. 32–6, pp.68–9. A number of recent statutes provide definitions of terms such as "broadcast" and "publish" and set out which persons are to be held responsible for breach of the statutory provisions – see Chap.7 below. In *DPP v Independent Newspapers* (above, n.215), Kelly J. acquitted the managing editor as he "was not the editor … nor did he have responsibility for the content" (at p.4 of the typescript).

6.7.1 Contempt and Tribunals

Contempt of court was extended to tribunals under the Tribunals of Inquiry Acts. It arose in the course of the Beef Tribunal. Concern was expressed at the "misreporting" of the first day of the Beef Tribunal, when a list of allegations, authorised to be read out by the tribunal, was presented in the media "as though they were accusations made under oath from the witness box, as though they had been stated as matters of fact".[241] Counsel's fear was for the client's good name, not fear of prejudice, as the chairman of the tribunal had asserted that he would not be influenced in any way by what was said by the press or anyone else. A number of factors were relevant to the question of whether the reporting amounted to or should be punishable as contempt. The first day's reporting in 1991 would long since be forgotten by the time the tribunal ended and its report was published in 1994. Besides, this was a tribunal, not a court of law.[242] Indeed, it was a public tribunal, a *public* inquiry, so that truth could be ascertained in the public interest. In those circumstances, and given that the primary source of danger was the decision of the tribunal itself to allow the rereading of the list of allegations, it would seem inappropriate to invoke the contempt power against the three national newspapers and RTÉ. The chairman ruled some three months later that they had not been in contempt.[243]

The issue of contempt arose again in *The Sole Member v Lawlor*,[244] when Liam Lawlor TD failed to comply with orders of the Flood Tribunal. A key issue in that case was the role of contempt, and whether it could be used in such a way as to achieve the goals of both civil and criminal contempt in one set of circumstances. In that sense, it marked an extension of contempt, and yet in reality it did little more than acknowledge and rationalise for the first time the distinctions, which were recognised as far back as *Keegan v de Búrca*,[245] as not always useful and becoming blurred.

6.7.2 Statutory Contempt

There are several statutes that provide for contempt-like powers, and their effect is open to question. For instance, section 4 of the Offences against the State Act 1972:

---

[241] *The Irish Times*, October 11–13, 1991.

[242] Because the tribunal was obviously going to last for a very long time and, in any event, was not a court of law administering justice, the argument put forward in *Wong v Minister for Defence* (above, n.228, as to the impact on the administration of justice in general) could hardly be said to apply. *Wong* itself may represent an extension of the contempt power.

[243] *The Irish Times*, January 15, 1992. The justification offered by Casey (James Casey, *Constitutional Law in Ireland* (3rd ed., Round Hall Sweet & Maxwell, Dublin, 2000, at p.552), that the individual's constitutional right of access to the courts must not unlawfully be obstructed, would be applicable in *Wong* (and *Desmond v Glackin*, which Casey points to) but not in the case of the Beef Tribunal, which was not a court, even if it did have certain statutory powers akin to those of the High Court.

[244] Supreme Court, December 12, 2001.

[245] Above, n.40.

"any public statement made orally, in writing or otherwise ... that constitutes an interference with the course of justice [or] if it is intended, or is of such a character as to be likely, directly or indirectly, to influence any court ... [is punishable by fine and/or imprisonment. However,] nothing in this section shall affect the law as to contempt of court."

This apparently leaves intact common-law contempt but creates a supplementary statutory offence of much wider application, as there is no requirement that the interference be serious, and it envisages punishment even where the interference is unintentional or indirect. Casey[246] believes that the section has never been invoked and hopes that it would be applied in accordance with the European Convention on Human Rights, rather than in a way that would imperil legitimate freedom of expression. Its overreach makes it suspect as being disproportionate to its apparent aim. The only thing that might save it is the need to show actual interference and the intention to, or likelihood of, influencing a court.

The Offences against the State Act 1939, which provides for the setting up of the Special Criminal Court, gives that court the same jurisdiction and powers in relation to contempt of court as the High Court "in the same manner and in the like cases" (section 43(e)). The issue arose in relation to a BBC Panorama programme and follow-up report in the *Daily Mail* about the Omagh bombing. The programme claimed to identify the people responsible for the bombing. A man charged with conspiracy to cause the bomb explosion contended that the programme and report jeopardised his right to a fair trial. The contempt issue was resolved on the basis that a statement be read out in court regarding the presumption of innocence.[247]

Other statutes provide for offences punishable "in like manner" as contempt of court. These offences are statutory forms of contempt, to be punished as in the case of contempt with unlimited fines and/or imprisonment. In so providing, the statutes are declining to set maximum limits. This would seem to be a retrograde step, when one would expect that statute law would seek to replace the unlimited punishment aspect of common-law contempt with fixed sentences, as the British Act of 1981 did. Statutes that have such provisions include the Criminal Justice Act 1999, section 9, which replaced section 17(2) of the Criminal Procedure Act 1967. Under the provisions inserted into the 1967 Act by the 1999 Act, the District Court judge may certify contravention of the publishing and broadcasting restrictions to the High Court. The High Court may inquire into the matter, hear witnesses, consider any statement offered in defence and punish or take steps to punish that person "in the like manner as if he had been guilty of contempt of the Court" (section 4J(3)). The Act also provides that any person who disobeys a witness order or a witness summons

---

[246] Above, n.243, at p.554. *The Report of the Committee to Review the Offences Against the State Acts 1939-1998 and Related Matters* (Government Publications, Dublin, 2002), para.6.179, states that s.4(1) is too broad and is at odds with the right of free speech in Article 40.6.1 of the Constitution, and that contempt of court offers sufficient protection (para. 6.182).

[247] *Murphy v BBC and Daily Mail* (*The Irish Times*, February 27, 2001, August 1, 2001).

without just cause will be guilty of contempt of court (sections 4K and 4L respectively).

Some statutes have extended the contempt power beyond the courts to a variety of tribunals.[248] Section 12 of the Defence (Amendment) Act 1987 creates an offence of contempt of a court-martial. The Law Reform Commission instanced several other statutes with "deemed contempt" provisions.[249] The Commission took the following view:

> "The generic criminalisation of conduct in relation to tribunals by reference to contempt of the High Court must surely be unconstitutional in view of the arbitrary imposition of criminal responsibility which it necessarily involves."[250]

Support for this view is to be found in the striking down of section 3(4) of the Committee of Public Accounts of Dáil Éireann (Privilege and Procedure) Act 1970 by the Supreme Court in *In re Haughey.*[251] Section 10(5) of the Companies Act 1990 went even further and was found by the Supreme Court in *Desmond v Glackin (No. 2)*[252] to be unconstitutional. The Act dealt with the appointment by the Minister for Industry and Commerce of inspectors to investigate the affairs of a company. The section empowered the inspector to certify the refusal of a witness to attend or answer questions to the High Court to be dealt with as if s/he were guilty of contempt of court.[253] Several recent Acts, such as the Committees of the Houses of the Oireachtas (Compellability, Privileges and Immunities of Witnesses) Act 1997, section 3(8)(e), and the Ethics in Public Office Act 1995, section 32(4)(d), have provisions which make it an offence to do anything which if done in relation to proceedings before a court would be contempt of court.

6.7.3 "Contempt of the Courts"

In *Quinn v Ryan,*[254] an extradition case, the court held that the plan of the gardaí to whisk Quinn out of the jurisdiction into Northern Ireland was "contempt of the courts", because its object was to circumvent the courts: "to eliminate the courts and to defeat the rule of law. ... Anyone who sets himself such a course is guilty of contempt of the courts and is punishable accordingly."[255]

---

[248] There is a worrying development of journalists being subpoenaed to appear before tribunals, disciplinary bodies, etc. For example, a freelance journalist was subpoenaed to appear before the Medical Council to reveal sources in relation to an article published in the *Sunday Independent* (*The Irish Times*, May 7, 1992). The "deemed contempt" provisions could apply to a journalist who refused to reveal sources to any of these bodies.

[249] Above, n.43, *Paper*, at Chap.9.

[250] *ibid.* at p.422.

[251] [1971] I.R. 217. See J.M. Kelly, *The Irish Constitution*, above, n.105, at p.369.

[252] [1993] 3 I.R. 67.

[253] See above, n.43, *Report*, at p.59.

[254] [1965] I.R. 70.

[255] *ibid.* at 122.

The gardaí explained their conduct and the matter was not pursued. For that reason, it remains unclear whether Ó Dálaigh C.J. intended that such conduct be brought within the existing sphere of common-law contempt or whether in using the form of words "contempt of the courts" rather than "contempt of court", he sought to distinguish this conduct from that covered by the common law of contempt or sought to widen the scope of the latter.

6.8 PROCEDURE

The procedure to be followed in contempt cases is set out in the Rules of the Superior Courts. Order 44 deals with attachment and committal. An order of attachment directs that the person be brought before the court to answer the contempt in respect of which the order is issued (Order 44, rule 1). An order of committal directs that the person be lodged in prison until s/he purges the contempt (Order 44, rule 2). With the exception of contempt in the face of the court, an order for attachment or committal can only be issued by leave of the court, following an application on notice to the person against whom the order is to be directed (Order 44, rule 3). Many of the cases referred to in the discussion of contempt in this chapter were more concerned with appropriate procedures than with other aspects of contempt. The long-time practice has been to try cases of contempt summarily, that is, without a jury, but still it causes considerable disquiet. There is the issue of the role of the court as party, judge, witness and jury in its own case in determining whether the court itself has been brought into contempt. There is the matter also of Article 38 of the Constitution, which asserts a right to trial by jury in all criminal cases except minor ones. Contempt, with its unlimited fines and imprisonment, is avowedly not minor.

The summary power was originally confined to cases of civil contempt and contempt *in facie curiae*. The current practice of dealing summarily with cases of constructive contempt, *i.e.* contempt committed outside of court, for example in the media, dates from the end of the eighteenth century. It has been challenged on constitutional grounds in this jurisdiction but upheld. All the judges in *AG v O'Kelly*[256] agreed that the High Court had jurisdiction to deal summarily with contempt, although Hanna J. stated that this power was discretionary: the matter could be sent to a jury, but where "for any good reason" the court thought it should determine the matter itself, it had the power to do so.[257] Summary proceedings were convenient but could never be endorsed just because their rapidity and simplicity might make them attractive to the Executive.[258] The summary procedure could be justified only by the urgent and imperative need of a prophylactic order from the High Court.[259]

Ó Dálaigh C.J. in *Keegan v de Búrca*[260] left open the question of jury trial,

---

[256] Above, n.98.
[257] *ibid.* at 332.
[258] Gavan Duffy P., above, n.97, at 218.
[259] *ibid.* See generally, Gerard McCormack, "The Right to Jury Trial in Cases of Contempt" (1983) G.I.L.S.I. 177 and 209.
[260] Above, n.40.

while Finlay P. in *The State (Commins) v McRann*[261] held that even if the contempt issue involved the trial of a criminal charge to which Article 38.5 of the Constitution *prima facie* applied, the terms of Article 34 constituted a qualification on the provisions of Article 38.5 and authorised the courts to adjudicate the issue of contempt in a summary manner.[262] Finlay P. presented a further argument in support of the summary power, an argument based on the tripartite division of power in the Constitution: if the person charged with contempt were to be entitled to trial by jury, then the court would have to wait for the Attorney General or Director of Prosecutions, *i.e.* a servant of the Executive, to present an indictment. It would thus be possible for the Executive, by a refusal to present an indictment, to paralyse the capacity of the courts to impose their will.[263]

O'Higgins C.J. endorsed Finlay P.'s argument in *The State (DPP) v Walsh and Conneely*.[264] Here the central argument was that the court did not have a summary jurisdiction in respect of contempt by scandalising, where speed or urgency were not factors. The Court held unanimously, but for different reasons, that the court did have summary jurisdiction, at least in a case such as this where no issues of fact arose. The independence of the judiciary as proclaimed by Article 35.2 of the Constitution and the protection of judicial proceedings required it. Henchy J. took the view that *O'Kelly* and *Connolly* were right but for the wrong reasons. Having established that there was a *prima facie* right to trial by jury by virtue of Article 38.5 of the Constitution for contempt which is a criminal offence, he concluded that where there were live and real issues of fact to go to the jury, then there was an entitlement to trial by jury:

> "it would not seem to be compatible with the constitutional requirement of fundamental fairness of procedures, or with the equality before the law guaranteed by Article 40, s.1, if contempt of court, which carries with it the risk of a fixed but unlimited term of imprisonment or an unlimited fine, were the only major offence which is exempt from the requirement of a determination by a jury of the controverted facts."[265]

This approach has certain attractions, but what are its practical implications? In the case of the media, it is difficult to envisage many situations where the facts will be in issue, as it is the fact of publication that constitutes the offence and the only issue is the tendency to obstruct, scandalise or prejudice. Nevertheless, it would seem that the summary procedure for criminal contempt is now so firmly entrenched in our law that, despite its unhealthy origins and irregular development, it is now seen as an inherent and necessary power and exercised as the norm but with a consciousness that it must be used with care and restraint. The arguments against it will not easily displace it.[266]

---

[261] Above, n.168.

[262] *ibid.* at 87.

[263] *ibid.* at 88.

[264] Above, n.50.

[265] *ibid.* at 439. The respective roles of judge and jury are that it is a matter for the judge to decide questions of law and for the jury to decide questions of fact.

[266] See above, n.43, *Paper*, at Chaps 7–8; *Report*, at Chap.3, which concludes that it should

6.9 Conclusions on Contempt

The area of contempt of court has given rise to considerable disquiet over the years because of its uncertain scope, the unlimited fines and terms of imprisonment that it can attract, the potential for arbitrary use by the courts, and the strict liability element, all of which have made it suspect on constitutional grounds. The distinctions between civil and criminal contempt have become blurred and unhelpful. Contempt as a criminal offence lacks many of the safeguards of the criminal law, such as a *mens rea* requirement and a right to jury trial. As the Canadian Law Reform Commission remarked, the end result is often a triumph of technicality over logic and clarity.[267] Many of the cases that arise are dealt with *instanter*, that is, on the spot, and are not reported except in the media. There are few written judgments and because judges nowadays often accept an apology rather than imposing fines or imprisonment, few cases are appealed. Aspects of the common law of contempt have already been found to be in breach of the European Convention of Human Rights in the *Sunday Times* case.[268]

Nonetheless, there has been considerable progress in recent years. The views of the Law Reform Commission[269] in relation to contempt of tribunals of inquiry have taken root and cases are now referred to the DPP for a decision on whether to proceed, rather than the tribunal itself dealing directly with the matter. In addition, since the Commission reported in 1994, the Supreme Court in *Irish Times Ltd v Judge Murphy* in 1998 and in *Kelly v O'Neill and Brady* in 1999, as outlined above, has brought greater clarity to the overall context in which contempt of court operates. In doing so, it has provided a value system in which to apply and assess the validity of contempt of court rules and objectives. It has introduced requirements of necessity and proportionality in line with the jurisprudence of the European Court of Human Rights. The rest is up to the legislature.

6.10 Injunctions

Another area of the relationship between the courts and the media is the use of court injunctions to prevent the media from publishing information, whether to safeguard the right to a fair trial or other rights of a private or commercial nature. Injunctions are orders sought from the courts to direct someone to do something (*mandatory* injunction) or to refrain from doing something (*prohibitory* injunction). An *interim* (or temporary) injunction, usually lasting for a few days, may be sought at short notice and *ex parte*, *i.e.* without notice to the party against whom it is being sought. It simply puts the situation on hold for a few days until the matter can be given a preliminary hearing in

---

be left to the Supreme Court in an appropriate case to clarify the problems left unsolved by *Conneely*.

[267] Above, n.28, *Working Paper*, at p.11.
[268] Above, n.29.
[269] Above, n.39.

court. An *interlocutory* injunction may be sought for a longer period, pending a full hearing of the case. However, notice must be given to the other party and a stateable case must be made out, *i.e.* the applicant must persuade the court that s/he has a reasonable chance of succeeding in the eventual hearing. The traditional test applied by the courts was the "balance of convenience" test: what the effect of granting an injunction would be if the applicant were eventually to succeed or fail and whether, on balance, it would be better to grant it or not. However, where freedom of expression is in issue, a stricter test applies.[270] Very infrequently a *perpetual* injunction is granted at the full hearing, such as the perpetual injunction preventing two Dublin clinics from giving abortion assistance in *SPUC v Open Door Counselling Ltd.*[271] In addition, a *quia timet* injunction may sometimes be required to prevent repetition of a harmful act or to prevent the occurrence of an event that it is feared will happen.

6.10.1 Injunctions Restraining Publication

In the media context an injunction could be sought to restrain publication of information that might damage reputation,[272] privacy or commercial interests, for example, or endanger the right to a fair trial. In 1994, an interim injunction was granted to four priests to prevent publication of a book, *Bless Me Father*, about what transpired between the author and the priests when the author went into the confessional box and pretended to confess as a hoax.[273] An interim injunction was also granted to the girl in the *X* case and her mother to prevent five newspapers publishing details of the case, other than matters that could lawfully be disclosed during the criminal prosecution of the man accused of sexual offences against the girl.[274] In 2001, the *Irish Examiner* was restrained from disclosing the whereabouts of a person relocated under the witness protection programme and whose life was said to be under threat. The interim order restrained them from making enquiries or taking any steps within or outside the state for the purpose of discovering the whereabouts of a person whom they knew, or reasonably suspected to be, a relocated witness under section 40(1) of the Criminal Justice Act 1999.[275]

The previous year, a financial company involved in the Irish film industry succeeded in getting an interlocutory injunction against a magazine on the grounds of confidentiality.[276] In another case, the owners of the copyright and serialisation rights of a book about Bishop Casey were granted an interim injunction to stop a number of newspapers publishing extracts from the book.[277] An interlocutory injunction was not granted. Instead, certain conditions were

[270] See discussion in Chap.4 above of *Reynolds v Malocco t/a 'Patrick' magazine* [1999] 1 I.L.R.M. 289; see also Chap.7 below.

[271] [1988] I.R. 593; [1987] I.L.R.M. 477.

[272] Injunctions in defamation cases have been discussed in Chapter 4.

[273] *The Irish Times*, May 10, 1994.

[274] *The Irish Times*, May 17, 1994; above, n.148.

[275] *The Irish Times*, May 1, 2001.

[276] *The Irish Times*, February 11, 25, 1993.

[277] *The Irish Times*, March 20, 1993.

imposed in relation to publication, but these respected the newspapers' rights to "fair dealing" under section 12 of the Copyright Act 1963, for example their right to carry reviews of the book.[278] In another case, the Bar Council, which was handling a complaint against a barrister, obtained an interlocutory injunction restraining a newspaper from publishing confidential information contained in a letter to the Chairman of its Professional Practices Committee until the hearing of the action.[279] The British tabloid newspaper, *The Sun*, its editor and a journalist were fined for publishing extracts from the letter in breach of the injunction.[280] Some weeks earlier, the *Sunday Business Post*, which was being sued for libel by Aer Rianta over allegations it had published concerning the State-owned authority's securing of overseas contracts, consented, on legal advice, to the making permanent of two interim orders, restraining it from repeating or publishing any further allegations about the company.[281]

Injunctions are sometimes sought on the grounds that publication would prejudice a fair trial. Thus injunctions have been granted to restrain publication of a magazine article and photographs while a criminal appeal was pending.[282] An application against RTÉ made in 1985 by two people awaiting trial in the Circuit Court resulted not in an injunction, but in a three-minute interview being removed from a "Today Tonight" programme dealing with attacks on elderly people in the west.[283] In a worrying development, a programme on the death in unusual circumstances of a priest was severely curtailed on the grounds that major segments of it could prejudice any possible court hearing in the case.[284] No charges had yet been preferred.

6.10.2 Injunctions as Prior Restraint

Injunctions have, therefore, been sought and granted quite regularly to prevent publication or broadcasting. As a prepublication restraint, they can have more serious implications for the media than a fine or an award of damages after the event. If the media cannot publish the information, the public cannot receive it. Even if the effect of the injunction is only to delay publication, the delay may mean that the information loses its newsworthiness or is overtaken by events. Depending on the scope of the injunction, it may be that the subsequent events may not be reported either, thus imposing a grave restraint on the media.

Breach of an injunction is liable to be punished as contempt of court. As a form of prior restraint, however, injunctions to prevent publication will not, and should not, be issued lightly. It was argued in the *Spycatcher*[285] case that

---

[278] *ibid.*

[279] *The Irish Times*, March 23, 1993.

[280] *The Irish Times*, March 31, 1993.

[281] *The Irish Times*, December 5, 1992, January 12, 1993.

[282] *The Irish Times*, November 30, 1993, re *Cullen v Tóibín*, above, n.121.

[283] *The Irish Times*, May 31, 1985; *Cf. The Irish Times*, December 4, 1986.

[284] *The Irish Times*, August 22, 1985; see also the *Gallagher* case, above, n.215.

[285] *The Observer and Guardian v UK*, European Court of Human Rights, Series A, No.216; (1992) 14 E.H.R.R. 153. See also *Vereiniging Weekblad Bluf! v The Netherlands* (1995) 20 E.H.R.R. 189.

the appropriate test for granting an injunction affecting freedom of expression is necessity and not the balance of convenience test outlined above and applied by the English courts on *American Cyanamid* principles.[286] The European Court of Human Rights in *Spycatcher* refused to review the *American Cyanamid* principles *in abstracto* and confined itself to determining whether the interference resulting from their application "was necessary having regard to the facts and circumstances prevailing in the specific case before it". While Article 10 of the European Convention on Human Rights does not prohibit the imposition of prior restraints as such,

> "the dangers inherent in prior restraints are such that they call for the most careful scrutiny on the part of the court. This is especially so as far as the press is concerned, for news is a perishable commodity and to delay its publication, even for a short period, may well deprive it of all its value and interest."[287]

In the US, the Supreme Court in the *Pentagon Papers* case[288] stressed the heavy presumption against the constitutional validity of any form of prior restraint, a presumption not reduced by the temporary nature of the restraint, because today's news is tomorrow's history.[289] In *CNN v Noriega*,[290] however, the Court did entertain a temporary injunction on the broadcasting of tapes of conversations between Noriega and his lawyers. The test applied by the US courts is one of a "clear threat" of "immediate and irreparable damage", in this case to the accused's right to a fair trial.[291] In Britain, an injunction imposed by the courts to prevent Channel 4 broadcasting a dramatic reconstruction of the appeal in the *Birmingham Six* case was lifted after the judgment in the appeal had been handed down.[292] On the other hand, a BBC Panorama

---

[286] [1975] A.C. 396, where Lord Diplock, at 407, held that the court must be satisfied that the claim is not frivolous or vexatious, that there is a serious question to be tried. O'Higgins C.J. in *Campus Oil v Minister for Industry and Energy (No.2)* [1983] I.R. 88, at 107, agreed, saying that the test to be applied is whether a fair *bona fide* question has been raised.

[287] Above, n.285, at para.60.

[288] *New York Times v United States* 403 U.S. 713 (1971).

[289] *Nebraska Press Association v Stuart* 427 U.S. 539, 559 (1976).

[290] 111 Sup. Ct. 451 (1990), 498 U.S. 976. See the dissenting judgment of Justice Marshall, who was joined by Justice O'Connor, regarding the heavy presumption against the constitutional validity of any prior restraint on expression, which means that those seeking to rely on it carry a heavy burden of justifying it. If the lower courts were correct in restraining publication in the *Noriega* case, then "it is imperative that we re-examine the premises and operation of *Nebraska Press* itself". The inconsistency in application of the prior restraint doctrine by the Supreme Court has created a chilling effect on publishers: Alberto Bernabe-Riefkohl, "Another Attempt of Solve the Prior Restraint Mystery: Applying the *Nebraska Press* Standard to Media Disclosure of Attorney-Client Communications" (2000) 18 Cardozo Arts & Ent. L.J. 307.

[291] *ibid.* See also Stephanie Izen, "Prior Restraints Revisited: Have the Courts Finally Shackled the Press?" (1992) 12 Loyola Ent. L.J. 535.

[292] *The Irish Times*, December 4, 1987, January 30, 1988. RTÉ had already shown it in part. See also *Hodgson v UK* (1988) 10 E.H.R.R. 503, concerning *R v Ponting* ([1985] C.L.R. 318, official secrets, discussed in Chap.10). A postponement order had been

programme, which named a number of people it alleged were suspects in the Omagh bombing, was allowed to go ahead. The Belfast High Court was not satisfied that there were risks to the individuals named but was satisfied that there was no interference with the presumption of innocence, arising from the content of the programme. Applying the Human Rights Act 1998, which incorporates the European Convention on Human Rights into Northern Irish law, Mr Justice Kerr held that the relevant sections of the Act meant that the balance fell firmly in favour of the broadcaster.[293]

In Ireland, Finlay C.J. in *SPUC v Grogan*[294] said that, where an injunction is sought to protect a constitutional right, the only matter which could properly be capable of being weighed in the balance against the granting of such protection would be another competing constitutional right. This, in the Chief Justice's view, replaces the ordinary concept of *status quo ante* arising in interlocutory injunction cases.

In practice, most judges tend to be pragmatic, and there have been many cases where injunctions against the media have been refused.[295] On occasion also, the need for an injunction will be obviated by an undertaking by the media to remove the offending material and then the remainder of the programme or publication can go ahead.[296] Nonetheless, even this lesser remedy is still an intrusion on press freedom and should have to be justified on specific grounds, such as privacy or fair trial. Even the threat of an injunction can have repercussions for the media or at least a chilling effect. An application for a High Court injunction in Northern Ireland by one political party candidate caused Ulster Television to cancel a series of European election broadcasts, in accordance with the provisions of the Representation of the People Acts, even though similar applications in connection with election broadcasts had previously been refused.[297] An injunction might not be granted to stop the broadcasts, but the fact that one party would not participate meant that there would not be proportionate representation from all lawful parties to meet the requirements of the Act.

6.10.3 Notice of injunction

Once an injunction has been granted, proper notice must be given to the person or persons to whom it is directed. The court order may state the terms to apply to "the defendants, their servants or agents" (*e.g.* the High Court order in *SPUC v Open Door Counselling and the Dublin Well-Woman Centre*[298]) or it

---

made under s.4(2) of the Contempt of Court Act 1981. The Commission rejected the complaint because the order only affected the manner in which the trial could be reported and the judge's evaluation of the risk of prejudice was reasonable in the circumstances. See Glatt, "Trial by Docudrama" (1990) 9 Cardozo Arts and Ent. L.J. 201–30.

[293] *The Irish Times*, October 10, 2000.

[294] [1989] I.R. 753, at 765; [1990] I.L.R.M. 350, at 357.

[295] See, for example, applications against RTÉ (*The Irish Times*, February 6, 1985, September 14, 1985); also the defamation cases referred to in Chap.4 above.

[296] See, for example, *The Irish Times*, March 29, 1985, December 4, 1986.

[297] *The Irish Times*, June 6, 1984.

[298] Above, n.271.

may be addressed to all those having notice of the order. Thus, when an injunction was granted against the *Sunday Business Post* and "any person with notice of the order", the British tabloid newspaper, *The Sun*, was fined for contempt for breaching the order. That was so even though the paper argued that it had not been served with the order; it was still bound.[299] Concern was voiced in *Spycatcher* and in the Scottish *Inside Intelligence* case[300] about the fact that an injunction granted against one publication was taken to apply to all publications within the jurisdiction.[301]

The case of *Agricultural Credit Corporation (ACC) v Irish Business*[302] involved an application for an injunction on the grounds of libel and the leaking of documents belonging to the ACC, on which it owned the copyright. The High Court order restrained the defendants, their servants and agents and "any person with notice" of the making of the order. The judge also gave liberty to the plaintiffs to notify any third party who would then be bound by it. Notice was served on all of the national newspapers and RTÉ. It stated that the hearing was by order of the judge held *in camera* and accordingly the making of the order could not be published.[303] Such a position was untenable in law and the ban was quickly lifted. There was no legal basis for it.[304] The order was later amended to remove the prohibition on publicity.[305] Nonetheless, while that prohibition remained, it led to caution on the part of all the media. The *Cork Examiner*, which had not received notice in time, published the whole story, but apart from that there was very little reporting of the fact of the hearing, only a short news item on RTÉ and a small piece in *The Irish Times*, which had heard independently that the hearing was to be held and had sent a journalist and photographer. A report on the ACC in the *Sunday Tribune* had to be withdrawn at the insistence of the printers and distributors, even though it had been cleared by the paper's own lawyers.[306]

In the subsequent application for an interlocutory injunction, the interests of open justice prevailed. An *in camera* hearing had again been sought, but this time was refused. This was not an urgent hearing like the first one and, therefore, the provision of section 45(1) of the Courts (Supplemental Provisions) Act 1961 permitting as an exception a private hearing in applications of an "urgent nature" for an injunction did not apply.[307]

The *ACC* case, it seems, was not an isolated incident, and the *Sunday Tribune* in an editorial, for example, informed readers that an injunction had been granted against it nine days previously "on a matter of considerable public

---

[299] *The Irish Times*, March 31, 1993.

[300] [1989] S.L.T. 705 (HL).

[301] See Andrew Halpin, "Child's Play in the Lords" (1991) N.L.J. at pp.173–4, Neil Walker, "Spycatcher's Scottish Sequel" (1990) P.L. 345.

[302] *Sunday Tribune*, August 4, 1985.

[303] *ibid.*

[304] LRC, *Consultation Paper on Defamation*, 1991, at pp.133, 365; Adrian Hardiman, "How ACC Halted Magazine Articles", *The Irish Times*, September 10, 1985.

[305] *Sunday Independent*, August 4, 1985.

[306] *The Irish Times*, August 5, 1985.

[307] Note that disclosure of the identity of the source who gave the documents to the magazine was also sought (*The Irish Times*, September 11, 1985). See further Chap.7.

interest."[308] It was reported also that a term of the injunction granted to four priests against publication of a book about what transpired in confessionals was that there should be no publication of the injunction.[309] One issue that this raises is how contempt of court could apply in a case where a newspaper, for example, publishes extracts from such a book, if the fact that the injunction had been granted was not known because the very fact of its existence was not to be published. In such circumstances there would be a technical contempt, but it would be unjust to punish the publisher. In the confessionals case, however, the ban on publication was lifted, following an application by the National Newspapers of Ireland (NNI), and a promise by them that they would not invade the privacy of the priests and would only comment on the case in a fair and proper manner without revealing any confidential matter.[310]

In the *X* case in 1992,[311] when an injunction was sought to restrain a 14-year-old pregnant girl from leaving the jurisdiction to have an abortion, the press and public were excluded from the court hearing. They were excluded also from the appeal. The newspapers and RTÉ sought permission to attend, giving assurances of confidentiality in their reporting, but were refused a hearing on the grounds that they had no standing (*locus standi*).[312] In 1988, the *Irish Press* supported by the *Irish Independent*, applied to the High Court to have reporting restrictions lifted in proceedings taken by a former Ryanair executive against the company. The application was refused by Costello J. on the grounds that the applicants had no *locus standi* to make it. Only the written judgment would be made available to them; affidavits, exhibits, the petition and any pleadings would be covered by the *in camera* order.[313] In some cases, there is no public interest involved, the information is of a private nature and an injunction is clearly warranted. In others, however, it is imperative that the media receive notice of the application for the injunction, an opportunity to oppose it and a swift and effective avenue of appeal if an injunction is granted.

---

[308] *Sunday Tribune*, July 26, 1987, also editorial, September 18, 1988. The paper claimed the basis of it was "now known to be without foundation", yet "the law" prevented the paper telling readers what it was about.

[309] *The Irish Times*, May 7, 10, 1994; *Irish Independent*, May 7, 1994.

[310] *The Irish Times*, May 7, 1994.

[311] *AG v X*, above, n.148.

[312] *The Irish Times*, February 25, 1992. The request was made on the grounds of the public interest and the media undertook to comply with all directions of the court if reporting were allowed. Finlay C.J. stated that they had no right of audience.

[313] *The Irish Times*, October 15, 1988. *Cf. RM v DM* [2001] 2 I.L.R.M. 369, where the High Court ruled that reports, documents and other evidence, including affidavit evidence, furnished in *in camera* hearings in judicial separation and divorce proceedings could not be disclosed without the consent of the court, or information derived from them produced in subsequent proceedings (see further Chap.7).

Further Reading

Boyle, Kevin and McGonagle, Marie, "Contempt of Court: The Case for Law Reform", in Marie McGonagle (ed.), *Law and the Media: The Views of Journalists and Lawyers* (Round Hall Sweet & Maxwell, Dublin, 1997), p.127.

Clayton, Richard & Tomlinson, Hugh, *Fair Trial Rights* (Oxford University Press, Oxford 2001).

Eady, D. & Smith A.T.H. (eds), *Arlidge, Eady & Smith on Contempt* (2nd ed., Sweet & Maxwell, London, 1998).

Jaconelli, Joseph, *Open Justice – A Critique of the Public Trial* (Oxford University Press, Oxford, 2002).

O'Dell, Eoin, "Speech in a Cold Climate: The 'Chilling Effect' of the Contempt Jurisdiction", in Liz Heffernan (ed.), *Human Rights – A European Perspective* (Round Hall Press, Dublin, 1994), p.219.

CHAPTER SEVEN

Reporting the Courts, Parliament and Local Government

7.1 REPORTING THE COURTS

The starting point for consideration of the privileges and restrictions that apply to court reporting is Article 34.1 of the Irish Constitution: "Justice shall be administered in courts established by law ... and save in such special and limited cases as may be prescribed by law, shall be administered in public".

As we have already seen in the last chapter, Article 34 provides for a system of open justice, with both the media and the public free to attend, and the media entitled to report. That is the norm.[1] The only exceptions are the "special and limited cases as may be prescribed by law" to which the Constitution refers. The fact that the limitations must be prescribed by law excludes the possibility of judicial discretion, which was a feature of pre-Constitution cases.[2] There is, however, an element of discretion built into some of the statutes that provide for restrictions on media reporting. Also, despite the fact that Article 34 refers to "special and limited cases" as an exception to the general rule of open justice, in reality statute law provides for quite a number of situations where the media and public can be excluded from the court altogether, or restrictions imposed on what may be reported. As can be seen in the following sections, restrictions on the media have been imposed quite frequently, and issues arising from media reporting have exercised the courts on a regular basis. The situation has been clarified to some extent by Supreme Court judgments in recent years and a greater awareness of the media role in informing the public has developed. In relation to court reporting, it is a role that the media need to exercise responsibly in the interests of the public.

7.1.1 Exclusion of the Media from the Court

The Courts (Supplemental Provisions) Act 1961 provides the basis for the exclusion of the public, though not necessarily the media, from the court. Each of the areas of restriction provided for will be considered in turn, to the extent that they affect the media. Section 45(1) of the 1961 Act states:

"Justice may be administered otherwise than in public in any of the

---

[1] See Walsh J. in *In re R* [1989] I.R. 126, at 134.
[2] See Carney J. in *DPP v WM* [1995] 1 I.R. 226, Irish Times Law Report, March 13, 1995.

following cases:

    (a) applications of an urgent nature for relief by way of *habeas corpus*, bail, prohibition or injunction;

    (b) matrimonial causes and matters;

    (c) lunacy and minor matters;

    (d) proceedings involving the disclosure of a secret manufacturing process".

Section 45(2) provides that these areas of restriction are in addition to any other cases prescribed by any Act of the Oireachtas. Section 45(3) has the effect of resurrecting to "full force and effect" any earlier statute that provided for the administration of justice otherwise than in public and that "is not in force solely by reason of its being inconsistent with the provisions of the Constitution". While the latter provision is peculiar, it does, as Carney J. pointed out in a case concerning provisions of the Punishment of Incest Act 1908,[3] enjoy a presumption of constitutionality, the validity of which was not and could not be challenged in the particular proceedings before him. To the extent, however, that section 5 of the 1908 Act provided that all proceedings were to be held in private, it appeared to be incompatible with the Constitution (see below).

7.1.1.1 Applications of an urgent nature

The two main issues under this heading that have caused uncertainty for the media in the past are bail applications and injunctions. In relation to bail hearings, the position has now been clarified by the Bail Act 1997. Reporters may remain in court and may report the proceedings. However, they must not publish or broadcast any information relating to the criminal record of the person applying for bail.[4] To do so would encroach on the person's right to have a fair trial and to be presumed innocent until proven guilty. The Act also specifies which persons shall be held responsible for a publication or broadcast that does publish such information and the penalties to be imposed.[5]

---

[3] *ibid.*

[4] The Bail Act 1997, s.4(2) and s.4(3). S.4(2) provides that a court "may" direct that the proceedings shall be heard otherwise than in public, or exclude from the court all persons except officers of the court, persons directly concerned with the proceedings, *bona fide* representatives of the press and other such persons if any as the court may permit to remain.

[5] S.4(4). In the case of a newspaper or periodical, it is any proprietor, editor and publisher, who will be held responsible. In the case of any other publication, it is the publisher. In the case of a broadcast, it is any person who transmits or provides the programme and any person having functions in relation to the programme corresponding to those of the editor of a newspaper. They shall be guilty of an offence and liable on summary conviction to a fine not exceeding £1,500 and/or to a term of imprisonment not exceeding 12 months, or on indictment to a fine not exceeding £10,000 and/or to imprisonment for a term not exceeding three years (s.4(4)(c)(i) and (ii)). The terms "broadcast" and "written publication" are both defined in s.4(5). Interestingly, the latter term includes a film, sound track and any other record in permanent form. A body corporate can also be proceeded against (s.4(6)).

The nature and scope of injunctions has already been explained in Chapter 6. The only aspect to be dealt with here, therefore, is the effect on the press when an injunction, usually an interim one, is sought as a matter of urgency. In that case, the injunction can be applied for at any time of the day or night and, if outside court hours, may be heard in the judge's own home. Application is generally made on an *ex parte* basis because there is no time to alert the other side or because it is more convenient not to.[6]

In Chapter 6 we were concerned mainly with injunctions granted against media organisations to prevent publication or broadcasting of particular matter, whereas in this chapter we consider the impact of injunctions granted to others in a situation in which the media are not allowed to attend or report. The media may be excluded either because they do not know that an application for an injunction is to be made at short notice or because the proceeding is to be heard *in camera*, that is, in private. An application might be held *in camera* because of the confidential nature of the subject-matter, for example. Otherwise, reporters would have to be admitted. The refusal to hear the application for an interlocutory injunction *in camera* in *ACC v Irish Business*[7] is a good example, as is *Maguire v Drury*.[8]

In that respect, it was disappointing that the courts denied the media a right to be heard when they applied to be allowed to report the Supreme Court argument in the appeal against the High Court injunction in the *X* case.[9] The hearing of the appeal was to be *in camera* with the press and the public excluded. The national newspapers and RTÉ requested permission to attend and gave assurances that they would respect the privacy of the parties and the directions of the court in their reporting. The court refused their request and, at that time, rejected any notion of a public representative function on the part of the media.

The position regarding *locus standi* generally was considered by Walsh J. in *SPUC v Coogan*:

> "[T]he Court will, where the circumstances warrant it, permit a person whose personal interest is not directly or indirectly presently or in the future threatened to maintain proceedings if the circumstances are such that the public interest warrant[s] it. In this context the public interest must be taken in the widest sense. ... In the last analysis it is a question reserved exclusively to the Courts to decide".[10]

Walsh J. was referring to the possibility of an "outsider" being able to maintain

---

[6] Even if the other side is present, it seems that there is no opportunity given for that side of the case to be heard at the interim stage. Apart from the time constraints, it is difficult to see why not. See *ACC v Irish Business* (above, Chap.6, nn.302–6; *The Irish Times*, September 10, 1985).

[7] *ibid.*

[8] [1995] I.L.R.M. 108. The Supreme Court also rejected an application for an *in camera* hearing, because of the momentous issues of great public concern involved, in a case of withdrawal of a life-support system from a woman in a near-vegetative state (*The Irish Times*, June 15, 1995).

[9] *The Irish Times*, February 25, 1992.

[10] [1990] I.L.R.M. 70, at 78–9.

an action. If the courts were prepared to contemplate that possibility, then there would seem to be no reason to refuse the media the right to be heard to make their case as to why they should be allowed to attend and report on proceedings.[11] Since then, in *Irish Times Ltd v Judge Murphy*[12] the Supreme Court has recognised the representative role of the media, as the eyes and ears of the public, which would appear to strengthen the media's position in such circumstances in the future.

Another issue, as pointed out in Chapter 6, is the scope of injunctions. A ban on the very fact of the granting of an injunction is an affront to the public. An injunction addressed to all the media has major implications for freedom of information and the public's right to know. Even injunctions not directly addressed to the media can cause problems. In the case of *AG (SPUC) v Open Door Counselling*,[13] for example, a perpetual injunction was granted by the courts restraining two clinics, their servants and agents, from assisting pregnant women in procuring abortions. RTÉ found itself answering a formal complaint to the Broadcasting Complaints Commission arising from live transmission of an interview with representatives of the clinics in the wake of the decision against them. RTÉ was not guilty of bias, according to the Commission, but was in breach of section 18 of the Broadcasting Authority Act 1960, insofar as remarks made by the interviewees could be construed as "being likely to promote or incite to crime". RTÉ was advised that there should be no discussion of abortion on live broadcasts and only discussion of the general merits of the law in recorded programmes. There was also a danger that contempt of court law would be invoked against the media while the Supreme Court appeal was pending. Protest marches against the High Court's ruling were either not covered at all or marchers were asked to remove banners displaying the telephone numbers of abortion clinics in Britain. Such was the level of confusion that it was believed the showing of such pictures might constitute defiance of the injunction and amount to civil contempt.[14]

7.1.1.2 Matrimonial Causes and Matters

In matrimonial causes and matters, proceedings may be held otherwise than in public. In addition, specific statutes provide that family law matters be held *in camera*. Reporting, likewise, is strictly curtailed in the interests of the privacy of the parties and family unit, which the Constitution expressly protects (Article 41). However, the terminology in the various Acts is not consistent and can

---

[11] The media also made a submission in connection with *In re R* (above, n.1) to have the hearing held in open court but were refused. Since then, the interventions in *Maguire v Drury* (above, n.8, the case of the man who was threatening to sue the Catholic Church over an alleged relationship between his wife and a priest) and in the case of the book *Bless Me Father* (*The Irish Times*, May 10, 1994, discussed in Chap.6 above) were more successful.

[12] [1998] 1 I.R. 359. See discussion in Chap.6.

[13] [1987] I.L.R.M. 477.

[14] See Marie McGonagle, "Freedom of Expression and Information" in Gerard Quinn (ed.), *Irish Human Rights Yearbook* (Round Hall Sweet and Maxwell, Dublin, 1995), p.31.

make it difficult for journalists to know what their entitlements are.[15] The Family Law (Maintenance of Spouses and Children) Act 1976, section 25(1) and the Family Home Protection Act 1976, section 10(6), provide that cases "shall" be heard "otherwise than in public" and, in the High Court and Circuit Court, "shall" be heard "in chambers" (sections 25(2) and 10(7), respectively). The Married Women's Status Act 1957, section 12(4), is discretionary rather than mandatory: "if either party so requests, the court may hear the application in private". Cases under the Marriages Act 1972 "may be heard and determined in private" (sections 1(3)(c) and 7(3)(c)). The Adoption Acts 1952–76 provide for the hearing of cases *in camera* (section 20(2) of the 1952 Act, regarding cases stated to the High Court). The Judicial Separation and Family Law Reform Act 1989, section 34, provides that proceedings shall be held otherwise than in public. The Family Law Act 1995, section 38(6), states that sections 33–36 of the Judicial Separation and Family Law Reform Act 1989 shall apply to proceedings under that Act too. Virtually the same provision is contained in the Family Law (Divorce) Act 1996, section 38(5). The Domestic Violence Act 1996, states at section 16(1) that civil proceedings under the Act "shall be heard otherwise than in public", which now seems to be the preferred formulation.

Whatever the variety of formulations in the legislation, the practice in the family law courts has been that all proceedings are heard *in camera*. The Working Group on a Courts Commission,[16] citing O'Higgins C.J. in *In re Kennedy and McCann*,[17] explains that family law cases are held in private "in order to preserve, for the sake of the children and their welfare, a decent privacy in relation to the disputes which have arisen between their parents". If that is the sole or primary reason for the *in camera* rule, it should follow that cases which involve couples who do not have children should not be held in private. At a minimum it supports the argument in favour of a more nuanced approach and the making of a distinction between types of family cases, rather than blanketing them all together as at present.[18]

Where statutes contain a mandatory provision, as in section 34 of the Judicial Separation and Family Law Reform Act 1989, which directs that all proceedings "shall be heard otherwise than in public", the judge has no choice but to exclude the media, and the media have to obey.[19] There is more scope

---

[15] For a discussion of the terminology used, see J.M. Kelly, *The Irish Constitution* (Gerard Hogan and Gerry Whyte (eds), 3rd ed., Butterworths, Dublin, 1994), at p.403 and Tom O'Malley, "The Criminal Law (Incest Proceedings) Act 1995" *Irish Current Law Statutes Annotated* (Sweet and Maxwell, Dublin, 1995).

[16] Working Group on a Courts Commission, *A Working Paper on Information and the Courts* (Government Publications, Dublin, November 1997), p.31.

[17] [1976] I.R. 382, at 385.

[18] For a discussion of the *in camera* rule in family law cases, see Rosemary Horgan, Brian Gallagher and Geoffrey Shannon, "Camera angles", *Law Society Gazette*, July/August 2002, p.26 and "Reform of the In Camera Rule" [2002] 7 B.R. 278 (same article in both periodicals, with minor editorial variations). Ironically, the statutory provisions regarding proceedings specifically involving children (see below), particularly the more recent ones, are more nuanced.

[19] The only other option open to them would seem to be to take a High Court action challenging the constitutionality of the legislative provision. *Locus standi* would be

for the media where the statutory provision is discretionary rather than mandatory. Representations can be made to the judge to hold the hearing in public in the public interest. In the constitutional challenge to the Judicial Separation Act in *F v F, Ireland and AG*,[20] for example, a submission to be allowed to report in the public interest was made by the National Newspapers of Ireland (NNI). Murphy J. relied on the mandatory provision of section 34 of the Act to exclude the media from part of the case in order "to protect the privacy and confidentiality of the husband and wife in relation to the facts concerning the marriage and the family law matters".[21] The remainder of the case, which dealt with the constitutionality issue, he heard in public. He acknowledged the public interest in the constitutional issue but asked that the names of the parties not be reported.

When a hearing is conducted in private, publication of any material from it is not automatically banned, but can be restrained by injunction or may be punished as contempt. In *Maguire v Drury*[22] – a case between a man and his wife, which was expected to be followed by an action by the man for damages against the Catholic Church on the grounds that the wife's alleged affair with a priest had caused the breakdown of the marriage in question, publication of any material taken from the *in camera* judicial separation proceedings was restrained by interim injunction. The order was limited to the *in camera* matter and did not prevent publication of the man's account of the proceedings he intended to bring against the Church. However, neither the woman nor the children were to be referred to by name, and no pictures of them were to be published. An interlocutory injunction was later refused on the grounds that the case did not concern the intimacies of married life or the marital communications between husband and wife, but rather allegations by the husband of an extramarital liaison entered into by his wife, which he wanted to publicise in order to give vent to his anger, and perhaps to make money. The courts are reluctant to intervene in such cases "in a manner which would entrench on the freedom of expression enjoyed by the press and by the media generally, merely to avoid the distress caused by publication of matters which show up a parent or parents in a sordid or unfavourable light".[23]

The purpose of these restrictions is overtly to protect the privacy of the parties and, in some cases, the privacy and identity of any children of the marriage. The status and protection accorded to the family and marriage in the Constitution is an important dimension of this.[24] However, the *in camera* nature of family law proceedings has its drawbacks in terms of public knowledge and in terms of public appreciation of the extent and nature of family law problems in the State. It also hampers the formation of precedent and guidance as to appropriate remedies. People do not know how family cases are handled away

---

required, and there is also a presumption of constitutionality that applies to all post-1937 legislation passed by the Oireachtas, so the task would be an uphill battle.

[20] *The Irish Times*, July 8, 1994.

[21] *The Irish Times*, July 7, 1994.

[22] *The Irish Times*, June 2, 1994.

[23] [1995] I.L.R.M. 108, at pp.114–15.

[24] See James Casey, *Constitutional Law in Ireland* (3rd ed., Round Hall Sweet & Maxwell, Dublin, 2000), at p.277.

from the spotlight of media attention. Practitioners themselves have suggested that improvements in the standard of presentation, in the degree of interest taken and in the general approach to family law cases, would result from media reporting. The Law Reform Commission, in its *Consultation Paper on Family Courts* in 1994,[25] accepted the dangers but regarded family law cases as:

> "a class different from other cases in that they frequently involve detailed discussion of personal and usually private relationships at a time when the parties concerned may be feeling hurt and vulnerable. It is rightly felt that family members should as far as possible be protected from the further stress which may be occasioned by publicity and by exposure of their personal lives to those having only a prurient interest. Even more so, where children are involved, there is a strong desire to maintain what O'Higgins C.J. described in *Re McCann v Kennedy* [*sic*] as 'a decent privacy', this being regarded as necessary to prevent harm or distress to the child".[26]

The Law Reform Commission, therefore, provisionally recommended against any change with regard to allowing access by the public or press.[27] The Working Group on a Courts Commission, however, further considered the purpose of the *in camera* rule and the practical implications of changing it, which would require amendment to a number of statutory provisions.[28] The Group took account of the anxiety of litigants to avoid publication of the facts of their cases on the one hand, and on the other the increasing criticism of the rule from practitioners and others who made submissions. It referred to the 1985 report of the Joint Oireachtas Committee on Marriage Breakdown, which had underscored the importance of public scrutiny as a check on arbitrary decision-making. Decisions taken in private can be misunderstood and that can diminish confidence in the fairness of the administration of justice. The group added that the rule can hide from the public the extent of marriage breakdown and consequent litigation, and prevent a proper evaluation of the situation.

The Working Group also considered the situation in other countries. In Canada, for example, the view has been taken that privacy and confidentiality should not be confused with total secrecy: "The public is entitled to know the way justice is administered in the courts; no court should be permitted to operate in secrecy".[29] In Australia also, the *in camera* rule was relaxed to allow publication of family cases, while protecting the identities of the parties. The reason was to allow for public debate concerning the work and performance of the court. The Working Group concluded that a balance must be found

---

[25] Law Reform Commission, *Consultation Paper on Family Courts*, 1994, at para. 7.44; *Report on Family Courts* (LRC 52–1996), at paras 1.11, 2.13.

[26] *ibid.*, *Paper*, at para. 7.43, reaffirmed in *Report* at para.10.43.

[27] *ibid.*, *Paper*, at para. 7.45. The LRC did recommend, however, that *bona fide* researchers and students of family law should be permitted to attend family proceedings (confirmed in *Report*, para. 10.44)

[28] Sixth Report of the Working Group on a Courts Commission, *Sixth Report* (Pn 6533, Stationery Office, Dublin, 1998) at para.5.12.

[29] Law Reform Commission of Canada, "The Family Court", *Working Paper No.1* (1974), p.36.

between the right to privacy of the litigants and children and the right to a fair, transparent and accountable system of justice in this area. "It is also clear", the group said, "that policy reform, research, accountability and provision of adequate services cannot take place without accurate statistics from the courts on a regular basis". It recommended, therefore, that a pilot project be set up, which would include the appointment of a qualified solicitor or barrister to *inter alia*:

- record and report on family law decisions and written judgments, without identifying the parties, for relevant legal publications
- assemble family court statistics for publication on a regular basis
- provide weekly or monthly articles reporting on current family law decisions, statistics and other relevant matters to be published by the Courts Service.

The group also supported the recommendation of the Law Reform Commission that *bona fide* researchers and students of family law be permitted to attend family proceedings.

In line with the recommendations of the Working Group, the Courts Service established a pilot project titled "The Family Court Recording Service". The aims of the project are to provide general information to the public as to what happens in the family courts, and to collect accurate statistics so that the court service can plan the future of the family courts. While both are admirable, it is submitted that they do not go far enough to address the problems.

Mr Justice Paul Carney of the High Court, who has had long experience of family law cases, speaking extra-judicially,[30] has said that there is a very strong case to be made that the citizen should be entitled to monitor and observe the fair administration of justice in their home through the contemporary technology of television. He also said that the news media could be trusted to report family law cases. The absence of reporting of family law cases was damaging to our understanding of the nature of our society. He said that it was only because of the centralisation of sexual abuse cases in the Central Criminal Court that we have an understanding of what is happening in that area. Such cases have been responsibly reported, with anonymity being properly protected. He went on to say that the restrictions the media are subjected to by the courts would seem to go beyond what the words "special and limited" meant in Article 34.1 of the Constitution.

The government plans to change the *in camera* rule in family law cases to allow general reporting of overall trends while continuing to respect the privacy of individuals involved.[31] Meanwhile the court recorder produces information bulletins on family law matters.[32]

---

[30] TCD conference, January 2000 (*The Irish Times*, January 24, 2000).

[31] *The Irish Times*, June 21, 2002, referring to Mr Brennan speaking in the Dáil for the Minister for Justice, Equality and Law Reform, Mr McDowell. The need arises because the barrister appointed to report on family law cases in accordance with the recommendations of the Working Group was unable to do so (*The Irish Times*, October 15, 2001), apparently as a result of legal advice to the Courts Service Board.

[32] *The Family Law Information Bulletin*, Vol.1, Issue 1 of October 2001 deals with the

While the intimacy and privacy of the family relationship requires protection, a blanket ban on reporting is difficult to justify. Family proceedings vary greatly in nature and likewise the role of the court in dealing with them. In some cases, the matter may not involve more than the administration of property or the variation of an order in relation to ancillary relief. In others, the welfare of children will be paramount. In any event, a distinction could be made at the extremes.

The European Court of Human Rights held by a majority in *B and P v UK*[33] that proceedings which concerned the residence of children following their parents' divorce or separation were prime examples of cases where the exclusion of the press and public might be justified to protect the privacy of the child and parties and to avoid prejudicing the interests of justice. To enable the deciding judge to gain as full and accurate a picture as possible of the advantages and disadvantages of the various residence and contact options open to the child, it was essential, the Court said, that the parents and other witnesses felt able to express themselves candidly on highly personal issues without fear of public curiosity or comment. Anyone who could establish an interest was able to consult or obtain a copy of the full text of the orders and/ or judgments of the courts in child residence cases in the UK, and judgments of the Court of Appeal were routinely published, enabling the public to study the manner in which the courts generally approach such cases and the principles applied in deciding them. Consequently there had been no breach of Article 6(1) of the European Convention on Human Rights, even though the parents in the particular case had requested a public hearing and been refused.

Some degree of privacy and confidentiality may be necessary, therefore, in certain types of family law cases, but privacy should not be confused with total secrecy. A test of proportionality would seem appropriate. Second, it is privacy that should be protected rather than fear of exposure or embarrassment. As the nature of judicial separation and divorce cases change from fault-based

---

Circuit Court; Issue 2, December 2001, deals with the District Court; Vol. 2, Issues 1 and 2, February and May 2002, deal with domestic violence. Vol. 1 Issue 2 explains the practical implications of the *in camera* rule in that only applicant and respondent, plus their legal representatives, if any (the majority are unrepresented), the District Court judge and registrar may be present.

[33] App. Nos 36337/97 and 35974/97, decision of April 24, 2001 (Chamber Judgment, 5 votes to 2). B's case in the UK had been heard *in camera* throughout, while in P's case the first hearing was *in camera* but the second application was heard in open court. In the UK, therefore, certain distinctions have been made. In *Re X (a minor) (restrictions on identification)*, (Fam. Div., Bracewell J., October 13, 2000), for example, it was held that there was a legitimate public interest in publishing information about the alleged controversial doctrines of a local authority in relation to the fostering of children, and in *Re Z (a minor) (identification: restriction and publication)* [1997] Fam. 1, a distinction was made between the protective and custodial roles of courts in relation to wards, while in *Clibbery v Allen* [2002] E.W.C.A. Civ. 45, [2002] 1 F.L.R. 565, it was held that open justice prevailed to the extent that a party (cohabitee, no children) to proceedings held in chambers could not be restrained from making revelations about the proceedings to the press. See also, in Ireland, Baby A case: *In the matter of an inquiry pursuant to Article 40.4.2 of the Constitution and in the matter of Baby A, an infant: Eastern Health Board v E, A and A* [2000] I.R. 430, below, n.47.

to "no fault" criteria, it may be argued that the same degree of protection is no longer needed and that much would be gained from allowing reporters access and imposing restrictions on reporting the identities of the parties instead. The Judicial Separation Act 1989, the Family Law Act 1995 and the Family Law (Divorce) Act 1996 make provision for property adjustments and other ancillary orders, for example, which could perhaps be determined in public and reported, while preserving the anonymity of the parties.[34] As the Law Reform Commission noted in a more general context: "If the principle of open justice is to be given full effect it should not be subject to limitations unless they are essential in the interests of justice".[35]

7.1.1.3 Minors

The media are generally excluded from hearings involving the care and custody of minors. In other cases involving the criminal prosecution of a minor, for example, the media may be admitted but reporting restrictions will be applied to preserve the anonymity of the minor concerned.

The Children Act 2001 repeals the Children Acts of 1908 and 1941 and generally updates the law on children, including the age of criminal responsibility and criminal proceedings involving children. The 2001 Act prohibits certain published or broadcast reports in a number of areas. It provides that no report shall be published or included in a broadcast in relation to the admission of a child to the diversion programme (a programme to which a child, who accepts his/her criminal responsibility, may be admitted, in order to direct him/her away from committing further offences). The same applies to the proceedings at any conference relating to the child, including the contents of any action plan for the child and the contents of the report of the conference. It also prohibits any information that would lead to identification of the child.[36]

The Act prohibits any identifying report or picture of a child involved in proceedings before the Children Court (section 93(1)), except where the court decides to dispense with the requirement for the purpose of avoiding injustice

---

[34] It was reported (*The Irish Times*, February 24, 2001) that the President of the Circuit Court intended to extend the *in camera* rule to cases involving home division disputes between cohabiting couples. It is not clear on what authority that decision could have been taken. While equality of treatment between married and cohabiting couples is desirable to the greatest extent possible within the constraints of the Constitution, the better course would appear to be to narrow the scope of the *in camera* rule (with safeguards for the privacy of the persons concerned) rather than extend it further.

[35] *Consultation Paper on Contempt of Court*, 1991, at p.248.

[36] Section 51. Section 51(1)(b) provides that the name, address or school of the child or any other information, including any picture, which is likely to lead to identification of the child may not be published or broadcast. There are exceptions for statistical information and *bona fide* research (s.51(2)). The section also stipulates who shall be liable if the provision is contravened (s.51(3)) and the punishment to apply on summary conviction (a fine not exceeding £1,500 and/or 12 months imprisonment) and on indictment (a fine not exceeding £10,000 and/or three years imprisonment). It is a defence that a person charged was not aware at the time and neither suspected nor had reason to suspect that the publication or broadcast in question was of a matter referred to in subs.(1). The terms "broadcast" and "publish" are defined in the section (s.51(6)).

to the child or where it is necessary for the purpose of apprehending a child unlawfully at large (section 93(2)). In either case the court must explain the reasons for its decision in open court (section 93(3)). The section applies also to appeals and proceedings by way of case stated (section 93(5)) but does not affect any enactment concerning the anonymity of an accused or the law relating to contempt of court. Section 94 of the Act provides that the court shall exclude from the hearing of any proceedings before it, all persons, except specified persons, directly concerned in the case and *bona fide* representatives of the press (section 94(1)(e)).

In any proceedings for an offence against a child or where a child is a witness, a similar prohibition on published or broadcast reports applies (section 252(1)). Again, the court can dispense with the requirement to any specified extent if satisfied that it is in the interests of the child to do so (section 252(2)), in which case the court must give its reasons in open court (section 252(3)). The section does not affect the law on contempt of court. In any proceedings for an offence where a child is called as a witness, the court can exclude from the court all persons except officers of the court, persons directly concerned in the proceedings, *bona fide* representatives of the press and such other person (if any) as the court may in its discretion permit to remain (section 257(1)). Those powers are in addition to any other powers the court may have to hear proceedings *in camera* or to exclude witnesses (section 257(2) and (3)).

Earlier legislation relating to children contained a variety of restrictions on reporting and power to hold proceedings *in camera*. The Status of Children Act 1987 provides that the court may direct that the whole or any part of the proceedings for a declaration of parentage shall be heard otherwise than in public and that an "application for a direction ... shall be so heard unless the Court otherwise directs" (section 36(4)). In practice, the courts do exclude the public from such cases.[37] Under the Child Care Act 1991, section 29, cases dealing with the protection of children in emergencies (Part III), care proceedings (Part IV) and children in the care of the Health Boards (Part VI), will be heard in private.[38] Proceedings under the Succession Act 1965, sections 56(11), 119 and 122, "shall be held in chambers".

The Guardianship of Infants Act 1964 makes no mention of excluding the media or holding proceedings in private, but because it relates to minors, it would come within the scope of section 45(1) of the Courts (Supplemental Provisions) Act 1961, which provides that matters relating to minors may be administered otherwise than in public. The same is true in relation to adoption,

---

[37] See William Duncan and Paula Scully, *Marriage Breakdown in Ireland: Law and Practice* (Butterworths, Dublin, 1990), at para. 18.024; also the Rules of the Circuit Court (S.I. No. 510 of 2001), Ord. 59, rr.1(8) and 2(9).

[38] The Child Care Act 1991, s.31 provides that no matter likely to lead members of the public to identify a child who is the subject of proceedings under Parts III, IV or VI shall be published or broadcast. S.31(3) details those who will be held responsible if there is a breach of s.31(1) and s.31(5) defines "broadcast" and "written publication" in the same terms as in the Bail Act 1997 – see above, n.5. A court, however, may dispense with that prohibition if satisfied that it is in the interests of the child to do so (s.31(2)). Section 31(4) further provides that nothing in the section shall affect the law as to contempt of court.

abduction and wardship proceedings.[39] At any rate provision is made in the rules of court[40] for applications under the Guardianship of Infants Act and certain other Acts to be heard in private. In *In re Kennedy and McCann*,[41] the editor and a journalist with the *Sunday World* newspaper were fined for publishing details of a hearing held *in camera* under the Guardianship of Infants Act. The report was found to be in contempt of court as it was inaccurate in a number of respects, the names of the parties were revealed and it was accompanied by pictures of the mother and children. The Adoption Acts 1952–76 also provide for *in camera* hearings, subject to rules of court (1952 Act, section 20(2)), and for the privacy of records (1976 Act, section 8), unless in the best interests of the child concerned.

The fact that a hearing is held *in camera* does not of itself mean that nothing can be reported in relation to the hearing, but anything that is reported runs the risk of being in contempt of court if inaccurate or otherwise prejudicial. In 1993 the High Court held that the *Sunday Tribune* had committed no offence in publishing a report relating to an *in camera* hearing. The court accepted the evidence given by the editor and journalist that they did not know that the case had been held *in camera* and accepted an apology.[42] In 1999, three tabloid newspapers were deemed to have identified, contrary to section 31 of the Child Care Act 1991, a child applicant in need of care. All three had referred to the child's age, had named the Health Board concerned and had identified the detention centre in which he was being held. Kelly J. in the High Court, while satisfied a *prima facie* contempt of court had been made out, was concerned that contempt proceedings would detract from the main concern, namely the welfare of the child, and referred the matter to the DPP. The remainder of evidence in the case was heard *in camera* and the decision given in open court.[43]

---

[39] See Alan Shatter, *Family Law in the Republic of Ireland* (4th ed., Butterworths, Dublin, 1997), at p.110; *The Irish Times*, July 4, 1994. An information booklet on wards of court was issued by the Department of Justice in July 1998 (available at *www.justice.ie*). In the UK, it was held that the media do not require leave of the court either to interview a ward of court or to publish or broadcast such an interview: *BBC v Kelly* (*The Times*, August 9, 2000). The publication of information about a ward, even if the child was known to be a ward, was not, of itself and without more ado, a contempt of court. Much depends on the role the court is exercising in relation to the ward, whether a merely protective role or a custodial role. In the latter, the child's interests would be paramount. The public interest in *Kelly* was clear, especially as the court had enlisted the media's assistance in tracing the ward, who had run away from home and joined a religious sect.

[40] The Circuit Court Rules, above, n.37. Ord. 59, r. 4(21) provides that proceedings under the Guardianship of Infants Act 1964 and various other family law statutes up to and including the Children Act 1997 shall be heard *in camera* save where the court directs.

[41] [1976] I.R. 382.

[42] *The Irish Times*, May 27, 1993.

[43] *The Irish Times*, August 18, 1999. Shatter, above, n.39, points out (at para. 2.37) that s.31 of the Child Care Act was until then the only provision in family law that provided for a fine and/or imprisonment for violation of a prohibition on the publication or broadcasting, in that case of any matter likely to lead members of the public to identify a child who is the subject of care proceedings. A fine not exceeding £1,000 or imprisonment for a term not exceeding 12 months, or both, are stipulated. See now also the Children Act 2001, above, n.36.

In a custody case in which a mother and child had disappeared, the *in camera* rule was lifted to allow an appeal by the father on The Late Late Show on RTÉ. The mother and child were located. It was right that the media should co-operate in tracing the child, the judge said, but that was the extent to which the media should intrude into the affairs of the family. Coverage should be restrained and, in the interests of the child, photographs should not be taken.[44] The interests of the child led to the imposition of fines for contempt of court in a child abduction case in 1995. In *PSS v JAS*,[45] the child's mother had given an interview to an *Irish Independent* reporter. RTÉ then broadcast extracts from the report on a radio programme, *Morning Ireland*. LM/FM Radio received a phone call from the child's grandmother and went on to broadcast an interview with her and the child's mother. The mother, all of the named media outlets, the relevant reporters and editors were held to be in contempt of court, in that they had breached the *in camera* rule.[46]

In a case known as the "Baby A case",[47] involving unlawful custody and adoption, the proceedings were held *in camera*. Laffoy J. said it was the "invariable practice" of the court to hold such cases *in camera*, although it did have a discretion as to whether or not to hear minor matters otherwise than in public. At the end of the proceedings, Laffoy J. made an order restricting publication of information concerning the proceedings, save by leave of the court, to that given in her specially edited judgment. The purpose of the order was to protect the identities of two babies, Baby A and Baby B. While others involved in the case, including the principals of the crisis pregnancy counselling agency, a barrister and a doctor, were not entitled to anonymity, she was concerned that if any of them were named there could be "slippage" leading to the identification of the babies.

The Irish Times, followed by a number of other media organisations, applied

---

[44] *The Irish Times*, January 18, 2000.

[45] Unreported, High Court, Budd J., May 19, 22, 1995.

[46] The mother, the court said, had "deliberately plucked away the shield which the law provides in order to protect children from publicity" and had done so "to stir up and orchestrate a popular campaign" against the court order made pursuant to the Hague Convention on Civil Aspects of International Child Abduction (at p.23 of the judgment). However, because of her distraught state, the trial judge accepted her apology with an admonishment. See Alan Shatter, above, n.39, at 2.35. The *Irish Independent* was fined £2,000, the editor £300, and the reporter £250, for articles that were grossly inaccurate and partisan accounts of the proceedings, accompanied by photographs of the parents and child, and constituted a "reckless travesty" of the court's judgment and order. Budd J. was concerned that publication of the story might deter prospective litigants from seeking the assistance of the courts to resolve disputes concerning custody of children for fear of the huge damage such publicity may do to the child's welfare (at p.25 of the judgment). RTÉ was admonished for its inadvertent breach of the *in camera* rule. LM/FM, who did not know that the case could not be discussed, were told that ignorance is no defence, merely a factor in mitigation (at p.97 of the judgment). Orders for costs were made against Independent Newspapers and the Independent Broadcasting Corporation t/a LM/FM. In a mark of how seriously it regarded the matter, the court also imposed a sentence of one month's imprisonment in the event of those fined not paying the fines due within a specified time (Shatter).

[47] *In the matter of an inquiry pursuant to Article 40.4.2 of the Constitution and in the matter of Baby A, an infant: Eastern Health Board v E, A and A* [2000] I.R. 430.

successfully to be allowed to name the agency involved.[48] The ban on disclosing other names was continued. McGuinness J., who heard the media application, said she was very conscious that it raised questions of constitutional rights, their balancing and priority: freedom of expression, the right to have justice done in public and the right of the infant children to be protected.[49] Disclosing the name of the agency was in the public interest, she said, as pregnant women seeking counselling should have the information and also other agencies who felt their name was under a cloud would be protected.[50] However, a further application by RTÉ and other media to be allowed name the general practitioner and barrister involved in the case was refused. Emphasising that the case was essentially about the children and the overriding need to protect their identity, McGuinness J. detailed the dangers of a "drip-feed" of information in the media which could lead to identification of the children. There was no particular danger that other pregnant girls in crisis situations would make contact with these particular individuals, and therefore the revelation of the individual names was "more a matter of public curiosity than of public interest in the true sense".[51] Meanwhile, the *Irish Independent* had disclosed the names of some of those involved and an application was made on behalf of the agency to attach and commit the editor, health correspondent and chief executive for contempt of court by breaching the court order (civil contempt).[52]

7.1.1.4 Disclosure of a Secret Manufacturing Process

Provision is made in the Companies Acts for *in camera* hearings in cases that involve the disclosure of a secret manufacturing process. In *In re R*,[53] the applicant company sought an order under section 205(7) of the Companies Act 1963:

> "If in the opinion of the court, the hearing of proceedings under this section would involve the disclosure of information the publication of which would be seriously prejudicial to the legitimate interests of the company, the court may order that the hearing of the proceedings or any part thereof shall be in camera".

The *Irish Press* and Independent Newspapers made a submission that proceedings should be in public and that they be allowed to attend on the grounds of public interest and freedom of speech. The court refused their request.[54] Then, in response to an application by the plaintiff himself, the

---

[48] *The Irish Times*, September 1, 3, 1999.

[49] *Ex tempore* ruling of August 31, 1999, followed by written judgment on application of RTÉ and other media, including *The Irish Times* and Independent Newspapers [2000] I.R. 451, at 453.

[50] *ibid.* at 455.

[51] *ibid.* at 455. She asked the media to give undertakings in relation to her order, which she made to apply to the media generally and anyone who has notice of its making (at 456).

[52] *The Irish Times*, September 9, 30, 1999.

[53] Above, n.1.

[54] *The Irish Times*, October 15, 1988.

Supreme Court directed that the proceedings be held in public on the grounds:

(a) that it was essential to the administration of justice that it be in public unless that requirement by itself operated to deny justice in a particular case, and

(b) that the company had failed to show that a public hearing would by itself so impede the doing of justice as between the parties that the judge ought in the exercise of his discretion to order that the proceedings be heard *in camera*.[55]

A similar decision was reached by the Supreme Court in *Irish Press plc v Ingersoll Irish Publications Ltd*.[56] Because much of the information was already in the public arena and there had been no reference to identifiable or particular documents likely to cause specific and identifiable damage of a serious kind such as would seriously prejudice the legitimate interests of the companies, the proceedings should be held in public. The fundamental constitutional right vested in the public, namely the administration of justice in public, must be considered and section 205(7) of the Companies Act 1963 should be strictly construed.[57]

Section 31 of the Companies (Amendment) Act 1990, also provides that: "The whole or part of any proceedings under this Act may be heard otherwise than in public if the court, in the interests of justice, considers that the interests of the company concerned or of its creditors as a whole so require".

Under this provision, an application by the examiner of Goodman International and related companies was heard *in camera* on the grounds that the disclosure of certain matters mentioned in an affidavit would be seriously prejudicial to the legitimate interests of the companies that were under the protection of the courts.[58] Later, in *In the matter of Countyglen plc*,[59] the High Court had to consider whether the application for an order by an inspector appointed under section 7(4) of the Companies Act 1990 to investigate the affairs of Countyglen plc could be heard in private. The decision hinged on whether the application was an *administrative* one only and therefore did not come within the requirements of Article 34(1) of the Constitution, which states that *justice* shall be administered in public.

While some of the directions sought by the inspector "were highly confidential and disclosure of the application would have been likely to prejudice the sensitive enquiries which he was then seeking to pursue, it was clear", Murphy J. said, "that the 1990 Act did not confer on the court any statutory power to hear the application otherwise than in public".[60] However, the particular direction sought and given was held not to constitute the

---

[55] *ibid.*
[56] [1993] I.L.R.M. 747.
[57] *ibid., per* Finlay C.J. at 754.
[58] *The Irish Times*, September 19, 1990.
[59] [1995] 1 I.L.R.M. 213.
[60] *ibid.* at 215.

administration of justice and accordingly, "was not required under the Constitution to be dealt with in public".[61]

This case marked a worrying development for the media. The argument on which it is based could be used to effectively bypass the constitutional requirement of openness in certain circumstances. One would expect that the hearing of an application for a court order is judicial by nature rather than administrative, regardless of the content of the order or the type of power it confers. Equally, the granting of an order through the court, one would have thought, must constitute a judicial function. In *Countyglen*, however, a distinction was made between an order and a mere direction to the inspector with a view to ensuring that his investigation was carried out as quickly and inexpensively as possible. Furthermore, there was significant precedent to support the contention that the fact that an order was to be made by a court did not, of itself, determine that it constituted the administration of justice. It may be desirable to dispose of administrative matters informally but the consequences for media reporting and consequently the information of the public should not be lost sight of.

7.1.1.5 Other Statutory Provisions

There are several statutes that provide for *in camera* proceedings in certain specified circumstances. These formerly included income tax matters by virtue of section 30 of the Finance Act 1949 and section 416(10) of the Income Tax Act 1967, whereby appeals reheard before the Circuit Court "shall be held *in camera*" and every hearing by the High Court or Supreme Court of a case stated shall "if the person ... so desires, be held *in camera*". However, following the enactment of section 9(b) of the Finance Act 1983, which deleted the latter provision of section 416(10) of the 1967 Act, the High Court refused an application to have proceedings arising out of a judge's tax appeal heard *in camera*. According to the court, the intention of the legislature was that any case stated after the 1983 enactment should be heard in public.[62]

Another example is section 12 of the Official Secrets Act 1963, which allows the prosecution to apply to have part of the hearing held in private on the basis that it would otherwise prejudice the safety or preservation of the State. If the prosecution applies "the court shall make an order to that effect". The court does not have a discretion in the matter, which seems to fly in the face of the whole principle of open justice and the role of the courts in that regard. However, the verdict and sentence, if any, shall be pronounced in public. The Official Secrets Act is currently under review. Its operation has been curtailed in recent years, primarily by the Freedom of Information Act 1997 and the new climate of openness that it enshrines.[63]

---

[61] *ibid.* at 217. See also *Brennan v Minister for Justice* [1995] 1 I.R. 612; [1995] 2 I.L.R.M. 206. Note also that the Defamation Act 1961, s.18(1), provides a privilege for fair and accurate reports of court proceedings where the court is exercising "judicial authority".

[62] *The Irish Times*, December 7, 1987.

[63] See further Chap.10 below. Other legislation also curtails the operation of the Official Secrets Act; for example, the Committees of the Oireachtas (Compellability, Privileges

Similarly court-martials are open to the public, but an order can be made by the convening authority or president of the court-martial under section 194 of the Defence Act 1954 to exclude the public where it is deemed "expedient in the interests of public safety, defence or public morals" for the whole or part of the trial. A mandatory provision occurs in section 8 of the Defamation Act in relation to applications for an order to bring a criminal prosecution for libel against a newspaper. An order must be obtained from a High Court judge sitting *in camera*. The constitutionality of the section has been questioned.[64]

In relation to criminal investigations and trials, there are certain restrictions that can be invoked in support of the right to a fair trial. For a period, section 20(1) of the Criminal Justice Act 1951 allowed the court to exclude the public from the preliminary examination of an indictable offence "if satisfied that it is expedient for the purpose of ensuring that the accused will not be prejudiced in his trial". That is no longer the case, except in relation to any proceedings of an indecent or obscene nature (section 20(3)). Preliminary examinations were later governed by the Criminal Procedure Act 1967, which provided that they should be in open court except "where the court is satisfied because of the nature or circumstances of the case or otherwise in the interests of justice" that it is desirable to exclude the public, though not the press (section 16(2)). Provision for the abolition of preliminary examinations was made in the Criminal Justice Act 1999.[65]

It has happened on occasion that the media have been admitted to court but asked to leave at some point during the hearing. In a High Court application for an *in camera* hearing in 1993, the media were asked to leave and not report on the proceedings in any form and to treat the matter as an *in camera* hearing, although reporting was allowed on what had been stated in court up until that point. The request was made in "highly unusual circumstances",[66] and by reference to the Supreme Court's decision in *AG v X*.[67] However, since the case involved an application for an *in camera* hearing and related to an alleged offence covered by rape legislation, the question must be asked as to whether the circumstances were so exceptional that the ordinary precautions for preserving the anonymity of the parties under the terms of the Criminal Law

---

and Immunities of Witnesses) Act 1997, s.16(2), provides that it shall not apply to evidence given or documents produced or sent to a committee pursuant to a direction.

[64] See Kelly, above, n.15, at footnote 32, p.403.

[65] The Act requires a Ministerial Order to bring the relevant sections into effect. S.10(5) repeals ss.14–18 of the 1967 Act. In practice, reporters often had difficulty distinguishing between bail applications (discussed above) and preliminary examinations. It is to be hoped that the new procedures and better information services in the courts will address that problem. The 1999 Act, s.9, inserting s.4I, provides that proceedings shall be in open court but that a court can, because of the nature or circumstances of the case, or otherwise in the interests of justice, exclude the public, but not *bona fide* members of the press. The general trend in Ireland as elsewhere, particularly in light of Art. 6 of the European Convention on Human Rights and the jurisprudence of the European Court, is for pre-trial proceedings to be held in public. That principle extends also to tribunals, disciplinary boards and other quasi-judicial bodies: see, for example, *Diennet v France* (1995) 21 E.H.R.R. 554.

[66] *The Irish Times*, May 28, 1993.

[67] [1992] 1 I.R. 1; [1992] I.L.R.M. 401.

(Rape) Acts did not suffice. It may be significant that the presiding judge declined to make an order of prohibition or injunction, which counsel sought. At any rate, the media can be excluded only where statute law so provides. Therefore, unless the present case concerned a minor, such an order, if granted, would have been open to challenge, particularly now in light of the Supreme Court judgments in *Irish Times Ltd v Judge Murphy*.[68] It is a different matter for the judge to ask the media in reporting on rape and sexual abuse cases to include in their reporting the reasons for suspending sentences, when given.[69] Such offences are so emotive that it is important for the public to know why a certain course of action is taken.

The question of the admission of reporters to incest trials was raised by Carney J. in *DPP v WM*.[70] The provision of section 5 of the Punishment of Incest Act 1908 appeared mandatory and left no scope for judicial discretion: "All proceedings under this Act are to be held *in camera*".[71] Following that case, the Criminal Law (Incest Proceedings) Act 1995 was introduced. Section 2 provides for the exclusion of the public but not the media, while section 3 prohibits the publication of any matter likely to lead members of the public to identify either the accused or the alleged victim once an individual has been charged. If any such matter is published or broadcast, the proprietor, editor and publisher, or their equivalents in the broadcast media, can be fined and/or imprisoned.[72]

7.1.2 Reporting Restrictions

A number of statutes impose reporting restrictions on the media. The Defamation Act 1961, section 18, on the other hand, confers a privilege in respect of fair and accurate reports of court proceedings held in public, provided the reports are published contemporaneously, *i.e.* while the court hearing is taking place or immediately after its completion. The privilege is, therefore, a

---

[68] [1998] 1 I.R. 359.

[69] See *The Irish Times*, June 19, 1999.

[70] Above, n.2.

[71] This contrasted with the provision made for other sexual offences under the Criminal Law (Rape) (Amendment) Act 1990, which allows the judge to exclude from the court all persons "except ... *bona fide* representatives of the press" (s.11). As Carney J. pointed out, total secrecy, so that the community at large would not even be entitled to know of the happening of the case or the sentence imposed, would be unacceptable and would not be in conformity with the constitutional scheme for the administration of justice. Neither would this be in conformity with the European Convention on Human Rights, which, at Art. 6, states that there is a right to a fair and public hearing of "any" criminal charge. See also generally Rec (2003) 13 of the Committee of Ministers to Member States on the provision of information through the media in relation to criminal proceedings, July 10, 2003 (available at *www.coe.int/cm*).

[72] Section 3 sets out the persons who will be liable, in similar terms to those listed in the Bail Act 1997, n.5 above. It also defines "broadcast" and "written publication" but in somewhat narrower and less expansive terms than in the Bail Act. The difference might have been explained by the fact that the Incest Act predated the Bail Act by two years, except that the Child Care Act which predated both, is in the same terms as the Bail Act (see n.5 and n.38 above). Section 4 provides for the same penalties as set out in the Bail Act 1997, n.5 above.

useful one for newspapers and broadcasters but, because of the requirement of contemporaneity, is of little benefit to book publishers, video or film makers or other media.[73] Moreover, the privilege does not extend to the publication or broadcasting of any "blasphemous or obscene matter" (section 18(2)), the concern being to protect public morals. This concern for the protection of public morals, even in the context of court reporting, can be seen, in particular, in the Censorship of Publications Act 1929. Part III of that Act is headed "Reports of Judicial Proceedings" and provides at section 14:

> "1. It shall not be lawful to print or publish or cause or procure to be printed or published in relation to any judicial proceedings—
>
> (a) any indecent matter the publication of which would be calculated to injure public morals, or
>
> (b) any indecent medical, surgical or physiological details the publication of which would be calculated to injure public morals".[74]

The section is anachronistic but does not apply to the reporting of cases in the official law reports or legal or medical publications (section 14(3)).

Several statutes contain provisions preventing publication of any material that would identify the parties. The Criminal Law (Rape) Acts 1981–90 prohibit the publication of any matter likely to lead members of the public to identify the victim or the accused, unless or until convicted, or under direction of the court. Even on conviction, the person may not be named if to do so would identify the victim (1990 Act, section 8(2)). As anonymity must be maintained, photographs may not be published. Two national newspapers and TV3 were fined for showing photographs of the former family home in a case where a man had raped and tortured his daughter and wife. Photographs of the defendant with his eyes blacked out had also been published in the newspapers. The

---

[73] The Defamation Act, s.2, defines "newspaper" as "any paper containing public news or observations thereon, or consisting wholly or mainly of advertisements, which is printed for sale and is published in the State or in Northern Ireland whether periodically or in parts or numbers at intervals not exceeding 36 days". Other statutes define "written publication" and "broadcast". See nn.5, 38 and 72 above.

[74] Subs. 2 has been repealed by s.3 of the Family Law (Divorce) Act 1996. It made it unlawful to print or publish or cause or procure to be printed or published any report, statement, commentary or other matter of or in relation to any judicial proceedings for divorce, nullity of marriage or judicial separation, other than the names and addresses of the parties and witnesses, names of court, judge and lawyers, a concise statement of the charges, defences, points of law raised and outcome. S.14 may have reflected the moral standards of its time but it was both outdated and largely academic, because the courts usually exclude the press from this type of proceeding anyway, thus making it impossible for them to report even to the very limited extent envisaged in the section. A prosecution had to be brought by the DPP and there appears to have been only one prosecution under the section, that being in 1971 when six national newspapers were fined a total of over £23,000 for publishing details of a "divorce *a mensa et thoro*" case (literally, divorce from bed and board, *i.e.* separation), *The Irish Times*, June 30, July 7, 1971, referred to in Alan Shatter, *Family Law in the Republic of Ireland* (2nd ed., Wolfhound Press, 1981), at p.21.

information, taken all together, could lead to the identification of the victims. The trial judge, in sentencing the man to 15 years imprisonment, had made an order that nothing should be published which would lead people to identify the victims.[75] The trial judge accepted that the publications performed important public functions in highlighting shortcomings in the social services, and that without media coverage, these issues might not have been dealt with. Responsible journalism performed a very valuable service for the community, but journalism which exploited the victims of sexual crimes for other reasons and often just for financial gain could not be tolerated, the judge said.[76]

With regard to criminal proceedings, the Criminal Justice Act 1999, *inter alia*, abolishes the preliminary examination procedure, whereby the evidence against an accused person was assessed in the District Court to see if s/he should be sent forward to a higher court to be tried. Section 9 of the 1999 Act amends the Criminal Procedure Act 1967 to provide that no person shall publish or broadcast or cause to be published or broadcast any information about a proceeding under Part III of the Act, where an accused person is before the District Court charged with an indictable offence, other than:

"(a) a statement of—
 (i)   the fact that the proceeding has been brought by a named person in relation to a specified charge against a named person, and
 (ii) any decision resulting from the proceeding, and
(b) in the case of an application under section 4E for the dismissal of a charge against the accused, any information that the judge hearing the application permits to be published or broadcast at the request of the accused".

If, on application by the prosecutor, it appears to a judge of the District Court that a person has contravened subsection (1), the judge may certify to that effect to the High Court. The High Court may inquire into the matter, hear witnesses, consider any statement offered in defence and punish or take steps to punish that person "in the like manner as if he had been guilty of contempt of the Court".[77]

---

[75] *The Irish Times*, July 14, 15, 29, 2000. A charge against *The Irish Times* was dropped; its publication had not breached the order.

[76] The judge also accepted that the standard of court reporting was very high – the problem arose not with the court reports but with subsequent articles. TV3 apologised to the court for its unintentional breach of the order (a shot of the victims' residence was used as a backdrop to a report on the wider social issues). Independent Newspapers told the court it had adopted new measures in relation to legal vetting of photographs prior to publication: *The Irish Times*, July 14, 29, 2000. See also *The Irish Times*, October 5, 2001, where RTÉ challenged a ruling by a District Court judge that the media should not name a man facing charges of indecent assault. RTÉ contended that reporters present in court had noted the judge's order that they should not publish anything that would identify the injured parties, but that the order did not specify the identity of the accused.

[77] The section (s.4J) that is inserted by the 1999 Act replaces s.17(2) of the Criminal Procedure Act 1967, which provided that: "No person shall publish or cause to be published any information as to any particular preliminary examination other than a statement of fact that such examination in relation to a named person on a specified

The purpose of the restriction is undoubtedly to protect the accused and ensure his/her right to a fair trial. However, it could be argued that it is phrased in very broad terms and is overly restrictive in its reach. In practice, the section that it replaces was constantly breached, not necessarily in a prejudicial manner but certainly in a technical sense.[78] The Law Reform Commission, however, recommended no change.[79] Whatever the exact scope of legal restrictions, the key for journalists is not to cause prejudice to the accused person's right to a fair trial.

In the *Nevin* murder trial (*DPP v Nevin*), Carroll J. banned newspapers from commenting on or photographing the accused for the duration of the trial. She did so because Mrs Nevin's right to a fair trial "far outweighed" the media's right to comment on her appearance or demeanour. Mrs Nevin was presumed innocent in law and was entitled to respect for her dignity.[80] The defence then sought to have the trial stopped permanently and several journalists were called to testify and reveal their sources. When they refused to reveal their sources, the defence asked Carroll J. to direct them to do so but she declined. An *Irish Times* application to be allowed to publish stock photographs of the accused was also refused.[81]

One of the difficulties with the restrictions imposed by the trial judge was that they applied only to the print media. They did not affect radio or television coverage, apparently because no complaint had been made by the defence with regard to the broadcast media.[82] In many respects the ban resembled that which had been imposed in *News Verlags v Austria*,[83] and which the European Court of Human Rights found to be a violation of Article 10 of the European Convention on Human Rights. (See the discussion in Chapter 6 above.)

It may be noted also that the Special Criminal Court, as a special court, is governed by Article 38 of the Constitution, not Article 34, as is the case with the regular courts. The court is established by government under Part V of the Offences against the State Act 1939. Section 41 of that Act provides that every Special Criminal Court has control of its own procedures, but that the practice and procedure that apply in the Central Criminal Court shall, as far as

---

charge has been held and of the decision thereon, unless the judge permits it at the request of the accused". S.4J(5) as inserted by the 1999 Act also defines the terms "broadcast" and "publish". Compare the definition of broadcast with that in other Acts, *e.g.* above, nn.5, 38, 72. S.10(5) of the Act repeals ss.14–18 of the 1967 Act.

[78] Above, n.77. The section was rarely invoked against the media. As long as nothing was published that interfered with the presumption of innocence, technical breaches, such as publishing non-prejudicial details of appearance or demeanour or events or observations regarding the court appearance, tended to be tolerated.

[79] See the discussion in *Paper*, above, n.35, at pp.343–7, and *Report on Contempt of Court* (LRC 47–1994) at para. 6.37.

[80] *The Irish Times*, February 10, 2000, April 12, 2000; *cf.* the reporting of the trial of Nora Wall, who was ultimately cleared of the charges against her, but who had to endure shock horror headlines and unflattering photographs during her trial. Also other female defendants – see Brenda Power, "When court 'appearance' has another meaning" *The Sunday Tribune*, February 13, 2000.

[81] *The Irish Times*, April 12, 2000. See further discussion of the case in Chap.6 above.

[82] *The Irish Times*, February 10, 2000.

[83] App. No.31457/96, judgment of January 11, 2000.

practicable, apply to the trial of a person in the Special Criminal Court also. The Special Criminal Court Rules provide that it shall be an open court "subject to such conditions as the court may from time to time impose", but that the court may impose restrictions on reporting in order to protect witnesses.[84]

Difficulties for reporters can also arise when there is a "trial within a trial", that is, when the jury is asked to leave the court while counsel argue a particular issue. The press may be excluded also or may be allowed to remain in court but ordered not to report.[85] This can lead to practical difficulties for them, because there is generally a pool or rota of court reporters, as it would be too expensive for each organisation to have its own reporters in court every day. A case may be adjourned during the argument in the absence of the jury, and a reporter on duty on the next occasion the court is sitting may not realise that s/he is not entitled to report. Again, an acknowledgment of the presence of reporters and an appreciation of their function and the courts' interest in the accuracy of reports would suggest that the nature of the proceedings should be made clear.

7.1.3 Access to Evidence

Court reporters are usually known to court officials and are often facilitated in an informal way with regard to information concerning cases. However, there is no formal recognition of the reporter's role and no specific right of access to court documents. In the UK in *Home Office v Harman*,[86] a solicitor was held to be in contempt of court for showing documents to a reporter after they had been read in open court. The House of Lords held, by a majority, that the journalist could not be assisted by direct access to the documents themselves. A complaint was lodged with the European Commission on Human Rights in Strasbourg, which found a *prima facie* breach of Article 10 of the Convention, which protects freedom of expression.[87] A friendly settlement was reached with the UK. Since 1999, Rules of Court make provision for access to claim forms and, while there is no right of access as such to other court documents, leave of the court can be sought to inspect them.[88]

---

[84] *Cf.* Criminal Law (Jurisdiction) Act 1976, ss.7(3), and 17(1).

[85] It has been a long-established practice in the criminal courts for evidence given in the absence of the jury not to be reported. Reporters may need to hear the evidence or argument in order to understand what is happening but if the purpose in excluding the jury is to prevent them hearing it for fear of prejudice, then it follows that the media should generally not report it. The Special Criminal Court ruled in the trial of Colm Murphy on charges related to the Omagh bombing that evidence from a trial within a trial should not be reported: *The Irish Times*, October 17, 2001. The concern is that such evidence could later be held to be inadmissible and its publication could prejudice the right to a fair trial.

[86] [1982] 1 All E.R. 532 (HL).

[87] *Harman v UK*, Eur. Comm. H.R. (1984) 38 Decisions and Reports 53, App. No.10038/82 (1984) 38 D.R. 53.

[88] See Geoffrey Robertson and Andrew Nicol, *Media Law* (4th ed., Penguin Books, London, 2002), at 472 (civil cases) and 479 (criminal proceedings). For the position in the United States, see Sherrie L. Wilson, "A Proposal for Media Access to Audiotapes and Videotapes Presented During Trials" (1999) *Communications and the Law* 45.

In Ireland, it has been recommended by the Law Reform Commission that in the interests of accuracy and avoiding simple errors of identity and fact, reporters should have access to charge sheets.[89] The position regarding other documents is less clear. The Newspaper Commission, which reported in 1996, recommended that there should be a simple and certain procedure for making available to *bona fide* journalists, exercising their rights to provide material for newspapers, the right to inspect court documents which have become part of a public hearing in the court.[90] The matter was referred by the government to the Working Group on a Courts Commission, which recommended, *inter alia*, the establishment of an information office and media liaison forum, the drafting of guidelines on public access to court documents and a rule of practice on constructively opened documents.[91]

The last-mentioned is of particular importance, as a problem can arise for reporters when in the course of a public hearing court documents are read in private by a judge and taken as read without actually being read into the public record in open court. Reporters are unclear as to whether they are then free to report details of such records. The President of the High Court has said that judges reading documents in private to save time were not strictly administering justice in public. Affidavits read in such a way, he said, should be treated as read in open court and should be made available to the press.[92] Otherwise, the press, as the watchdog of the public, is prevented from informing the public and no one other than the parties has any idea what is going on. It was held by the Supreme Court in *In re R*[93] that a stipulation that "proceedings" be held *in camera* includes the pleadings, affidavits, exhibits, as well as oral testimony and the judgment in the case.

7.1.4 Forms of Reporting

At present cameras are not permitted in court, although the Law Reform Commission has recommended that the possibility be considered.[94] Cameras

---

[89] *Consultation Paper on the Civil Law of Defamation*, 1991, para. 256.

[90] *Report of the Commission on the Newspaper Industry* (Pn 2841, Stationery Office, Dublin, 1996), para. 7.61.

[91] Above, n.28, at para. 4.25, Recommendations. The Courts Service, which would implement the recommendations, was established in November 1999, under the Courts Service Act 1998. See also, Lord Irvine of Lairg, "Reporting the Courts: The Media's Rights and Responsibilities" (1999) xxxiv Ir. Jur. 1 at pp.16–17, regarding publication by his Department of *The Media: A Guide for Judges* and his view that "the way forward is mutual co-operation between courts and the media in pursuit of public interests upheld by both".

[92] *The Irish Times*, September 17, 2002.

[93] Above, n.1, Finlay C.J. at 131 and Walsh J., at 136.

[94] Above, n.79, *Report*, at paras 4.45–49. Mr Justice Paul Carney of the High Court, speaking at a conference (above, n.30), said that there was a very strong case to be made that the citizen should be entitled to monitor and observe the fair administration of justice in their home through the contemporary technology of television. See also comment in the *Sunday Tribune*, July 23, 2000 arguing in favour of televising of courts and tribunals as a means to ensure that the public can see what is going on. This followed the huge demand from the public to attend the Nevin murder trial when many people could not get in or if they did were extremely cramped and could not see or hear.

were allowed into the Supreme Court for the first time for the opening of the argument on the Abortion Information Bill 1995.[95]

The use of tape recorders, video recorders, television cameras or the taking of photographs in court is not regulated by statute in this jurisdiction. The practice has been to allow reporters to take notes and designated artists to sketch, but the courts have not been prepared to allow anything more than that[96] although, as the Law Reform Commission[97] says, the courts have inherent jurisdiction to regulate their own procedure. Considerations include whether use of recorders or cameras would cause interference with court proceedings, whether they would intimidate witnesses, invade their privacy or be used out of court for other purposes, such as to coach future witnesses. It may be argued that all of these negative uses and effects can be dealt with by regulation.[98] Reporters, at present, are not entitled to report everything that is said. In some cases, as we have seen, they are excluded from the court altogether, in others limitations are imposed on what they can report. Journalists and broadcasters maintain that there is no difference between editing on paper and editing on film.[99]

In support of audio or visual recordings, it can be said that they would enhance accuracy in reporting and reduce the potential for disputes as to whether proceedings were accurately reported.[100] It is also likely, as the technology develops and the public becomes more of a participant in the media, that many of the fears expressed at present, such as the fear of the effects on witnesses, will disappear. Many of the misgivings felt by members of the Dáil and Seanad about the televising of proceedings in the Houses of the Oireachtas have proven unfounded. It is probable that the tight restrictions imposed at present will gradually be relaxed as members and viewers become more accustomed to the coverage. Televising the proceedings of certain of the Oireachtas Committees has already proven popular and has not given rise to any disquiet.

---

[95] *The Irish Times*, April 5, 1995. The President, under the power conferred on her by Art. 26 of the Constitution, referred the Bill to the Supreme Court to test its constitutionality. The Regulation of Information (Services Outside the State for Termination of Pregnancies) Bill 1995 was found to be constitutional: *In the matter of Article 26 of the Constitution and in the matter of the reference to the court of the Regulation of Information (Services Outside the State for Termination of Pregnancies) Bill 1995* [1995] 2 I.L.R.M. 81.

[96] Compare the situation in the UK where the Criminal Justice Act 1925, s.41, prohibits the taking of photographs or the making with a view to publication of a sketch in the court or its precincts. S.41 does not apply in Scotland. On the role of sketches, see Katherine Krupp, "Journalism Meets Art – Courtroom sketches convey subjective elements beyond the range of the camera", *Media Studies Journal*, below, n.106.

[97] Above, n.35, at pp.8–9.

[98] In the United States, for instance, it was held in *US v Kleinman* 107 F. Supp. 407 (DDC 1952) that witnesses could refuse to testify before the camera where that would increase the danger of error or the probability of prosecution for perjury. On January 9, 2002 an application by the BBC to televise the appeal in the Lockerbie case was granted, without the need to obtain the consent of those involved or to have the footage approved. There were, however, a number of conditions, including that no audio-visual images would be supplied of any evidence taken from witnesses (*IRIS* 2002–2, p.10).

[99] Coverage can be subject to rules and supervision; see Geoffrey Robertson, *Freedom, the Individual and the Law* (7th ed., Penguin Books, London, 1993), p.347.

[100] Above, n.35, at pp.248–55.

In England, section 9 of the Contempt of Court Act 1981 forbids the use of tape recorders except by leave of the court. Practice Directions have indicated that there is no objection to the use of tape recorders in court in principle and that use by the media should be given sympathetic consideration.[101] The tape cannot, however, be broadcast (section 9(1)(b)). Unauthorised use can result in contempt of court and forfeiture of machine and tapes (section 9(3)). Televising the courts is effectively precluded by section 41 of the Criminal Justice Act 1925, but the General Council of the Bar is in favour of television broadcasting.[102] Nevertheless, fears have been expressed in various quarters that only notorious criminal trials would be broadcast and that editing would result in sensationalism and distortion. However, as Robertson and Nicol[103] point out, "present television news reporting, in sixty-second 'slots' with breathless presenters pictured outside court quoting snatches of evidence, sometimes over inaccurate 'artists' impressions' of the courtroom is of minimal value". The same authors also point out that the public is genuinely interested in significant court cases and that the arguments in favour of open justice apply with even greater force to aural or visual coverage.[104] The *Pinochet* case in 1998 was the first case in which an English court announced its decisions live on television, gave the first "judicial sound-bites in English legal history" and the first "televised judicial press release".[105] Contrary to popular belief, experience of televising court cases in the United States has not been all negative. Bar associations, initially hostile to the whole idea, report that lawyers are better prepared, judges better behaved and the public better informed as a result of cameras in court.[106]

---

[101] Robertson and Nicol, above, n.88, at pp.470–1.

[102] See Public Affairs Committee of the General Council of the Bar, *Televising the Courts*, 1989; Brian McConnell, "Cameras in Court" (1990) 140 N.L.J. 1622. Cameras have been permitted in certain of the Scottish courts since 1993 under a practice direction of 1992 ("Television in the Courts", August 7, 1992, cited in petition of the BBC of March 7, 2000 and available at *www.scotcourts.gov.uk* under "opinions"). However, two applications (in March and April 2000) in the Scottish courts by the BBC to be allowed to broadcast the Lockerbie trial were refused – see Robertson and Nicol, above, n.88 at pp.484–5, and *IRIS* 2000–4, p.7. The trial was of two Libyans charged with bombing a plane, which crashed over Lockerbie in Scotland. The trial took place in the Netherlands but under Scottish law. An application by the BBC to televise the appeal in the case, in real time, and also streamed on its website, with a simultaneous Arabic translation, and with edited highlights on regular news bulletins and on BBC News 24, succeeded: *IRIS* 2002-2, p.10. In Canada, the constitutionality of a provision banning cameras in court was upheld in *R v Squires* (1992) 11 O.R. (3d) 385 (C.A.), but in practice the Federal Court of Appeal regularly allows video recordings of its proceedings and the Supreme Court has allowed them on a number of occasions also – see Robert Martin, *Media Law – Essentials of Canadian Law* (Irwin Law, Ontario, 1997), at p.68.

[103] Above, n.88, at p.484. For a survey of the views of Irish judges, see Paul Lambert, "Courtroom Television Broadcasting" (1997) 2(5) *Communications Law* 180.

[104] *ibid*. The authors refer (at p.483) to New Zealand, where appeal hearings are routinely televised without any damage to the administration of justice.

[105] [1998] 3 W.L.R. 1456. See Joshua Rozenberg, "The *Pinochet* case and cameras in court" [1999] P.L. 178.

[106] See above, n.99, at 346; n.102, Public Affairs Committee, at para. 4.1. On the situation in the US and Canada, see *Free Press, Fair Trial* (1998) *Media Studies Journal* (full issue, The Media Studies Center and Freedom Forum, New York, Winter 1998).

Dramatic reconstructions of courtroom scenes and docudramas are not covered by legislation but may be suspect on contempt grounds if transmitted during the proceedings. It is difficult to envisage what kind of prejudice could result when the programme obviously involves actors and dramatic techniques. As audiences can clearly differentiate between news and documentaries on the one hand and pure entertainment or dramatic portrayal on the other, it would seem appropriate to assess any possible threat to the courts in the context of the particular medium or programme format.[107]

7.2 REPORTING TRIBUNALS

Tribunals established by statute are open to the public but may be authorised by statute to hold sittings or part of sittings in private. The Industrial Relations Act 1946, which established the Labour Court, provides that the court "may hold any sitting or part of a sitting in private" (section 20(7)). The Industrial Relations Act 1969 is more confined: an investigation of a trade dispute shall be conducted in private unless otherwise requested by a party to the dispute (section 8(1)), in which case any part of the investigation dealing with the matter that should, in the interests of a party to the dispute, be treated as confidential, may be conducted in private (section 8(2)). An investigation by a Rights Commissioner shall be conducted in private (section 13(8)), except in the case of disputes under the Payment of Wages Act 1991, as shall an appeal to the court from the Commissioner's decision (section 13(9)). The provision for private hearings under the Industrial Relations Acts is therefore very wide.

Tribunals of Inquiry are open to the public unless the tribunal itself is of the opinion that it is in the public interest to exclude the public because of the subject matter of the inquiry or the nature of the evidence.[108] It appears somewhat incongruous to think of a public tribunal of inquiry excluding the

---

Robertson and Nicol, *op. cit.*, at p.483, also cite a study by the *Wall Street Journal* of the effect on the US justice system of televising the O.J. Simpson trial. The study concluded that there were two effects: (1) It caused an amazing drop in the number of people who wanted exemptions from jury service: citizens wished, much more than before, to play their part in justice, and (2) It caused those who did serve on juries to pay much less attention to lawyers and their arguments, and concentrate their deliberations on facts proved in evidence.

[107] See Cunningham, "The Maxwell Musical: a Contempt of Court or the Mere Exercise of the Right to Free Speech" [1994] 2 ENT. L.R. 65; G. Stuart Adam, "The Thicket of Rules North of the Border – Canadian perspectives on a free press and fair trials" *Media Studies Journal*, above, n.106, at 29, referring to a docudrama, *The Boys of St. Vincent*, on the sexual abuse of young males by priests, which was to be broadcast by the Canadian Broadcasting Corporation just before the trial of a priest accused of similar behaviour. See also Ch. 6 above.

[108] Tribunals of Inquiry Act 1921, s.2(a). For discussion, see Gallagher, "Tribunals and the Erosion of Privacy" (1999) B.R. 406. Gallagher argues that there is insufficient protection in the relevant statutes for privacy and reputation and suggests, *inter alia*, that the courts could review the constitutionality of s.2(2) of the 1921 Tribunals of Inquiry Act, which requires evidence to be heard in public, to see if it goes further than is necessary in the encroachment of the rights to privacy (at p.412).

public, but it is conceivable in an inquiry such as the Kerry Babies Tribunal that the public could be excluded on the grounds of individual privacy. Whether individual privacy would equate with the public interest, which is the only ground in the Act for exclusion, is another matter. There have been instances of tribunals of inquiry holding some sessions in private for specific purposes.[109] The Supreme Court in *Haughey and others v Moriarty and others*[110] held that a tribunal is entitled to hold its preliminary investigations in private in order to determine what evidence is relevant and what evidence should be given orally. On the other hand, the Supreme Court held unanimously in *Redmond v The Sole Member (Flood Tribunal)*[111] that allegations of corruption against the former Dublin County Manager should be heard in public.

Inquests, which are carried out in accordance with the Coroners Act 1962, can be attended and reported but are problematic in a number of respects. They are limited in terms of what they can do and the verdict they can bring in. Questions of civil or criminal liability cannot be considered or investigated; the inquest is confined to ascertaining the identity of the person, and how, when and where death occurred (section 30). As a result, a finding of death by suicide could not be brought in where a death occurred before 1993, as suicide was a crime until decriminalised by the Criminal Law (Suicide) Act of that year. There is still some uncertainty about returning a verdict of suicide, as such a verdict can be considered to go beyond the proximate cause of death – the "how, when and where" to which the inquest is confined by the 1962 Act.

The 1962 Act also provides that there must be no note of censure or exoneration, although recommendations of a general character may be made, where designed to prevent further fatalities (section 31). The Act does, however, give the coroner very wide discretionary powers in conducting inquests. S/he can decide to sit with or without a jury "as he thinks proper", unless the manner of death brings it within certain specified categories, for example, murder, infanticide, manslaughter (section 39). There is a right of access to documents but it generally only accrues after the inquest (section 29(3)), whereas it would be much more useful to all concerned to have information regarding witnesses to be called, evidence to be given and so forth before the inquest. The coroner in the inquest which followed the shooting dead of John Carthy by gardaí in Abbeylara requested the media – he did not have power to compel them – not to publish the names or photographs of the members of the Garda Emergency

---

[109] The Moriarty Tribunal went into private session in December 2001 on the grounds that people could be mentioned who might have no bearing on the proceedings (*The Irish Times*, December 18, 2001). A decision of the Flood Tribunal to take evidence in private in Guernsey from an old and infirm witness was challenged successfully by a number of media organisations (*The Irish Times*, September 25, 29, 1999). In the UK, it was deemed irrational and contrary to the principles of freedom of expression and public hearings that the Shipman inquiry (murder of patients by Dr Shipman) be held in private – *R v Secretary of State for Health, ex parte Wagstaffe* [2001] 1 W.L.R. 292.

[110] [1999] 3 I.R. 1.

[111] [1999] 3 I.R. 79; [1999] 1 I.L.R.M. 241. Arguments centred on the constitutional right to privacy and the exigencies of the common good when such inquiries are necessary to preserve the purity and integrity of public life. The tribunal had not exceeded its jurisdiction or failed to observe fair procedures.

Response Unit (ERU), who came to the inquest voluntarily to give evidence in person in open court.[112]

A report on the Coroners' Service, published at the end of 2000, made many recommendations on the operation of the service, including the introduction of a code on media reporting of inquests.[113] It recognised the right of the media to report but emphasised the need for sensitivity and respect for the bereaved in the difficult circumstances surrounding inquests. As a result of the report, amending legislation is to be introduced to increase the powers of the coroner and to modernise the system.[114]

The Defamation Act 1961 (section 24 and Second Schedule) confers a qualified privilege on fair and accurate reports of tribunals of inquiry in foreign states, or of any judicial or arbitral tribunal deciding matters in dispute between states. Fair and accurate reports of proceedings at any public meeting or sitting of judicial authorities, other than courts, and of any commission, tribunal, committee, or statutory inquiry, within the State or Northern Ireland are privileged, subject to explanation or contradiction. (See Chapter 4 above.)

7.3 REPORTING PARLIAMENT

The right to report parliament was hard won, but, once established, became an important part of the media apparatus (see Chapter 3). Parliamentary reports became a significant feature of newspaper content. It was in respect of parliament that the principle of free speech was first recognised, and members given immunity for what they said there.[115] The right of journalists to be present

---

[112] *The Irish Times*, October 10, 2000. Witnesses can be compelled to attend but the penalty for not doing so is paltry and can lead to problems in practice – see, for example, the experiences of the Dublin City Coroner (*The Irish Times*, April 18, 2003) and Jim O'Callaghan, "Refusals to attend and give evidence at inquests: the constitutionality of section 38(2) of the Coroners Act 1962" (2001) 6(5) B.R. 310.

[113] Report of the Working Group on the Review of the Coroner Service, December 2000 (available at *www.justice.ie*), Rec.73, p.68. The Working Group also recommended *inter alia* that the jurisdiction of the coroner should be clarified to include the investigation not only of the medical cause of death but also the circumstances surrounding the death and to allow suicide verdicts to be returned whenever it has been established beyond a reasonable doubt that a person has taken their own life (Recs 49–53, p.63). It further recommended that a Rules Committee be established (pp.62–3 and Appendix J) and that guidelines be provided regarding the reaching and wording of verdicts (p.63).

[114] The new legislation is the Coroners (Amendment) Bill 2003. The Coroners (Amendment) Bill (No.12 of 1995) was not enacted. The new legislation will allow a coroner to investigate the circumstances as well as the medical cause of death, which the Supreme Court held in *Greene v McLoughlin* (January 26, 1995) was not permitted under the 1962 Act. Following disquiet at the rise in the number of suicides and the media portrayal of some of them, a booklet entitled *Media Guidelines on the Portrayal of Suicide* was issued by the Samaritans and the Irish Association of Suicidology (*The Irish Times*, January 20, 2000, *www.samaritans.org*, *www.ias.ie*).

[115] For an historical analysis, see *Dillon v Balfour* (1887) 20 L.R. Ir. 600. For a more recent examination of the scope of that privilege, see *Goodman International v Hamilton (No.1)* [1992] 2 I.R. 542, [1992] I.L.R.M. 145, and *(No.2)* [1993] 3 I.R. 307; *(No.3)* [1993] 3 I.R. 320. In *Young and Ó Faoláin v Ireland* (App. Nos. 25646/94 and 29099/

and report on what was said and done took longer to be recognised. However, both parliamentary privilege and the right to report are enshrined in Article 15.12 of the Irish Constitution: "All official reports and publications of the Oireachtas or of either House thereof and utterances made in either House wherever published shall be privileged".

The Article does not declare a right to report as such but does establish that all official reports and publications wherever published shall be privileged, as will any utterances made in either House. The Irish language version makes clear that publications and utterances each attract a privilege: "Gach tuarascáil agus foilseachán oifigiúil … maille le caint ar bith dá ndéantar", *i.e.* all official reports and publications … as well as "any" utterances. They are privileged wherever published, including in the mass media, and there may not be a suit or prosecution for publishing them ("táid saor ar chúrsaí dlí"). The privilege may, therefore, be wider than had previously been believed and may offer more scope to the media. For instance, the privilege is wide enough to extend to book publishers, as there is no requirement of contemporaneity such as there is in the case of court reports (Defamation Act, section 18).

The Law Reform Commission regarded the law as uncertain and recommended that there be an express statutory defence for fair and accurate reports published contemporaneously or within a reasonable time after the proceedings.[116] The Commission also pointed out that the reference to "utterances" would seem to exclude written statements, which are not actually read out.[117] Additionally, the Constitution does not distinguish between absolute and qualified privilege. It is to be assumed, therefore, that the privilege in Article 15.12 is absolute, given that the Defamation Act, in section 24 and Schedule 2, Part 1, makes provision for a qualified privilege in respect of fair and accurate reports of the proceedings of foreign legislatures. The Constitution further provides that sittings of both Houses shall be in public (Article 15.8.1), except in cases of special emergency, with the assent of two-thirds of the members present (Article 15.8.2).

Utterances made in parliamentary committees are also privileged by virtue of the Committees of the Houses of the Oireachtas (Privilege and Procedure) Act 1976. Section 2 confers privilege on members of either House in respect

---

95, [1996] E.H.R.L.R. 326, the European Commission on Human Rights rejected a complaint under Arts 6 and 8 of the Convention that the immunity granted to parliamentarians denied the complainants an effective remedy in Irish law in respect of statements made by TDs in the Dáil. The Commission took the view that the protection of free debate was a legitimate aim and that the measure was proportionate. See the views of the European Court of Human Rights in *A v UK* (App. No.35373/97, December 17, 2002). In 1999, the Reverend Ian Paisley used parliamentary privilege in Westminster to name 20 people he claimed were involved in republican paramilitary violence (*The Irish Times*, January 29, 1999).

[116] Above, n.79, *Report*, at para. 6.26. In the UK, a fair and accurate report of proceedings of either House or of a parliamentary committee has qualified privilege in defamation and contempt of court proceedings. Comment is also privileged provided it is based on an accurate account of statements made in parliament – see Nicol, Millar, Sharman, *Media Law and Human Rights* (Blackstone Press Ltd, London, 2001), at p.150.

[117] Law Reform Commission, *Consultation Paper on the Civil Law of Defamation*, 1991, at para. 96; *Report* (LRC 38–1991) at para. 4.10.

of any utterance made in or before a committee. The privilege extends to documents of the committee or of its members, all official reports and publications of the committee and utterances made in committee by members, advisers, officials and agents of the committee, wherever published. A doubt as to whether the privilege extended to witnesses was removed in relation to one committee in 1994 by the Select Committee on Legislation and Security of Dáil Éireann (Privilege and Immunity) Act 1994 and to committees in general by the Committees of the Houses of the Oireachtas (Compellability, Privileges and Immunity of Witnesses) Act 1997.[118]

Section 32(11) of the Ethics in Public Office Act 1995 states that documents, reports and statements by members or officials of the Commission appointed under the Act shall be absolutely privileged, wherever published. Section 32(8) states that witnesses before the committee or the commission shall be entitled to the same privileges and immunities as a witness in a court. Section 32(9) of the Act states that sittings of a committee or the commission for the purposes of an investigation by it under the Act "may be held in private". Immunity for complainants is also provided for by section 5 of the Standards in Public Office Act 2001.

Another aspect of parliamentary privilege, the right of members of the Oireachtas to protect their confidential sources, has arisen in the context of the Beef Tribunal and more recently the Morris Tribunal. In the former case, the Supreme Court ruled that deputies had not only a right but a duty to protect members of the public providing information as long as they acted responsibly.[119] In the latter instance, two senior politicians received information about allegations of corruption by a number of gardaí in Donegal, which the Morris tribunal was later established to investigate. The deputies alerted the then Minister for Justice to the information they had received. The gardaí sought access to their telephone records and the tribunal subsequently ruled that the Deputies must reveal their sources and hand over the documents concerned.[120] Morris J. held that the tribunal had been greatly hampered by its

---

[118] In the investigation by the Committee on Legislation and Security in 1994 into delays in processing sexual abuse cases involving a priest and regarding what the Taoiseach and government ministers had told the Dáil about the matter, the Attorney General, Eoin Fitzsimons, required privilege before testifying. A bill to clarify privilege before Committees of the Oireachtas was introduced in the Dáil in November 1995: the Committees of the Houses of the Oireachtas (Compellability, Privileges and Immunities of Witnesses) Bill (No. 45 of 1995), which resulted in the Act of 1997.

[119] *AG v Hamilton (No.2)* [1993] 3 I.R. 227, [1993] I.L.R.M. 821. Legislators had to be free to represent their constituents without fear of sanctions or penalties. The deputies could not be compelled to reveal the source of their allegations because their allegations were identical to their utterances in the Dáil. However, the ambit of parliamentary privilege was not unlimited and did not extend to statements made to the tribunal itself. See also *Goodman International v Hamilton (No.3)* [1993] 3 I.R. 320, High Court, May 27, 1993, Geoghegan J., where it was decided that the deputies were entitled at common law to protect their confidential communications with the public.

[120] See *The Irish Times*, December 23, 2002 (access sought by gardaí to deputies' telephone records), February 11, 2003 (legal representation at the tribunal granted to two committees of the Oireachtas, and question raised regarding discoverability of papers and records of members of the Oireachtas), February 19, 2003 (defending the tribunal's right to serve orders of discovery).

inability to establish the identity of the politicians' informants. He was also concerned that innocent people could have been convicted on the basis of unlawfully obtained evidence.[121] The politicians were granted leave to apply by way of judicial review for an order quashing the tribunal's direction to produce the information.[122]

Of more direct interest to the media is the televising of the Dáil, which was agreed in principle in 1988,[123] after a successful period of radio broadcasting and shortly after a similar decision was taken in Britain to televise the House of Commons.[124] The rules governing the televising of the Dáil were drawn up by an all-party committee and approved by the Dáil itself. The rules included a ban on showing close-ups of official documents and a "recommendation" against showing wide shots of the chamber when it was relatively empty. They also included a requirement to focus on the Ceann Comhairle when he was speaking and whenever there were scenes "of disorder or unparliamentary behaviour".[125] The Standing Orders[126] provide that the Committee on Procedure and Privileges shall make recommendations to the Joint Committee on Broadcasting and Parliamentary Information on the rules of coverage for the televising of proceedings of Dáil Éireann and its Committees. The role of the Joint Committee is to discharge the necessary monitoring, administrative and financial arrangements for in-house televising and for sound and televised broadcasting of Dáil Éireann and its committees and to review and modify rules of coverage.[127]

7.4 Reporting Local Government

The right of the media to attend and report on meetings of local authorities is more recent than that of parliament. Until 2001, it was governed by section 15

---

[121] February 28, 2003, *The Irish Times*, March 1, 2003.

[122] Unreported, High Court, O'Neill J., March 24, 2003, *The Irish Times*, March 25, 2003. The government does not intend to indemnify the two politicians in their court action: *The Irish Times*, April 9, 2003.

[123] *The Irish Times*, May 18, 1988.

[124] Television broadcasts of the Commons began as an experiment in November 1989, just a couple of months before the Dáil: *The Irish Times*, November 21, 1989.

[125] See *The Irish Times*, October 22, 1990, January 26, 1991. In New Zealand, in 1991 the government floated a proposal to charge the media for their accommodation in the press gallery from where they report parliament. In so doing, the government was signalling that use of the parliamentary galleries was not a right but a service for which payment could be demanded and ultimately denied altogether. Representations were made by the media and the proposal was abandoned: Karl du Fresne, *Free Press, Free Society*, Newspaper Publishers' Association of New Zealand, 1994. In *Prebble v Television New Zealand Ltd* [1994] 3 N.Z.L.R. 1, the issue also arose as to whether the media could rely on statements made in the legislature in defending a defamation action. The NZ Court of Appeal held that they were precluded from doing so by the terms of parliamentary privilege; consequently the interests of justice required that the action be stayed. For the position in the UK prior to *Reynolds v Times Newspapers* [1999] 3 W.L.R. 1010, [1999] 4 All E.R. 609, see Andrew Sharland and Ian Loveland, "The Defamation Act 1996 and Political Libels" [1997] P.L. 113.

[126] June 2002, s.97(1)(f).

[127] *ibid.*, ss. 101(1)(a) and (b).

of the Local Government (Ireland) Act 1902.[128] The situation was unclear and unsatisfactory in many respects and required updating. Part 6 and Schedule 10 of the Local Government Act 2001 now provide for meetings and proceedings of local authorities. Section 45 provides for the attendance of the public and media at meetings.[129] Although the public and media are entitled to attend meetings, the Authority may, by resolution, decide to meet in committee because of the special nature of the meeting, or an item of business to be or about to be considered at the meeting, or for other special reasons. It may do so for the whole or a part of the meeting concerned, where such authority "considers that such action is not contrary to the overall public interest" (section 45(3)).

The most effective way for a local authority to exclude the press in practice is by deciding to go into committee. The "overall public interest" criterion in the new provisions is, therefore, a welcome improvement on the previous position and gives the media a basis for challenging such a decision if the need arises.[130] Further safeguards are provided in section 45(4). First, there is a requirement that at least one-half of the total number of members of the local authority concerned vote in favour of the resolution. Second, the resolution must indicate in a general way the reasons for the resolution and those reasons must be recorded in the minutes of the meeting.

As before, local authorities can make their own standing orders and use them to regulate attendance of the public and the media in terms of available space and to deal with misconduct. They can also make rules in relation to the taking of photographs and the use of any means for recording or relaying the proceedings as they take place or at a later stage (section 45(5)). However, they can not use any of those factors as a means to prohibit the attendance of representatives of the media (section 45(6)). Prior to the entry into force of the 2001 Act there was some disquiet among the media about decisions of some local authorities to go into committee and exclude the press, but overall there

---

[128] S.15 of the 1902 Act, which was repealed by the Local Government Act 2001, stated: "No resolution of any council, board or commissioners to exclude from its meetings representatives of the press shall be valid unless sanctioned by the Local Government Board in pursuance of by-laws which the Local Government Board are hereby empowered to frame, regulating the admission of the representatives of the press to such meetings". This was followed in 1903 by an Order of the Local Government Board which merely provided for the admission of members of the press on production of a document signed by the newspaper proprietor or editor (now a press card), stating that the person seeking admission was a representative of the press. It also reiterated that any decision of a council, board or commissioners to exclude the press would, if sanctioned by the Local Government Board, be valid, although it did not stipulate on what basis such exclusion might be sanctioned. See, generally, Richard Woulfe, "Local Authorities and the Press", *The Media and the Law*, Incorporated Law Society Seminar, Dublin, 1985.

[129] The term "media" is defined in the section to include "accredited representatives of local and national press, local and national radio and local and national television" (s.45(1)). In referring to local television, the Act is very much up to date as local television is still in its infancy in Ireland.

[130] Formerly, the situation was governed by the Local Government Act 1955, ss.60–62, which were repealed by the Local Government Act 2001. The Minister for the Environment had the power to make regulations regarding meetings and procedures, but the power did not seem to be used (s.61(1)). A local authority had power to make standing orders for the regulation of their proceedings (s.62).

was not thought to be any great impediment to journalists in reporting local authority meetings.[131] Indeed, even prior to the Act, some broadcasting of local authority meetings had been taking place.[132]

Until the passing of the Freedom of Information Act 1997, there was no general right to inspect documents of local authorities, only limited rights under specific statutes. For example, the Local Government (Planning and Development) Acts and acts relating to specific services, provided for the keeping of registers and for inspection and purchase of certain documents, including development plans. The current legislation is the Planning and Development Act 2000, which replaces various earlier provisions.[133]

Section 110 of the Environmental Protection Agency Act 1992 provides that the Minister for the Environment shall, following consultation with any other government minister concerned, make regulations for public authorities to make available to any person on request specified information relating to the environment. The Minister made regulations in 1993, in order to give effect to an EC Directive.[134] However, access to information was still limited, and the exceptions whereby information could be withheld were extensive.[135] The issue of access to information held by local authorities, as well as government departments and a host of other public bodies, has been greatly strengthened by the enactment of the Freedom of Information Act 1997, which is discussed

---

[131] There had been complaints from journalists in the past and, even though the situation had improved over the years, the updating and safeguards provided in the 2001 Act were necessary and overdue. Even in recent years there have been incidents where the media have been excluded from specific meetings of local authorities, such as area meetings and Special Policy Committee meetings: *The Irish Times*, January 18, 2001. Strategic Policy Committee meetings and Area meetings are now governed by Part VII of the Local Government Act 2001. S.54(1) states that the Minister may make regulations providing for the attendance of members of the public and representatives of the media at meetings of joint committees or committees other than those specified in the regulations, or at which the local authority concerned, in accordance with such procedures as may be specified in the regulations, determines such attendance is not permitted. Ss.45(3) and (4) shall apply to such attendance – s.54(1)(c).

[132] See *The Irish Times*, January 24, 2001, referring to WLR FM's broadcasts of the monthly meetings of Waterford City Council and Waterford County Council.

[133] S.7 sets out in detail the requirement to keep a register. S.16 provides for copies of development plans and reports of the manager of the planning authority to be made available to the public. S.38 sets out the documentation to be made available to the public in respect of planning applications. Ss.113(3)(c) and (d), respectively, state that nothing shall prevent disclosure of information in accordance with the Freedom of Information Act 1997 and the European Communities Act 1972 (Access to Information on the Environment) Regulations 1998, and any amending provisions of them.

[134] EC Directive 90/313/EEC [1990] O.J. No. L158/56, which came into force on January 1, 1993; Access to Information on the Environment Regulations 1993 (S.I. No. 133 of 1993).

[135] See *The Irish Times*, December 13, 1994. Information could be refused if it affected international relations, national security, if the matter was *sub judice* or was the subject of an inquiry or investigation. It could be refused also if it involved the confidentiality of the deliberations or proceedings of public authorities, or commercial and industrial confidentiality. Most far-reaching was the right to refuse information where a study or report was incomplete or in preliminary or draft form: S.I. No. 133 of 1993, s.6(1). New regulations were made in 1998 — the Access to Information on the Environment Regulations 1998.

in detail in Chapter 10 below. A further EC Directive on public access to environmental information has been agreed by the Parliament and Council.[136]

A general note should be added that the Defamation Act 1961, section 24 and Schedule 2, make provision for a qualified privilege for a fair and accurate copy of or extract from any register kept in pursuance of any law which is open to inspection by the public or of any other document which is required by law to be open to inspection by the public. A similar privilege, subject to explanation or contradiction, attaches to a fair and accurate report or summary of any notice or other matter issued for the information of the public by, or on behalf of, any government department, local authority or the Commissioner of the Garda Síochána, or their counterparts in Northern Ireland.

Further Reading

Alexander, S.L., *Covering the Courts: A Handbook for Journalists* (University of America Press, Lanham, MD, 1999).
Goldfarb, Ronald L., *TV or Not TV: Television, Justice, and the Courts (A Twentieth Century Fund Book)* (New York University Press, New York, 2000).
Lord Irvine of Lairg, "Reporting the Courts – The Media's Rights and Responsibilities" (1999) xxxiv *Irish Jurist* 1.

---

[136] Directive 2003/4/EC, November 8, 2002. The Directive, which will replace Directive 90/313/EC, is the first step towards EU ratification of the international convention on access to information, public participation in decision-making and access to justice in environmental matters (Aarhus, Denmark, June 1998; *The Irish Times*, June 26, 1998). The Directive is due to be implemented by Member States in 2004.

CHAPTER EIGHT

Public Order and Morality

"What is freedom of expression? Without the freedom to offend, it ceases to exist".*

8.1 THE CONSTITUTION AND INTERNATIONAL INSTRUMENTS

The primary concerns of Article 40.6.1.i of the Irish Constitution are public order and morality. The central value guaranteed by the Article may well be freedom of expression but the emphasis is very much on the importance of maintaining and safeguarding public order and morality. Even before the right itself is mentioned, there is a warning that it will only be available subject to public order and morality: "The State guarantees liberty for the exercise of the following rights, subject to public order and morality ...". Then in the reference to the "rightful liberty of expression" of the organs of public opinion (the media), the state is required to ensure that: "... organs of public opinion, such as the radio, the press, the cinema ... shall not be used to undermine public order or morality ...". In addition, a tailpiece to Article 40.6.1.i specifies that certain types of publication constitute an offence: "The publication or utterance of blasphemous, seditious or indecent matter is an offence which shall be punishable in accordance with law".

While the formulation of the Article is clumsy and repetitive, there is no doubt that it gives prominence to public order and morality.[1] In fact it treats them almost as a unit, and there are indeed various areas of overlap. Historically, when the burning concern was to prevent criticism of State institutions, including the established church, public order and morality were often interwoven. So, too, was the area of sedition and seditious publications. In fact, the tailpiece to Article 40.6.1.i of the Constitution represents the historical position.

It is also the case that there is a considerable overlap between public order, sedition and "the authority of the State", which is an additional area of restriction on the freedom of the press and organs of public opinion, specified in Article

---

*Salman Rushdie, *Weekend Guardian*, February 10, 1990.

[1] See J.M. Kelly, *The Irish Constitution* (Gerard Hogan and Gerry Whyte (eds), 3rd ed., Butterworths, Dublin, 1994), at pp.921–5, for the significance of the phrase, its interpretation by the Supreme Court as a control mechanism in *The State (Lynch) v Cooney* [1982] I.R. 337, [1983] I.L.R.M. 89, and its limitation to public order in this State alone by the High Court in *AG for England and Wales v Brandon Book Publishers Ltd* [1986] I.R. 597, [1987] I.L.R.M. 135.

40.6.1.i of the Constitution. "The authority of the State" will be the subject of discussion in Chapter 10. Chapter 9 will deal with morality. The present chapter concentrates on restrictions imposed on the media in the interests of public order and may, therefore, be taken in conjunction with both Chaps 9 and 10.

The maintenance of public order is seen as a legitimate reason for limiting freedom of expression, not only in Ireland but in the international human rights instruments also. For example, Article 10(2) of the European Convention specifically includes "the prevention of disorder or crime" among the areas of restriction. Under the Convention, however, only those measures which are prescribed by law and necessary in a democratic society may be invoked to restrict the central right, which is freedom of expression. Public order is also recognised as a legitimate basis for restriction in Article 19 of the International Covenant on Civil and Political Rights. The expression "public order" (*ordre public*) as used in the Covenant may be defined as: "the sum of rules which ensure the functioning of society or the set of fundamental principles on which society is founded. Respect for human rights is part of public order (*ordre public*)".[2]

It is therefore very broad and could be said to be the source of legitimacy for a variety of restrictions imposed on the media, including those imposed in the interests of reputation by defamation law.[3] That is the case in other European countries, where defamation is part of the criminal law because of its public order element, in the broad sense.[4] In the international human rights instruments, however, protection of the reputation and rights of others is usually given separate recognition. In the Irish Constitution, Article 40.6.1.i does not specifically mention reputation, but the fact that Article 40.3.2 mentions good name has generally been relied on as the source of the right and the constitutional basis for defamation law. Since defamation law is almost exclusively part of the civil law in Ireland, it was dealt with separately in Chapter 4. The residual aspect of defamation, which still forms part of the criminal law, will be discussed below.

8.2 Restrictions in the Interests of Public Order

In Ireland the restrictions imposed on the media in the interests of public order, in the narrower sense of the phrase, of preventing disorder, may be divided into three main categories: general criminal-law sanctions, general statutory restrictions and specific media-oriented restrictions. Each of the categories is outlined first and then considered in more detail.

The first category, general sanctions of the criminal law, comprises such crimes as those relating to libel, incitement, conspiracy and unlawful assembly.

---

[2] Syracusa Principles, No.22 (1985) 7 H.R.Q. 1.
[3] See James Casey, *Constitutional Law in Ireland* (3rd ed., Round Hall Sweet & Maxwell, Dublin, 2000), at p.543.
[4] European countries also have an integrated approach to privacy and personal rights as seen in their civil codes and in the development of a personality right, for example, in the German Constitution (*Grundgesetz*), Arts 1–2.

These are not specifically directed at the media but may apply to the media as to anyone else.

The second category consists of restrictions imposed by statute that are of general application and are not directly or necessarily media-related, although sometimes they may be pressed into action to deal with problems arising in the media. Section 4 of the Prohibition of Forcible Entry and Occupation Act 1971, for example, was intended to prevent the encouragement of squatting and, although generally applicable, was specifically aimed at the activities of a newspaper at the time. The Post Office Act 1951 was pressed into action to deal with a hoax telephone call made to a national radio show on August 31, 2000. The person concerned was charged with making a telephone call, which he knew to be false, for the purpose of causing annoyance, inconvenience or needless anxiety to others, contrary to section 13(1)(b) of the Post Office (Amendment) Act 1951.[5] The prankster, pretending to be the captain of the Galway hurling team, made disparaging remarks about women involved in Gaelic games, particularly camogie, and suggested they stick to hockey and golf.

A more recent example is the Prohibition of Incitement to Hatred Act 1989, which makes it an offence to publish or distribute written material or show or play a recording of visual images or sounds that are threatening, abusive or insulting and are intended, or likely, to stir up hatred. Section 3 of the Criminal Damage Act 1991, makes it an offence in certain circumstances to threaten to damage property. Sections 6 and 7 of the Criminal Justice (Public Order) Act 1994 deal with threatening, abusive or insulting behaviour with intent or recklessness to provoke a breach of the peace and the distribution or display in public of threatening, abusive, insulting or obscene material.[6] It has been used

---

[5] April 25, 2001, Galway District Court (*The Irish Times*, April 26, 2001, *IRIS – Legal Observations of the European Audiovisual Observatory* 2001–4:13 (*www.obs.coe.int*)). The Post Office Act was used because specific broadcasting legislation is aimed primarily at the obligations and responsibilities of broadcasters rather than individual callers. Other generally applicable provisions aimed at public order include the Offences against the Person Act 1861 (s.16) and the Malicious Damage Act 1861 (s.50): offence to send letters threatening murder and malicious damage, respectively. The Criminal Law Act 1976 made it an offence to join or take part in, support or assist the activities of an unlawful organisation. A Sinn Féin councillor was jailed for five years for inciting people to join the IRA. The maximum sentence under the Act was ten years (see *The Irish Times*, July 30, 1989). Another case of a Sinn Féin activist selling pro-IRA t-shirts in Galway was dealt with at District Court level under the Casual Trading Act. He was fined £1,000 (*The Sentinel*, September 16, 1990; *The Irish Times*, September 19, 1990). The Criminal Law Act 1976 was part of the emergency legislation resulting from the period of violence in Northern Ireland. The government ended the state of emergency in 1995.

[6] A number of nineteenth-century Acts, such as the Dublin Police Act 1842, s.14, contained similar provisions. It has been suggested in Kelly, above, n.1, at p.932, that statutory provisions that criminalise the use of abusive or insulting language are unconstitutional unless justified by the need to prevent a breach of the peace. The Law Reform Commission in its *Report on Offences Under the Dublin Police Acts and Related Offences* (LRC 14–1985) recommended that the old provisions be replaced by a new offence requiring intent or likelihood to cause a breach of the peace (paras 7.7–7.10). S.14(13) of the Dublin Police Act 1842 was repealed by the Criminal Justice (Public Order) Act 1994.

against public demonstrations[7] and contains a prohibition on the advertising of brothels and prostitution (section 23), which has been used against certain of the media (see further below).

The third category consists of those restrictions directly aimed at the media, for example, public order provisions in section 11 of the Wireless Telegraphy Act 1926, and in the Broadcasting Acts 1960–1993. The former makes it an offence to transmit any message or communication subversive of public order. The latter prohibit the broadcasting of anything likely to promote or incite to crime and require the broadcasting authority to be mindful of the need for understanding and peace in the whole island.[8] Provisions in the Broadcasting Acts, which apply to RTÉ, and the Radio and Television Act 1988, which applies to the independent radio and television stations, prohibit advertising that is directed towards a political or religious aim or that is in furtherance of a trade dispute. Such areas were regarded as contentious and likely to produce strong feelings and sectarianism. There have been a number of challenges to those bans and one such case, *Roy Murphy v Ireland*, has been taken to the European Court of Human Rights.[9] In addition, a court challenge was taken to RTÉ's allocation of airtime to the opposing sides in referenda.[10]

8.2.1 Criminal Libel

Of the generally applicable laws, the one that had most implications for the media historically but less so today is the common-law offence of criminal libel. Criminal libel has been given statutory recognition and been somewhat modified in relation to the media by Part II of the Defamation Act 1961.[11] Part II of the Act contains specific references to newspapers but makes no reference to broadcasting. In fact, Part II is not made to apply to broadcasting at all. Whether this was deliberate policy on the part of the legislators or simply an oversight is not clear.[12] In any event, the statutory provisions and safeguards provided for newspapers in the Act do not apply to broadcasting, which would,

---

[7] For example, members of the anti-abortion group, Youth Defence, were convicted of breaching the Act but had their convictions overturned by the Circuit Court (*The Irish Times*, July 11, 2000).

[8] For a discussion of ss.18 and 31 of the Broadcasting Authority Act 1960, as amended, see Chap.10.

[9] App. No.44179/98, judgment of July 10, 2003. See further discussion below. A complaint relating to a blanket ban on political advertising was rejected by the European Commission on Human Rights in *X and Association of Z v UK*, App. No.4515/70, July 11, 1971, on the basis of the licensing provision in Art. 10(1) of the Convention. However, that was an early decision taken before commercial broadcasting emerged.

[10] *Coughlan v RTÉ* [2000] 3 I.R. 1. A number of court challenges have led to changes in the conducting of referenda: for example, Government spending on referenda in *McKenna v An Taoiseach & Ors (No.2)* [1995] 2 I.R. 10, and in *Hanafin v Minister for the Environment* [1996] 2 I.R. 321.

[11] It was carried over from the Law of Libel Amendment Act 1888, s.8.

[12] The Dáil Debates on the Defamation Bill reveal that existing statutory provisions were carried over in what was seen merely as a "tidying-up" exercise (188 *Dáil Debates*, Col. 1644). The NI High Court in *Monteith v Clarke and others* [1993] N.I. 376 says simply that the definition of "newspaper" in the Law of Libel Amendment Act 1888 had never been amended so as to include television or radio broadcasts.

therefore, it seems, be governed by common-law rules. There does not appear to be any plausible reason for differentiating between broadcasting and the print media in this way.[13] However, because the situation has become so rare, it is no longer considered a threat by the media.

Originally intended to protect the government of the day from harmful criticism, criminal libel developed to take several different forms: blasphemous libel, seditious libel, obscene libel and, finally, defamatory libel, where there was a threat or likelihood of a breach of the peace. Prosecutions for criminal libel in this last form became an effective deterrent to duelling to protect one's honour. It was introduced by the Star Chamber as a measure to suppress duelling and to promote public peace and order.[14] It also became an effective weapon for curtailing the excesses of the press.

Prosecutions for criminal libel in any of its forms are very rare nowadays.[15] In recent years there have been only three applications to prosecute newspapers and all have failed. The first, in 1976, was brought against the *Irish Independent* by Eddie Gallagher, who had been jailed for his part in the Dr Herrema kidnapping.[16] The second in 1990 arose out of a piece in the *Phoenix* magazine, in which it was alleged that the Rev. Stephen Hilliard, a Church of Ireland rector who had been killed by an intruder in his home, had been involved many years earlier in IRA activities.[17] The judgment of Gannon J. in the High Court was instructive. His analysis of the common-law rules, the statutory provisions and the anomalies they contain present a challenge to the legislature

---

[13] Geoffrey Robertson and Andrew Nicol, *Media Law* (3rd ed., Penguin, London, 1992), at p.101, say that the same tests should be satisfied in relation to libels that have appeared elsewhere, not just in a newspaper or periodical. See also the discussion in Geoffrey Robertson and Andrew Nicol, *Media Law* (4th ed., Penguin, London, 2002), pp.147–150, particularly regarding the "loophole" that journalists do not have the benefit of the safeguard that publishers of newspapers cannot be prosecuted for criminal libel except by leave of the High Court (see text of provision below). An application for leave to prosecute was not necessary in order to prosecute the journalist concerned in *Monteith v Clarke* (above, n.12).

[14] See J.R. Spencer, "Criminal Libel – A Skeleton in the Cupboard (1)" [1977] Crim. L. Rev. 383. See also J.R. Spencer, "Criminal Libel – A Skeleton in the Cupboard (2)" [1977] Crim. L. Rev. 465, and Law Reform Commission, *Consultation Paper on the Crime of Libel*, 1991, at Chap.1 "Historical Development of the Crime of Libel".

[15] The non-media case of *DPP v Fleming* (*The Irish Times*, November 23, 1989), involving indecent phone calls and graffiti, will be discussed briefly in Chap.9 below. There has not been a public prosecution of the media in Britain for criminal libel for many years, although there have been rare examples of private prosecutions: see Nicol, Millar, Sharland, *Media Law and Human Rights* (Blackstone Press Ltd, London, 2001), at p.76. The first case of criminal libel in Northern Ireland in 1993, *Monteith v McPhilemy and Others* (above, n.12), concerned an application to prosecute a newspaper and the producer of a controversial television programme, which had alleged collusion between RUC officers and loyalist death squads. The application against the newspaper was refused, as the "extreme sanction of prosecution for criminal libel" was not required in order to satisfy the public interest. The application to prosecute the newspaper journalist and programme producer was not necessary, as it only applies to those responsible for the publication of a newspaper.

[16] Unreported, High Court, 3 July 1978, Finlay P., cited by Gannon J. in *Hilliard v Penfield Enterprises Ltd* [1990] 1 I.R. 138.

[17] *Hilliard v Penfield Enterprises Ltd*, above, n.16.

to repeal the provisions of the 1961 Act or introduce amending legislation.[18] The third application, which concerned blasphemous libel, also raised a number of anomalies and resulted in an appeal to the Supreme Court in 1999.[19]

The Law Reform Commission in its *Consultation Paper on the Crime of Libel* (as they preferred to call criminal libel, to avoid confusion in the public mind) concluded that the offence in its present condition is highly unacceptable: "It runs contrary to many modern principles of criminal liability and fair trial, and threatens freedom of speech to a high degree, in theory if not in practice, so long as it continues to exist in its present state".[20]

The Commission, however, did not recommend abolishing the offence altogether. Its use in a recent case, the Commission argued, demonstrated that "its abolition would deprive the criminal law of a valuable weapon". It was felt that this form of criminal procedure might still have a useful, although limited, function.[21] The Commission's argument does not take account, however, of the various statutory measures available. Those measures have since been augmented by sections 6 and 7 of the Criminal Justice (Public Order) Act 1994. The case to which the Commission referred, *DPP v Fleming*,[22] in which Fleming was convicted for writing graffiti about a woman on telephone boxes all around Ireland, could probably now be prosecuted under the 1994 Act. The Act extends to the distribution or display in public of threatening, abusive, insulting or obscene material, with an intention (or recklessness) to cause a breach of the peace.[23]

More recently, use has been made of criminal libel to address attacks on reputation on the internet. In each case, the attacks were of a serious nature and were intended to cause harm. They therefore bore a close resemblance to *DPP v Fleming*,[24] but it does not appear that they could be accommodated in the same way by the Criminal Justice (Public Order) Act 1994. Section 3 of that Act defines a public place to include a highway, outdoor area, or premises to which the public have access. It is therefore delineated by reference to physical space and does not appear to encompass the virtual world of the internet. The first of two reported cases concerned a message sent by a man to bulletin boards and by e-mail, alleging that one of his former teachers was a paedophile.[25] In the second case, *DPP v Kenny*, a businessman was convicted

---

[18] *ibid.* at 147.

[19] *Corway v Independent Newspapers* [1999] 4 I.R. 484. The case is considered in Chap.9 below.

[20] Above, n.14, *Paper*, at para. 178.

[21] *Report on the Crime of Libel* (LRC 41–1991) at Chap.2. The Commission recommended retention of the offence in a more confined form.

[22] Above, n.15.

[23] The argument that statute law adequately dealt with the type of situation covered by criminal libel was one of the considerations that led the New Zealand Committee on Defamation in its 1977 report to recommend abolition of the common-law offence. The most compelling reason was the adequacy of the civil action for defamation. See discussion in above, n.14, *Paper*, at pp.142–3.

[24] Above, n.15.

[25] *DPP v X*, Dublin Circuit Criminal Court, *The Irish Times*, December 21, 1999. The man, whose name was not released by direction of the judge, had continued to send such messages while on bail pending trial and later admitted that he had published them

of libelling a business competitor. He had placed a notice on the internet indicating that she was providing prostitution services.[26] The Defamation Act 1961, which contains provisions on criminal libel, provides that anyone who maliciously publishes any defamatory libel, knowing it to be false, shall be liable to a fine of up to IR£500, or imprisonment not exceeding two years, or to both fine and imprisonment (section 12).

Although criminal libel proved useful in the above cases, it is problematic in many respects and would be better repealed. It could be replaced, if necessary, by a narrowly-drawn offence, which would have all the hallmarks and safeguards of the criminal law. Section 23 of the Electronic Commerce Act 2000, however, has breathed new life into criminal libel. It provides that all provisions of existing defamation law shall apply to all electronic communications within the State, including the retention of information electronically.

From the point of view of the media, the case of *Hilliard v Penfield Enterprises*[27] illustrates all the elements of criminal libel, the difficulties and anomalies. The *Phoenix* magazine published what purported to be an account of the funeral of the Rev. Stephen Hilliard, a former *Irish Times* journalist, who had become a Church of Ireland rector and had been killed by an intruder in his home in January 1990. The *Phoenix* made a number of allegations about the deceased's having been involved in criminal activities of a subversive nature many years previously.[28] Mrs Hilliard, the wife of the deceased, applied to the High Court, pursuant to section 8 of the Defamation Act, for an order to bring a prosecution against the *Phoenix*. Section 8 states:

"No criminal prosecution shall be commenced against any proprietor, publisher, editor or any person responsible for the publication of a newspaper for any libel published therein without the order of a judge of the High Court sitting *in camera* being first had and obtained, and every application for such order shall be made on notice to the person accused, who shall have an opportunity of being heard against the application".

The *Phoenix* qualified as a newspaper under the definition given in the Defamation Act 1961. Gannon J. considered the application on the basis of

---

maliciously, knowing them to be false. A two and a half year prison sentence was handed down.

[26] *DPP v Kenny*, Circuit Court, March 27, 2001; *The Irish Times*, March 28, 2001. Following conviction, the defendant offered to pay £10,000 compensation to the victim. The judge, however, deemed it insufficient. In a civil action she would probably be awarded a much higher sum. A "substantial" sum was later offered. See Chap.4 above.

[27] Above, n.17. See discussion of case in Marie McGonagle, "Criminal Libel" (1990) 12 D.U.L.J. 138.

[28] Gannon J., above, n.17, at 141, described it thus: "It is difficult to believe that ... the ... respondents [*i.e.* the editor, proprietor and publisher of the *Phoenix*] could stoop so low as to present or adopt such a mean, spiteful and wounding attack upon a deceased under the guise of a commentary on his funeral.... It would be impossible to describe a libel which accuses a person of having been twenty years ago an intelligence officer for the IRA and of providing contacts to lead to massive bank robberies, or of setting fire to houses and cars on behalf of the IRA as being of a trivial character ... it can only be described as most serious...."

principles laid down by Wien J. in *Goldsmith v Pressdram*,[29] which had been approved by Finlay P. in the 1978 application of Eddie Gallagher (judgment not circulated). Those principles are:

(a) there must be a clear *prima facie* case;

(b) the libel must be a serious one, so serious that it is proper for the criminal law to be invoked;

(c) a likelihood of a breach of the peace is not necessary, though it may be relevant[30]; and

(d) the judge must ask himself whether the public interest *requires* the institution of criminal proceedings.[31]

In *Hilliard*, Gannon J. found that a *prima facie* case could be made out. On the question of seriousness, the test is the likely effect of the publication on a significant section of law-abiding citizens. Furthermore, it is the damage to the good name and repute of the vilified party in the esteem of other people that is important and not self-esteem.[32] A tendency to cause a breach of the peace would signal the seriousness of the libel but proof of the existence of such a tendency is no longer necessary. If such a tendency does exist, it may be relevant. If it does not, it is of no great significance.[33] Because a clear *prima facie* case could be made out in *Hilliard* and the matter was a serious one, the remaining question to be considered was whether the public interest required a prosecution. That entailed consideration of the public interest in having crime properly investigated and bringing criminals to justice. The nature and circumstances of the libel had to be considered in that light and not obscured by the right of a party who has been wronged to a remedy.[34]

---

[29] [1976] 3 W.L.R. 191, [1977] 2 All E.R. 557; cited in above, n.17, at 142.

[30] As held by the Court of Appeal in *R v Wicks* [1936] 1 All E.R. 384. In *Gleaves v Deakin* [1979] 2 All E.R. 497, at 508–9, Lord Scarman said that it is the gravity of the libel that matters; it must be such as to provoke anger or cause resentment, and breach of the peace is but one factor that contributes to the gravity of the libel.

[31] Since s.23 of the Electronic Commerce Act 2000 says that all provisions of existing defamation law are to apply to all electronic communications, any libel on an internet publication by a newspaper would be subject to s.8 of the Defamation Act 1961, and therefore a judge would have to give leave for a prosecution.

[32] Above, n.17, at 143. Historically, when the emphasis was very much on the tendency to cause a breach of the peace, publication to a third party was not necessary. See above, n.27, McGonagle, at p.143.

[33] Above, n.17, at 143.

[34] A further issue that arose was the question of libel of the dead. Historically, there had been some instances of prosecutions being brought in respect of libel of the dead, and some evidence to suggest that if the libel were intended to injure the victim's posterity, it would be indictable. (See above, n.14, Spencer, at pp.385, 466, which cites the case of the successful prosecution of John Hunt for defamatory libel on the dead King George III. The libel was allegedly contained in a poem by Byron – a lampoon on an official eulogy, which Hunt had published and for which he was imprisoned.) Gannon J., however, came down on the side of *R v Ensor* ((1887) 3 T.L.R. 366, quoting from the judgment of Lord Kenyan in *R v Topham* (1791) 4 Tem. Rep. 126, 100 E.R. 931), to the effect that libel of the dead was not part of our law. If the law was to be extended to accommodate

confidential report compiled at the request of the EC Commission, questioned the determination of the Moroccan authorities, and principally the king, to combat the increase in drug-trafficking on Moroccan soil. The European Court of Human Rights noted that public opinion, in particular in France, had a legitimate interest in being informed of the EC Commission's assessment of the drugs problem in a country, Morocco, that was seeking admission to the EU. In accordance with its own previous jurisprudence, the Court considered that it was reasonable for *Le Monde* to have relied on the report without checking its accuracy. It noted also that, unlike in defamation proceedings, there was no defence of truth to the offence of insulting foreign heads of state under French law. It was therefore a disproportionate means of protecting reputation and it did not correspond to a pressing social need. Besides, the conferring on heads of state of a special status could not be reconciled with modern practice and political conceptions.

8.2.2 The Criminal Justice (Public Order) Act 1994 and other General Legislation

The most publicised use of the Criminal Justice (Public Order) Act 1994 against the media occurred when the publisher of *In Dublin*, the listings magazine, pleaded guilty to ten sample charges under section 23(1) of the Criminal Justice (Public Order) Act 1994 and was fined £50,000.[47] The Act makes it an offence to publish or distribute an advertisement for brothels or prostitutes and provides for fines of up to £1,000 (€1,269.74) on summary conviction and £10,000 (€12,697.40) on indictment for each offence. It is a defence for the publisher or distributor to show that the advertisement was received in the ordinary course of business and they did not know and had no reason to suspect, that it related to a brothel or a prostitute.

In the *In Dublin* case, the Censorship of Publications Board (see further, Chapter 9) had received a complaint that the advertisements contained indecent and obscene material, and had entered into correspondence with the publisher in relation to it, eventually imposing a six months' ban on the magazine.[48] The publisher sought a judicial review of the decision in the High Court, claiming that the Board's decision was unconstitutional and in breach of fair procedures of natural and constitutional justice. He also circumvented the ban by publishing an almost identical magazine called *Dublin*.[49] Initially, the High Court granted an injunction lifting the ban imposed by the Censorship Board, describing it as reprehensible and incredible. The court was critical of the Board for refusing to meet with the publisher and for repressing the fact that it had pre-determined the fate of the magazine while conducting a correspondence as to its future.[50] However, a subsequent garda investigation led to the charges

---

[47] *The Irish Times*, October 19, 2000. He was originally charged with 53 offences.

[48] *The Irish Times*, August 19, 1999.

[49] *ibid.* O'Donovan J. in the High Court said he deplored the fact that Mr Hogan had published and distributed the *Dublin* magazine but he did not consider it a contempt of court. While it may have been contrary to the spirit of the law, it was not unlawful, he said (*The Irish Times*, August 20, 1999).

being brought.[51] It seems preferable in a case like this to rely on precise provisions of the criminal law, such as section 23(1) of the Public Order Act, rather than to engage the inherently flawed machinery of the Censorship Board. Indeed, as far back as 1967, the then Minister, Brian Lenihan, who set about reforming the censorship legislation, advocated doing away with the Censorship Acts altogether, leaving pornography to the criminal law.[52]

8.2.2.1 The Prohibition of Incitement to Hatred Act 1989

There have been few cases taken under the Prohibition of Incitement to Hatred Act 1989 and none against the media. Those that have been taken have related to travellers and immigrants but have resulted mostly in acquittals.[53] The legislation is currently under review, due mainly to disquiet that the threshold (intention or likelihood to stir up hatred[54]) is too high and means that few cases will result. While experience may indicate that that is so, and incitement to hatred needs to be addressed, the legislature must be careful to ensure that adoption of a lower threshold[55] will not unjustifiably intrude on freedom of

---

[50] *The Irish Times*, August 20, 1999.

[51] The *Examiner* newspaper, which had carried advertisements for health clubs and massage parlours and such like for ten years, decided to drop them in light of this case (*The Irish Times*, August 19, 1999). However, it was reported the following year that an Irish website and a British magazine on sale here were publishing the same ads as those at issue in the *In Dublin* case (*The Irish Times*, May 2, 2000).

[52] See John Bowman's review of the newly-released cabinet papers in "Lenihan Saw Laws as an Embarrassment", *The Irish Times*, January 1, 2, 1997.

[53] For example, a Mayo county councillor, who had made derogatory remarks about travellers at a Western Health Board meeting, was acquitted in 1999: *DPP v Flannery* (*The Irish Times*, March 2, 1999). The local media had reported the remarks accurately but the national media were criticised by the judge for inaccuracies. A bus driver who was convicted under s.2 of the Act for remarks made to a Gambian man had his appeal upheld: *DPP v O'Grady* (*The Irish Times*, September 15, 2000). The appeal judge ruled that however appalling Mr O'Grady's remarks were, they were not intended or likely to stir up hatred (*The Irish Times*, March 14, 2001).

[54] In Britain, incitement to hatred is dealt with under Part III of the Public Order Act 1986. The test is similar to that in Ireland: intention or likelihood that racial hatred will be stirred up. Prosecutions can only be brought with the consent of the Attorney General and are relatively infrequent – see above, n.13, Robertson and Nicol, 2002, p.218. See also the Public Order (Northern Ireland) Act 1987. There is also race relations legislation (Race Relations Acts 1976–2000) in Britain. On the legal regulation of incitement and the effectiveness of enforcement, see Ruth Gavison, "Incitement and the Limits of Law" in Robert C. Post (ed.), *Censorship and Silencing: Practices of Cultural Regulation* (The Getty Research Institute, Los Angeles, 1998), at p.43. For a view of ways in which the Irish legislation might be reformed, see Conor Keogh, "The Prohibition of Incitement to Hatred Act 1989 – A Paper Tiger?" (2000) 6 (1) B.R. 178.

[55] In the UK, the Broadcasting Act 1990 amends s.22 of the Public Order Act 1986, and broadcasters can be convicted regardless of intention if "having regard to all the circumstances racial hatred is likely to be stirred up" – a change in the law described as "undesirable" by Robertson and Nicol, above, n.13, 2002, p.218. See also David Feldman, "Content Neutrality" in Ian Loveland (ed.), *Importing the First Amendment* (Hart Publishing, Oxford, 1998), at p.148: one cannot restrict speech solely on the grounds that it causes hurt feelings, offence or resentment, but only if calculated to provoke fear and violence (at p.152), and one cannot sever the link between the content of speech, the

expression. The Constitution Review Group, for example, in a statement that related to religious feelings but could equally apply to protection against racism, has said that "this is best achieved by carefully defined legislation along the lines of the Prohibition of Incitement to Hatred Act 1989 which applies equally to all religious groups, but which at the same time took care to respect fundamental values of freedom of speech and freedom of conscience".[56]

It should also be considered that a small number of court cases, or a number of unsuccessful cases, does not necessarily mean that an Act is flawed or not meeting its objectives; it could be effective also as a deterrent. Besides, a criminal prosecution is not always the best solution, and civil actions, rights of reply and retraction and the airing of the issues in public, through the media, can be equally effective in some circumstances.[57] Whether those considerations are valid or sufficient in the Irish experience of more than a decade of the Incitement to Hatred Act requires investigation. The role of the media in portraying difference and diversity is also crucial.

Todorov speaks of the need for a form of media representation which "recognises the diversity of peoples and the unity of the human race at one and the same time".[58] The tendency is otherwise, veering towards the marginalisation or demonisation of others.[59] The media often reflect, and may even encourage, public fears of the unknown or less known. The social and political contexts often determine the treatment.

---

context in which it takes place and the social dangers to which it is intrinsically likely to give rise. On racial speech face-to-face and assault, see W. Sadurski, "Racial Vilification, Psychic Harm and Affirmative Action" in Campbell and Sadurski (eds), *Freedom of Communication* (Dartmouth Publishing Company, London, 1994), at p.88.

[56] *Report of the Constitution Review Group* (Pn. 2632, Dublin, May 1996), p.297.

[57] Recommendation No.R(97) 20 of the Committee of Ministers of the Council of Europe, for instance, advocates, among other governmental actions, the use of civil law actions, providing for compensation for victims of hate speech and the possibility of court orders allowing victims a right of reply or order for retraction (Principle 2). Both the UN Special Rapporteur and the UN Human Rights Committee have called for affirmative action, including awareness-raising and educational initiatives, to redress cultural stereotypes for marginalized groups and to facilitate and enhance their participation in public affairs. See Report of the Special Rapporteur (Mr Abid Hussain) on the promotion and protection of the right to freedom of opinion and expression, submitted in accordance with Commission Resolution 1999/36: Addendum, Report on the Mission to Ireland, E/CN.4/2000/63/Add.2, para. 90; Concluding Observations of the Human Rights Committee: Ireland, CCPR/CO/69/IRL., para. 23. Gavison, above, n.54, at p.60 says that we "should not abolish laws simply because they do most of their work by guiding behaviour without the need for prosecution".

[58] Tzvetan Todorov, *On Human Diversity* (Harvard University Press, London, 1993), p.353, cited in Robert Ferguson, *Representing Race: Ideology, identity and the media* (Arnold, London, 1998), at p.257. Robert Post, "The Social Foundations of Defamation Law: Reputation and the Constitution" (1986) 74 California L.R. 691, at p.736, says: "Tolerance is the art of living with diversity, of finding commonality in the face of difference. The essence of tolerance is the refusal to draw boundaries that shut out the deviant". But, we cannot tolerate everything: "A community without boundaries is without shape or identity; if pursued with single-minded determination, tolerance is incompatible with the very possibility of a community". See also Robert Post, "Racist Speech, Democracy and the First Amendment" (1991) 32 William and Mary L.R. 267.

[59] Ferguson, above, n.58, at p.256.

What the media do not say about issues of race is also of crucial importance. As Ferguson points out, media silence can also serve power relations.[60] When qualities of "otherness" cannot be sustained because the possibility of a shared humanity threatens to become dominant, the media may ignore an issue or sandwich it in such a way as to neutralise its humanising potential.[61] In an observation that is universally applicable, Ferguson says: "For white and named is at one end of a representational spectrum, at the other end of which is black and unnamed. The new globalisation, the new internationalism, the new sensitivity to war is highly colour (in)sensitive".[62]

Race issues have come centre-stage in Ireland only in recent years.[63] The track record of the Irish media to date has been somewhat uneven, with almost all media organisations being singled out for criticism at one time or another, particularly for sensationalism or poorly-documented alarmist reports. In 1996, the Director of Public Prosecutions (DPP) decided not to prosecute journalist Mary Ellen Synon under the Prohibition of Incitement to Hatred Act.[64] The *Sunday Independent* journalist had written an article critical of the life and culture of the travelling community. It could be argued that the article was highly abusive and perjorative, rather than inciting as such.[65] While the travellers' group, Pavee Point, was disappointed at the decision not to prosecute, a spokesperson rightly identified the issue as one which highlighted the need for strong equal status legislation,[66] as much as or even more so than the need for a review of the 1989 Act.

---

[60] *ibid.* at p.242. For discussion of theories, objectives and effectiveness of hate speech laws, see Tarlach McGonagle, "Wresting (Racial) Equality from Tolerance of Hate Speech" (2001) 23 D.U.L.J. 21.

[61] Above, n.58, at p.252.

[62] *ibid.* at p.256.

[63] The issue was addressed at the Second Annual NGO Forum on Human Rights organised by the Department of Foreign Affairs, June 26, 1999, and at the Third Forum, July 1, 2000. The issue of racism and the media was also discussed at the Third Forum. (Conference proceedings are published by the Human Rights Unit, Dept of Foreign Affairs, Dublin.) See also Andy Pollak, "An invitation to racism? Irish daily newspaper coverage of the refugee issue", in Damien Kiberd (ed.), *Media in Ireland: The Search for Ethical Journalism* (Open Air, Dublin, 1999), p.33. ECRI, the European Commission against Racism and Intolerance, in its Second Report on Ireland (Doc. No.CRI (2002) 3, April 23, 2002, available at *www.coe.int/T/E/Human_Rights/Ecri/1-ECRI/2-Country-by-country_approach/Ireland/PDF_CBC2-Ireland.pdf*) noted, at para. 63, that although some media report widely and in a responsible fashion on issues of racism and intolerance concerning minority groups, others have tended to adopt a very negative attitude, particularly towards asylum seekers and refugees and towards members of the Travelling Community. Since that fuels public prejudices and misconceptions, ECRI urged media professionals to adopt codes of self-regulation.

[64] *The Irish Times*, September 3, 1996.

[65] The article was headed (presumably by a sub-editor) "Time to get tough on tinker terror 'culture'" and described the life of travellers as, *inter alia*, "worse than the life of beasts … without the ennobling intellect of man or the steadying instinct of animals". In keeping with normal practice, no reason was given by the DPP for the decision not to prosecute, but it was widely felt that difficulties in proving intention or likelihood contributed to it.

[66] *The Irish Times*, September 3, 1996. Ms Synon also drew the ire of the public when she wrote a very derogatory article in the *Sunday Independent* on the subject of the paralympic games: *Sunday Independent*, October 22, 2000. Advertisers threatened to withdraw

Strong equal status legislation, the Equal Status Act 2000, is now in place. Ireland ratified the International Covenant on Civil and Political Rights in 1989, and therefore took on the obligations of Article 20, which requires that any advocacy of, *inter alia*, racial hatred that constitutes incitement to discrimination, hostility or violence, shall be prohibited by law. In addition, Ireland finally ratified the International Convention on the Elimination of All Forms of Racial Discrimination (ICERD) in December 2000, once the Equality Act and Equal Status Act had been enacted to provide the necessary framework. Various bodies now also have codes, for example the anti-racism protocol for political parties and candidates at elections, drawn up by the National Consultative Committee on Racism and Interculturalism (NCCRI), a body which was established in 1998 to advise the government on policy issues and raise public awareness.[67]

The National Union of Journalists elaborated its guidelines on reporting the traveller community in 1995, and has since adopted guidelines on reporting refugees and asylum seekers, as well as other vulnerable groups.[68] RTÉ has a diversity policy document and also includes sections on "Respect for Diversity" and "Recognising Marginalised Groups" in its *Programme Makers' Guidelines*, 2002. The Advertising Standards Authority of Ireland (ASAI), a self-regulatory body, which governs all forms of advertising, upheld a complaint in 2001 in relation to an anti-racism campaign run by Amnesty International. It was claimed that the billboard campaign, which featured the Taoiseach, Tánaiste and Minister for Justice, portrayed them as racist.[69] The ASAI ruled that the advertisement exploited the three political leaders in a manner that was humiliating and offensive. The prior written permission of the three leaders had not been sought.

The perceived harm attaching to racist speech, therefore, can be tackled at various levels. It can be tackled broadly under anti-discrimination and equality laws, or as part of the prevention of crime and disorder generally. It can also be tackled in a more direct manner through specific anti-racism laws and measures. At EU level, for instance, Article 13 of the Treaty of Amsterdam, which came into force in 1999, gives the European Union competence to introduce anti-discrimination laws. In the field of broadcasting, the EC Television without Frontiers Directive also contains a provision, Article 22a, which requires Member States to ensure that broadcasts do not contain any incitement to hatred on grounds of race, sex, religion or nationality.

Under the Council of Europe machinery, Protocol No. 12 of the European

---

advertising from the paper, the *Sunday Independent* published an apology, made a donation, and Ms Synon resigned.

[67] *The Irish Times*, July 3, 2000.

[68] Available at *www.nuj.org.uk*; also Art. 10 of the Code of Conduct, which states that a journalist shall only mention, *inter alia*, a person's race, colour, creed, gender or sexual orientation if this information is strictly relevant, and shall not encourage prejudice or hatred on any of those grounds. The guidelines on the reporting of traveller issues were drawn up by the NUJ with the help of the Irish Travellers' Movement (see *The Irish Times*, April 15, 1996).

[69] The accompanying slogan read "Some say they are involved in racism. Others say they are doing nothing about it". See *The Sunday Tribune*, September 2, 2001.

Convention on Human Rights gives greater protection for equality, while a recommendation of the Committee of Ministers deals specifically with hate speech.[70] The European Convention on Transfrontier Television, Article 7, requires broadcasters to ensure that broadcast services do not give undue prominence to violence or be likely to incite to racial hatred. In the European Court of Human Rights, the prevention of crime and disorder were considerations in cases such as *Lehideux and Isorni v France*[71] and *Witzsch v Germany*,[72] both of which centred on Holocaust denial. Many of the cases taken against Turkey[73] involved incitement to hatred and race propaganda.

The issue of racism in the media has given rise to a volume of cases at national level in many countries. For example, a French court in October 2002 cleared a novelist, Michel Houellebecq, who is resident in Ireland, of incitement to racial hatred. He had criticised the Koran and the Islamic religion in a magazine interview.[74] Racism in the media has also arisen in a number of cases before the European Court of Human Rights. The Convention does not contain any separate right not to be subjected to racism, although the issue may be dealt with under Article 10, in relation to freedom of expression. In addition, Article 14 provides that the rights set out in the Convention shall be secured without discrimination on grounds such as sex, race, colour, language, religion, political or other opinion, national or social origin, association with a national minority, property, birth or other status. Similarly, Protocol No. 12 requires the enjoyment of the rights set out in the Convention without discrimination. Article 17 provides that nothing in the Convention can be

---

[70] Above, n.57, Recommendation No.R(97) 20 of the Committee of Ministers of the Council of Europe on "Hate Speech". The principles set out in the recommendation apply to hate speech, in particular hate speech disseminated through the media. It defines "hate speech" and sets out seven principles advocating measures to combat racist speech, but with due consideration for freedom of expression and the role of the media; also Rec No.R(97) 21 on the media and the promotion of a culture of tolerance.

[71] Judgment of September 23, 1998; (2000) 30 E.H.R.R. 665. The case concerned an advertisement in *Le Monde* newspaper, seeking to rehabilitate the memory of Marshal Philippe Pétain, who had been sentenced to death in 1945 for collusion with Germany. However, the applicants (a former Minister in Pétain's government and his defence lawyer) had not attempted to deny or revise the facts, which they referred to, *inter alia*, as "Nazi atrocities and persecutions". The Court of Human Rights considered their criminal conviction disproportionate, and, as such, unnecessary in a democratic society.

[72] App. No.41448/98, Court decision of April 20, 1999. The case, which concerned a conviction for denying the reality of the Holocaust, was declared inadmissible. There have also been cases of hate speech under the UN machinery, for example *Faurisson v France* (UN Doc C.C.P.R./C/58/D/550/1993).

[73] See, for example, the five judgments of July 8, 1999, and *Ozturk v Turkey* (judgment of September 28, 1999 – incitement to hatred), *Erdogdu v Turkey* (judgment of June 15, 2000 – propaganda). On hate propaganda, see also the decision of the Canadian Supreme Court in *R v Keegstra* [1996] 3 S.C.R. 667.

[74] *The Irish Times*, October 23, 2002. M. Houellebecq's lawyer interpreted the decision as recognising freedom of expression and the right to attack ideologies, distinguishing between an ideology and an ethnic group. See also *R v Chief Metropolitan Stipendiary Magistrate, ex parte Choudhury* [1991] 1 All E.R. 306, [1991] 1 Q.B. 429, discussed in Chap.9 below and *Irving v Penguin Books Ltd* [2000] E.W.H.C. Q.B. 115 (defamation case arising out of criticisms of David Irving's denials of the Holocaust).

interpreted as implying that any state, group or person has any right to engage in any activity or perform any act aimed at the destruction of any of the rights and freedoms set out in it.[75]

In a case against Austria (*Unabhangige Initiative Informationsvielfalt v Austria*),[76] the Court found a breach of Article 10. The case concerned a leaflet, which referred to "racist agitation" by Jorg Haider's Freedom Party. It provided a list of contact numbers of party members and invited readers to tell them what they thought of their policy. The Austrian courts granted an injunction to prevent repetition of the offending remarks by the publisher. The European Court of Human Rights, however, took the view that the matter had to be placed in the context of a political debate and that it contributed to a discussion on matters of public interest, such as immigration and the legal status of aliens in Austria. In *Ceylan v Turkey*,[77] the Court found that a newspaper article criticising anti-terrorist measures taken against the Kurds was strong political invective rather than hate speech. In *Jersild v Denmark*,[78] the Court held that a conviction of a journalist for merely reporting but not endorsing racist activities would amount to a breach of Article 10.

In recent years, Holocaust denial and racism on the internet have become growing concerns, which have increased awareness of the need for effective deterrents and sanctions. In France, for example, a court ordered the search engine *Yahoo!* to either remove Nazi memorabilia from its US-based auction website or to block French access to that site. *Yahoo!* appealed the case in the US and won.[79] A French court later cleared *Yahoo!*.[80]

---

[75] It has been used to refuse support for holocaust denial – see, for example, the discussion in *Lehideux and Isorni v France*, above, n.71. See generally, Nicol, Millar, Sharland, above, n.15, Chap.7 "Racial Hatred"; McGoldrick and O'Donnell, "Hate-speech laws: consistency with national and international human rights law" (1998) 18 *Legal Studies* 453; Jonathan Cooper and Adrian Marshall Williams, "Hate Speech, Holocaust Denial and International Human Rights Law" [1999] E.H.R.L.R. 593, and Aernout Nieuwenhuis, "Freedom of Speech: USA v Germany and Europe" *Netherlands Quarterly of Human Rights*, Vol. 18/2, 195–214, 2000.

[76] App. No.28525/95, judgment of February 26, 2002.

[77] Judgment of July 8, 1999, (1999) 30 E.H.R.R. 73.

[78] Series A, No.298, (1994) 19 E.H.R.R. 1. *Jersild* appears to be the first case where the Court considered, albeit summarily, the compatibility of freedom of expression with the obligations of state parties under ICERD, Art. 4 to criminalise acts and utterances of a racist nature. The Court stated (at para.30) that it was not for it to interpret the "due regard" clause in Art. 4, but that its interpretation of ECHR, Art.10 in the present case was "compatible" with Denmark's obligations under the UN Convention. ICERD, Art. 4 states: "States Parties condemn all propaganda and all organizations which are based on ideas or theories of superiority of one race or group of persons of one colour or ethnic origin, or which attempt to justify or promote racial hatred and discrimination in any form, and undertake to adopt immediate and positive measures designed to eradicate all incitement to, or acts of, such discrimination and, to this end, with due regard to the principles embodied in the Universal Declaration of Human Rights and the rights expressly set forth in article 5 of this Convention ...". Art. 5 includes the right to freedom of opinion and expression.

[79] See Kyu Ho Youm, "US court refuses to recognise French judgment in *Yahoo!* on grounds that it violates the free speech clause of the First Amendment to the US Constitution" (2002) 7 *Communications Law* 15.

[80] *The Irish Times*, November 8, 2002, *The Guardian*, February 12, 2003.

In response to those concerns, the Council of Europe's Committee of Ministers adopted an Additional Protocol to the European Convention on Cybercrime. The Protocol widens the scope of that Convention to cover acts of a racist or xenophobic nature. It does so on the basis that they "constitute a violation of human rights and a threat to the rule of law and democratic stability" and that "national and international law need to provide adequate legal responses to propaganda of a racist and xenophobic nature committed through computer systems". That said, the Additional Protocol also recognises that "computer systems offer an unprecedented means of facilitating freedom of expression and communication around the globe".

"Racist and xenophobic material" is defined in the Additional Protocol as:

> "[A]ny written material, any image or any other representation of ideas or theories, which advocates, promotes or incites hatred, discrimination or violence, against any individual or group of individuals, based on race, colour, descent or national or ethnic origin, as well as religion if used as a pretext for any of these factors".

In particular, parties are called upon to criminalise, when committed "intentionally and without right", the dissemination of such material through computer systems (Article 3), as well as racist and xenophobic threats and insults (Articles 4 and 5 respectively), and denial or gross minimisation, approval or justification of genocide or crimes against humanity (Article 6).[81]

The European Commission against Racism and Intolerance (ECRI), in its Second Report on Ireland,[82] noted as a particular problem the use of radio phone-in programmes by members of the public as a platform for airing prejudices and racist views. ECRI urges the application of self-regulatory codes to address the problem (para.63). Media portrayal of asylum-seekers is also addressed (para.79).

8.2.2.2 The Refugee Act 1996

Section 19 of the Refugee Act 1996 contained a provision which required the print[83] and broadcast media to get the written consent of the Minister for Justice before they could identify asylum-seekers. The measure, which came into effect in November 2000, was intended to protect the rights of asylum-seekers but acted as a restriction on their freedom of expression as well as that of the

---

[81] The text of the Convention is available at *www.conventions.coe.int*. It was opened for signature in Budapest, November 23, 2001. The Additional Protocol was opened for signature in Strasbourg on January 28, 2003 and at the time of writing has been signed by 17 Member States including Ireland.

[82] Above, n.63, Doc. No.CRI (2002) 3. In 2003, ECRI issued general policy recommendation No.7 on national legislation to combat racism and racial discrimination (CRI (2003) 8). It is addressed to the governments of Member States and urges, *inter alia*, that the law should provide for "effective, proportionate and dissuasive sanctions" (paras 12, 23).

[83] A "written publication" is stated to include a film, sound track and any other record in permanent form.

media.[84] While the Minister could not unreasonably withhold consent, failure to obtain consent could lead to fines of up to £1,500 (€1,905) and/or one year's imprisonment. A challenge to the constitutionality of the section, on the grounds that it conflicted with the freedom of expression guarantee of Article 40.6.1.i and also with the open justice principle of Article 34.1, was rejected on its own facts. The application was "moot" because the applicant had already been named in the media and she had not established that her interests had been adversely affected by the provision of the Act. [85] Following representations from the NUJ and others, an amendment to the section was included in the Immigration Bill 2002. The consent of the Minister would no longer be required but that of the asylum seeker would still be required for the written publication or broadcast of any matter likely to lead members of the public to identify that person (section 6(g)).

8.2.3 The Broadcasting Acts

There are a number of provisions in the Broadcasting Acts that have a public order dimension. Of particular interest are those dealing with political and religious advertising, and the provision of airtime for party political and referendum broadcasts. Provisions more concerned with the authority of the State will be discussed in Chapter 10.

8.2.3.1 Political Advertising

The Broadcasting Acts in Ireland, like those in many other western European countries, prohibit political advertising, or more precisely advertising which is directed towards a political end.[86] Party political broadcasts, for which free airtime is allocated, are permitted,[87] but paid-for political advertising is not. It is not altogether clear why political broadcasting is banned but in *Colgan v IRTC*,[88] it was stated to be because it is a divisive issue. In other countries, where similar provisions apply, the rationale is linked to equality and non-

---

[84] The National Union of Journalists criticised the section as a restriction on the freedom of expression of asylum-seekers and as censorship of the media. The Minister said that the section, which was brought in by a previous government, was intended to protect the privacy of asylum-seekers and the confidentiality of the asylum process. He said (February 6, 2001, as reported in *The Irish Times*, February 7, 2001), however, that he had reviewed the matter and would amend the section. The media would no longer need to obtain the consent of the Minister, only that of the applicant for asylum.

[85] *Jonathan v Ireland*, High Court, May 31, 2002, reported in *The Irish Times*, May 4, 2002, June 1, 2002. An appeal is pending.

[86] The Broadcasting (Authority) Act 1960, s.20(4), and the Radio and Television Act 1988, s.10(3). Advertisements pursuant to a trade dispute are also prohibited. The Referendum Act 1998, s.5, however, provides that the above sections shall not apply to advertisements broadcast at the request of the Referendum Commission (established by the Act) concerning a referendum.

[87] Broadcasting Authority Act 1960, s.18(2) and Radio and Television Act 1988, s.9(2).

[88] [2000] 2 I.R. 490, at 508; [1999] 1 I.L.R.M. 22, at 41: "these sensitive and divisive areas" and "giving advantage to rich men" (relying on Barrington J. in *Roy Murphy v IRTC* [1999] 1 I.R. 12; [1998] 2 I.L.R.M. 360, at 370).

discriminatory practice.[89] The belief is that wealthier parties and candidates could buy more advertising and thus gain an electoral advantage. On the contrary, in some Eastern European countries political advertising is regarded as an integral part of the right to freedom of expression and information, which allows new candidates to buy recognition and a profile. However, in those countries there are limits on the duration, frequency and charges.[90]

Two important questions arise: how is political advertising defined and what constitutes political advertising. It would appear that it is not confined to election campaigns, or indeed to political parties or candidates, but may encompass other wider public interest issues. The term "political" is not defined in the Irish legislation, but the court in *Colgan* stated that the phrase "political end" in section 10(3) of the Radio and Television Act 1988 means that it is directed towards furthering the interests of a particular political party or towards procuring changes in the laws of this country or of a foreign country, or countering changes in those laws or procuring a reversal of government policy or of particular decisions of governmental authorities. It is not therefore confined to a "party political end"; nor is it so broad as to include public affairs generally.[91]

There are distinctions to be made between political advertising and information for the electorate. For instance, the practice has developed of televising debates between candidates for political office, which play an increasing role in election coverage. Here a further distinction can be made between "television debates" and "televised debates".[92] Also, the role of opinion polls in the run-up to an election has to be considered. In some countries, such as France, opinion polls are banned in the period immediately before polling day but such polls have still been available on the internet.[93] In 2001, the Irish government tried to push through a Bill to ban the carrying out and publishing of opinion polls in the seven days immediately before polling day. (The proposal was made at the committee stage of the Electoral (Amendment) Bill 2000.) The move was opposed on freedom of expression grounds and subsequently dropped. An *Irish Times* editorial[94] described opinion polls as

---

[89] Sydney Kentridge, "Freedom of Speech: Is it the Primary Right?" (1996) 45 I.C.L.Q. 253, at p.259, says that the object of laws on political advertising is to protect the fairness and equality of the political process.

[90] See Emmanuelle Machet, Working Paper, EPRA/2000/02, available on *www.epra.org*. See also, the Council of Europe's Recommendation No.(99)15 on measures concerning media coverage of election campaigns, and in Ireland the BCI election guidelines at *www.bci.ie*.

[91] *Colgan*, above, n.88, at 504 and 37 respectively.

[92] The distinction is of particular relevance to the situation in the US: Kyu Ho Youm, "Editorial Rights of Public Broadcasting Stations vs. Access for Minor Political Candidates to Television Debates" (2000) 52 *Federal Communications Law Journal* 687.

[93] The French Cour de Cassation, September 4, 2001, found that the ban on publishing, circulating and commenting on opinion polls during the week preceding an election was not compatible with ECHR, Art.10 – see *IRIS* 2001–9:15 (*www.obs.coe.int*).

[94] *The Irish Times*, July 7, 2001; see also *The Irish Times*, July 12, 2001: the Government said it had decided to drop the provision because there was not all-party consensus on it, while the Opposition claimed it was because it was flawed.

"merely a modern tool of political science", which have never been shown to have distorted the results. They are, in fact, the paper said "the most independent material to be put before voters towards the end of a campaign as truth often becomes the casualty of the spins of politicians and parties".

There is no right of access to the airwaves as such.[95] It is clear from the case law of the European Court of Human Rights, however, that advertising relating to issues at the heart of political debates can be regarded as "political". As such, it must not be restricted, unless the restriction is necessary in a democratic society, in response to a pressing social need.[96] In *VgT v Switzerland*,[97] a television advertisement regarding animal welfare had been rejected on the grounds that it had a clear political character. The advertisement compared the conditions in which pigs were kept in small pens to concentration camps. The European Court of Human Rights found that there had been a violation of Article 10, as the restriction was not necessary in a democratic society. It appears, therefore, that advertisements, which are a means of participating in an ongoing general debate, must be permitted. Similarly, it may be argued even more strongly that if they are merely information notices, for example, of a meeting of a political party, and not urging a vote or setting out a particular party line, they should be allowed.[98]

The issue in *Colgan v IRTC*[99] was an "information project" organised by Youth Defence, an anti-abortion group, in 1996. The project involved, *inter alia*, radio broadcasts, which the IRTC, the regulatory authority for the commercial radio sector, refused to accept. It did so on the basis of the statutory provision, namely section 10(3) of the Radio and Television Act 1988: "No advertisement shall be broadcast which is directed towards any religious or political end or which has any relation to an industrial dispute".

---

[95] See, for example, *Haider v Austria* App. No.25060/94 (1995) 83 D.R. 66. Candidates who were refused access to the airwaves were also unsuccessful in *Huggett v UK* (App. No.24744/94) and *Tete v France* (App. No.11123/84) (1987) 54 D.R. 52.

[96] See, for example, *Bowman v UK* (1998) 26 E.H.R.R. 1, a case concerning the distribution of campaign literature about abortion at election time: "Free elections and freedom of expression, particularly freedom of political debate, together form the bedrock of any democratic system. The two rights are inter-related and operate to enforce each other: for example, as the Court has observed in the past, freedom of expression is one of the 'conditions' necessary 'to ensure the free expression of the people in the choice of the legislature'. For this reason it is particularly important in the period preceding an election that opinions and information of all kinds are permitted to circulate freely" (para.42). In *Haider v Austria*, above n.92, it was held to be in the interests of political debate for journalists interviewing candidates to put critical and provocative points of view to them since they have an immediate opportunity to respond.

[97] App. No.24699/94, (2001) 34 E.H.R.R. 159.

[98] In 2001, the IRTC banned radio advertisements by pro- and anti- Nice Treaty activists, but advertisements from the Referendum Commission were excepted because they were providing a public information service and were a neutral voice: *The Irish Times*, June 2, 2001; above, n.86. In *Coughlan* (below), Barrington, J. took the view that it is "clearly proper that such groups of citizens should be given an opportunity, if practicable, to use the national airwaves to place their views before their fellow citizens" (at para.105), although it does not appear that he had paid advertisements in mind.

[99] Above, n.88.

The applicant, a committee member of Youth Defence, sought a judicial review of the IRTC's decision and also claimed that if the Act authorised the prohibition of the advertisement, it was an unconstitutional infringement on his freedom of expression. The court had to decide whether the advertisement was simply a form of communication of information, as contended by the applicant, or an advertisement directed towards a political end, as stipulated in section 10(3) of the Act. In concluding that it was an advertisement directed towards a political end, O'Sullivan J. described it as "a powerful advertisement clearly directed against the evil of abortion and proclaiming itself to be sponsored by a group itself clearly identified with a campaign for a new referendum and a change in the law". The advertisement was, therefore, inextricably bound up with the project of bringing about a change in the law – a political aim. On the constitutional issue, O'Sullivan J. relied on the Supreme Court judgment in *Roy Murphy v IRTC*[100] and declined to find section 10(3) repugnant to the Constitution. Consequently, *Colgan* was not appealed to the Supreme Court. However, the Supreme Court decision in *Roy Murphy v IRTC* itself resulted in an application to the European Court of Human Rights (see further below).

Meanwhile developments had taken place in some common law juris-dictions. In *Australian Capital Television v Commonwealth of Australia*,[101] for example, the High Court by a majority struck down both the ban on political advertising and the requirement that broadcasters offer free airtime for referenda and national elections. The Radio Authority in the UK refused to broadcast an Amnesty International advertisement intended to highlight the atrocities in Rwanda[102] but while the case was pending before the European Court of Human Rights,[103] the Radio Authority reversed its decision and thus the Article 10 issues were not argued before the court. In *Prolife Alliance v BBC*,[104] a case similar in some respects to *Colgan v IRTC* (above), the Court of Appeal in London had to address the question as to whether the *content* of a party election broadcast (PEB) by a registered political party could be restricted. The anti-abortion group, Prolife Alliance, which was contesting a general election, made a video for broadcasting as a PEB. The video showed the products of a suction abortion and the BBC and other terrestrial broadcasters refused to accept it on the grounds of taste and decency. Having reviewed the case law of the European Court of Human Rights, the court concluded that, provided they were truthful and unsensational, it was only in the rarest of circumstances that PEBs could properly be rejected. "Almost always the balance will fall to be struck in favour of the free communication of political aims and ideas" (at para.63). The House of Lords has since overturned the ruling of the Court of Appeal.[105]

---

[100] Above, n.88.
[101] (1992) 108 A.L.R. 577.
[102] *R v Radio Authority, ex parte Bull* [1998] Q.B. 294 (CA).
[103] *Amnesty International (UK) v UK* App. No.38383/97, January 18, 2000.
[104] [2002] E.W.C.A. Civ. 297, [2002] 2 All E.R. 756, March 14, 2002.
[105] April 10, 2003. See further Chap.9.

8.2.3.2 Religious Advertising

The provisions relating to religious advertising are the same provisions as those that relate to political advertising and are detailed above. The leading case is *Roy Murphy v IRTC*.[106] Pastor Roy Murphy wished to advertise the showing of a video on the resurrection at a location in Dublin during Easter Week. The IRTC refused to accept the advertisement in accordance with section 10(3) of the Radio and Television Act 1988. The High Court upheld their decision. On appeal, the Supreme Court addressed the constitutional issues, namely freedom of religion (Article 44), freedom of expression (Article 40.6.1) and freedom to communicate (Article 40.3.1). Barrington, J., on behalf of the Court said that, as the provision extended to any and all religions, it was not discriminatory. It was directed at material of a particular class and not at people who profess a particular religion. It could not therefore be regarded as an attack on a citizen's right to practise his religion but could constitute a limitation on the manner in which the citizen could profess his religion.[107] While it did amount to a restriction on the constitutional rights to freedom of expression, religion and communication, it was justified as it had a legitimate aim and was proportionate. The only restriction placed upon the applicant's activities was that he could not advance his views by a paid advertisement on radio or television. The restriction on his constitutional rights was very slight; the ban was rationally connected to the objective of the legislation and was not arbitrary, unfair or based on irrational considerations, the Court said.[108] The presumption of constitutionality, which attached to the Radio and Television Act 1988, as an Act of the Oireachtas passed after the Constitution came into force, was not rebutted. The Court therefore upheld the decision of the High Court and dismissed the applicant's appeal.

The applicant then brought his case to the European Court of Human Rights, which decided in 2003 that there had been no breach of Article 10. The Court classified the advertisement in question as religious, rather than commercial, expression but placed considerable weight on the fact that, as advertising, it had a distinctly partial objective and, since advertising time was purchased, would lean in favour of unbalanced usage by religious groups with larger resources. The "extreme sensitivity" of religious advertising in Ireland, the fact that the prohibition related only to broadcasting and that there was no uniform consensus across Europe, led the Court to conclude that the State had

---

[106] Above, n.88.

[107] *ibid.* at 23. The judgment is important for its analysis of the relationship between Art. 40.3 (the right to communicate) and Art. 40.6.1 (freedom of expression). See Chap.2 above. The court held that the applicant was entitled to invoke both.

[108] Above, n.88, at 26–7. The argument that a blanket ban on religious advertising was "proportionate" and only a "very slight" restriction on the applicant's constitutional rights raises questions. A similar argument was advanced and accepted by the European Commission on Human Rights in *Purcell v Ireland* (the s.31 broadcasting ban relating to Sinn Féin in 1991), but the background and context were very different and also the outcome might have been different if the case had proceeded to the court – see further discussion in Chap.10.

demonstrated "relevant and sufficient" reasons to justify the interference with the applicant's freedom of expression.[109]

The *Roy Murphy* case was not the only case of a religious advertisement being refused in Ireland. In 1999, an advertisement for the *Irish Catholic* newspaper was refused by the IRTC[110] and another advertisement for the same newspaper was refused by RTÉ and the BCI in December 2002.[111] This was despite the fact that the Broadcasting Act 2001 had modified the ban on religious advertising slightly, in view of the rejection of the first advertisement for the *Irish Catholic* and that for the showing of Roy Murphy's video. Section 65 of the 2001 Act provides that nothing in the existing provisions (section 20(4) of the Broadcasting Authority Act 1960 and section 10(3) of the Radio and Television Act 1988) shall be construed as preventing the broadcasting of a "notice" of the fact:

"(a) that a particular religious newspaper, magazine or periodical is available for sale or supply, or; (b) that any event or ceremony associated with any particular religion will take place if the contents of the notice do not address the issue of the merits or otherwise of adhering to any religious faith or belief or of becoming a member of any religion or religious organisation".

On foot of that amendment, RTÉ initially accepted advertisements for a campaign, backed by prominent businessmen, called "Power to Change".[112] The advertisements featured a number of well-known figures promoting religion. RTÉ, on legal advice, subsequently withdrew its acceptance.[113] In September 2002, the High Court refused an injunction compelling RTÉ to show the advertisements, on the grounds that to do so would effectively be

---

[109] App. No.44179/98, judgment of July 10, 2003. *VgT v Switzerland* (above, n.97) was distinguished, as it concerned a matter of public interest to which a reduced margin of appreciation applied (para.67). As *Murphy* concerned religious expression, a wider margin of appreciation applied (para.70). See, in particular, paras 71-82.

[110] *The Irish Times*, February 19, 1999. Part of the advertisement ran: "The *Irish Catholic* – a lively and provocative family newspaper that connects the issues of today with the teachings of the church".

[111] *The Irish Times*, November 10, 2002, December 5, 7, 2002. The issue was raised in the Seanad on December 4, 2002 (*www.gov.ie/oireachtas*), where the ban was variously described as "offensive and an affront to pluralism" (Sen. Ryan) and "an inverted form of pluralism" (Sen. O'Rourke). The advertisement contained the words "these are hard times for the Catholic Church, so hard that it's easy to forget all the good the church does". Lawyers for RTÉ and the BCI interpreted this as addressing the merits and promoting religion, and therefore in breach of s.65.

[112] *The Sunday Tribune*, August 18, 2002, *The Irish Times*, September 20, 21, 24, 2002, *IRIS* 2003-2:11. The campaign was interdenominational and endorsed by the four main Christian churches in Ireland. The advertisements were described as spiritual in content, rather than religious.

[113] *The Irish Times*, September 20, 2002. It was believed that the advertisements breached s.65 of the Broadcasting Act 2001, in that they were not just notices of a religious event or newspaper, magazine or periodical but involved an element of persuasion. The advertisements invited viewers to call for a free book and CD.

disposing of issues set down for determination by the court at a full trial.[114]
Following negotiations, a modified version of the advertisements was accepted
and broadcast.[115]

8.2.3.3 Referenda Broadcasts

The allocation of airtime for referenda broadcasts has given rise to some disquiet
in recent years. *Coughlan v BCC and RTÉ*[116] concerned the 1995 referendum
on divorce. All of the political parties were in favour of a "Yes" vote and all
were given airtime by RTÉ for party political broadcasts advocating a "Yes"
vote. The Broadcasting Authority Act 1960, section 18(1), as replaced by
section 3 of the Broadcasting Authority (Amendment) Act 1976, required RTÉ
in its broadcast treatment of current affairs and matters of public controversy
and debate, to be fair to all interests concerned and to ensure that broadcast
matter is presented in an objective and impartial manner and without any
expression of the Authority's own views. If fairness cannot be achieved in a
single programme, it may be done in two or more programmes.[117] Allowance
is made for party political broadcasts.[118]

   The applicant complained to the Broadcasting Complaints Commission
(BCC) that RTÉ had infringed section 18 of the Act and, in effect, provided a
one-sided, unbalanced presentation of the referendum issue. RTÉ responded,
inter alia, that it allocated time to the political parties on the basis of well-
established guidelines but had no role in relation to the content of such
broadcasts. The High Court had found immediately prior to the referendum[119]
that RTÉ was entitled under section 18(2) to allocate time for party political
broadcasts at the time of the referendum. The BCC accordingly held against
the applicant in that respect but did accept that another broadcast by the Right
to Remarry group, which was not a party political broadcast, was not

---

[114] High Court, September 23, 2002, *The Irish Times*, September 24, 2002.

[115] *The Irish Times*, October 3, 2002. In March 2003 (*The Irish Times*, March 3, 2003) the
Minister for Communications, Marine and Natural Resources announced his intention
to review the legislative provisions in relation to religious advertising and initiated a
consultation process (*www.marine.gov.ie*).

[116] Above, n.10. Previous cases concerning the referendum process included *Hanafin v
The Minister for the Environment* [1996] 2 I.R. 321, *McKenna v An Taoiseach (No.2)*
[1995] 2 I.R. 10, *Crotty v An Taoiseach* [1987] I.R. 713. Other complaints upheld by
the Broadcasting Complaints Commission (BCC) include one from the Workers Party
that RTÉ was unfair to it in its coverage of the Amsterdam Treaty referendum (*The Irish
Times*, August 27, 1999) and one from an individual that a radio programme had been
unfair in its coverage of the divorce referendum (*The Irish Times*, October 21, 1999).
See also the annual reports of the BCC.

[117] S.3(1)(b) and 3(1)(c) respectively.

[118] S.18(2). Walsh, J. had pointed out in *The State (Lynch) v Cooney* [1982] I.R. 337 that
RTÉ is under no statutory or other obligation to transmit political broadcasts but is
entitled to do so. In the case of party political broadcasts, RTÉ exerts no editorial control
over the content, except to ensure that there is no breach of any law by which RTÉ is
bound. As Barrington, J. pointed out in *Coughlan* (at 37), political parties are not
expressly mentioned in the Constitution.

[119] *Patrick Kenny v RTÉ*, High Court, Laffoy J., November 20, 1995.

counterbalanced and did breach section 18(1) of the Act. Mr Coughlan sought a judicial review of the BCC's decision.

In the High Court, Carney J. held that RTÉ's approach had "resulted in inequality amounting to unconstitutional [*sic*] unfairness, which would not have arisen had their starting point been to afford equality to each side of the argument to which there could only be a YES or NO answer". He therefore quashed the decision of the BCC. The Supreme Court dismissed the appeal. Hamilton C.J. held that in deciding to transmit party political broadcasts, RTÉ must have regard to fair procedures and exercise its power in a constitutional manner. "In the case of a referendum which has as its objective the amendment of the Constitution", the Chief Justice said, "fair procedures require that the scales should be held equally between those who support and those who oppose the amendment".[120] Political parties have no right, whether under the statute or under the Constitution, to be afforded the opportunity by RTÉ to make party political broadcasts. It is purely a matter for the discretion of RTÉ.[121]

Denham J. stressed the importance of the referendum process as a tool for direct democracy and the difference between the referendum process and that of an election. In a referendum, unlike an election, there is a single issue, and the presentation of that issue to the public is different to that in an election. As a tool of direct democracy, the system should be fair, equal and impartial. However, mathematical equality was not a requirement of constitutional fairness and equality. It might be necessary to hold no party political broadcasts in a referendum campaign.[122] Both Keane J. and Barron J., also dismissing the appeal, discussed the legislative basis for party political broadcasts and uncontested broadcasts by other identifiable groups, pointing out the fact that RTÉ allowed non-political parties to make uncontested broadcasts similar to party political broadcasts, although they appeared to have no power to do so.[123]

Only Barrington J. dissented. Interestingly, in his commentary on the statutory provisions and the various types of broadcasts involved, he remarked that RTÉ might be "under a constitutional obligation to observe some kind of pro-

---

[120] *Coughlan*, at 25.

[121] *ibid.*

[122] *ibid.* at 28, 30–1; *cf.* Barrington J. at 42–43. Looking to the future, Denham J. remarked that constitutional principles of equality and fairness would continue to be important as narrowcasting is developed, as methods of communication which can be retrieved and viewed individually and repeatedly through electronic communication such as the internet, are developed (at 32).

[123] Keane, J. at 51–2, Barron, J. at 60. Also on the issue of referenda, the European Commission in *Bader v Austria* (App. No.26633/95, (1996) 22 E.H.R.R. CD 213) rejected a complaint that the Austrian authorities had supplied insufficient information to the electorate to enable them to vote in a referendum on accession to the EU. It did so on the basis of the Court's case law on access to information in *Gaskin v UK* ((1989) 12 E.H.R.R. 36) and *Leander v Sweden* ((1987) 9 E.H.R.R. 433). See also *Guerra v Italy* (judgment of February 19, 1998), where the applicants complained that the state had not informed the population of the risks run or the measures to be taken in the event of an accident at a nearby chemical plant. Art.10 was not applicable because the public's right to receive information does not impose positive obligations on the state to gather and disseminate information.

portionality" in the allocation of time to private citizens collectively and to political parties.[124] Describing a referendum as "the ultimate act of sovereignty", he identified the need for the people to be well-informed and therefore the need for RTÉ in its allocation of airtime not to play down or neutralise the role of political leaders in favour of committed amateurs, which would be "unwise".[125] He concluded that there was "no constitutional inequality or unfairness and no breach of democratic values in allowing political leaders access to the airwaves at referendum time on conditions dissimilar to those granted to private citizens but related to their social function as political leaders of the people".[126]

Further Reading

Council of Europe, *Media and Elections Handbook* (Council of Europe Publishing, Strasbourg, 1999).

Esposito, Gianluca, "Racist and Xenophobic Content on the Internet – Problems and Solutions: The Additional Protocol to the Convention on Cybercrime", I.J.C.L.P. Web-Doc, July 9, 2003 (International Journal of Communications Law and Policy, *www.digital-law.net/IJCLP/7_2003/ijclp_webdoc_9_7_2003.htm*).

Rorive, Isabelle, "Racist and Xenophobic Content on the Internet – Problems and Solutions: Strategies to Tackle Racism and Xenophobia on the Internet – Where are we in Europe?" I.J.C.L.P. Web-Doc, July 8, 2003 (*www.digital-law.net/IJCLP/7_2003/ijclp_webdoc_8_7_2003.htm*).

---

[124] *ibid.* at 39, although he did not elaborate the precise point.

[125] *ibid.* at 43. See also his remarks (at 44) on RTÉ's role in ensuring that the people are well informed ("by upholding 'the democratic values enshrined in the Constitution, especially those relating to rightful liberty of expression'") and on the major role of radio and television in our democratic society (at 45).

[126] *ibid.* at 46. The High Court (February 24, 2003) rejected a claim by the Green Party to a court order requiring RTÉ to provide live coverage of its Árd Fheis. Miss Justice Carroll pointed out that this was not a referendum and that it was not for the courts to lay down the criteria that should apply (*The Irish Times*, February 25, 2003).

CHAPTER NINE

Moral Censorship of the Media

"[T]he public is the real censor".[1]

9.1 INTRODUCTION

As we have already seen, the Constitution in Article 40.6.1 lays considerable emphasis on public order and morality, repeating the phrase in its specific reference to the press and adding a tailpiece indicating that the publication or utterance of blasphemous, seditious or indecent matter is an offence, punishable in accordance with law. The Article does not create an offence; it merely acknowledges that such publication or utterance is an offence, which is capable of being punished ("punishable") by law. Article 9 of the 1922 Constitution had also guaranteed freedom of expression "for purposes not opposed to public morality".

Public morality is still regarded today as a legitimate reason for restricting freedom of expression, although perceptions of what will offend against public morals have undoubtedly changed since 1937. All the international human rights documents recognise the protection of public morals as a legitimate restriction, but the respective courts accept that the concept of morality changes over time and from one culture to another, so that states must be entitled to some latitude, a "margin of appreciation", in deciding their own standards and requirements. Nonetheless, a state that invokes public morality as a ground for restricting freedom of expression bears the onus of demonstrating that the restriction in question is essential to the maintenance of respect for the fundamental values of the community.[2] The European Court of Human Rights has emphasised repeatedly that the domestic margin of appreciation is not unlimited and goes hand in hand with a European supervision of both the aim of the measure, as adopted and applied, and its necessity.[3]

9.2 OFFENCES AGAINST PUBLIC MORALITY

In assessing the extent of restrictions in Ireland in the interests of public morality, consideration must be given first to the offences referred to in the tailpiece to

---

[1] G.B. Shaw, *The Shewing-up of Blanco Posnet* (Penguin Books, London, 1987), p.38.
[2] Siracusa Principles (Principles on the Limitation and Derogation of Provisions in the International Covenant on Civil and Political Rights, Annex, UN Doc E/CN.4/1984/4 (1984)), No.27 "public morals" (1985) 7 H.R.Q. 1.
[3] *Handyside v UK* (1979) 1 E.H.R.R. 737, at 49.

Article 40.6.1.i of the Constitution. Blasphemous and indecent matter will be discussed here and seditious matter will be covered in Chapter 10.

9.2.1 Blasphemy

Blasphemy has both a public order dimension and a moral dimension. Indeed, blasphemy at one time could be equated with sedition, when the Church was regarded as an institution of the State, which was not to be subjected to criticism. Equally, any criticism of the Church or Christian doctrine was regarded as blasphemous, even if put forward in good faith and in all seriousness and expressed in temperate language. Even the author of a book entitled *A Humble Inquiry into the Scripture Account of Jesus Christ*, published in Dublin in 1702, was prosecuted, not for blasphemy but for sedition.[4] His inquiry was later described as "candid", and it was decided that he had not spoken with irreverence of Christ, so he could not be convicted on that ground. Punishment was severe – in this case a fine of £1,000, a colossal amount of money at the time, and a year's imprisonment, as well as security for good behaviour for life. The law merely reflected prevailing attitudes and values. Students might be interested to know that an undergraduate at Trinity College Dublin was expelled in 1794 "for expressing heretical and blasphemous opinions to the effect that Christ was not the son of God, that the mode of creation described in Genesis was unreasonable, and that Hell did not answer his conception of a future state".[5] Fortunately, moral principles and values change.[6]

9.2.1.1 Definitions

In relation to blasphemy, the Constitution seems to contemplate two offences: publication and utterance. Common law, in addition, contemplated blasphemous acts, such as burning the Bible. Statute law, on the other hand, appears more concerned with publication,[7] although a number of nineteenth-century Acts penalised the singing of profane songs in public and the use of profane language. However, it is not clear whether they meant blasphemous language or merely language that was offensive.[8] The Criminal Justice (Public Order) Act 1994, for instance, is concerned, *inter alia*, with offensive language and conduct (sections 5–7).

One advantage that statute law has over common law is that it provides for limits on penalties, whereas common law treated all blasphemy as an indictable misdemeanour subject to imprisonment for a fixed but unlimited period. There

---

[4] See Paul O'Higgins, "Blasphemy in Irish Law" (1960) 23 M.L.R. 151, at p.159.

[5] *ibid.*, p.160, citing R.B. McDowell, *Irish Public Opinion 1750–1800* (Faber & Faber, London, 1944).

[6] See generally, Neville Cox, "Sacrilege and Sensibility: The Value of Irish Blasphemy Law" (1997)19 D.U.L.J. 87, at p.99.

[7] See, for example, the Defamation Act 1961, ss.13 and 18, which confer a privilege for court reporting that does not extend to the publication of blasphemous matter.

[8] For example, the Dublin Police Act 1842, Indecent Advertisements Act 1889, Towns Improvement (Ireland) Act 1854.

is, however, no statutory definition of blasphemy and little by way of enlightenment from the courts.[9] In fact, the English Law Commission[10] has acknowledged that there is no single, comprehensive definition of the crime of blasphemy, and the Irish Law Reform Commission has concluded that there is no certainty as to its precise scope and essential ingredients.[11]

A definition offered by Smith and Hogan is that, at common law, "matter is blasphemous if it denies the truth of the Christian religion or of the Bible or the Book of Common Prayer or the existence of God", and a publication is blasphemous "if it is couched in indecent or offensive terms likely to shock and outrage the feelings of the general body of Christian believers in the community".[12] The offence in English law, therefore, relates only to the feelings of Christians and intention or motive is not relevant; it is enough that the publication is "likely to" cause shock and outrage. In the Irish context, Ó Síocháin defined it as "to speak or write offensively about God or religion as to deny the existence of God, or to bring God or religion into contempt, ridicule or disbelief",[13] while Murdoch says it consists of "indecent and offensive attacks on Christianity, or the Scriptures, or sacred persons or objects calculated to outrage the feelings of the community.... The mere denial of Christian teaching is not sufficient to constitute the offence".[14]

The Supreme Court in *Corway v Independent Newspapers*[15] in 1999 pointed out that there was no definition of blasphemy in the Constitution or in legislation, although section 7(2) of the Censorship of Films Act 1923, and section 13(1) of the Defamation Act 1961, assume its existence without defining it. The task of defining blasphemy, the Court said, is a matter for the legislature, not for the courts. It did say, however, that, in keeping with Article 44 of the Constitution, it must extend beyond the confines of the Christian religions.[16]

---

[9]   See, for example, above, n.4, pp.163–4. The Supreme Court judgments in *Corway v Independent Newspapers* ([1999] 4 I.R. 484, discussed below) highlight the uncertainties and anomalies and the impossible task of determining the scope of the crime of blasphemy.

[10] *Report on Offences against Religion and Public Worship* (No.145, 1985).

[11] *Report on the Crime of Libel* (LRC 41–1991), at p.11.

[12] See J.C. Smith and B. Hogan, *Criminal Law* (9th ed., Butterworths, London, 1999), at pp.714-715 [citations omitted], citing early case law and the House of Lords in *Whitehouse v Gay News Ltd and Lemon* [1979] A.C. 617, [1979] 1 All E.R. 898, [1979] Crim L.R. 311. From the nineteenth century the emphasis began to be placed on the language and manner of the publication, the tendency to "shake the fabric of society and to be a cause of civil strife" (*Bowman v Secular Society Ltd* [1917] A.C. 406, at 466, Lord Sumner). See also *Blackstone's Criminal Practice 2002* (OUP, Oxford, 2002), B19.7 "Blasphemy and Blasphemous Libel", and *Corway v Independent Newspapers*, above, n.9, at 495-6.

[13] *The Criminal Law of Ireland* (7th ed., Foilseacháin Dlí, Dublin, 1981), at p.307. This definition is regarded by O'Higgins, above, n.4, at pp.165-6 as "not very helpful", "circular and not of much value".

[14] *Dictionary of Irish Law* (Topaz Publications, Dublin, 1988; 3rd ed., 2000). Walsh, J. in *Quinn's Supermarket v Attorney General* [1972] I.R. 1, stated that Art.44 of the Constitution does not refer exclusively to the Christian deity. Art.8 of the 1922 Constitution, which provided for freedom of conscience and religion, expressly stated that "no law may be made either directly or indirectly to endow any religion, or prohibit or restrict the free exercise thereof or give any preference, or impose any disability on account of religious belief or religious status ...".

[15] Above, n.9.

[16] *ibid.* at 501.

The Constitution Review Group (CRG) in 1996 made the point that Article 44.2.3 could provide a basis for widening the application of blasphemy laws to encompass other religions but concluded that they would be better abolished than extended.[17]

9.2.1.2 Applicability

The English *Gay News* case, which first addressed the problems of blasphemy law in a modern-day context, concerned a poem in a journal for homosexuals, depicting Christ as a homosexual in explicit detail.[18] Leave to commence a criminal prosecution[19] had been granted by a judge pursuant to section 8 of the Libel Act 1888, the equivalent of section 8 of the Defamation Act 1961 in Ireland, but the Director of Public Prosecutions declined to take over the prosecution. The charge was that the *Gay News* had "unlawfully and wickedly published or caused to be published a blasphemous libel concerning the Christian religion, namely an obscene poem and illustration vilifying Christ in his life and crucifixion".[20] The last such case to be tried in Britain had been in 1921-2.[21]

In *Gay News* the court was taken up with questions of intention. The trial judge ruled that "intention to publish" was all that was required.[22] The publisher was accordingly fined £1,000 and sentenced to nine months' imprisonment, suspended for eighteen months. The editor was fined £500. The Court of Appeal rejected the appeal and the case went to the House of Lords on a point of law only: the question of intention. There it was decided by a majority that an intention to blaspheme was not necessary, just an intention to publish.[23] In other words, blasphemous libel was a strict liability offence, and once the matter was published, motives – good, bad or indifferent – were irrelevant. At the same time, reasoned argument or a mere denial of the existence of God was insufficient, the Court said, as the offence encompasses "any contemptuous, reviling, scurrilous or ludicrous matter relating to God, Jesus Christ, or the Bible, or the formularies of the Church of England".[24] As with other forms of

---

[17] *Report of the Constitution Review Group* (Pn. 2632, Dublin, May 1996), p.297. The European Court of Human Rights found it anomalous that the notion of an offence of blasphemy confined to the Christian religions could persist in a modern, multi-denominational society: *Wingrove v United Kingdom*, November 25, 1996, Reports of Judgments and Decisions, 1996–V (1996) 24 E.H.R.R. 1, para.50.

[18] *R v Lemon* [1979] 2 W.L.R. 281. The poem was accompanied by a drawing illustrating its subject matter.

[19] A private prosecution was brought by Mrs Mary Whitehouse, a veteran campaigner for high moral standards in the media. The case was, therefore, known in the first instance as *Whitehouse v Lemon* (above, n.12) and variously as *R v Lemon* or *R v Gay News* [1979] A.C. 617; [1978] 68 Cr. App. R 381.

[20] *ibid.* at 620.

[21] *R v Gott* (1922) 16 Cr. App. R. 87, cited in *Gay News*. See also Geoffrey Robertson, *The Justice Game* (Vintage, London, 1999), p.137.

[22] Above, n.19, at 620.

[23] *ibid.* at 665.

[24] *Per* Lord Scarman, quoting Art.214 of Stephens' *Digest of the Criminal Law* (9th ed., 1950).

criminal libel, it was no longer necessary to prove a tendency to cause a breach of the peace. The Law Lords did agree, however, that the law of blasphemous libel was unclear.[25]

When the case went to the European Commission of Human Rights,[26] the British government invoked three separate grounds of justification for the restriction on freedom of expression imposed by the prosecution for blasphemous libel, namely, the prevention of disorder, the protection of morals, and the rights of others. The Commission found that there had been no violation of Article 10 of the Convention and that the restriction imposed had the legitimate purpose of protecting the rights of citizens not to be offended in their religious feelings by publications.[27] Offensiveness, therefore, was the key and the justification for the restriction on freedom of expression, although the Commission did not elaborate on this point.[28] Provided the principle of proportionality inherent in Article 10(2) was respected, it was a matter for the state concerned how it wished to define the offence. The common-law offence of blasphemous libel did not seem disproportionate to the Commission, despite the fact that it was a strict liability offence and did not take account of the intended audience, nor was there any defence for literary or artistic merit.[29]

9.2.1.3 Blasphemous Libel

The decision in *Gay News* had major repercussions several years later when Salman Rushdie's book *The Satanic Verses* was published and provoked a Muslim backlash. The book deeply offended many Muslims and was banned in all Muslim countries. There were public demonstrations in the UK and other countries, a number of people died as a result and a "fatwa", or death threat, was issued against the author. The Muslim community in the UK wanted Rushdie prosecuted for blasphemy but as the common-law offence of blasphemous libel had been held to apply only to Christian religions, the court action failed.[30]

The case raised questions not only about the scope of the common-law offence of blasphemous libel but also about the desirability of a blasphemy law and its implications for freedom of speech. If Mr Rushdie's right to freedom of expression was to prevail and the Muslim community was not entitled to protection under the law, then the same standards would have to apply to the rights of the Muslims to freedom of expression. Thus the question of banning

---

[25] *ibid.* at 633 and 657.

[26] *Gay News and Lemon v UK*, App. No.8710/79, (1983) 5 E.H.R.R. 123.

[27] *ibid.* at 130.

[28] *ibid.*

[29] *ibid.*

[30] *R v Chief Metropolitan Stipendiary Magistrate, ex parte Choudhury* [1991] 1 All E.R. 306, [1991] Q.B. 429. The court would not extend the offence to cover other religions because it would be "virtually impossible by judicial decision to set sufficiently clear limits to the offence and other problems involved are formidable" (at 318). *Choudhury* was declared inadmissible by the European Commission of Human Rights (*Choudhury v UK*, App. No.17439/90, March 5, 1991, (1991) 12 H.R.L.J. 172), just as *Gay News* had been.

a film, *International Guerrillas* (1990), that depicted Rushdie as a drunkard, a sadist, a torturer and a murderer, who at the end of the film was murdered by God, could not be entertained, as Rushdie himself was first to recognise. How could one insist on freedom to publish *The Satanic Verses* and then advocate the banning of a film demonising the author?[31] When the question of a new paperback edition of *The Satanic Verses* was drawing further ire from the Muslims in Britain and elsewhere, the Muslim community in Ireland was quoted as saying that they would prefer if the publisher did not go ahead with the paperback edition because they would see it as an insult to Muslim "feelings" rather than as the upholding of free speech.[32] It is arguable, therefore, that the essence of the offence of blasphemy is offensiveness and hurt to religious feelings rather than an attack on God or religion as such.

These developments in England have prompted questions as to whether blasphemous libel should be abolished altogether or extended to protect the feelings of people of other religions. Blasphemous libel is a form of criminal libel and contains all the same uncertainties and anomalies as the other forms (defamatory, obscene and seditious libel). That being so, it is arguable that there is nothing to be gained from retaining it in any shape or form, and if it is already problematic, there can be no value in extending it to other religions.

In Ireland, the Law Reform Commission has concluded that there is no place for an offence of blasphemous libel in a society that respects freedom of speech.[33] However, the Commission does not think it is possible to abolish blasphemous libel without a referendum because of the constitutional requirement in the tailpiece to Article 40.6.1.i.[34] At any rate, prosecutions for blasphemous libel are now virtually unknown, although occasionally attempts are made or threats issued. In one case,[35] the High Court was told that a series of posters carrying messages like "Kill God", which had been displayed on billboards around Dublin, had been removed, so no injunctive relief was granted. The applicant had complained that display of the posters constituted the offence of blasphemy, as well as blasphemous libel.[36]

---

[31] The story-line, briefly, was that a character named Salman Rushdie wanted Pakistan, the stronghold of Islam, to fall. To that end, he planned to spread vice and debauchery, but three brothers (God's soldiers) set out to foil his plans and destroy him before he would manage to destroy all virtue and decency on the planet. On the freedom of expression issues involved, see Ellen Hazelkorn and Patrick Smyth (eds), *Let in the Light: Censorship, Secrecy and Democracy* (Brandon Book Publishers, Dingle, 1993), particularly the chapter by Rushdie himself, p.26, at pp.35-6, where he concludes that "[I]t has to be the thing you loathe that you tolerate, otherwise you don't believe in freedom of speech".

[32] *The Irish Times*, January 20, 1990. The tone and language of the novel gave offence. If offensiveness is the essence of blasphemy, then it is arguable that statute law aimed at public order and incitement to hatred would suffice to protect against it. See above Chapter 8. The European Court of Human Rights in the later case of *Wingrove v UK* ((1996) 24 E.H.R.R. 1) rejected such an argument on the basis that the other laws referred to in that case pursued related but distinct aims and did not specifically provide protection against seriously offensive attacks on matter regarded as sacred by Christians (at para.57).

[33] Above, n.11, at p.11.

[34] *ibid.*

[35] *O'Mahony v Levine*, unreported, High Court, October 17, 1994.

[36] A small percentage of complaints to newspapers from time to time allege blasphemy, but

The whole issue of blasphemy in Irish law was considered by the Supreme Court in 1999 in *Corway v Independent Newspapers*,[37] the first case of blasphemy in Ireland since 1855. Leave to prosecute for blasphemous libel had been sought in the High Court pursuant to section 8 of the Defamation Act 1961 and had been refused. The complaint concerned a cartoon published in the *Sunday Independent* in November 1995, depicting a priest and three prominent politicians, under the caption "Hello progress – bye bye Father". The caption was a play on the slogan "Hello divorce – bye bye Daddy", used during the November 1995 divorce referendum by some anti-divorce campaigners. The priest was holding a host in one hand and a chalice in the other. The applicant complained that the cartoon and caption were calculated to insult the feelings and religious convictions of readers generally by treating the sacrament of the Eucharist and its administration as objects of scorn.

The Supreme Court, having traced the evolution of the crime of blasphemy in England and Ireland, reviewed it in light of the 1922 Constitution. The Court concluded that the guarantees of freedom of conscience, religion and expression in Articles 8 and 9 of the 1922 Constitution were wide enough to cover all religions and none:

> "The tenets of any one religion do not enjoy greater protection in law than those of any other. There can be no question therefore of the mere publication of an opinion on a religious matter constituting a criminal offence unless the publication is such as to undermine public order or morality.
>
> Article 73 [of the 1922 Constitution] carried forward the laws of the previous regime:
>
> > "Subject to this Constitution and to the extent to which they are not inconsistent therewith".
>
> It is debatable to what extent, if at all, it carried forward the common law in relation to blasphemy".[38]

---

the term is used in a very broad sense by complainants to cover anything critical of the Church or religious beliefs or devotions. See generally on newspaper complaints, Kevin Boyle and Marie McGonagle, *Media Accountability: The Readers' Representative in Irish Newspapers* (National Newspapers of Ireland, Dublin, 1995).

[37] Above, n.9.

[38] *ibid.* at 499–500, Barrington J. The Court went on to say that if the Church of England had been disestablished and if England had introduced a secular Constitution it was highly probable that the debate in the House of Lords in *R v Lemon* (the *Gay News* case, above, nn.18, 19) would have taken a different course. As a result, the *Gay News* case did not appear to be a safe guide for the Court to follow in the present case. For a commentary on the *Corway* case, see Stephen Ranalow, "Bearing a Constitutional Cross: Examining Blasphemy and the Judicial Role in *Corway v Independent Newspapers*" (2000) 3 *Trinity College Law Review* 95. Freedom of conscience and the free profession and practice of religion are protected, subject to public order and morality, in the Irish Constitution 1937, Art.44.2.1, and are widely protected also in the international human rights instruments, *e.g.* Art.18 of the Universal Declaration of Human Rights, Art.18 of the ICCPR (and HRC General Comment No.22 (48/1993)), Art.9 of the ECHR. Art.44.2.3 of the Irish Constitution provides that the State shall not impose any disabilities or make any discrimination on the ground of religious profession, belief or status.

Furthermore, it was difficult to see how, related as it was to an established church (the Church of Ireland was disestablished in 1869), it could survive in the framework of the 1937 Constitution. The effect of Articles 44 (religion) and 40.1 (equality) of the 1937 Constitution was to guarantee:

> "Freedom of conscience, the free profession and practice of religion and equality before the law to all citizens, be they Roman Catholics, Protestants, Jews, Muslims, agnostics or atheists. But Article 44 goes further and places the duty on the State to respect and honour religion as such. At the same time the State is not placed in the position of an arbiter of religious truth. Its only function is to protect public order and morality. ... [I]t is difficult to see how the view of the majority in the House of Lords in *R v Lemon* that the mere act of publication of blasphemous matter without proof of any intention to blaspheme is sufficient to support a conviction of blasphemy would be reconciled with a Constitution guaranteeing freedom of conscience and the free profession and practice of religion" (at 501).

In the absence of legislation and in the present uncertain state of the law, the Court could not see its way to authorising the institution of a criminal prosecution for blasphemy. The cartoon may indeed have been in very bad taste but the Court concluded that no insult was intended, and dismissed the appeal. Thus, despite the reference in the Constitution to the publication or utterance of blasphemous matter, it is unlikely, in the absence of legislation, that future applications for prosecutions for blasphemous libel will be entertained in the Irish courts.

9.2.1.4 Statute Law

Existing statutes that make reference to blasphemy include the Censorship of Films Act 1923. The film censor can refuse a certificate for a film on the grounds, *inter alia*, that it is blasphemous (section 7), but the Act does not define what is meant by blasphemous, nor does it set out criteria for the censor to apply. The censor has exercised this power in relation to a number of films, such as Monty Python's "Life of Brian", which was banned in 1979 on grounds of blasphemy, but later released following resubmission to the censor.[39] Some films, like Jean-Luc Godard's "Hail Mary", were not even submitted to the censor because of the expectation that they would not receive a certificate.[40]

It is perhaps surprising that there is no reference to blasphemy in the Wireless Telegraphy Act 1926,[41] nor in the Censorship of Publications Acts 1929–67, as a ground for banning books or periodicals. It is even more surprising that blasphemy should have been included in the Censorship of Films Act 1923

---

[39] *The Sunday Tribune*, August 16, 1987. A ban lasts for seven years under the Censorship of Films (Amendment) Act 1970.

[40] *The Irish Times*, February 22, 1987.

[41] The omission may be due to how radio was viewed and controlled at the time as a state "service", *i.e.* a cultural and educational medium, rather than an entertainment medium.

and not a few years later in the Censorship of Publications Act 1929,[42] although it has to be said that there are other surprising differences between the two Acts. For instance, provision was made in the former for an appeal from the film censor's decision, whereas in the latter, no provision for appeal was made until an amending Act was brought in in 1946.

The Defamation Act 1961 makes it an indictable offence to compose, print or publish any blasphemous libel (section 13), an offence punishable by a maximum fine of £500 and/or two years' imprisonment, or seven years' penal servitude. It also makes provision for seizure by the gardaí of all copies of the libel. The severity of these penalties provided for in the Act indicates the seriousness with which the offence was viewed at one time.[43] The fact that a person who "composes" a libel can be guilty of the offence in the same way as anyone who prints or publishes a libel suggests that publication to a third party is not a necessary element of the offence.[44] All of Part II of the Act, which deals with "criminal proceedings for libel", applies to blasphemous libel, as a form of criminal libel, except where the section specifically deals with defamatory libel only, for example, sections 6, 11 and 12. An order of a judge of the High Court is needed, therefore, for the prosecution of a newspaper (section 8).[45] It should be remembered that Part II does not apply to broadcasting. Nor do the Broadcasting Acts make any reference to blasphemy, even though the Broadcasting Authority Act 1960 was passed just one year before the Defamation Act. It may also be noted that the privilege that attaches to fair and accurate reports of court proceedings in section 18(1) does not extend to the publication of any blasphemous matter that might arise therein. The subsection does not prevent the publication of blasphemous matter, but it is at least conceivable that a reporter who omitted such matter from a report could lose the privilege on the grounds that the report was not then fair and accurate.[46]

There is no mention of blasphemy, as such, in the Video Recordings Act 1989, section 3, which allows the censor to refuse a certificate if the video would, among other things, be likely to stir up hatred against a group of persons on account of their religion. This reflects a more modern interpretation of the essence of blasphemy and the type of harm the law seeks to prevent. In 1989 the first video to be banned in England for blasphemy by the British Board of Film Classification (BBFC) was "Visions of Ecstasy", a short film containing images of St Teresa of Avila partly naked and writhing in ecstasy before Christ

---

[42] Apparently a reference to blasphemy was dropped from the original Censorship of Publications Bill because of the fear of anti-Protestant or anti-Semitic crusades: see *The Irish Times*, February 9, 1985. It is unlikely that it was intended that blasphemy should come under the general rubric of material that was indecent or obscene.

[43] The Defamation Act 1961 was intended primarily as a consolidating act, carrying over provisions of various nineteenth-century Acts.

[44] The House of Lords in *R v Gay News* (above, n.19) found that an intention to publish was required. The term "composes", which is not defined in the Act, may refer to the setting up of the type, as a stage in the printing process.

[45] As to the criteria that apply, see Ch. 8 regarding *Hilliard v Penfield Enterprises*.

[46] It is not clear what the subsection actually achieves. It attempts to discourage reporters from including blasphemous or obscene matter in court reports.

on the cross.[47] At that time the Irish Video Recordings Act had not yet come into force.

The underlying concerns of blasphemy appear in the modern context to have been largely replaced by concerns to protect people from religious hatred. As seen in Chapter 8 above, the Prohibition on Incitement to Hatred Act 1989 defines hatred as including hatred against a group of persons in the State or elsewhere on account of their religion (section 1). The Act is wide enough to cover words and images in both print and audiovisual media which "are threatening, abusive or insulting and are intended or, having regard to all the circumstances, are likely to stir up hatred" (section 2(1)).

As mentioned at the start of this discussion, the Constitution says that the publication or utterance of blasphemous matter is an offence punishable by law. Depending on how one defines the essence of blasphemous matter, particularly with reference to the modern-day context, it could be argued that the common-law offence of blasphemous libel could be abolished. It could be abolished because existing statutory provisions meet the requirements to protect against religious discrimination and speech that is threatening, abusive or insulting and intended to, or likely to, stir up hatred. If necessary, the statutory provisions could be strengthened, or recast, to protect from outrage or attack the feelings of religious groups, if that is seen as an appropriate aim and a justifiable reason for curtailing free speech. However, it is arguable that the real harm to be guarded against is not so much injury to feelings as the stirring up of religious hatred, with its implications for public order. Injury to feelings may be a rather tenuous and anomalous basis on which to restrict freedom of expression.[48] A reconsideration of existing law should be undertaken in accordance with Ireland's international obligations.

Religious hatred is included in some but not all of the international instruments. The International Convention on the Elimination of All Forms of Racial Discrimination (ICERD) 1966 does not define "racial discrimination" to include religious hatred (Article 1). Article 20(2) of the International Covenant on Civil and Political Rights, on the other hand, declares that "Any advocacy of national, racial or religious hatred that constitutes incitement to discrimination, hostility or violence shall be prohibited by law". The European Convention on Human Rights 1950 does not expressly mention religious hatred, although Article 10 (freedom of expression) can be restricted on the basis of "the rights of others" and Article 14 ensures that the rights and freedoms provided for in the Convention shall be secured without discrimination, *inter alia*, on the grounds of religion. The European Convention on Transfrontier Television 1989 requires respect for human dignity and the fundamental rights of others in programme services and specifically mentions racial hatred, though not religious hatred (Article 7).[49] The EC Television without Frontiers Directive

---

[47] A full description is given in paras 9 and 61 of the judgment of the Strasbourg Court: *Wingrove v UK* (1996) 24 E.H.R.R. 1.

[48] See Law Reform Commission, *Consultation Paper on the Crime of Libel*, 1991, at p.170.

[49] Programme services shall not be indecent and in particular shall not contain pornography (Art.7(1)(a)), or give undue prominence to violence or be likely to incite to racial hatred (Art.7(1)(b)).

1989, as amended, requires Member States to ensure that broadcasts do not contain any incitement to hatred on grounds of race, sex, religion or nationality (Article 22a).

There would appear to be adequate protection, therefore, against hatred, including religious hatred, in both national and international law, without the need to retain blasphemous libel, "an offence which originated in a period of religious intolerance and was governed by different conceptions of the role of the Church in State matters [... and so] would be totally incompatible with modern conditions".[50] Other aspects of racism and the media are discussed in Chapter 8 above.

9.2.1.5 European Court of Human Rights

The views of the European Court of Human Rights in *Jersild v Denmark*,[51] although dealing with racial hatred, are instructive in this regard. The Court upheld the right of the journalist to broadcast an interview with a racist group as part of the information role of the media. The remarks might well have been offensive to many but the journalist's aim and the effect of the programme were not to promote those ideas or to stir up hatred but merely to inform the viewing public of an ill that existed in their society. The real difficulty lies in trying to square the decision in *Jersild*, which concerned racist speech, with that in *Otto-Preminger Institut v Austria*,[52] which concerned blasphemy. The case involved a film, based on a play written in 1894, which portrayed God the Father as old, infirm and ineffective, Jesus Christ as a "mummy's boy" of low intelligence and Mary, who is obviously in charge, as an unprincipled wanton. The story line was their decision to punish mankind for its immorality by causing men and women to infect each other with a sexually transmitted disease - a punishment suggested by the devil - but to leave the possibility of redemption. The film was to be shown in the applicant's cinema in Innsbruck to members of the public over seventeen years of age. An application for the seizure of the film and later for its forfeiture was granted by the Austrian courts.[53]

The European Court of Human Rights found that the authorities had not violated Article 10 when they seized the film. The fact that the film was to be shown in a predominantly Roman Catholic area meant that the authorities had acted to ensure religious peace in the region. The national authorities were in a better position to assess the need for such a measure in the circumstances than an international court.[54] In other words, the Court continued its stance of

---

[50] Law Reform Commission, *Report on the Crime of Libel*, above, n.11, at p.11. The Commission also concluded that "it might well be that any problems in the area [covered by blasphemous libel] which might exist were adequately covered by these provisions [of the Prohibition of Incitement to Hatred Act]".

[51] *Jersild v Denmark*, Series A, No.298, (1995) 19 E.H.R.R. 1.

[52] Series A, No.295-A, (1995) 19 E.H.R.R. 34. See also Eamonn Hall, "Blasphemy" (1994) GILSI 361. The restraint in *Jersild* was held to constitute a violation of Art.10, while that in *Otto-Preminger* was not.

[53] *ibid.* at para.12.

[54] *ibid.* at para.56.

allowing States a wide margin of appreciation in cases involving issues of public morals. Three dissenting judges accepted that the showing of the film might have offended people but felt that, as the nature of the showing had been announced in advance and admission was confined to over-seventeens, the seizure and forfeiture of the film was not proportionate to the legitimate aim pursued.[55]

The key difference between *Jersild* and *Otto-Preminger*, it would seem, from the judgment of the Court, is that whereas the interview with the racist group in *Jersild* was part of a serious news programme and contributed information to the public, the film in *Otto-Preminger* was "gratuitously offensive" and did not "contribute to any form of public debate capable of furthering progress in human affairs".[56] As there was no discernible consensus throughout Europe as to the significance of religion in society, States must have a margin of appreciation, the Court said, but because of the importance of the freedoms involved and the necessity for any restriction to be convincingly established, the Court's supervision of that margin must be strict.[57] However, the Court accepted the arguments of the Austrian government that it needed to preserve the peace and prevent people feeling that their religion was the subject of unwarranted attacks, and that it had taken account of the "freedom of artistic expression" guaranteed by Article 10.[58]

It is clear from the later case of *Wingrove v UK*,[59] which concerned a video, that the Court places more weight on political speech than on artistic expression, at least in the area of morals and religion:

> "Whereas there is little scope under Article 10(2) of the Convention for restrictions on political speech or on debate on questions of public interest … a wider margin of appreciation is generally available to the Contracting States when regulating freedom of expression in relation to matters liable to offend intimate personal convictions within the sphere of morals or, especially, religion".[60]

In *Wingrove* the Court considered the British laws of blasphemy. It observed

---

[55] *ibid.* at para.11 of the joint dissenting opinion of Judges Palm, Pekkanen and Makarczyk. The Commission had taken a similar view but the majority of the Court was of the opinion that because the film was widely advertised it was sufficiently "public" to cause offence (at para.54). The decision that there had been no violation of Art.10 was by six votes to three.

[56] *ibid.* at para.49. The dissenting judges rejected this argument, as such a decision was bound to be tainted by the authorities' idea of "progress".

[57] *ibid.* at para.50. The dissenting judges pointed out that a right to protection of religious feelings was not expressly guaranteed by the Convention but "may" be a legitimate ground for restriction if necessary in a democratic society; *ibid.* at para.6 of the joint dissenting opinion.

[58] *ibid.* at para.56. *Cf. Muller v Switzerland*, Series A, No.133; (1991) 13 E.H.R.R. 212. See also David Pannick, "Religious Feelings and the European Court" (1995) P.L. 7.

[59] App. No.17419/90, (1997) 24 E.H.R.R. 1.

[60] *ibid.* at para.58. Judge Lohmus in his dissenting judgment referred to the different applications of the margin of appreciation and expressed the view that "it is difficult to ascertain what principles determine the scope of that margin of appreciation". The Court held by seven votes to two that there had been no breach of Art.10.

that strong arguments had been advanced in favour of the abolition of blasphemy laws, for example, that such laws may discriminate against different faiths or denominations, or that legal mechanisms are inadequate to deal with matters of faith or individual belief. However, the fact remains, the Court said, that:

> "[T]here is as yet not sufficient common ground in the legal and social orders of the member states of the Council of Europe to conclude that a system whereby a State can impose restrictions on the propagation of material on the basis that it is blasphemous is, in itself, unnecessary in a democratic society and thus incompatible with the Convention".[61]

The Court continued:

> "Moreover, as in the field of morals, and perhaps to an even greater degree, there is no uniform European conception of the requirements of "the protection of the rights of others" in relation to attacks on their religious convictions. What is likely to cause substantial offence to persons of a particular religious persuasion will vary significantly from time to time and from place to place, especially in an era characterised by an ever growing array of faiths and denominations. By reason of their direct and continuous contact with the vital forces of their countries, State authorities are in principle in a better position than the international judge to give an opinion on the exact content of these requirements with regard to the rights of others as well as on the "necessity" of a "restriction" intended to protect from such material those whose deepest feelings and convictions would be seriously offended" (para.58).

Hence the justification for leaving to participating states a wider margin of appreciation, subject to supervision. In *Wingrove*, the fact that it involved refusal of a certificate by the British Board of Film Classification meant that it was a form of prior restraint, and thus called for special scrutiny.[62] Nonetheless, the Court accepted that English law does not prohibit the expression of views hostile or offensive to the Christian religion but rather the manner in which the views are advocated. The high degree of profanation that must be attained, the Court said, constitutes, in itself, a safeguard against arbitrariness.[63] It appears also that the Court places more weight on the news and information

---

[61] *ibid.* at para.57. This statement appears to envisage a different test, a negative form of justification. A finding that there is not sufficient ground to conclude that something is unnecessary is not the same as a positive finding that a restriction was necessary in a democratic society in that it corresponded to a pressing social need, which is the normal test. Use of the qualifying words "as yet", however, appears to leave the door open for future cases to be decided differently. See further, Sandy Ghandhi and Jennifer James, "The English Law of Blasphemy and the European Convention on Human Rights" [1998] E.H.R.L.R. 430.

[62] *ibid.* at para.58. Judge de Meyer in his dissenting judgment took the view that this was a pure case of prior restraint, which was unacceptable in the field of freedom of expression.

[63] *ibid.* at para.60. On the issue of the protection of the English law of blasphemy extending only to the Christian religions, Judge Pettiti, in a separate judgment, said that it was

role of the media than it does on artistic expression in the form of film, video and what might collectively be called the entertainment media.[64] Most complaints involving restrictions in the interests of public morals that have been sent to Strasbourg have been found not to violate Article 10. A notable exception was *Open Door Counselling v Ireland*[65] which, unlike *Jersild* did not concern the media, but which did, like *Jersild*, concern information, in that case, abortion information.

While the distinction drawn by the Court is interesting, the reality is that there are few prosecutions for blasphemy nowadays. Nonetheless, the threat remains and material is sometimes withheld or excised, particularly from plays and films for television viewing, rather than run the risk of prosecution. That is to say, the continued existence of the offence in its uncertain state leads to a degree of self-censorship. It is possible also that the Christian principles underlying blasphemy have been internalised to such an extent that anything likely to constitute blasphemous matter will be suppressed, consciously or otherwise, even on grounds of good taste.[66] To the extent that blasphemy in its modern context appears to target offensiveness and outrage rather than doctrinal matters, the best form of protection seems to lie in the Prohibition of Incitement to Hatred Act 1989. The Act is wide enough to protect minority religions and ethnic groups. It also requires intention to incite, which incorporates the *mens rea* principle of criminal law, and respects the need for a threshold for freedom of expression: speech that falls short of incitement will not be restricted. As the dissenting judges in *Otto-Preminger* said:

> "The need for repressive action amounting to complete prevention of the exercise of freedom of expression can only be accepted if the behaviour concerned reaches so high a level of abuse, and comes so close to a denial of the freedom of religion of others, as to forfeit for itself the right to be tolerated by society".[67]

---

regrettable, because such a limitation makes no sense now that we have the UN and UNESCO instruments on tolerance. The ECHR does not prohibit such laws but does leave scope for reviewing them under Art.14. Judge Pettiti was not inclined to consider the matter in terms of blasphemy. He found it was the combination of an ostensibly philosophical message and wholly irrelevant obscene and pornographic images that was particularly shocking.

[64] In *Wingrove* the Court considered the fact that although the video was only of short duration and unlikely to have a large audience in the way that a full-length feature film would, videos could be copied, lent, rented, sold and viewed in different homes. However, it did not consider the medium of the video *per se*. Judge Pettiti took the view that the sale of videos in supermarkets is even more dangerous than the sale of books, as it is more difficult to ensure that the public are protected. He also pointed to the boundaries between literature, obscenity and pornography. Judge Lohmus, in his dissenting judgment, remarked, *inter alia*, that "Artistic impressions are often conveyed through images and situations which may shock or disturb the feelings of a person of average sensitivity". See further Paul Kearns, "The Uncultured God: Blasphemy Law's Reprieve and the Art Matrix" [2000] E.H.R.L.R. 512.

[65] Series A, No.246; (1993) 15 E.H.R.R. 244.

[66] See, generally, Richard Webster, *A Brief History of Blasphemy* (The Orwell Press, Southwold, 1990).

[67] Above, n.52, at para.7 of the joint dissenting opinion.

To sum up, the Australian Press Council, supporting the proposal of the New South Wales Law Reform Commission to abolish blasphemy, has said: "Blasphemy is an anachronistic and uncertain offence which is more likely to cause problems between groups than to prevent them".[68]

9.2.2 Indecent Matter and obscenity

The poem in the *Gay News* case was also described in the charge as obscene. The Irish Constitution refers to indecent matter; there is no mention of obscenity. The Censorship of Publications Act 1929 refers to both but defines only the word "indecent" which: "shall be construed as including suggestive of or inciting to sexual immorality or unnatural vice or likely in any other similar way to corrupt or deprave" (section 2).

Cockburn J. in *R v Hicklin*,[69] in 1868, put forward the following test for obscenity:

> "I think that the test of obscenity is this, whether the tendency of the matter charged as obscenity is to deprave or corrupt those whose minds are open to such immoral influences and into whose hands a publication of this sort may fall".

This test focused on the effect on the most vulnerable members of society. It was rejected in the United States in 1934, in favour of a standard focusing on the effect on the average person of the dominant theme of the work as a whole.[70] The test in *Hicklin* was later supplanted by a statutory definition in Canada and in the UK. The Canadian definition focused on the "undue exploitation" of sex or sex combined with violence: "Any publication, a dominant characteristic of which is the undue exploitation of sex, or of sex and any one of the following subjects, namely, crime, horror, cruelty and violence, shall be deemed to be obscene".[71]

The British legislation is the 1959 Obscene Publications Act. In that Act "indecent" means offensive, shocking, disgusting or revolting, whereas "obscene" means matter whose effect, if taken as a whole, is such as to tend to deprave and corrupt persons who are likely in all the circumstances to read, see or hear the matter contained or embodied in it (section 1).

The Irish definition of "indecent", therefore, is closer to the English definition of "obscene". Indeed, the two terms are used rather indiscriminately in Irish law.

The *Hicklin* test was examined in Ireland in 1959 in *AG v Simpson*,[72]

---

[68] Australian Press Council Submission to the Law Reform Commission of New South Wales on Blasphemy, April 14, 1992, *APC News*, May 1992.

[69] (1868) LR 3 Q.B. 360.

[70] See *US v One Book called 'Ulysses'* 5 F.Supp. 182 (1934); *Roth v US* 354 U.S. 476 (1957). The *Ulysses* standard was further refined in *Miller v California* 413 U.S. 15 (1973).

[71] An Act to Amend the Criminal Code, S.C. 1959, c.40 s.11.

[72] (1959) 93 I.L.T.R. 33. For the background to and details of the episode, see Gerard Whelan and Carolyn Swift, *Spiked: Church-State Intrigue and The Rose Tattoo* (New

where the District Justice quoted heavily from the English and American authorities, particularly *Roth v US*,[73] in which Brennan J. found that the *Hicklin* test was "unconstitutionally restrictive" of the freedoms of speech and press. In *Simpson*, Dublin theatre producer Alan Simpson was prosecuted for having produced for gain the Tennessee Williams play "The Rose Tattoo", the objection being that the performance was indecent, profane and obscene. The District Justice found that no *prima facie* case had been made out and Simpson was discharged.

9.2.2.1 Obscene Libel

Obscene libel is a common-law offence, a form of criminal libel, and all that has previously been said about criminal libel in any of its forms applies. In fact, the Defamation Act treats blasphemous libel and obscene libel almost identically. In Ireland, there has been no case law on obscene libel since 1929, because obscene publications have been dealt with under the Censorship of Publications Act of that year. Obscenity in the audiovisual media is also governed by statute.[74] The only prosecutions for obscene libel in recent years have been in the non-media sphere. In *DPP v Fleming*,[75] for example, a farmer was prosecuted on a number of charges of defamatory and obscene libel for writing graffiti about neighbours (giving their telephone number and suggesting that sex was available) in public toilets, on road signs and in telephone boxes around the country.

Obscene libel is, therefore, largely redundant in practice,[76] as are a number of other common-law offences, which surface only occasionally. For instance, the offence of conspiracy to corrupt public morals surfaced fleetingly in *AG (SPUC) v Open Door Counselling*,[77] while in the 1959 case of *AG v Simpson*[78] the prosecution contended that a play being staged in Dublin, "The Rose Tattoo", outraged the public interest, was contrary to public morals and was obscene. The charge was of showing for gain an indecent and profane performance.[79]

A case that was to raise and help clarify certain aspects of the legal regulation

---

Island Books, Dublin, 2002). In practice, there was relatively little censorship of plays in Ireland (Brian Fallon, *An Age of Innocence – Irish Culture 1930-1960* (Gill & Macmillan, Dublin, 1998) p.204.

[73] Above, n.70, *Roth*, at 489.

[74] The Censorship of Films Acts, Broadcasting Acts and Video Recordings Act.

[75] *The Irish Times*, November 18, 1986, November 23, 1989, November 6, 1990; LRC, above, n.48, at p.93. He was sentenced to imprisonment of nine months and twenty-one months (of which fourteen months were suspended). There have been a few recent prosecutions for libel on the internet but they were treated as defamatory libel rather than obscene libel. See above Chs 4 and 8.

[76] See above, n.11, *Report*, at p.13, which says that obscene libel is virtually obsolete and should be abolished.

[77] [1988] I.R. 593, [1987] I.L.R.M. 477. *Cf.* in England, *Shaw v DPP* [1962] A.C. 220, [1961] 2 W.L.R. 897.

[78] Above, n.72.

[79] *ibid.* See further, above, n.48, at paras 129–32.

of speech for the protection of public morals was *Handyside v UK*.[80]
Controversy arose over the *The Little Red Schoolbook*, translated from Danish
and published by the plaintiff in the UK and, after translation, in about twenty
other countries. Some English newspapers published accounts of the book's
contents and a number of complaints were received. The DPP asked the police
to investigate. They got a warrant to search and seize copies but somehow
missed 18,800 copies of the 20,000 print run. In a subsequent court action, the
publisher was fined £50 and ordered to pay £110 costs. An order was made
also for the destruction of the books. The appeal failed. The book cost thirty
pence, contained 208 pages and had an introduction entitled "All grown-ups
are paper tigers". It had chapters on education, learning, teachers, pupils and
"the system". The chapter on pupils, however, contained a twenty six-page
section on sex, which included subsections on everything from masturbation
to menstruation, from "dirty old men" to pornography, from VD (venereal
disease) to methods of abortion. Marriage was largely ignored. The book was
intended as a reference book for schoolchildren from the age of twelve upwards.
It contained passages like the following:

> "Porn is a harmless pleasure if it isn't taken seriously and believed to be
> real life. Anybody who mistakes it for reality will be greatly disappointed.
>
>   But it's quite possible that you may get some good ideas from it and
> you may find something which looks interesting and that you haven't
> tried before".[81]

Because the book was for twelve-year-olds upwards and the year was 1976, it
is not surprising that the court concluded that, looked at as a whole, the book
would tend to deprave and corrupt a significant proportion of the children
likely to read it.

The European Court of Human Rights found that the conviction of Mr
Handyside was a justifiable interference with his right to freedom of expression
and that there had been no violation of Article 10 of the Convention. As it is
not possible to find in the domestic law of the various contracting states a
uniform European conception of morals, the Court said, Article 10(2) of the
ECHR leaves to the contracting states a margin of appreciation.[82] That domestic
margin of appreciation goes hand in hand with a European supervision. That
is to say that because the concept of morals varies from state to state, the
European Court of Human Rights will be less inclined to second-guess a
national authority. The Court was at pains to point out that freedom of
expression, however, applies:

> "not only to 'information' or 'ideas' that are favourably received or
> regarded as inoffensive, but also to those that offend, shock, or disturb

---

[80] Above, n.3.

[81] *ibid.*, para.32, at pp.747-8.

[82] Above, n.3, at para.59, p.760. In the absence of a European-wide standard, national and
    local standards in individual states become relevant and governments' views of such are
    rarely second-guessed.

the State or any section of the population. Such are the demands of that pluralism, tolerance and broadmindedness without which there is no 'democratic society'. This means, among other things, that every 'formality', 'condition', 'restriction' or 'penalty' imposed in this sphere must be proportionate to the legitimate aim pursued".[83]

In the particular circumstances of *Handyside*, however, the restriction was justifiable in that the book was intended for children. Nonetheless, the Court's decision should not be taken to mean that the appropriate test is what would tend to deprave or corrupt children or adolescents. Whereas such a test was justified in *Handyside* because the intended readership was children and adolescents, that test should not be applied generally to the whole population, to publications intended for an adult readership, which is what happened in Ireland with the operation of the censorship machinery. Repeatedly, in the Dáil and elsewhere, concern was expressed with the need to protect the youth and "ordinary" people of the country from the unwholesome literature that was flooding into the country mainly from the US and the UK. Although the censorship exercised by the Censorship of Publications Board has been less contentious in recent years, the Board does continue to operate. In 1990 a book intended for six to eight-year-olds, *Jenny Lives with Eric and Martin*, published in London and the cause of protests and controversy in Britain, was banned by the Board.[84]

9.2.2.2 *Statute Law*

A number of nineteenth-century statutes contained provisions restricting or prohibiting the publication of indecent or obscene matter, including songs, representations and advertisements. They penalised the sale and distribution or exhibition in public of indecent or obscene publications,[85] and their importation,[86] as well as indecent or obscene speech or acts.[87] They have been largely replaced by the Criminal Justice (Public Order) Act 1994, discussed in Chapter 8 above.

(i) Censorship of Films

In addition to the nineteenth-century Acts, a number of measures were introduced shortly after the emergence of the new State, beginning with the

---

[83] *ibid.* at para.49, pp.754–5. See Luzius Wildhaber, "The right to offend, shock or disturb? Aspects of freedom of expression under the European Convention on Human Rights" (2001) xxxvi Ir. Jur. 17.

[84] *The Irish Times*, July 30, 1990. The book was about a little girl living with a homosexual couple.

[85] Dublin Police Act 1842; Indecent Advertisements Act 1889.

[86] Customs Consolidation Act 1876.

[87] Dublin Police Act 1842; Towns Improvement (Ireland) Act 1854. The Obscene Publications Act 1857, which was aimed at preventing the sale of obscene publications, permitted seizure and destruction of such matter but did not define obscenity.

Censorship of Films Act 1923.[88] The Act provided for the appointment of a
film censor. The censor was to grant a certificate for the public showing of a
film. He could refuse a certificate, however, on the grounds that the film or
part of it was indecent, obscene or blasphemous or would tend to inculcate
principles contrary to public morality or would otherwise be subversive of
public morality (section 7(2)). Films that have been banned in this way include
"Whore" (1991), "Working Girls" (1986) and "Personal Services" (1987), all
dealing with prostitution.[89] The ban on "Personal Services" was later lifted by
the Appeal Board.[90] Violence is not specifically mentioned in section 7(2) but
rather incitement to crime, which led to the censor's decision in October 1994
not to grant a certificate to Oliver Stone's "Natural Born Killers",[91] which
was passed uncut and granted an over-eighteens certificate in Britain. A planned
showing of the film at the Irish Film Centre was abandoned when it appeared
that an injunction was to be sought to prevent it.[92]

A further twist in the saga occurred when TV3 announced in 1999 that it
intended to broadcast *Natural Born Killers*.[93] The Department of Justice

---

[88] It seems surprising that a newly independent state should pass a censorship of films act
at such an early stage. The reason, it seems, was that local authorities, who had
responsibility for the showing of films in their areas, lobbied the government for a
centralised system. Louisa Burns-Bisogno, *Censoring Irish Nationalism* (McFarland &
Co. Inc., North Carolina and London, 1997) explains the background: Cinematography
came to Ireland in 1896 and the first film of any length was made in 1900 (at p.9).
Indeed, an American production team made films in Ireland from 1910-1914 (at p.19).
The British exerted control within 2 years of the advent of the new medium: the licensing
of theatres had been in place under the Disorderly Houses Act of 1751; also, the nitrate
film used was highly inflammable, so control was required in the interests of public
safety (at p.12). The Cinematographers Act 1909 provided for control over film production
and required the licensing of all cinemas, including those in Ireland. To that end a
supervisory power was vested in local authorities, who used the Act to censor the "living
pictures" as they were then called (at p.12). The major motivation behind British
censorship in Ireland, according to Burns-Bisogno, was, from the earliest, the containment
of the rising tide of Irish nationalism (p.12).

[89] *The Irish Times*, October 11, 1991; *The Sunday Tribune*, March 29, 1987. On film
censorship in other countries, see Ruth Petrie (ed.), *Film and Censorship – The INDEX
Reader* (Cassell/Index on Censorship, London, 1997) and *www.indexoncensorship.org*.

[90] *The Irish Times*, May 14, 1987.

[91] *The Irish Times*, October 27, 1994. The ban was upheld by the Films Appeal Board in
January 1995. Other films banned included "Showgirls" (1995) and "From Dusk till
Dawn" (1995), starring George Clooney.

[92] *The Irish Times*, February 24, 1995; April 1, 1995. An injunction had been granted by
Cork Circuit Court in 1994 to prevent the screening and distribution of a David Puttnam
film, "War of the Buttons", when the parents of one of the children in the film complained
that he had been filmed in the nude, contrary to their moral and religious beliefs: *The
Irish Times*, July 2, 1994. On the censorship of films generally see Ciaran Carty,
Confessions of a Sewer Rat (New Island Books, Dublin, 1995); see also Louisa Burns-
Bisogno, above, n.88. Following the enactment of the Freedom of Information Act 1997,
the film censor handed over all records relating to the censorship process to the national
archive, where they could be promptly catalogued and made available. Under the
censorship process, some 3,000 films had been banned and 8,000 had been "cut" (scenes
removed) by the early 1970s, from which time the numbers greatly decreased.

[93] TV3, the national commercial broadcaster, planned to broadcast an edited "made for
television" version of the film late at night (10:45 p.m.) in January 2000. That version

threatened to seek a court injunction to prevent it from being broadcast, contending that a film banned by the Censor could not be broadcast. However, since the Censorship of Films Acts apply only to the exhibiting of films "in public by means of a cinematograph or similar apparatus", it appeared that the Minister had no authority to intervene. Instead, the appropriate authority, since it related to broadcasting, was the Independent Radio and Television Commission (IRTC).[94] The Act which established the IRTC, the Radio and Television Act 1988, requires it to ensure that broadcasters do not broadcast anything which may reasonably be regarded as offending against good taste or decency, or likely to incite to crime. The IRTC had already established procedures and practices for considering certain television programme material. Additional procedures and practices for the assessment of exceptional television programme material were subsequently adopted by the IRTC. TV3 was advised of the new procedures and it was then a matter for it to decide whether to proceed with the broadcast. In any event, the ban was lifted and the film was finally broadcast on TV3 late on Saturday 25 August 2001.

The Censorship of Films (Amendment) Act 1925 extended the provisions of the 1923 Act to publicity material, posters, trailers, and such like. The poster of the film "Striptease", starring Demi Moore, was banned from billboards and confined to the foyers of cinemas and newspaper advertisements for the film in 1996, because it showed the actress in a nude pose.[95] Age classifications, as a guide for parents on the suitability of content of films were introduced in the industry generally and in Ireland in the 1960s and are displayed in the censor's certificate and advertising of films. The over 12 and 15 categories were changed by the film censor in 2001 to "12PG" (that is, suitable for the over 12 age group, under 12 accompanied by an adult) and "15 PG" respectively. The other categories, general, PG (Parental Guidance) and 18 remain in operation.

The Censorship of Films Act 1923 was followed by the Wireless Telegraphy Act 1926, which made it an offence to send any message of an indecent, obscene or offensive character or subversive of public order (section 11). Later statutes include the Defamation Act 1961, which contains provisions on obscene libel (Part II), the Radio and Television Act 1988 (section 9(1)(d)), which requires

---

had removed the most offensive sequences and was to be preceded by regular warnings to viewers. The day before the planned broadcast, the Department of Justice threatened to seek a court injunction to prevent it. TV3 reluctantly decided to withdraw the film (see *IRIS* 2001-8:11).

[94] TV3 took the view that the IRTC – and not the Film Censor – had jurisdiction over material broadcast on television. The IRTC's own legal advice supported that view. In 2001, shortly before TV3 showed the "made-for-television" version, *Natural Born Killers* was released on video in Ireland, seven years after it had been banned by the Film Censor. Videos intended for use in broadcasting are included in the definition of "exempted supply" in s.2(e) of the Video Recordings Act 1989. The IRTC has now become the Broadcasting Commission of Ireland (BCI) under the Broadcasting Act 2001.

[95] *The Irish Times*, September 19, 1996. The poster for the film *The People versus Larry Flint* (1996) came under threat in France because of its offensive depiction of a crucifix. The Advertising Standards Authority in the UK banned the poster for Ali G's movie *Ali G In Da House* following complaints that it involved a nude pose which caused offence (March 26, 2002).

broadcasters to ensure that nothing is broadcast "which may reasonably be regarded as offending against good taste or decency". The Video Recordings Act 1989 extended the remit of the film censor to videos and section 3(1) allows him to refuse a supply certificate if the viewing of the video would, *inter alia*, be likely to stir up hatred or would tend, by reason of the inclusion of obscene or indecent matter, to deprave or corrupt.[96] The Act also provides for classification according to suitability for persons generally or of certain ages: under twelves accompanied, over fifteens, over eighteens (section 4), and for a labelling system indicating contents (section 12).[97] An appeal from a refusal of a certificate by the censor or in respect of the classification granted can be made within three months to the Censorship of Films Appeal Board (section 10).[98] The most far-reaching measures, however, were contained in the Censorship of Publications Act 1929 as amended.

(ii) Censorship of Publications

There was obviously a great deal of concern with public morals in the early part of the century but no clear legal regime for dealing with it, no clear standards or tests to apply. The common-law approach was confusing and the nineteenth-century legislation in force was mainly concerned with the sale or public exhibition of indecent or obscene publications. From 1911 there had been a movement in favour of censorship, the Irish Vigilance Association. This Association was supported by religious groups and was given impetus in 1923 by the Geneva Convention for the Suppression of the Circulation and Traffic in Obscene Publications, held under the auspices of the League of Nations. Three years later, the Committee on Evil Literature was established by the Minister for Justice. The Committee examined existing legislation in other countries and the obligations under the Geneva Convention, to which

---

[96] Few films are banned nowadays but in 1999 the Censor banned the release on video of *The Idiots* (directed by Lars Von Trier) on the grounds that "the viewing of it would tend, by reason of the inclusion in it of obscene or indecent matter, to deprave or corrupt persons who might view it" (*The Sunday Times*, October 24, 1999). Stanley Kubrick's *A Clockwork Orange*, originally banned in 1973, was passed without cuts and given an 18-Certificate in 2000. The 33-year ban on *Ulysses* (directed by Joseph Strick), was also lifted and given a 15 certificate: *The Irish Times*, September 27, 2000; November 11, 2000.

[97] Changes to the labelling system were introduced in 1996 (S.I. No. 407 of 1996) to enhance the age classifications categories (PG, 12s) and the appearance of the labels displaying them. A voluntary system was agreed with the distributors in respect of video games in 2000. The Act did not appear to cover video games. In a new initiative in 2000, the ELSPA (European Leisure Software Providers Association) rating system, applied to all computer games distributed in Europe, was to be highlighted as a means of giving clear information to parents regarding content. Prominent symbols would appear on both the packaging and the games themselves. In addition, the distributors recommended to their members that all games which were rated in either of the age categories "Over 15" or "Over 18" should be submitted to the Film Censor for classification and certification. See *www.justice.ie* (under "speeches"), *IRIS* 2001–2:13. The changes to the age categories in respect of films (above, and *IRIS* 2001–7:11) do not apply to videos.

[98] In accordance with the Act, these measures came into force in 1994 by virtue of Statutory Instruments: S.I. Nos 133–137 of 1994.

Ireland had acceded in 1924. It heard representations from all interested parties within the State and reported to the Minister at the end of 1926.[99] The Committee found that the ordinary law for dealing with indecent publications had broken down and that the few criminal charges being laid each year were making no impact on the flow of objectionable matter into the country. Many of the Committee's recommendations were included in the Censorship of Publications Bill, which was introduced in 1928.

The political and moral climate at the time was conducive to censorship and the zeal with which censorship was espoused was not wholly attributable to the desires of the newly formed State to shake off the legacy of the past and the harmful influences from outside. There was nothing exceptional about the enactment of censorship legislation at the time. Many European countries, including Britain, were worried about the effects of the spread of objectionable literature and had introduced legislation to address it. However, the scheme adopted by the Irish legislature was to become notorious because of the manner in which it was applied. It was used as authorisation for widespread prior restraint in a paternalistic exercise designed to protect the morals of both the "youth" and "ordinary people" of the country and to insulate them from "unwholesome" external influences.[100]

One of the difficulties with the law prior to the 1929 Act was that, as most authors and publishers were outside the jurisdiction, the only possibility was to prosecute booksellers and distributors. Such a course of action was not desirable in itself as the law was uncertain and, as was argued in the Dáil, the nature of "indecent" matter was so wide and variable as to make it virtually impossible in many cases for a bookseller or distributor to know whether the handling of particular books or periodicals would constitute an offence.[101] The only real alternative, therefore, it was thought, was to prevent the material from coming into the country in the first place. There were already facilities for doing that under the Customs Consolidation Act 1876 and the Post Office Act 1908. In practice, however, the respective officials were dealing with such a vast range and quantity of matter coming into the country that it would have been impossible for them to concentrate to any significant extent on indecent books or periodicals. Besides, there were no statutory criteria that they could apply, with the result that forfeiture was entirely arbitrary and a matter of chance.[102] Instead of recommending a strengthening of the existing law, the

---

[99] Michael Adams, *Censorship – The Irish Experience* (University of Alabama Press, Alabama, 1968), at p.34. For the records of the Committee on Evil Literature, which were made available to the public in January 1995, see *www.nationalarchives.ie/evil_article_1.html*. The Committee comprised three laymen and two clerics: one Roman Catholic and one Church of Ireland. It heard and considered submissions from a variety of individuals, organisations and institutions. (The website also contains material on birth control literature – see further below.)

[100] Both groups are constantly referred to throughout the Dáil Debates on the Censorship of Publications Bill 1928, vols 26, 28.

[101] 28 *Dáil Debates*, Cols 273, 699; 12 *Seanad Debates*, Cols 112-13.

[102] The 1946 Act, s.5, provides that a customs officer "may" detain on importation any book which in his opinion ought to be examined by the Board. In the US, the customs law was amended in 1930 (Tariff Act of 1930, 19 USC, s.1305 (a)) to specifically

Committee on Evil Literature had recommended a new system of prevention rather than prosecution. Hence, the purpose of the Censorship of Publications Act 1929, as set out in the long title, was to provide for:

> "[T]he prohibition of the sale and distribution of unwholesome literature and for that purpose to provide for the establishment of a censorship of books and periodical publications, and to restrict the publication of reports of certain classes of judicial proceedings".[103]

The way the Act was applied in practice, to the detriment of works of literature, has been well documented elsewhere,[104] and so the present study will concentrate instead on the substantive law, its aims and its failings.

The Act, which as a bill had been the subject of prolonged debate and was not lightly passed, envisaged a type of prior restraint, in the form of interference with the channels of distribution. It established a censorship board, which was to receive complaints from the public, "examine" (not necessarily "read") the publication complained of and report to the Minister.[105] The Board was to have regard to the literary, artistic, scientific or historic merit of the particular publication, its language and general tenor, the nature and extent of publication, the class of reader addressed and any other matter it considered relevant. If the Board reported that a particular publication was in its general tendency indecent, obscene or unduly devoted to crime in the case of a periodical, the Minister could make an order prohibiting its sale and distribution within the State. All of these provisions, contained in Part II of the 1929 Act, were repealed and replaced by the Censorship of Publications Act 1946, which, according to its long title, was intended to "make further and better provision for the censorship of books and periodical publications".

There were various problems with the 1929 Act. First, it failed to make provision for an appeal, which was remedied by the 1946 Act (section 3). It also enabled books, though not periodicals, to be banned forever, a defect that was not remedied until a further Act of 1967, which imposed a twelve-year limit. Until 1979, when the Health (Family Planning) Act was passed, books

---

except classics and works of literary merit and to build in procedural safeguards, including the requirement of a court order for seizure.

[103] Books were included even though the Committee on Evil Literature had warned of the dangers. Besides, the Irish people at the time were a "newspaper-reading people", not a book-reading people: 26 *Dáil Debates*, Col.630.

[104] See, for example, Adams, above, n.99; Kieran Woodman, *Media Control in Ireland* (Galway University Press, Galway, 1985); Julia Carlson, *Banned in Ireland* (Routledge, London, 1990); Brian Fallon, "The Literary Censorship", in *An Age of Innocence – Irish Culture 1930–1960* (Gill & Macmillan, Dublin, 1998); *The Bell*, vol.9, 1945, *passim*. On the legal issues, see Kevin Boyle and Marie McGonagle, "Censorship of Publications – Irish Style" (1989) 10 JMLP 87 (forerunner of (Tolley's) *Communications Law*); Jerome O'Callaghan, "Censorship of Indecency in Ireland: A View from Abroad" [1998] 16 *Cardozo Arts and Entertainment Law Journal* 53. On the censorship of Irish-language publications, see Tarlach Mac Congáil, "Gobán sa Bhéal" 58 *Comhar* (No.4, April 1999) 7 and (No.5, May 1999) 21.

[105] The role of the Customs and Excise service under the 1929 Act just happened, but it was affirmed and developed by s.5 of the 1946 Act.

and periodicals could be banned on the basis that they advocated contraception, and the printer, publisher, seller or distributor could be prosecuted.[106] As late as 1989 a prosecution was brought against the Irish Family Planning Association for unlawfully selling condoms at the Virgin Megastore in Dublin, contrary to section 4(1)(4) of the Health (Family Planning) Act 1979, as amended by section 2 of the Health (Family Planning) (Amendment) Act 1985. A fine of £400 was imposed.[107] The legislation, a liberalising measure at the time, imposed an age limit of eighteen and abolished the need for a prescription for contraceptives, which could lawfully be sold by chemists and health boards only.

The censorship of publications that advocate abortion remained unchanged until 1995, when the Regulation of Information (Services outside the State for Termination of Pregnancies) Act 1995 was passed to regulate abortion information. The ban on the advocacy of abortion, in the Censorship Acts 1929-67, caused problems in the period following the right-to-life amendment to the Constitution in 1983 (Article 40.3.3) and the court cases that ensued. The Censorship Board gave the British magazine *Cosmopolitan* an ultimatum in September 1989 to withdraw its advertisements for abortion clinics within six months or face being banned in Ireland. The magazine complied. In February 1990 another British magazine, *Company*, removed a supplement on abortion from copies distributed in Ireland. FÁS, the national employment training authority, removed references to abortion from its guide for young people emigrating to Britain. Two books on women's health were removed from the shelves of public libraries in Dublin following complaints.[108]

The difficulties with the legislation and its application are legendary. Control was exercised on the basis of standards that were vague and imprecise; the terminology was tentative and often inconsistent. Even the definition of "indecent", which one would have thought was central to the Act, was inserted only at a late stage, when the bill was recommitted to the Dáil. The scope of the Act was so wide and uncertain that how it would operate depended entirely on the personnel, the five part-time, anonymous, ministerially-appointed, "fit and proper" citizens, meeting in secret, who would comprise the Board.[109] Most of the publishers affected by the decisions were outside the country and sales in Ireland were meagre anyway, so there was little likelihood of a challenge to decisions of the Board. Besides, to be banned often gave an added sales

---

[106] In 1929 when the Act became law, contraception was viewed as race-suicide. See, for example, 12 *Seanad Debates*, col.123. See generally, John Horgan, "Saving us from ourselves: contraception, censorship and the 'evil literature' controversy in 1926" [1995] 5 Ir. Comms. Rev. 61.

[107] *The Irish Times*, September 9, 1989, May 16, 1990. The Misuse of Drugs Act 1984 also made it an offence to publish, sell or distribute books, periodicals or other publications which advocate or encourage, or include advertisements for, the use of any controlled drug (section 5).

[108] *The Irish Times*, October 1, 1991, October 16, 1991.

[109] The names of the members of the board are published on appointment but no information is given about them or their fitness or qualifications for holding office (*The Sunday Business Post*, August 15, 1999). The term "fit and proper" was included in the 1929 Act, but not in the 1946 Amendment Act.

boost. In England, *Lady Chatterly's Lover* is said to have sold three million copies in the three months following its prosecution in 1961.[110]

For these reasons, the operation of the Board and its decisions were not subjected to scrutiny for fifty years. It would have been open to an individual author, publisher or reader personally affected by a decision to take a constitutional challenge, but this did not happen. The only case that resulted was *Irish Family Planning Association v Ryan*,[111] which involved the banning by the Board of an information booklet on birth control. The case was decided on natural justice principles rather than freedom of expression. The Supreme Court said that the Board ought to have exercised their discretion to communicate with the publisher, as the publisher was readily contactable, and the book was purely factual, not advocating any course of conduct and not obscene.[112]

There was a further flurry of activity in 1987, when the Board banned Dr Alex Comfort's *The Joy of Sex* and *The Erotic Art of India*, a title in Thames and Hudson's acclaimed art series. The latter had already been out of print for two years and the publishers had no plans to reissue it. After that the Board became less visible and contentious.[113] The ban on *The Joy of Sex* was lifted by the Appeal Board.[114] In 1988, in response to a complaint intended to show how ludicrous the system was, the Board refused to ban the *Bible*.[115]

In Dublin magazine was the subject of a six months' ban imposed by the Board in 2000. The Board had received a complaint with regard to advertisements for escort agencies and massage parlours, which were a front for brothels and prostitution. In this instance the Board had entered into correspondence

---

[110] Geoffrey Robertson and Andrew Nicol, *Media Law* (4th ed., Penguin Books, London, 2002), at p.155. On theories and effects of censorship see Judith Butler, "Ruled Out: Vocabularies of the Censor" in Robert C. Post (ed.), *Censorship and Silencing: Practices of Cultural Regulation* (Getty Research Institute, L.A., 1998), at p.247.

[111] [1979] I.R. 295. On the question of the constitutionality of the Board, see James Casey, *Constitutional Law in Ireland* (3rd ed., Round Hall Sweet & Maxwell, Dublin, 2000), at pp.571–2.

[112] *ibid.* at 314–5, O'Higgins C.J.

[113] It emerged from subsequent interviews with the judge who chaired the Board that the concern of the Board was for the protection of children, so that a juvenile standard was being imposed on the whole community (*The Sunday Tribune*, February 15, 1987). In the US, in *Butler v Michigan* 352 U.S. 380 (1957), Justice Frankfurter had said: "The State insists that, by thus guaranteeing the general reading public against books not too rugged for grown men and women in order to shield juvenile innocence, it is exercising its power to promote the general welfare. Surely, this is to burn the house to roast the pig.... [It] is to reduce the adult population of Michigan to reading only what is fit for children". For similar reasons, in *Bantam Books, Inc. v Sullivan* 372 U.S. 58 (1963) the Court declared unconstitutional a Rhode Island scheme creating a commission on youth morality to educate the public concerning any book containing obscene, indecent or impure language, or manifestly tending to the corruption of the youth.

[114] *The Irish Times*, September 27, 1989. The ban on *Playboy* magazine imposed in 1959 was lifted by the Appeal Board in September 1995 (*The Irish Times*, September 29, 1995; *The Sunday Tribune*, October 1, 1995).

[115] *The Irish Times*, March 8, 1988. Madonna's book *Sex* (Warner Books, 1992) was banned in 1992 but sold a large number of copies in the 23 days between its arrival and the ban.

with the publisher beforehand.[116] He then sought a judicial review of the decision in the High Court, claiming that the Board's decision was unconstitutional and in breach of fair procedures of natural and constitutional justice. He also circumvented the ban by publishing an almost identical magazine called *Dublin*.[117] A more appropriate vehicle than the flawed censorship legislation in such a case would be a law specifically aimed at advertising. In the event, the case was finally disposed of under the Criminal Justice (Public Order) Act 1994.[118]

The British magazine *Loaded* was also removed from circulation in 2000, when gardaí brought it to the attention of the distributors, Easons, that it contained advertisements for so-called escort agencies.[119] The Board had not received any complaints about *Loaded* magazine and had not therefore acted to ban it. It later refused to consider a complaint that the *Examiner* newspaper should be banned because it, too, carried advertisements for adult massage.[120] The refusal led to a High Court application for judicial review, intended to highlight the operational inconsistencies of the Censorship Board. Leave was also sought to challenge the constitutionality of the Censorship of Publications legislation but the application was refused.[121]

Nonetheless, the legitimacy of the Board's continued existence is open to question. The Law Reform Commission has recommended that the legislation on obscene and indecent matter and the various schemes of censorship be reviewed to determine whether they are consistent with the requirements of the Constitution as to freedom of speech, to determine whether they are appropriate in modern conditions, and to formulate, if necessary, changes to the existing law.[122] The UN Human Rights Committee also recommended in 1993 that "steps should be taken to repeal strict laws on censorship and ensure judicial review of decisions taken by the Censorship of Publications Board".[123] The UN Special Rapporteur on freedom of expression in turn recommended that the Irish Government "consider reviewing or even repealing the law concerning the censorship of publications and of films and videos", and "that the Censorship of Publications Board operate in public and make its decisions open to public scrutiny".[124]

---

[116] *The Irish Times*, August 19, 1999. The Court was critical of the procedures followed by the Board (above, Chap.8).

[117] *ibid.*

[118] See Chap.8 above.

[119] *The Irish Times*, May 22, 2000.

[120] *The Irish Times*, February 22, 2000.

[121] *The Irish Times*, February 23, 2000. Another application to the High Court sought the exclusion of two pages containing telephone sex lines from a new Golden Pages Directory. The application was brought on the grounds of indecency and the concern that children would have easy access to sex chat lines. Kearns J. adjourned the case generally when Eircom, the publishers of the telephone book, gave undertakings to ensure increased vigilance in the monitoring of calls to such sex chat lines and to implement measures restricting access thereto: "Sex chat, porn access lines closed", *The Irish Times*, July 15, 2000.

[122] Above, n.48, at Chap.9 and p.190; n.11, at para.22.

[123] Concluding Observations of the Human Rights Committee, Ireland, August 8, 1993, CCPR/C/79/Add.21 (Concluding Observations/Comments), para.21.

[124] Report of the Special Rapporteur (Mr. Abid Hussain) on the promotion and protection

(iii) Other Aspects of the Censorship Acts

As noted in Chapter 7, the Censorship of Publications Act 1929 also restricts reporting of judicial proceedings in the interests of morals (section 14). The provisions were taken over from the British Judicial Proceedings (Regulation of Reports) Act 1926, section 1, which was aimed at controlling detailed reports of divorce proceedings. The provisions were accepted without challenge in the Dáil. The test in each case is whether the matter would be calculated to injure public morals.[125]

9.2.3 Pornography

The difficulty with the Censorship of Publications Acts in this country is not that they fail to filter out pornography but rather that they are so flexible as to filter out important works of literature as well. The main difficulty is that sufficiently precise standards are not easy to formulate. There is ample evidence of a thriving pornography industry but little consensus on what constitutes pornography of a kind that requires regulation. The problem is accentuated by developments in technology, which mean that pornographic material can appear in all media from print to video to computer. Pornographic material in film and video can be refused a certificate by the censor in accordance with the Censorship of Films Acts and the Video Recordings Acts. The problem is how to define pornography. The film "Bad Lieutenant" (1992) was reported to have been refused a certificate because it was demeaning to women,[126] and the film "Dangerous Game" (1993), by the same director (Abel Ferrara) and featuring Madonna, because of a violent scene of anal rape.[127] The question is whether either conforms to our idea of pornography? Is matter that is demeaning to women or that contains sexual violence sufficient to constitute pornography, or is something more required? Must both degradation and sexual violence occur to take a film out of the category of simply bad taste or indecency and place it in the category of pornography?

Much has been written about pornography and whether it should be considered outside the constitutional guarantee of free speech on the grounds that it does not constitute "speech" that is deserving of protection or whether it should be outlawed on the basis of the avoidance of identifiable harm. A causal relationship has always been difficult to establish. It is not the portrayal of sex as such that is objectionable in today's world but the violence, objectification, degradation and subordination that may accompany it and the effect that the combination may have on attitudes to and treatment of the "victims", who are usually women and children. Conservative, liberal and feminist theories have

---

of the right to freedom of opinion and expression, submitted in accordance with Commission Resolution 1999/36: Addendum, Report on the Mission to Ireland, 1999, E/CN.4/2000/63/Add.2, at para.87.

[125] Subsection 2 of s.14 has been repealed by s.3 of the Family Law (Divorce) Act 1996.

[126] That in itself, however, is not one of the specified grounds for refusing a certificate: see Jerome O'Callaghan, above, n.104, at 74, indicating that the censor regarded the film as blasphemous and profane.

[127] *The Irish Times*, November 23, 1994. The film was originally known as "Snake Eyes".

prevailed at different times but the essence of the problem remains elusive. Should pornography be curtailed and, if so, on what theory, what test? Is it offensiveness, as has been canvassed in the case of blasphemy, that is the key to objections, or is it the stirring up of hatred and other negative responses to the women and children it objectifies?[128] If so, it might be argued that incitement to hatred legislation could provide an adequate model for response. If not, is the appropriate test or standard that of community tolerance, *i.e.* the moral standards of the community? It may be that standards developed in the context of sex discrimination could be applied. Another possibility is that it could be encompassed within the theory of human dignity, protected by national constitutions. In a broad framework, pornography can be viewed as a denial of human dignity. Article 7 of the European Convention on Transfrontier Television, for example, requires respect for human dignity and specifically mentions pornography:

> "1. All items of programme services, as concerns their presentation and content, shall respect the dignity of the human being and the fundamental rights of others".

In particular, they shall not:

> "(a) be indecent and in particular contain pornography;
>
> (b) give undue prominence to violence or be likely to incite to racial hatred".

The Council of Europe's Standing Committee on Transfrontier Television issued a Statement in September 2002 on the need for television programmes to uphold human dignity and the rights of others. The Statement, which is particularly concerned with programme formats, is addressed to regulators and urges them, *inter alia*, to avoid contractual arrangements which oblige participants in programmes to waive or relinquish substantially their right to privacy, as this may represent an infringement of human dignity.[129]

The Video Recordings Act 1989 does not specifically mention pornography as such but allows the censor to refuse a certificate if the viewing of the video:

---

[128] It has been argued that offensiveness is only a secondary element and not the real root of the problem, which is the influence of pornography on people who use it and the resulting harm to women and children. See Catherine Itzen (ed.), *Pornography: Women, Violence and Civil Liberties* (OUP, Oxford, 1992), and Catherine Itzen, "Pornography, Harm and Human Rights – the European Context" (1995) 16 JMLP 107. See also Catharine A. McKinnon, "Pornography as Defamation and Discrimination" in T. Morawetz (ed.), *Law and Language* (Ashgate, Aldershot, 2000); Rae Langton, "Subordination, Silence, and Pornography's Silence" in Post, above, n.110, at p.261.

[129] Statement on Human Dignity and the Fundamental Rights of Others, September 12–13, 2002, available at *www.coe.int/T/E/human_rights/media*. On the concept of human dignity, see generally David Feldman, "Human Dignity as a Legal Value – Part I (1999) P.L. 682, and Part II (2000) P.L. 61. The concept of human dignity and of privacy is of particular relevance to reality television, the "Big Brother" genre of broadcast programmes (see Ch. 5 above).

"(a)(iii) would tend, by reason of the inclusion in it of obscene or indecent matter, to deprave or corrupt persons who might view it,

(b) it depicts acts of gross violence or cruelty (including mutilation and torture) towards humans or animals". (section 3)

The association representing most of the international video companies operating in Ireland before the Act was passed said that the industry was threatened by two major problems: piracy and pornography.[130]

European Community law also has relevance to this issue. The 1989 EC Television without Frontiers Directive, as amended in 1997, obliges Member States, *inter alia*, to ensure freedom of reception for programmes "retransmitted" from other Member States (Article 2), unless such a programme seriously and gravely infringes Article 22, which is designed to protect minors, particularly from "pornography or gratuitous violence". If that is the case, the Member State may "provisionally suspend retransmissions" (Article 2). The application of the Directive to the retransmission of satellite services was tested in the Red Hot Dutch case, *R v Continental Television*[131] in 1992. Red Hot Dutch was to transmit encrypted films of a pornographic nature into the UK, uplinked from the Netherlands. The relevant domestic law in the UK was the Broadcasting Act 1990, which imposed obligations on broadcasters to exclude matters that offended against good taste and to observe a code on the portrayal of sex and nudity. The Act allowed the Secretary of State to make an order proscribing a foreign satellite service that failed to comply with the provisions of the Act. In March 1993 the UK government announced its intention to make such an order. The Dutch company sought judicial review of the decision. The argument centred firstly on the meaning of "retransmission" in the Directive and the contention that it could not be said to cover a satellite service originating in another Member State. Secondly, it raised the scope of Article 22 and its reference to steps taken to ensure that minors will not normally hear or see the broadcasts. The Red Hot Dutch films were to be transmitted between the hours of 11 p.m. and 4 a.m. each Saturday night. The views of the European Court of Justice were sought but not given as the company went out of business and did not pursue the issue before the ECJ. The Directive itself is under review.[132]

In recent years there has been particular concern with pornography on the internet. The Child Trafficking and Pornography Act 1998 was introduced to prohibit trafficking and the use of children for purposes of sexual exploitation. It also makes it an offence to produce, disseminate, handle or possess child pornography.[133] For the purposes of the Act, a child is a person under

---

[130] *The Irish Times*, April 24, 1986. Much of the concern since then has centred on children. The primary responsibility remains with parents but in order to provide guidance for them in relation to content, age classification and labelling systems have been improved (above, n.97).

[131] [1993] 2 C.M.L.R. 333, C–327/93. See further, Phillip Dann, "The Red Hot Channel: Pornography without Frontiers" (1993) 6 ENT L.R. 191; Stuart Dowis, "Still Red-Hot: Pornography; Freedoms and Morality" [1995] 5 ENT L.R. 201.

[132] See further Chap.11 and *www.europa.eu.int/comm/avpolicy*.

[133] For example, a man was sentenced to two and a half years' imprisonment for advertising child pornography over the Internet: *DPP v Muldoon* (*The Irish Times*, July 31, 2002).

the age of seventeen. "Child pornography" includes both visual and aural representations of children, or persons depicted or represented as children engaging in or witnessing sexual activity. It also covers those representations that advocate sexual activity with children or imply that children are available to be used for sexual exploitation. The Act mentions various specific forms of representation, including books, periodicals, films, videos,[134] photographs, tapes, computer disks and graphics. It also has catch-all phrases to allow for the development of new technologies.[135] Sanctions range from life imprisonment for trafficking to 14 years on indictment for knowingly producing, distributing, importing, selling or showing child pornography.[136] Knowingly possessing child pornography can lead on indictment to a fine not exceeding £5,000 or to a term of imprisonment not exceeding five years or both.[137] There are a number of exceptions in the Act, including *bona fide* research, a defence on which journalists researching a story should also be able to rely.[138]

In addition to the specific statutory offences dealing with child pornography on the internet, a self-regulatory system of monitoring is in place. The system comprises an advisory board[139] and a hotline,[140] which operates in co-operation with an international association of hotlines (INHOPE)[141] to combat child pornography on the internet. As part of the self-regulatory system, the Internet Service Providers Association of Ireland published its first Code of Practice and Ethics in January 2002.[142] The Council of Europe has also issued a Recommendation on self-regulation and user protection against illegal or harmful content on new communications and information services.[143] Article

---

[134] In each of these cases (books, periodicals, films, videos), the Act (s.2(1)(d)(I), (II) and (III)) expressly excludes any that have been examined and permitted under the censorship machinery, *i.e.* the Censorship of Publications Board under the Censorship of Publications Acts 1929-67, the Film Censor under the Censorship of Films Acts 1923-92 or the Video Recordings Acts 1989 and 1992. The Censorship of Films (Amendment) Act 1992 made provision for assistant censors, given the increased role of the office under the Video Recordings Act.

[135] For example, "any representation, description or information produced by or from computer-graphics or by any other electronic or mechanical means" (s.2(1)(d)).

[136] S.5 covers a number of such offences, punishable on summary conviction by a fine not exceeding £1,500 and on indictment by a fine or imprisonment for a term not exceeding 14 years or both. Knowingly publishing or distributing advertisements is also included.

[137] S.6; on summary conviction, a fine not exceeding £1,500 or imprisonment not exceeding 12 months. The Act also provides for entry, search and seizure (s.7). A number of prosecutions have resulted.

[138] S.6(3). An exception is made also for those carrying out official duties, *i.e.* the film censor and Censorship of Publications Board, and those engaged in the prevention, investigation or prosecution of offences under the Act (s. 6(2)).

[139] *www.iab.ie*. These measures resulted from the recommendations of the report of the Working Group on the Illegal and Harmful Use of the Internet (Pn. 5231, Stationery Office, Dublin, 1998), available at *www.justice.ie*.

[140] *www.hotline.ie*.

[141] *www.inhope.org*.

[142] *www.ispai.ie*, *www.iab.ie*, under "publications". See also, Tarlach McGonagle, "Ireland: Milestones in Online Self-Regulation" (2002) 3 *Computer und Recht International* 93.

[143] Rec. (2001)8 of the Committee of Ministers of the Council of Europe on self-regulation concerning cyber content (self-regulation and user protection against illegal or harmful

9 of the European Convention on Cybercrime 2001, which Ireland signed in February 2002, requires each State party to adopt legislation and other measures to establish criminal offences with regard to child pornography. Child pornography is defined (Article 9(2)) and a range of offences indicated, from producing to offering or making available, distributing or transmitting, procuring or possessing, child pornography through a computer system (Article 9(1)).

9.3 TASTE AND DECENCY OBLIGATIONS

As noted above, broadcasters in Ireland have statutory duties in relation to matters of taste and decency under section 18 of the Broadcasting (Authority) Act 1960, as amended, and section 9(1)(d) of the Radio and Television Act 1988. Section 19 of the Broadcasting Act 2001 requires the Broadcasting Commission of Ireland to draw up a code specifying standards to be complied with, and rules and practices to be observed, in respect of taste and decency, and, in particular, in respect of the portrayal of violence and sexual conduct. As the RTÉ guidelines state,[144] standards of taste and decency are not immutable; they change with time and place and, therefore, they cannot be legislated for or regulated in any rigid way. Particular attention has to be given to the portrayal of violence and sexual conduct, as well as the use of language and even, on occasion, the manner and tone of a broadcast. It is not possible to avoid offending all sections of the community at all times and, therefore, the main concern is not to cause gratuitous offence. Particular regard is paid also to children, hence the operation of the watershed in relation to television programming: programmes up until 9 p.m. are regarded as family viewing, after that more adult material is permitted. Such measures are authorised by the EC Television without Frontiers Directive 1989, as amended in 1997.[145]

---

content on new communications and information services; available at *www.coe.int/T/E/Committee_of_Ministers* under "documents"). The Recommendation recalls earlier recommendations on the distribution of videograms (Recommendation No. R(89) 7), on video games with a racist content (No. R(92) 19), on the portrayal of violence in the electronic media (No. R(97) 19), on hate speech (No. R(97) 20), as well as Art.4 ICERD (discussed in Chap.8 above). The Recommendation encourages Member States to establish self-regulatory organisations, content descriptors (indicating, *inter alia*, violent and pornographic content), content selection tools, content complaints systems, and to create mediation and arbitration mechanisms, as well as encouraging the development of user information and awareness.

[144] RTÉ Programme-Makers' Guidelines, 2002, p.37.

[145] Art.22(2) speaks of ensuring "by selecting the time of the broadcast or by any technical measure, that minors in the area of transmission will not normally hear or see such broadcasts". Art.22(3) goes on to say that "when such programmes are broadcast in unencoded form Member States shall ensure that they are preceded by an acoustic warning or are identified by the presence of a visual symbol throughout their duration". The Directive (Art.22b) provides for an investigation of further measures to facilitate control by parents over the programmes that children may watch. Ireland was included in the EU study on parental control co-ordinated by the Programme in Comparative Media Law and Policy at the University of Oxford. The overall findings of the report are available at *www.europa.eu.int/comm/avpolicy*; Communication from the

Article 7(2) of the Council of Europe's Convention on Transfrontier Television also requires that all items of programme services which are likely to impair the physical, mental or moral development of children and adolescents shall not be scheduled when, because of the time of transmission and reception, they are likely to watch them.

Questions of taste and decency will not of themselves give rise to court actions,[146] although they may well be considerations in cases taken on other grounds. In England in *Pro-life Alliance v BBC*, a case somewhat similar to *Colgan v IRTC*,[147] the Court of Appeal held that any refusal to transmit a political message, which was also part of a general election campaign, would only be sanctioned in the most extreme of cases, involving factors such as dishonesty or gratuitous sensationalism.[148] The video, submitted by the Pro-Life Alliance, a registered political party, which was contesting seats in the general election, contained images of the products of a suction abortion. The BBC contended that transmitting it would have conflicted with its obligations in respect of taste and decency,[149] even if transmitted late at night and preceded by a warning. Laws L.J., however, found that although it was graphic and disturbing, there was nothing gratuitous or sensational or untrue in the intended broadcast. The censorship was therefore not justified, particularly in the context of a general election. Since the image was the message, it could not be accepted that the applicant should be entitled merely to tell what happens in an abortion, rather than show it. Free political expression was the pressing imperative and "considerations of taste and decency cannot prevail over free speech by a political party at election time save wholly exceptionally".[150] However, the House of Lords overruled the decision by a five to four majority in April 2003.[151]

Commission relating to the Study on Parental Control of Television Broadcasting (COM (1999) 371 final, July 19, 1999. RTÉ introduced on-screen icons indicating programme content in 2002 (see *The Irish Times*, January 19, 2002, *IRIS* 2002–2:12).

[146] They may give rise to a complaint to the Broadcasting Complaints Commission.

[147] [2000] 2 I.R. 490, [1999] 1 I.L.R.M. 22, and Chap.8 above.

[148] [2002] EWCA Civ 297, March 14, 2002.

[149] The relevant provisions were, in the case of the BBC, para.5(1)(d) of the BBC's Agreement and its Producers' Guidelines, chapter 6; in the case of the independent broadcasters, s.6(1)(a) of the Broadcasting Act 1990 and the Programme Code of the Independent Television Commission (ITC), s.1, in relation to taste and decency. The BBC and independent broadcasters also had a joint document "Guidelines for the Production of Party Election Broadcasts". The content of the video, the BBC (on behalf of all the terrestrial broadcasters) concluded, would be offensive to very large numbers of viewers. Interestingly, Lord Simon Brown in his judgment looked at some of the decisions taken in matters of taste and decency by the Independent Television Commission and the Broadcasting Standards Commission under their codes. The Human Rights Act 1998, which brought the ECHR within domestic law in the UK, makes provision for such codes to be considered.

[150] *ibid.* at para.44. See also *Bowman v UK* (1998) 26 E.H.R.R. 1, which concerned the distribution of campaign literature about abortion at election time.

[151] It gave its reasons for doing so on May 15, 2003 [2003] U.K.H.L. 23. In short, it found that "it is not for the courts to find that broadcasters acted unlawfully when they did no more than give effect to the statutory and other obligations binding on them (Lord Nicholls at para.16).

When Channel 4 broadcast a satirical programme about paedophilia and its treatment in the media, the regulatory body, the Independent Television Commission (ITC) in the UK, required it to broadcast an apology. The channel was found to be in breach of the requirement of the ITC's Programme Code to avoid "gratuitous offence" and to "issue clear and specific warnings" where some viewers might find the programme disturbing or offensive.[152] In Ireland, RTÉ expressed regret that it had carried an advertisement publicising an *Ireland on Sunday* newspaper article, which referred to a convicted rapist as a "beast". The man committed suicide after hearing the radio advertisement.[153] Questions of taste and decency in the printed press are usually dealt with in-house or at NUJ level or through self-regulatory schemes, such as that operated by the Press Complaints Commission in the UK, in conjunction with its editors' code.[154]

9.4 ADVERTISING

Advertising in the media, whether print,[155] broadcasting,[156] film,[157] video,[158] on billboards or in public places,[159] is restricted, *inter alia*, in the interests of public morals. In addition to the specific legal requirements, the Advertising Standards Authority of Ireland (ASAI), a self-regulatory body, operates a Code of Standards, with which members are required to comply. It covers virtually all forms of commercial advertising, including internet advertising.[160]

---

[152] *www.itc.org.uk.*

[153] *The Irish Times*, June 21, 2000.

[154] *www.nuj.org.uk, www.pcc.org.uk.*

[155] The Censorship of Publications Act 1929, s.17 includes advertisements that relate or refer to any sexual disease, complaint or infirmity or to the prevention or removal of irregularities in menstruation or abortifacients. A reference to contraceptives was removed by the Health (Family Planning) Act 1979, s.12(2).

[156] Broadcasting Authority Act 1960, Radio and Television Act 1988 (Pt III) (s.10), prohibiting the carrying of advertisements directed towards any religious end.

[157] Censorship of Films (Amendment) Act 1925, applying essentially the same provisions as those of s.7(2) of the principal Act of 1923 regarding matter that is "indecent, obscene or blasphemous" or that would "convey suggestions contrary to public morality or would be otherwise subversive of public morality" to advertising by extract from a film (s.3(2)). The Act, according to the long title, relates to "pictorial advertisements of cinematograph pictures".

[158] The Video Recordings Act 1989 is mainly concerned with the supply and importation of video recordings. It exempts works that, taken as a whole, are designed to inform, educate or instruct; that are concerned with religion, music or sport; or are video games. Videos used in broadcasting are governed by the Broadcasting Acts.

[159] Indecent Advertisements Act 1889. It is also an offence under the Misuse of Drugs Act 1984 to publish, sell or distribute printed matter, which includes advertisements for any controlled drug (s.5).

[160] The ASAI is an independent self-regulatory body set up and financed by the advertising industry and has no mandate to act as a censor or arbiter of public morals. Its codes are administered primarily in the interests of consumers. There are other industry codes, such as the Drinks Industry Code, that of the Irish Pharmaceutical Healthcare Association and the Medical Council's Guide to Ethical Conduct (Advertising and the Media).

In relation to broadcast advertising, section 4 of the Broadcasting Act 1990 requires that a code of advertising standards be drawn up and amended from time to time by the Minister in consultation with the broadcast regulators, then the RTÉ Authority and the IRTC. The current Code, which was drafted in 1995, and updated in 1999,[161] contains various provisions relating to the content, identification and insertion of advertisements. All broadcast advertising must comply with the respective statutory provisions,[162] with the Code, with Articles 10–16 of the Television without Frontiers Directive (TWF), and with any additional restrictions imposed by statute on various types of advertising. In accordance with the Directive, the Code provides that advertising shall not prejudice respect for human dignity, include any discrimination on grounds of race, sex or nationality, be offensive to religious or political beliefs, or encourage behaviour prejudicial to the protection of the environment.[163] In addition, all forms of advertising for cigarettes, cigars and other tobacco products is prohibited,[164] and strict controls are imposed on the advertising of alcohol.[165] There are detailed provisions regarding advertising and children's programmes.[166] The Code also contains protection for the privacy of the individual (Article 16) and applies the ban on political, religious and industrial relations advertising contained in the broadcasting legislation (discussed in Chapter 8 above). The Broadcasting Complaints Commission has power to hear complaints that an advertisement contravened the Code of Standards.[167]

---

[161] It was updated by the Department of Arts, Heritage, Gaeltacht and the Islands to provide a new definition of advertising and to introduce restrictions governing teleshopping, in line with the EC Television without Frontiers Directive (97/36/EC). The full text of the Code, including the 1999 revision, is available at *www.bci.ie* under "publications". Previously, RTÉ adopted and implemented its own codes. Under a former code in 1993, and following a long period in which advertisements for contraceptives were prohibited by law (see above, nn.106-7), RTÉ was not prepared to accept advertisements for contraceptives and, as a result, was unwilling for quite some time to accept advertisements for the use of condoms as part of the Health Education Bureau's campaign to combat AIDS (see *The Irish Times*, May 14, 1993).

[162] S.20 of the Broadcasting Authority Act 1960, as amended, in the case of RTÉ, and section 10 of the Radio and Television Act 1988, in the case of commercial broadcasters.

[163] Art.5.1, repeating Art.12 TWF, except that the latter refers to "television" advertising and that its reference to behaviour prejudicial to health or to safety is included separately in the Irish code in Art.11. Both documents extend to the regulation of sponsorship and teleshopping also.

[164] Art.13 in both documents. The advertising of medicinal products and medical treatment available only on prescription is prohibited by the Directive (Art.14), while the Code refers to separate procedures in relation to those and other areas of advertising (Art.18.1).

[165] Art.15 in both documents.

[166] Art.14 of the Code and Art.16 of the Directive, which says that "television advertising shall not cause moral or physical detriment to minors". To that end it shall not exhort minors to buy a product or service by exploiting their inexperience or credulity, directly encourage them to persuade their parents or others to purchase the goods or services, exploit the special trust minors place in parents, teachers or others, or unreasonably show minors in dangerous situations.

[167] Broadcasting Authority (Amendment) Act 1976 (s.4(e)(a)), as amended by s.8(3) of the Broadcasting Act 1990.

There are many additional legal provisions that govern particular types of advertising. Many are designed to protect the consumer by requiring truth and honesty and that advertising not be misleading. Some relate to particular products and services, where there is the potential to cause harm. The regulations concerning the advertising of medicines and treatments, and harmful products such as tobacco and alcohol are extensive. Increasingly, they are governed by European law, by individual Directives[168] and by the general rules and principles on advertising, sponsorship and teleshopping set out in the Television without Frontiers Directive. Advertising aimed at children is particularly circumscribed.[169] In *Konsumentenombudsmannen v de Agostini*[170] the European Court of Justice in Luxembourg had to consider the Swedish Broadcasting law prohibiting advertising aimed at children under the age of twelve. The Court held that the prohibition could not be applied to broadcasters established in another Member State but serving the Swedish market, because the Television without Frontiers Directive already contains a complete set of provisions on advertising, including advertising aimed at children. Consequently, there would be double control if the Swedish measures were also to apply to them.

The IRTC, in its new guise as the BCI, has additional duties in regard to advertising under section 19 of the Broadcasting Act 2001. It is required to draw up a code of standards to be complied with, and rules and practices to be observed, in respect of advertising, teleshopping, sponsorship and other forms of commercial promotion employed in broadcasting services. Additionally, it must draw up a code on similar issues that relate to matters likely to be of direct or indirect interest to children.[171] The codes are to provide for matters required under the Television without Frontiers Directive.[172] The Act also makes provision for review of the codes and for enforcement by the BCI.[173]

---

[168] For example Directive 98/43/EC on the advertising and sponsorship of tobacco products, although that particular Directive, which contained a general prohibition on advertising and sponsorship relating to those products, was annulled (*Germany v European Parliament and Council of the EU*, ECJ, Case C–376/98, October 5, 2000).

[169] In 1996, RTÉ took steps to cut down on the number of commercial messages around its programming for children. Since then, no commercial breaks have been permitted before, during or immediately after programmes for pre-school children and there has been a decrease in the frequency of advertising breaks in programmes for older children: see Bob Collins, "Respect of Minors", European Broadcasting Union (EBU), *Diffusion* 2001/2, p.11. On the long-running debate that preceded those steps, see Bob Quinn, *Maverick – A Dissident View of Broadcasting Today* (Brandon Books, Dingle, 2001). On other aspects of children's advertising, see the remaining articles in *Diffusion* 2001/ 2, Reinhold Bergler, "The effects of commercial advertising on children" (1999) 18 *International Journal of Advertising* 411, and Els de Bens, "Does it make sense to restrict or ban TV advertising to children?" (2001) *The Journal of Advertising and Marketing Policy in the European Community* 6.

[170] Joined cases C–34/95 and C–36/95, July 9, 1997.

[171] Ss.19(1)(b) and (c) respectively. The BCI announced its plans to develop a code on children's advertising in April 2003 (*www.bci.ie*). See also the research undertaken by the Independent Television Commission in the UK (*www.itc.org.uk*) and at EU level (*http://europa.eu.int/comm/avpolicy*).

[172] S.19(4).

[173] Ss.19(10) and 21(1)(b) respectively.

Section 20 refers to codes of standards with respect to the transmission of information by any electronic means other than broadcasting, and including the internet. The BCI may co-operate or give assistance in the preparation of such codes.

The BCI will have to take account of developments arising from the digital environment.[174] It will also need to take account of changes brought about by the periodic revision of the Television without Frontiers Directive. The current review of the Directive involves advertising and is informed by two independent studies, one on the impact of television advertising and teleshopping on children, and the other on the development of new advertising techniques.[175] With regard to the issues of public morality, which is the subject of this chapter, Article 12 of the present version of the Directive provides that advertising and teleshopping shall not prejudice respect for human dignity, include any discrimination on grounds of race, sex or nationality, be offensive to religious or political beliefs, encourage behaviour prejudicial to health or safety, or encourage behaviour prejudicial to the environment. Article 16 further provides that television advertising and teleshopping shall not cause moral or physical detriment to minors. The Council of Europe's Convention on Transfrontier Television of 1989, and the Protocol of 1998 amending it, also includes provisions relating to children's advertising.[176]

Further Reading

Adams, Michael, *Censorship – The Irish Experience* (University of Alabama Press, Alabama, 1968).

Carlson, Julia (ed.), *Banned in Ireland* (Routledge, London, 1990).

Colliver, Sandra (ed.), *Striking a Balance: Hate Speech, Freedom of Expression and Non-discrimination* (ARTICLE 19, International Centre Against Censorship, London, 1992).

Cox, Neville, *Blasphemy and the Law in Ireland* (Edwin Mellen Press, New York, 2000).

---

[174] See, for example, under the EU machinery, the European Council's Recommendation on the protection of minors and human dignity in the audiovisual and information services industry (COM (2001) 106 final), the Communication from the Commission on the Principles and Guidelines for the Community's Audiovisual Policy in the Digital Age (COM (99) 657 final), and the Council's conclusions of December 17, 1999 on the protection of minors in the light of the development of digital audiovisual services (OJ C 8/9, January 12, 2000).

[175] The studies are available at *http://europa.eu.int/comm/avpolicy/stat/studi_en.htm*. See also the Fourth Report from the Commission to the Council, the European Parliament, the European Economic and Social Committee and the Committee of the Regions on the application of Directive 89/552/EEC "Television without Frontiers", Brussels, January 6, 2003, COM(2002)778 final.

[176] ETS 132, May 5, 1989 and ETS 171, October 1, 1998. Art.15 provides that Art.11 will include a stipulation that "[a]dvertising and tele-shopping addressed to or using children shall avoid anything likely to harm their interests and shall have regard to their special susceptibilities" and that "[t]ele-shopping shall not exhort minors to contract for the sale or rental of goods and services". The Protocol applies to tele-shopping essentially the same restrictions that already apply to advertising. At the time of writing, Ireland has not yet ratified the Convention on Transfrontier Television.

Jones, Derek (ed.), *Censorship: A World Encyclopedia*, 4 vols (Fitzroy Dearborn Publishers, London and Chicago, 2001).

Mahoney, Kathleen E., "Obscenity, Morals and the Law: Challenging Basic Assumptions" in Rosalie Abella and Melvin L. Rothman (eds), *Justice beyond Orwell* (Les Editions Yvon Blais, Montréal, 1985).

Murphy, John A., "Censorship and the Moral Community" in Farrell, Brian (ed.), *Community and Communications in Ireland* (Mercier Press, Dublin and Cork, 1984), p.51.

O'Callaghan, Jerome, "Censorship of Indecency in Ireland: A View from Abroad" [1998] 16 *Cardozo Arts and Entertainment Law Journal* 53–80.

Post, Robert C. (ed.), *Censorship and Silencing: Practices of Cultural Regulation* (The Getty Research Institute for the History of Art and the Humanities, Los Angeles, 1998).

CHAPTER TEN

The Authority of the State

"That the people shall know".[1]

10.1 INTRODUCTION

In 1927, Brandeis J. in the United States Supreme Court wrote that "public discussion is a political duty", that "the greatest menace to freedom is an inert people".[2] At that time, his was still a minority view, but by 1971, Harlan J. was to write for the Court:

> "The constitutional right to free expression is powerful medicine. ... It is designed to remove governmental restraints from the arena of public discussion ... in the hope that use of such freedom will ultimately produce a more capable citizenry and more perfect polity. [In this sense it is] not a sign of weakness but of strength."[3]

Harlan J. regarded freedom of expression as a sign of a self-confident society and a powerful protection against the growing power and intrusiveness of the State.

In the United States that freedom has led to a press that exposes *real* official wrongs, a press that helped force a president from office, candidates from presidential campaigns, nominees from appointment to the Bench of the Supreme Court itself. That is the kind of press that arouses resentment, particularly from politicians who feel victimised, but also from the public who fear that the press is too powerful, arrogant and intrusive. Why should a self-appointed group of people, engaged in a commercial enterprise with a profit ethic, have the power to select its victims, to expose wrongdoing and goings-on in the corridors of power? In answer to that question, Anthony Lewis,[4] celebrated columnist with the *New York Times*, cites three cases:

1. *New York Times v Sullivan*[5] where an attempt was made to use the law of

---

[1] Former logo of Columbia Graduate School of Journalism; *cf.* the biblical reference John 8:32: "And ye shall know the truth and the truth shall make you free".

[2] *Whitney v California* 274 U.S. 357, at 375 (1927).

[3] *Cohen v California* 403 U.S. 15, at 23–5 (1971).

[4] Anthony Lewis, John Foster Memorial Lecture 1987, 9 *London Review of Books* No. 21, 26 (November 1987); see also Anthony Lewis, *Make No Law* (Vintage Books, New York, 1992).

[5] 376 U.S. 254 (1964).

libel for a new purpose, a political purpose, to frighten news organisations from covering the racial struggle in the South. If that had been allowed to happen, it would have made a great difference to that struggle, because most Americans were not aware of the cruel reality of racism until the news reports of the 1950s and 1960s confronted them with it. The impact of television was particularly powerful and a major player in the quest for new equal rights laws and social change. The US Supreme Court held that the First Amendment to the Constitution allowed robust and uninhibited speech about public life. As politicians have parliamentary privilege for what they say in the course of their duties, there must be a corollary public privilege to criticise, to assert meaningful control over the political process, and the means to effect that control is through the media.

2. *Near v Minnesota*,[6] which concerned a newspaper that made crude attacks on public officials, accusing them of corrupt alliances with gangsters. The paper was also viciously anti-Semitic. The Minnesota legislature introduced a law to close down newspapers that were a public nuisance, but the US Supreme Court by a five to four majority found that the legislation violated the First Amendment. Open public discussion was necessary to prevent abuse of official power; therefore, there should be no prior restraint.

3. *New York Times v US*,[7] the "Pentagon Papers" case, in which the *New York Times* and *Washington Post* published excerpts from a secret official history of the Vietnam war while the war was still going on. The government sought an injunction against further publication, on the grounds of the threat it posed for national security. The injunction was refused. The government had shown no threat of vital breaches in security, only the possibility of embarrassment. The federal judge sympathised with the government but said:

> "[A] cantankerous press, an obstinate press, a ubiquitous press must be suffered by those in authority in order to preserve the even greater values of freedom of expression and the right of the people to know."[8]

Cases in Britain and in Ireland have raised similar issues but not all, as we shall see, with similar results.

10.2 THE IRISH CONSTITUTION

In the United States the constitutional development of freedom of the press has been clear, although not untroubled. In Ireland the constitutional formulation does not appear as positive or forthright. The absolutist nature of the former – "Congress shall make no law abridging ... the freedom of the press" – can be

---

[6] 283 U.S. 697 (1931).

[7] 403 U.S. 713 (1971).

[8] *New York Times v US* 328 F. Supp. 324 (1971), Gurfein J. at 331.

contrasted with the very tentative nature of Article 40.6.1.i, where freedom of the press could be said to be conceded rather than declared:

> "[T]he State shall endeavour to ensure that organs of public opinion, such as the radio, the press, the cinema, while preserving their rightful liberty of expression, including criticism of Government policy, shall not be used to undermine ... the authority of the State."

In the US the state must not interfere with freedom of the press, while in Ireland the constitutional mandate is the reverse: the State has a duty to ensure that the press will not overstep the mark. The only saving grace is the fact that Article 40.6.1.i talks of actually undermining the authority of the State, rather than "tending to" undermine it, but in case there was any doubt, the tailpiece reminds us that the publication or utterance of seditious matter is an offence punishable by law.

Another issue that arises in this formulation is the meaning of the term "the rightful liberty" of the press. Mr de Valera wished to prevent "liberty degenerating into licence".[9] There was no room, he said, for anarchy or anarchical principles.[10] Freedom of the press was freedom within the bounds of the common good and, in particular, within the requirements of the preservation of the State. The press clause attracted a lot of attention in the Dáil during the debate on the draft constitution, where views ranged from a belief that it was harmless and therefore should not be there at all, to a belief that it completely negated the right the article purported to guarantee. However, the inclusion of the phrase "including criticism of government policy" was the only concession Mr de Valera was prepared to make. While it is inconceivable in a democracy that the freedom of the press should not extend to criticism of government policy, nonetheless the phrase could be of considerable significance in qualifying and restricting the scope of the mandate on the State not to let the media be used to undermine the "authority of the State". The concept of the "authority of the State" is so wide that, if it were not circumscribed in this way, it could be used to suppress or punish mere expressions of dissent or criticism of State institutions and officials. The "authority of the State" certainly appears broader than the security or preservation of the State.

The Constitution has not often been invoked in this regard in cases relating to the media. An exception was *AG for England and Wales v Brandon Book Publishers*,[11] concerning publication of a book about the British secret service. Also in *The State (Lynch) v Cooney*[12] the Court was concerned with the "duty of the State" under Article 40.6.1.i to intervene to prevent broadcasts on radio or television which would endanger the authority of the State. However, the Court recognised that:

> "These ... are objective determinations and obviously the fundamental

---

[9] 68 *Dáil Debates*, Col.425 (Report stage).
[10] 67 *Dáil Debates*, Col.1634.
[11] [1986] I.R. 597; [1987] I.L.R.M. 135 (discussed below).
[12] [1982] I.R. 337; [1983] I.L.R.M. 89.

rights of citizens to express freely their opinions and convictions cannot be curtailed or prevented on any irrational or capricious ground. It must be presumed that when the Oireachtas conferred these powers on the Minister it intended that they be exercised only in conformity with the Constitution."[13]

In setting out Article 40.6.1.i, a tailpiece was added that made the "publication or utterance of blasphemous, seditious, or indecent matter" a punishable offence. Blasphemous and indecent matter were discussed in Chapter 9, leaving seditious matter to be discussed here.

10.3 SEDITIOUS MATTER

Since the sixteenth century there has been concern to prevent the publication of seditious matter, which in reality often meant any matter critical of the government or the institutions of the State. The main weapon used against the press was the common-law offence of seditious libel. Prosecutions and threatened prosecutions were very frequent, especially from the end of the eighteenth century when the growth of the Volunteer Movement brought the press into conflict with the administration.[14] The offence of seditious libel was originally intended to protect the government and prevent loss of confidence in it. In the early days even trivial criticisms could be punished and the threat of prosecution proved an effective deterrent. It seems that, unlike blasphemous and other forms of criminal libel, intention – in this case an intention to subvert public order or government – was required.[15] Otherwise, the statutory provisions of Part II of the Defamation Act 1961 apply to seditious libel as to the other forms of criminal libel.

The editor of the *Irish Press* was prosecuted and fined for seditious libel under the Constitution (Amendment No.17) Act 1931 arising out of a series of

---

[13] *ibid.*, O'Higgins C.J., at 361 and 94 respectively. Reference was also made to the Constitution by O'Flaherty J. in *O'Toole v RTÉ* [1993] I.L.R.M. 458, at 467; and by Keane J. in *Carrigaline Community Television v Minister for Transport, Energy and Communications* [1997] 1 I.L.R.M. 241, at 288-290.

[14] See Brian Inglis, *The Freedom of the Press in Ireland 1784–1841* (Faber and Faber, London, 1954).

[15] Peter F. Carter-Ruck and Harvey Starte, *Carter-Ruck on Libel and Slander* (5th ed., Butterworths, London, 1997), pp.216-7. Seditious libel punished as a crime any speech "that may tend to lessen [the King] in the esteem of his subjects, may weaken his government, or may raise jealousies between him and his people" (W. Blackstone, *Commentaries on the laws of England*, 123); Robert C. Post, "The Social Foundations of Defamation Law: Reputation and the Constitution" (1986) 74 Cal.L.Rev. 691, at p.702, note 67, also refers to W.B. Odgers, *A Digest of the Law of Libel and Slander* 479-98 (4th ed., 1905), and includes a quote from 1724 to the effect that while libel on private persons tends to create bad blood and to cause a disturbance of the public peace, it is a very high aggravation of a libel that it tends to scandalize the Government, by reflecting on those who are intrusted with the administration of public affairs, which does not only endanger the public peace ... but also has a direct tendency to breed in the people a dislike of their governors and incline them to faction and sedition.

articles alleging police brutality towards Republican sympathisers.[16] Apart from that, the common-law offence has hardly been used in modern times. One could thus conclude that the common-law offence of seditious libel is no longer necessary in Irish law. Firstly, the original rationale of the offence, namely to protect government from criticism, is no longer a valid aspiration. It belonged to a pre-democratic age. Now, with the constitutional recognition of the press's right to criticise government policy, an offence of seditious libel can ultimately play only a residual role, if any, in protecting the State from such criticism as is calculated or intended to undermine the authority of the State, but not the authority of the government of the day. Secondly, the common-law offence is rendered unnecessary by the existence of statutory provisions governing a variety of forms of sedition.[17]

10.3.1 Statute Law

A number of statutes, especially in the 1920s and 1930s, contained provisions relating to seditious libel. The Public Safety Act 1927, for example, provided for the suppression of and prohibition of the importation of periodicals containing seditious libel (sections 10 and 11(1)).[18] The Constitution (Amendment No.17) Act 1931 removed the requirement of the leave of a High Court judge for the prosecution of a newspaper for seditious libel.[19] The Emergency Powers Act 1939 empowered the government to make orders prohibiting the publication or dissemination of subversive statements and propaganda (section 2(2)(i)). All of these Acts should be seen as emergency legislation, occasioned, if not necessitated, by the unsettled period following the foundation of the State.

The Censorship of Films Act 1923, which was not emergency legislation and which is still in force with slight amendments, did not contain any reference to seditious matter. The Wireless Telegraphy Act 1926, the Act that provided the foundation for radio broadcasting, authorised ministerial control of wireless telegraphy in time of national emergency (section 10). The short-lived Public Safety Act 1927 contained provisions relating to newspapers, which were to be picked up again in the Constitution (Amendment No.17) Act 1931 and the Offences against the State Act in 1939. The offences provided for included possession of documents relating to unlawful organisations[20] and the

---

[16] John Horgan, "State Policy and the Press" (1984) 8(2), *Media and Popular Culture, The Crane Bag* 51.

[17] See also Law Reform Commission, *Report on the Crime of Libel* (LRC 41–1991), at p.10 and *Report of the Constitution Review Group* (Pn.2632, Government Publications, Dublin, 1996), pp.297–9, recommending that the reference to "seditious" matter be deleted from Art. 40.6.1.i of the Constitution.

[18] The Act was short-lived. It was passed in response to the killing of the Minister for Justice and was repealed the following year.

[19] S.33. This Act, which established a military tribunal to try offences, totally undermined the 1922 Constitution then in force. The military tribunal banned *An Phoblacht*, the *Irish Worker*, the *Worker's Voice* and even some foreign publications (John Horgan, *Irish Media – A Critical History Since 1922* (Routledge, London, 2001) p.31).

[20] S.6 of the 1931 Act and s.21 of the 1939 Act, respectively.

publication by newspapers of statements by or on behalf of or emanating from an unlawful organisation.[21]

Indeed, military censorship in the first years of the new State,[22] during which even the *Irish Independent* and *Evening Herald* were temporarily banned because of their support for the irregulars,[23] gave way to wartime censorship. The Emergency Powers Act 1939 was a temporary wartime measure which was renewed annually and expired in 1946. It allowed the government to make emergency orders to

> "[A]uthorise and provide for the censorship, control, or partial or complete suspension of communication … (section 2(2)(h)),
>
> [and to]
>
> make provision for preserving and safeguarding the secrecy of official documents and information and for controlling the publication of official information and for prohibiting the publication or spreading of subversive statements and propaganda, and authorise and provide for the control and censorship of newspapers and periodicals." (section 2(2)(i))

Wartime censorship was vigorously enforced.[24] Copy had to be submitted to the official censor who was authorised to delete paragraphs and to suggest amendments.[25] The neutrality of the State had to be safeguarded, but media censorship went well beyond that. Weather reports were censored, as were reports of parliamentary debates.[26] A number of newspapers were banned and radio reports were tightly controlled. In addition, import duties were levied on all foreign publications as a budgetary measure in 1933 and maintained until 1971.

10.3.1.1 Offences against the State Act 1939

The Offences against the State Act 1939, which is still in force,[27] contains

---

[21] S.9 of the 1931 Act and s.23(1) of the 1939 Act, respectively.

[22] Official Notice of Military Censorship of Newspapers and Publications, July 2, 1922. See *Collected Orders*, Part 1, p.67; 1 *Dáil Debates*, Cols 797–8.

[23] See above, n.16, at p.52. On wartime censorship see generally, Donal Ó Drisceoil, *Censorship in Ireland 1939–1945 – Neutrality, Politics and Society* (Cork University Press, Cork, 1996).

[24] See Kieran Woodman, *Media Control in Ireland, 1923–1983* (Galway University Press, Galway, 1985), pp.75–6; Hugh Oram, *The Newspaper Book: A History of Newspapers in Ireland, 1649–1983* (MO Books, Dublin, 1983); above, n.16, at p.54; Joe Carroll, *The Irish Times*, August 7–13, 1983 (series of six articles) and Ó Drisceoil, above, n.23, at Chaps 4 and 5.

[25] 89 *Dáil Debates*, Cols 715-721.

[26] 24 *Seanad Debates*, Col.2573.

[27] Ss.10–14 of the 1939 Act contain prohibitions on publications, possession of treasonable, seditious or incriminating documents and the obligation to print the printer's name and address on public documents. An informal consolidation of the legislation 1939–1998 is included in the *Report of the Committee to Review the Offences against the State Acts 1939–1998 and related matters* (Government Publications, Dublin, 2002), p.359.

provisions in relation to unlawful associations, seditious matter and seditious documents. The Act makes it an offence to set up in type, print or publish any seditious document (section 10(1)). The term "seditious document" is defined in the Act as including a document containing matter calculated or tending to undermine public order or the authority of the State; or which alleges, implies or suggests that the government in power under the Constitution is not the lawful government; or that the military forces maintained under the Constitution are not the lawful military forces of the State; or a document in which words, abbreviations or symbols, referable to a military body are used in referring to an unlawful organisation (section 2).

It is an offence under the Act to send or contribute seditious matter to any newspaper or periodical and for the proprietor to publish any letter, article or communication which is sent or contributed by, or on behalf of, an unlawful organisation (section 10(2)). The scope of the section is very broad. Punishment includes fines and imprisonment, as well as forfeiture of every copy and of printing machinery (section 10(3)). The forfeiture of printing machinery was always the greatest deterrent because it had the potential to deprive a person of his or her livelihood. It is an offence also to refuse to hand up such a document or publication if requested to do so by a garda (section 10(4)). In the case of seditious matter printed outside the State, the Minister can authorise the Gardaí to seize and destroy all copies or can prohibit its importation (section 11(1)).

Even to have a treasonable, seditious or incriminating document in one's possession, without printing it, is an offence under the Act, regardless of one's purpose (section 12(1)). In that case, it is a good defence for a newspaper proprietor, editor or "chief officer" to destroy the document within twenty-four hours of receipt without making any copy of it (section 12(5)). The emphasis, therefore, is on suppression of such a document rather than evaluation or consideration of its content or the underlying problem. The definition of "incriminating" document in the Act is extremely broad[28] and it is arguable that the present peace process could have been seriously hampered if such provisions had been invoked. Contributions at various points in time from the UDA and IRA might not have been published. In practice, of course, many of these provisions have simply been ignored. Unlawful organisations were denied access to broadcasting but their statements were fully reported and analysed in the print media.

One provision of the Offences against the State Act that is of general application and unrelated to sedition is the requirement that the printer's name and address be on all documents — not just seditious documents — printed and intended for the public, with the exception of newspapers printed on their own premises (sections 13 and 14). The latter is not an unusual provision.[29]

---

[28] An "incriminating document" is defined in the Act as one issued by, or emanating from, an unlawful organisation, or appearing to be so issued or so to emanate or purporting or appearing to aid and abet any such organisation or calculated to promote the formation of an unlawful organisation (s.2).

[29] The provision in the Offences against the State Act 1939 may have been taken over from the Newspapers, Printers and Reading Rooms Repeal Act 1869, which did not apply to Ireland. That provision was originally intended to suppress certain treasonable and seditious societies in existence during the Napoleonic Wars. See Colin Manchester, "The

Other countries, such as France, have similar provisions in their law. Such a provision may have made sense at a time when the printer had control over what he printed but with modern technology that is no longer the case. Nowadays many books, periodicals and newspapers are printed outside the State and there can be little argument for requiring the printer to put his/her name and address on them without requiring the author, editor or publisher to do so, as they are the people who have control over content.

In this and other respects, the Offences against the State Acts go far beyond what is necessary for the protection of the State in a modern democracy and could be open to challenge on constitutional grounds.[30] The UN Human Rights Committee expressed concern about aspects of the Acts and recommended in particular that the need for the Special Criminal Court be examined to ensure its conformity with the International Covenant on Civil and Political Rights.[31] The Law Reform Commission also urged reform.[32] A Committee established to review the Offences against the State Acts 1939-1998 reported in 2002.[33] Among the many other provisions of the Acts considered were the provisions concerned with "information offences". The Offences against the State (Amendment) Act 1972, for example, contains a wide-ranging provision making it an offence to issue a public statement, orally, in writing or otherwise, that constitutes an interference with the course of justice (section 4). The provision has been criticised by the Review Committee as being too broad and

---

Newspapers, Printers and Reading Rooms Repeal Act 1869: A Case for Repeal?" (1982) 2 LS 180.

[30] James Casey, *Constitutional Law in Ireland* (3rd ed., Round Hall Sweet & Maxwell, Dublin, 2000), at p.558, says that in the US such a sweeping statute would be unconstitutional.

[31] UN Human Rights Committee, *Comments of the Human Rights Committee*, July 28, 1993, paras 11, 19. See also the Report of the UN Special Rapporteur on Human Rights, E/CN.4/2000/63/Add.2, January 10, 2000, available at *www.unhchr.ch* under "Issues", "Freedom of opinion and expression", "Documents", "Report". Part V of the 1939 Act, which allows the government to pass a resolution establishing a special court when the ordinary courts are inadequate to handle a particular situation, is part of the emergency legislation. The present Special Criminal Court dates from 1972. The decision of the Dáil to rescind the state of emergency (448 *Dáil Debates*, Cols1538–1587) did not affect these aspects of the Offences against the State Acts, which are part of the ordinary law rather than emergency law.

[32] Law Reform Commission, *Consultation Paper on the Crime of Libel*, 1991, rec.25. The LRC took the view that the scheme of censorship, the Censorship Acts and the Offences against the State Act 1939 should be examined: "Many of these provisions are outdated and may be inconsistent with modern views on what is required in the public interest. Others may be constitutionally suspect. Some are confusing and ambiguous". See also above, LRC, *Report*, n.17, rec.30.

[33] *Report of the Committee to Review the Offences against the State Acts 1939–1998* (Government Publications, Dublin, 2002), also known as "The Hederman Report", as the committee was chaired by a former Supreme Court judge of that name. Its recommendations have not yet been acted upon, but the Criminal Justice (Terrorist Offences) Bill 2002 was published in December 2002. It adds to the measures contained in the Offences against the State Acts, and is, therefore, itself open to criticism, in terms of overbreadth and disproportionality — see Donncha O'Connell, "Anti-terror laws go too far" (2003) 12(3) *Metro Éireann* (available at *www.metroeireann.com/contents/donncha.htm*).

at odds with the right of free speech in Article 40.6.1.i of the Constitution.[34] Similarly, section 8 of the 1998 Act, which creates an offence of unlawful collection of information, was considered by the majority of the Committee to be far too widely drawn. The majority instanced journalists writing a profile of a politician or publishing a "Who's Who", who might find themselves technically in breach of the section and having to meet the burden of proof in respect of an offence which carries the possibility of up to ten years imprisonment. [35]

Other statutes make it an offence to advocate the commission of the offence of forcible entry,[36] to recruit, incite or invite others to join, support or assist an unlawful organisation.[37] The Prohibition of Incitement to Hatred Act 1989 makes it an offence to incite hatred on grounds of race, colour, nationality, origins, membership of the travelling community or sexual orientation.

The Broadcasting Authority (Amendment) Act 1976 prohibits the broadcasting of matter likely or tending to undermine the authority of the State (section 3(1)(a)). The ministerial order required to implement the ban on interviews with spokespersons or representatives of certain listed organisations, resulting from section 31 of the Broadcasting Authority Act 1960, as amended by section 16 of the 1976 Act, was not renewed after January 1994. It was finally repealed by the Broadcasting Act 2001. Discussion of the section 31 ban is therefore largely academic but because it reflects a very important time in recent Irish history, some explanation of its history and failings is appropriate.

10.3.1.2 The Broadcasting Bans

The Broadcasting Authority Act 1960, which heralded the advent of television broadcasting, contained a provision at section 31:

> "The Minister may direct the Authority in writing to refrain from broadcasting any particular matter of any particular class and the Authority shall comply with the direction."

This section, which was originally intended as a fallback measure, that is, a reserve power for use in emergency situations, went unnoticed for over a decade until 1971. In that year the first ministerial directive was issued in accordance with section 31, in response to a "7 Days" current affairs programme on RTÉ, which included interviews with members of an illegal organisation, the IRA. In the previous years there had been government interference with programming on a number of occasions,[38] and in 1966 Taoiseach Seán Lemass had said in a Dáil speech:

---

[34] Above, n.33, *Report*, at paras 6.176–6.181.
[35] Above, n.33, *Report*, at paras 6.163–6.172.
[36] Prohibition of Forcible Entry and Occupation Act 1971, s.4(1).
[37] Criminal Law Act 1976, s.3, which was introduced in response to the violence in Northern Ireland and therefore is emergency in nature.
[38] See Leila Doolan, Jack Dowling, and Bob Quinn, *Sit Down and Be Counted: The Cultural Evolution of a Television Station* (Wellington Publishers, Dublin, 1969), at p.55; 227 *Dáil Debates*, Col.1661; 228 *Dáil Debates*, Cols 1002–3.

"[T]he Government reject[s] the view that Radio Teilifís Éireann should be, either generally or in regard to its current affairs and news programmes, completely independent of Government supervision. As a public institution supported by public funds and operating under statute it has the duty … to sustain public respect for the institutions of Government. … The Government will take such action by way of making representations or otherwise as may be necessary to ensure that RTÉ does not deviate from the due performance of this duty."[39]

Section 31 was to become a central feature of Irish broadcasting, as ministerial orders invoking it were renewed annually from 1976 onwards. The scope of the provision was narrowed by section 16 of the Broadcasting Authority (Amendment) Act 1976.[40] The intended effect of the section 31 orders was to deny airtime to the IRA and other organisations banned in the State and in Northern Ireland, to deprive them of the oxygen of publicity and the air of legitimacy that it was believed appearing on the broadcast media would accord them. Sinn Féin, which was not a banned organisation, was later added to the list and, although it was to become a legally registered political party in the State, was prohibited from making a party political broadcast in the run-up to the general election of 1982, in which it was fielding candidates.[41] The Supreme Court in *State (Lynch) v Cooney*,[42] in which Sinn Féin challenged the section 31 order, applied the presumption of constitutionality, *i.e.* that all statutes passed by the Oireachtas since the coming into force of the Constitution in 1937 are presumed to be in conformity with the Constitution:

"The basis for any attempt at control must be, according to the Constitution [Article 40.6.1], the overriding considerations of public order and public morality. The constitutional provision in question refers to organs of public opinion and these must be held to include television as well as radio. It places upon the State the obligation to ensure that these organs of public opinion shall not be used to undermine public order or public morality or the authority of the State. It follows that the use of such organs of public opinion for the purpose of securing or advocating

---

[39] 224 *Dáil Debates*, Cols 1045–6.

[40] It stated (s.16(1)): "Where the Minister is of the opinion that the broadcasting of a particular matter or any matter of a particular class would be likely to promote, or incite to, crime or would tend to undermine the authority of the State, he may by order direct the Authority to refrain from broadcasting the matter or any matter of the particular class, and the Authority shall comply with the order." An order under the section was to remain in force for up to twelve months and could be extended by further orders of similar duration (s.16(1A)). An order could be annulled by either House of the Oireachtas (s.16(1B)) but this never happened. One of the safeguards pointed to when the amending legislation was being introduced was the provision for regular parliamentary scrutiny. In fact, that never happened. There was no parliamentary debate and very few parliamentary questions about s.31. Those that were asked drew very little response.

[41] Keane J. in *Coughlan v BCC and RTÉ* [2000] 3 I.R. 1 (discussed in Chap. 8 above) pointed out that the registration of political parties began in 1963 under the Electoral Act of that year (at para.148).

[42] Above, n.12.

support for organisations which seek by violence to overthrow the State or its institutions is a use which is prohibited by the Constitution. Therefore it is clearly the duty of the State to intervene to prevent broadcasts on radio or television which are aimed at such a result or which in any way would be likely to have the effect of promoting or inciting to crime or endangering the authority of the State. These, however, are objective determinations and obviously the fundamental rights of citizens to express freely their convictions and opinions cannot be curtailed or prevented on any irrational or capricious ground. It must be presumed that when the Oireachtas conferred these powers on the Minister [*i.e.* to make orders invoking section 31] it intended that they be exercised only in conformity with the Constitution."[43]

Section 31, therefore, was not unconstitutional. That did not necessarily mean that the State was obliged to keep it in force, but merely that the Constitution did not prevent such a measure. Needless to say, the State took the Court's decision as the green light to continue the ban. This occurred despite the fact that the ban was impractical, given that the British channels, which were not affected by the ban, could be received in Ireland.

The ban also created a climate of repression and self-censorship within RTÉ. The tendency was always to err on the safe side, and it was easier not to make programmes that might cause problems. Besides, the Supreme Court had said, *inter alia*, in *Cooney* that the fact that the text of the broadcast might be innocuous was not relevant to the issues before the Court.[44] This led to some confusion and a tendency to interpret the ban more widely than was ultimately decided to be necessary. RTÉ excluded from the airwaves anyone who was a member of Sinn Féin, regardless of the topic on which s/he was to speak. Mushroom-growing, local water schemes, trade union matters and a strike in a factory were all excluded because the intended interviewees were members of Sinn Féin. The orders invoking section 31, however, referred only to spokespersons for, or representatives of, Sinn Féin. It would later be held in *O'Toole v RTÉ*[45] that RTÉ had interpreted the ban too broadly, and that the order did not prevent ordinary members of Sinn Féin speaking on an innocuous subject on the airwaves. The Broadcasting Complaints Commission rejected a complaint about section 31 in 1988. The Commission did not give any reasons but in effect upheld the extension of section 31 to ordinary members of Sinn Féin speaking on innocuous subjects.[46]

Meanwhile, election coverage was also affected. When Gerry Adams won his seat at Westminster, he could be interviewed on broadcast stations all over the world. On RTÉ only the losing candidate could be interviewed.[47] Section

---

[43] *ibid.* at 94, O'Higgins C.J.

[44] *ibid.* at 97.

[45] Above, n.13.

[46] *The Sunday Tribune*, November 8, 1987, April 24, 1988, and Annual Report of the BCC for 1988.

[47] By 1984 Sinn Féin had won over one hundred thousand votes in the North and about thirty local council seats in the Republic, yet the electorate was not allowed to hear them interviewed on RTÉ. Voters could not have their views or grievances expressed on radio

31 continued to operate until January 1994, despite the fact that the Broadcasting Authority (Amendment) Act 1976 already offered a viable alternative in section 3, substituting section 18(1)(A) of the 1960 Act:

"The Authority is hereby prohibited from including in any of its broadcasts or in any matter referred to in paragraph (c) of subsection (1) [*i.e.* news, current affairs] of this section anything which may reasonably be regarded as being likely to promote, or incite to, crime or as tending to undermine the authority of the State."

This section had been relied on to prevent interviews with Martin Galvin of Noraid in 1984[48] and with journalist Nell McCafferty in 1987.[49]

It seems peculiar that an Act would have two separate sections dealing with the same problem. Section 31, as amended, required a ministerial order of limited duration to implement it, while section 18(1)(A) is permanent and automatic. The same remedy attached to both: a complaint that either section had been breached could be made to the Broadcasting Complaints Commission. One advantage that section 18(1)(A) has over section 31 is that it incorporates a standard of reasonableness: the authority is prohibited from broadcasting any matter which "may reasonably be regarded" as likely to promote or incite to crime or as tending to undermine the authority of the State. The ministerial orders implementing section 31, on the other hand, were directed at specified organisations and confined mainly to interviews or reports of interviews with representatives of, or spokespersons for, them. It is true that the original section 31 of the 1960 Act was of broader scope and could have been invoked by a minister to prevent the broadcasting of totally unrelated matter, but since the amendment in the 1976 Act that was no longer the case; sections 31 and 18 covered essentially the same ground.

Section 31, as amended, was extended to the local radio stations by the Radio and Television Act 1988 (section 12). In the same year Jenny McGeever, a journalist with RTÉ, who breached section 31, lost her job. She had included a few words from Martin McGuinness, a leading member of Sinn Féin, in her report for the "Morning Ireland" radio programme on the funeral of three alleged IRA members killed in the Gibraltar shooting.[50] Some months later, in October, the British government announced its decision to introduce a similar, though less restrictive, ban. The British ban did not extend to elected representatives,

---

or television by their elected representatives. The right of the public to information on a whole host of issues, including the political situation in the North, was denied in this way. This effect was at its most poignant during the Hume-Adams talks, which were crucial to the development of the peace process. Gerry Adams could not be interviewed about these talks, or about his defeat in the Westminster elections of 1992.

[48] *The Irish Times*, August 24, 1984.

[49] *The Irish Times*, November 23, 1987. It also caused transmission of a programme "Irish America Report" to be deferred. An edited version of the programme, which reported on the activities of Irish-American groups in relation to Northern Ireland, was later transmitted (*The Irish Times*, March 30, 1988).

[50] Journalist Jenny McGeever's subsequent High Court action against RTÉ was settled (*The Sunday Tribune*, September 18, 1988).

election campaigns or parliamentary proceedings. Only words spoken by a person appearing on a programme were covered; therefore, films or stills with voice-overs were permitted.[51] Both bans became the subject of (separate) complaints to Strasbourg.

10.3.2 European Commission on Human Rights

10.3.2.1 Purcell v Ireland

A challenge to section 31 was taken to Strasbourg by a number of RTÉ and Raidió na Gaeltachta journalists. The European Commission on Human Rights in *Purcell v Ireland*[52] accepted that section 31 constituted an interference with the journalists' right under Article 10 of the European Convention on Human Rights to receive and impart information and ideas but was satisfied that the restrictions were prescribed by law and that the aim pursued was legitimate. The applicants had not disputed the seriousness of the terrorist threat in Ireland, and section 31 did not prohibit the reporting of the activities of the listed organisations, only interviews with their spokespersons:

> "[I]t thus prohibits the use of the broadcast media for the purpose of advocating support for organisations which seek to undermine, by violence and other illegal means, the constitutional order and the fundamental rights and freedoms it guarantees."[53]

The restriction was necessary in a democratic society, the Commission said, as there was evidence of a pressing social need. Besides, states have a margin of appreciation in assessing whether such a need exists. It was not the Commission's role to determine whether other measures were more appropriate or to assess the expediency and efficiency of the measures taken. The Commission's role was rather to determine:

(i) whether the reasons adduced for the section 31 restrictions were relevant and sufficient under Article 10(2), and

(ii) whether the Minister had convincing reasons for assuming the existence of a pressing social need.[54]

In a situation where politically-motivated violence was a constant threat to the lives and security of the population and where the advocates of this violence seek access to the mass media for publicity purposes, it is particularly difficult to strike a fair balance, the Commission said.[55] The Commission was satisfied

---

[51] See ARTICLE 19, *Censorship, Secrecy and the Irish Troubles* (ARTICLE 19, London, 1989). In compliance with the terms of the Representation of the People Act, the ban was lifted during the run-up to local, general and European elections to allow candidates to be asked about election issues only (*The Irish Times*, April 11, 1989).

[52] (1991) 12 H.R.L.J. No.6-7, 254. RTÉ producer Betty Purcell's name was given to the case.

[53] *ibid.* at p.259.

[54] *ibid.* at p.260.

[55] *ibid.*

that section 31 was designed to deny the possibility of using the broadcast media as a platform for advocating an organisation's cause, encouraging support and conveying the impression of their legitimacy. The restrictions might cause the broadcasters "inconvenience" but they were not incompatible with Article 10(2).

The decision was a disappointing one for a number of reasons. The Commission seemed to be swayed by the level of violence, the particular impact of television and the fact that the complainants did not reject the government's argument that Sinn Féin was closely linked to the IRA. It is a pity that the case did not clear the first hurdle and go to the Court, especially in light of the Court's subsequent decision in *Jersild v Denmark*.[56] In *Jersild*, the Court emphasised again the important role of the print and broadcast media. It was for journalists, not courts, to decide what techniques of reporting should be adopted. Furthermore:

> "News reporting based on interviews, whether edited or not, constitutes one of the most important means whereby the press is able to play its vital role. ... The punishment of a journalist for assisting in the dissemination of statements made by another person in an interview would seriously hamper the contribution of the press to discussion of matters of public interest and should not be envisaged unless there are particularly strong reasons for doing so."[57]

It is possible that the scale of the problem in Northern Ireland at the time would have constituted a "particularly strong" reason. One telling difference between the presentation of the case before the Court in *Jersild*, compared with that in *Purcell*, was that in the former it was possible to show the court footage of the programme containing the interviews with the racist Green-jackets. In the case of *Purcell*, on the other hand, it was not as easy to do so because the section 31 ban, as a form of prior restraint, had prevented the broadcasting of interviews.[58]

10.3.2.2 Developments after Purcell

Following the Commission's decision that *Purcell* was manifestly ill-founded, it was perhaps inevitable that the *Brind*[59] case on the British ban would also be declared inadmissible.[60]

---

[56] *Jersild v Denmark*, Series A, No.298; (1995) 19 E.H.R.R. 1; see also *Castells v Spain*, Series A, No.236; (1992) 14 E.H.R.R. 445 and *Surek v Turkey*, App. Nos 23927/94, 24277/94, judgment of March 3, 1999, July 8, 1999. See further below.

[57] *ibid.* at para.51.

[58] Unlike the censorship of film or publications, the way s.31 operated meant that there was no paper or footage trail. John Horgan (*Irish Media – A Critical History Since 1922*, Routledge, London, 2001, at p.123) says that the s.31 ban left a yawning gap in the electronic media archive for more than twenty of the politically most significant years in twentieth-century Ireland, and led to a consistent tendency to underestimate the strength of Sinn Féin at election times.

[59] *R v Secretary of State for the Home Department, ex parte Brind* (1991) 1 A.C. 696,

Meanwhile in 1990, when the *Purcell* case was still pending before the European Commission of Human Rights, Larry O'Toole, the chairman of a strike committee at the Gateaux bakery in Dublin, had been interviewed on a number of occasions by RTÉ about the strike. The first interview was broadcast but the remainder were not, because it had emerged that Mr O'Toole was a member of Sinn Féin. In the High Court action that followed,[61] it was held that RTÉ was wrong on three counts in its interpretation of the ministerial order invoking section 31:

(i) RTÉ had misinterpreted the Ministerial order by applying it to ordinary members of Sinn Féin, when it was clearly confined to representatives of, and spokespersons for, Sinn Féin.[62]

(ii) The obligations of fairness and impartiality in respect of news and current affairs imposed on RTÉ by the Broadcasting Authority Acts were infringed by the refusal on arbitrary grounds to allow the views of the workers in a major industrial dispute which was arousing widespread public attention,

---

[1991] 2 W.L.R. 588 (HL). The British broadcasting ban was upheld by the High Court in Belfast in 1990, when an application for judicial review was refused. A Sinn Féin City Councillor had argued that the ban breached the NI Constitution Act 1973, which prevents government ministers from discriminating against groups or individuals on grounds of religious belief or political opinion (*The Irish Times*, September 8, 1990; Irish Times Law Report, November 26, 1990). Some months earlier, a song by the Pogues about the Guildford Four was banned from the airwaves under the British ban (*The Sunday Tribune*, October 22, 1989). The British ban was extended in December 1990 to cover cable and non-domestic satellite television services (*The Irish Times*, December 20, 1990). In 1994 Bernadette McAliskey lost a High Court action challenging the BBC's decision to use subtitles instead of her voice in broadcasting a studio debate on political violence. She had never been a member of any of the listed organisations. In the televised debate she had said she understood why violence occurred (*The Irish Times*, May 28, 1994). As in *Purcell*, the challenge to the British ban was rejected by the European Commission: *Brind v UK* (App. No.18714/91, (1994) 77 D.R. 42). Nonetheless, *Brind* was useful, at least for lawyers, in the sense that it provided the opportunity to fight the case in the Court of Appeal and House of Lords with reference to the European Convention on Human Rights and the principles and standards it enshrines. *Purcell* was also useful in that it focused attention on s.31 and demanded, for the first time in its contentious history, that its use be justified by the authorities. The victory for the government was a hollow one and the first step in the dismantling process of s.31. As one of the lawyers involved in the case said: "This decision [*Purcell*] … seemed to effectively reverse the special status of political speech acknowledged in earlier decisions of the Commission and Court. But there is the basis of a jurisprudence which can be built on that recognises the role of the media which Irish and British courts ought to be encouraged to follow." (Kevin Boyle, lecture given at the Irish Centre for European Law, Trinity College Dublin, 1992; edited version, "Freedom of Expression and Democracy" in Liz Heffernan (ed.), *Human Rights. A European Perspective* (Round Hall Press, Dublin, 1994), p.211, at p.212 (n.4)).

[60] *The Irish Times*, May 25, 1994.

[61] Unreported, High Court, July 31, 1992; *O'Toole v RTÉ* [1993] I.L.R.M. 454 (Sup Ct).

[62] *ibid.*, High Court, at pp.7-8 of the typescript. O'Hanlon J. relied on the judgment of O'Higgins C.J. in *The State (Lynch) v Cooney* [1982] I.R. 337 at 364: "the order is not directed against a broadcast by a particular person as an individual, or against any group of individuals, as such. It is directed against a broadcast on behalf of Sinn Féin or by any person or persons purporting to represent that organisation."

to be put forward on their behalf by the person they had appointed to be their spokesman.[63]

(iii) While access to broadcasting was not a right, a decision to single out a particular person or group and impose a blanket prohibition against his or their views on any topic whatever, expressed in their personal capacity and not as spokesman for or as representing any organisation, would have to be justified on very substantial grounds.[64]

The High Court's decision was appealed to the Supreme Court by RTÉ, apparently for purposes of clarification, and was upheld. The section 31 order only applied to spokespersons for, and representatives of, Sinn Féin, and not to ordinary members speaking on an innocuous subject, who "should be treated equally with others when [their] views do not transgress either the Constitution or the law".[65]

The Irish Government in the *Purcell* case had argued that allowing airtime to Sinn Féin would lend validity and respectability to their cause and activities. It may be argued that accessibility itself does not necessarily lend credibility. A similar argument prevailed, however, in the application by Brandon Book Publishers for judicial review of the decision by RTÉ and the IRTC not to permit the broadcasting of pre-recorded advertisements for Gerry Adams's book, *The Street and Other Stories*.[66] The independent radio stations had already interviewed Gerry Adams about his book and the ban on it.[67] Carney J. in the IRTC case accepted that there was evidence to support the broadcasters' view that:

> "Mr Adams could not be separated from his office as President of Sinn Féin and that any broadcast by him on any topic would have the *de facto* effect of advocating support for Sinn Féin."[68]

Their decision not to permit the advertisement could only be interfered with if it were perverse, irrational or malicious, the judge said, and none of those considerations arose.[69] A somewhat unexpected boost to the fight against

---

[63] *ibid.*, High Court, at p.8 of the transcript. A ministerial order prohibiting all access to members of Sinn Féin would, in the judge's view, have been open to considerable doubt as a valid exercise of the powers conferred on the Minister under s.31, as amended.

[64] *ibid.*, High Court, at p.9 of transcript.

[65] *ibid*, Supreme Court, at 467, O'Flaherty J.

[66] *Brandon Book Publishers Ltd v RTÉ* [1993] I.L.R.M. 806; *Brandon Book Publishers Ltd v IRTC*, unreported, High Court, October 29, 1993. RTÉ has a copy clearance department that vets copy before broadcasting.

[67] *The Irish Times*, August 19, 1992.

[68] Above, n.66, IRTC, at p.17 of transcript.

[69] *ibid.* at p.17 of the transcript, Carney J., relying on the principles of *The State (Keegan) v Stardust Victims Compensation Tribunal* [1986] I.R. 642; [1987] I.L.R.M. 202. It may be noted that Lord Diplock in *GCHQ* (*Council of Civil Service Union v Minister for the Civil Service* [1985] A.C. 375, 410) identified illegality, irrationality and procedural impropriety as grounds for judicial review and suggested that the European test of proportionality (deriving from administrative law and applied in such cases as *Sunday*

section 31 came from the UN Human Rights Committee in 1993. Ireland had ratified the International Covenant on Civil and Political Rights in November 1989 and was required to submit a report to the Committee concerning the implementation of the Covenant in Ireland. In response to that report, the Committee stated that the section 31 ban infringed the freedom to receive and impart information under Article 19, paragraph 2 of the Covenant[70] and that the State should take the necessary measures to ensure that Article 19 was complied with.[71]

In January 1994 the Irish government decided not to renew the order implementing section 31,[72] and as previously stated, the section has since been repealed by the Broadcasting Act 2001. The British ban was lifted shortly after the Irish one, as the peace process developed and the cessation of violence came to be accepted as genuine. However, before the British ban had been lifted, an interview with Gerry Adams on CNN in the United States caused some controversy, not because of its content, but because it was dubbed (voice-over), not only for broadcast in Britain, but for the rest of Europe as well, as the signal was uplifted to CNN's satellite from Britain.[73]

Over time, the public became accustomed to seeing and hearing Sinn Féin and all shades of opinion in Northern Ireland on Irish radio and television. As the peace process continued and the level of paramilitary violence gradually decreased, the spirit of reconciliation and forgiveness inherent in the Good Friday Agreement prevailed. Section 31 was gradually relegated to the status of a memory and the political process was allowed to continue undeterred. However, despite the relative peace, the decision by RTÉ to broadcast a lengthy interview with Brighton bomber, Patrick Magee, on September 6, 2000, in which he attempted to justify violence, led to a public outcry.[74]

10.3.3 European Court of Human Rights

The question of political violence and terrorism has been considered by the European Court of Human Rights in a number of cases. It arose in *Castells v*

Times v UK) might be added as a fourth ground in due course. The Court of Appeal was invited to adopt proportionality as a ground in *Brind*, the British broadcasting ban case, but refused to accept it as anything more than a criterion for assessing one of the three grounds identified in *GCHQ*. The House of Lords concurred but left open the possibility of future development: *R v Secretary of State for the Home Department, ex parte Brind* [1991] 1 A.C. 696, [1990] 1 All E.R. 469, at 480; [1991] 2 W.L.R. 588, [1991] 1 All E.R. 720.

[70] UN Human Rights Committee, *Comments of the Human Rights Committee*, July 28, 1993, at para.15.

[71] *ibid.* at para.21. Ireland has also ratified the Optional Protocol to the International Covenant under which individual complaints can be taken to the Committee in a similar way as to the European Commission and Court. Ireland was required to submit a further report in March 1996 and at three-year intervals after that.

[72] The first televised party political broadcast on behalf of Sinn Féin, a one-minute video for the European elections, was transmitted on May 26, 1994, some few months after the decision not to renew the Ministerial order activating s.31.

[73] *The Irish Times*, February 7, 1994, May 25, 1994.

[74] *The Irish Times*, September 7, 2000.

Spain,[75] where the threat came from the Basque separatists, whom Castells represented as a senator. In a magazine article he accused the government of not investigating crimes carried out by armed groups on Basque citizens. In fact, he went so far as to accuse the government of instigating the attacks. The article was published during a particularly violent period and Mr Castells was sentenced to imprisonment and disqualification from public office for one year. Nevertheless, the European Court of Human Rights made clear that governments must tolerate criticism and scrutiny, even more so than politicians, and that it is only in the most exceptional circumstances that a government may resort to the criminal law to punish criticism of itself:

> "In a democratic system the actions or omissions of the Government must be subject to the close scrutiny ... of the press and public opinion." (para.46)

In *Thorgeirson v Iceland*,[76] in which a journalist alleged that the incidence of police brutality was increasing, the Court found that the journalist's main purpose had been to promote reform and, because the conduct of the police was a legitimate matter of public concern, he consequently deserved a higher level of protection. More recently in *Surek v Turkey*,[77] the Court gave its views on the role of the media in situations where violence is being perpetrated against the state. In an important statement confining use of the criminal law against the media to the dissemination of hate speech and the promotion of violence, it said:

> "The Court stresses that the 'duties and responsibilities' which accompany the exercise of the right to freedom of expression by media professionals assume special significance in situations of conflict and tension. Particular caution is called for when consideration is being given to the publication of the views of representatives of organisations which resort to violence against the state lest the media become a vehicle for the dissemination of hate speech and the promotion of violence. At the same time, where such views cannot be categorised as such, contracting states cannot with reference to the protection of territorial integrity or national security or the prevention of crime or disorder restrict the right of the public to be informed of them by bringing the weight of the criminal law to bear on the media." (para.63)

The Court also considered the question of official secrets and breach of confidence in the *Spycatcher* case.[78] The intended publication in Australia in

---

[75] Above, n.56.
[76] Series A, No.239; (1992) 14 E.H.R.R. 843.
[77] Above, n.56. A large number of cases concerning conflict and national security were taken against Turkey under Art. 10 of the ECHR by Kurdish people who had been prosecuted or victimised. Some of the cases are referred to in Chap.8 above. All are available on the ECHR website (*www.echr.coe.int*) and discussed in all the leading human rights textbooks.
[78] *The Observer and The Guardian v UK*, Series A, No.216; (1992) 14 E.H.R.R. 153. See

1985 of the memoirs of Peter Wright, a former member of the British Secret Service (MI5), triggered a series of actions against publication of the book itself and against newspaper articles about the book, serialising it or containing information from it. Among the allegations made by Mr Wright were that MI5 had conducted unlawful activities calculated to undermine the Labour government in the 1970s, had burgled and "bugged" the embassies of allied and hostile countries and had planned and participated in other unlawful and covert activities at home and abroad.[79] In 1987 the book was published in the United States.

The case eventually made its way to the European Court of Human Rights, which found that there had been a violation of Article 10 during the period when the injunctions against publication were continued by the English courts after the information had been published in the United States. During the earlier period the injunctions were found to be justified for two reasons: firstly, because of the need to maintain the authority of the judiciary during the period up to the hearing of the claim for permanent injunctions; and, secondly, to protect national security, in the sense of the integrity of the Security Service.[80]

In Ireland the most far-reaching protection was contained in the Official Secrets Act 1963. The Act is still on the statute books but under review and due to be replaced.[81] In practice, it has been largely superseded by the Freedom of Information Act 1997.

10.4 THE OFFICIAL SECRETS ACT 1963

The Official Secrets Act 1963 was passed as part of the government's plan to consolidate laws and pass indigenous laws to replace those of earlier legislatures, in this case the British Official Secrets Acts of 1911 and 1920.[82]

---

also *Vereniging Weekblad Bluf! v Netherlands* Series A, No.306-A, (1995) 20 E.H.R.R. 189.

[79] *ibid.* at para.11.

[80] *ibid.* at para.56. Indeed, the protection of national security is widely recognised in international human rights instruments as an area of restriction on freedom of expression and media activities but safeguards are required to prevent governments from using it to prevent embarrassment or exposure of wrongdoing and such like. *The Johannesburg Principles on National Security, Freedom of Expression and Access to Information* (ARTICLE 19, London, 1996), based on international and regional law and practice, were drafted, *inter alia*, to "promote a clear recognition of the limited scope of restrictions on freedom of expression and freedom of information that may be imposed in the interest of national security, so as to discourage governments from using the pretext of national security to place unjustified restrictions on the exercise of these freedoms".

[81] Dáil Éireann, Select Committee on Legislation and Security, *Report on Review of the Official Secrets Act 1963* (Stationery Office, Dublin, 1997). The Criminal Justice (Protection of Confidential Information) Bill is currently being drafted (No.35 on legislative programme of government) and is due to be published in 2004.

[82] Several deputies asked why it was necessary to do so in this case and the explanation they were given was that examination papers had been leaked by an apprentice printer and therefore legislation was necessary to deal with such leaks (194 *Dáil Debates*, Cols 599–600, 603). The remedy, if it was a remedy, was to pass a full-scale official secrets act. The reality of the times, however, suggests that the IRA campaign of the 1950s may have been a more significant factor in the decision.

It was pointed out in the Dáil that it was unsatisfactory to have to rely on British legislation, especially when, as in this case, it was unsuitable and defective. The British Act of 1911 had been rushed through as emergency legislation and had passed all stages in a single day.[83]

The 1963 Act was extremely wide in its application, protecting virtually every document connected with the running of the country.[84] It bound public servants to secrecy, to safeguard official information and not to divulge it under pain of criminal sanctions. Perhaps the most disturbing feature of the Act was the provision that a Minister could certify that any document was secret or confidential. Once issued, that certificate was to be conclusive evidence of the fact that it was secret or confidential – not *prima facie* evidence, but "conclusive" evidence (section 2(3)), thus precluding the courts from inquiring into the nature of the certified document.

The Act made it an offence to communicate such information unless authorised to do so or under a duty to do so as a holder of public office or in the interest of the State (section 4(1)). It applied to all civil servants, in fact to anybody, by making it a criminal offence to communicate any information, no matter how trivial and no matter to whom, unless there was authorisation to do so. The wide definition of "official secret" and the severity of the sanctions that could be imposed meant that its chilling effect was extensive.

There have been surprisingly few prosecutions under the Act, although its impact in creating and maintaining a culture of secrecy has been no less real as a result. Section 13 of the Act prohibits the possession of any document containing, or any record whatsoever of, information relating to the operations of An Garda Síochána (police). It was invoked against a "Today Tonight" current affairs television programme on the leaking of an official Garda memorandum on the security of the British Ambassador during his holiday in Sneem, Co. Kerry. The decision to invoke the Act was an attempt to prevent the media from detailing the precise nature of the leak. It appears that the document had been marked "confidential" but did not carry a "secret" or "top secret" classification; in other words, it was sensitive but routine information.[85]

---

[83] The British Official Secrets Acts of 1911 and 1920 remained in force in Ireland in the form adopted in 1928 under the Adaptation of Enactments Act 1922, until repealed by s.3 of the 1963 Act. However, when one considers that there had been only one prosecution brought in Ireland under the British Acts and that it had been in 1933 and unsuccessful, it is still difficult to explain why the new Act was passed in 1963 and especially in the form in which it was passed.

[84] Official information, for instance, was defined in s.2 as "any secret official code word or password, and any sketch, plan, model, article, note, document or information which is secret or confidential or is expressed to be either and which is or has been in the possession, custody or control of a holder of public office, or to which he has or had access by virtue of his office, and includes information recorded by film or magnetic tape or by any other recording medium". The term "public office" was defined in the Act and it, too, was very broad, extending to "appointment to or employment under any commission, committee, tribunal or inquiry set up by the government or a Minister" (s.2(1)).

[85] See *The Irish Times*, August 15, 17, 20, 1987; *The Sunday Tribune*, August 16, 1987. The DPP decided not to bring charges against journalist Emily O'Reilly over the publication in November 1993 of the government's draft policy document on the North.

However laudable its purpose, the wording of the section is unduly wide. Section 12 of the Act also allows the prosecution – not the court – to apply to have any part of a hearing under the Act held *in camera* on the grounds that it would be prejudicial to the safety or preservation of the State and "the court shall make an order to that effect".[86]

The only successful prosecutions of the media under the Act in recent years have both been against Independent Newspapers. The first, the "Shergar" case involved the *Irish Independent* and its editor.[87] Shergar was a racehorse that had been kidnapped, and the newspaper and its editor were each fined £100 in the District Court on charges of breaching the Official Secrets Act by publishing Garda identikit pictures of two suspects in the case. They had obtained and communicated to the public confidential information (*i.e.* the pictures), reproduced from a Garda bulletin which was stamped "confidential", although the pictures themselves were not. About fifteen hundred copies of the bulletin had been circulated to Garda stations throughout the State, to the Department of Justice, and to police forces abroad. Added to that was the fact that daily press conferences had been held during the Garda investigations. In those circumstances, counsel asked, how could the pictures be regarded as secret and confidential?[88]

The Act was invoked against the media again in 1995 at the very time when it was under official review and when the government's plans to introduce freedom of information legislation were at an advanced stage. Journalist Liz Allen and Independent Newspapers were prosecuted for publishing a confidential Garda document which purported to show that the force had prior knowledge of the multi-million pound Brinks-Allied Bank robbery in January 1995. The case was heard in the District Court in March 1996 and fines were imposed.[89]

Other cases in which aspects of the Official Secrets Act or the authority of the State were invoked against the media include *AG for England and Wales v*

A Garda investigation into the leak was ordered by the Tánaiste and Minister for Foreign Affairs, Mr Spring (*The Irish Times*, April 28, 1994).

[86] The Select Committee recommended that any decision to hold proceedings *in camera* should be entirely a matter for the judiciary, not the parties (above, n.81). For a discussion of *in camera* proceedings, see Chap. 7.

[87] *DPP v Independent Newspapers* (*The Irish Times*, February 8, July 20, 1984: *Irish Independent*, July 31, 1984). Casey, above, n.30, at p.568, mentions that *The Irish Times* was also threatened with prosecution in 1976 when it was about to publish details of a proposed deal between the State and Bula Mining Ltd., but that no proceedings ensued.

[88] Could it not be argued also that the Official Secrets Act should be reserved for important matters of State, not for minor matters before the District Court? Because the ambit of Part II of the Act is extremely wide, it lacks a central focus and unity of purpose. The serious and the trivial are lumped together and given blanket protection at the expense of the rights of the individual and the public's right to disclosure. Even on its widest interpretation, the constitutional interest in the "authority of the State" could not justify blanket protection of this kind. At a minimum, the scope of s.4 in particular needs to be precisely delimited. The Select Committee recommended that criminal sanctions should apply only in respect of disclosure of certain narrow categories of information and that there should be a public interest defence. The conviction was upheld on appeal.

[89] *The Irish Times*, November 8, December 16, 1995.

Brandon Book Publishers.[90] Carroll J. in the High Court refused an injunction to prevent distribution of a book, *One Girl's War*, about the wartime exploits of the British Secret Service. The war had ended more than thirty years previously and the book posed no threat to the authority of this State, which would have been the only reason under our Constitution for granting the injunction as a restriction on freedom of expression. Because no considerations of public interest arose in this jurisdiction, the case was based solely on the principle of confidentiality deriving from the employment of the author of the book. Importantly for the media, Carroll J. cited with approval the dicta of Mason J. in the Australian case of *Commonwealth of Australia v John Fairfax and Sons Ltd*[91] to the effect that:

> "[I]t is unacceptable in our democratic society that there should be a restraint on the publication of information relating to government when the only vice of that information is that it enables the public to discuss, review and criticise government action."

Accordingly, the Court will determine the government's claim to confidentiality by reference to the public interest. Unless disclosure is likely to injure the public interest, it will not be protected. Carroll J. also recognised that:

> "[W]hat is at stake is the very important constitutional right to communicate now and not in a year or more when the case has worked its way through the courts."[92]

In another development in 1988, An Foras Forbartha was abolished and replaced by the Environmental Research Unit. The Unit was wholly within the Department of the Environment, with the result that staff had to abide by the Official Secrets Act.[93] The dangers that such a restriction poses for the public interest in information on such a sensitive issue as the environment is all too clear. In 1990 the Dáil Committee on Public Accounts was told that it could not see a consultancy report prepared for government prior to its sale of its share in Tara Mines. The reason given was that it contained confidential commercial information, which could not be disclosed under a clause inserted in the original agreement between the government and Tara Mines in 1975.[94]

---

[90] Above, n.11. Under the British legislation, a public interest immunity certificate was signed by the Secretary of State for Northern Ireland banning access to the Stalker report in the interests of national security. Mr John Stalker had been appointed to inquire into allegations of a shoot-to-kill policy in the North (*The Irish Times*, May 20, 1994). See also *R v Shayler* [2002] U.K.H.L. 11, March 21, 2002, regarding the compatibility of the UK Official Secrets Act 1989 with Art. 10 of the ECHR.

[91] (1980) 147 CLR 39, at 51, cited by Carroll J. at 136–7; See also Gerard Hogan, "Free Speech, Privacy and the Press in Ireland" (1987) P.L. 509.

[92] Above, n.11, at 602 and 138 respectively.

[93] *The Irish Times*, September 10, 1988.

[94] *The Irish Times*, February 16, March 2, 1990. It was also reported that workers in a State-sponsored body, Shannon Airport Marketing, were asked to sign the Act as part of their employment contract (*The Irish Times*, February 8, 1995).

The main difficulties with the Official Secrets Act, therefore, have been its all-embracing scope, the fact that it was liable to be invoked to deal with the most trivial of situations as well as those of national importance and, most worrying of all, the culture of secrecy that it emanated from and in turn engendered. The case for freedom of information legislation was all the more pressing as a result. A culture of secrecy pervaded Irish society and the media had a role to play in breaking it down.[95] The Official Secrets Act is the epitome of a culture of secrecy, but it is not the only element contributing to that culture. For instance, the libel laws in Britain allowed Robert Maxwell to carry out frauds over decades with impunity. In the new culture of openness that has resulted from the introduction of freedom of information legislation, the whole machinery of censorship and secrecy needs to be reviewed and reformed.

10.5 THE FREEDOM OF INFORMATION ACT 1997

The Freedom of Information Act was passed in 1997 and was heralded as an important first step in the quest to achieve greater openness and transparency in society. It embodied a recognition of the public's right of access to government-held information and presented an opportunity to move away from the long-established culture of secrecy that surrounded public life in Ireland.

The process of change began with legislation such as the Ombudsman Act 1980 and the National Archives Act 1986,[96] but the Freedom of Information Act was the major initiative, as it gave the public *direct* access to information held by government departments and public bodies. That entitlement created the need for a sea-change in the whole ethos and work practice of the public service, which had previously been trained to safeguard information and keep it from the public, in accordance with the letter and spirit of the Official Secrets Act 1963. It was clear, therefore, from the beginning, that the mammoth change that was envisaged in the Act would not happen easily or automatically. Progress to openness and transparency in government would take time. Change would not come of its own accord; it would have to be worked for.

It was clear also that a measure of the strength or weakness of the Act would be its overall scope and, in particular, the extent of the exemptions: the wider they were drawn, the less the likelihood of the Act working successfully

---

[95] The Greencore or Telecom scandals would not have become public if it had not been for the media, who persisted in their investigations despite threats from lawyers (see Sam Smyth, *Sunday Independent*, September 15, 1991). More is known about the activities of certain Irish companies from the information they have to reveal to the authorities in the US under legislation there than they have ever revealed here (see *The Irish Times*, March 27, 1992).

[96] Also, the Ethics in Public Office Act 1995, the Electoral Act 1997, the Data Protection Act 1988, the Local Elections (Disclosure of Donations and Expenditure) Act 1999 and other such legislation, particularly local government planning legislation, opened up facets of public life and increased access to information. The first of the Tribunals of Inquiry set up by Government also gave impetus to the freedom of information campaign. Regulations providing for access to information on the environment were made in 1993 in accordance with EC Directive 90/313; [1990] O.J. L158/56. See further below and McDonagh, below, n.97, at p.404.

in practice. In the event, one of the factors that was to prove invaluable in the Irish experience was the willingness of the government minister charged with steering the legislation through the parliament to engage in wide and meaningful consultation throughout the drafting stage.[97] Minister Eithne Fitzgerald, who has become synonymous with the Freedom of Information Act, consulted widely not only with interest groups within the State but with legislators and operators of similar legislation in other countries, particularly Australia, New Zealand and Canada.[98]

Secondly, the Act was introduced incrementally. It was not intended to try to force all public bodies to operate it immediately.[99] All government departments and certain public bodies listed in the Act were given one year from the date of the passing of the Act to get their record-keeping system in order, to appoint Freedom of Information officers, and to prepare information booklets on their internal structures and on the types of records they held.[100] Local authorities and health boards were given eighteen months to prepare, and since then, other public and semi-state bodies have been brought within

---

[97] A group called "Let in the Light", composed mainly of journalists and academics, was formed in 1992 to campaign for freedom of information. The group campaigned throughout the next five years, holding seminars, workshops and national conferences with guest speakers, including the Minister and campaigners and officials from other countries. The addresses from their inaugural conference in January 1993 are published in Ellen Hazelcorn and Patrick Smyth (eds), *Let in the Light: Censorship, Secrecy and Democracy* (Brandon Books, Dingle, 1993). When the Act was passed in 1997, "Let in the Light" organised further workshops and conferences to raise awareness, as well as training sessions in the use of the Act, in conjunction with the NUJ, IRTC, and various groups in the voluntary sector at national and local level for journalists, broadcasters, the voluntary sector and the public at large. For an account of the lead up and background to the Act, see Patrick Smyth and Ronan Brady, *Democracy Blindfolded: The Case for a Freedom of Information Act in Ireland* (Cork University Press, Cork, 1994); Brendan Ryan, *Keeping us in the Dark: Censorship and Freedom of Information in Ireland* (Gill and Macmillan, Dublin, 1995); Dermot Keogh (ed.), *Irish Democracy and the Right to Freedom of Information (Ireland: A Journal of History and Society)* (Dept of History, UCC, Cork, 1995); Ronan Brady, "As Transparent as Glass?" in Marie McGonagle (ed.), *Law and the Media: The Views of Journalists and Lawyers* (Round Hall Sweet & Maxwell, Dublin, 1997), p.27, and Maeve McDonagh, *Freedom of Information Law in Ireland* (Round Hall Sweet & Maxwell, Dublin, 1998).

[98] See generally, Maeve McDonagh, *ibid.*

[99] A list of public bodies who came under the Act in April 1998 (Government Departments and other bodies) and in October 1998 (local authorities) is contained in the Schedule to the Act. Many other bodies have been added periodically since. They include RTÉ, BCI, FÁS, and the universities. The total initially was 65 and is now in the region of 400. The Garda Síochána are mentioned in the Schedule and could be brought under the Act but that has not been done to date. The Information Commissioner, in his annual report for 2002, identifies the failure to bring the Garda Síochána under the Act as the "only substantial omission". That and other reports, as well as a full list of the bodies that come under the Act is available on the Information Commissioner's website: *www.oic.gov.ie.*

[100] The information booklets are known as s.15 and s.16 manuals, as they are mandated under those sections of the Act. S.15 manuals were required to give details of the structures and organisation of the public body, as well as the classes of records held by it. S.16 manuals were required to give details of the rules, procedures, practices, guidelines, and interpretations used by the public body in its decision-making. Most such manuals are available on-line as well as in hard copy.

the Act on an on-going basis. A strength of the Act lies in the fact that this can be done with minimum bureaucracy and delay through ministerial regulations.[101]

Another key factor in the successful implementation of the Act was the extensive training provided by the Government for public servants and by non-governmental organisations and representative groups for potential users, journalists and the voluntary sector in particular. The Government established a central policy unit, located in the Department of Finance, a crucial ministry, to monitor implementation of the Act, to advise information providers and to produce guidelines on specific issues, with a view to developing best practice.[102]

Perhaps the most important element of all in this carefully constructed bulwark to the operation of the Act was the provision for an Information Commissioner, whose role is discussed in detail below.

10.5.1 The Freedom of Information (Amendment) Act 2003

In February 2003 the Government announced its intention to bring in an amending Act to ensure that sensitive records would not become available on a rolling basis after five years, as provided for in section 19(3)(b) of the 1997 Act. It subsequently emerged that the Government intended to amend other provisions of the Act also. The decision caused widespread consternation, both because the 1997 Act was to be rolled back and because there had been no public consultation.[103] The irony was that the Freedom of Information Act, the epitome of openness and transparency in government, was being curtailed by government in a process shrouded in secrecy.[104]

The Information Commissioner, who had not been consulted about the proposed amendments, published his own suggested amendments to the Act in February 2003, based on his experience of the operation of the Act and on judicial decisions in relation to, for example, discovery and court documents. He also reported to government on his concerns about the need for a "personal safety" clause in the Act and about the interaction between Data Protection legislation and Freedom of Information legislation.[105]

---

[101] The Act at s.3 enables the Minister to make regulations, *inter alia*, to bring other bodies within the Act.

[102] See *www.foi.gov.ie*.

[103] See, for example, *The Irish Times*, February–April 2003, particularly February 15 (article by Maeve McDonagh), and March 10 (article by Eithne Fitzgerald). The Government was concerned at the implications of the five year rule for the functioning of Cabinet and the inclusion of ministerial views in government memoranda. It also seized the opportunity to remedy what it saw as some of the difficulties that had arisen in practice, for example, large volumes of requests from certain individuals and requests that they believe cause substantial and unreasonable interference.

[104] The Joint Committee on Finance and Public Service subsequently held a special meeting at which it heard submissions from the Information Commissioner, the NUJ, NNI, ICCL and others before the Bill completed its passage through the Seanad. However, very few changes to the Bill resulted from its deliberations. The most significant was in relation to personal information.

[105] See the Commissioner's website. The Data Protection (Amendment) Act 2003 was also

The main changes brought about by the 2003 Act relate to cabinet papers, communications between Ministers, certification by Secretary-Generals of government departments that the information is part of an on-going deliberative process and therefore cannot be released, the imposition of up-front charges for freedom of information requests and applications for review and mandatory exemptions for documents related to international relations. As far as possible the amendments are included in the account of the provisions of the legislation, which follows.

10.5.2 The essence of the Freedom of Information legislation

The Freedom of Information legislation provides first and foremost a right of access. Its purpose is to enable members of the public to obtain access to information in the possession of public bodies to the greatest extent possible, consistent with the public interest and the right to privacy.[106] The presumption, therefore, is clearly in favour of access, which is a right, not merely a privilege, and which is to be denied only to the extent that it is justified by reference to one of the exemptions relating to public interest or individual privacy. Access means essentially a right to inspect documents or to receive a copy of them.[107] The Act also says that access is the right of "everyone"[108] and that access is to "any record"[109] held by a public body.

The Act makes provision for access to both personal information and non-personal information,[110] but only that in the hands of *public* bodies. It does

---

passed in April 2003. It is discussed briefly in Chap. 5 above. The Commissioner also spoke of the interaction of data protection and freedom of information in his annual report for 2002.

[106] As stated in the long title to the Act.

[107] When making a request for access under the Act, the applicant can specify what form of access s/he requires: inspection, paper copies, diskette, etc.

[108] It is not therefore confined to citizens. The same is true of the legislation of other countries, for example the United States and Sweden. For a brief resumé of the Freedom of Information Act 1997, see the NNI Factsheet (National Newspapers of Ireland, Dublin, 1997, available at *www.irishmedialaw.com*) and David Meehan, "Freedom of Information Act 1997: Public and Private Rights of Access to Records held by Public Bodies" (1997) I.L.T. 178 and David Meehan, "The Freedom of Information Act in Context" (1997) I.L.T. 231.

[109] The term "record" is broadly defined in the Act. However, there is a limitation in that if a body does not keep a particular record, then such a record cannot be accessed. Nor can a body be obliged to start keeping such a record. However, it has been established in practice that where the information itself is available, though not in the particular form requested, it must still be made available. Furthermore, where the failure to keep particular records is seen as undesirable, pressure can be brought on the body concerned via the Central Policy Unit, the Information Commissioner or, indeed, the media. The Information Commissioner stated his intention to draw up a code of best practice based on the experience of the first two years of operation of the Act. He reviewed compliance by public bodies in the third year of operation of the Act.

[110] Personal information refers to records or files directly concerning an individual, which that individual may access and have corrected, if necessary, under the Act. See the definitions in s.2 of the Act. (The Data Protection Act 1988 already enabled individuals to access personal records held on computer but not those held manually. See also the speech of the Information Commissioner "Data Protection and Freedom of Information

not extend to private bodies. This limitation can lead to anomalies. For instance, it transpired in practice that patients who had attended public hospitals were entitled to access their medical records under the Act, while those in private hospitals were not. A grey area remained in the case of privately-run hospitals that were nonetheless in receipt of public funding. These institutions were quickly brought within the Act by ministerial regulation.[111] A further issue may arise in relation to private bodies that are given public functions, as when public services are privatised. Private bodies exercising public functions under a statutory provision can be brought within the Act.[112]

In the case of personal records, there is no time restriction. An individual is entitled to access to records going back to the time they began to be held. In the case of non-personal records, however, it is only those created after the commencement of the Act that are included, except as prescribed by the Minister, or where access to earlier records is necessary in order to understand records created after the commencement.[113]

While access is to "any record" and the term "record" is defined very broadly in the Act,[114] there are certain specified exemptions.[115] There are certain records

– Is there a Contradiction?", March 5, 2002, available at *www.oic.gov.ie/23ba_3c2.htm*.) Personnel records are also covered by the Act. Non-personal information refers to all other information that governments and public bodies hold in pursuit of their functions and that may be sought by anyone, but perhaps more likely, by journalists, environmentalists, writers, historians, opposition politicians, commercial interests.

[111] The issue was clarified by Ministerial order (S.I. No. 329 of 1999).

[112] First Schedule, s.1(5)(f): "any other body, organisation or group on which functions in relation to the general public or a class of the general public stand conferred by any enactment", in which case, according to s.2, they "shall be a public body only as respects functions referred to in [s.1(5)(f)]". Freedom of Information laws usually cover only public bodies but the issue of privatisation was addressed in ARTICLE 19, *A Model Freedom of Information Law* (ARTICLE 19, London, July 2001, available at *www.article19.org*). Art.6 of the Model Law defines "private body" to include "any body, excluding a public body, that: a) carries on any trade, business or profession, but only in that capacity; or b) has legal personality". A body is a "public" body only to the extent of its statutory or public functions, although any body that carries out a public function may be designated a public body. (The Model Law, however, is only a "model" based on best international practice.)

[113] S.6(5). The Information Commissioner has interpreted this to mean that earlier records can be accessed only where "necessary" to understand later ones and not where they would simply enhance or broaden understanding. See, for example, Case No.98117, February 18, 1999 and Case Nos 99347/99357, December 21, 1999, available on the Commissioner's website *www.oic.gov.ie* under "Index to Decisions", and *Salve Marine Ltd v Information Commissioner*, High Court, July 19, 2000, in which Kelly J. held that the Information Commissioner had correctly interpreted s.6(5)(a), that he had done so in a manner which gave effect to the object of the Act in a purposeful and meaningful way. The time limitation was introduced for pragmatic and organisational reasons only and the then Minister, Eithne Fitzgerald, who steered the legislation through Parliament, has said that she hopes it will be possible over time to remove such time restrictions. S.6(4) would enable the Minister to allow for such earlier access.

[114] "Record" includes any memorandum, book, plan, map, drawing, diagram, pictorial or graphic work or other document, any photograph, film or recording (whether of sound or images or both), any form in which data (within the meaning of the Data Protection Act 1988) are held, any other form (including machine-readable form) or thing in which information is held or stored manually, mechanically or electronically and anything that is part of a copy, in any form, of any of the foregoing or is a combination of two or more

which the head of a public body "may" refuse and others which s/he "shall" refuse. The records that "may" be refused included, under the 1997 Act, certain submissions made to Government or key personnel, including Ministers and the Attorney General, that is, the submissions and information for consideration, but not the decisions, of Government. Those records now fall within the "shall" refuse category. Their range has also been extended to include communications between members of the Government and groups of members.[116] The definition of Government is extended to include committees.[117]

While a request for information concerning the deliberative process of a public body "may" be refused, it "shall" be refused if the Secretary General has issued a certificate stating that it contains matter relating to the deliberative process of a Department of State. Such a certificate shall be final and preclude an internal review or review by the Information Commissioner.[118]

The head of a public body has no discretion and "shall" refuse access to records concerning statements made at government meetings (section 19(2)) or records that would be exempt from production in court or would if disclosed constitute contempt of court (section 22).[119] The category extends to the private

---

of the foregoing (s.2 of the 1997 Act) and a copy, in any form, of a record shall be deemed, for the purposes of this Act, to have been created at the same time as the record (2003 Act). The Data Protection Act 1988 has itself been amended by the Data Protection (Amendment) Act 2003.

[115] Part III of the Act is headed "Exempt Records" and it has undergone substantial amendment under the 2003 Act. In the case of submissions and advice to Government for their consideration or for use at meetings of Government, if the head of a public body is of the opinion that it would be contrary to the public interest to disclose whether such a record existed or not, s/he can refuse to do so (s.19(5)).

[116] S.19(1)(aa)(i) and (ii), on matters under consideration by the Government or proposed to be submitted to the Government or a group of members. The subsection does not apply to factual information relating to a decision of the Government that has been published to the general public, or relating to a decision of Government or communication that was made more than ten years before receipt of the request (s.19(3)).

[117] S.19(6). A committee in this section may consist of members of Government or one or more members together with one or more Ministers of State and /or the Attorney General; or it may consist of officials appointed by the Government to assist it in a particular matter, or that is requested to report to it, or which is certified by the Secretary General to be a committee to which the section applies. "Officials" includes civil servants, special advisers and any others so prescribed. The Secretary General is required each year to furnish to the Information Commissioner a report in writing specifying the number of certificates issued by him/her under the section. In all, this provision removes a very wide range of information from the public reach and is one of the most far-reaching and significant claw-backs contained in the 2003 Act. Information that until 2003 was readily available under the 1997 Act will now be refused.

[118] S.20(1). A certificate shall be revoked when the Secretary General of the Department concerned is satisfied that the deliberative process has ended. While s.20(3) gives some leeway, the section overall gives undue power to the Secretary General of each Department and if s/he invokes a certificate unnecessarily or does not revoke a certificate when warranted, it is difficult to see what can be done since a review is precluded. Vigilance on the part of users and the Information Commissioner will be the only solution.

[119] On the application of s.22(1)(b) in relation to discovery and contempt of court, see *EH and EPH v The Information Commissioner*, High Court, O'Neill J., April 4, 2001 (*www.oic.gov.ie/231e_3c2.htm*). S. 22(1)(b) has been amended by the insertion of the words: "[the record] is such that the head knows or ought reasonably to have known that its [disclosure would constitute contempt of court]".

papers of MEPs, members of local authorities or health boards, to opinions, advice and recommendations, or the results of consultation considered by either House of the Oireachtas (parliament) or a committee of either House. Included also is information given to a public body in confidence (section 26),[120] as well as commercially sensitive information, except, for example, where the relevant person has consented or where disclosure is necessary in order to avoid a serious and imminent danger to the life or health of an individual or the environment (section 27). Access must be refused also where it would involve the disclosure of personal information (section 28(1)) or where it is mandated by other legislation (section 32).

In the "may" refuse category are matters which, if disclosed, could prejudice the effectiveness of tests or investigations, or adversely affect the performance of their management functions or disclose positions taken for the purpose of negotiations carried out or to be carried out by or on behalf of the Government or a public body (section 21). The "may" refuse category also includes records which could reasonably be expected to prejudice or impair an aspect of law enforcement (section 23), or endanger the life or safety of any person,[121] and information that could prejudice research or the well-being of a cultural, heritage or natural resource, or a species of flora or fauna (section 30). Likewise, information may be excluded if its disclosure could have a serious adverse effect on the financial or economic interests of the State (section 31).

Added to the "may" refuse category by the 2003 Act are records relating to the appointment or proposed appointment, business or proceedings of tribunals of inquiry and other tribunals or bodies established by Government, or by a Minister or by either or both Houses of the Oireachtas.[122] It is interesting to note that included within this discretionary "may" category (rather than in the compulsory "shall" category) are matters that could be prejudicial to law enforcement, security, defence, international relations and matters relating to Northern Ireland.[123] However, an addition to the relevant section provides

---

[120] An addition, s.26(4), inserted by the 2003 Act, allows the non-disclosure to the requester of whether or not such a record exists. A similar provision has been inserted in relation to commercially sensitive information (s.27(4)) and in relation to personal information (s.28(5A)). The Government refused to release, on the grounds that they were "commercially sensitive", documents relating to the compensation deal reached with the religious orders over child abuse in residential institutions, *The Irish Times*, February 6, 2003.

[121] S.23(1)(aa), as inserted by the 2003 Act.

[122] S.22(1A). It does not apply to the general administration of tribunal offices.

[123] Freedom of Information Act 1997, s.24. In relation to these last-mentioned matters, a Government Minister, if satisfied that the record requested is of sufficient sensitivity or seriousness to justify his/her doing so, may issue a certificate that the record is an exempt record (s.25). While this power is far-reaching, there are certain safeguards built in, for example a copy of the certificate and a written statement of the reasons must be given to the requester (s.25(6)(b)). The certificate may be revoked by the Minister (s.25(9)), but, if it is not, it will be reviewed by the Taoiseach (Prime Minister) every 12 to 24 months (s.25(7)(a)). Under the 1997 Act , the review period was every 6 to 12 months, but that has been changed by the 2003 Act. A certificate will expire after 2 years (s.25(13)) but as long as it is in existence, it is conclusive; the Information Commissioner cannot review the decision; the only possible redress is by way of appeal

that information relating to intelligence in respect of the security or defence of the State, or to the tactics, strategy or operations of the defence forces, or to the detection, prevention or suppression of activities calculated or tending to undermine the public order or the authority of the State "shall" be refused.[124]

10.5.3 Procedures

10.5.3.1 Making a request

Access is by request, in writing or other forms as may be determined.[125] It must be stated that the request is being made under the Freedom of Information Act.[126] Sufficient particulars must be given to enable the record to be identified. It is important to give as precise indications as possible, not least to cut down on search time, which in the case of non-personal information may be charged for.[127] Indeed, a request may be refused altogether on the grounds that it does

---

to the High Court (s.25(3)(a) and (b)). In the year 2000 two such certificates were issued by the Minister for Justice, one relating to international relations and Northern Ireland and the other relating to state security (Annual Report of the Information Commissioner, Appendix II, available at *www.oic.gov.ie/report00/21e6_262.htm*). In 2001, one certificate was issued, relating to law enforcement and state security (Annual Report, Appendix II, at *www.oic.gov.ie/report01/21e6_20a.htm*). In 2002, two such certificates were issued by the Department of Justice (Annual Report, Appendix II, at *www.oic.gov.ie/252a_3c2*).

[124] S.24(2)(a). The remainder of the subsection, relating to diplomatic matters and confidential communications involving person(s) outside the State or international organisations, now moves from the "may" to the "shall" refuse category.

[125] S.7(1). The experience in practice has been that e-mail is the most expeditious means of requesting access, particularly for journalists, as it is fast and allows easy tracking of requests.

[126] The Act states that the request must be made to the head of the public body concerned (s.7(1)) but the bodies themselves have been flexible on this. Requests, at any rate, are usually directed in the first instance to the Freedom of Information Officer, specially designated in each body to handle freedom of information requests.

[127] S.47 of the Act deals with fees. The Government fixed the rate under the 1997 Act at IR£16.50 per hour, but the first half hour was not charged for in practice and charges were only to be levied for efficient searches (s.47(3)(a)). If the search was going to cost more than £40, the requester must be informed and, at his/her request, assistance must be given in amending the request so as to reduce the cost (s.47(7) and (8)). If it can be shown that the information being sought will assist in the understanding of a matter of national importance fees may be reduced or waived (s.47(5)). The fee set for copies of records was 3 pence per page. For cases relating to fees, see Case Nos 99060, 99151 and 99003, available on the Information Commissioner's website *www.oic.gov.ie* under "Index to decisions". Fees were not a major issue under the 1997 Act. Indeed, the Commissioner in his Annual Report for 2002 stated that reviews of decisions to charge fees "continued to represent a very small percentage of applications received ranging from 1 per cent to 0.5 per cent over the period". The imposition of a basic up-front fee envisaged in the 2003 Act, s.47(6A), is a retrograde step from the point of view of the public, as it is likely to act as a deterrent to genuine requests as well as frivolous or vexatious requests, at which it is purportedly directed. There is provision, however, for different amounts for different classes of requester (s.47(6A)(d)). The fees introduced in July 2003 were: €15 for each request, €75 for each internal review and €150 for a review by the Information Commissioner.

not contain sufficient particulars to enable it to be identified or that it is so voluminous as to cause a substantial and unreasonable interference with or disruption of the other work of the public body concerned.[128]

Reasons for requiring the information need not be given, however, and, indeed, even if they are given, the public body is directed not to take account of them.[129] Thus, it should have no bearing on the decision to grant or refuse information whether the records are required, for example, by journalists pursuing a story, or by a client who wants to sue the organisation in the courts. In fact, regardless of the purpose for which access is requested, the public body must give the requester reasonable assistance in identifying the records required. Sometimes it can be difficult for a requester to know whether a particular public body holds the information required. The manuals that had to be prepared in accordance with the Act are a help and most are now available on-line, but where a requester still has difficulty identifying the appropriate body or records, or has a disability, s/he is entitled to reasonable assistance in doing so.[130] The requester may also stipulate the form or manner of access required: disk, hard copy, transcript, decodified form or simply a reasonable opportunity to inspect.[131]

10.5.3.2 The time-frame

The head of the public body concerned must acknowledge receipt of the request "as soon as may be" but not later than two weeks following receipt. If a requester sends the request to the wrong body, the head of the body addressed has a duty under the Act to pass on the request within two weeks to the appropriate body, if s/he knows which, and inform the requester accordingly.[132]

Not later than four weeks after receipt of the request, the head must notify the requester as to whether access is to be granted, indicating the person dealing with the request.[133] If the request is granted the notice must indicate the day on which, and the manner in which, access is to be granted, for how long, and the amount of fee, if any, to be charged. If the request is refused or deferred, in whole or in part, the notice must give reasons and normally also specify any

---

[128] A request may also be refused if it is frivolous or vexatious (s.10).

[129] S.8(4)(a) and (b).

[130] S.6(2)(a) and (b).

[131] S.7(1)(c).

[132] S.7(2) and following. The time frame has been clarified in the 2003 Act, so that "week" means a period of 5 consecutive weekdays and, in determining such a period, Saturdays and Bank Holidays are to be disregarded. The time frame for reviews can be extended by up to two weeks where a number of records or of persons are concerned in cases where notice has to be given (s.29(2A)). There is also provision for extension in relation to reviews by the Commissioner (s.34(3) and (4)).

[133] S.8 of the Act. Overall rates of granting access are not very impressive. In 2001 50 per cent of the requests dealt with by the public bodies were granted in full, while a further 20 per cent were part-granted. The Commissioner found, however, that the public had a better understanding of the business of government, thanks in part to the media as a conduit of information, and that the public service was more accountable, more open in its dealings with the citizen and more willing to explain its actions and activities. The culture in the public service is changing, slowly but surely, but more needs to be done.

matter relating to the public interest that has been taken into account in reaching the decision, as well as particulars of rights of review and appeal.[134] The giving of reasons is crucial to enable appropriate use of the review and appeals procedures.

10.5.3.3 The review and appeals system

If access is refused, the first step is to seek an internal review. This must be carried out within three weeks by a person higher in the organisation than the person who handled the original request.[135] If the internal review is also unsuccessful, the requester may apply to the Information Commissioner for a further review.

10.5.3.4 The role of the Information Commissioner

The Information Commissioner has wide powers under the Act[136] and this has proved to be one of the great strengths of the Act in practice. The Commissioner can review decisions on access. When requested to do so, s/he must carry out the review within four months of receipt of the application, as far as practicable, unless a settlement is reached before then. If the Commissioner considers that the reasons given for refusing or limiting access are inadequate, s/he can direct the head of the body concerned to supply further information. Part of the Commissioner's remit includes a periodic review of the operation of the Act. S/he can carry out an investigation "at any time" into the practices and procedures adopted by any public body in compliance with the Act and report on them. In fact, the Commissioner is obliged to carry out an investigation in relation to public bodies generally not later than three years after the commencement of the Act. This is in addition to the annual report and any commentaries s/he may wish to publish on the practical application and operation of the provisions of the Act. The brief also requires the Commissioner to foster and encourage the publication of information in the public interest. Reviews and investigations are to be carried out in as informal a manner as possible.

Clearly, it is not in anybody's interest to refer trivial or hopeless matters to the Commissioner and thus clog up the schedule. Nonetheless, it is imperative that recourse to the Commissioner is used, and used well, to provide the substance that will enable him/her to invoke the full range of powers available to the office under the legislation. Hindrance or obstruction of the Information Commissioner is the only action to attract criminal penalties under the Freedom of Information Act. Fines to a maximum of £1,500 (approximately €1,900)

---

[134] S.8(2)(d) and (f). The failure of some public bodies to give sufficient reasons for their decisions was noted by the Information Commissioner on a number of occasions, for example in his Fourth Annual Report, June 2002.

[135] S.14. There is also provision for the withdrawal of requests for review (s.14(8)).

[136] Part IV of the Act, *i.e.* ss. 33–40, deals with the powers and functions of the Information Commissioner.

and/or prison sentences of up to six months may be imposed for such conduct.[137]

Decisions of the Information Commissioner can be appealed to the High Court but only on a point of law. There has been a small number of such appeals to date.[138] There was no provision in the 1997 Act for a further appeal to the Supreme Court but that has been included in the 2003 Act.[139]

10.5.3.5 Implementation

One of the things most crucial to the successful implementation of the Freedom of Information Act was the preparation, particularly by the public bodies concerned. The fact that they had to draw up handbooks describing the classes of records they hold, as well as the rules, procedures, guidelines, interpretations and precedents used by them in making decisions and recommendations, was beneficial both to themselves and to the public. Secondly, the extensive training undertaken both within the public service and among potential users, including the media, was also vital to the successful implementation of the Act. In both sectors it helped to spread awareness and foster commitment.[140] A third element of importance was the establishment of the Central Policy Unit in the Department of Finance to guide and support the preparations for implementation of the Act. This Unit, which continues to offer guidance and propose strategies for handling freedom of information issues, is an expert advisory service for the public service as a whole. Implementation of the Act was further enhanced by the setting up of networks of information providers and advisory groups representing the business community and citizens, as a forum for dialogue and a mechanism for furthering understanding of freedom of information.

---

[137] S.37(7).

[138] In 2002 there were nine appeals, bringing to ten the total number pending at the time of publication of the Information Commissioner's annual report. One of the cases pending involved RTÉ. See further below and the Information Commissioner's website. The Commissioner's website is regularly updated and provides detailed information on the role and operation of his office, including decisions and settlements made in relation to reviews (in 2002, 25 per cent of all reviews were settled). See also Cathleen Noctor, "The Freedom of Information Act in the High Court" [2001] I.L.T. 81, and below, n.157, *Minister for Justice v The Information Commissioner*.

[139] S.42(6)(c).

[140] See address of the Information Commissioner, *Delivering Freedom of Information in Scotland*, November 19, 1999, available at *www.oic.gov.ie*. It is interesting to note that the Scottish legislature announced its intention to bring in legislation modelled on the Irish Freedom of Information Act (*The Irish Times*, August 31, 2000). The resulting legislation is the Freedom of Information (Scotland) Act 2002. A Freedom of Information Act was also passed in England and Wales in November 2000 and will be phased in over a five-year period.

10.6 EXPERIENCE OF THE FREEDOM OF INFORMATION ACT IN PRACTICE

10.6.1 Strengths and weaknesses

10.6.1.1 General

Some of the strengths of the Freedom of Information Act have already been outlined in the course of the discussion above. In general terms, experience of the Freedom of Information Act in practice over the early years has shown that it is important, first and foremost, to create awareness of the Act and to familiarise the general public with the scope and workings of the Act. Education as to the workings of government at both central and local level is the *sine qua non* for optimal use of the Act. The wide dissemination of leaflets and handbooks in hard copy and on-line, in readable and digestible form, at mainstream points of contact, is fundamental.[141]

In addition, it is necessary always to be vigilant to ensure that the exemption clauses are not invoked in a blanket fashion and that reasons given for refusing access to information are both sufficient and justified in accordance with the provisions of the Act.[142] To resolve any doubt, it is important to use the review and appeals mechanisms provided. If one wishes to access a record that appears to come under the discretionary "may refuse" category, it is still worth trying for it because, if access is refused, reasons for the refusal must be given. Armed with the reasons, the requester will then be in a position to decide whether the reasons are sufficient or whether it is worthwhile proceeding to seek a review. The reasons for refusal must be stated in precise form; it is not enough to give a cursory reference to the "public interest". The experience in other countries and to a degree in Ireland in the early days of the operation of the Act has been for the authorities to try to invoke the exemptions to the Act in blanket form, so it is important to challenge any such practice or ruse.[143]

On the other hand, there is no point in seeking records that are clearly in the compulsory "shall refuse" category. However, it is not always clear that a particular record does belong to that category and again there is evidence of a tendency in many jurisdictions of authorities using categories such as "commercially sensitive" information in a blanket way.

The issue of fees is important with regard to public usage of the Act. If fees are set at a level that would discourage or preclude widespread use of the Act, they will effectively undermine the Act itself and amount to a denial of access. As the Australian Law Reform Commission observed, it is

---

[141] The Information Commissioner has published a study of the manuals or handbooks published by the various bodies. Awareness of them was not as high as one might have expected or hoped but where there was awareness, the manuals had been found helpful. The study of the s.15 and s.16 manuals is available at the Information Commissioner's website or in hard copy from the Office of the Information Commissioner.

[142] One of the findings of the Information Commissioner in his Report on Compliance by Public Bodies in 2001 (*www.oic.gov.ie/report01/227A_20A.htm*) was that there was a widespread failure to give proper reasons.

[143] The Information Commissioner in his Report on Compliance by Public Bodies found that some public bodies were resorting unnecessarily to certain exemptions.

counterproductive to "encourage involvement in government but effectively disqualify citizens from participating by imposing prohibitive charges".[144] In Ireland, there is no charge for access to personal information (section 47(4)). With the advances of technology in recent years and the investment in technology for record keeping in public bodies, search and retrieval time required to access records is much reduced. As a result, fees were rarely incurred for non-personal information under the 1997 Act prior to its amendment in 2003. It was only where large volumes of information were requested or where information was requested in a form other than that in which it was held by the body, that fees were levied. The 2003 Act introduced provision for an up-front fee for non-personal information and for a request to be refused for reasons of non-payment.[145] Demands for fees can be appealed to the Information Commissioner (section 34(1)(c)) but under the 2003 Act the fee will have to be paid in advance. In any event, fees can be reduced or waived altogether where it can be shown that the information sought would aid in the understanding of a matter of national importance (section 47(5)). That provision should be available to journalists researching major stories, among others. The 2003 provision also allows for different levels of fees for different categories of requesters. The voluntary sector and various categories of individuals should benefit. In some countries, the news media, because of their function in informing the public, are accorded special status as regards fees.[146]

The imposition of fees for non-personal information came in response to concern in government over the years about large-scale use of the Act by one

---

[144] Australian Law Reform Commission, Report No.77/Administrative Review Council, Report No.40, *Open Government: a Review of the Federal Freedom of Information Act 1982* (Australian Government Publishing Service, Canberra, 1995) para.14.2, cited in McDonagh, above, n.97, at p.76. For the charges introduced in July 2003, see above, n.127.

[145] S.47(6A) states that the head of a public body or the Information Commissioner "shall" refuse to accept the request or application if the fee is not paid.

[146] In the US, for example, news media status is recognised for the purposes of FOIA requests. The categories were introduced under the FOI Reform Act 1986. Representatives of the media receive a waiver of copying costs for the first 100 pages provided and a full waiver of research fees. That waiver is automatic but they can also ask for public interest fee waivers for any additional pages. The waiver applies to those "actively gathering information about current events or of current interest to the public as an entity organised and operated to publish or broadcast news to the public" (1987 regulations). In Ireland, in *The Irish Times v Judge Murphy* ([1998] 1 I.R. 359, discussed in Chap. 6 above), the Supreme Court has acknowledged in very clear terms the importance of the media role in informing the public. All of the judges recognised *the public's right to know* and the importance of the media role in assuring that right in practice. Reference was made to "the great security of publicity". In particular, Denham J. acknowledged that we live in a modern democracy in the age of information technology. In a modern democracy, information is brought into the public domain by many routes, she said, but in reality most people receive their information from the press: "Thus any curtailment of the press must be viewed as a curtailment of the access of the people". Judges Barrington and Keane referred to the press as "the eyes and ears of the public": "In modern conditions, the media are the eyes and ears of the public and the ordinary citizen is almost entirely dependent on them for his knowledge" (Keane J. at 409).

or more individuals for commercial purposes.[147] Use of the Act by business and commercial interests is one of the prices to be paid for making access available to all. It is not surprising either that the Act will be found to be a useful alternative or addition to discovery in certain court proceedings.[148] Journalists and others may find also that there is a certain amount of "piggy-backing", that is, requests being made for access to the records or list of records requested by fellow journalists, employees, and so forth. Journalists also find it irksome that the "scoop" value may be diluted by the information being made available to more than one news organisation at the same time, or where it is released at a time that conveniences one organisation's deadlines but not another's, for example on a Monday, which suits a newspaper that publishes on a Tuesday but not one that publishes on a Sunday.[149] That may be a downside from the point of view of journalists but not necessarily from the point of view of the overall objective of getting the information to the public.

Experience has shown that it is vitally important to use the good offices of the Information Commissioner, not only to resolve specific refusals of access, but even more importantly to clarify matters of doubt and to establish good practice generally. The first Commissioner, Kevin Murphy, who was appointed for a term of six years, was already established in the role of national Ombudsman and continued to act in that capacity. His experience in that role stood him in good stead. It was invaluable to the successful implementation of the Act that he was so determined and courageous in his application and promotion of freedom of information. During his term as Information Commissioner he took a number of initiatives, including a study of the manuals[150] and of the general practices of public bodies, with a view to drawing up a code of best practice. His successor, Emily O'Reilly, a former journalist, took up her posts of Information Commissioner and Ombudsman on June 1, 2003.[151]

The fact that the range of the Act can be extended quickly by way of ministerial regulations is also a bonus. Already, many additional bodies have been brought within it and several matters of doubt clarified. For instance, it was not altogether clear in the beginning what the position was regarding parents seeking access to their children's records or relatives seeking access to records of deceased persons. The issue was clarified by ministerial regulation and later inserted into the Act that parents may access information relating to their children, provided it is in the children's best interests.[152] Similarly, spouses, next-of-kin, personal representatives or legally appointed functionaries in

---

[147] See *The Irish Times*, August 19, October 7, 1999; February 17, April 7, 2000.

[148] See, for example, TJ McIntyre, "Supplementing Discovery: Using the Freedom of Information Act to Obtain Documents for Litigation Purposes" (2002) 9(6) C.L.P. 127.

[149] See, for example, *The Sunday Tribune*, December 19, 1999 (Comment).

[150] See above, n.100.

[151] Ironically, that appointment too lacked openness. There was no public competition or appearance before a Dáil committee; the Minister for Finance simply introduced a Dáil motion recommending the appointment and the resolution was approved without a vote (April 10, 2003, *The Irish Times*, April 11, 2003).

[152] S.I. No. 47 of 1999 and s.17(6) as inserted by the 2003 Act.

respect of a deceased's estate may access information relating to dead family members.[153]

A constant concern since the Freedom of Information Act came into force was that Ministers and government officials would be reluctant to commit information and views to writing. The Commissioner himself noted that there was some evidence of this happening.[154] He pointed out that less comprehensive records may be a double-edged sword and may lead to a distorted view of contributions, as well as doing a disservice to future analysis by historians. He urged the Department of Finance, therefore, to have regard to the duty on public servants to create such records as are necessary to document, adequately and properly, the Government's objectives, policies, decisions, procedures and transactions.

A weakness in the Act is that the Garda Síochána (police) are not covered. However, they are listed in the schedule to the Act and may be brought within it by ministerial regulation. All that is needed is the political will to do so but so far that will has not manifested itself.[155] Certain other bodies are excluded and cannot be brought within the scope of the Act at all. These include the courts and tribunals of inquiry.[156] In *Minister for Justice v The Information Commissioner*[157] access to a number of records relating to a court case were refused. On application to the Information Commissioner, access was granted to certain of the records, but the Minister for Justice appealed the decision to the High Court. Section 46(1)(a) of the Freedom of Information Act states that the Act does not apply to the courts, except (I) records relating to proceedings in a court held in public but not created by the court and whose disclosure to the general public is not prohibited by the court, or (II) records relating to the general administration of the courts or the offices of the courts.[158] Applying the section, Finnegan J. found that the Act does not apply to the shorthand note and transcript of a case prepared by the official stenographer, or to the

---

[153] *ibid.* Guidelines for information providers on how to apply these provisions have been drawn up by the Central Policy Unit in the Department of Finance (*www.foi.gov.ie*).

[154] Speech entitled *Freedom of Information Now*, available at *www.oic.gov.ie/225a_3c2.htm*.

[155] It may still be possible to get certain information concerning the Garda Síochána through requests to the Department of Justice; similarly in relation to the Prison Service (for example, prison officers' expenses, *Sunday Independent*, December 3, 2000). Journalists and others using the Act need to be inventive and try to find ways of getting around any blockage. See below, for example, in relation to league tables of schools.

[156] S.46. Further categories have been added by the 2003 Act. They are records relating to costing, assessment or consideration of any proposal of a political party and records given by a public body to a member of the Government or a Minister of State for the purposes of any proceedings in either House of the Oireachtas or any committee or subcommittee of either House, and including parliamentary questions (s.46(1)(da) and (db)). The Courts Service came under the Act from March 9, 2000. For the position regarding records held by a court and the application of s.46(1) of the Act, see *In re FOIA* (Irish Times Law Report, May 14, 2001).

[157] [2002] 2 I.L.R.M. 1.

[158] The section also applies to tribunals of inquiry and to records held or created by the Attorney General and DPP, as well as various other offices and personnel, including the private papers of members of the Oireachtas.

book of evidence[159] or witness statements. On documents relating to fees for medical reports, the Information Commissioner had rightly granted access, having regard to the presumption in section 34(12)(b) of the Act, to the effect that a refusal of access has to be justified by the head of the public body to the satisfaction of the Commissioner.[160]

Although the decision of the Information Commissioner was largely overturned in that case, in many instances a review by his office can bring rewards.[161] Also, while the gardaí, courts and tribunals, and certain other bodies are outside the scope of the Act or not yet brought within it, that does not mean that no information regarding them can be accessed using the Act. It may be that direct access is precluded but there may be other indirect means. Information concerning the gardaí might be obtained via the Department of Justice or other public bodies with whom they are involved contractually. For instance, *The Sunday Tribune* was able to use the Act to get information concerning a row between the Air Corps, the gardaí and senior civil servants that led to increased costs and delays in acquiring a second garda helicopter.[162]

The limiting of access to non-personal information to records created after April 21, 1998 is a drawback also. Yet, it has to be acknowledged that it was probably necessary at the time to allow the Act to come into operation in a gradual and orderly way, rather than being overwhelmed at the outset by requests for information from an earlier period when record-keeping was slower and more cumbersome.[163] The lead-in time of one year or eighteen months for public bodies, likewise, was probably necessary in practice. One positive development, in terms of retrospection, that was expected to take effect from April 21, 2003, was the provision of section 19(3)(b). This subsection applied

---

[159] As it, and the documents contained in it, are prepared by the DPP, whose records are excluded by s.46(1)(b).

[160] Recommendation Rec(2002)2 of the Committee of Ministers of the Council of Europe on access to official documents states that Member States should examine the extent to which the principles of the recommendation could be applied to information held by legislative bodies and judicial authorities.

[161] For example, *The Sunday Times* sought the names of all the TDs who had petitioned the Minister for Justice to drop or reduce court penalties against their constituents. The request was refused. The Information Commissioner overturned the decision (*The Sunday Times*, January 21, 2001). The following year the Information Commissioner was able to report that since the case there had been no further requests (*The Irish Times*, June 13, 2002).

[162] *The Sunday Tribune*, July 8, 2001. The same paper succeeded in accessing information regarding expenditure at the Moriarty and Flood Tribunals from the Department of the Taoiseach and Department of the Environment, respectively. In those cases, the information would appear to come under the exception in s.46(1) in any event but now, see above, n.122.

[163] As noted above, it is possible to access earlier non-personal information where it can be shown that it is necessary to enable understanding of current information. In some cases, public servants have decided that the earlier records should not be released but have provided a background briefing to assist understanding. It is possible that such a briefing is sufficient in some cases but in others it may be necessary to appeal the decision and attempt to get the records themselves. It is possible sometimes also to get lucky, as for instance when certain records were released accidently by the Department of Foreign Affairs (*The Irish Times*, September 24, 2002).

to records relating to decisions of the Government made more than five years before the receipt of a freedom of information request for them. From 2003 onwards records, which previously were retained and became available only after a thirty-year period, were to become available after five years. The Government, however, decided to amend the Act to remove that possibility and substitute a period of ten years.

A potential weakness is the possibility of the Government introducing legislation that could conflict with the Freedom of Information Act and undermine it.[164] For instance, a number of newspapers sought information from the Department of Education that, if released, would allow them to draw up league tables of schools' academic performance. Teachers' unions and others opposed such tables. The Department of Education refused to release the information on the basis of section 21 of the Freedom of Information Act, since access to the records, it contended, could reasonably be expected to prejudice the effectiveness of the Leaving Certificate examinations and could have a significant adverse effect on the performance by the Department of its functions relating to management (including industrial relations and management of its staff).[165] Furthermore, section 53 of the Education Act 1998 applied, the Department argued, even though it was passed subsequent to the Freedom of Information Act. The Education Act contained an express provision (section 53), which came into force on February 5, 1999, that the Department of Education could refuse information that would assist in drawing up league tables. Therefore, in the Department's view, the section meant that the records should have been refused in accordance with section 32(1) of the Freedom of Information Act. The decision led to a review by the Information Commissioner, who decided that the information should be released for the year 1998, that is, the year before section 53 of the Education Act came into force, but with certain safeguards to protect the privacy of individual students.[166] His decision was appealed by the Department of Education to the High Court, which reserved judgment until 2001.[167]

The central issue for the High Court was whether section 53 of the Education Act had any application to a request for information, and subsequent appeal to the Information Commissioner, made pursuant to the Freedom of Information Act prior to the coming into force of section 53. The essence of the court's decision was that the application of section 53 of the Education Act was "retroactive" rather than "retrospective" because the Information Com-

---

[164] The Freedom of Information Act, Sch.3, lists 36 earlier Acts containing secrecy or non-disclosure provisions which are excluded from the application of s.32. S. 32 states that the head of a public body "shall refuse to grant a request" if the disclosure of the record concerned is prohibited by any enactment other than a provision specified in the third schedule.

[165] S.21(1)(a) and (b).

[166] Case 98104, 98130, 98024, *The Sunday Times, The Sunday Tribune and the Kerryman* newspapers and the Department of Education and Science (available at *www.oic.gov.ie/2246_3c2.htm*).

[167] *Minister for Education and Science v The Information Commissioner*, High Court, July 31, 2001, Ó Caoimh, J.

missioner's decision had not actually been taken until after the section had come into force.[168]

The decision is disappointing on a number of grounds. First of all, the finding that a review by the Information Commissioner was by way of a hearing *de novo* meant that the relevant facts and circumstances were those applying at the date of the review and not at the date of the original decision. Hence the distinction between "retroactive" and "retrospective": if the relevant facts and circumstances had been those applicable to the original decision, section 53 could not have applied unless it had a retrospective effect.

Secondly, the court determined that the newspapers had no vested right to the information, that while the Act confers a *prima facie* entitlement to information, it involves an application for the information in question and a positive determination to entitlement of the right. The right, the Court said, is only a right to apply for the information and does not vest until a decision has been made, notwithstanding the terms of the Act itself.[169] It is submitted, however, that the terms of the Act itself would suggest that there is a right to the information itself, unless justifiably refused on specific grounds in support of other rights and interests, as set out in the Act itself.[170] Indeed, the presumption in the Act is very much in favour of access.[171]

---

[168] At p.29 of the transcript. The Commissioner expressed regret that it had not been possible for him to reach his decision within the time limits specified in the FOIA (which predated the coming into force of s.53 of the Education Act 1998). If it had been possible, the requesters' right to the records would have become a vested right at that time; consequently, the requesters lost that right: see *www.oic.gov.ie/report01/226E_20A.htm*. However, newspapers later sought records from the universities, which enabled them to show which schools were getting most pupils into third level education: see, for example, *The Irish Times*, October 28, 2002.

[169] At pp.29-30 of the transcript.

[170] The long title to the Act speaks of enabling the public "to obtain access", of providing "a right of access", of "exceptions to that right" and of decisions "relating to that right". Exceptions and decisions, one would think, cannot refer to a right merely to apply, but rather to a right to the information itself. S.2 of the Act defines "determined" in terms of the "needs" of the requester and says that "the right of access shall be construed in accordance with s.6". S.6(1) in turn states: "Subject to the provisions of this Act, every person has a right to and shall, on request therefore, be offered access to any record held by a public body and the right so conferred is referred to in this Act as the right of access." S.6, therefore, appears to distinguish between the right itself and the *exercise* of the right, which requires a request to be made. Indeed, s.7(1) clearly differentiates between the two when it says that: "A person who wishes to *exercise* the right of access shall make a request" (emphasis added). For instance, although the term "right of access" is used liberally throughout the Act, s.6(2) does not use the term in relation to the duty of a public body to give reasonable assistance to a person who is seeking a record, while s.6(7) does use the term to state that "Nothing ... shall be construed as applying the right of access to an exempt record". It cannot be the case that one cannot apply for an exempt record, but rather that one has no right of access to it.

[171] See, for example, s.34(12)(a) which states that a decision to grant a request shall be presumed to have been justified unless the person concerned shows to the satisfaction of the Commissioner that the decision was not justified, and (b) which states that a decision to refuse to grant a request shall be presumed not to have been justified unless the head concerned shows to the satisfaction of the Commissioner that the decision was justified.

The court judgment also exposed a potentially dangerous loophole in the Act to the extent that it sanctioned a measure designed to exclude the Act in situations where the Government did not wish it to apply.[172] The opportunity, therefore, is there to undermine the Freedom of Information Act. The High Court decision also closed off one avenue for journalists in pursuit of particular information about schools but a subsequent request to the universities, when they were brought under the Act at the end of 2001, was granted and that allowed journalists to show the schools providing students to each of the universities in the State.

10.6.1.2 Media usage

The Freedom of Information Act is an important *additional* tool for journalists. It is not a substitute for tried and tested means of getting information, for the reliable source, or the list of contacts, on which journalists depend. Indeed, the two methodologies can be used in tandem, as contacts well placed in an organisation are often helpful in alerting journalists to the existence of particular records or in helping them to identify relevant records. As journalists in other countries have observed, the art and practice of leaking has not gone away; on the contrary, it is still a growth industry.

One of the lessons that journalists need to learn early on in their use of the Act is to be persistent. They should not be discouraged by refusals, by documents received but so heavily blacked out as to be virtually useless, or by attempts to frustrate their efforts and wear them down.[173] There are obstacles. They may arise because a sea-change in the culture of the public service does not happen overnight. Public servants were steeped in a culture that required them to guard information, not to release it. With appropriate training, many public servants have responded positively and wholeheartedly to the new openness. Others may take longer. Some local authorities, in particular, may have been less organised and less enthusiastic than central government, although figures released by the Information Commissioner in his annual report for 2002 show that local authorities now have a better record for releasing information in full than central government. With a new Act that seeks to bring about a major cultural change, teething problems inevitably arise. Situations not altogether contemplated may present themselves and lead to persisting doubts, until clarified through use of the machinery of the Act, notably

---

[172] The Court found that the intention of the provision was such that it should apply to the situation pertaining in the case and have transitional effect as the Oireachtas did not intend to leave a lacuna (at p.30 of the transcript).

[173] For an overview of the first year of operation of the Act, including examples of journalists' and others' experiences of using it, see *FOI Reports*, available from School of Communications, Dublin City University, Dublin 9. The NUJ itself had some success in use of the Act on behalf of its members (question of contract with retiring head of Bord Fáilte in relation to publication of its magazine – see *FOI Reports*). However, its request for details of the complainant(s) to the Censorship Board regarding advertisements in *In Dublin* magazine (see Chapter 8 above) was refused (*The Sunday Tribune*, September 12, 1999). Later, in relation to a similar request to know the complainants in respect of the *Weekly Sport* newspaper, the High Court accepted the State's submission that the identity of the complainant(s) was irrelevant.

the office of the Information Commissioner. It is a learning process for information provider and requester alike. Journalists new to the methodology may not formulate or direct their requests in the manner set out in the Act. Some mutual understanding and flexibility is needed, therefore, in the early days until a routine practice is established.

For these or other reasons, take-up by journalists in Ireland was slow at first.[174] Journalists working for weekly newspapers, especially Sunday newspapers, embraced the Act more quickly than their counterparts in the broadcast media and daily newspapers, ostensibly because they had more time at their disposal. It was estimated by individual journalists in the first year of operation of the Act that one in ten requests produced a story of substance; that 5-6 produced information, much of which was not relevant or worth including in copy, and that the remaining 3 were either refused or so heavily "censored" as to be unusable.[175] However, even a 1 in 10 success rate was considered worthwhile, and to be able to ascertain in some cases that there is no story is acknowledged by journalists as better than pursuing a story for months in the erroneous belief that there was something there.

Editors and media proprietors need to be prepared to invest in the Act in financial terms and in terms of staff time. While journalists researching stories should be able to avail of the fees waiver outlined above, there may be a need to request a large amount of information or information in a form other than the one in which a public body normally holds it. In either case, fees may be demanded. For instance, a newspaper sought access to information concerning the expenses incurred by all elected representatives. That information was held in an itemised form under different headings. In response to the request, it had to be assembled from the various locations and fees in the order of £1,000 were demanded.[176] The options for the newspaper, if it wanted to pursue the request, were either to seek the waiver or to pay up in order for the request to continue being processed and later challenge the demand for fees by

---

[174] By 1999, journalists comprised 14 per cent of requesters, having made 1,612 of the total 11,531 requests made in the second year of the operation of the Act. See the *Second Annual Report of the Information Commissioner*, available at *www.oic.gov.ie/report99*. The Fourth Annual Report, published on June 12, 2002 revealed that the media had made 3,123 requests in 2001, a rise of 23 per cent over 2000 and a rise of almost 94 per cent over 1999. The Commissioner advocated the development of a balanced approach from both the media and from public bodies, firstly from the media, which should not confuse their own self-interest with the public interest; and, secondly, from public servants who should seek to develop professional and confident relationships with individual members of the media in the context of their requests for information. In 2002 the number of requests from journalists fell back to 12 per cent of all requests, compared to 20 per cent in 2001 and 19 per cent in 2000.

[175] Information supplied to training workshop organised by "Let in the Light" and the National Union of Journalists, February 19, 1999. The Information Commissioner, in his report for 2001, said that 50 per cent of requests are granted in full, 20 per cent in part, but that that rate falls short of the rate in Australia, where the legislation is very similar. The figures for 2002 are 46 per cent granted in full, 21 per cent part-granted.

[176] The case concerning *The Sunday Tribune* and the expenses of elected representatives is Case No.99168, available on the Commissioner's website. See also *The Sunday Tribune*, December 19, 1999; *The Irish Times*, May 4, 2002 – TDs volunteered to release details of their own expenses.

appealing to the Information Commissioner. Use of the Freedom of Information Act may necessitate some financial and time investment, therefore, but it also provides a tool whereby small media outlets can rival and even "scoop" larger organisations.

A barrier to the use of the Act has been erected by the imposition by Government from July 2003 of fees of €15 for each request, €75 for each internal review and €150 for each review by the Information Commissioner. Fees of that level amount to a serious disincentive and, therefore, curtailment of the use of the Act. There is also a danger that public servants, safe in the knowledge that requesters may be unable or disinclined to pay the substantial fees to be levied for reviews, may be more inclined to refuse the information sought. Journalists, particularly those, unlike freelances, who have the cushion of working for a media organisation with some resources, have a duty to continue making judicious use of the Act and seeking to establish a waiver of fees under section 47(5) of the Act, in respect of their role of bringing matters of national importance to the public.

The time factor, though tight by public service standards, militates against journalists who work to constant, strict deadlines. A request made today will not usually[177] produce copy for tonight's main news bulletin or tomorrow's newspaper. However, some stories do run on and it is worth putting in a request at the earliest possible moment in case the story does run on. The request may well produce information that will add a new dimension or counter an existing one at some future stage in the development of the story. It may add new depth or corroboration to an ongoing story.[178] Some of the usage of the Act by journalists in the first five years, however, was to access information of a trivial nature, while some unearthed stories of major importance to the public and others that caused considerable embarrassment to the Government. The Information Commissioner reported that civil servants were concerned at the selective, unfair or sensationalist use of information by journalists.[179]

It is also heartening to find that some public bodies and individual public servants are becoming much more proactive in releasing information.[180] Whereas before they could be prosecuted under the Official Secrets Act 1963 for unauthorised disclosure of "official secrets", they are now in a position

---

[177] Sometimes it will in that the public body may decide to issue the information straight away without the need for going through all the procedures. An example was the request from RTÉ's "Morning Ireland" programme in April 2002 for access to information on contacts made by a Government Minister to the Minister for Justice in relation to a court case involving one of his constituents. A story had broken about the Government Minister contacting a judge to inquire about delivery of a letter concerning a constituent who was before the courts, and the Act was used to elicit information regarding related correspondence (*The Irish Times*, April 13, 2002).

[178] See examples in *FOI Reports*, above, n.173.

[179] Annual Report 2001. Journalists, on the other hand, detail experiences of inconsistencies in the release of information, often depending on the government department's own agenda, and of information being refused and then "leaked" a few weeks later (*The Irish Times*, March 1, 2003 (Weekend Review section)).

[180] However, the Information Commissioner in his Report on Compliance by Public Bodies (above, n.143) states that more information could be released without resorting to the Act.

under the Freedom of Information Act to release all information covered by the Act or that can reasonably be believed to be covered by it.[181]

Some users, including journalists and the Minister who steered the Act through parliament, have reported best results by telephoning the public body and asking if they can have specified information or if they need to make a request under the Act. That way, a considerable amount of information is being made available forthwith, without the necessity to go through the process stipulated by the Act.[182] In addition, where the same information is repeatedly requested by different users, the public body may decide to release it routinely in future. Such was the case with the report of the tax strategy group, the Charter on Public Procurement, and politicians' expenses.[183]

As stated above, the time-frame provided for in the Act for handling requests may seem unnecessarily long to journalists and it is to be hoped that the period for responding to requests will gradually be reduced. Indeed, there is evidence that, in many cases, responses are received well within the limits. A stage where significant delays have been experienced, however, is that of reviews by the Information Commissioner. Due to large numbers of applications for review and staff shortages in his office, the Commissioner had to announce that delays beyond the four-month limit set in the Act were already occurring by 1998-9.[184] However, additional staff were appointed and the Commissioner adopted a strategy of dealing with new cases first as they come in and then working to clear the backlog as quickly as possible.

Overall, the Irish Freedom of Information Act is seen as a success.[185] While certain shortcomings are apparent, as noted above, so too are certain strengths, which offer the potential for further extending the scope and influence of the Act. When it first began to operate in April 1998, *The Irish Times* newspaper in its leader stated: "For now, the Government has opened a window. But it still has to let in the light." The culture had to change, both within the public service and also in the public domain in general. People have to assert their rights. They have to be made aware of them and then prompted to avail of them.

Journalists have a particularly important role to play in this process. As the Information Commissioner stated:

[181] The Freedom of Information Act 1997, s.48, amends the Official Secrets Act 1963 accordingly.

[182] *The Irish Times* (Finance section), January 29, 1999.

[183] *ibid.*, *The Irish Times*, October 5, 1999; *The Sunday Times*, December 19, 1999. The Minister for Communications began to place all FOI documents on the departmental website (*www.dcmnr.ie*) from April 15, 2003. The move was designed to increase public access to official documents and to deflect from the heavy criticism of the restrictions in the new Act. Requests and releases referring to personal information are exempt (*Sunday Business Post*, April 6, 2003). The Data Protection Commissioner questioned the decision on the grounds that to include the names of the requesters could amount to a breach of the Data Protection Act (*The Sunday Times*, May 18, 2003).

[184] See the *Second Annual Report of the Information Commissioner*, available at *www.oic.gov.ie/report99*; *The Irish Times*, June 6, 2000.

[185] See, for example, the Annual Report of the Information Commissioner for 2002, and the furore that greeted the Government's announcement that it was to curtail the Act in 2003 (above, n.103).

"[E]ffective use of the Act by members of the media is important. In the longer term, the Act has a significant role to play in terms of encouraging transparency and democratic participation. These benefits can, however, be realised only in a limited way as a result of individual requests by private citizens. In a modern democracy one vital means of bringing information about the business of government into the public domain is through the media. It is important that the media's capacity to do this should not depend solely on channels where the choice of information, and the timing of its release, is at the discretion of the party providing it. The Act, by giving a statutory right of access to information, shifts the initiative to the requester. Hence the importance that the media avail of this right on behalf of the community."[186]

Journalists therefore have an obligation to the public not only to use the Act but also to highlight and detail their use of it, the gains and the losses, as a way of monitoring and documenting the operation of the Act, so as to bring about any necessary changes to it.[187]

The path to openness has been established. So, too, has administrative accountability. The public has direct access to a whole range of public bodies in a way it never had before. That new relationship between government and citizen now has to be fostered and strengthened. The 2003 Act has curtailed the scope of the 1997 Act to some extent but there is still a lot of value to be gained from using what remains of it.

10.7 Freedom of Information in Other Countries

Ireland was certainly not the first country to embrace freedom of information laws and principles. Sweden is credited as the first country to do so as far back as 1766. In modern times, other Scandinavian countries were the first to introduce such laws.[188] Canada, Australia and New Zealand passed laws in 1982,[189] on which the Irish Freedom of Information Act 1997 was modelled. Prior to its amendment in 2003, the Irish Freedom of Information Act 1997 had itself become a model for other countries, particularly in Eastern Europe.[190]

---

[186] *First Annual Report of the Information Commissioner*, available at *www.oic.gov.ie/ report98*.

[187] In New Zealand, for example, journalists' organisations (for example, the Commonwealth Press Union (New Zealand Section)) produced dossiers on their experience in using similar legislation there and the Act was subsequently reviewed by the Law Commission.

[188] Finland in 1951, Denmark in 1964 and Norway in 1970. France and the Netherlands introduced FOI laws in 1978. See generally, John Doyle, "Freedom of Information: Lessons from the International Experience" (1996–7) 44 *Administration* 64.

[189] See Robert Hazell, "Freedom of Information in Australia, Canada and New Zealand" (1989) 67 *Public Administration* 189 and *passim* McDonagh, above, n.97. The FOI website maintained by Maeve McDonagh at University College Cork (*www.ucc.ie/law/ lawonline/freedom*) includes links to FOI in almost all of the countries listed in this section, as well as Germany, Hong Kong, South Africa and the EU.

[190] It is regarded in Poland, for example, as encompassing the "best possible legislative

While legislation already existed in most western European countries, the UK Freedom of Information Act was not passed until November 30, 2000 and will be phased in over a period up to November 30, 2005. Prior to that, various pieces of legislation in the UK had opened up particular meetings and records to the public and a Code of Practice on Access to Government Information was introduced in 1994 and revised in 1997. [191]

In the United States the Freedom of Information Act was passed in 1966 and amended periodically,[192] with further revision in 1996, which requires agencies to be pro-active and make material affecting the public available through public reading rooms and on the internet. The primary users of FOIA became the business and commercial interests, whose potential use of the Act had been little considered. Journalists also made considerable use of the legislation and many significant stories have been broken as a result.[193] The Government in the Sunshine Act 1976 requires that meetings of government agencies, such as the Federal Trade Commission, Copyright Royalties Tribunal and a host of other councils and commissions, be open to the public, unless there were proper reasons why they should not. Following the atrocities of September 11, 2001, however, some States sought to limit access in the interests of security.[194]

Information is specifically mentioned in Article 19 of the Universal Declaration of Human Rights and of ICCPR, as well as Article 10 of the ECHR. There are also a number of international documents specifically dealing with access to official information. The UN Convention on Access to Information, Public Participation in Decision-making and Access to Justice in Environmental Matters, for example, was adopted in Aarhus, Denmark on June 25, 1998.

---

ideas", which would be used to form the basis of the drafting of the Polish legislation (see *www.freepress.org.pl/english/index.htm*).

[191] For a brief account, see Tom Crone, *Law and the Media* (4th ed., Focal Press, Oxford, 2002), Chap. 14, p.212. The text of the English Act is available at *www.legislation.hmso.gov.uk/acts/acts2000/20000036.htm* and the Codes of Practice are available on the Lord Chancellor's website *www.lcd.gov.uk/foi/codesprac.htm*. See also the Campaign for Freedom of Information (*www.cfoi.org.uk*). For a comparison of various aspects of the UK legislation with those of the Irish and other countries' legislation, see Maeve McDonagh, above, n.97, and "FOI and Confidentiality of Commercial Information" [2001] P.L. 256. In Scotland, the Freedom of Information Act was passed in 2002. It was modelled on the Irish Act and the text is available at *www.scottish.parliament.uk*.

[192] In 1974, 1976 and 1986 (FOI Reform Act 1986), as well as technical adjustments from time to time. The text of the US legislation (often referred to as "FOIA" from its initials) and a guide to its use are available on the Department of Justice website *www.usdoj.gov/ oip/foia*. The Guide (2002) has a useful introduction, which outlines the background and development of the Act.

[193] A number of organisations, which promote freedom of information, document usage of the Act and practical developments as they arise, as well as offering FOI assistance. See, for example, the Electronic Journalist FOI Center (*www.foi.missouri.edu*), the Reporters Committee for Freedom of the Press (*www.rcfp.org*), the Society of Professional Journalists (*www.spj.org/foia*) and the National FOI Coalition (*www.nfoic.org*).

[194] See, for example, (2002) 26(1) *The News Media and The Law* 28, available at *www.rcfp.org* (The Reporters Committee for Freedom of the Press).

Access to information at EU level was slow to develop.[195] On occasion, when information relating to environmental issues was not forthcoming from Brussels, use was made of the Swedish Freedom of Information Act[196] or recourse was had to the European Ombudsman.[197] A right of access to information on the environment was introduced in 1990.[198] The Ombudsman has played an important role in prompting European Union institutions to release documents. The Commission, Parliament and Council have all been subject to rules governing access to information since 2001 in accordance with Regulation (EC) No.1049/2001.[199] The right of access to documents is now guaranteed in Article 255 of the Amsterdam Treaty and in Article 42 of the Charter of Fundamental Rights of the European Union:

> "Any citizen of the Union, and any natural or legal person residing or having its registered office in a Member State, has a right of access to European Parliament, Council and Commission documents."[200]

---

[195] See, for example, *Carvel and Guardian Newspapers Ltd. v Council of Ministers*, case T–194/94 ECJ, October 19, 1995; *Journalisten Tidningen*, case T–174/95; *Green Paper on Public Sector Information in the Information Society* (Com(98)585 final, adopted on January 20, 1999) and *Access to Commission Documents* (available at *www.europa.eu.int*); James Michael, "Freedom of information comes to the European Union" [1996] P.L. 31, Michael O'Neill, "In search of a real right of access to E.C.-held documentation" [1997] P.L.446.

[196] See generally *www.statewatch.org* and *www.freedominfo.org*.

[197] *www.euro-ombudsman.eu.int*. See also *www.statewatch.org* and *IRIS – Legal Observations of the European Audiovisual Observatory* 2001–9:5 (*www.obs.coe.int*).

[198] EC Directive 90/313; [1990] O.J. L158/56. The Directive had to be implemented in Member States by December 1992. It was implemented in Ireland by the EC (Access to Information on the Environment) Regulations 1993 (S.I. No.133 of 1993). There was a lot of dissatisfaction with the Regulations, particularly the scope of the grounds for refusing access. See, for example, Geraldine O'Brien, "Freedom of access to information on the environment – the reality in Ireland" (1995) 5 *Irish Communications Review* 68. Following a review, new Regulations were introduced in 1996 (S.I. No.185 of 1996) and again in 1998 (S.I. No.125 of 1998). See further, McDonagh, above, n.97, at p.404.

[199] O.J. L145, May 31, 2001. The Regulation is based on Art. 1 of the Amsterdam Treaty (that decisions will be taken as openly as possible and as closely as possible to the citizens), and Art. 255 of the Treaty (the right of access to documents). The exceptions are those which would undermine (a) the public interest (specifically public security, defence and military matters, international relations and the financial, monetary or economic policy of the community or a Member State) and (b) privacy and the integrity of the individual, in particular in accordance with Community legislation regarding the protection of personal data (Art. 4). It also deals with the treatment of sensitive documents (Art. 9). For the experience of journalists in accessing documents since the Regulation came into force, see the publications of the International Federation of Journalists (www.ifj.org/publications). One of the conclusions of an IFJ survey was that the growing electronic availability of documents in general together with the Council's document register have made it easier to identify and request documents and that transparency for journalists has increased. However, the survey did not indicate that the accessibility of the requested documents had increased correspondingly. See also, Tony Bunyan, "Secrecy and Openness in the European Union: the Ongoing Struggle for Freedom of Information" at *www.freedominfo.org/case/eustudy.htm*.

[200] The drafting of the Charter was concluded in December 2000. The right of access is included in Chapter V, Citizens' rights. The text of the charter is available at *www.europa.eu.int*.

In addition, Article 43 gives a right to contact the Ombudsman:

> "Any citizen of the Union and any natural or legal person residing or
> having its registered office in a Member State has the right to refer to the
> Ombudsman of the Union cases of maladministration in the activities of
> the Community institutions or bodies, with the exception of the Court of
> Justice and the Court of First Instance acting in their judicial role."[201]

Gradually, the European Court of Justice in Luxembourg (ECJ) has built up a
body of case law securing the right and clarifying its scope. The Court in 2001
upheld a decision of the Court of First Instance annulling the Council of the
EU's refusal to grant access to a report on arms exports.[202] The refusal was on
the grounds that it was sensitive information which could be harmful for the
EU's relations with non-Member States. Article 4 of Council Decision 93/
731/EC provides that public access shall not be granted where its disclosure
could undermine, *inter alia*, public security and international relations. The
ECJ, however, held that Decision 93/731 was intended to provide the public
with the widest possible access to documents held by the Council, so that any
exception to the right of access must be interpreted strictly.[203]

At the Council of Europe level, progress has been gradual also, with a
certain amount of "soft" law building up but a seeming reluctance to embrace
any binding provision on the right of access. Article 10 of the ECHR does not
expressly address the right of access to official information. The case law of
the Court has stopped short of interpreting Article 10 to include such a general
right. In *Leander v Sweden*[204] and *Gaskin v UK*[205] the Court found that there
had been no violation of Article 10. In *Guerra v Italy*,[206] the applicants
complained that the state had not informed the population of the risks run or
the measures to be taken in the event of an accident at a nearby chemical plant.
The Court found that Article 10 was not applicable because the public's right
to receive information does not impose positive obligations on the state to
gather and disseminate information.

The Committee of Ministers of the Council of Europe did acknowledge a
right to seek information in its *Declaration on the Freedom of Expression and*

---

[201] This right is the right guaranteed by Articles 21 and 195 of the EC Treaty. In accordance
with Art. 52(2) of the Charter, it applies under the conditions defined by the Treaty.

[202] Case C–353/99 P, *Council of the European Union v Heidi Hautala*, judgment of the
ECJ, December 6, 2001.

[203] See generally, TJ McIntyre, "Freedom of Information in Europe" (1999) 5(1) B.R. 41;
Noel Travers, "Access to Documents in Community Law: on the Road to a European
Participatory Democracy" (2000) xxxv Ir. Jur. 164; Maeve McDonagh, "Freedom of
Information in Ireland and Europe: Progress and Regression" (2001) 29(2) *International
Journal of Legal Information* 256 and "The Interaction of European Community Law
and National Access to Information Laws: An Irish Perspective" (2000) 9(2) *Irish Journal
of European Law* 216.

[204] Series A, No.116, (1987) 9 E.H.R.R. 433. The case involved refusal of access on the
grounds of national security.

[205] Series A, No.160, (1989) 12 E.H.R.R. 36. The case involved refusal of access to a case
record held by a local authority when the applicant was a minor under their care.

[206] Judgment of February 19, 1998.

Information adopted in 1982. Since then the Committee has also drafted a number of Recommendations.[207] Its Recommendation on Access to Official Documents (2002) sets out key principles of law and practice for the guidance of Member States.[208] The Recommendation recognises the "importance in a pluralistic, democratic society of transparency of public administration and of the ready availability of information on issues of public interest". The rationale is that wide access to official documents:

> "allows the public to have an adequate view of, and to form a critical opinion on, the state of the society in which they live and on the authorities that govern them, whilst encouraging informed participation by the public in matters of common interest;
>
> fosters the efficiency and effectiveness of administrations and helps maintain their integrity by avoiding the risk of corruption;
>
> contributes to affirming the legitimacy of administrations as public services and to strengthening the public's confidence in public authorities."

Freedom of information, therefore, is of central importance to the promotion of transparent and accountable government.

Further Reading

(1993) 22 *Index on Censorship*, Nos 8 & 9 (Re. Ireland).
McDonagh, Maeve, *Freedom of Information Law in Ireland* (Round Hall Sweet & Maxwell, Dublin, 1998).
McDonald, John, and Others, *The Law of Freedom of Information* (OUP, Oxford, 2003).
Ó Drisceoil, Donal, *Censorship in Ireland 1939–1945 – Neutrality, Politics and Society* (Cork University Press, Cork, 1996).

---

[207] Recommendation No. R(81) 19 on the access to information held by public authorities, as well as Recommendation No. R(91) 10 on the communication to third parties of personal data held by public bodies, Recommendation No. R(97) 18 concerning the protection of personal data collected and processed for statistical purposes and Recommendation No. R(2000) 13 on a European policy on access to archives.

[208] Rec(2002)2, adopted on February 21, 2002. The Principles constitute a minimum standard and cover definitions, scope, possible limitations, requests for access, processing of requests, forms of access, charges, review procedure and complementary measures and initiatives. The general principle (No.III) is: "Member States should guarantee the right of everyone to have access, on request, to official documents held by public authorities. This principle should apply without discrimination on any ground, including that of national origin." See also, the international principles drafted under the auspices of ARTICLE 19, the Global Campaign for Free Expression: *The Public's Right to Know: Principles on Freedom of Information Legislation* (ARTICLE 19, London, June 1999) and *A Model Freedom of Information Law* (ARTICLE 19, London, July 2001). Both are available at *www.article19.org*.

CHAPTER ELEVEN

Media Structures and Regulation Present and Future

"To begin with, the era of free speech is closing down".[1]

11.1 INTRODUCTION

The purpose of this chapter is to set the scene pertaining to Media Law at the beginning of the twenty-first century. At the outset, the situation at the close of the twentieth century is recalled, and key issues arising at that time are identified. Such has been the growth of Media Law in recent years, that it is not possible to do justice in a single chapter to all of the detailed and finely nuanced legal and policy developments and discussions that have been taking place at national, European and international level, as a result of technological advances, competition in the marketplace, and competing rights and theories. The chapter aims, therefore, to give an overview of key developments, to outline some of the more important considerations and to provide some signposts to encourage students, researchers and media personnel to pursue some of the issues more fully and to follow future developments as they occur.

11.2 THE MEDIA IN THE TWENTY-FIRST CENTURY

As outlined in Chapter 3 above, the twentieth century saw the rise and expansion of the audio-visual media. Towards the end of the century, digital technology augmented still further the range of media and information services available. As a result, the number of broadcast channels across Europe rose to 666 in 2001, and is now in excess of 800, with an increasing number received in more than one EU country.[2] As the growth of multi-channel and digital services

---

[1] George Orwell, writing in the *New Leader*, June 24, 1938, in Sonia Orwell and Ian Angus (eds), *The Collected Essays, Journalism and Letters of George Orwell* (Vol. 1, Penguin Books, Reading, 1968), p.373.

[2] "What changes will be made to the Community's audiovisual policy? Work programme for reviewing the 'Television without Frontiers' Directive", Press Release, Brussels, January 7, 2003. Despite the huge increase in the number of channels, the average viewer's behaviour shows little change: there has been no switch to new media at the expense of television viewing (*ibid.*). New media services are supplementing rather than replacing existing forms of television viewing. For some further statistical data, see Fourth Report from the Commission to the Council, the European Parliament, the European Economic

continues, both public service and private commercial broadcasting free-to-air are maintaining their audience share so far but their financial strength is decreasing. Subscription services, offering access to special and major events, specialist and niche programming and interactive services, are increasing. Yet, there is progressive concentration, and despite the proliferation of channels and choice, just 50 channels share 75 per cent of the European market.[3] To feed all the new services, the need for content has greatly increased. Quotas have been put in place at national and European level in respect of programme content produced by independent producers, and most channels comply with states' requirements on independent production.[4]

The greatest challenge facing legislators and regulatory authorities at the beginning of the twenty-first century, therefore, was convergence. Convergence was creating problems for pluralism and diversity, for regulation and for regulators.[5] Were regulation and regulators also to converge? Key issues for discussion and decision included whether to maintain separate regulation for public service and private commercial broadcasting or move to uniform regulation, given that the impact on the audience was the same, and uniform regulation was necessary to protect advertisers and sponsors. Also to be decided was whether uniform regulation was feasible or desirable across all sectors. Could existing or modified broadcasting regulation be applied also to the new media? Would deregulation result or would existing legal regulation cede to forms of co-regulation[6] and self-regulation? Underlying all the arguments advanced was the recognition that broadcasting and information media are not just a commodity like cars or carpets, but have an important cultural dimension and social value, which must be safeguarded.[7] The central role they play in a modern democracy remains crucial.

At another level, the aftermath of the terrorist attacks of September 11th has had consequences for journalism and media, with the rush to legislate to combat terrorism, and new rules chipping away at freedom of expression and

---

and Social Committee and the Committee of the Regions (COM(2002) 778 final, Brussels January 6, 2003) and the Yearbooks (*Film, Television, Video and Multimedia in Europe*) of the European Audiovisual Observatory (for details, see *www.obs.coe.int*).

[3] EPRA conference, Ljubljana, October 23–25, 2002 (*www.epra.org*, background papers).

[4] *ibid.* Quotas on European content are also in place under the Television without Frontiers Directive (see below).

[5] See, for example, European Commission Report, *Audiovisual Media and Authorities: Tasks and challenges for regulators in an evolving media landscape in Europe* (Vienna, November 1998); *Convergence in European Digital TV Regulation* (Chris Marsden & Stefaan Verhulst (eds), Blackstone Press Ltd, London, 1999).

[6] See Carmen Palzer, "Co-Regulation of the Media in Europe: European Provisions for the Establishment of Co-regulation Frameworks" *IRIS plus* (*IRIS–Legal Observations of the European Audiovisual Observatory* 2002–6); Tarlach McGonagle, "The Potential for Practice of an Intangible Idea: Co-Regulation of the Media in Europe" *IRIS plus* (*IRIS* 2002–10); Tony Prosser, "Self-Regulation, Co-Regulation and Reform of Media Regulation in the UK", *Co-regulation of the Media in Europe* (IRIS Special, Strasbourg: European Audiovisual Observatory, 2003), p.59.

[7] These values are repeatedly referred to in the recitals and preambles to the policy documents of the EC and Council of Europe in the field. See, in particular, the preamble to the European Convention on Transfrontier Television (discussed below).

other civil liberties, including privacy, through increased surveillance and data retention.[8] All pointed to an even greater need to maintain and develop as wide a range of alternative sources of information as possible, to actively encourage and promote pluralism and diversity in the media, editorial independence and awareness of human rights.

The war in Iraq in 2003 also raised serious questions about the role and future of journalism and the media. The ratings war, the commodification of news, the widespread use of "spin", the question mark over the reliability of information from whatever source and the impartiality of the reporting of "embedded" journalists, all gave rise to disquiet.[9] This form of reality television reached new heights but showed up its inadequacies. The public migrated in large numbers from printed newspapers and television to the internet, particularly newspaper and television-based sites.[10]

11.3 REGULATION OF BROADCASTING

In the past, the regulation of broadcasting has been considered necessary for two main reasons. Firstly, in the early days, access to the electromagnetic spectrum was limited. The allocation of frequencies was the subject of international negotiation between governments and was therefore seen as the preserve of governments. It was treated as part of the State's communications apparatus. Technological developments since have opened up access and the so-called "scarcity argument" no longer holds much weight. Secondly, broadcasting, particularly television broadcasting, which is still relatively new, has been regarded somewhat apprehensively as a powerful medium, especially because it is almost universally available and brought directly into people's homes. As a result, its impact is immediate.[11] Governments therefore perceived the need to introduce laws to regulate both structure and content.

---

[8] The Criminal Justice (Terrorist Offences) Bill 2002 is intended to give effect in Irish law to the EU Framework Decision on Combating Terrorism, the International Convention Against the Taking of Hostages, the Convention on Prevention and Punishment of Crimes Against Internationally Protected Persons including Diplomatic Agents, the International Convention for the Suppression of Terrorist Bombings and the International Convention for the Suppression of the Financing of Terrorism. That is in addition to the Offences against the State Acts 1939–1998, which have themselves been the subject of criticism (see above Chap.10). Further legislation involving control and interception of e-mails and other forms of communication is contemplated (above Chap.10).

[9] See Michael Foley, "Perspective on the war provided by Irish journalists is uniquely valuable", *The Irish Times*, April 1, 2003: "If this war has taught us anything, it is that instant, real-time modern television coverage is very bad at covering war. Television just does not have the subtlety to explain complexity. It forces the viewer to make sense of what is often a series of unconnected images". Foley also recalls that journalists are meant to witness, interrogate and interpret and that journalism at its best cannot exist without trust. See also Helen Shaw, "Serious news in US early victim of Iraq war", *The Irish Times*, May 14, 2003.

[10] See *The Irish Times*, April 16, 2003.

[11] Ironically, the opposite argument was used to justify film censorship in the early part of the twentieth century, when cinematographic film was the main entertainment form. The

As the European Commission has put it:

> "The broadcast media play a central role in the functioning of modern democratic societies, in particular in the development and transmission of social values. Therefore, the broadcasting sector has, since its inception, been subject to specific regulation in the general interest. This regulation has been based on common values, such as freedom of expression and the right of reply, pluralism, protection of copyright, promotion of cultural and linguistic diversity, protection of minors and of human dignity, consumer protection".[12]

Furthermore, broadcasting is generally perceived as a reliable source of information and represents, for a not inconsiderable proportion of the population, the main source of information. It thus enriches public debate and ultimately ensures that all citizens participate in public life.[13]

As outlined in Chapter 3 above, the first manifestation of government intervention came in the form of a requirement to have a licence to broadcast and a licence to receive broadcasting. This was established by law in the Wireless Telegraphy Act 1926, followed by the Broadcasting Acts 1960–93, and was applied to the commercial stations by the Radio and Television Act 1988.[14] The RTÉ Authority and the Independent Radio and Television Commission (IRTC) were established under the respective legislation as the regulatory bodies with responsibility for both structural and content regulation. They were required to establish and oversee broadcasting in accordance with the statutory regime and to ensure that the statutory obligations of broadcasters were met.[15] Their role was complemented by that of the Broadcasting Complaints Commission (BCC), established under the Broadcasting Authority (Amendment) Act 1976, to hear complaints of breaches by RTÉ, and later by the commercial stations, of their statutory obligations.

The role of the IRTC was as licensor and regulator of the commercial sector. As well as issuing licences in accordance with the 1988 Act, the IRTC had a duty to monitor compliance with the conditions of the contracts awarded. A number of its decisions resulted in judicial review in the courts. In each case,

---

argument was made that, since people went to see films *en masse*, the influence and impact was all the greater.

[12] Commission of the European Communities, COM (2000) 580 final, p.35.

[13] Commission of the European Communities, Communication on state aid (Com 2001/C 320/04, O.J. C 320/5), p.2, para.8 (available at *www.europa.eu.int/comm/avpolicy/legis/com_en.htm*).

[14] There are various other wireless telegraphy acts and orders; see Eamonn Hall, *The Electronic Age: Telecommunication in Ireland* (Oak Tree Press, Dublin, 1993), Table of Statutes, at p.526.

[15] RTÉ's statutory obligations in respect of programme content are set out in s.18 of the 1960 Act, as amended. RTÉ, the national public service broadcaster appeared to breach its own guidelines, the terms of the current code on advertising, and the statutory regulations with regard to news broadcasts, when it carried, in a news bulletin, a live interview with one of the judges in its "Popstars" series. The judge, who is the originator of pop bands such as Boyzone and Westlife, was interviewed holding a bottle of Fanta. Fanta were the sponsors of the series (*The Irish Independent*, February 22, 2002).

except the withdrawal of the licence in the TV3 case, the allegations of objective bias were rejected and the fairness of the procedures adopted by the IRTC upheld.[16] Among the cases taken was the Supreme Court appeal in 2001 against a High Court decision upholding the awarding of a Dublin "youth" radio licence to a consortium called "Spin FM".[17] A rival consortium, "Storm FM" had claimed that there was objective bias against it on the part of a member of the IRTC, who had made inquiries to the gardaí regarding reports of drug abuse in a nightclub owned by a member of the "Storm FM" consortium. The Court said that once a Commission (IRTC) member became aware that the chairman of one of the consortiums applying for a radio licence was the owner of a nightclub about which there were adverse reports concerning abuse of drugs, he was put on legitimate inquiry as to the suitability of the applicant in question. The evidence disclosed no more than that the member of the IRTC had grounds for making the inquiries, the Court said.

In its role as content regulator, the IRTC also had to deal with TV3's decision to broadcast a made-for-television version of the violent film *Natural Born Killers*. The 1988 Act requires the Commission to ensure that broadcasters do not broadcast anything which may reasonably be regarded as offending against good taste or decency, or likely to incite to crime.[18] The IRTC also had to take decisions regarding the acceptability of certain advertisements under the 1988 Act, which prohibits advertisements of a political or religious nature.[19] A slight

---

[16] *TV3 v IRTC*, Supreme Court, October 26, 1993; see above, Chap.3. See, for example, *Dublin and County Broadcasting v IRTC*, unreported, High Court, May 12, 1989, where it was held that the decision of the IRTC was not vitiated by bias; *Radio Limerick One Ltd v IRTC* [1997] 2 I.R. 291; [1997] 2 I.L.R.M. 1, which involved the withdrawal of a licence due to persistent breaches of the contract obligations; and *Maigueside Communications Ltd v IRTC* [1998] 4 I.R. 115, which involved a decision to award a licence to another applicant. Further challenges resulted from decisions in 2002–3 to award licences to new entrants in preference to existing players in Sligo and Kilkenny, albeit in the context of newly designated franchise areas. See, for example, *The Irish Times*, May 2, 2003, May 27, 2003 (Minister to review the radio licensing regime before the BCI is re-established next year as the Broadcasting Authority of Ireland (BAI)). A report (Report No.5, May 2003) of the Joint Oireachtas Committee on Communications, Marine and Natural Resources was critical of *inter alia* the lack of transparency and accountability of recent BCI decisions. It advocated *inter alia* an independent non-judicial appeals mechanism, independent verification of claims made by applicants for licences, the automatic roll-over of licences where holders are in general compliance with their contracts and an examination of the cost of the licensing process (see *www.oireachtas.ie* and *The Irish Times*, May 29, 2003). The High Court, July 31, 2003, Ó Caoimh J. upheld the decisions of the BCI in the Sligo and Kilkenny cases.

[17] *Spin Communications Ltd t/a Storm FM v IRTC* [2002] 1 I.L.R.M. 98.

[18] TV3 took the view that the Commission – and not the Film Censor, who had banned the original version of the film for public showing – had jurisdiction over material broadcast on television, and the Commission's own legal advice supported that view. In any event, the ban was lifted and the film was finally broadcast on TV3 late on Saturday August 25, 2001. See above Chap.9.

[19] Its decision not to allow an advertisement for the showing of a video on the Resurrection was upheld by the Supreme Court in *Roy Murphy v IRTC* [1999] 1 I.R. 12; [1998] 2 I.L.R.M. 360. See also *Colgan v IRTC* [2000] 2 I.R. 490, [1999] 1 I.L.R.M. 22, and the refusals to allow advertisements for the *Irish Catholic* newspaper and for the *Power to Change* campaign, all of which are documented above in Chap.8. The IRTC had also

change in the position regarding religious advertising is contained in the final part of the 2001 Act.[20]

11.3.1 The Broadcasting Act 2001

The role of all three regulatory authorities has been changed by the Broadcasting Act 2001, an Act primarily concerned with the introduction of digital terrestrial television (DTT). Considering the extent of convergence that was taking place at the turn of the century, and the opportunity the new legislation would afford for the restructuring of broadcasting in light of technological developments, a rationalisation of the role and structure of the regulatory bodies might have been expected. The UK[21] and Italy, for example, were already on their way to establishing "one-stop" authorities.[22] As technologies converged, overlaps and inconsistencies developed in the regulatory framework and so the regulatory bodies converged too.

Ireland was not ready to take such a step at that time. Instead, under the Broadcasting Act 2001 the IRTC became the Broadcasting Commission of Ireland (BCI), with an extended remit. The BCC retained its name but it too was given an extended remit, a more stable basis and a potentially higher

---

refused to allow the broadcast of an advertisement for a book of short stories by Sinn Féin President Gerry Adams in 1993, under s.9 of the 1988 Act, which replicated s.31 of the Broadcasting Authority Act 1960, as amended (*Brandon Book Publishers Ltd v IRTC*, unreported, HC, October 29, 1993; see above, Chap.10). Other examples include concern over an advertisement on Highland Radio in Donegal for recruitment to the then RUC, the police force in Northern Ireland (*The Irish Times*, November 5, 9, 1994).

[20] Broadcasting Act 2001, Pt VII covers miscellaneous matters including fees, offences and various amendments, among them s.65 which permits the broadcasting of a notice that a particular religious newspaper, magazine or periodical is available for sale or that a particular religious event or ceremony will take place, provided the contents of the notice do not address the issue of the merits of any religion or of becoming a member of any religion or religious organisation. The Minister announced a consultation process with a view to removing the ban on religious advertising in March 2003. The European Court of Human Rights found that the ban did not breach Art.10 ECHR (judgment of July 10, 2003).

[21] In 1999 the British Government published a Green Paper, *Regulating Communications: The Way Ahead*, which set out the case for a reduced regulatory role in respect of media and telecommunications, a "lighter touch" approach. A White Paper, *A New Future for Communications*, in preparation for the introduction of a Communications Bill, was published in December 2000. It recommended that a single regulator, to be called OFCOM, and encompassing the existing regulators, be created to regulate the media and telecommunications. OFCOM was established under the Office of Communications Act 2002 (See *IRIS* 2002–7:12). A certain amount of rationalisation had already taken place in the UK with the merger in 1996 of the Broadcasting Complaints Commission and the Broadcasting Standards Council, for instance, to become the Broadcasting Standards Commission, and with the development of co-operation between OFTEL, the Director-General of Fair Trading and the Monopolies and Mergers Commission. See Thomas Gibbons, *Regulating the Media* (2nd ed., Sweet & Maxwell, London, 1998), pp.19, 264.

[22] For details of the single regulator model in these and other countries, see *www.epra.org*. For a detailed account of the background to media regulation in the UK and Ireland, see Marie McGonagle and Candelaria Van Strien-Reney, "Media ownership issues in the UK and Ireland" (1999) 4 *Mediaforum* 100.

profile. The position of the RTÉ Authority in the new regime has also been clarified, expanding its public service role to include local, community and regional broadcasting services, as well as special interest subscription or pay-for-view services and electronic transmission.[23] In the overall scheme of things, however, the BCI became the central authority and the RTÉ Authority was to have a subsidiary role, focusing on public service programming and largely technical and operational matters.

The Broadcasting Act 2001 emerged after a protracted period of planning.[24] It made provision primarily for the introduction of digital television but also for a host of new analogue and digital radio and television services. Part II of the Act deals with the supply and transmission of programme material. It puts in place a system to accommodate the needs of digital technology, the measures necessary for transmission by digital means, including the establishment of a transmission company[25] and a multiplex company.[26]

Part II of the Act also establishes the name and remit of the BCI, which includes making arrangements for the provision of additional broadcasting services and ensuring that the broadcasting services made available "best serve the needs of the people of the island of Ireland, bearing in mind their languages

---

[23] Other than by broadcasting: Broadcasting Act 2001, ss.29 and 30 respectively.

[24] The process began with the publication of the Government's Green Paper on Broadcasting: *Active or Passive? Broadcasting in the Future Tense* (Government Publications, Dublin, 1995). That was followed by *Clear Focus – The Government's Proposals for Broadcasting Legislation* (Pn 3648, The Stationery Office, Dublin, 1997). The Bill was introduced in 1999 but did not become law until March 2001.

[25] S.5. The principal objects of the transmission company are to transmit by analogue means radio and television broadcasting services on behalf of the existing service providers (RTÉ, Teilifís na Gaeilge, which is to become independent of RTÉ, and the commercial services provided in accordance with the 1988 Act) and to transmit by digital means programme material and related and other data in a digital form in accordance with arrangements entered into with the multiplex company established by the Act. It is also to promote the development of multimedia services and electronic information services, including those provided by means of the internet. Licences for the operation of the apparatus by RTÉ and the transmission company are to be issued by the Director for Telecommunications Regulation, now the Commission for Communications Regulation (ComReg) (s.6). Similarly, a DTT licence will be issued to the company (s.7). ComReg is the Commission for Communications Regulation. Its role is discussed below.

[26] S.8. The principal objects of the multiplex company are to establish and operate six digital multiplexes, *i.e.* electronic systems which combine programme material and related and other data in a digital form for the purposes of having it transmitted by the transmission company, and to enter into arrangements with the programme service providers (RTÉ, Teilifís na Gaeilge, and the commercial stations established under the 1988 Act) for the transmission of programme material and data in digital form. Like the transmission company, it is to promote the development of multimedia services and electronic information services, including those provided by means of the internet. It is to have a digital multiplex licence, issued by ComReg (s.9). Conditions may be attached to the licence. RTÉ was allocated one multiplex, Teilifís na Gaeilge and TV3 one half each. Neither the transmission company nor the multiplex company shall be responsible for programme content, since their function is merely one of facilitating the transmission. They will not, therefore, be liable, for example, for copyright infringement or defamation arising from programme content (s.15).

and traditions and their religious, ethical and cultural diversity".[27] The BCI is also given the role of entering into digital content contracts for the supply of programme material and electronic programme guide contracts for the provision to the public of information on programme schedules.[28] In both cases, the contracts will be subject to certain conditions. In the case of digital content contracts, a condition of the contracts will be compliance with the codes and rules that the Commission is required to draw up under section 19 of the Act in relation to programme standards, and in relation to advertising, teleshopping and sponsorship, in particular as regards children. A further condition is that the contract may be terminated if it contravenes Articles 22 or 22A of the Television without Frontiers Directive or a provision of the Incitement to Hatred Act 1989 or if it constitutes an incitement to commit an offence.[29] In the case of electronic programme guides, the contractor will be required to comply with the guidelines to be drawn up by the BCI in consultation with ComReg under section 17.[30] A further condition is to ensure that information regarding RTÉ, Teilifís na Gaeilge and TV3 services, as well as those provided in and receivable throughout Northern Ireland, is easily accessible.[31]

Part III of the Act deals with standards in broadcasting. The mechanism to be used for ensuring programme standards is the drafting of codes relating to taste and decency, portrayal of violence and sexual conduct, which are to be prepared by the BCI on the direction of the Minister. These and the proposed codes of advertising standards and rules on the amount of advertising allowable in any one day or given hour are designed to comply with the Television without Frontiers Directive.[32] In drafting the codes, priority is to be given to a code of advertising, teleshopping and sponsorship, which "relate to matters likely to be of direct or indirect interest to children". The BCI embarked on the drafting of a children's code in April 2003.[33] Rules requiring each broadcaster to provide facilities for the deaf and blind are also mandated.[34] While the BCI's role is mainly in relation to broadcasting, it may also co-operate or give assistance in the drafting of codes or standards with respect to the transmission of information by electronic means, including the internet.[35]

---

[27] Ss.10–11. The "additional services" envisaged in the Act are discussed below.

[28] Ss.12 and 16 respectively.

[29] S.12(5).

[30] S.16(4).

[31] S.16(5). The Commission may invite expressions of interest for such contracts (s.16(7) and (8)).

[32] Section 19(4). Procedures, including provision for inspection of draft codes is included in s.19(5) and (6).

[33] See *www.bci.ie*. In relation to children, the Commission is authorised (s.19(8)) to conduct research, to take account of any guidelines issued by any body dealing with the welfare of children and to consider the merits or feasibility of prohibitions (s.19(7)). The first phase of the consultation process was completed in June 2003 (see *The Irish Times*, June 16, 2003) and the code itself is expected to be completed by June 2004. The code is then to be reviewed every three years (s.19(10)).

[34] S.19((11),(12),(13)).

[35] S.20. It is not to be involved, however, with codes relating to the technical aspects of such transmission (s.20(2)).

11.3.2 The Broadcasting Complaints Commission

The Broadcasting Complaints Commission (BCC) is reconstituted with an enhanced remit under the 2001 Act.[36] It was originally established under the Broadcasting Authority (Amendment) Act 1976 to deal with complaints against RTÉ and later had its role extended to the private commercial sector by the Radio and Television Act 1988.[37] Its new structure is set out in the 2001 Act. Its membership, term of office, remuneration, the complaints to be dealt with and the procedures for dealing with them are all set out in the Act.[38] A new link is forged between it and the BCI, insofar as the latter "may" supply services, accommodation or facilities and defray its expenses.[39] A complaints' body by definition should be independent of broadcasters and regulators alike. The arrangements envisaged in the 2001 Act are therefore not ideal.[40]

The BCC, as before, is to hear complaints of breaches of the statutory role of broadcasters, both public service and commercial, and those involved in the new services envisaged in the Act. They can hear, therefore, complaints of breaches of the provisions, *inter alia*, that news be reported in an impartial and objective manner without expression of the broadcasters' own views, that current affairs be fair to all sides, or complaints of failure to comply with a provision of a code under the 2001 Act itself or under the Broadcasting Act 1990.[41] Where the Complaints Commission finds in favour of the complainant

---

[36] The Government's Green Paper on Broadcasting in 1995 (above, n.24) questioned whether the structures under which the BCC then operated were adequate, whether they were the most effective and efficient for current needs and to cater for broadcasting into the next century. It had a minimum membership of three, was part-time, appointed by the Government for a period of five years, operated from a box number and determined if there had been a breach of their statutory obligations by broadcasters. It could not impose any sanctions, other than publication of its adjudications. It was not highly visible and, as its annual reports reveal, it handled only a small number of complaints each year.

[37] In February 2002, for example, the Broadcasting Complaints Commission upheld a complaint against TV3, the national commercial television station. The station had through "human error" broadcast a cartoon with an adult storyline and containing unsuitable language at 9 a.m. on a Sunday morning when small children could be expected to be viewing. TV3 was asked to make a public apology.

[38] Sections 22–24. The membership is set at not less than seven and not more than nine (s.22(3)). The procedures allow for those who are the subject of a complaint to be afforded the opportunity to comment on the complaint or to make a submission in the case of an advertisement. Consideration of a complaint by the BCC, however, is to be carried out in private (s.24(9)).

[39] The BCC is currently housed in the same premises as the BCI and the latter is providing secretarial support.

[40] The Government's Green Paper on Broadcasting in 1995 considered the case for merging the policy and regulatory functions of the RTÉ Authority and IRTC to form "one over-arching Authority that would assume overall responsibility for broadcasting policy", a "Super Authority". It was to include the BCC, which caused disquiet because of the need for the latter to be independent. For the thinking behind the restructuring of broadcasting and the increased role of the BCC under the Broadcasting Act 2001, see the Government's Green Paper on Broadcasting 1995, para.5.10 and para.5.3. Under the new arrangement, the BCI will be required to take decisions regarding aspects of programme content, compliance with codes and such like, which may themselves be the subject of complaints to the BCC.

[41] The 1990 Act, s.4 made provision for a code of advertising. The code, as drafted in 1995

in whole or in part, the broadcaster will be required to broadcast the decision and to correct any inaccurate facts or information relating to the individual concerned at a time and in a manner corresponding to that in which the offending broadcast took place. The correction of facts or inaccuracies relating to attacks on a person's honour or reputation is a remedy in the nature of a "right of reply" as required by the Television without Frontiers Directive.[42] As before, the BCC will be required to submit an annual report to the Minister.[43]

Part IV of the Act addresses the issue of public service broadcasting and confirms its validity. The term "public service broadcasting" is not defined in the Act but some of its characteristics are referred to in section 28.[44] It is to continue as a free-to-air service, universally available, providing a comprehensive range of programming, including news and current affairs, that reflects the linguistic and cultural diversity of the whole island. Part VI of the Act and the Second Schedule deal with the establishment of Teilifís na Gaeilge, now known as TG4, as an independent entity.[45] The provisions relating to public service broadcasting and to TG4 are discussed in some detail below.

In addition to free-to-air broadcasting services, provision is made in Part V of the Act for television programme service contractors to provide a variety of services, including community, local and regional services, subject to the authorisation of the BCI. In the case of satellite television, as with digital television, a content contract is required. The BCI is authorised to enter into satellite content contracts under the same kind of conditions as digital content contracts. Such contracts are subject to payment of a fee to the BCI.[46] In the case of cable and MMDS transmissions, where licences are granted by the ODTR, now ComReg (see below), the programming must come from RTÉ, TG4, TV3, the holder of a digital or satellite content contract or an excepted person, pursuant to a local, community or cable-MMD content contract.[47]

---

and updated in 1999, in accordance with s.4, was still in operation when the 2001 Act was passed.

[42] Article 23, EC Directive 89/552/EEC, October 3, 1989, as amended in 1997. Article 8 of the European Convention on Transfrontier Television also enshrines a right of reply. The obligation to provide a form of right of reply in accordance with the Directive and Convention was incorporated into the Broadcasting Act 1990, s.8 (see 399 *Dáil Debates*, cols 1579–1582, June 7, 1990; 126 *Seanad Debates*, cols 290–1, July 12, 1990). Section 24(11) of the Broadcasting Act 2001 specifically refers back to s.24(2)(f) regarding honour and reputation.

[43] S.25. The Minister is then to lay copies of it before both Houses of the Oireachtas.

[44] As commonly understood, public service broadcasting refers to broadcasting that is independent of Government, publicly funded (usually by a licence fee levied on viewers), that provides a wide range of programming intended to inform, educate and entertain the whole community, including catering for minority interests. See further below.

[45] Teilifís na Gaeilge was originally established, for reasons of speed and convenience, under the legislation pertaining to RTÉ. It was relaunched as TG4 in 1999, mainly for practical reasons to secure a high placing on the ever-increasing number of channels in the lead-up to the introduction of digital.

[46] S.36.

[47] S.37. "Excepted person" is defined in the Act as "a person who is under the jurisdiction of another Member State of the European Union or another Member State of the EEA and, for the purposes of this definition, the provisions of the Council Directive shall apply for the purpose of determining the state (whether it be a Member State of the

The Act reflects the ethos and character of community broadcasting, namely that it be provided by persons representative of the community, that it specifically address the interests of the community concerned, involve active participation of the community and that it be non-profit-making.[48] It is interesting to note that in relation to local content contracts, the BCI must be satisfied that the programme material will be made by the person entering into the contract or will be commissioned by that person and that a substantial proportion of that material will be made in the locality or will be of such a character as to be of special interest to persons living in the locality. In entering into a cable-MMD content contract also, the BCI must be satisfied that the contract will result in "the range and diversity of broadcasting available in the relevant area being increased".[49] The BCI, in drawing up and implementing its policy on pluralism and diversity, in accordance with the 1988 Act, and now the 2001 Act as well, was conscious of the need to preserve the local ethos of broadcasting. Its consultation process, carried out in 2001–2, and detailed below, revealed a clear support for maintaining the local broadcasting ethos, which it was claimed could be achieved through conditions imposed in relation to programming, in the manner provided for in the 2001 Act, rather than by local ownership as such.[50]

11.3.3 Pluralism and diversity

The 2001 Act also addresses the issue of diversity of sources and content of programming.[51] In relation to local services, for example, it provides that the

European Union or of the EEA) under the jurisdiction of which the person falls". The EEA includes the EU, Norway, Liechtenstein and Iceland. S.37 also deals with retransmission by cable or MMD system. The term "Retransmission" as used in the section means simultaneous, unaltered and unabridged transmission (s.37(14)).

[48] S.39(2)–(6). The term "local community" is defined as the community of a town or other urban or rural area (s.39(8)). The BCI has a role in establishing procedures for liaison with local communities, surveying programme material and assessing the needs of the community in respect of broadcasting (ss.39(4), (6) and 40).

[49] S.41(2). "Relevant area" is defined in s.41(3), and s.41(4) stipulates that a condition of such a contract will be that as respects the programme material supplied, the provisions of the TWF Directive in relation to European works will be complied with; see below.

[50] The BCI stressed its support for the view, widely espoused by respondents to its consultation paper, that the maintenance of a local ethos (as distinct from local ownership) was a key objective. See *www.bci.ie* for the Consultation Paper, responses to it and the policy statement which eventually emerged. Section 38 sets out a number of conditions which may be imposed by the BCI in local content contracts in relation to programming.

[51] Diversity is important for the public to have access to a wide range of information sources. Gibbons identifies three levels of pluralism or diversity: of content, of source, of outlet (delivery). Pluralism or diversity of source and outlet will not necessarily guarantee diversity of content, although they can provide conditions that are favourable to achieving diversity of content. The converse is also true: concentration in the hands of a few large players is likely to minimise the opportunities for diversity of content and thereby increase their influence on the audience. The main concern with achieving diversity of content lies in the fact that the media are the primary sources of knowledge about the world for the public (Thomas Gibbons, "Concentrations of Ownership and Control in a Converging Media Industry" in Chris Marsden and Stefaan Verhulst (eds), *Convergence in European Digital TV Regulation* (Blackstone Press Ltd, London, 1999), p.155, at p.157.

BCI in awarding local content contracts shall have regard to whether entering into such a contract would operate against the public interest and, in particular, shall have regard to:

> "(a) the desirability of allowing any person, or group of persons, to have control of, or substantial interests in, an undue amount of the communications media in the locality served by the cable or MMD system proposed to be used to transmit that material, and
>
> (b) the desirability of promoting diversity in the sources of information available to the public and in the opinions expressed in the communications media".[52]

In October 2001, the BCI announced details of its new ownership and control policy. The Radio and Television Act 1988 required the BCI (then the IRTC) to formulate and apply a policy that would take account of plurality of ownership and diversity of content in broadcasting. In terms of structures, the 1988 Act did not impose any ban on newspaper involvement in ownership of the new stations. It was left to the IRTC to take whatever steps were needed regarding cross-ownership in order to ensure pluralism and diversity. The IRTC initially imposed a 25 per cent limit on newspapers' share, later extended to 27 per cent, with a reciprocal limit on local radio's holdings in newspapers.[53] As a result, newspapers became involved in many of the new stations and, indeed, with cable companies and the new distribution system, MMDS.[54]

Subsequent events in the newspaper industry, in particular the dominance of Independent Newspapers, served to confirm misgivings about that involvement and its capacity to become a source of danger to pluralism and diversity.[55] Indeed, it may have proved detrimental that for so long debate

---

[52] S.38(6). To that purpose, the BCI may require the person(s) concerned to furnish information regarding proprietary or financial interests held, or control exercised, in any of the communications media, including newspapers, magazines and journals (s.38(7)).

[53] In 2001, the IRTC initially refused to allow Ulster Television to take over County Media, the owner of three independent local radio stations in Cork. Under the Radio and Television Act 1988, s.6(2), the IRTC was required to have regard *inter alia* to the character, expertise and experience of the applicant, as well as the desirability of having a diversity of services in the geographical area concerned. The policy of the IRTC since 1988 had been to prevent any existing media outlet from holding more than a 27 per cent stake in any other media concern and to retain a strong local presence in the ownership of local stations. To allow UTV to buy County Media would have marked a fundamental change in that policy. The Minister for Enterprise, Trade and Employment cleared the UTV deal under national mergers and takeovers legislation and the deal was concluded. (See *The Irish Times*, January 30, 2001 and *www.entemp.ie/press/htm*, respectively). For further details of developments in practice, see the Consultation Paper at *www.bci.ie*.

[54] MMD or MMDS signifies the multi-point microwave distribution system, introduced in 1988 to provide television services in more sparsely populated areas of the country, where cable, which was used in the cities, would not be practicable.

[55] The demise of the Irish Press titles in 1995 and findings of the Competition Authority, for example (see above, Chap.3). In September 1995 the Government established a commission to examine the newspaper industry, which reported in 1996. Its first term of reference was "The need to guarantee plurality of ownership, to maintain diversity of editorial viewpoints necessary for a vigorous democracy and to promote cultural diversity

centred mainly on questions of licences, personnel and advertising revenue, rather than on the complex practical and philosophical issues surrounding the whole future of broadcasting in general. The larger long-term questions of control, supervision and the implications of satellite broadcasting, for example, had not been addressed to any great extent until the publication of the Government's Green Paper on Broadcasting in 1995,[56] which eventually led to the 2001 Act and the revision of the BCI's policy on pluralism and diversity.

The BCI's revised policy sets out its guiding regulatory principles, statutory obligations, policy objectives and policy details. The guiding principles recognise the importance of the BCI being in a position to respond flexibly and adequately to the unforeseen and often complex questions that will emerge in the developing broadcasting landscape, particularly with digital technology. In fulfilling its statutory obligations, the BCI aims to put the public into a position which gives them access to a diversity of programming from a variety of sources. It is required by the 2001 Act to endeavour to ensure that "the number and categories of broadcasting services" made available in the State "will best serve the needs of the people of the island of Ireland, bearing in mind their languages and traditions and their religious, ethical and cultural diversity".[57] The BCI's overall objective was to develop and operate a simple, flexible but comprehensive regulatory scheme, capable of responding to technological and market developments, as well as national and local conditions.

The BCI took the view that it would be acceptable for any one investor to have control or substantial interests in a number equivalent to 15 per cent or less of the total number of commercial sound broadcasting services licensed under the 1988 Act. A number equivalent to 15–25 per cent would require more careful consideration, while over 25 per cent would be unacceptable. The BCI also set out the criteria it would apply in order to determine what constitutes a reasonable share of all the communications media available to audiences in a particular franchise area, as required by the Act. Non-EU applicants would be required to have their place of residence or registered office within the EU or as otherwise required by EU law.[58] The BCI would also have regard to any reciprocal arrangements in place with other states. It would take account of interests and control but, whereas previously it imposed maximum percentages on holdings in broadcast companies, under its new policy it would consider allowing 100 per cent ownership as long as all the criteria set out in its revised policy were met.[59]

The key objectives to be achieved and the duties of the BCI in achieving

---

in the industry". The Commission found that there was a clear link between plurality of ownership and diversity of editorial viewpoint and of cultural content but that it was not an automatic connection, nor was plurality of ownership the only feature contributing to such diversity. Plurality of titles was also a significant factor, particularly in circumstances where a good standard of editorial independence was maintained (*Report*, 1996, paras 1.4 and 1.5).

[56] Above, n.24.

[57] S.11(2) of the 2001 Act.

[58] See above, n.47.

[59] The revised policy is available at *www.bci.ie*.

them are embodied in the legislation of 1988 and 2001. The principles and objectives underlying the legislation are clear but the method of achieving them is left to the Commission to determine as a matter of policy. Increasingly, however, in line with technological and market developments, the BCI needs to take cognisance of both competition law and telecommunications law. Competition law can be used to ensure that no obstacles are created on either side, but there is an argument that ordinary competition law is no longer sufficient, that a special competition law is needed for the audiovisual sector.[60] There is a consensus at any rate that technology must not dominate and competition legislation must not overshadow other considerations and values. The importance of the democratic role of the media is such that there is a need for specific rules additional to those enshrined in competition law.

At European level, the European Court of Human Rights has said that "[Imparting] information and ideas of general interest ... cannot be successfully accomplished unless it is grounded in the principle of pluralism".[61] The European Convention on Transfrontier Television of the Council of Europe refers to the importance of broadcasting for the development of culture and free formation of opinions in conditions "safeguarding pluralism and equality of opportunity among all democratic groups and political parties". It regards an increasing range of choice of programme services for the public as enhancing Europe's heritage and developing its audiovisual creation. On media pluralism, Art.10*bis* requires parties to the Convention to endeavour to avoid endangering media pluralism. A review of the Convention, in light of convergence and new media services, is contemplated.[62]

The Committee of Ministers of the Council of Europe has adopted Recommendation No. R(99) 1 on measures to promote media pluralism, in particular those concerning media ownership rules, access to platforms and diversity of media content. Other Recommendations enshrine or recall the principles of media pluralism and diversity.[63] The Recommendation on measures to pro-

---

[60] See, for example, European Commission Report, *Audiovisual Media and Authorities: Tasks and challenges for regulators in an evolving media landscape in Europe* (Vienna, November 1998). The EC Treaty in 1993 made specific reference to the audiovisual sector (Art.128(2)). It placed an onus on the Community to encourage co-operation between Member States and to take cultural aspects, artistic and literary creation, including in the audiovisual sector, into account in its actions under the provisions of the Treaty. A consultation process followed publication of the Green Paper in 1997: *Working Paper on results of consultation, 1998, "Audiovisual Policy: next steps"* (July 1998); *Report of the High Level Group on Audiovisual Policy, "The Digital Age: European Audiovisual Policy"* (October 1998); *Communications: Results of the public consultation on the Green Paper*, 1999. A coherent set of principles emerged from the process: *Communication on Principles and Guidelines for the Community's Audiovisual Policy in the Digital Age*, (Com(1999)) 657. See generally, *www.europa.eu.int/comm/dg10/avpolicy/index_en.html*.

[61] *Informationsverein Lentia v Austria* (Series A, No.276; [1993] 17 E.H.R.R. 93, at para.38).

[62] See Andreas Grünwald, *Report on possible options for the review of the European Convention on Transfrontier Television* (Standing Committee on Transfrontier Television, April 24, 2003, available at *www.coe.int/T/E/human_rights*).

[63] For example, Recommendation Rec(2000) 23 on the independence and functions of regulatory authorities for the broadcasting sector. See also, Advisory Panel on Media

mote the democratic and social contribution of digital broadcasting recommends that governments of Member States, *inter alia*, "create adequate legal and economic conditions for the development of digital broadcasting that guarantee the pluralism of broadcasting services and public access to an enlarged choice and variety of quality programmes" and "protect and, if necessary, take positive measures to safeguard and promote media pluralism, in order to counterbalance the increasing concentration in this sector".[64]

11.3.4 The 2001 Act and beyond

The 2001 Act reconfigured broadcasting structures in the State. RTÉ was entitled under the Act to have one full multiplex and signalled its intention to establish three additional digital channels at an estimated running cost of €50 million per year. However, RTÉ did not at first receive from Government the size of increase in the licence fee that it had requested in order to fund the new channels. When it finally did, the increase was to be performance-related and conditional on RTÉ operating a code of fair trading.[65] RTÉ was to be restructured and a Charter drawn up by the Government, setting out the principles under which RTÉ as a public service broadcaster would be required to operate and become more accountable to its audience.[66]

As outlined above, the remit of the BCI now covers digital content contracts, electronic programme guides and various other services. The extension of their remit placed the BCI is a superior position to the RTÉ Authority. For instance, in order for RTÉ to enter into an agreement with Sky television to have its programmes relayed on Sky's satellite service, RTÉ was required to obtain a licence from the BCI.[67] This was the first instance in which the BCI assumed

Diversity, *Media Diversity in Europe*, H/APMD (2003) 1, which looks at *inter alia* media ownership regulations and trends, public service broadcasting, new technologies and diversity issues. *Cf.* ARTICLE 19, *Access to the Airwaves: Principles on Freedom of Expression and Broadcast Regulation* (International Standards Series, ARTICLE 19, London, 2002), particularly Principle 3: Promoting Diversity.

[64] Recommendation Rec(2003) 9.

[65] RTÉ faced an economic crisis following the refusal of successive governments to increase the licence fee. The fee was raised by €43 to €150 per annum as from 2003 but RTÉ was required to publish an annual statement of proposed programming (a Statement of Commitments), which would then be independently reviewed at the end of each year. See press release of May 7, 2003, available at *www.dcmnr.gov.ie/press releases*.

[66] See the proposals of the Forum on Broadcasting and the Department's Report to the Minister on the Report of the Forum on Broadcasting (November 2002, available at *www.dcmnr.ie*), which accepted *inter alia* that RTÉ's performance of its public service commitments should be measured and subject to greater public accountability; see also *The Sunday Times*, May 18, 2003. RTÉ agreed to the Charter and content regulation as long as their editorial independence was assured. RTÉ also proposed the setting up of a listeners/viewers council. Advertisements for members of the council were placed at the end of May 2003 (*The Irish Times*, May 24, 2003).

[67] In November 2001 RTÉ announced that it planned to offer its television and radio channels on the Sky digital platform in the Republic and Northern Ireland from April 2002. UK broadcasters were believed to have paid very large sums of money to Sky for carriage rights on its satellite platform but records obtained under the Freedom of Information Act revealed that RTÉ had agreed carriage terms similar to those it already had with

a role in relation to RTÉ. It will assume further responsibilities in relation to codes and subtitling under the Broadcasting Act 2001.

11.3.5 ComReg

In a parallel development, responsibility for telecommunications, including the infrastructure and licensing of cable and MMDS, was first transferred from the relevant Government Minister to the Office of the Director of Tele-communications Regulation (ODTR) in 1996.[68] However, in 2002, legislation was introduced to restructure that office from a single director to a commission, and to rename it the Commission for Communications Regulation (ComReg).[69]

ComReg has a role in regulating electronic communications (tele-communications, radio communications and broadcasting) and the postal service. It has responsibility for the radio spectrum and allocation of frequencies. In relation to broadcasting, its main role is in relation to licensing of radio and television distribution, by cable, MMDS, and deflector.[70] ComReg may, therefore, be said to be the infrastructure regulator for communications in the State, while the BCI is the structure and content regulator for broadcasting and related services.

Regulation of delivery systems lay with the ODTR, as it then was, and one of the issues it inherited on its establishment in 1996 was the problem of licensing the deflector systems, which were providing low-cost access to British television channels by deflecting their signals (see above, Chap. 3). In response to the problem, the Director granted the deflector operators short-term licences, pending the expiry of the "exclusive" MMDS licences and the introduction of digital television. She also considered limiting the period of exclusivity of the MMDS licences to five years, after which other television delivery systems could compete with the MMDS providers.[71] Licences, subject to annual

---

cable operators throughout the country, who must carry RTÉ's programmes without charge (*The Irish Times*, January 5, 2002). The BCI contended that RTÉ required a licence under s.36 of the 2001 Act in order to enter into the deal with Sky. The BCI awarded a satellite retransmission contract, since what was involved was the unaltered, unabridged and simultaneous transmission of existing services (*The Irish Times*, January 24, 2002, February 20, 2002).

[68] Telecommunications (Miscellaneous Provisions) Act 1996.

[69] Communications Regulation Act 2002. The Commission, consisting of three commissioners, was established on December 1, 2002. For the functions of ComReg, see *www.odtr.ie*, particularly publications such as "Response to Department of Public Enterprise's Invitation to comment on Review of legislation relating to the licensing and use of the radio spectrum" (Document No. ODTR 01/07, February 2001) and "Response to the outline legislative proposals in relation to the regulation of the communications sector published by the Department of Public Enterprise" (Document No. ODTR 00/74, September 2000).

[70] It issues the radio equipment and spectrum licences for transmission purposes for broadcasting services authorised by the RTÉ Authority and the BCI. See *www.odtr.ie*. The deflector services (UHF Television Programme Retransmission Systems) are considered below. ComReg announced a new legal enforcement campaign against pirate radio stations in March 2003, following complaints of interference with air traffic control (*The Sunday Tribune*, January 19, 2003).

[71] Successive governments were unwilling to grant licences to the deflector operators and

renewal, were issued under the Wireless Telegraphy (UHF Television Programme Retransmission) Regulations 1999, pending the restructuring of broadcasting under the 2001 Act, which also gave the ODTR, now ComReg, a role in the licensing of regional and digital television.[72]

11.3.6 The Forum on Broadcasting 2002

The Forum on Broadcasting, established by the Government in March 2002, reported in August of that year.[73] Many individuals and organisations, including RTÉ, the BCI and the ODTR, made written submissions to the Forum. The ODTR set out the current position regarding broadcasting services in Ireland and the future under the new EU Framework Directives. The BCI set out all the relevant statutory provisions and assessed various aspects of the current position regarding the range and types of broadcasting services. It supported many of the present arrangements, accepted the appropriateness of public/ private partnerships in the context of the development of new channels, and made the case for a single content regulator.

The main conclusions of the Forum centred on the importance of fostering and strengthening public service broadcasting. Funding and requests for a greater increase in the licence fee had been major issues over the years, particularly with the planned introduction of digital television. The Forum took the view that funding should be sufficient to allow RTÉ, as the designated public service broadcaster in the State, to fulfil its obligations and plan for the future on a realistic level. Increased public funding for RTÉ should be conditional, however, on RTÉ's fulfilment of its public service obligations and on its efficient operation, which should be monitored in accordance with a Charter. Transparency was identified as a key requirement in various specified areas of its operation, including commissions from the independent production sector.

The Forum also recommended the establishment, by legislation, within three years, of a new single regulator for broadcasting in Ireland to be called the Broadcasting Authority of Ireland (BAI), to assume the existing regulatory functions of the BCI and the RTÉ Authority. An autonomous Broadcasting Complaints Commission should remain and the ODTR should continue to

---

a number of court cases followed (*e.g. Carrigaline Community Television Broadcasting v Minister for Transport, Energy and Communications* [1997] 1 I.L.R.M. 241; *South Coast Television Services v Minister for Communications*, High Court, March 11, 1998, in which a decision of the Minister refusing a broadcast licence to a television deflector operator was quashed; *Cable Management (Ireland) Ltd v Comhlacht Phobal Teilifíse Thír Chonaill Teo*, High Court, June 17, 1998; *Cable Management (Ireland) Ltd v Ardara Community Piped Television Ltd*, High Court, June 17, 1998).

[72] See *The Future of TV Transmission in Ireland: The Way Forward*, July 1998, and *Television Transmission Licensing for Cable and MMDS Systems*, December 1998 (Office of the Director of Telecommunications Regulation, Dublin, available at *www.odtr.ie*). A Consultation Paper on the future for regional and local television delivery services was published in 2001 (01/69). Those services were envisaged as a potential route to digital services for deflector licensees.

[73] The text of the Report is available at *www.dcmnr.gov.ie/files/BroadcastingFinal.doc*.

regulate distribution platforms, but with formal liaison between the ODTR and the BAI.

Other recommendations include the promotion of community broadcasting as a stated policy objective of the Government and regulatory authorities. Irish language broadcasting should be enhanced and incentivised and children's programming should be encouraged in the case of all broadcasters. In addition, the Government should promote, at a European level, clear and enforceable policies in relation to children's advertising.

11.3.7 The Broadcasting Authority of Ireland

Further changes to the roles of the existing regulatory bodies are envisaged in the Report of the Forum on Broadcasting 2002.[74] Following publication of the report, the Minister announced his intention to implement the recommendation of the Forum and set up a single regulator, the Broadcasting Authority of Ireland (BAI).[75] Legislation to that effect is to be introduced in the Autumn of 2003. Under the new structure, the public service remit of RTÉ and its licence fee will continue to be sanctioned by Government but subject to the BAI approving the delivery of specified outputs as outlined in the multi-annual business plans, which RTÉ will be required to draw up.[76] The legislation will have to determine the exact allocation of functions of the BAI in the overall scheme. One of the BAI's roles will be to stimulate meaningful competition in the commercial sector and in that regard its policy on ownership and control of commercial broadcasters will be reviewed after three years.

11.4 THE FUTURE OF BROADCASTING

11.4.1 Public Service Broadcasting

11.4.1.1 Public service remit

The overall goal of public service broadcasting, as originally conceived, was to provide high quality programming that would be available to all sectors of the public and would perform a public service function by informing, educating and entertaining the population. Key characteristics, as identified by Barendt are:

---

[74] RTÉ is to become a commercial State company with its own board of directors. For a critique, see Muiris Mac Conghail, "Public-service broadcasting still threatened", *The Irish Times*, May 8, 2003.

[75] The majority of the submissions made in response to the Report of the Forum on broadcasting favoured the concept of a single content regulator (Report to the Minister, above, n.66).

[76] Report to the Minister on the Report of the Forum on Broadcasting, above, n.66. The BAI will monitor RTÉ's performance on an on-going basis, and pending the establishment of the BAI, the Minister has arranged for independent monitoring of RTÉ's performance to be carried out.

(i) General geographical availability (now sometimes referred to in the context of the new media as "universal access")

(ii) Concern for national identity and culture

(iii) Independence from both the State and commercial interests

(iv) Impartiality of programmes

(v) Range and variety of programmes (now usually referred to as "diversity" of content)

(vi) Substantial financing by a general charge on users (*i.e.* a licence fee).[77]

Today, the attainment of those objectives and the future of public service broadcasting is under threat. Each of the characteristics is being undermined either by competition, by developments in technology, by lack of finance or by the fragility of the new world-order that has emerged since the terrorist acts of September 11, 2001. Of particular concern are the financing of such a service to ensure its independence and the delivery of diversity of content to ensure alternative viewpoints and news sources.

In common with other European countries, Ireland has had a long commitment to public service broadcasting. The importance of the public service ethos has been brought into focus by the development of private commercial broadcasting. The maintenance of that ethos in face of the profit ethic of commercial broadcasting has justified a more interventionist role on the part of the regulators. That creates a tension, however, since the possibilities offered by new technology and the growing internationalisation, indeed globalisation, of the media strengthen the argument for deregulation. The competition from American media, where deregulation has already occurred, conspires with the convergence of the various forms of media — audiovisual, satellite, electronic, multimedia — to add to the complexity of the problem. It may be argued that what needs to be safeguarded, from a national cultural point of view, are the *values* of public service broadcasting, not necessarily the particular means.[78]

---

[77] Eric Barendt, *Broadcasting Law: A Comparative Survey* (Clarendon Press, Oxford, 1993), p.52. See generally, Toby Mendel, *Public Service Broadcasting: A Comparative Legal Survey* (ARTICLE 19, London, 2000), ARTICLE 19, *Access to the Airwaves: Principles on Freedom of Expression and Broadcast Regulation* (International Standards Series, ARTICLE 19, London, 2002), Section 10: "Public Service Broadcasters", and Jackie Harrison and Lorna Woods, "Defining European Public Service Broadcasting" (2001) 16(4) *European Journal of Communication* 477.

[78] See Monroe Price, "Public Broadcasting and the Crisis of Corporate Governance" [1999] 17 Cardozo Arts and Ent LJ 417; Michael Tracey, *The Decline and Fall of Public Service Broadcasting* (OUP, Oxford, 1998). Recommendation Rec(2003) 9 of the Committee of Ministers of the Council of Europe on digital broadcasting refers to the remit of public service broadcasting as "including a basic general service that offers news, educational, cultural and entertainment programmes aimed at different categories of the public" (Principle 19). This may include new specialised channels and new interactive services. Universality is regarded as fundamental for the development of public service broadcasting in the digital era. Therefore, it must "be present on the different digital platforms (cable, satellite, terrestrial) with diverse quality programmes and services that are capable of

Those values include independence from political and commercial pressures, wide access to news and views, and the social and cultural responsibilities that require the provision of a comprehensive service. They are recognised, affirmed and elaborated in some detail in the Broadcasting Act 2001:

> "(1) The national television and sound broadcasting service required to be maintained by the Authority [*i.e.* RTÉ] under section 16 of the Act of 1960 shall have the character of a public service, continue to be a free-to-air service and be made available, in so far as it is reasonably practicable, to the whole community on the island of Ireland and the Authority shall have all such powers as are necessary for or incidental to that purpose.
>
> (2) ... the Authority shall ensure that the programme schedules of the broadcasting service referred to ...
>
>   (a) provide a comprehensive range of programmes in the Irish and English languages that reflect the cultural diversity of the whole island of Ireland and include, both on television and radio ... programmes that entertain, inform and educate, provide coverage of sporting, religious and cultural activities and cater for the expectations of the community generally as well as members of the community with special or minority interests and which, in every case, respect human dignity,
>
>   (b) provide programmes of news and current affairs in the Irish and English languages, including programmes that provide coverage of proceedings in the Houses of the Oireachtas and the European Parliament, and
>
>   (c) facilitate or assist contemporary cultural expression and encourage or promote innovation and experimentation in broadcasting".[79]

---

uniting society, particularly given the risk of fragmentation of the audience as a result of the diversification and specialisation of the programmes on offer" (Principle 20). In this connection, given the diversification of digital platforms, the must-carry rule should be applied for the benefit of public service broadcasters as far as reasonably possible in order to guarantee the accessibility of their services and programmes *via* these platforms (Principle 21).

[79] S.28(1) and (2). It is interesting to note that the coverage of Parliament, which at one time was forbidden and then deemed a privilege, has now become an obligation. While the section does not go so far as to require live coverage, it does require coverage of proceedings, which, it may be argued, implies the use of cameras. As indicated in Chap.7 above, the introduction of television cameras was met initially with some trepidation by parliamentarians and led to the imposition of considerable rules and regulation. The position of RTÉ in that regard is now strengthened, it would seem, by the Act. In any event, TG4, which has existed under the umbrella of RTÉ, has been providing coverage of Committees of the Oireachtas also. The inclusion of the European Parliament in the section is novel and it too is mandatory, although to date RTÉ has not covered it to any great extent. The reference to "human dignity" is reminiscent of Art.7 of the European Convention on Transfrontier Television. Finally, the requirement to encourage or promote innovation and experimentation in broadcasting is perhaps surprising, given the financial

For the purpose of ensuring the public service character of service, the Minister "may" specify categories of programmes (section 28(3)(a)), although he may not interfere with the manner of making any such programme or with the editorial process (section 28(5)). Certain other safeguards regarding notice and consultation by the Minister are set out in section 28(6), as well as the need for approval by each House of the Oireachtas.[80]

A further purpose of the Broadcasting Act 2001 is to establish on an independent footing the Irish-language television station, Teilifís na Gaeilge, since renamed TG4.[81] The station has been operating since 1996, but was placed temporarily under the legislation that applies to RTÉ.[82] Teilifís na Gaeilge, like RTÉ, is to have the character of a public service, is to be free-to-air and made available as far as reasonably practicable to the whole community on the island of Ireland.[83] It, too, is to meet the above programming requirements, primarily in the Irish language.[84] Its duties as regards culture, peace and the democratic values enshrined in the Constitution are set out in section 46 of the 2001 Act.[85]

Other European countries have shared those values inherent in public service broadcasting but differed in the detailed approach to implementing them.[86] The EU and the Council of Europe have introduced measures aimed at dealing with the overspill of broadcasting across national boundaries and at promoting competition but maintaining minimum standards. The Protocol to the Amsterdam Treaty, which refers to public service broadcasting, recognises its importance in preserving media pluralism.[87] The Television without Frontiers Directive and the corresponding Convention on Transfrontier

---

constraints under which RTÉ has always operated and the role in that regard of the BCI (formerly the IRTC) in its "New Adventures in Broadcasting" scheme (details at *www.bci.ie*), which is to be maintained and expanded as resources permit, on the recommendation of the Forum on Broadcasting (above, n.73). The exhortation to RTÉ is to encourage innovation in "broadcasting" rather than "broadcast programming" and so may refer instead to embracing the extra possibilities offered by digital.

[80] Ss.28(3)–(7).

[81] See above, n.45. Part VI of the Act deals with Teilifís na Gaeilge.

[82] Records obtained under the Freedom of Information Act (*The Irish Times*, February 24, 2003) revealed differences between the Government and RTÉ over the future direction and control of TG4. One of the proposed models was that TG4 would come under the control of the government department which deals with Irish language matters rather than the department with responsibility for broadcasting. The continuance of TG4's links with RTÉ was also a matter of dispute. TG4's Irish-language programming is subsidised by the State (RTÉ supplies €10 million worth of programming to it per year) but its non-Irish programming is funded entirely from advertising revenue. The station has almost 3 per cent of the national audience.

[83] S.45 of the 2001 Act.

[84] S.45(4). It may acquire programmes in other languages also (s.45(5)).

[85] S.46. The public service obligations set out in the Broadcasting Authority Acts 1960–1976 in respect of RTÉ are extended to TG4 by s.50 of the 2001 Act.

[86] See generally Eric Barendt, *Broadcasting Law*, above, n.77; Wolfgang Hoffmann-Riem, "Trends in the development of broadcasting law in Western Europe" (1992) 7 Eur Jl Comm 147; Mendel, above, n.77.

[87] The Protocol, which came into force in May 1999, is annexed to the consolidated version of the Treaty establishing the European Community and is therefore an integral part of it.

Television of the Council of Europe do not explicitly refer to public service broadcasters but apply to all television broadcasters across frontiers. Under the Council of Europe machinery, a Resolution on the future of public service broadcasting was adopted in 1994[88] and a Recommendation on the guarantee of the independence of public service broadcasting was adopted in 1996.[89] The importance of public service broadcasting for social, democratic and cultural life was also reaffirmed in an EC Resolution of 1999.[90]

The recitals of Recommendation Rec(2003) 9 on digital broadcasting also refer to the specific role of the broadcasting media, and in particular that of public service broadcasting, in modern democratic societies. Its role is "to support the values underlying the political, legal and social structures of democratic societies and in particular respect for human rights, culture and political pluralism". The specific role of public service broadcasting is described as a "uniting factor capable of offering a wide choice of programmes and services to all sections of the population", and as "an essential factor for the cohesion of democratic societies". As a result, public service broadcasting should be maintained in the new digital environment under a secure funding framework which guarantees public service broadcasters the means necessary to accomplish its remit in that new environment.[91]

Given the advances in technology and changes in the media in the past decade or so, it is natural that public service broadcasting, as originally defined and structured, should be coming under scrutiny. The sector has been under siege for some time, as it tries to compete financially and in terms of audience-share with the burgeoning commercial sector. RTÉ's dependence on a licence fee as well as income from advertising has caused great difficulty in the run-up to the introduction of digital broadcasting.[92]

---

[88] Resolution No.1, adopted at the 4th European Ministerial Conference on Mass Media Policy, Prague, December 7–8, 1994.

[89] Committee of Ministers, Recommendation No. R(96) 10.

[90] Resolution of the Council and of Representatives of the Governments of the Member States (1999/C30/01, January 25, 1999). The Resolution stresses that "broad public access, without discrimination and on the basis of equal opportunities, to various channels and services is a precondition for fulfilling the special obligation of public service broadcasting". The Resolution also recognises the need for public service broadcasting to benefit from technological progress, to bring the public the benefits of the new audiovisual and information services and the new technologies and to undertake "the development and diversification of activities in the digital age" (O.J. C 30, February 5, 1999, p.1).

[91] Recommendation on measures to promote the democratic and social contribution of digital broadcasting, Rec(2003)9. The Recommendation is very strong on the need for public service broadcasting to play a central role in the transition to terrestrial digital broadcasting. The Principles relating to public service broadcasting are Principles 19–22 and cover its remit, universal access to it and finance.

[92] The system of dual funding, necessary in a small economy, created tensions from an early date, between the public service ethos and commercial pressures. Those tensions increased with the rise of competition and globalisation of the sector, with the result that RTÉ has been struggling for some years. Its ability to produce home-grown programmes has been affected, as has its ability to compete in the international arena for major series, films, football rights, etc.

11.4.1.2 Financing and "state aid"

The financing of public service broadcasting has been an issue in Ireland and in other countries.[93] The 2001 Act addresses the use to which public monies may be put by RTÉ and TG4. The amount paid to RTÉ every year under s.8 of the Broadcasting Authority (Amendment) Act 1976[94] may be used only for public service programming, as set out above, for complying with its duty towards the Irish language and national culture,[95] for exercising its powers under s.16(2) of the 1960 Act,[96] and for providing services other than broadcasting services for the benefit of the public.[97] As before, provision is made for RTÉ to carry advertisements, which now include teleshopping, in accordance with the EC Television without Frontiers Directive.[98] RTÉ is also to continue to provide the equivalent of one hour per day of programme material to TG4 and the maximum and minimum amounts are to be fixed by the Minister.[99]

Public service broadcasting in other countries has faced similar problems and new ways of providing such a service, or at least an alternative to private commercial broadcasting, are being examined. One approach that has been considered is that of imposing public service obligations on private broadcasters. In Ireland, that approach was adopted from the inception of private commercial broadcasting under the Radio and Television Act 1988. Another approach in some countries has been to try to find alternative ways of providing

---

[93] Principle 22 of Recommendation Rec(2003)9 (above, n.91) provides that "In the new technological context, without a secure and appropriate financial framework, the reach of public service broadcasters and the scale of their contribution to society may diminish". Member States should, therefore, give public service broadcasters the possibility of having access to the necessary financial means to fulfil their remit.

[94] S.8 deals with the annual amounts to be paid to the Authority by the Minister, which is an amount equal to the total receipts in that year in respect of broadcast licence fees, less any expenses and grants (s.8(a)), and an amount equal to the total of the receipts in that year in respect of wired broadcast relay licence fees, less expenses certified by the Minister as having been incurred by him in the collection of those fees. The amount payable to Teilifís na Gaeilge is provided for in s.51 of the 2001 Act.

[95] Broadcasting Authority Act 1960, s.17. The amount payable to TG4 may only be used for the purposes of performing its function as a public service and exercising the powers conferred on it by the 2001 Act (s.45(6)).

[96] The subsection includes the installation and operation of apparatus, procuring programmes, making contracts, acquiring copyrights, subscribing to news services, and such like. S.30 of the 2001 Act inserts new subsections into s.16(2) of the 1960 Act, to allow RTÉ to provide special interest pay-per-view services and electronic programme guides, but these new services are excluded from the range of activities for which public monies may be expended. The Authority is required to make an annual report on expenditure of public monies. Ss.32 and 33 also deal with aspects of expenditure under the 1960, 1976 and 1993 Acts, particularly the allocation of funding to independent producers.

[97] In accordance with its powers under the Broadcasting Acts 1960–2001.

[98] S.31 of the 2001 Act. Teleshopping has the same meaning as it has in s.19 of the Act, the section which deals with codes: "teleshopping material means material which, when transmitted, will constitute a direct offer to the public for the sale or supply to them of goods or other property (whether real or personal) or services" (s.19(18)).

[99] S.47 and s.48 of the 2001 Act. A similar provision in respect of TG4 is contained in s.49.

and funding public service broadcasting, in order to ensure that social and cultural aims are met. The principal methods have been to devise schemes for funding independent producers and requiring broadcasters to allocate a percentage of their budget or output to programmes supplied by independent producers. In Ireland, provision was first made for this in the Broadcasting Act 1990 (section 5). In 2002, when a sizeable increase in the licence fee was agreed, a condition was attached that 5 per cent be allocated to a fund, for which other broadcasters can tender, to enable them to make public service programmes.[100] However, the overall trend, in Ireland and in many other countries is to relax regulation across the board, which itself has implications for public service obligations.

An issue, which has given rise to considerable debate across Europe, is that of state aid to public service broadcasters. A Communication from the Commission in 2001 set out the principles which apply.[101] Public service broadcasters have traditionally been funded either by state funding exclusively, in the form of grants or licence fee or both, or by a system of dual funding, through state funding and income from advertising. RTÉ is dual funded. When the market was opened to competition, Member States of the EU considered that public service broadcasting ought to be maintained as a way of ensuring the coverage of areas and provision of the kind of services to the public that private operators would not necessarily fulfil to the optimal extent. Private operators, however, complained that they were not given a level playing pitch because of the public funding schemes in existence in favour of public service broadcasters. The issue fell to be determined on the basis of the application of Articles 87 and 88 (state aid) and Article 86 (application of rules) of the EC Treaty.[102]

---

[100] The licence fee increase for RTÉ was announced in December 2002 in the context of a major reform of public service broadcasting, as outlined above. The fund will be administered by the BAI, and in the interim by the BCI. There is also a proposal to introduce a commercial television licence for premises such as licensed premises (Report to the Minister, above, n.66).

[101] Communication from the Commission on the Application of State Aid Rules to Public Service Broadcasting, above, n.13. See generally, Andreas Bartosch, "The Financing of Public Service Broadcasting and EC State Aid Law: An Interim Balance" (1999) 4 *European Competition Law Review* 197 and Lidia Márton, "The Impact of EU Competition Law on the Financing of Public Service Broadcasters" (2001) 6 *Communications Law* 56.

[102] The key provision, Art.86(2), makes public service undertakings subject to the rules of the Treaty, in particular competition rules, insofar as the application of those rules does not obstruct the performance of their particular tasks, and states that the development of trade must not be affected to such an extent as would be contrary to the interests of the Community. The European Commission approved the funding through licence fees of the BBC's News24 channel. The funding did amount to State aid within the meaning of Art.87(1) of the EC Treaty but was compatible with the common market under Art.86 (No.NN 88/98, UK, decision of the Commission December 14, 1999 in complaint filed by BskyB). See also approval of BBC's nine new digital television and radio channels, Commission decision of May 22, 2002 – no real advantage conferred on the BBC because the compensation paid was not disproportionate to the net costs of the new channels, which form part of the BBC's public service obligation. The measure, therefore, did not constitute state aid within the meaning of Art.87(1) of the EC Treaty, and even if it had

Public service broadcasting, in this regard, is stated to be special in that no other public service has *at the same time* access to such a wide sector of the population, provides it with so much information and content, and by doing so conveys and influences both individual and public opinion.[103] The question, therefore, is whether it can be treated as an exception to the rules on state aid.[104] The Protocol to the Amsterdam Treaty states that:

> "The provisions of the Treaty establishing the European Community shall be without prejudice to the competence of Member States to provide for the funding of public service broadcasting insofar as such funding is granted to broadcasting organisations for the fulfilment of the public service remit as conferred, defined and organised by each Member State, and insofar as such funding does not affect trading conditions and competition in the Community to such an extent which would be contrary to the common interest, while the realisation of the remit of that public service shall be taken into account".

It is the effect of state funding, therefore, rather than its purpose that is the decisive element. It must not affect trading conditions and competition contrary to the common interest. The fact that the realisation of the public service remit can be taken into account in assessing the impact means that a clear and precise definition of that remit is required and that it is the realisation or performance of that remit that is significant.[105] The public service functions of the broadcaster must therefore be clearly distinguished from its other activities and independent monitoring of performance carried out to verify that trade and competition are not adversely affected. Public service broadcasters must, therefore, give a detailed account of the sources and amount of all income accruing from the performance of non-public service activities.[106] As a result,

---

done, it would have been compatible with the common market. TV3 lodged a complaint against the Irish Government in 1999 (*The Sunday Tribune*, January 30, 2000) over the payment of the licence fee to RTÉ and also opposed the rise in the licence fee announced in 2002 (*The Irish Times*, March 13, 2003). It blamed the licence fee for its decision to close its Belfast office (*The Irish Times*, July 31, 2003).

[103] Com 2001/C 320/04, above, n.13, at para.6. The Communication (para.8) also quotes a statement from the Oreja High Level Group on Audiovisual Policy ("The digital age European Audiovisual Policy. Report from the high level group on audiovisual policy", 1998) to the effect that public service broadcasting "has an important role to play in promoting cultural diversity in each country, in providing educational programming, in objectively informing public opinion, in guaranteeing pluralism and in supplying, democratically and free-of-charge, quality entertainment".

[104] Article 87(1) states: "Save as otherwise provided in this Treaty, any aid granted by a Member State or through State resources in any form whatsoever which distorts or threatens to distort competition by favouring certain undertakings or the production of certain goods shall, insofar as it affects trade between Member States, be compatible with the common market."

[105] Communication, above, n.13, at paras 32, 37.

[106] Communication, above, n.13, at para.54. Hence the provisions relating to RTÉ in the Broadcasting Act 2001, above, nn.79 and 84. As a result, the compatibility of State aid to public service broadcasters can only be assessed on a case-by-case basis.

the compatibility of state aid to public service broadcasters can only be assessed on a case-by-case basis.[107]

To sum up, the value of public service broadcasting in the new technological environment has not diminished with changed conditions; if anything it has increased. However, in order to discharge its obligations and meet its objectives, it needs to be able to operate independently, which in turn requires the provision of sufficient funding, subject to public accountability.[108] The new broadcasting regime in Ireland, under the Broadcasting Authority of Ireland, must enshrine those basic requirements if public service broadcasting is to be maintained and if the public is to reap the full benefits.

11.4.2 Regulating broadcasting and print media in the age of convergence

The fact that both public service and private commercial broadcasting are regulated by sector-specific laws and the print media are not remains an anomaly.[109] The difference in approach is difficult to justify now that the core argument – the limits of the electromagnetic spectrum – which allowed governments to keep control of broadcasting and operate a monopoly, no longer holds up. There are, of course, other arguments stemming from the different nature, scope and functions of the print and broadcast media, but the divergent approach is also difficult to implement in practice as the two forms of media coalesce. Online newspapers, teletext services on television, Internet television and webcasting are becoming increasingly established. Digital and interactive services are coming on stream.

With the arrival of those new services, technology and market forces have combined on a global scale to threaten the continued existence of the smaller and more traditional media. Large newspaper and multimedia groups are swallowing up small newspapers and broadcasting stations across the world, leading to problems of concentration of ownership and cross-ownership, and fears of lack of diversity in media content.[110] The future of public service broadcasting, as discussed above, is under threat also. To continue divergent regulatory regimes in that environment seems impractical and undesirable, unless justified at the level of principle.

The practical aspect of the problem tends to suggest deregulation as one

---

[107] Communication, above, n.13, para.60. See also, the Report of the Forum on Broadcasting (above, n.73) at p.11 on the Transparency Directive of 2000 on state aid generally and the impact it may have on state aid in the broadcasting sphere (Directive 2000/52/EC, July 26, 2000 on the transparency of financial relations between Member States and public undertakings).

[108] See above, n.77, Mendel, at p.50 and Tarlach McGonagle, "Changing Aspects of Broadcasting: New Territory and New Challenges" in *Key Legal Questions for the Audiovisual Sector* (*IRIS plus* Collection, European Audiovisual Observatory, Strasbourg, 2003), p.40, at p.44.

[109] See, for example, Barendt, above, n.77, at p.7.

[110] See generally *Television and Media Concentration: Regulatory Models on the National and the European Level* (IRIS Special, European Audiovisual Observatory, Strasbourg, March 2001).

answer, as has happened in the US, for example, and allow the market to dictate, subject to the supervision of Competition law. In terms of principle and democratic values, however, that would be questionable. Another possibility, which would be difficult to justify, either in terms of principle or practice, would be to adopt a statutory framework for the print media as well. That would be a regressive step and would spell the death knell for the most prized freedom of the press. It would also overlook the fact that the printed press, while not subject to a specific sectoral regime, is already subject to a host of statutory provisions, including strict laws of defamation. The solution to the problem may lie in the clear preference for self-regulation evidenced in the new media and the trend towards elements of self-regulation and co-regulation in the broadcast media (discussed below). A more co-ordinated and co-operative approach by regulatory bodies, using a variety of regulatory models and instruments, across the various sectors, may bring dividends.[111]

The European Commission[112] has made a number of abortive attempts to regulate media ownership but has been hampered by a lack of will and by the *status quo* – the dominance in the Italian market by the Berlusconi empire, for example. Meanwhile, the EC Television without Frontiers Directive 1989, which governs certain aspects of television broadcasting as between Member States, and was revised in 1997, is currently under review again.[113] Issues of pluralism and diversity are constantly monitored, as the EU remains fearful of the giant American multinational media conglomerates that continue to saturate the market.

11.4.2.1 Digital broadcasting

Technological, social and economic changes have brought about the need to examine whether existing regulatory structures and responses are adequate for the new digital age. As one commentator remarked, "Though the future is digital, our thinking about regulation is analogue".[114] A lot of the arguments that have dominated the debate have been technology and economics driven. However, a general consensus appears to have emerged that the need goes beyond the purely technological and economic, given the democratic and social deficit which technological and market developments may entail.[115] Regulation

---

[111] See Alexander Scheuer and Peter Strothman, "Media Supervision on the Threshold of the 21st Century—What are the Requirements of Broadcasting, Telecommunications and Concentration Regulation?" in *Key Legal Questions for the Audiovisual Sector*, above, n.108.

[112] In the fields of broadcasting and convergence, the EC issued a Green Paper in 1984 on the establishment of a common market in broadcasting, followed in 1997 by a Green Paper on the Convergence of the Telecommunications, Media and Information Technology Sectors (Com(1997)623)).

[113] See above, n.2. The Television without Frontiers Directive (89/552/EEC, as amended by Directive 97/36/EC) was implemented in Irish law by means of the European Communities (Television Broadcasting) Regulations 1999 (S.I. No. 313 of 1999), which revoked the previous regulations (S.I. No. 251 of 1991).

[114] Beth Noveck, "Analogue Thinking; Digital Television: Recrafting Content Regulation", in Chris Marsden and Stefaan Verhulst (eds), above, n.51, p.37 at p.38.

[115] See, for example, the recitals to Recommendation Rec(2003) 9 of the Committee of

must focus on and embrace free speech and democracy arguments, as well. The European Parliament has said in this regard that cultural products cannot be dealt with in the same way as other products.[116]

A leading legal commentator, Thomas Gibbons, also argues that it is important not to be driven by technical developments, that just because methods of communication are changing does not mean that the character of the media itself is altering too. The public interest in media activity is no less important; there will continue to be concern about free speech and editorial independence, together with the demands of quality and accountability. What convergence does, Gibbons states, "is [to] challenge us to examine the grounds for traditional regulation and to ask whether it is based on old forms rather than some broader and enduring principles".[117]

A combination of competition law, media ownership rules and other measures will be necessary to meet the public interest objective of media pluralism and diversity. Competition law alone will not be sufficient, as it is primarily concerned with the operation of economic markets rather than with pluralism objectives. Media ownership rules alone will not suffice either to ensure pluralism.

A Recommendation on the Democratic and Social Impact of Digital Broadcasting was adopted by the Committee of Ministers of the Council of Europe in 2003.[118] It notes that digital technology opens new possibilities for the public and broadcasters, that it offers advantages but also presents risks. As a result, adequate preparations must be made for it so that it is carried out in the best possible conditions in the interests of the public, broadcasters and the audiovisual industry as a whole. A number of features of the technology are noted, including the multiplication of the number of channels, and the potential to bring the information society into every home. The latter raises the need to avoid exclusion, notably by the availability of free-to-air services and transfrontier television services, and to safeguard essential public interest objectives, including freedom of expression and access to information, cultural diversity, the protection of minors and human dignity, consumer protection and privacy.

The Recommendation calls for a well-defined strategy that would ensure a carefully thought-out transition to digital, to maximise its benefits and minimise

---

Ministers of the Council of Europe on measures to promote the democratic and social contribution of digital broadcasting. According to the Recommendation, a balance must be struck between economic interests and social needs, clearly taking a citizen perspective.

[116] Also COM (1999) 657 final, above, n.60.

[117] Thomas Gibbons, "Concentrations of Ownership and Control in a Converging Media Industry" in Chris Marsden and Stefaan Verhulst, *Convergence in European Digital TV Regulation*, above, n.51, p.155, at p.156; *Key Legal Questions for the Audiovisual Sector* (Susanne Nikoltchev (ed.), European Audiovisual Observatory, Strasbourg, 2003). For background and development see, *Media Policy: Convergence, Concentration and Commerce* (Denis McQuail and Karen Siune (eds), Sage Publications, London, 1998).

[118] Above, n.115. The text of the Recommendation is available at *www.coe.int/T/E/ Human_Rights/media*. See also the Report of the Forum on Broadcasting (above, n.73) on digital broadcasting (pp.14–15) and the impact of digital broadcasting (p.21).

its possible negative effects. The strategy should promote co-operation between operators, complementarity between platforms, the interoperability of decoders and the availability of a wide variety of programmes. Given that simultaneous analogue and digital broadcasting is costly, there should be a rapid changeover to digital, while making sure that the interests of the public and broadcasters are taken into account. Services on offer should be many and varied.[119] Media literacy is regarded as a key factor in reducing the risk of a digital divide and so proper information on the media should be made available to the public and suitable training courses provided on the use of digital equipment.[120]

In Ireland, the map is only beginning to be drawn, with the implementation of the Broadcasting Act 2001 and the planned restructuring of broadcasting in light of the Report of the Forum on Broadcasting 2002.[121] The initial attempt to establish Digital Terrestrial Television (DTT) ended with the sole applicant withdrawing from the process.[122] The introduction of DTT was seen by the Forum on Broadcasting as a desirable policy objective and that view is shared by the Department for Communications, Marine and Natural Resources, which set about considering other options for achieving it.[123] The impact of digital broadcasting on RTÉ will also be kept under review.

11.4.2.2 Advertising

With regard to advertising, RTÉ had traditionally been in competition with the national newspapers and, to a lesser extent, with the provincial press.[124] Now, local broadcasting stations are dependent on advertising too and stations broadcasting from Northern Ireland are attracting cross-border advertising.

---

[119] Costs of equipment to the consumer should be kept to a minimum.

[120] Principles 12–14 deal with Electronic Programme Guides (EPGs). Other principles deal with copyright, economic interests, piracy, conditional access, the importance of free-to-air services, in view of the increase in pay-per-view services and various aspects of public service broadcasting (see above). The European Convention on the Legal Protection of Services based on, or consisting of, Conditional Access 2001 entered into force July 1, 2003 (ETS No.178). It makes illegal a number of activities which give unauthorised access to protected services (*e.g.* pay television), on the basis that these activities threaten the economic viability of the organisations providing broadcasting and information society services and, in consequence, may affect the diversity of programmes and services offered to the public.

[121] Above, nn.66 and 73.

[122] *The Irish Times*, January 11, 2002. RTÉ was to sell its transmission network and the DTT project was premised on the Government facilitating the establishment of a DTT platform by the market (see Report to the Minister, above, n.66). The Minister for Communications, Marine and Natural Resources remained committed to an all-island TV rollout, whether by digital or satellite (Press Release, April 4, 2003).

[123] Report to the Minister, above, n.66.

[124] RTÉ had a decided advantage over the newcomers at first in that it had had a monopoly for so long and also had and continues to have the safety-net of income from licence fees. The 1990 Broadcasting Act set about "levelling the playing-pitch" by placing a "cap", an upper limit, on the amount of advertising income RTÉ could accept (s.3). The section was repealed by the Broadcasting Authority (Amendment) Act 1993, which also obliged RTÉ to spend a percentage of its income in commissioning independent television programmes (s.4).

New services, including satellite and internet services, are also competing for advertising. The broadcasting stations operate under a code of advertising drawn up in accordance with legislation.[125] The Code takes account of the EC Television without Frontiers Directive, as amended in 1997. For instance, the definition of advertising in the code was updated in 1999 to read:

> "[A]ny form of announcement broadcast whether in return for payment or for similar consideration or broadcast for self-promotional purposes by a public or private undertaking in connection with a trade, business, craft or profession in order to promote the supply of goods or services, including immovable property, rights and obligations, in return for payment".[126]

Under the revised Code, certain provisions relating to advertising and sponsorship were extended to teleshopping in line with the Directive. In a further development, the BCI is required by section 19 of the Broadcasting Act 2001 to draw up a range of new codes, which will apply to RTÉ, the independent broadcasters and the providers of new broadcasting services. The BCI began a process of consultation in April 2003. The new codes will cover advertising, sponsorship and teleshopping, and there will be a separate code dealing with children's advertising.[127] It is expected that emerging areas, such as virtual advertising and webvertising, will be addressed later, following, and in accordance with, the revision of the Television without Frontiers Directive.[128]

That Directive is currently undergoing further periodic review, and as part of the process a study has been carried out on the application of the rules on advertising.[129] The rules contained in the Directive concern *inter alia* the amount of advertising permitted (the daily and hourly limits), the number of and form of advertising breaks, the rules applicable to the content and

---

[125] A code was drafted in 1995 in accordance with s.4(1) of the 1990 Act. It was revised on October 7, 1999, by the Minister for Arts, Heritage, Gaeltacht and the Islands, who had responsibility for broadcasting, to take account of changes made to update the TWF Directive. In drafting and updating the code, the Minister was obliged by s.4(3) of the 1990 Act to consult with the RTÉ Authority and the IRTC, now the BCI. The Advertising Standards Authority of Ireland (ASAI), comprising advertising companies, operates a voluntary code covering all forms of advertising (*www.asai.ie*).

[126] See also the interpretation of "advertising" in *Radio Limerick One v IRTC* [1997] 2 I.L.R.M. 1 (SC).

[127] Some aspects of children's advertising are addressed in Chap.9 above. See also Christopher Preston, "The unintended effects of advertising upon children" (1999) 18 *International Journal of Advertising* 363 and Chris Preston, "Are children seeing through ITC advertising regulations?" (2000) 19 *International Journal of Advertising* 117 (both of which have extensive reading lists attached).

[128] For a brief consideration of webvertising from the point of view of consumer protection, see Jan-Malte Niemann, "Webvertisements Covered By Art.5(2) Rome Convention?" (2000) 5 *Communications Law* 99.

[129] The detail of the review and the findings of the various studies carried out as part of the process are contained in the Fourth Report from the Commission to the Council, the European Parliament, the European Economic and Social Committee and the Committee of the Regions (COM(2002) 778 final, Brussels, January 6, 2003).

presentation of advertising messages and specific rules on sponsorship.[130] A number of studies were commissioned as part of the review. The first dealt with the impact of television advertising and teleshopping on minors.[131] It showed extensive use of self-regulation in this area, that television is more heavily regulated in this regard than other media and that the number of complaints was very low, showing that the Directive, as implemented in the Member States, works effectively.[132]

The second study concerned new advertising techniques. As well as techniques such as product placement and spot advertising, with which audiences are already familiar, the study looked at techniques of interactive and virtual advertising, as well as the use of split screens and banner adverts. The situation differed considerably from one Member State to another. The UK was the only state to have specific rules on interactive advertising, and Germany was the only one to have specific rules on split-screen advertising, although a number of States have a ban on it.[133] Overall, these techniques were only in their infancy and therefore very few specific rules existed at the time of the review.[134] The study also found that a wide range of sponsorship techniques exist and that they differ substantially from the classic TV-sponsorship form that existed when the rules in the Directive were drafted.

The detail of the advertising provisions of the Television without Frontiers Directive and the jurisprudence of the European Court of Human Rights on advertising (commercial speech) under Article 10 of the ECHR are discussed below.

---

[130] The rules are contained in Arts 10–18, Directive 89/552/EEC, as amended by Directive 97/36/EC (O.J. L 298/23, October 17, 1989 and O.J. L 202/60, July 30, 1997, respectively) and are considered in more detail in the section on the Directive below. The European Convention on Transfrontier Television (Council of Europe, 1989, as amended by Protocol ETS No. 171, October 1, 1998) also contains provisions on television advertising.

[131] All of the studies are available at *www.europa.eu.int/comm/avpolicy/stat/studi_en.htm.*

[132] Fourth Report, above, n.129 at p.13. The study showed also that the framework provided in the Directive was both adequate and flexible and that there were a remarkable number of differences at Member State level, ranging from the age limits in definitions to specific provisions on certain sectors, *e.g.* financial activities or alcohol advertising. Sweden, for example, has a complete ban on advertising aimed at minors below the age of twelve, Greece has a ban on toy advertising and Belgium, Italy and Denmark have certain restrictions on advertising around children's programming. The majority of states, including Ireland (see above and Chap.9), do not restrict advertising aimed at children but do have detailed rules as to the content of such advertising (*e.g.* not encouraging children to enter strange places or converse with strangers). The Swedish provision was the subject of a case before the ECJ (*Konsumentenombudsmannen v Agostini Forlag and TV-Shop I Sverige*, Cases C–34, 35, 36/95), which held that the prohibition on advertising aimed at children could not be applied to broadcasters established abroad but also serving the Swedish market. It would amount to a double control since the TWF Directive already contains provisions on advertising aimed at children.

[133] *ibid.* at p.14. Several states ban virtual advertising.

[134] The case law of the ECJ concerning advertising is considered in brief below.

11.5 European Community Law and the Media

11.5.1 The European Court of Justice

The judgment of the European Court of Justice in *Italy v Sacchi*[135] in 1974 first established the relevance of the Treaty of Rome (the EEC Treaty) to the media. The case concerned the unauthorised broadcasting of foreign programmes into Italy, *via* cable, and the monopoly that existed in television programming in that country at the time. The transfer of television programmes transnationally was held to constitute a service and therefore to fall within the Treaty's concept of free movement of services. In the same way, trade in films, sound recordings, apparatus and products used for the transmission of television signals is subject to the rules relating to the free movement of goods. The distinction made in the early cases between goods and services in this field is, however, somewhat artificial given the developments that have taken place in technology since then and the arrival of multimedia technologies.

The *Coditel*[136] and *Debauve*[137] cases in 1980 were found to involve the application of non-discriminatory rules (*i.e.* they applied to domestic and foreign services alike), which were permissible "in the absence of harmonisation". *Coditel* concerned the application to foreign transmissions of Belgian copyright rules and *Debauve* the application of a ban on television advertising. The ban on advertising in the *Dutch Advertisers* case,[138] however, was found to be discriminatory, as it was aimed at the retransmission of foreign satellite programmes only. The Court held that it could not be justified on public policy grounds, as its aim was to prevent advertising except through a public agency, which had a monopoly.[139] These cases formed the background and gave the impetus to the EC Television without Frontiers Directive of 1989, which sought to at least co-ordinate, if not actually to harmonise, national rules.

Other cases since then have addressed issues such as jurisdiction,[140]

---

[135] Case C–155/73, [1974] 1 E.C.R. 409.
[136] *Coditel v Ciné Vog Films*, Case C–62/79, [1980] 2 E.C.R. 881.
[137] *Procureur du Roi v Debauve*, Case C–52/79, [1980] 2 E.C.R. 833.
[138] *Bond Van Adverteerders (Dutch Advertisers' Association) v The State (Netherlands)*, Case C–352/85, (1989) 3 C.M.L.R. 113.
[139] *ibid.* at 155.
[140] In *Commission of the European Communities v UK*, Case C–222/94, concerning satellite broadcasters, the Court confirmed that a broadcaster comes within the jurisdiction of the state in which it is established. See also *TV 10 SA v Commissariaat Voor de Media* Case C–23/93, (1994) ECJR 1-4795, regarding place of establishment of broadcasters and the concept of "provision of services". In *VT4 v Flemish Community of Belgium*, Case C–56/96, the Court decided that when a broadcaster is established in more than one state, it comes under the jurisdiction of the state in which it has its centre of activity and in which, in particular, its scheduling decisions are taken. In *Paul Denuit v Belgium*, Case C–14/96, the Court held that a state cannot object to the retransmission on its territory of programmes broadcast by a television broadcaster within the jurisdiction of another Member State. On the question of jurisdiction, see Tarlach McGonagle and Ad van Loon, *Jurisdiction over Broadcasters in Europe* (IRIS Special, European Audiovisual Observatory, Strasbourg, Council of Europe, 2002), which contains *inter alia* an analysis of and excerpts from the relevant ECJ case law.

licensing systems[141] and advertising.[142] More recent cases have dealt with aspects of the newer technologies. The ECJ has held, for example, that a prior authorisation procedure for the marketing of decoders, digital transmission and reception systems, and related conditional access services for digital television, restrict the free movement of goods and services, but may be justified if they pursue a public interest objective and are proportionate.[143] Similarly, a tax on satellite dishes in Belgium was found to be contrary to the freedom to provide services.[144] Other cases have found individual Member States guilty of failure to transpose Directives or to apply them correctly.[145]

11.5.2 The Television without Frontiers Directive

11.5.2.1 The overall context

As a Directive, the Television without Frontiers Directive (TWF) is part of the binding law of the EU and, as with any Directive, Member States are required to transpose it into their domestic law. The TWF was designed to ensure freedom of transmission in broadcasting, in line with the overall objectives of the Treaty establishing the common market. It was recognised in the Recitals to the Directive, however, that there is a much broader principle at stake in television broadcasting than just freedom to provide goods and services. That freedom is also a "specific manifestation in Community law of a more general principle, namely the freedom of expression as enshrined in Article 10(1) of the Convention for the Protection of Human Rights and Fundamental Freedoms". For that reason, freedom in relation to broadcasting and television programmes under the Directive must be in accordance with Article 10(1) of the ECHR and subject only to the limits set by Article 10(2) of the Convention and Article 56(1) of the Treaty. In a Greek case,[146] the Court of Justice examined exclusive rights to broadcasting in light of Article 10.

---

[141] In *Commission of the European Communities v Belgium*, Case 11/95, the Court condemned a preliminary licence system as a form of second control which amounted to a denial of the principle of free circulation.

[142] For example, *RTI v Ministerio delle Poste e Telecomunicazioni*, Case C–320/94; *Konsumentenombudsmannen v Agostini Forlag and TV-Shop I Sverige*, Cases C–34, 35, 36/95, regarding misleading advertisements and advertisements aimed at children; *ARD v Prosieben Media AG*, Case C–6/98, regarding the calculation of advertising breaks in scheduled transmission times for films; *Germany v European Parliament and Council of the EU*, Case C–376/98, annulling Directive 98/43/EC on the advertising and sponsorship of tobacco products.

[143] *Canal Satelite Digital SL v Administracion General dal Estado*, Case C–390/99, January 22, 2002.

[144] *François de Coster v College es bourgmestre et echevins de Watermael*, Case C–17/00, November 29, 2001.

[145] For example, Ireland was found guilty of failure to transpose the 1992 Directive on rental and lending rights into Irish law (ECJ, October 12, 1999), while the European Commission took infringement proceedings against Spain for its poor implementation of the TWF Directive (*IRIS* 2001–4:3). See also Cases C–119/00, C–207/00, 140/99 and 145/00, regarding the TWF Directive.

[146] *Elliniki Radiophonia Tileorassi–Anonimi Etairia v Dimotiki Etairia Pliroforissis*, Case No. C–260/89; judgment of June 18, 1991, [1991] E.C.R. I–2925.

The European Community's audiovisual policy, therefore, has a dual aim:

> "On the one hand, it concerns the internal market and the industry itself, the objective being to ensure the free movement of programmes within the Community and strengthen the European audiovisual industry. However, it also has a cultural and social objective, since it is also designed to protect certain general interests, both of the population as a whole and of specific social groups".[147]

The Television without Frontiers Directive, adopted in 1989 and amended in 1997, establishes, within that wider context, a legal framework for the free movement of television broadcasting services in the EU. The main issue to be addressed in 1989 was that terrestrial and satellite broadcasting, in conjunction with cable delivery systems, had the capacity to spill over national boundaries, with the result that Member States were not in a position to regulate them. The Directive therefore set out rules regarding transmission and reception of services, and jurisdiction.[148]

11.5.2.2 Quotas for European works

The Directive also seeks to promote the development of a European market in broadcasting and related activities, such as the production of audiovisual programmes and television advertising.[149] Concern was felt at the time that American programmes would swamp the European market; hence Article 4 of the Directive placed a duty on Member States to ensure that broadcasters reserved the majority of transmission time for European works. The types of programmes excluded from the Article 4 provision (news, sports events, games, advertising, teletext services and teleshopping) indicates that the concern was for the European film industry. The duty was somewhat watered down, however, by the use of such phrases as "where practicable" and "to be achieved progressively". Article 5 aims to safeguard the smaller independent sector. It requires Member States to ensure, where practicable, that broadcasters reserve at least 10 per cent of their transmission time or budget for European works created by producers who are independent of broadcasters.[150]

---

[147] Commissioner Viviane Reding, above, n.2, Press Release.

[148] Article 2(3) states that broadcasters under the jurisdiction of a Member State are those established in that Member State, and "established" means that they have their head office there or that editorial decisions are made there. Other broadcasters shall be deemed to be under the jurisdiction of a Member State if they use a frequency granted by that State, use a satellite capacity appertaining to that State or use a satellite up-link situated in that State (Art.2(4)). Article 2a deals with freedom of reception and retransmission. Directive 93/83/EEC dealt with cable and satellite delivery.

[149] See *www.europa.eu.int/avpolicy/regul/regul_en.htm*. For an assessment of the operation of the Directive, see Emanuelle Machet, "A Decade of EU Broadcasting Regulation", *Mediafact* (European Institute for the Media, Dusseldorf, 1999) and B.J. Drijber, "The Revised Television without Frontiers Directive: is it fit for the next century?" (1999) 36 *Common Market Law Review* 87.

[150] Article 6 sets out the meaning of "European works" and how the origin of the works is to be established by reference to the residence of authors and workers, and where

11.5.2.3 Television advertising

The Directive was also concerned with the harmonisation of television advertising. [151] Articles 10 to 19, as amended in 1997, lay down the rules relating to advertising, sponsorship and teleshopping. Television advertising and teleshopping must be readily recognised as such and kept separate from other parts of the programme service by optical and/or acoustic means. Subliminal techniques or surreptitious advertising are not to be used (Article 10). [152] Advertisements shall normally be inserted between programmes but may be inserted during programmes, provided the integrity and value of the programme is not prejudiced. Natural breaks, such as the interval in a sports event, should be used for advertising slots. Feature films are to be interrupted on the basis of duration, once for each complete period of 45 minutes. [153] In other programmes, a period of at least 20 minutes should elapse between advertising breaks. There should be no breaks in the broadcast of religious services, and none in news, current affairs, documentaries, religious or children's programmes, unless the programmes are of at least 30 minutes' duration (Article 11).

Advertising must respect human dignity and must not discriminate, be offensive, be prejudicial to health, safety or the environment (Article 12). A number of prohibitions are also detailed. The advertising of and teleshopping for tobacco products (Article 13) [154] and prescription medicines (Article 14) are prohibited. Advertisements and teleshopping for alcohol are restricted (Article 15). Particular regard must be had for minors (Article 16), [155] and

---

producers are established or the production of works supervised or controlled or, in the case of co-productions, the contribution made to the total production costs. "Authors" appears to include the director and writers of the screen-play and music, and "workers" would include actors and film crew. In this respect, the Directive is protectionist. As stated in the Recitals to the Directive, it aims to "promote markets of sufficient size for television productions in the Member States to recover necessary investments, not only by establishing common rules opening up national markets but also by envisaging for European productions where practicable and by appropriate means, a majority proportion in television programmes in all Member States".

[151] Copyright, however, was omitted as no agreement could be reached, and was left to be dealt with by subsequent legislation. See further below, n.218.

[152] The definition of advertising in Art.1 of the Directive was extended in 1997 to cover surreptitious advertising, sponsorship and teleshopping (Art.1(d), (e) and (f)).

[153] A debate emerged as to the method of calculation, whether gross or net: see above, n.142, *ARD v Prosieben*, where the ECJ held that as Art.11(3) imposes a restriction on broadcasting, it must be narrowly interpreted and therefore the gross principle applies. The Court went on to say, however, that Member States would not be precluded from applying the net principle for advertisements to television broadcasters within their jurisdiction, provided such rules are compatible with other relevant provisions of Community law (at paras 42–3).

[154] An EC Directive prohibiting all advertising and sponsorship of tobacco products (98/43/EC) was successfully challenged in the European Court of Justice and subsequently annulled: *Germany v European Parliament* (Case C–376/98), *R v Secretary of State for Health, ex p. Imperial Tobacco Ltd* (Case C–74/99). The Court found that it could not be justified by reference to the Treaty provisions. It has been replaced by Directive 2001/37/EC.

[155] Advertising (and teleshopping) must not directly exhort minors to buy a product or

special requirements are laid down for sponsored programmes (Article 17).[156] Total amounts of advertising within the hourly and daily programming are fixed (Article 18), and Member States are free to lay down stricter periods if they wish (Article 19).

11.5.2.4 Protection of minors

A key provision of the Directive is Article 22, which provides for the protection of minors and public order. Member States are required to take appropriate measures to ensure that television broadcasters under their jurisdiction do not broadcast any programmes which might seriously impair the physical, mental or moral development of minors, in particular programmes that involve pornography or gratuitous violence. Where programmes are likely to be harmful but not to a serious extent, measures must be taken to ensure that minors will not normally see or hear them. Such measures include the time of broadcast (after the watershed) or technical measures, being preceded by an acoustic warning or visual symbol.[157] Incitement to hatred is also prohibited.[158]

With respect to minors, an EU-wide study on parental control in broadcasting was carried out following the 1997 amendment of the Directive.[159] The most recent report found that rating systems varied widely as between countries and even within countries and consequently a study of the ratings practices is being conducted. The adoption of a pan-European rating system for video games was welcomed. [160]

11.5.2.5 Right of reply

Article 23 makes provision for a right of reply or "equivalent remedies" for those whose legitimate interests, in particular reputation and good name, have been damaged by an assertion of incorrect facts in a television programme.[161]

---

service by exploiting their inexperience or credulity; it shall not directly encourage them to persuade their parents or others to purchase the goods or services; it shall not exploit the special trust they place in their parents, teachers or others and must not show minors in dangerous situations.

[156] Television programmes may not be sponsored by tobacco companies. News and current affairs programmes may not be sponsored.

[157] RTÉ introduced visual symbols in 2002, indicating programme content suitable for children, parental supervision, young adult, general audience and mature audience. See *The Irish Times*, January 19, 2002, *IRIS* 2002–2:12. The "watershed" is a rule of thumb whereby programmes listed before a certain time (9 p.m. in Ireland) are regarded as suitable for family viewing, while those after the watershed are more adult.

[158] Section 22(a). See above, Chs 8 and 9.

[159] The study is available at *www.europa.eu.int/comm/avpolicy/legis/key_doc/ parental_control/index_en.htm*. It was followed by a communication from the Commission (COM(1999)371).

[160] See above, Chap.9. The European rating system was adopted in Ireland in 2000 (*The Sunday Times*, June 3, 2001), at which time, the Film Censor also changed his title on film certificates from "censor" to "scrúdaitheoir", an Irish-language word signifying "inspector" or "examiner".

[161] A right of reply "or equivalent remedies" must be provided and transmitted within a reasonable time subsequent to the request being substantiated.

Whether the provision in the Broadcasting Act 1990 or that in the Broadcasting Act 2001, regarding recourse to the Broadcasting Complaints Commission and the broadcasting of its findings, is sufficient to meet Ireland's obligations in this regard is open to question. Although intended to comply with the Directive, the measure, involving the BCC, could not be said to constitute a right of reply and it is debatable whether it is sufficient to constitute an "equivalent" remedy.[162]

11.5.2.6 Review

Article 26 of the Directive, as amended in 1997, provides for two-yearly reports on the application of the Directive and, where appropriate, further proposals to adapt it to developments in the field of television broadcasting. The latest review of the existing rules takes account of economic and technological developments up to 2002. The Report[163] covers three main areas: the broadcasting of events of major importance to society, the application of the rules on protection of minors, and the application of the rules on advertising. A separate report was published on the application of Articles 4 and 5 relating to quotas of European programming.[164]

The review, and indeed all of the provisions of the Directive are of immense importance in the context of the imminent accession to the EU of a number of Central and Eastern European states. They form part of the *acquis communitaire*, or package of EU laws and policies, which acceding states are required to embrace in order to become members of the common market.

The overall picture that is emerging so far from the review seems to be that application of the Directive in Member States is generally satisfactory. Following a consultation process on key issues, the review will be completed and a final communication or package of proposals presented.[165]

11.5.2.7 Coverage of major events

With regard to the other major topic covered in the review, several Member States have made use of the power conferred by Article 3a of the Directive that:

---

[162] See above, n.42.

[163] Fourth Report from the Commission, above, n.2.

[164] Fifth Communication from the Commission to the Council and the European Parliament on the application of Arts 4 and 5 of Directive 89/552/EEC "Television without Frontiers", as amended by Directive 97/36/EC, for the period 1999–2000, COM(2002)612 final, Brussels, November 8, 2002, available at *www.europa.eu.int/ comm/avpolicy/regul/twf/art45-intro_en.htm*. The Report concludes that application of Arts 4 and 5 in the Member States is generally satisfactory, and that there is a "positive and dynamic trend in the broadcasting of European works, including those by independent producers, in the context of a general increase in the number of channels over the reference period, thereby contributing to the promotion of cultural diversity in Europe". (The Directive itself provides for two separate types of reports: the first, under Art.26 covers the application of the rules of the Directive in general; the second, under Art.4(3) involves the monitoring of the application of Arts 4 and 5 regarding European works and independent producers.)

[165] See above, n.2, Press Release and Fourth Report.

"Each Member State may take measures in accordance with Community law to ensure that broadcasters under its jurisdiction do not broadcast on an exclusive basis events which are regarded by that Member State as being of major importance for society in such a way as to deprive a substantial proportion of the public in that Member State of the possibility of following such events via live coverage or deferred coverage on free television. If it does so, the Member State concerned shall draw up a list of designated events, national or non-national, which it considers to be of major importance for society".[166]

The cost of acquiring rights to sports events, in particular, has soared to such an extent that it is very difficult for individual broadcasters and particularly public service broadcasters to compete.[167] Hence the protective measures permitted by Article 3a. In response, the Irish Government introduced legislation in 1999. The Broadcasting (Major Events Television Coverage) Act 1999 paved the way for the drawing up of a list by the Minister for Communications of designated events to be protected for showing on free-to-air television.

However, that list did not emerge until 2002.[168] It was prompted by the decision of the Football Association of Ireland (FAI) to sell the rights for Ireland's home internationals to Sky Television, a subscriber-only channel.[169] The list includes Ireland's home and away soccer matches in the European championship and World Cup qualifiers and finals, All-Ireland Gaelic football and hurling finals, the Olympics, the Irish rugby team's matches in the Six Nations and Rugby World Cup and, in horse racing, the Irish Grand National and Irish Derby.

The Minister then signalled his intention to introduce amending legislation, effectively to provide a mechanism to deal retrospectively with deals such as the FAI/Sky deal and to strengthen the existing legislation. The Broadcasting (Major Events Television Coverage) (Amendment) Act was passed in April 2003. Section 2 of the Act makes clear that the Act applies to events designated

---

[166] *Cf.* The European Convention on Transfrontier Television (as amended by Protocol ETS No. 171, which entered into force on March 1, 2002), Art.9*bis*.

[167] As a result, in 1993 the EBU (European Broadcasting Union), an association of radio and television broadcasters, was exempted from the competition provisions of Art.85(1) of the EEC Treaty and allowed to collectively acquire rights, subject to granting access to third parties (Commission decision of June 11, 1993, O.J. L 179, July 22, 1993, p.23). See also John Enser, "The Commission's Decision in the Eurovision Case: A Triumph of Pragmatism over Principle?" [1993] 6 ENT. L.R. 193. For a more recent assessment of the issues, particularly in the UK, see R. Craufurd Smith and B. Bottcher, "Football and Fundamental Rights: Regulating Access to Major Sporting Events on Television" (2002) 8(1) *European Public Law* 107.

[168] October 2002. The Government indicated that the delay was due in the first instance to the need to pass the Broadcasting Act 2001 and then to engage in a period of consultation. A question arose then as to whether the other requirements of Art.3a were met, namely that the list of such events be drawn up in a clear and transparent manner *in due and effective time* (emphasis added). Notification to the Commission is also required (Art.3a(2)).

[169] A summary of the situation is reported in *IRIS* 2002–10: 9–10. The FAI/Sky deal led to protracted debate and controversy.

both before and after the passing of the Act, whether or not an agreement or arrangement has been entered into between the event organiser and a broadcaster. An agreement or arrangement entered into before the passing of the Act is covered, provided it was entered into after the publication of the Television without Frontiers Directive and concerns an event taking place after November 13, 1999, the date on which Article 3a of the Directive was given effect to in Ireland by the Broadcasting (Major Events Television Coverage) Act 1999.

The High Court is given a central role in implementing the new legislation (section 4). Qualifying broadcasters (that is, free-to-air broadcasters like RTÉ and TV3) can apply to the High Court for an order to allow them to provide coverage of a designated event upon terms to be fixed by the Court. The Court can appoint an arbitrator to determine reasonable market rates, in accordance with the criteria set out in the Act (section 6). The inclusion of an arbitration mechanism was urged by many sporting organisations during the consultation process.

Where the High Court has fixed the terms and there is more than one qualifying broadcaster interested, the event organiser can choose which of them shall have the rights. In situations where an existing contract is in place between an event organiser and a non-qualifying broadcaster (that is, one that is not free-to-air), as in the FAI/Sky case, the High Court, on application to it by a qualifying broadcaster, shall decide to whom and in what proportion monies in respect of reasonable market rates should be paid. The Court may, if it considers it necessary, adjust an existing agreement or arrangement. In the FAI/Sky case, a settlement was reached without the need to have recourse to the Court.[170] The Act also provides for periodic review of designated events and the designation of events (section 9).

11.5.2.8 Short reports of events

An issue not covered by the Television without Frontiers Directive, but now under consideration, is that of access to short extracts of events that are subject to exclusive rights.[171] The European Convention on Transfrontier Television, on the other hand, as amended by the Protocol, has such a provision:

---

[170] Sky decided to vary its exclusive deal with the FAI (May 22, 2003) and a settlement was reached by the FAI with RTÉ (*The Irish Times*, May 28, 2003). The issue of listed events for the UK was addressed by the House of Lords in *R v Independent Television Commission*, July 25, 2001, [2001] UKHL 42.

[171] Work Programme for the review of the Television without Frontiers Directive, annexed to Fourth Report, COM(2002) 778 final (above, n.2), Theme 6, Issue not covered by the Directive: access to short extracts of events subject to exclusive rights. The text states: "Bearing in mind the interests at stake (event organisers, rights holders, agencies, television broadcasting bodies, the public) and taking into account the fact that some Member States have already adopted specific provisions on the subject, in the interest of having as broad an information base as possible, this new question should be addressed with a view to analysing whether the absence of Community provisions creates obstacles to the internal market".

"Each party shall examine and, where necessary, take legal measures such as introducing the right to short reporting on events of high interest for the public to avoid the right of the public to information being undermined due to the exercise by a broadcaster within its jurisdiction of exclusive rights for the transmission or retransmission, within the meaning of Article 3, of such an event".[172]

The Council of Europe's Group of Specialists on the democratic and social implications of digital broadcasting has prepared a Draft Recommendation on the right to short reporting on major events where exclusive rights have been acquired.[173]

11.5.3 The Human Rights Dimension

As noted above, broadcasting is not just a commodity to be regulated by reference to the market. It also has an important cultural, social and democratic role, which must be recognised and safeguarded. The human rights dimension, and in particular the freedom of expression aspect, is therefore of central importance. While the European Convention on Human Rights sets out the broad principles, other instruments address the specifics of broadcasting as a trans-European communications medium.

11.5.3.1 The European Court of Human Rights

The European Court of Human Rights over the years has considered the compatibility of the licensing of broadcast services with the freedom of expression guarantee of Article 10 of the ECHR. Article 10(1) states that "this Article shall not prevent States from requiring the licensing of broadcasting, television or cinema enterprises". In a series of cases in the 1990s, the Court took the view that national licensing systems were necessary for the orderly regulation of broadcasting enterprises, but were subject to the requirements of para.2 of Article 10.

In *Groppera Radio AG v Switzerland*,[174] a ban on cable retransmissions in Switzerland of broadcasts from Italy was justified under Article 10(2), as it pursued the legitimate aims of prevention of disorder in telecommunications and protection of the rights of others by ensuring a fair allocation of frequencies internationally and nationally.[175] In *Autronic AG v Switzerland*,[176] however, the Court found that the Swiss authorities had breached Article 10 by preventing a private company from picking up signals from a Soviet satellite for

---

[172] Article 9. The amending Protocol to the European Convention on Transfrontier Television entered into force on March 1, 2002. At national level, the News Access Code of Practice in operation among broadcasters in the UK is of interest: see Tom Simpson, "Exclusive Sports Broadcast Rights and Fair Dealing" [2001] ENT. L.R. 207.

[173] MM-S-DB (2003)003, April 16, 2003.

[174] Series A, No.173; (1990) 12 E.H.R.R. 321.

[175] *ibid.* at para.70. The measures taken by the Swiss authorities had not overstepped the margin of appreciation (at para.73).

[176] Series A, No.178; (1990) 12 E.H.R.R. 485.

rebroadcasting into Switzerland. Article 10 applied not only to the content of information, the Court said, but to the mode of transmission or reception as well. To restrict the mode of transmission or reception was to interfere with the right to receive and impart information in Article 10.[177]

In the Austrian radio cases *Informationsverein Lentia v Austria*,[178] the Court found that Austria had breached Article 10 of the Convention by retaining a State monopoly over broadcasting and refusing to license other stations. The Court stressed the fundamental role of freedom of expression and of the press in a democratic society, which "cannot be successfully accomplished unless it is grounded in the principle of pluralism, of which the State is the ultimate guarantor" (para.38).

As a result of the technical progress made over the last decades, the Court said, justification for not granting licences could no longer be found in considerations relating to the number of frequencies and channels available. Other countries had either granted licences subject to specified conditions or had made provision for forms of private participation in the activities of the national corporation.[179]

Ireland was among the countries that had removed the monopoly long held by RTÉ and, as outlined above, the Broadcasting Act 2001 has opened up the broadcasting sector still further in response to the technological realities. In Europe, the focus has shifted in recent years to the eastern states and the need for them to bring their media laws and practice into line with the ECHR. However, even long-established democratic states need to review their laws and practice, as some remnants of older laws and practice sit awkwardly with the ECHR. Luxembourg, for example, has recently drafted a new law on freedom of expression in the media, to replace a law dating from 1860s. Ireland, too, has old and inappropriate laws and needs to take note.[180]

The jurisprudence of the European Court of Human Rights in relation to various aspects of broadcasting and other media has been addressed in earlier chapters. The place of advertising within the freedom of expression guarantee of Article 10 of the European Convention on Human Rights has been examined in a number of cases by the Strasbourg Court, a few of them involving the media. In *Markt Intern and Beermann v Germany*,[181] for example, the European

---

[177] *ibid.* at para.47.

[178] Series A, No.276, judgment of November 24, 1993.

[179] *ibid.* at para.39. Austria's refusal to do so was disproportionate to the aim pursued and, accordingly, was not necessary in a democratic society (at para.43). Since then, the Court has had to deal with several other cases from Austria, where the monopoly did not end until 1997. See generally John O'Dowd, "Broadcasting Policy and European Law" in McGonagle (ed.), *Law and the Media* (Round Hall Sweet & Maxwell, Dublin, 1997), p.257, who concludes that Irish law was "already broadly in conformity with the requirements of the European Convention on Human Rights as interpreted in the *Lentia* case" (at p.300).

[180] Such as blasphemous libel, see discussion of that and other anomalous or antiquated laws in earlier chapters.

[181] Series A, No.165, (1990) 12 E.H.R.R. 161. The dissenting judgments gave greater weight to commercial speech: "It is just as important to guarantee the freedom of expression in relation to the practices of a commercial undertaking as it is in relation to the conduct of a head of Government ... In order to ensure the openness of business

Court of Human Rights found no breach of Article 10. Although Article 10 did apply to commercial speech, the publication in question, which reported the dissatisfaction of a consumer with a mail-order firm, was found to be premature, as the firm had agreed to investigate the matter. The premature publication would have had adverse effects on the firm's business.

In 1993 the European Commission on Human Rights declared inadmissible a complaint that a fine imposed in respect of indirect commercial publicity (pictures of Coca Cola bottles and other brand products in a children's news programme) constituted an unnecessary interference with the broadcaster's freedom of expression.[182] Then in 1996 in *Lindner v Germany*,[183] the Court declared the particular application inadmissible but emphasised the importance of advertising as a means for the citizen to discover the characteristics of products and goods offered to him. Nevertheless, advertising may sometimes be restricted, especially to prevent unfair competition and untruthful and misleading advertising. Even when true and accurate it may be restricted in order to ensure respect for the rights of others. However, any such restrictions must be closely scrutinised by the Court.

Such is the centrality of the ECHR as a point of reference within the EU system that in an ECJ case on tobacco advertising, the then Advocate General, Niall Fennelly (now a judge of the Irish Supreme Court) considered arguments based not only on the relevant EC Directive but also on Article 10 of the ECHR. He took the view that freedom to promote commercial activities derives not only from the right to engage in economic activities in a market based on free competition but also from the entitlement as human beings to "express and receive views on any topic, including the merits of goods or services which they market or purchase".[184]

11.5.3.2 The European Convention on Transfrontier Television (ECTT)

The European Convention on Transfrontier Television 1989, as amended by the 1998 Protocol, contains provisions on advertising. All advertisements must be fair and honest, must not be misleading and, if addressed to children, must

---

activities it must be possible to disseminate freely information and ideas concerning the products and services proposed to consumers" (at 177). In an earlier case, *Barthold v Germany*, Series A, No.90 (1985) 7 E.H.R.R. 383, at 407–8, Judge Pettiti in a concurring judgment made clear that commercial speech is directly connected to and included in the sphere of freedom of expression protected by Art.10.

[182] *Nederlandse Omroepprogramma Stichting v the Netherlands* App. No.16844/90, decision of October 13, 1993. See generally Dirk Voorhoof, "Restrictions on Television Advertising and Article 10 of the European Convention on Human Rights" (1993) 12 *International Journal of Advertising* 189. See also *Casado Coca v Spain*, Series A, No.285, (1994) 18 E.H.R.R. 1. In Ireland, an interview on an RTÉ news bulletin with pop-music impresario, Louis Walsh, holding a bottle of "Fanta" to the camera, when "Fanta" had been the sponsors of a pop-music competition series on RTÉ, would give rise to similar questions (*The Sunday Tribune*, January 20, 2002).

[183] App. No. 32813/96, March 9, 1999.

[184] *Germany v European Parliament* (Case C–376/98), *R v Secretary of State for Health, ex p. Imperial Tobacco Ltd* (Case C–74/99), above, n.154, at para.154.

have regard to their interests and susceptibilities. Advertisers must not exercise any editorial influence over the content of programmes (Article 11).

Other measures, similar to those in the EC Television without Frontiers Directive relate to the content, duration, form and presentation of advertising, and the insertion of advertisements between and within programmes. Surreptitious advertising and subliminal techniques are prohibited. Split-screen advertising is not specifically mentioned in the Convention but an Opinion on split-screen advertising was adopted by the Standing Committee on Transfrontier Television of the Council of Europe on April 29, 2002, acknowledging that this form of advertising was covered by the Convention term "other forms of advertising".[185]

Overall, the European Convention on Transfrontier Television, as revised by the Protocol of 1998, covers much the same ground as the EC Television without Frontiers Directive, including a right of reply (Article 8), major events (Article 9*bis*), advertising, sponsorship and teleshopping (Articles 11–18). It also contains provisions on cultural objectives and media pluralism (Article 10) and establishes a Standing Committee to *inter alia* make recommendations concerning the application of the Convention, suggest any necessary modifications, and use its best endeavours to secure a friendly settlement of any difficulty referred to it (Article 21).

11.5.4 Competition Law

The emergence of large media companies and economic pressures generally have led to a situation of concentration of ownership and cross-ownership, that is, the same person(s) owning or having a controlling interest in both newspapers and broadcasting stations, sometimes also in advertising, print and distribution companies.[186] In such a situation there is a greater opportunity for a company to cut its own costs or drive up competitors' costs. It also puts the company in a stronger position to outbid rivals in the pursuit of lucrative sports coverage or the rights to show top films and to take on the dominance of the American conglomerates. Some degree of strength over and above that wielded by smaller companies may well be desirable in some respects, but there is also a danger that over-concentration will force out competitors and lead to a lack of diversity in news and current affairs coverage. The key issue is not so much ownership as such but how to maintain a diversity of sources in

---

[185] Article 12(1). The Standing Committee is established under Art.20 of the Convention. See *IRIS* 2002–6:3.

[186] Concentration may take a number of forms: *Horizontal Media Concentration, i.e.* ownership and capital integration on the part of companies operating in the same market, *e.g.* television broadcasters; *Vertical Media Concentration, i.e.* ownership and capital integration where a company combines with other companies, upstream or downstream in production or trading terms, *e.g.* among broadcasting companies and their associated production and distribution markets; *Diagonal Media Concentration, i.e.* ownership and capital integration among companies that do not belong to the same market or stand in a supplier-purchaser relationship, *e.g.* among broadcasting companies and other media, such as print and internet. See Susanne Nikoltchev, "Introduction", *Television and Media Concentration*, above, n.110.

the face of economic factors militating against it. One of the devices used to try to counteract these forces is competition law.

European Community law, in particular Articles 81 and 82 (formerly Articles 85 and 86) of the Treaty of Rome, have provided a basis for Member States to take action to eliminate anti-competitive practices. Article 81 is concerned with agreements that would prevent, restrict or distort competition, while Article 82 prohibits abuse of a dominant position in the market. These articles were given force in Irish law by the Competition Acts 1991–2002.[187] It was under the provisions of the 1991 Act that the Competition Authority in 1994 was asked by the Minister for Enterprise and Employment to investigate the situation in the Irish newspaper industry following Independent Newspapers' acquisition of a 24.9 per cent share-holding in the Irish Press group.[188] The Authority was concerned with two main issues: the question of transfrontier competition in the industry and the issue of dominance in the industry.[189] The Authority concluded, that regardless of how the market was viewed, Independent Newspapers had a dominant position and was clearly capable of inflicting considerable harm on most of its rivals and could force them out of the market altogether.[190]

It is not, of course, the fact of a dominant position that is relevant but rather the abuse of a dominant position. Predatory pricing, that is, below cost selling in order to weaken or eliminate competitors, can usually only be engaged in by a dominant firm and is indicative of abuse of that dominant position.[191] The Authority concluded that English newspaper companies operating in the Irish market were not engaged in predatory pricing and that the fall-off in

---

[187] Ss.4 and 5 of the 1991 Act; s.5 of the 2002 Act deals with dominant position and s.7 with related offences.

[188] In accordance with the Competition Act 1991, s.11 (see above Chap.3). The Competition Authority, established by the Competition Act 1991, also officially revoked the licence for the operation of the British Net Book Agreement in June 1994. The agreement, which allowed price-fixing of books and protected smaller book sellers, was found to contravene the Act. It followed a ruling of the EC Court of First Instance in Luxembourg *(Publishers Association v EC Commission*, Case T-66/89, Court of First Instance, July 9, 1992) that the agreement contravened Art.85 of the EEC Treaty. See Ciaran Walker, "Court of First Instance Judgment on the Net Book Agreement: Implications for the Irish Book Market" [1992] 6 ENT. L.R. 215 and, more recently, Council Decision of February 12, 2001 on the application of national fixed book-price systems (2001/C 73/03, O.J. C73/5, March 6, 2001, which invites the Commission *inter alia* when applying competition rules on the free movement of goods to take account of the "specific value of a book as a cultural object and the importance of books in promoting cultural diversity, and the cross-border dimension of the book market").

[189] Competition Authority, *Interim Report of Study on the Newspaper Industry* (The Stationery Office, Dublin, 1995). The situation as found by the Authority was one in which English newspapers formed only 7 per cent of overall sales in Ireland. However, the tabloid percentage of this market had been increasing, while the quality market had been falling (para.8.32).

[190] *ibid.* at para.8.34.

[191] The Competition Act 2002, s.4 deals with anti-competitive practices, decisions and concerted practices, including price-fixing. S.6 deals with offences in relation to such practices. Another measure used to assess dominance is the presence of "significant market power" (SMP), see European Commission Guidelines on Market Analysis and Assessment of Significant Market Power, July 11, 2002, O.J. C165/6.

sales of Irish newspapers was attributable to other causes, such as the high cost structure and price gap.[192] The acquisition by Independent Newspapers of a stake in the Irish Press group, on the other hand, was found to be designed to prevent a rival acquiring control of the Press newspapers.[193] It was adjudged to have prevented the emergence of more intense competition in the various segments of the market and therefore to amount to abuse of a dominant position.[194] It was an abuse of a dominant position contrary to section 5 of the Competition Act 1991 and an anti-competitive agreement contrary to section 4 of the same Act.

In one of the longest running battles on competition law, the European Court of Justice ruled in 1995 that RTÉ and Independent Television Publications (ITP) had abused a dominant position in not allowing other companies to publish full listings of television programmes.[195] The relevant market in this case was deemed by the Court to be the market in television listings. The Court ruled that *Magill* and other interested companies should be allowed to publish full listings subject to payment of a reasonable level of royalties.[196]

---

[192] *ibid.* at para.8.51.

[193] *ibid.* at para.8.53.

[194] *ibid.* at para.8.55. The Irish Press titles closed in 1995. At the time, Independent Newspapers was providing ongoing finance to the *Sunday Tribune* to enable it to continue operating. Although it was outside the Authority's remit to pronounce on it, the Authority did express the view that if the provision of finance was designed to inflict damage on rival newspapers, then that too would amount to abuse of a dominant position (para.8.57).

[195] *RTÉ & ITP v Commission*, Cases C–241-242/91P, [1995] E.C.R. I–743, [1995] 4 C.M.L.R. 718. In March 1985, when *Magill* first announced its intention to publish a weekly TV guide, RTÉ entered into negotiations with *Magill* and offered a very restrictive licence to which *Magill* reluctantly agreed (*RTÉ v Magill TV Guide Ltd* [1988] I.R. 97). Under the terms and conditions of that licence, *Magill* was to be entitled to publish RTÉ's programme schedules for the day of issue only, *i.e.*, Thursday's programmes each week or Friday and Saturday's programmes or Saturday and Sunday's. In addition, it could refer briefly to not more than twelve programmes each from RTÉ 1 and RTÉ 2's programmes for the coming week. Viewers who wanted to know the week's programming schedule had no alternative but to buy the weekly guides published by the television stations themselves. Some time later when the conditions of the licence were breached, Costello J. in the High Court granted an interlocutory injunction restraining the defendants from publishing their *TV Guide*, pending the trial of the action ([1988] I.R. 97). The *Sun* newspaper was also prevented by injunction from publishing RTÉ's listings for the ten days of Christmas (see *The Irish Times*, December 4, 1992). The competition issue was investigated by the EC Commission, which found a breach of the Community's rules. The Commission's decision was upheld by the Court of First Instance in 1991, and that ruling was in turn appealed to the Court of Justice.

[196] The copyright aspects of the case are discussed below. For the implications of the decision in *Magill*, particularly with regard to compulsory licensing, see the more recent case law of the ECJ and the commentary in leading textbooks, such as Paul Craig & Gráinne de Búrca, *EU Law: Text, Cases and Materials* (OUP, Oxford, 2003) p.1014, or for the competition aspects, Alison Jones & Brenda Sufrin, *EC Competition Law: Text, Cases and Materials* (OUP, Oxford, 2001) p.403; Ulrika Båth, "Access to Information v. Intellectual Property Rights" [2002] E.I.P.R. 138.

11.5.5 The Competition Act 2002 and media mergers

The Commission on the Newspaper Industry in 1996 made a number of recommendations with regard to competition, including amending the law on merger controls and below cost selling.[197] The competition issues raised in the report were referred by the Government to the Competition and Mergers Review Group of the Department of Enterprise, Trade and Employment. It recommended that specific provision be made for media mergers in Competition legislation.[198] The Competition Act 2002, s.23, now provides the procedures to be adopted in relation to media mergers. The powers and functions of the Authority in relation to mergers and acquisitions generally are set out in section 22.

Section 23 basically provides for notification that a merger is considered to be a media merger, in which case, if the Authority makes a determination, the Minister may, within ten days, direct the Authority to carry out an investigation under section 22. A number of "relevant criteria" are set out, by reference to which the Minister may decide, notwithstanding the determination of the Competition Authority (section 23(4)), either that the merger may be put into effect, or put into effect subject to certain conditions, or not put into effect. The "relevant criteria"[199] include consideration of the strength and competitiveness of media businesses indigenous to the State, the extent to which ownership and control is spread among individuals and other undertakings, the extent to which "diversity of views prevalent in Irish society is reflected through the activities of the various media businesses", and finally the market share in any media business held by any individual or undertaking involved or with an interest in the media merger. A limited right of appeal to the High Court and to the Supreme Court on a point of law only is provided.[200] Ministerial orders on foot of the "relevant criteria" shall be laid before each House of the Oireachtas, and either House can, by resolution within 21 days, annul such order and the determination of the Authority shall have effect.[201] Various terms such as "broadcasting service", "cable system", "media business", "programme material" and "providing a broadcasting services platform" are defined in the section.[202]

The Competition Act 2002 also provides for co-operation agreements between the Competition Authority and other statutory bodies, including the

---

[197] *Report of the Commission on the Newspaper Industry* (Pn 2841, The Stationery Office, Dublin, 1996), Chs 3 and 4, Recommendations 2, 7–9.

[198] Competition and Mergers Review Group, *Final Report* (Pn.8487, Department of Enterprise, Trade and Employment, Dublin, 2000).

[199] S.23(11).

[200] S.24(2) and (9) respectively.

[201] S.25(1) and (2).

[202] S.23(10). "Media business", for instance, means the publication of newspapers or periodicals consisting substantially of news and comment on current affairs, the provision of a broadcasting service or the provision of a broadcasting services platform. "Broadcasting service" is widely defined to include cable, MMDS, satellite and other transmission systems, but not the internet. On the internet, see Stephen Dodd, "Competition law and the Internet" (2000) 6 B.R. 133, Phillip Ruttley, "EC Competition Law in Cyberspace: An Overview of Recent Developments" (1998) 19 E.C.L.R. 186.

BCI and ComReg.[203] The provision recognises the fact of convergence and the resulting overlap in the work of the various regulatory authorities. The purpose of co-operation is to allow for consultation, the sharing of information, ensuring consistency and avoiding duplication.

As noted above, there is wide acceptance that Competition law is not sufficient on its own to address all the issues arising in the media sector, as it is primarily concerned with the operation of economic markets rather than with pluralism objectives. Media ownership rules alone will not suffice either to ensure pluralism.[204] Competition law can be used to ensure that no obstacles are created to new entrants into the market but a combination of competition law, media ownership rules and other measures will be necessary to meet the public interest objective of media pluralism and diversity.[205] Following a period of reflection at European level, the Commission has recognised that media regulation is still necessary to safeguard the non-economic rights and democratic values of freedom of expression and information.[206]

11.5.5.1 The Framework Directives

The EC has also been heavily engaged in drawing up a framework for electronic communications in the light of convergence. The most recent process, begun in 1999,[207] resulted in the publication of a number of proposals for Directives and Decisions,[208] and a Regulation of the European Parliament and Council on Unbundled Access to the Local Loop, December 5, 2000. The "Framework" Directives came into force in 2002.[209] They were followed by a new Directive

---

[203] S.34. As technologies and markets are rapidly converging, the BCI likewise has to take cognisance not only of broadcasting law but of competition law and telecommunications law as well. A co-operation agreement between the Competition Authority and the BCI has been drawn up (see *www.bci.ie*).

[204] Council of Europe, *Report on Media Pluralism in the Digital Environment*, October 2000 (*www.humanrights.coe.int/media*).

[205] On the application of competition law to the media, see generally, Laurent Garzaniti, *Telecommunications, Broadcasting and the Internet: E.U. Competition Law and Regulation* (Sweet & Maxwell, London, 2000).

[206] The first Directive on competition in the telecommunications field, Directive 90/388/EEC, was amended by five further Directives issued between 1994 and 1999 (Directive 1999/64/EC, O.J. L 175, July 10, 1999).

[207] *Communication: Towards a new framework for electronic communications and infrastructure and associated services: The 1999 Communications Review* (COM (1999) 539).

[208] *Results of the public consultation on the 1999 Communications Review and Orientations for the new regulatory framework, 2000*: Com(2000)384, 385, 386, 392, 393, 407

[209] They consist of a package of five Directives: the Framework Directive (2002/21/EC, O.J. L 108/33, April 24, 2002), the Access Directive (2002/19/EC, O.J. L 108/7, April 24, 2002), the Authorisation Directive (2002/20/EC, O.J. L 108/21, April 24, 2002), the Universal Service Directive (2002/22/EC, O.J. L 108/51, April 24, 2002) and the Directive on Privacy and Electronic Communications (2002/58/EC, O.J. L 201/37, July 31, 2002), all available at the EU website, *www.europa.eu.int/information_society*. For a discussion of the Directives and their implications, see Nico van Eijk, "New European Rules for the Communications Sector", *IRIS plus* (IRIS 2003–2, European Audiovisual Observatory, Strasbourg) and Brian Gormley, "Regulation of the Electronic Media: Ireland's Future Approach to Issues of Convergence" (2002) 2 *Technology and*

on competition in the markets for electronic communications networks and services.[210] The liberalisation process and gradual opening up of the telecommunications markets necessitated the adjustment of earlier Directives in order to reflect the latest technological developments and the convergence phenomenon that has shaped the information technology, media and telecommunications industries over recent years. Even the terminology has changed from "telecommunications" services and networks to "electronic communications" services and networks.[211] The Directive provides for the removal of restrictions and a prohibition on exclusive or special rights for electronic communications networks or services (Article 2). General authorisations, which have replaced licences, must be based on objective, non-discriminatory, proportionate and transparent criteria (Article 3). Other articles deal with vertical integration, use of frequencies, directory services, universal service obligations, satellites and cable television networks.

11.6 COPYRIGHT AND RELATED RIGHTS

The *Magill* case also raised issues of copyright in television listings. The law of copyright protects original or creative work from being unfairly exploited, without the permission or authorisation of those who created it. Copyright, originally devised as the right to make copies,[212] means the exclusive right to use and authorise others to use a work, that is, to reproduce, publish, perform in public, broadcast, cause to be transmitted or make an adaptation of the work in question. In other words it acts as a restraint on plagiarism or unfair exploitation of another's work. In the audiovisual field, for example, it acts as a measure to tackle piracy[213] and the bootlegging of music, film or video.[214]

Entertainment Law Journal 2. ComReg sought to regulate BskyB under the Directives, but the Minister for Communications has indicated that if that is not possible he will seek to have the Television without Frontiers Directive amended to that effect (*The Irish Times*, December 20, 2002, February 8, 2003, March 14, 2003).

[210] Directive 2002/77/EC, September 16, 2002.

[211] *ibid.*, Arts (6) and (8).

[212] Historically, copyright entailed a form of censorship, in that it authorised a monopoly of printing. In order to print a restricted range of books, for example, a printer in Ireland had to have a patent or licence, issued by the King (see above, Chap.3). Lord Macauley said that copyright was "a tax on readers for the purpose of giving a bounty to writers". (Macauley, Speech in the House of Commons, February 5, 1841).

[213] On music piracy, see Karen Murray, "Protecting Intellectual Property by Technological Measures" (*www.ictlaw.com*). The Committee of Ministers of the Council of Europe passed Recommendation Rec(2001)7 on measures to protect copyright and neighbouring rights and combat piracy, especially in the digital environment.

[214] On bootlegging, the ECJ in the Phil Collins case (Cases C–92 and C–326/92, [1994] 1 E.I.P.R. D–22), had to deal with the problem that a concert given by Phil Collins in the US was recorded without his consent and CDs of the recording were imported into Germany. German copyright law gave full protection to German citizens but did not give protection to foreign artists in respect of works effected outside Germany. The Court held that under Art.7 of EC Treaty, a Member State cannot discriminate against citizens of another Member State. Therefore, nationals of another Member State have the right to enjoy the longer term of protection under German copyright law.

For the media, therefore, it is a two-edged sword. At one level, it provides much-needed protection for economic interests in published or broadcast works. A good idea can be very lucrative; it can have immense commercial value. It may generate not only profitable individual works but entire series of profit-making publications as well as substantial other revenue, for example, from merchandising or film, television or electronic exploitation.[215] The law of copyright recognises the originality and the skill, the investment of time and effort in putting the idea into concrete form, as well as the risk that, once reduced to tangible, concrete form, the idea can then be copied by others, especially nowadays with technology. So the law acts to protect this investment, to provide the incentive and to minimise the risk. Copyright law will provide protection, but it may do so at the expense of freedom of expression and the right to report.[216] Key issues that arise in relation to copyright protection, therefore, from the point of view of the media, include the nature and scope of original or creative work, who is entitled to the protection of the law in relation to the work and what is the extent of the protection.

Up until the year 2000, copyright in Ireland was governed by the Copyright Act 1963, which was modelled on the British Act of 1956. With advances in technology[217] and developments in European[218] and international law,[219] by the end of the century that Act had become outmoded in many respects and was in serious need of updating. Some adjustments were made prior to 2000. The Intellectual Property (Miscellaneous Provisions) Act 1998, for example, amended the 1963 Act to strengthen the position of the rights-holder in civil actions for copyright infringement and substantially increased the penalties, as well as providing for criminal prosecutions.

Such is the complexity of copyright nowadays[220] that the Copyright Act

---

[215] See Hugh Jones, *Publishing Law* (Routledge, London, 1996), p.3.

[216] For a discussion of the tension between the two in the UK context, see M.D. Birnhack, "Acknowledging the Conflict between Copyright Law and Freedom of Expression under the Human Rights Act" [2003] ENT. L.R. 24.

[217] For example, in *Mandarin Records Ltd v Mechanical Copyright Protection Society (Ireland) Ltd* (High Court, October 5, 1998), Barr J. had to consider whether power CDs constituted "records" and therefore fell within the 1963 Act. Also in *Universal City Studios Inc v Mulligan* [1998] 1 I.L.R.M. 438, Laffoy J. had to consider whether video cassettes were cinematographic films for the purposes of the Act. The Report of the Information Society Steering Committee (*Information Society Ireland: Strategy for Action*, March 1997) noted that the 1963 Act did not regulate adequately the issues arising in the information age.

[218] European Directive 91/250/EEC on the legal protection of computer programs, Directive 92/100/EEC on rental and lending rights, Directive 93/83/EEC on cable and satellite, Directive 93/98/EEC on the term of copyright, Directive 96/9/EC on the legal protection of databases.

[219] The WTO Agreement on Trade Related Intellectual Property Rights (the TRIPS agreement) 1994, the Berne Convention for the Protection of Literary and Artistic Works (Paris 1971, amended 1979), the Rome Convention 1960, the World Intellectual Property Organisation (WIPO) Copyright Treaty 1996 and the WIPO Performances and Phonograms Treaty 1996.

[220] Even at the beginning of the twentieth century, Mark Twain complained: "Only one thing is impossible for God: to find any sense in any copyright law on the planet" (Notebook, May 23, 1903). Given the complexity of copyright law, the present text can

2000 was a very long time in preparation, which led to infringement proceedings against Ireland in the European Court of Justice for failure to transpose the EC Directive on rental and lending rights in time.[221] The Act, as it finally emerged, contains 376 sections, is divided into seven parts, subdivided into chapters, and three schedules, which are also divided into parts.[222] As well as generally updating the law and taking account of international obligations, the Copyright Act 2000 also introduced some entirely new concepts, including moral rights, which had long been a feature of the civil law system in other European states but not of the common law system. It also adds new provisions on performers' rights[223] and provides a range of civil and criminal measures to deal with copyright infringement and other matters. Virtually all of the provisions of the Act came into force on January 1, 2001.

11.6.1 The Copyright Act 2000

Part I of the Act deals with definitions and the interpretation of various terms and concepts, as well as a number of procedural matters and the jurisdiction of the courts. The term "broadcast" is defined, as are the terms "cable programme" and "cable programme service".[224] The meaning to be attributed to "encrypted broadcasts"[225] and to the "making and protection of broadcasts"[226] is also set

---

only pinpoint and outline some of the more salient rules and principles, with particular reference to the media. For a detailed analysis of the law, see the annotated version of the Act (Adele Murphy and Colm Kelly, *Copyright and Related Rights Act 2000* (Round Hall Sweet & Maxwell, Dublin, 2002)) and leading textbooks, such as Robert Clark, *Irish Copyright and Design Law* (Butterworths, Dublin, 2001), and in Britain, *Copinger and Skone James on Copyright* (Sweet & Maxwell, London, 1999), and Laddie, Prescott, Vitoria, *The Modern Law of Copyright and Designs* (3rd ed., Butterworths, London, 2000).

[221] See above, n.145. The Court did not accept Ireland's argument that the delay was due to the fact that it was engaged in a major revision of copyright law.

[222] See the annotated version of the Act, above, n.220. For discussion of various aspects of the Bill, prior to enactment, see David Vaver, "Moral Rights: the Irish Spin" (1999) 3(3) I.I.P.R. 3; Mr Justice Hugh Laddie, "Copyright Law: Perspectives from a Neighbouring Island" (1998) 2 (1) I.I.P.R. 5; Colm O'Dwyer, "Copyright and Related Rights Bill, 1999 and the Music Industry" (2000) B.R. 350; and for a short overview of the Act, Terence Coghlan, "The Copyright & Related Rights Act 2000" (2001) B.R. 294 or Raymond Byrne and William Binchy, *Annual Review of Irish Law 2000* (Round Hall Sweet & Maxwell, Dublin, 2001), p.25.

[223] See, Colm Kelly, *Performers' Rights*, unpublished LL.M. thesis, NUI, Galway, 2001.

[224] "Broadcast" is defined in s.2 as a "means of transmission by wireless means, including by terrestrial or satellite means, for direct public reception or for presentation to members of the public of sounds, images or data or any combination of sounds, images or data, or the representations thereof, but does not include MMDS service".

[225] S.5 explains the circumstances in which encrypted broadcasts will be considered to come within the definition of "broadcast" in s.2, notably where the decoding equipment is made available by, or with the authority of, the person making the broadcast. It therefore addresses the situation that arose in *News Datacom v Lyons* [1994] 1 I.L.R.M. 450. The defendant began selling at a much lower cost a smart card not produced or authorised by the plaintiffs but which could unscramble the plaintiffs' television signals transmitted *via* satellite in a scrambled form. The plaintiffs sought an injunction to prevent sale of the card on the basis that the only way the defendant could produce such a card was by copying the plaintiffs' card, *i.e.* by breach of copyright.

out. Part II contains the main substance of the Act. It addresses the issues of subsistence of copyright, authorship, duration, rights of copyright owner, exceptions, moral rights, dealings, infringements and remedies, copyright licensing schemes and associated miscellaneous matters. Part III deals with performers' rights and Part IV with performers' moral rights. Part V deals with the law on databases, Part VI with the jurisdiction of the Controller and Part VII with Technological Protection Measures.

As Murphy and Kelly[227] note, copyright is a negative right that affords copyright owners the right to prevent others from carrying out certain acts, such as copying, distributing, lending or interfering in another manner with the subject-matter of the copyright. It is defined in section 17(1):

> "Copyright is a property right whereby, subject to this Act, the owner of the copyright in any work may undertake or authorise other persons in relation to that work to undertake certain acts in the State, being acts which are designated by this Act as acts restricted by copyright in a work of that description".[228]

The first thing to note about the definition is that it categorises copyright as a "property" right. It has long been recognised as a form of intellectual property, but Keane J. in *PPI v Cody*[229] viewed it as part of the right to private property under the Constitution, when he held:

> "The right of the creator of a literary, dramatic, musical or artistic work not to have his or her creation stolen or plagiarised is a right of private property within the meaning of Article 40.3.2 and 43.1 of the Constitution, as is the similar right of a person who has employed his or her technical skills and/or capital in the sound recording of a musical work ... [It] is the duty of the organs of the State, including the courts, to ensure, as best they may that these rights are protected from unjust attack and, in the case of injustice done, vindicated".

A second observation of practical importance is that the right is automatic and does not have to be registered in any formal sense, although when copyright is contested, some proof of "creation" or ownership may be necessary in

---

[226] S.6 covers broadcasts both within the EEA and outside it; *cf.* Broadcasting Act 2001, s.37 (above, n.47) and Art.2(3) of the Television without Frontiers Directive (above, nn.140, 148).

[227] Above, n.220. While the definition provides that copyright is the exclusive right to do certain things, the reality is that copyright is the exclusive right to prevent other people doing certain things (see Judge McCracken, "Copyright in Ireland – The State of Play – Statutory Provisions", The Copyright Association of Ireland Inaugural Seminar 1996).

[228] The "acts" referred to are set out in ss.37–42. They include a reproduction right, making available right, distribution right and rental and lending right. Certain infringements and secondary infringements are set out in ss.43–8.

[229] [1994] 2 I.L.R.M. 241, at 247. Barrington, J. in *Coughlan v BCC and RTÉ* (above, Chap.8) said that equality in Art.40 of the Constitution refers to equality of persons not ideas, that ideas have no rights under our Constitution or otherwise because rights (including political rights) pertain to persons not to ideas (at para.132).

evidence.[230] The right attendant on ownership of copyright is the right to "authorise" others to make certain use(s) of the "work". Copyright, therefore, applies not to ideas as such but to ideas expressed in some tangible or concrete form.[231] Copyright law applies not to an idea but to a "work", that is, something that is printed or recorded in some other way.[232] Furthermore, the Act authorises use of the work "in the State". It is therefore of national application but operates within the framework of EC law and international co-operation.[233]

Copyright, as so defined, subsists in the types of work listed in section 17(2):

"(a) original literary, dramatic, musical or artistic works;
(b) sound recordings, films, broadcasts or cable programmes;
(c) the typographical arrangement of published editions;
(d) original databases".

Those categories will be considered in turn. First, though, it may be noted that the word "original", which is defined in the Act only in the context of "origi-

---

[230] Even when there is evidence, there can be difficulties. See, for example, the US case, *Repp v Webber* 1994 (858 F.Supp. 1292, 1301 (SDNY 1994)), where Ray Repp, a composer of religious music, published as sheet music, performed at concerts, etc., gave a handmade cassette of some of his work to Bobby Vee, a mutual friend of his and of Julian Lloyd Webber, brother of Andrew. Later, when the song "Phantom Song" came out and was featured in *Phantom of the Opera*, Repp claimed copyright infringement. He claimed that Webber had had access to his material, but the court held that he had not established that Webber had had a reasonable opportunity to hear the prior song. Webber's admitted fondness for religious music was not sufficient proof either. The court also found that the songs were not strikingly similar. Webber produced uncontradicted evidence of independent creation, namely the evidence of Sarah Brightman of collaboration on it. However, the appeal court reversed, and sent the issue for trial (132 F.3d 882, 891 (2d Cir. 1997)).

[231] Claims for "idea theft" are not uncommon in the US, particularly in relation to successful films. There were over 20 idea-submission claims in respect of the film *ET* (Extra-Terrestrial) for example (E. Whetmore, *Media America* 154 (3d ed., Wadsworth Publishing, Belmont, CA, 1985), cited in Arthur Campbell, *Entertainment Law: Cases and Materials* (Austin & Winfield, London, 1994) at p.165).

[232] Section 17(3) states: "Copyright protection shall not extend to the ideas and principles which underlie any element of a work, procedures, methods of operation or mathematical concepts and, in respect of original databases, shall not extend to their contents and is without prejudice to any rights subsisting in those contents". It reflects the position under the 1963 Act (see, for example, *Gormley v EMI Records (Ireland) Ltd* [1999] 1 I.L.R.M. 178) and embodied in TRIPS, which states at Art.9(2): "Copyright protection shall extend to expressions and not to ideas, procedures, methods of operations or mathematical concepts as such".

[233] The central principle of the international conventions is that each contracting state grants the same protection to the citizens of the other contracting states as it does to its own. The nature, extent and duration of the protection, therefore, depend on national law but the Conventions also lay down minimum standards so that at least there is some level of uniformity. Some states give higher levels of protection than others; therefore, there are some weak links and there is also the difficulty that not all states are parties to the conventions. Thus uniformity or harmonisation between states is an important goal for players in the entertainment industry.

nal database" and computer program,[234] applies only to those and to literary, dramatic, musical or artistic works. Secondly, it may be noted that to the traditional areas of copyright in (a) original literary, dramatic, musical or artistic works, and (b) sound recordings, films, broadcasts or cable programmes, are added (c) typographical arrangements of published editions and original databases. Thirdly, it may be noted that, in the context of the media, particularly the audiovisual or entertainment media, there may be multiple copyright involved. In a television programme, for instance, there may be separate copyright owners in the case of each of the various components (the script, screenplay, theme or background music, not to mention photographs, archive and other material that might be used, as well as the film and the programme itself once it is broadcast).[235] In relation to music also, there can be separate copyrights existing in the words of a song, in the music of a song, and in the actual recording of a song. There is no copyright in news, as such, although there could be in the presentation or format. A media organisation cannot, therefore, have exclusive rights to the reporting of events of public importance.[236]

11.6.1.1 Original literary, dramatic, musical or artistic works

The authors of literary, dramatic, musical and artistic works have a proprietary interest in their work and under copyright law can authorise or license its use and take legal action if their rights are infringed.[237] Since it is the author who has the right to authorise use of the work, the rules on authorship are of particular interest. The "author" is the person who creates the work. In most cases it is clear who the author is. In the case of a photograph, for example, it is the photographer. In the case of a sound recording, it is the producer; in the case of a film, the producer and principal director.[238] The author of a work is said to be the first owner of the copyright, except when the work is made by an employee in the course of employment, or the work is the subject of Government or Oireachtas copyright, or that of a prescribed international organisation, or

---

[234] S.2. In both contexts it is defined as the author's "own intellectual creation". The degree of originality required is generally not very high. In the *Magill* case (above, n.195), for example, it was accepted by the courts that copyright exists in television listings, that they constitute an original work and therefore attract copyright protection. Normally, it is sufficient to show that skill, labour and judgment have been expended.

[235] In fact any work that involves skill, labour and judgment, whether in the research, writing or translation, or in the putting together and presentation of a film, video, broadcast or publication, may attract copyright protection. There is no copyright in retransmission, for example, by cable television, unless the content is altered (s.20)). For an American perspective with regard to Internet TV, see Baoding Hsieh Fan, "When Channel Surfers Flip to the Web: Copyright Liability for Internet Broadcasting" (2000) 52(3) *Federal Communications Law Journal* 619.

[236] See, further, the discussion in Robertson and Nicol, *Media Law* (4th ed., Penguin Books, London, 2002), pp.296–8 and the discussion below of s.23 of the 2000 Act.

[237] The interpretation of "author" is addressed in s.21 of the Act and the acts which can be "authorised" or restricted are detailed in s.37.

[238] For the other main categories, see s.21. The term "producer" is defined in the Act. For a commentary on the section, see Murphy and Kelly, above, n.220, pp.41–2 and Robertson and Nicol, above, n.236, pp.324–6.

is conferred on some other person by an enactment.[239] The situation of journalists in the employment of media organisations is considered below.

Copyright in literary, dramatic, musical or artistic works lasts for the lifetime of the author and for 70 years after his/her death, regardless of when the work is first published. In the case of anonymous or pseudonymous works, copyright lasts for 70 years after the work is first lawfully made available to the public.[240] The period under the 1963 Act was 50 years. The extension of the period in 1995 in accordance with EC law, caused certain difficulties. For instance, it meant that some works that were out of copyright prior to 1995, under the 50-year rule, had the copyright period revived under the 70-year rule.

An example is the works of James Joyce. In *Sweeney v National University of Ireland Cork t/a Cork University Press*,[241] an interlocutory injunction was granted by the High Court, preventing the inclusion of extracts from the works of James Joyce in an anthology of twentieth century Irish literature. Copyright in the works of James Joyce had lapsed under the 50-year rule in 1992 but was revived under the EC Term Directive.[242] The regulations giving effect to the Directive provided that any person who before October 29, 1993 undertook the exploitation of the literary work or made preparations of a substantial nature to exploit such work when such work was not protected would not be liable to the owner of the copyright as revived.[243] Smyth J. stated:

> "the estate [the Joyce estate which owned the copyright] seeks to protect the integrity of the reputation of James Joyce as a major literary figure, and to protect the spirit, letter and integrity of his works ... this matter is not simply about the amount of a licence fee for the use of a given set of extracts; it is more importantly about the source of the material for the extracts and the input the estate would have in relation to the treatment of those works".[244]

In the judge's opinion this alleged loss was not quantifiable or capable of being compensated by an award of damages; therefore, the injunction was

---

[239] S.23(1). Government copyright is retained in the Act, although, in Europe, only Ireland and the UK recognise government copyright in this way. Government copyright lasts for 50 years (s.191), Oireachtas copyright also for 50 years (s.193) and similarly that of international organisations (s.196).

[240] S.24. The duration of copyright was harmonised upwards in the EC Duration of Copyright ("Term") Directive EC 93/98. In the case of literary, dramatic, musical and artistic works it was raised from the 50-year period pertaining under the 1963 Act to 70 years.

[241] [2001] 1 I.L.R.M. 310. See also Anthony Robinson, "Copyright in Joyce's Ulysses: an Act for the Discouragement of Learning?" [2002] ENT. L.R. 177.

[242] Directive 93/98/EEC, first implemented in Ireland by the European Communities (Term of Protection of Copyright) Regulations of 1995, and now by s.24 of the 2000 Act. Joyce died in 1941; therefore copyright expired under the 50-year rule on January 1, 1992. Copyright was revived from July 1, 1995 under the 70-year rule.

[243] Article 14 of the Regulations of 1995 (above, n.242). A number of new texts were prepared or published during that time. The edition at issue in *Sweeney* was by Danis Rose and was published in 1997.

[244] On the "moral right" to integrity, see further below.

granted. The anthology was published without the extracts.[245] In a separate case, *The Irish Times* settled a copyright claim arising out of a webcast of James Joyce's *Ulysses*. The webcast, to celebrate Bloomsday on June 16, 1998, involved a global reading by well-known personalities of *Ulysses* over the internet, carried on the Irish Times' website, *www.ireland.com*. The Joyce estate argued that the webcast was a breach of copyright and instituted High Court proceedings against *The Irish Times* and the main sponsor, Irish Distillers. However, the court proceedings were settled out of court, prior to the hearing, on the basis of a payment of costs and damages and agreement to a permanent injunction, which would prevent any future webcast.[246]

(i) Literary works

A literary work is defined as "a work, including a computer program, but does not include a dramatic or musical work or an original database, which is written, spoken or sung" (section 2(1)). The Act does not elaborate further but case law under the 1963 Act had established some of the parameters. Thus in *Magill*,[247] Lardner J. in the High Court held that the term "literary work" in sections 2 and 8 of the Copyright Act 1963 was not confined to work exhibiting literary art or style but had the broad sense of any written or printed composition. Furthermore, the requirement of originality related to the expression of matter in writing or print rather than the ideas expressed. A compilation for the purposes of section 2 would entitle its author to copyright under section 8 if the written or printed work was an original composition and involved labour, time and skill in its compilation. The television listings at issue in *Magill* were, therefore, "literary works" within the sense of the Act and the television stations were entitled to copyright, which had been infringed by *Magill*.[248] In *Gormley v EMI*,[249] however, the judge held that the skill, labour and judgment necessary to create a literary work had not been demonstrated.[250]

---

[245] *The Irish Times*, February 19, 2001. The James Joyce estate, which owns the copyright, also stopped a musical adaptation at the Edinburgh Fringe Festival in July 2000 (*The Sunday Times*, September 17, 2000).

[246] *The Sunday Times*, July 15, 2001. *Cf. Joyce Estate v Macmillan Publishers* (*The Irish Times*, November 23, 2001), an English case which held that an edition of James Joyce's *Ulysses*, by Irish scholar, Danis Rose, was in breach of copyright.

[247] Above, n.195, [1989] I.R. 554, [1990] I.L.R.M. 534. Lardner J. also considered the competition issue (see above).

[248] *ibid.* at 563. The definition of "literary work" in the 1963 Act included any written table or compilation. The express inclusion of computer programs in the definition of "literary work" in the 2000 Act is, however, an innovation and is in accordance with European and international obligations; see Annotated version of the Act, above, n.220. See further ss.80–2 of the Act and Pt II of the Second Schedule, which repeals earlier regulations governing the categorisation of computer programs and para.9(2) of the First Schedule, which provides that the Act applies to all computer programs, irrespective of the date of their creation.

[249] Above, n.232.

[250] Case law has established other examples falling within the scope of "literary work", for example, letters [including letters to newspapers], game rules, newspapers, telegrams, exam papers, and a list of words used as a telegraph code: see *Copinger and Skone James on Copyright*, above, n.220, Vol.1, para.3.11. Also, football fixture lists, opinion polls, railway timetables: see Robertson and Nicol, *Media Law*, above, n.236, at p.292.

Copyright will generally not subsist in names, titles or slogans. Thus, in *Warner Bros v CBS*,[251] concerning a mystery-detective story called "The Maltese Falcon", a publishing contract was entered into and later certain defined and detailed exclusive rights passed to Warner Brothers by contract to use "The Maltese Falcon" in motion pictures, radio and television. The use of the characters and their names were not specified, so a question arose as to whether Warner Brothers had an exclusive right to their use or whether others could contract to use them also. It was shown by reference to custom and practice that writers do not usually part with these, so Warner Brothers lost the case.

While a literary work does not have to be in writing, "writing" is defined as including "any form of notation or code whether by hand or otherwise and regardless of the method by which, or medium, in or on which, it is recorded" (section 18(2)(1)). In *Gormley v EMI*, which concerned a tape-recording ("Give up yer aul sins") of children telling Bible stories taught to them by their teacher, Barron J. agreed that no distinction in principle existed between taking down speech in shorthand and recording it on tape. Nonetheless, he held that "the symbol which comprises the notation must be capable without more of being understood. This is not so with a magnetic trace. As a result, it is not entitled to protection as a literary work".[252]

(ii) Dramatic, musical and artistic works

Dramatic, musical and artistic works must also be original. To be "original" they must involve an element of independent labour, skill or judgment. A "dramatic work" is defined as including "a choreographic work or a work of mime". It does not have to be in writing but must be capable of being physically performed,[253] and a key element appears to be action or human movement.[254] It thus includes plays, sketches and screenplays, but not unscripted "gags" or "routines", unless recorded in some fashion,[255] or mere stage props or wardrobe, although some of these may be protected in other ways.[256]

---

[251] 216 F.2d 945 (9th Cir. 1954), 348 U.S. 971 (1955). The main character was Detective Sam Spade. Character names may be protected instead by trade mark, *e.g.* Disney characters. See, Reuben Stone, "Copyright Protection for Titles, Character Names and Catch-phrases in the Film and Television Industry" [1996] 5 ENT. L.R.178. See also the long-running saga on the ownership of "James Bond", discussed in Keith Poliakoff, "License to Copyright: the Ongoing Dispute over the Ownership of James Bond" (2000) 18(2) Cardozo Arts & Ent. L.J. 387.

[252] Above, n.232, at 185. Had this case been decided following the passage of the 2000 Act, it is possible that a different conclusion would have been reached; see Terence Coghlan, "The Copyright & Related Rights Act 2000" (2001) 6(5) BR 294 at 295.

[253] An example is the English case *Norowzian v Arks Ltd* [1999] F.S.R. 79, Court of Appeal, November 11, 1999, concerning the very successful Guinness advertisement featuring a man dancing to music with a Guinness glass in the foreground.

[254] See *Creation Records v News Group Newspapers Ltd* [1997] E.M.L.R. 444; *Nine Network Australia Pty Ltd v Australian Broadcasting Corporation* (2000) 48 I.P.R. 333.

[255] Section 18 provides that copyright shall not subsist in a literary, dramatic or musical work or database until that work is recorded in writing or otherwise by or with the consent of the author. Copyright can then subsist in both the recording and the work that is recorded.

[256] For example, performers' rights are protected in the Act. As to whether costume designs

A musical work is defined as "a work consisting of music but does not include any words or action intended to be sung, spoken or performed with the music". The words or lyrics are considered separately, therefore, as are the sound recordings, the records, CDs or DVDs. As noted above, therefore, there can be separate copyrights existing in the words of a song, in the music of a song, and in the actual recording of a song.[257] A piece of recorded music, which has been broadcast, may have three separate copyrights involved: in the music itself, in the recording and in the broadcast.

An artistic work is defined as including "irrespective of their artistic quality", such works as (a) photographs, paintings, drawings, diagrams, maps, charts, plans, engravings, etchings, lithographs, woodcuts, prints or similar works, collages or sculptures (including any cast or model made for the purposes of a sculpture), (b) works of architecture ... and (c) works of artistic craftsmanship.[258] A resale right for the benefit of the author of an original work of art has been recognised in an EC Directive of 2001.[259] It enables the authors of graphic and plastic art to have an economic interest in the subsequent sales of their work, which can sometimes be for prices far in excess of the original price. The right lasts for 70 years after the death of the artist.

11.6.1.2 Sound recordings, films, broadcasts or cable programmes

This category concerns certain forms of delivery of audiovisual services. As such, they do not have the same requirement of originality as literary, dramatic, musical and artistic works. Sound recordings are defined in the Act as "a fixation of sounds, or of the representations thereof, from which the sounds are capable of being reproduced, regardless of the medium on which the recording is made, or the method by which the sounds are reproduced". As Murphy and Kelly point out,[260] the definition is technology neutral, an important consideration in Media Law generally, given the rapid pace of technological development and the consequent risk of laws becoming quickly out of date. Sound recordings are normally associated, particularly in the case law, with the production of music, but apply more widely.

Copyright in sound recordings lasts for 50 years after it is made or, if it is lawfully made available to the public during that period, copyright will run for 50 years from the date on which it is made available.[261] There is a right to play

---

and stage sets are protected as artistic craftsmanship, see D. Michael Rose, "Copyright in Stage Production Elements: Requirements of Originality and Record under English Law" [1998] ENT. L.R. 30. Other rights may be protected by contract law or by the tort of "passing off".

[257] The words may constitute a literary work. The term "sound recording" is defined in the Act (s.2(1)). See also s.19, and ss.97–8 in relation to the playing of sound recordings.

[258] See Murphy and Kelly, above, n.220, particularly the case law regarding film sets. The term "photograph" is defined in s.2(1) of the Act. *Re* digital photographs, see Susan Corbett, "The Digital Photograph: intellectual property of ... whom?" (2001) 6(2) *Communications Law* 46.

[259] Directive 2001/84/EC, O.J. L 272/32, October 13, 2001.

[260] Above, n.220, at p.35.

[261] S.26. In any event, the terms under the 2000 Act, in accordance with the Directive, run from the beginning of the next calendar year, *i.e.* January 1.

sound recordings in public or include them in a broadcast or cable transmission service, provided notice is given to the relevant licensing bodies and payment is made.[262]

Film, the major entertainment medium of the early part of the twentieth century, involves huge investment and high risk. Nowadays, films are often co-productions and have complex financial arrangements. However, the definition of film in the 2000 Act is much broader than just cinematographic film. The Act defines a film as "a fixation on any medium from which a moving image may, by any means, be produced, perceived or communicated through a device". The Act recognises the nature and structure of film-making. Films, therefore, are considered "a work of joint authorship",[263] unless the producer and principal director happen to be the same person.[264] Copyright in film lasts for 70 years after the death of the principal director or author of the screenplay, dialogue or specially commissioned music, whichever of them is last to die.[265]

Despite the fact that film was a major entertainment medium early in the twentieth century, and its content regulated in Ireland since the enactment of the Censorship of Films Act 1923, no copyright in film, as such, was recognised prior to the 1963 Copyright Act.[266] The inclusion of "cinematographic film" in the 1963 Act was relied on in *Universal City Studios*[267] in order to determine whether a new technology, that of the video cassette, was covered by the Act. The court held that it fulfilled all the basic requirements of the definition of cinematographic film in the Act and therefore could be treated as such for the purposes of copyright.

Copyright in broadcasts lasts for 50 years.[268] As the Copyright Act 1963

---

[262] The details of the requirements are set out in s.38, as are the procedures for referring the matter to the Controller (of Patents, Designs and Trade Marks) if agreement cannot be reached. There were not very many cases taken under the 1963 Act, considering that it was in operation for nearly 40 years, but, of those that were, a number concerned payments and some involved the Controller, as the 1963 Act did not give a right to play such recordings in public or include them in a broadcast; it only gave a record company a right to remuneration. See, for example, *PPI v Cody* [1994] 2 I.L.R.M. 241 and *PPI v Controller of Industrial and Commercial Property* (1993) 1 I.R. 267, (1996) 1 I.L.R.M. 1 (SC). PPI (Phonographic Performance (Ireland) Ltd) is a copyright collection agency. Pt VI of the 2000 Act deals with the jurisdiction of the Controller.

[263] The principle of joint authorship applies to "work produced by the collaboration of two or more authors in which the contribution of each author is not distinct from that of the other author or authors" (s.22(1)).

[264] Section 22(2).

[265] Section 25(1). If the film is lawfully released to the public during the 70-year period following the death of the last of those persons, the copyright will run for 70 years from the date of release (s.25(2)). Once the copyright has expired there is no infringement.

[266] Films made prior to October 1, 1964 could be considered original dramatic works under the Industrial and Commercial Property Act 1927, and remain in that category under the 2000 Act (Sch.1, Pt I, para.5). See also para.6 regarding the soundtracks of such films. The First Schedule to the 2000 Act, Pt I sets out transitional provisions, while Pt II sets out the provisions applying to works made before July 1, 1912.

[267] Above, n.217.

[268] Section 27(1). The copyright in a repeat broadcast expires at the same time as the copyright in the original broadcast and no copyright subsists after that date (s.27(2)). For the definition of broadcast and other aspects of the Act dealing with broadcasts, see above, nn.224–6. The Committee of Ministers of the Council of Europe adopted

was passed shortly after television broadcasting began in Ireland, only RTÉ had copyright under it. When the new commercial stations came on stream in 1989, following the enactment of the Radio and Television Act 1988, copyright was extended to them, not by the 1988 Act, as might have been expected, but by a statutory instrument in 1991.[269] Under the 2000 Act, broadcasting means transmission by wireless means, but excluding MMDS. Cable transmission, by wire (not wireless), is considered separately but the same period of copyright protection applies (50 years).[270] A cable programme service is defined as:

> "a service, including MMDS, which consists wholly or mainly of sending sounds, images or data or any combination of sounds, images or data, or the presentations thereof, by means of a telecommunications system–
>
> (a) for reception at 2 or more places (whether for simultaneous reception or at different times in response to requests by different users), or
> (b) for presentation to members of the public".[271]

Accordingly, the internet has been considered to come within the definition of a cable programme, although the definition also lists a number of exclusions, which would cover *inter alia* interactive services and real-time chat rooms.[272]

Of interest to book and newspaper publishers is the provision on typographical arrangements. This protection is separate from content and covers layout, presentation and design. It recognises the labour and skill expended in

---

Recommendation Rec(2002)7 on measures to enhance the protection of the neighbouring rights of broadcasting organisations (September 11, 2002).

[269] S.I. No. 101 of 1991. S.45 of the 1963 Copyright Act allowed the Government to extend, by order, the provisions of the Act relating to sound or television broadcasts, which RTÉ had under the Act, to others.

[270] S.28. See also ss.99–105 for other aspects of copyright relating to broadcasts and cable. Irish operators of cable and MMDS networks were required to obtain the permission of owners of copyright in any foreign broadcasts, including the British stations, that were to be transmitted by cable or MMDS in Ireland. Due to the difficulty in acquiring all these necessary authorisations, a standard form copyright licensing agreement was adopted to represent the terms upon which licences would be granted to cable and MMDS operators in Ireland. The European Commission took a favourable view of the agreement (*Re BBC Enterprises Ltd* [1993] 5 C.M.L.R. 300). The EC Directive on satellite broadcasting and cable retransmission (Directive 93/83/EEC O.J. L 248, October 6, 1993, p.15), which requires certain minimum standards of protection, provides that the right of copyright owners to grant or refuse authorisation can be exercised only through a collecting agency. See also, Report on the Application of Council Directive 93/83/EEC on the Co-ordination of Certain Rules Concerning Copyright and Rights Related to Copyright Applicable to Satellite and Cable Retransmission, COM(2002) 430 final, July 26, 2002. Section 174 of the 2000 Act deals with cable retransmission rights.

[271] S.2(1). A telecommunications system is stated to mean "a system for conveying sounds, data or information or any combination of sounds, images, or information, or the representations thereof, by means of a wire, beam or any conducting device through which electronically generated programme-carrying signals are guided over a distance".

[272] See Murphy and Kelly, above, n.220, at pp.36–7 and Baoding Hsieh Fan, above, n.235, regarding internet broadcasting.

designing the format and is therefore a more restricted right than that applying to content. Whereas copyright in content (literary or dramatic work) lasts for 70 years, copyright in typographical arrangements lasts only 50 years.[273]

In the case of a work not previously made available to the public during the copyright term, a person who then makes it available acquires rights for a 25-year period.[274]

11.6.2 Journalists' copyright

Of particular interest to journalists is section 23(2) of the Act, which deals with ownership of copyright in the case of journalists employed by a newspaper or periodical. In general, the author is the owner of the copyright, unless the work is made by an employee in the course of employment, in which case the employer is the first owner. However, in the case of journalists employed in a newspaper or periodical, the journalist remains the author but there is a restriction with regard to usage:

> "Where a work, other than a computer program, is made by an author in the course of employment by the proprietor of a newspaper or periodical, the author may use the work for any purpose, other than for the purposes of making available that work to newspapers or periodicals, without infringing the copyright in the work".

The subsection is the result of a compromise reached during the passage of the Bill.[275] It restricts journalists' use of their work but ensures that the interests of proprietors are safeguarded, at least to the extent of not having journalists passing on work for which they have been paid by the newspaper to other or rival newspapers or periodicals. The provision also gives journalists some window of opportunity by enabling them to use their material for other purposes, such as writing a book or appearing on radio or television.

The position of freelance journalists, who are not employees, is not directly addressed by the section.[276] As freelance journalists are not employees as

---

[273] S.29. On the other hand, copyright in computer-generated works lasts for 70 years (s.30). S.31 deals with works published in volumes, parts, instalments, issues or episodes.

[274] Other than moral rights (s.34). Moral rights are discussed below.

[275] The position is similar to that which pertained under the 1963 Act, s.10(2), though the wording is different and the emphasis is now on the author. However, newspaper proprietors had sought a form of exclusivity as a protection to ensure that journalists would not be able to encroach on or undermine their market. The nub of their argument was that the work of journalists in other branches of the media belongs to the employer, as it does in the case of British newspapers competing in the Irish market, which would put the Irish newspapers at a disadvantage *vis-à-vis* print and electronic competitors. They were concerned that an employee could sell the consequences of a newspaper's investment to someone else first. See Dáil and Seanad Debates on the Bill, particularly May 6, 1999 and October 13, 1999 (Seanad), referring to the objections of the NUJ.

[276] The NUJ announced that it was to take action on behalf of freelance journalists, who claimed that their work was used by the *Examiner* on its website without permission (*The Irish Independent*, February 22, 2002). The US Supreme Court ruled in 2001 in *New York Times v Tasini* (533 U.S. 483 (2001), June 25, 2001) that freelance journalists retain their copyright to articles put on newspaper databases. The *New York Times* said

such, they appear to fall outside the scope of the section.[277] The situation regarding use by newspaper proprietors of journalists' work on the internet is another important question.[278] Technically, as the journalist, and not the publisher, is the author, s/he has the right to authorise or refuse to authorise the use of his/her work on the internet. Whether a journalist will be entitled to give his/her work to an online newspaper or periodical will depend on the interpretation of the phrase "making available that work to newspapers or periodicals". Since the online editions of newspapers, in particular, are now common extensions of the printed version, it may be that they will be considered an integral part of the newspaper.[279] In practice, most of these matters will probably be resolved by inclusion in the terms of the contract with the journalist.

11.6.3 Fair dealing

Another area of interest is the exemption afforded for "fair dealing" with a copyright work. The term encompasses research and private study, criticism and review, incidental inclusion of copyright material, educational, library and archive use, and public administration.[280] Fair dealing for criticism and review, which are of importance to the media, requires sufficient acknowledgment, as does the reporting of current events.[281] The test for incidental inclusion is whether the interests of the copyright owner are unreasonably prejudiced.[282]

---

it would delete all such from the Lexis/Nexis database because negotiating individual charges with 27,000 freelances was not practical (*The Irish Times*, June 27, 2001). See also "Who owns this photograph? A free-lance photographer vs. *The New York Times*" (2001) CJR May/June 60, a short comment on freelance photographers' ownership of their photos, and Séamus Clarke, "Remuneration for Digital Content: the Rights of Authors in an On-line World" (1999) 3(3) IIPR 10.

[277] They are "independent contractors" (with a contract for services, rather than a contract of service, see *Re Sunday Tribune* [1984] I.R. 505); therefore their work is not normally done "in the course of employment" by a newspaper or periodical.

[278] For the situation in other countries, see Bernt Hugenholtz & Annemique de Kroon, "The Electronic Rights War" in *Focus: Copyright Law in the Digital Age* (European Audiovisual Observatory, Strasbourg, 2000), p.9.

[279] Murphy and Kelly suggest otherwise (above, n.220, at p.42). It should be noted also that the subsection entitles the author to use the work "for any purpose" other than for the purposes of making the work available to newspapers or periodicals.

[280] Ss.50–77.

[281] S.51 sets out the detail. See also Murphy and Kelly, above, n.220, for the background and case law; in particular see *Pro Sieben Media AG v Carlton UK Television Ltd* [1999] F.S.R. 610, *Associated Newspapers Group v News Group Newspapers* [1986] R.P.C. 515 and *Ashdown v Telegraph Group* [2001] 4 All ER. 666.

[282] S.52(3). An example from the US is *Amsinck v Columbia Pictures*, 862 F.Supp. 1044, 1050 (5 DNY 1994). A teddy bear mobile appeared in the background in several scenes of a Columbia Pictures film (1 min 36 sec in total). Columbia Pictures had obtained permission to use other copyrighted materials but not the mobile. The court held that it was fair use (the term used in the US for fair dealing), as it was fleeting and impermanent, there was no demonstrable harm, and it may even have benefited the designer; the mobile and film were not directly competing uses, the mobile was not used in ads for the film, and so the defendants were not seeking to profit directly from the plaintiff's creativity. See generally, Susanne Nikoltchev & Francisco Javier Cabrera Blásquez, "Movies Online: Balancing Copyrights and Fair Use" (*IRIS plus* 2002–4).

Likewise, the use of quotes or extracts from a work that has lawfully been made available to the public does not infringe copyright, provided it does not prejudice the interests of the copyright owner and a sufficient acknowledgment is given.[283] Of importance also in the realm of internet publication is the provision relating to transient and incidental copies.[284]

11.6.4 Moral rights

The inclusion of moral rights in the Act is an innovation. Moral rights developed from *droit moral* in French law. Moral rights are non-economic rights that authors have in relation to their works. They are widely recognised in civil law countries, which see copyright not just as an economic matter or means of commercial exploitation of an author's work, but as protection of a work that is a manifestation of the author's creative ability and form of expression, an extension of the author's personality. It was commonly believed that common law countries did not recognise or protect moral rights at all. However, it has been argued, by Dworkin for example, that these rights were protected to some extent indirectly by other branches of law.[285]

---

[283] S.52(4). An interesting question is whether parody comes under this element of the fair dealing doctrine. Directive 2001/29/EC (see further below) specifically mentions caricature, parody and pastiche (Art.5.3(k)). In the US, in *Campbell v Acuff-Rose Music Inc.* (62 USLW 4169 (1994), 510 US 569 (1994)), the Supreme Court held unanimously that a rap version by 2 Live Crew of Roy Orbison's 1960s song "Oh Pretty Woman", made more famous by the movie "Pretty Woman" came within the fair use doctrine. It recognised the value of parody as a form of humorous criticism and comment and gave leeway to the parodist to copy enough to effectively skewer the original, but not so much as to eat into the copyright owner's legitimate rights. See Sherri L. Burr, "Artistic Parody: a Theoretical Construct" (1996) 14 Cardozo Arts & Ent L.J. 65.

[284] S.87. See also s.89 on the use of notes or recordings of spoken words in certain cases, and s.90 on the public reading or recitation of works. For an analysis of recent and current international and European issues relating to the audiovisual media and new technologies, see *Focus: Copyright Law in the Digital Age* (European Audiovisual Observatory, Strasbourg, 2000) and Henning Wiese, "Copyright protection on the Internet – the main legal battles" (2002) 7(4) *Communications Law* 111.

[285] For example, by contract or the torts of passing off, injurious falsehood, defamation. See Gerald Dworkin, "The Moral Right of the Author: Moral Rights and the Common Law Countries" (1995) 19 *Columbia-VLA Jl of Law and the Arts* 229 and Adolf Dietz, "The Moral Right of the Author: Moral Rights and the Civil Law Countries" (1995) 19 *Columbia-VLA Jl of Law and the Arts* 199. An example of passing off is the old case of *Landa v Greenberg* (Chap.1908, Eng.), in which a journalist, who had built up a reputation using a *nom de plume*, was able to use the tort to prevent the paper continuing to produce articles under that *nom de plume* after she had left. American courts have also expanded privacy and personality rights to cover this area, *e.g.* John Lennon, of the Beatles, was able to stop the distribution of a recording of his music on the grounds that poor editing and an unartistic cover design amounted to mutilation of his work (*Big Seven Music Corp. v Lennon* (554 F.2d 504 (2d Cir.1977)). *Cf. Gilliam v ABC* (538 F.2d 14, 2d Cir.1976 – the mutilation of the Monty Python shows, sold by the BBC to ABC, when they were edited to allow for ad. breaks); also *Midler v Ford Motor Co.* (849 F.2d 460 (9th Cir.1988)) and similar cases, where the singer was able to get protection against deceptive exploitation in TV commercials of "sound-alike" renditions of music with which the singer was closely associated. Australia introduced moral rights in the Copyright Amendment (Moral Rights) Act 2000.

Article 6 of the Berne Convention (1971) states:

> "(1) Independently of the author's economic rights, and even after the transfer of the said rights, the author shall have the right to claim authorship of the work, and to object to any distortion, mutilation or other modification, or other derogatory action in relation to the said work, which would be prejudicial to his honour or reputation.
>
> (2) The rights granted to the author … shall, after his death, be maintained, at least until the expiry of the economic rights …
>
> (3) The means of redress for safeguarding the rights granted by this Article shall be governed by the legislation of the country where protection is claimed".[286]

The rights included as moral rights in the 2000 Act are the paternity right, integrity right, the right against false attribution and the right to privacy in photographs and films.[287] The paternity right is the right of the author of a work to be identified as the author. There are certain exceptions to the right. It does not apply, for instance, in the case of a work made for the purpose of reporting current events or for the purposes of a newspaper or periodical, encyclopaedia, dictionary, yearbook or other collective work of reference, or in the case of government copyright.[288]

The integrity right is the right of the author to object to any distortion, mutilation or other modification of, or other derogatory action in relation to the work, which would prejudice his or her reputation.[289] A corollary right to that right is the right to object to false attribution, to being falsely attributed as the author of a work which is not your own, or as the author of a work in an altered state when you did not effect the alterations.[290] The right to privacy in photographs and films applies where such works are commissioned and copyright subsists in the resulting work.[291] All of the moral rights, except the

---

[286] The UK introduced moral rights, so as to conform with the Berne Convention, in the Copyright, Designs and Patents Act 1988, although in limited form.

[287] Ss.107–114. See general commentary, Murphy and Kelly, above, n.220, at pp.109–112.

[288] S.108.

[289] S.109, and exceptions s.110, including the duty of authorised broadcasters and cable programme service providers to exclude material that is likely to offend public morality (s.110(2)(b)(iii)). Well-known cases involving the integrity right include *Morrison Leahy Music Ltd v Lightbond Ltd* [1993] E.M.L.R. 144, in which singer George Michael obtained an injunction to prevent the release of "Bad Boys Megamix", featuring snippets from his songs, and *Huston v Turner Entertainment* [1992] ECC 334, in which the broadcast of a colourised version of the film "Asphalt Jungle", directed by John Huston, was prevented.

[290] S.113. This right was already recognised in s.54 of the Copyright Act 1963. As noted above (n.285), one could also sue for defamation, passing off, etc. The singer Dorothy Squires got £100 damages for false attribution when the *News of the World* in an interview about her marriage to Roger Moore attributed certain remarks to her ([1972] 1 Q.B. 441). The £100 was in addition to libel damages (the case occurred before the 1988 Act in the UK).

[291] S.114. Some examples of situations where this right might apply are given in Chap.5 above, for example, the Sammy Wilson holiday photographs case and Michael Douglas and Catherine Zeta-Jones wedding photographs case. Remedies for infringement of moral rights are set out in s.137.

false attribution right, last for the same period of time as the copyright. The false attribution right lasts for 20 years after the death of the person on whom the right is conferred. All of the rights can be waived, but cannot be assigned or alienated.[292] Part III of the Act deals with rights in performances and performers' rights, including moral rights.[293]

11.6.5 EC Copyright Directive 2001

After the passing of the 2000 Act, a new EC Copyright Directive was finalised.[294] It gives effect, *inter alia*, to the World Intellectual Property Organization (WIPO) Copyright Treaty 1996 and extends core copyright concepts to digital media. The Recitals to the Directive recognise a right of communication to the public, which would cover all forms of communication, including broadcasting and interactive on-demand transmission. It also provides a range of exemptions and defences, which states can tailor to their own needs, provided they satisfy the three-step test set out in Article 9(2) of the Berne Convention. That is, they must apply only in special cases, must not conflict with normal exploitation of the work, and must not unreasonably prejudice the legitimate interests of the author. Article 5(1) of the Directive classifies ISPs as "intermediaries" and exempts them from the reproduction right. Article 6 seeks to ensure that those who benefit from exemptions and defences do not exploit them to keep information out of the public domain, for example, by firewalling or encryption.[295]

---

[292] Ss.115–118. Subsequent provisions of the Act deal with assignment and licences, licensing bodies, offences, and various other matters.

[293] For a detailed study of the topic, see Colm Kelly, above, n.223.

[294] EC Directive 2001/29/EC on the harmonisation of certain aspects of copyright and related rights in the information society, O.J. L 167/10, June 22, 2001 (Infosoc Directive). It was to come into effect in Member States in December 2002, but to date only a very small number of states have implemented it. For an overview of copyright law and the trend apparent in the Directive, see Jan Peter Mussig and Alexander Scheuer, "European Copyright Law and the Audiovisual Media: Are We Moving Towards Cross-Sectoral Regulation?" *IRIS plus* (Supplement to *IRIS* 2003–4), and for trenchant criticism of the Directive itself, see Bernt Hugenholtz, "Why the Copyright Directive is unimportant, and possibly invalid" (2000) 11 E.I.P.R. 501. The Committee of Ministers of the Council of Europe also adopted a Recommendation on measures to protect copyright and neighbouring rights and combat piracy, especially in the digital environment Rec(2001)7, September 5, 2001.

[295] Under Art.6(1), "Member States shall provide adequate legal protection against the circumvention of any effective technological measures", where the person concerned knows or has reasonable grounds to know, that he or she is pursuing that objective. Technological measures are defined as: "… any technology, device or component that, in the normal course of its operation, is designed to prevent or restrict acts, in respect of works or other subject-matter, which are not authorised by the rightholder of any copyright or any right related to copyright as provided for by law or the *sui generis* right provided for in Chapter III of Directive 96/9/EC". Included in the definition are "encryption, scrambling or other trans-formation of the work or other subject-matter or a copy control mechanism, which achieves the protection objective". For a brief review of Ireland's attempts under s.40(1) of the 2000 Act to prevent the introduction of Napster-type services, see Denis Kelleher, "Is Ireland out of tune on copyright?", *Law Society Gazette*, April 2001, 24; *The Irish Times*, May 10, 2002 and August 16, 2002, and for

11.7 ACCOUNTABILITY AND ACCESS

As the media have become more powerful in economic terms, and more pervasive in people's lives, attention has turned in recent years to questions of media accountability. Openness, transparency and accountability have become important factors in the composition and delivery of media regulation also.[296] Decision-making by independent bodies on the basis of readily accessible and clearly articulated principles and criteria has become the accepted standard. The key issues for legislation, as set out in the Council of Europe's Recommendation on the independence of regulators are: precise rules and procedures for appointment and dismissal, independence (including financial independence), transparency, powers and competence (including the adoption of regulations and guidelines, the granting of licences, monitoring of content, handling of complaints and imposing proportionate sanctions).[297]

The accompanying memorandum identifies the importance of being able to respond flexibly and adequately to questions that may be unforeseen and are often complex. It also points out that the primary task of regulatory bodies is not to "police" the broadcasting sector, but rather to ensure that it functions smoothly by establishing a climate of dialogue, openness and trust in dealings with broadcasters. The more the sector expands, and the more complex and dynamic it becomes, the more it needs well-considered and proportionate regulation to ensure that it functions properly.[298]

In the climate of openness and dialogue that has emerged in recent years, access of the public to complaints mechanisms and rights of reply have gained stature. Technology has also supported the direct involvement of the public in the media *via* phone-ins, e-mails, online and mobile polls and discussion programmes. The focus has shifted, therefore, away from the providers of services to some extent to audiences and consumers. Representative organisations and citizens' bodies concerned with various aspects of media coverage have introduced monitoring fora or produced guidelines. For example, the Equality Authority and the Combat Poverty Agency, launching their report, *Perception is Power – Social Exclusion and the Media*, announced that they

---

the role of technological measures in combating music piracy, see Karen Murray, above, n.213. On the wider issues, see Henning Wiese, "The Justification of the Copyright System in the Digital Age" [2002] E.I.P.R. 387

[296] For the basic concepts and their application to the print media in Ireland, see Kevin Boyle and Marie McGonagle, *Media Accountability: The Readers' Representative in Irish Newspapers* (NNI, Dublin, 1995).

[297] Rec(2000)23 of the Committee of Ministers. *A priori* control is specifically ruled out in s.19. The Recommendation seeks to guard against the possibility of arbitrary decision-making: All decisions taken and regulations adopted by the regulatory authorities should be duly reasoned, in accordance with national law; open to review by the competent jurisdictions according to national law and made available to the public (at para.27). See also ARTICLE 19, *Access to the Airwaves: Principles on Freedom of Expression and Broadcast Regulation* (ARTICLE 19, London, 2002), particularly s.4 on Regulatory and Complaints Bodies and s.5 on Licensing.

[298] Council of Europe, Explanatory Memorandum to Recommendation Rec(2000) 23 on the independence and functions of regulatory authorities for the broadcasting sector.

would set up a media forum to raise awareness of social exclusion and encourage journalists to reflect on their coverage of marginalised groups.[299]

While input from ground level is a positive development in the maintenance of standards and responsiveness to the public, the overall effect of the change in focus has been the growth of multi-layered regulation, with a proliferation of licensing, standards, complaints and monitoring bodies, some statutory, some self-regulatory.[300] Most formal regulators operate, within an overall legal framework, on the basis of codes. As a result, regulation has increasingly shifted from direct state regulation to forms of co-regulation, enforced self-regulation (a contradiction in terms) or semi self-regulation.[301] Indeed, the preamble to the Recommendation on the independence of regulators notes that "technical and economic developments, which lead to the expansion and the further complexity of the sector, will have an impact on the role of these authorities and may create a need for greater adaptability of regulation, over and above self-regulatory measures adopted by broadcasters themselves."[302]

The role of the BCI in drawing up codes and that of the BCC in handling complaints of breaches of both statutory obligations and the codes, has been discussed above. Forms of self-regulation in the print,[303] internet[304] and advertising[305] sectors are discussed in earlier chapters.[306] These include the

---

[299] *The Irish Times*, May 16, 2000. The Samaritans and Association of Suicidology also launched their *Media Guidelines on Portrayal of Suicide* (*www.samaritans.org*, *www.ias.ie*).

[300] As the system became unwieldy, some rationalisation was necessary to bring coherence to the converging media industries. See above, n.21 *re* UK.

[301] The use of the terminology still lacks precision. The term "semi-self-regulation" is used in Tom Crone, *Law and the Media* (4th ed., Focal Press, Oxford, 2002) p.258.

[302] Above, n.297.

[303] In 1989 all the national newspapers in Ireland appointed in-house Readers' Representatives to deal with communications and complaints from readers. They were to act on the readers' behalf, to channel complaints to the appropriate person(s) within the organisation and, where necessary, to elicit a suitable remedy. The majority of complaints received since 1989 concerned inaccurate or misleading reporting and, in those newspapers where the system worked well, corrections or clarifications were published, often in the next issue. Only a very small percentage of complaints was left unresolved. See Boyle and McGonagle, above, n.296. The system required a high level of visibility, so that readers would know about it and be in a position to use it, and the co-operation of management, editorial staff and particularly journalists. In the provincial newspapers, which are smaller, mainly weekly publications that are closer to their own community, it is often possible for the editor to handle readers' complaints himself/ herself.

[304] Chapters 5 and 9. The drawing up of codes is encouraged, for example in the EC Directive (2000/31/EC) on Electronic Commerce.

[305] The Advertising Standards Authority of Ireland (ASAI) also operates in co-operation with its counterparts in other European countries to deal with cross-frontier complaints (EASA, *www.easa-alliance.org*).

[306] Chs 4, 5 and 9. The National Union of Journalists (NUJ), with members in both print and broadcast journalism, has a code of conduct and disciplinary system, which was used, for example, in relation to the report in *The Phoenix* magazine which gave rise to the case of *Hilliard v Penfield Enterprises* (see Chap.8). Articles disparaging to the traveller culture (Chap.9) and to the paralympics, published in the *Sunday Independent* (October 22, 2000), gave rise to distress and offence among the public. Neither complaint could be handled by the disciplinary system of the NUJ as the journalist in question was

adoption of ratings systems and on-screen information, primarily as guidance for parents as to the suitability of content for children of various ages.[307] The proposal of the Minister for Justice, to bring in a statutory Press Council in conjunction with defamation law reform,[308] however, goes very much against the trend in the print media across Europe. Press Councils deal with ethics, not law, and in most European countries they remain subject to self-regulation. The form of regulation which seems to be envisaged by the Minister, whereby a Press Council, appointed by Government in accordance with legislation, would devise its own code of standards, is an example of traditional regulation by law, rather than co-regulation or self-regulation.[309]

The advantages of co- and self-regulation, particularly in light of the speed of technological change, lie primarily in their flexibility and adaptability, when compared to law. The ability of the law, particularly at national level, to meet the problems perceived in existing and potential media technology may be rather limited. Legal rules, if difficult to enforce with respect to satellite and digital broadcasting, for example, would be even more so with respect to internet and multimedia services, even if there were agreement as to what the scope and objectives of those legal rules should be.[310] That is to assume, of course, that law has a role to play in this regard and that regulation by law, or by a combination of law and other measures is necessary, which may not be the case. Co- and self-regulatory models also have the advantage of involving the various players concerned, and are premised on consensus-building and enhanced dialogue, shared, collective and individual responsibility, rather than control by law.[311]

However, the European Commission in its White Paper on European Governance[312] sounded a note of caution:

"Co-regulation implies that a framework of overall objectives, basic rights, enforcement and appeal mechanisms, and conditions for monitoring compliance is set in legislation. It should only be used where

---

one of only of a small percentage of journalists in Ireland who are not members of the NUJ. However, a number of voluntary organisations, health boards and local authorities refused to advertise in the paper after the publication concerning the paralympics. The apologies of the journalist and the *Sunday Independent* were carried on the front page of that paper. The paper offered to pay £50,000 to the Paralympic Council of Ireland (*The Irish Times*, October 25, 30, 2000, *The Sunday Times*, November 26, 2000).

307 See Chap.9.

308 Report of the Legal Advisory Group on Defamation, March 2003, available at *www.justice.ie* under "publications". The Newspaper Commission in 1996 recommended self-regulation in the form of a Press Ombudsman (*Report of the Commission on the Newspaper Industry* (pn.2841, The Stationery Office, Dublin, 1996), paras 7.17–7.26).

309 See Report of the Legal Advisory Group on Defamation, above, n.308, at pp.13–19.

310 See generally, Tarlach McGonagle, "Does the Existing Regulatory Framework for Television Apply to the New Media?" *IRIS plus* (*IRIS* 2001–6) and Tarlach McGonagle, "Changing Aspects of Broadcasting: New Territory and New Challenges", *IRIS plus* (*IRIS* 2001–10).

311 See Marie-Laure Lulé, "Self-Regulation and Co-Regulation: a Broadcasting Perspective" in *Co-Regulation of the Media in Europe* (European Audiovisual Observatory, Strasbourg, 2003), p.87, at p.92.

312 European Governance – A White Paper, COM(2001) 428 final.

it adds value and serves the general interest. It is only suited to cases where fundamental rights or major political choices are not called into question. ... Equally, the organizations participating in it must be representative, accountable and capable of following open procedures in formulating and applying agreed rules. This will be a key factor in deciding the added value of a co-regulatory approach in a given case".

One of the worries that arises in the current climate is the overload of regulation, referred to above. However light-touch each layer of that regulation may be, the more layers there are the greater the burden on the sector and ultimately the user.[313] While the BAI may be intended to be the overarching authority for broadcasting and related services in Ireland, it in turn will be subject to the constant twin-track flow of law and policy, however useful, coming from the EU and Council of Europe. Even within Ireland, the BAI will not be able to act on the basis of broadcasting regulation alone, whether legislative or co-regulation. It must act in tandem with not only the players in the broadcasting sector but also with the regulators in the field of telecommunications (ComReg) and competition law (the Competition Authority).

Another worry is the overkill of information with which the public is being constantly bombarded. That necessitates a navigational tool. Just as the best of the search engines assist in navigating the internet, so EPGs or second generation EPGs will need to be honed to do likewise with broadcast programme schedules, webcasts and related services.[314] Interactive television brings the citizen/consumer more into the picture and allows him/her to exercise choice, but in order to do so in a meaningful way, the means available must be straightforward, and access barriers must be kept to a minimum. The interoperability of the necessary equipment is therefore a key issue and control or regulation of technological gateways and bottlenecks[315] seems inevitable, unless technology can find its own solution. The future of regulation, therefore, will be coloured to some extent by the progress of the new media.

11.7.1 The new media

The creation of the World Wide Web in 1993, with the addition of sound and moving images (film) in 1996, has revolutionised the communications media. It was the single biggest advance in the technology of the media since the

---

[313] The "who guards the guardian" syndrome, which leads to a chain of regulation and builds up unnecessary bureaucracy.

[314] The Committee of Ministers of the Council of Europe has spoken of public authorities trying to support citizens in reaching for reliable and comprehensive information through all media and avoiding the real dangers of confusion and abuse, not by censorship but by education for discernment and exemplary public information (Message to the World Summit on the Information Society (WSIS), issued June 24, 2003).

[315] Fair and non-discriminatory access to electronic programme guides (EPGs), Application Programme Interfaces (APIs), conditional access systems, pay-TV and such like, is a goal to be pursued. See generally, *Co-Regulation of the Media in Europe* (European Audiovisual Observatory, Strasbourg, 2003).

invention of the printing-press by Gutenberg in the fifteenth century.[316] By the beginning of 2003, the search-engine Google, had indexed over three billion individual pages. Information had been internationalised, indeed globalised, and the technology is still expanding with the advance of wireless connectivity.

Internet technology, which involves publishing and distribution, enables point to multipoint and point to point communication on a vast scale, with the result that national laws to regulate or curtail it are less effective.[317] Many of the assumed truths of the traditional or classical media era are turned upside-down. Even the definition of journalism and journalist is called into question, and the issue of censorship takes on a new meaning.[318] Censorship and regulation in the traditional senses are no longer practical. Nonetheless, censorship by imposed blocking or requested blocking is still employed, the former by Governments in China and certain other countries, the latter by various bodies, usually to protect children.[319] Regulation, in the sense of standard setting, is mostly in the form of self-regulation or co-regulation, since laws often prove too rigid and lack the flexibility to adjust quickly to developing technologies and complex technological issues.[320] Self-regulation and co-regulation are the preferred methods of internet regulation in Europe.[321]

The Committee of Ministers of the Council of Europe, for example, adopted a Recommendation on self-regulation concerning cyber-content in 2001[322] and a Declaration on freedom of communication on the internet in 2003.[323] The

---

[316] See above, Chap.3. It must rank on a par with the development of literacy in the nineteenth century, which paved the way for mass circulation, except that the internet developed at a much faster rate.

[317] That is, from one computer terminal to many (multipoint) and from one to one, otherwise known as peer to peer communication. For an overview of the technology and issues arising, see Karin Spaink, Introduction, *From Quill to Cursor – Freedom of the Media in the Digital Era* (OSCE, Vienna, 2003).

[318] As Spaink, above, n.317, at pp.13–14, explains, the internet perceives censorship (whether by governments or as a result of libel or copyright laws) as damage to the system and routes around it, as do users, through the use of "mirroring", for example. "Mirroring" is the method by which website owners use their contacts to make copies of pages under threat of censorship and publish them elsewhere in a more secure place where they are less likely to be challenged.

[319] *ibid.* at p.18.

[320] Spaink, above, n.317, at pp.20–21, advances a number of arguments critical of self-regulation. See also, Sandy Starr, "The Diminishing Importance of Constitutional Rights in the Internet Age" in *From Quill to Cursor—Freedom of the Media in the Digital Era* (above, n.317), at p.57.

[321] For a brief review of approaches to regulation of the Internet in Europe, see Franz C. Mayer, "Europe and the Internet: The Old World and the New Medium" (2000) 11(1) EJIL 149, and Páll Thórhallsson, "Freedom of the Media and the Internet" in *From Quill to Cursor – Freedom of the Media in the Digital Era* (above, n.317), p.49.

[322] Recommendation Rec(2001)8 on self-regulation concerning cyber content (self-regulation and user protection against illegal or harmful content on new communications and information services), September 5, 2001. The Recommendation favours codes and the monitoring of compliance with the codes, and the application of existing self-regulatory standards, as far as possible, to the new communications and information services. It contains principles on content descriptors and content selection tools, as well as complaints mechanisms, mediation and arbitration and the development of user information and awareness.

[323] May 28, 2003, available at *www.coe.int*, under "basic texts".

Declaration encourages self-regulation and co-regulation, as opposed to content rules.[324] Principle 3 opposes prior state control, through blocking or filtering measures, which would deny the public access to information and other communication on the internet. However,

> "Provided that the safeguards of Article 10, paragraph 2, of the Convention for the Protection of Human Rights and Fundamental Freedoms are respected, measures may be taken to enforce the removal of clearly identifiable Internet content or, alternatively, the blockage of access to it, if the competent national authorities have taken a provisional or final decision on its illegality".[325]

The Declaration also promotes the removal of barriers (Principle 4), the freedom to provide services *via* the internet (Principle 5) and the limited liability of service providers for internet content (Principle 6). Service providers should not be obliged to monitor content to which they give access, that they transmit or store, and should not be held liable for content when their function is limited to transmitting information or providing access to the internet. Where the functions of service providers are wider and they store content emanating from other parties, they can be held co-responsible if they do not act expeditiously to remove or disable access to information or services as soon as they become aware of their illegal nature. The freedom of expression of those who made the information available in the first place and the corresponding rights of users of the information must be respected. On-line anonymity must be respected, although Member States may take measures to trace those responsible for criminal acts (Principle 7).

In the new media environment it is imperative not only that legislation keep apace with technological change but also that outmoded legal provisions from previous centuries or decades which still apply in Ireland be revised and updated. Those provisions include sections of the Defamation Act, Emergency Powers Acts, Offences against the State Acts, Official Secrets Act and many common-law rules, some of which may not be invoked very often but which do cast a shadow over media activities and are in urgent need of reform.

---

[324] Principle 2 espouses self-regulation and co-regulation, while Principle 1 states that Member States should not adopt content rules which go further than those applied to other means of content delivery. A Draft Recommendation on a right of reply for on-line services has been prepared by the Group of Specialists on on-line services and democracy of the Council of Europe (MM-S-OD, June 27, 2003). It sees a right of reply as a particularly appropriate remedy in the on-line environment due to the possibility of instant correction of contested information and the technical ease with which replies from concerned individuals can be attached to the contested information. One stipulation is that professional on-line media should make the name and contact details of a person responsible for handling requests for replies easily available (Principle 4).

[325] Principle 3, para.2.

11.8 CONCLUSION

Advances in technology have taken the media, in the space of a few decades, from a situation of monopoly, through a period of diversity of old and new services, to the point of convergence. In the broadcasting sphere, the progression has been from public service broadcasting, with its emphasis on democratic values and social objectives, and its focus firmly on the citizen, to private/ commercial broadcasting, where the guiding factors are market forces and competition, and with the focus on the consumer. The course of that development has brought broadcasting from the national stage to the transfrontier, international and eventually global arena. Now, as the technologies have continued to develop at a rapid pace, the thrust is towards convergence of the once separate platforms and players. The new technologies of internet and digitisation have spawned new services and new delivery platforms, which have changed the way newspapers, film, video and music can be delivered, and opened up new forms and markets for advertising, archiving and other forms of information storage and delivery. Increasingly, the delivery of media is becoming more customised and individualised. The individual customer can pre-select, can opt for specific news and information sources or exclude them altogether and opt for niche or special interest services. The future of the media may no longer be as "mass" media at all or may be so to a lesser extent. The capacity of personally tailored media to provoke or inform public debate may be considerably less than it is today. Such a development would have obvious consequences both for regulation, based as it is on democratic theory and on the impact of the (mass) media on public opinion, and for information management, which is more an issue now than ever before.

Key concerns that have accompanied this development have been, first of all, how to reconcile public service broadcasting with independent (private commercial) broadcasting, and all existing media with the new technologies. Underlying this is the desire to preserve and promote the intrinsic qualities of each. The goals of public service broadcasting: ensuring diversity, promoting language and culture, etc., are central to democracy. The desired effects of independent broadcasting: consumer choice, opening up the market, promoting competition, and preventing monopoly, are central to a modern economy. The privately-owned media and the open-ended internet straddle both sets of goals and values. The question is how best to accommodate them in the light of developments in technology.[326]

In order to meet overall objectives, including, and especially, the wider democratic values of freedom of expression, a combination of Competition Law and Media Law will be required. In the interests of speed and flexibility, other forms of regulation will also have to be contemplated. Consideration will have to be given also to introducing, or increasing elements of, co-regulation and self-regulation. The value of the last-mentioned forms of regulation is to provide the necessary flexibility, reduce direct intervention by the state and allow industry players to buy into the scheme, engage with the

---

[326] See generally Marie McGonagle, *Trends in Broadcasting Regulation*, EPRA Meeting, Ljubljana, Slovenia, October 23–25, 2002, available at *www.epra.org*.

regulatory bodies and take day-to-day control. In any such regime, clear and well-articulated principles, and fair and transparent procedures that are accessible to all are necessary.

The EU/EC has been involved in the debate and agenda-setting in this area for decades. The Council of Europe has also been active in the field for decades, providing principles and guidance. For instance, the Committee of Ministers of the Council of Europe, in 2001, adopted the European Convention for the Protection of the European Audiovisual Heritage with a Protocol on the Protection of Television Productions – the first binding international instruments on those matters.[327] The primary purpose is "to ensure the protection of the European audiovisual heritage and its appreciation both as an art form and as a record of our past by means of its collection, its preservation and the availability of moving image material for cultural, scientific and research purposes, in the public interest".

Have there been any particular trends over the past few years? The period has been one of reflection, of review, of coming to terms with new technologies, their potential and their implications. That has brought us back to basic principles, to reviewing existing regulation, the purposes of regulation. It has involved (i) separating out forms of regulation and objectives of regulation, and (ii) taking a more positive view of the role of regulation, as promoting and facilitating rather than simply restricting, but at the same time safeguarding key values and objectives. The trend, therefore, to the extent that there is one yet discernible, can be said to be towards safeguarding key objectives and maintaining focused regulation, but with a more proportionate or lighter-touch approach.[328]

The UK Government's White Paper (1999) perhaps sums it up, when it states among its goals:

> "to ensure the widest possible access to a choice of diverse communications services of the highest quality;
>
> to safeguard the interests of citizens and consumers;
>
> to make sure that the right balance is struck between freedom of speech and basic standards of decency and quality".[329]

The hope must be that media in the twenty-first century will be characterised by reliability of information, ease of access and meaningful choice. While much of the discussion above has been centred on structural regulation and the impact or potential impact of technology, it is important not to lose sight of the essence of the media, that is the news and information function and the journalists who endeavour to supply it. It is perhaps fitting, therefore, to end with the Guerin principles, adopted by the NUJ and organisations representing

---

[327] September 19, 2001.

[328] The European Commission (COM (1999) 657 final) states: "The principle of proportionality requires that the degree of regulatory intervention should not be more than is necessary to achieve the objective in question".

[329] Above, n.21.

media managements in 1996, following the murder of journalist, Veronica
Guerin, crime correspondent with the *Sunday Independent*:

- "The existence of a fair, free and independent media is essential to
  democracy
- The state must ensure that a constitutional and legislative environment
  exists to facilitate freedom of expression and a free media.
- Media organisations must continue to provide the resources necessary
  for investigative journalism.
- Media organisations must ensure workers are given the maximum
  protection in the pursuit of their duties
- Media workers resolve to resist any attempt at intimidation in whatever
  form and from whatever quarter".[330]

Further Reading

Barendt, Eric, *Broadcasting Law* (Clarendon Press, Oxford, 1993).
Gibbons, Thomas, *Regulating the Media* (2nd ed., Sweet and Maxwell, London,
    1998).
Kiberd, Damien (ed.), *Media in Ireland – The Search for Diversity* (1997),
    Media in Ireland – The Search for Ethical Journalism (1999), and *Issues
    in Broadcasting* (Open Air, an imprint of Four Courts Press, Dublin, 2002).
Nikoltchev, Susanne (ed.), *Focus – Copyright in the Digital Age* (European
    Audiovisual Observatory, Strasbourg, 2000); *Co-Regulation of the Media
    in Europe* (2003) and *Key Legal Questions for the Audiovisual Sector*
    (2003).

---

[330] The principles, which were endorsed by the NUJ, AIRS, NNI and RNAI, were formally
    launched on October 9, 1996 (*www.indigo.ie/~nujdub/guerinp.htm*).

Select Bibliography

Adams, Michael,
Censorship: The Irish Experience (The University of Alabama Press, Alabama, 1968).

Agre, Philip E. and
Rotenberg, Marc (eds),
Technology and Privacy: The New Landscape (MIT Press, Cambridge, Mass. & London, England, 1997).

Barendt, Eric,
Freedom of Speech (OUP, Oxford, 1996), reprint with additions.

Barendt, Eric,
Broadcasting Law (Clarendon Press, Oxford, 1993).

Barendt, Eric, and
Hitchens, Lesley,
Media Law: Cases and Materials (Longman, Harlow, England, 2000).

Barendt, Eric (ed.),
Privacy (Ashgate Publishing Ltd, Aldershot, Hants, 2001).

Barendt, Eric, and
Firth, Alison (eds),
The Yearbook of Copyright and Media Law (OUP, Oxford, annually 1995–2002).

Beatson, Jack, and
Cripps, Yvonne (eds),
Freedom of Expression and Freedom of Information: Essays in Honour of Sir David Williams (OUP, Oxford, 2000).

Birks, Peter (ed.),
Privacy and Loyalty (Clarendon Press, Oxford, 1997).

Blackburn, Robert, and
Polakiewicz, Jorg (eds),
Fundamental Rights in Europe: The European Convention on Human Rights and its Member States 1950–2000 (OUP, Oxford, 2001) – chapter on Ireland by Donncha O'Connell, p.423.

Burns-Bisogno, Louisa,
Censoring Irish Nationalism: The British, Irish and American Suppression of Republican Images in Film and Television, 1909–1995 (McFarland and Co. Inc., North Carolina and London, 1997).

Byrne, Raymond, and
Binchy, William,

Annual Review of Irish Law (Round Hall Sweet and Maxwell, Dublin).

Carlson, Julia (ed.),

Banned in Ireland: Censorship and the Irish Writer (Routledge, London, 1990).

Cassidy, Eoin, and
McGrady, Andrew G.,

Media and the Marketplace: Ethical Perspectives (Institute of Public Administration, Dublin, 2001).

Clayton, Richard and
Tomlinson, Hugh,

Privacy and Freedom of Expression (OUP, Oxford, 2001).

Coliver, Sandra (ed.),

Striking a Balance: Hate Speech, Freedom of Expression and Non-discrimination (ARTICLE 19 and University of Essex, Essex, 1992).

Coliver, Sandra and
Hoffman, Paul and
Fitzpatrick, Joan and
Bowen, Stephen (eds),

Secrecy and Liberty: National Security, Freedom of Expression, and Access to Information (M. Nijhoff Publishers, The Hague, 1999).

Courtney, Catherine, and
Newell, David, and
Rasaiah, Santha,

The Law of Journalism (Butterworths, London, 1995).

Crauford-Smith, Rachael,

Broadcasting Law and Fundamental Rights (Clarendon Press, Oxford, 1997).

Crone, Tom and Alberstat,
Philip and Cassels, Tom
and Overs, Estelle (eds),

Law and the Media (4th ed., Focal Press, Oxford, 2002).

Euromedia Research Group,
(Ostergaard, Bernt
Stubbe (ed.)),

The Media in Western Europe (2nd ed., Sage Publications, London, 1997).

Fallon, Brian,

Age of Innocence: Irish Culture 1930–1960 (Gill and Macmillan, Dublin, 1998) – chapter 15: "The Literary Censorship". (Paperback edition 1999).

Ferguson, Robert,

Representing Race: Ideology, Identity and the Media (Arnold, London, 1998).

Fisher, David I.,

Defamation via Satellite: A European Law Perspective (Kluwer Law International, The Hague, 1998).

Gibbons, Thomas, *Regulating the Media* (2nd ed., Sweet & Maxwell, London).

Goldberg, David, and Prosser, Tony, and Verhulst, Stefaan G., *Regulating the Changing Media: A Comparative Study* (Clarendon Press, Oxford, 1998).

Goldberg, David, and Prosser, Tony, and Verhulst, Stefaan G., *EC Media Law and Policy* (Longman, Harlow, 1998).

Greene, Marilyn J. (ed.), *New Code Words for Censorship* (World Press Freedom Committee, Virginia, 1999, updated 2000).

Hall, Eamon, *The Electronic Age: Telecommunication in Ireland* (Oak Tree Press, Dublin, 1993).

Harris, David J., and O'Boyle, Michael and Warbrick, Colin, *Law of the European Convention on Human Rights* (Butterworths, London, 1995).

Hazelcorn, Ellen and Smyth, Patrick (eds), *Let in the Light: Censorship, Secrecy and Democracy* (Brandon Books, Dingle, 1993).

Heffernan, Liz (ed.), *Human Rights: A European Perspective* (The Round Hall Press, Dublin, 1994).

Hooper, David, *Reputations Under Fire: Winners and Losers in the Libel Business* (Little, Brown and Company, London, 2000).

Horgan, John, *Irish Media: A Critical History Since 1922* (Routledge, London and New York, 2001).

Humphreys, Peter J., *Mass Media and Media Policy in Western Europe* (Manchester University Press, Manchester, 1996).

Inglis, Brian, *Freedom of the Press in Ireland 1784–1841* (Faber and Faber, London, 1954).

Jakubowicz, Karol, and Others, *Media and Democracy* (Council of Europe Publishing, Strasbourg, 1998).

Jones, Derek (ed.), *Censorship: A World Encyclopedia* (Fitzroy Dearborn, London and Chicago, 2001), 4 volumes.

Keogh, Dermot (ed.),   *Irish Democracy and the Right to Freedom of Information (Ireland: A Journal of History and Society)* (Dept of History, UCC, Cork, 1995).

Kiberd, Damien (ed.),   *Media in Ireland: The Search for Diversity* (Open Air, an imprint of Four Courts Press, Dublin, 1997).

Kiberd, Damien (ed.),   *Media in Ireland: The Search for Ethical Journalism* (Open Air, an imprint of Four Courts Press, Dublin, 1999).

Kiberd, Damien (ed.),   *Media in Ireland: Issues in Broadcasting* (Open Air, an imprint of Four Courts Press, Dublin, 2002).

Kuner, Christopher,   *European Data Privacy Law and Online Business* (OUP, Oxford, 2003).

Lessig, Lawrence,   *Code and other Laws of Cyberspace* (Basic Books, New York, 1999).

Lichtenberg, Judith (ed.),   *Democracy and the Mass Media* (Cambridge University Press, Mass., 1993).

Loveland, Ian,   *Political Libels: A Comparative Study* (Hart Publishing, Oxford, 2000).

Loveland, Ian (ed.),   *Importing the First Amendment: Freedom of Expression in American, English and European Law* (Hart Publishing, Oxford, 1998).

Marsden, Chris,   *Regulating the Global Information Society* (Routledge, New York, 2000).

Marsden, Chris and   *Convergence in European Digital TV Regu-*
  Verhulst, Stefaan,   *lation* (Blackstone Press, London, 1999).

Mendel, Toby,   *Public Service Broadcasting: A Comparative Legal Survey* (UNESCO, Asia Pacific Institute for Broadcasting Development, Kuala Lumpur, 2000).

McDonagh, Maeve,   *Freedom of Information Law in Ireland* (Round Hall Sweet & Maxwell, Dublin, 1998).

McDonald, Marc,   *Irish Law of Defamation* (2nd ed., The Round Hall Press, Dublin, 1989).

McGonagle, Marie (ed.),   *Law and the Media: The Views of Journalists and Lawyers* (Round Hall Sweet & Maxwell, Dublin, 1997).

McHugh, Damian,   *Libel Law: A Journalist's Handbook* (2nd ed., Four Courts Press, Dublin, 2001).

Munter, Robert,   *The History of the Irish Newspaper 1685–1760* (Cambridge University Press, Cambridge, 1967).

Murphy, Yvonne,   *Journalists and the Law* (2nd ed., Round Hall Sweet and Maxwell, Dublin, 2000).

Nicol, Andrew, and Miller, Gavin, and Sharland, Andrew,   *Media Law and Human Rights* (Blackstone Press, London, 2001).

Ó Drisceoil, Dónal,   *Censorship in Ireland 1939–1945: Neutrality, Politics and Society* (Cork University Press, Cork, 1996).

Parkinson, David,   *History of Film* (Thames and Hudson, London, 1995).

Pine, Richard,   *2RN and the Origins of Irish Radio* (Four Courts Press, Dublin, 2002).

Robertson, Geoffrey and Nicol, Andrew,   *Media Law* (4th ed., Sweet & Maxwell, London, 2002; Penquin Book, 2002).

Sadurski, Wojciech,   *Freedom of Speech and its Limits* (Kluwer Academic Publications, Dordrecht and Boston, 1999).

Savage, Robert J.,   *Irish Television: The Political and Social Origins* (Cork University Press, Cork, 1996).

Schauer, Frederick,   *Free Speech: A Philosophical Enquiry* (Cambridge University Press, Mass., 1982).

Shannon, Richard,   *A Press Free and Responsible: Self-Regulation and the Press Complaints Commission 1991-2001* (John Murray, London, 2001).

Skouris, Wassilios (ed.),   *Advertising and Constitutional Rights in Europe* (Nomos Verlagsgesellschaft, Baden-Baden, 1994).

Sunstein, Cass R.,   *Republic.com* (Princeton University Press, Princeton, N.J., 2001).

Tugendhat, Michael and   *The Law of Privacy and the Media* (OUP, Christie, Iain (eds.),   Oxford, 2002).

Van Dijk, P. and   *Theory and Practice of the European Con-* Van Hoof, G.J.H.,   *vention on Human Rights* (3rd ed., Kluwer Law International, The Hague, 1998).

Wacks, Raymond (ed.),   *Privacy* (Vol. 2, Dartmouth, Aldershot, Hants, 1993).

Wichmann, Manfred (ed.),   *Freedom of Expression and Human Rights Protection* (Friedrich-Naumann-Stiftung, Brussels, 1997).

Woodman, Kieran,   *Media Control in Ireland* (Galway University Press, Galway, 1985).

ARTICLES

Louise Arbour J., Supreme   "Exposing Truth while Keeping Secrets: Court of Canada,   Publicity, Privacy and Privilege" (2000) xxxv Ir. Jur. 17.

Eric Barendt,   "Press and Broadcasting Freedom: Does Anyone Have Any Right to Free Speech?" (1991) 44 C.L.P. 63.

                                "What is the point of Libel Law?" [1999] 52 *Current Legal Problems* 110.

Gerard Brennan,   "The third branch and the fourth estate" (1997) xxxii Ir. Jur. 62.

Katrin Schatz Byford,   "Privacy in Cyberspace: Constructing a Model of Privacy for the Electronic Communications Environment" [1998] 24 *Rutgers Computer and Technology Law Journal* 1.

Desmond Clarke,   "Section 31 and Censorship: A Philosophical Perspective" (1994) 12 I.L.T. 53.

Jonathan Cooper and Adrian   "Hate Speech, Holocaust Denial and Inter- Marshall Williams,   national Human Rights Law" [1999] E.H.R.L.R. 593.

Neville Cox, "Sacrilege and Sensibility: The Value of Irish Blasphemy Law" (1997) 19 D.U.L.J. 87.

Thomas Gibbons, "Freedom of the Press: Ownership and Editorial Values" (1992) P.L. 279.

"Defamation Reconsidered" [1996] 16 *Oxford Journal of Legal Studies* 587.

"Protection of Journalistic Sources" (2002) *Communications Law* 124.

Gerard Hogan, "Free Speech, Privacy and the Press in Ireland" (1987) *Public Law* 509.

W.S. Holdsworth, "Defamation in the Sixteenth and Seventeenth Centuries" (1924) 40 L.Q.R. 397.

Lord Irvine, "Reporting the courts: the media's rights and responsibilities" (1999) xxxiv Ir. Jur. 1.

Lawrence Lessig, "The Law of the Horse: What Cyberlaw Might Teach" (1999) 113 *Harvard Law Review,* No.2, 501.

Anthony Lewis, "Law and the press: a deadly embrace" (1998) xxxiii Ir. Jur. 34.

Gerard McCormack, "Corrupting the Criminal Process" (1985) 1 I.L.T. 6.

"The Right to Jury Trial in Cases of Contempt" (1983) G.I.L.S.I. 177 and 209.

Maeve McDonagh, "Freedom of Information in Ireland and Europe: Progress and Regression" (2001) 29(2) *International Journal of Legal Information* 256.

"The Interaction of European Community Law and National Access to Information Laws: An Irish Perspective" (2000) 9(2) *Irish Journal of European Law* 216.

R. B. McDowell, "Irish Newspapers in the Eighteenth Century" (1984) 8(2) *Media and Popular Culture, The Crane Bag* 40.

Tarlach McGonagle, "Wresting (Racial) Equality from Tolerance of Hate Speech" (2001) 23 D.U.L.J. 21.

Colin R. Munro,   "The value of commercial speech" [2003] C.L.J.
                                    134.

Úna Ní Raifeartaigh,   "Fault issues and Libel Law - A Comparison
                                    between Irish, English and United States Law"
                                    (1991) 40 I.C.L.Q. 763.

                                    "Defences in Irish Defamation Law" (1991) 13
                                    D.U.L.J. 76.

Jerome O'Callaghan,   "Censorship of Indecency in Ireland: A View
                                    from Abroad" [1998] 16 *Cardozo Arts and
                                    Entertainment Law Journal* 53.

Sandra Day O'Connor,   "Copyright law from an American perspective"
                                    (2002) xxxvii Ir. Jur. 16.

Eoin O'Dell,   "Does Defamation Value Free Expression?"
                                    (1990) 12 D.U.L.J. 50.

                                    "Reflections on a Revolution in Libel" (1991)
                                    I.L.T. 181.

Michael O'Neill,   "In search of a real right of access to E.C.-held
                                    documentation" [1997] P.L. 446.

M. Pollard,   "Control of the Press in Ireland through the
                                    King's Printer's Patent 1600-1800" (1978-80)
                                    14 *Irish Booklore* 79.

Robert C. Post,   The Social Foundations of Defamation Law:
                                    Reputation and the Constitution" (1986) 74
                                    Calif.L.Rev. 691.

                                    "The Social Foundations of Privacy: Com-
                                    munity and Self in the Common Law Tort"
                                    (1989) 77 Calif.L.Rev. 957.

                                    "Racist Speech, Democracy and the First
                                    Amendment" (1991) 32 William and Mary L.R.
                                    267.

Thomas Scanlon,   "A Theory of Freedom of Expression" (1972)
                                    1 *Philosophy and Public Affairs* 204.

Frederick Schauer,   "Principles, Institutions, and the First Amend-
                                    ment" (1998) 112 *Harvard Law Review* 84.

Frederick Schauer,   "Internet Privacy and the Public-Private Dis-
                                    tinction" 38 *Jurimetrics* 555.

Noel Travers,   "Access to documents in Community law: on
                             the road to a European participatory democracy"
                             (2000) xxxv Ir. Jur. 164.

Van Vechten Veeder,   "The History and Theory of the Law of
                             Defamation – Part I" (1903) 4 Colum. L. Rev.
                             546, Part II (1904) 4 Colum. L. Rev. 33.

Luzius Wildhaber,   "The right to offend, shock or disturb? Aspects
                             of freedom of expression under the European
                             Convention on Human Rights" (2001) xxxvi Ir.
                             Jur. 17.

S.D.Warren and   "The Right to Privacy" 4 Harv. L.R. 193 (1890).
   L.D. Brandeis,

OFFICIAL REPORTS (IRELAND)

Competition Authority, *Report of the Investigation of the Proposal whereby
   Independent Newspapers plc would increase its shareholding in the
   Tribune Group from 29.9% to 53.09%* (Stationery Office, Dublin, 1992).

Competition Authority, *Interim Report of Study on the Newspaper Industry*
   (The Stationery Office, Dublin, 1995).

Report of the Commission on the Newspaper Industry, (Pn 2841, Stationery
   Office, Dublin, 1996).

Constitution Review Group, *Report of the Constitution Review Group*
   (Stationery Office, Dublin, 1996).

Department of Arts, Culture and the Gaeltacht, *Clear Focus: The Government's
   Proposals for Broadcasting Legislation* (Pn 3648, Stationery Office,
   Dublin, 1997).

Competition and Mergers Review Group, *Final Report* (Pn 8487, Department
   of Enterprise, Trade and Employment, Dublin, 2000).

Law Reform Commission: *www.lawreform.ie/publications/publications.htm*

                    Consultation Paper on the Civil Law of Defamation (March
                    1991)

                    Report on the Civil Law of Defamation (LRC 38–1991)

                    Consultation Paper on the Crime of Libel (August 1991)

                    Report on the Crime of Libel (LRC 41–1991)

                    Consultation Paper on Contempt of Court (July 1991)

                    Report on Contempt of Court (LRC 47–1994)

Consultation Paper on Privacy: Surveillance and the Interception of Communications (September 1996)

Report on Privacy: Surveillance and the Interception of Communications (LRC 57–1998)

Working Group on a Courts Commission, Sixth Report, November 1998. *www.courts.ie/Home.nsf/Content/Press+Releases+Opening*

Report of the Forum on Broadcasting, August 2002. *www.dcmnr.gov.ie/files/FINLREPT3.DOC*

Report of the Legal Advisory Group on Defamation, March 2003. *www.justice.ie* under "publications".

INTERNATIONAL PRINCIPLES

ARTICLE 19, London: *www.article19.org*

The Johannesburg Principles on National Security, Freedom of Expression and Access to Information, 1996.

The Public's Right to Know: Principles on Freedom of Information Legislation, 1999.

Defining Defamation: Principles on Freedom of Expression and Protection of Reputation, 2000.

International Mechanisms for Freedom of Expression, 2001.

A Model Freedom of Information Law, 2001.

Access to the Airwaves: Principles on Freedom of Expression and Broadcast Regulation, 2002.

Virtual Freedom of Expression Handbook.

European Audiovisual Observatory, Strasbourg (details at *www.obs.coe.int*):

Nikoltchev, Susanne (ed.),   *Focus – Copyright in the Digital Age* (2000).

Television and Media Concentration (2001).

Jurisdiction over Broadcasters in Europe (2002).

Co-Regulation of the Media in Europe (2003).

Key Legal Questions for the Audiovisual Sector (2003).

USEFUL WEBSITES

Ireland

www.ireland.com (*The Irish Times*) (requires subscription)

www.unison.ie/irish_independent (*Irish Independent*) (requires subscription)

www.examiner.ie (*Irish Examiner*)

www.oireachtas.ie (Acts and Bills passed since 1998)

www.oic.gov.ie (Office of the Information Commissioner)

www.irishstatutebook.ie (Irish Statute Book, Acts and Bills 1922-1998)

www.bailii.org, www.irlii.org (British and Irish legislation, case law, journals)

www.irishlaw.org/legislation (Law Faculty, UCC)

www.lawreform.ie (Law Reform Commission)

www.nationalarchives.ie (National Archives of Ireland)

www.irtc.ie, www.bci.ie (Independent Radio and Broadcasting Commission, now the Broadcasting Commission of Ireland)

www.odtr.ie (Office of the Director of Telecommunications Regulation, now the Commission for Communications Regulation)

www.dataprivacy.ie (Data Protection Commissioner)

www.ispai.ie (Internet Service Providers Association of Ireland)

www.hotline.ie (Hotline regarding child pornography on the Internet, supervised by the Internet Advisory Board.)

www.iab.ie (Internet Advisory Board)

www.asai.ie (Advertising Standards Authority for Ireland)

www.nuj.org.uk (National Union of Journalists in Britain and Ireland)

http://indigo.ie/~nujdub (National Union of Journalists – Dublin branch)

Northern Ireland

www.northernireland-legislation.hmso.gov.uk/ (NI legislation)

European

www.europa.eu.int (European Union)

http://curia.eu.int/en/index.htm (European Court of Justice of the European Communities)

http://europa.eu.int/comm/avpolicy (European Commission Audiovisual Policy)

http://europa.eu.int/information_society/index_en.htm (European Commission

Information Society)

www.europarl.eu.int (European Parliament)

www.euro-ombudsman.eu.int (European Ombudsman)

www.statewatch.org (Monitor of the State and Civil Liberties in the European Union)

www.coe.int (Council of Europe)

www.echr.coe.int (European Court of Human Rights)

www.coe.int/T/E/human_rights/media (Media Division of the Human Rights Directorate of the Council of Europe)

www.obs.coe.int (European Audiovisual Observatory)

www.epra.org (European Platform of Regulatory Authorities – Broadcasting)

www.aipce.org (Alliance of Independent Press Councils of Europe)

www.easa-alliance.org (European Advertising Standards Authority)

www.inhope.org (Association of Internet Hotline Providers in Europe)

www.euroispa.org (European Internet Service Providers Association)

www.ivir.nl (Institute for Information Law, University of Amsterdam)

www.cvdm.nl/pages/english.asp (English language version of Dutch Broadcasting Commission)

www.seenapb.org/legislation (Broadcasting legislation in S.E. Europe)

www.7am.com (Variety of news sources, including BBC World, Reuters World, Guardian and Newsday)

International

www.unhcr.ch (UN Human Rights Committee)

www.ifj.org (International Federation of Journalists)

www.icfj.org (International Center for Journalists, Washington D.C.)

www.ijclp.org (online journal, *International Journal of Communications Law and Policy*)

http://elj.warwick.ac.uk/jilt (online journal, *Journal of Information Law and Technology*)

Index

(references are to paragraph numbers)